BULLETIN

OF THE

PUBLIC MUSEUM OF THE CITY OF MILWAUKEE

Vol. 15, Pp. 1-608   November 6, 1933

POMO MYTHS

By

S. A. Barrett

S. A. Barrett
Editor

Ira Edwards
Assistant Editor

MILWAUKEE, WIS., U. S. A.
Published by Order of the Board of Trustees

Printed by the
CANNON PRINTING COMPANY
Milwaukee, Wis.

POMO MYTHS

CONTENTS

INTRODUCTION

TERRITORY AND ENVIRONMENT

The Pomo Linguistic stock, as has been elsewhere[1] very fully discussed by the author, comprised in aboriginal times seven dialectic divisions.   One of these, the Northeastern dialect, occupied a very small territory on the extreme western margin of the Sacramento Valley. The other six occupied a territory roughly ninety by sixty miles in extent in Mendocino, Lake and Sonoma counties, all within the Coast Range Mountain region, immediately north of San Francisco Bay. This is a territory of very diverse environmental conditions, reaching from the coastline of the Pacific Ocean, across two relatively low ranges of mountains with innumerable valleys, and over to the Clear Lake basin.

Along the immediate coastline there was a belt of dense redwood forest which, combined with the sea life, gave this a very special environment. Then came the many intermountain valleys, large and small; and finally, there was the highly specialized environment due to Clear Lake and its various associated bodies of water.

This whole territory was, in aboriginal times, abundantly provided with the native vegetal foods, particularly the several species of oaks, the acorns from which provided the main food supply. The mountains and forests abounded in game, and the streams and lakes were bountifully stocked with fish of many species. In fact this region was an ideal "Indian country", and here there was developed a special culture, with certain variants in each of the environmental units. Such variations are reflected even in the mythology of the people.

In the course of rather extensive studies of the Pomo, made first for the University of California, and later extended for the Milwaukee Public Museum, the author collected quite an extensive series of myths in three of these dialectic areas, the Central, Northern, and Eastern, which give a very good cross-section of this subject from the coast to the Clear Lake region and which cover all three of these environmental units. The work for the University of California was conducted primarily between 1903 and 1906, while that for the Milwaukee Public Museum was carried on in 1914 and 1915.

---

[1] Ethnogeography of the Pomo Indians, Univ. Calif. Publ. Arch. Ethn., Vol. 6, pp. 1-322, 1908.

In those days there still existed many of the older Indians to whom tribal customs and beliefs really meant something, a fact of the highest importance in a study like that of mythology. Most of the myths here recorded were obtained from the older people who acquired them from their elders long before, and when they were in much more complete and detailed form than could possibly be found at the present time, after upwards of thirty additional years of the so-called civilizing process. Many are in all probability as fully detailed as they ever were given in the days before the advent of the white man. A few are fragmentary, and represent the abbreviated and sketchy versions recalled by some individual whose memory for that sort of thing was not of the best; but even these often show interesting variants of myth themes; and often such a fragmentary version throws an important light on some particular point. It has seemed best, therefore, to utilize every one collected, whether it be fully detailed and told with all the elaborate circumstance of its ancient recounting, or whether it be a sketchy, abbreviated account.

RECORDING OF MYTHS

The myths here recorded were in a large measure taken down in full long hand, and as free translations directly from the informant if he could speak English with sufficient ease. If not, then it was taken in the same manner through an interpreter. Some were taken in text form with interlinear, and also with free translations. The free translations only are here given, since it is the subject matter only of the myths which concern us, rather than any linguistic consideration. Those interested in the Pomo language as such should consult the able treatment of that subject by Dr. A. L. Kroeber who, in his discussion of "The Languages of the Coast of California North of San Francisco",[2] gives a short text in the Eastern Pomo dialect, of the well-known myth theme, the theft of the Sun. This text with its interlinear translation forms part of a section dealing with a discussion and analysis of the Pomo language.

In preparing these free translations of Pomo myths for publication, it has been necessary to revise them to a considerable extent in order to put them into good, clear and understandable form. In no case, however, has the sense of any passage been altered, and the full Indian

---

[2]Univ. Calif. Publ., Amer. Arch., Ethn., Vol. 9, pp. 343-346, 1911.

form, with its many repetitions, has been preserved. While many cases
of verbosity may appear it should be remembered that this was the
Indian tendency, and in order to give the myths their proper aboriginal
cast such repetitions and verbosity are needed.

In order to facilitate work with these myths it has seemed best to
insert, after the title of each, a list of the subtitles or titles of its con-
stituent incidents. Immediately following each subtitle there is a list
of the characters, including supernatural tokens and devices, actively
concerned with that particular myth incident.

As far as possible, Indian names have been eliminated from the
text. This will make for smoothness in reading. Where no English
equivalent is known, then the Indian term must, of course, be retained.
Should the Indian term in any particular dialect be desired this can be
found in the special glossary of Indian terms.

Also, there is in the index a full list of myth incidents and elements
and through this the reader may locate all occurrences of any incident
or element in which he is interested.

CHARACTERISTICS OF MYTHS

In their full forms some of these myths show considerable variation
in details and often in the sequence of incidents. This is probably due,
to some extent at least, to the marked tendency among the Pomo to
recount their myths in composite form. This tendency was pointed out
by the author in a previous article.[3]

It is quite the rule among the Pomo to recount a myth in the form
of a long continued story, incident following incident at great length.

In some of these there is a continuity of the action which is made
possible by carrying on one or more of the mythical characters throughout all the incidents. This is particularly noticeable in such myths as the
creation or destruction myths in which Coyote is one of the chief actors.
In such a myth we find each incident connected specifically to the one
preceding it by some detailed statement that Coyote then did so and so.
In a few instances we find Coyote reappearing in the next incident but
the informant is careful to explain that this is not the same Coyote who
was concerned with the preceding incident. In quite a number of these
myths we find a considerable series of these incidents successively
recounted without any apparent connection one to the other. Some-

---

[3] A Composite Myth of the Pomo Indians, Journ. Amer. Folk-Lore, XIX, pp. 37-51, 1906.

times the successive incidents are so unrelated in subject matter and in characters that one would be tempted to separate them completely and to consider each as an independent myth, were it not for the fact that the informant recounted them in this consecutive manner and that he specifically considered them as forming a unit.

CLASSIFICATION OF MYTHS

The composite nature of these myths presents one serious difficulty, namely that of classification. For instance, an informant may give as the title of a myth what is really the title of one only of its several incidents, making no mention of any of the others. Furthermore this title for the whole myth may relate to some really minor incident and that by no means the first in order of narration. How then shall this myth be classified? It can obviously be placed in only one group. It has been deemed best to classify it according to the title given, except where some other incident is so predominantly important as to warrant doing otherwise.

In this sort of a system we are bound to find a myth, which might with almost equal propriety be classified in half a dozen groups, in one place only. When we take up the group of creation myths we will really find only a few of the creation incidents there. Others will be found in the group dealing with destruction and so on. All this is, of course, due to the composite nature of these various accounts. To correct this condition a rather elaborate system of cross-references has been prepared. Reference to this will enable the reader to find each myth incident of any desired class, no matter where it is located. Furthermore, a similar method of indicating the location of each component element of each myth incident will be found very helpful.*

While in the main these myths are composite there is a certain group of simple tales each recounting a single incident only. These, of course, are easily classified and will be found, each with its particular group. A few of these are apparently independent subjects as used by some informant, but most of them may be found in use by others as parts of composite myths.

SUBJECT MATTER OF MYTHS

In the main the subject matter of Pomo myths has to do with the

---

*All such data are included in the index. Here will be found, myth titles, incidents, elements, characters, and catch-words with full page references.

"Bird-people" and the many supernatural beings which inhabited the earth in those earlier times before the creation of the present race of human beings. It was in those remote times when there was darkness upon the earth that the sun was stolen from its keepers over in the east. Then it was that the great World-fire and the Deluge occurred, and there were innumerable contests between culture heroes and monstrous supernatural beings, and there were extensive journeys attended by all kinds of perils from which the hero escapes or to which he finally falls a victim, only to be restored to life.

In those early days conditions were very different from those of the present and many tales accounting for the transformation to present conditions are told. Some have to do with important physiographic features such as the creation of Clear Lake, the form of such an important feature as Mt. Kanaktai and the like. Others are simple etiological tales which account for the shortness of Meadowlark's tail, the whiteness of Woodrat's front paws, and the like.

THE CULTURE HERO

The culture hero is quite prominently featured. In Coyote we find the one who is responsible for changing many things to their present form, for creating foods, inventing implements and instituting customs. According to certain versions some of these are credited to certain other characters, but Coyote is responsible for a very large share of the culture hero features and changes.

THE TRICKSTER

The trickster is fairly prominent in Pomo Mythology. Several tricksters are found but Coyote again takes first rank. Sometimes he plays pranks on others and sometimes he takes the brunt of the trick. Not infrequently we find within the same myth both of these features in successive incidents, thus making Coyote appear first as a sagacious planner outwitting some one and winning his point, and immediately following this by showing him as a gullible fool who is being imposed upon by some very simple and obvious piece of trickery.

THE POSITION OF POMO MYTHOLOGY IN THE CALIFORNIA AREA

It may be appropriate at the outset to definitely locate the Pomo in relation to other groups of California Indians and to state the characteristics of the mythological unit to which they belong.

In discussing the religion of the Indians of California,[3a] Dr. Kroeber very clearly presents the fundamentals underlying the religious and mythological concepts of California and shows that there were in aboriginal times three very distinct areas: the small Northwestern area; the Southern area, lying south of Tehachapi Pass and Point Concepcion; and the Central area, comprising the remainder, about two-thirds, of the state. Thus it will be seen that, as Dr. Kroeber states, "as an ethnographic province the greater part of California plainly forms a unit."

Within this greater "Central area" there are certain variations which warrant its subdivision into a North Central and a South Central sub-area, the dividing line being about the latitude of San Francisco.

The mythology of this Central area in general displays the following characteristics:

1. The absence of migration or historical accounts.

2. The presence of true creation motifs. The creation of the world from some pre-existing substance, by pre-existing creators on a primeval ocean. The creation of human beings from some particular objects, such as sticks or feathers.

3. The existence of an original "bird people" who were later transformed into the present birds, mammals, etc.

4. The presence of rather elaborate hero tales and accounts of adventure and of destroyers.

5. An abundance of animal characters and a relative scarcity of deified inanimate objects. Chief among these animal characters is Coyote.

6. The abundance of trickster and etiological tales.

7. The presence of an elaborate series of Coyote stories.

8. The presence of detailed accounts of the destruction of the world by fire or by deluge or both.

The presence of a creator and of a relatively consistent account of creation is almost unique for the whole of California.

The importance of Coyote and the diversity of his attributes, often dual and antithetical one to another, should be remarked. 1. He may appear as an actual creator, or, as an assistant who in part cooperates and in part thwarts the true creator. 2. He may be a beneficent cul-

---

[3a]Kroeber, 1907, Univ. Calif. Publ. Am. Arch. Ethn., Vol. 4, pp. 320-356.

ture hero improving the world in one way or another for man, or he may be a malevolent being who institutes certain of the ills of man, such as death. 3. He may be an all-wise, powerful shaman able to succeed in any endeavor, or he may be a credulous fool who can be duped by anyone in the most obvious or trivial undertaking. 4. He also appears as a crafty trickster, and as the butt of ridicule.

Upon comparison of the characteristics of the mythologies of the two sub-areas of Central California certain rather important incidents or characters present in the one are found to be wholly lacking or rare in the other. The creation idea is much more developed in the north than in the south. In the north there is usually a non-animal creator while in the south the creation is often by a combination of three animal characters of more or less equal importance. The hero and transformer stories of the north are largely lacking in the south. The prominence of magic aids in combat or in games between mythical personages is much greater in the north than in the south. When we compare the Coyote of the two regions we find that in the north this character is more important and stories concerning him are more diverse than in the south.[3b]

Pomo mythology clearly belongs to the northern sub-area of the Central California area.[3bb]

POMO RELIGIOUS CONCEPTS
THE UNIVERSE

The Pomo universe consisted of three worlds: the Earth proper upon which human beings now live and which was formerly inhabited by a supernatural "Bird-people" (including mammals). Then there is the first Upper World called Kalī'mīnaū, the abode of the chief diety Madū'mda; and the second Upper World which bore no special name and which was the particular abode of Madū'mda's younger brother, Tsīko'lkol. These two upper worlds, together with their inhabitants are fully described in speaking of the creation.

The earth or human world, which we know, is comprised, of course, only of that part of the earth's surface which was known definitely to the Pomo. It is surrounded by the unknown or mythical portions of the

---

[3b]For a fuller discussion of this subject see Kroeber, 1907B, pp. 195, 198. Also Kroeber, Handbook, 1925, pp. 898-918. It is also treated by Gifford and Block, 1930, pp. 15-75.

[3bb]For further discussion of the "Relation of Pomo Mythology to that of other Tribes of Central California" see pages 465-491.

earth's surface lying beyond the known. According to some informants, the only water boundary of the known world was toward the west, this being the Pacific Ocean. According to other informants, the Abode of the Dead lay beyond the southern boundary of the known world and was separated from it by a narrow body of water. According to still others, however, this separation was indicated solely by an imaginary line.

The six cardinal directions were inhabited by special supernatural beings. Toward the south lived Gū'ksū. Toward the east lived Ca'lnis. Toward the North lived Sūū'padax (Whirl-wind). Toward the west lived Xa'matūtsi ("water-occupation"). Above lived Kalī'matūtsi ("sky-occupation"). Below lived Ka'i matūtsi ("earth-occupation").

Informants are by no means wholly in agreement on these several supernatural inhabitants of the various places nor indeed upon the places themselves. According to some informants the inhabitants of the eastern edge of the world were the Sun-people, chief among whom was Sun-man, whose attributes were quite similar to those given to Gī'lak. Numerous stories of contests with Sun-man are so like others related concerning Gī'lak that we might be quite warranted in assuming that the two beings are one and the same individual. Full descriptions of them will be given when discussing supernatural beings.

Toward the north we find in one version that this world ends in a broad and turbulent river, beyond which there is another land or outer world. Beyond the ocean, on the west, there is another outer world to which miraculous journeys have been made. Also there are islands out in the ocean concerning which interesting stories are told.

A very different picture of the southern edge of the world is given by another informant. Here there exists a great stone wall reaching to the sky, through which is a single opening which opens and closes. This is a vertical wall and just this side of it there lives Stone-woman. On the opposite side of this stone wall there is a great valley in which lives Arrow-man.

In his discussion of Pomo religion[3e] Dr. A. L. Kroeber says: *"Guksu* was thought to live in a large dance house at the south end of the world; *Shalnis* or *Madumda* at the east; while the corresponding gods at the

---

[3e]Handbook of the Indians of California, Bur. Amer. Ethn., Bull. 78, p. 261, 1925.

north, west, above, and below were whirlwind, water, sky or thunder, and earth occupant or spirit."

CREATION

Pomo ideas concerning the creation of the universe differ somewhat. Some informants maintain that the Earth has always existed while others maintain that there was a definite creation and relate the circumstances under which this took place.[4] In every case, however, comparatively little importance is attached to the creation itself, and to the creator, much more weight being attached to the culture hero, Coyote. In fact, by some it is maintained that he is the real creator, that at first, he floated about in space upon a cloud, carrying with him in his hunting sack a small amount of earth. He finally tired of floating about in this manner, took the earth into the palm of his hand and commanded it to grow.

In another version we find Coyote creating the Earth in quite a different manner. We are told that there was nothing but water. Coyote swam around and tried to find some land where he might live. By and by, he found a little island upon which, there was some dirt. He scraped around on this little island and finally succeeded in getting some dirt under his finger-nails. Then he scraped this dirt out and told it to grow and become the World, and it did.

Still another version shows Coyote creating the Earth with the assistance of Spider. We are told that Coyote was let down from the zenith by Spider. He had previously created both of the upper worlds. In his hunting sack when he came down he had clouds, the sun, moon, water, etc. He had also a very small amount of earth wrapped up in some pendant moss. He first took a little of this earth and blew it out of his hand into the air. Then he laid down and went to sleep in order that he might dream. He could not dream, however. Then he ordered Spider to spin a web and, when he had done so, to look in the other direction. Coyote then spread the remaining earth on the web and told Spider to look around and see the Earth. Spider did this and the Earth stretched out before him. Coyote then made everything in the world and finally he made human beings.

The order in which these creations of Coyote were accomplished is as follows:

---

[4]No detailed myth of world creation was obtained by the author.

He first made the uppermost of the upper worlds. Then he created Madū'mda and brought him down into the lower of the upper worlds which he created at this time. He then created the Earth, with water, mountains and valleys. Then he created all of the mammals, and then he created one of the fishes, Mala'x, who in turn created all the rest of the different species of fish. Coyote next created the various supernatural beings. He then created waterdogs, lizards, snakes and birds; and finally he created people.

Tsīko'lkol was not created at this time, not in fact until after the Earth had been destroyed by fire. He was then created and was placed in the uppermost of the two upper worlds to preside there.

In this version of the creation it will be noted that all the creating is done by Coyote and that the uppermost of the upper worlds is the first one created.

However, Madū'mda is usually considered to be the master creator, although no account of specific creations by him has yet been secured. In fact, his origin and activities seem quite vague in the minds of most informants. One informant stated that Madū'mda was Coyote's younger brother. His origin is, however, entirely unaccounted for. It is simply related that this younger brother appeared to Coyote; and that after a time, for no stated reason, he created Tsīko'lkol from a hawk feather. This, however, was not until after Madū'mda had left the earth and gone up into the first or original upper world to reside. Coyote came up here at will but proved very disgusting to Tsīko'lkol on account of the fact that he eats raw flesh and particularly on account of his destruction of the world by fire. In order, therefore, to satisfy Tsīko'lkol, Madū'mda created a second upper world above his own as a residence for Tsīko'lkol, thus placing him out of any danger of contact with Coyote. That is, as matters now stand, each of these three dieties resides in a separate world over which he especially rules, though Madū'mda is recognized as the principal ruler of the universe.

A very different conception of the earth and of its creation is recorded by Loeb[48] whose work among the Pomo was done between 1921 and 1925, after some twenty additional years of white influence upon the Pomo. His informants were of a later generation and it is

    [48]Loeb, E. M., Pomo Folkways, Univ. Calif. Publ., Amer. Arch. Ethn., Vol. 19, pp. 300-304, 1926.

quite likely that we have from them versions which have been considerably modified. His informants state that the earth floats upon water and the Coast Central Pomo conceive that each of its four corners is supported by a pole, "each pole had a deity whose duty it was to keep the earth firmly in position." This earth was created "from a ball of gum taken from the armpits of Kuksu, the first man, and Marumda, the creator."

Loeb then observes, in speaking about the Eastern Pomo conception of Creation, "Coyote was only briefly mentioned in the creation story which I received and he entered the plot in the guise of a trouble maker. The Coast Central and Northern Pomo, on the other hand, knew nothing of Marumda, but conceived of Coyote as the creator and benefactor of mankind." In a footnote he states that one informant stated that "he believed Coyote and Marumda to be one and the same." Had he pursued this idea a little further he would have found this to be the universal conception among the older and more well-informed of the Pomo generally. In fact, I myself found this to be the case twenty years earlier, for it was customary in those days for narrators to refer to the creator as Madū'mda or Iwī'Madūmda (Creator or Coyote Creator) interchangeably, especially whenever narrating creation incidents. When referring to Coyote as a trickster or in other ordinary incidents he was referred to either as Coyote or Coyote Old Man. In substantiation of this we need only cite Loeb's chief informant, Will Benson, who says[4b] "Everybody knows that *Marumda* is the same as *Coyote*."

Thus it seems quite clear that in reality there is no lack of accord between our findings and the later ones of Loeb so far as the universality of the belief in Coyote as the great Creator of the Pomo is concerned. However, the idea that the earth is supported by four poles and that it was created with the assistance of Kuksu is entirely at variance with our information.

Elaborating upon this idea of creation among the Pomo Loeb[4c] gives three myths. The first two were secured from a single "Coast Central Pomo" informant. In the first of these Coyote appears as the creator but the whole tale is very different from any of those obtained in the earlier investigation upon which our present work is based.

[4b] de Angulo, J. and Benson, W. R., The Creation Myth of the Pomo Indians, Anthropos. Vol. XXVII, p. 262, 1932.
[4c] Loeb, E. M., "The Creator Concept among the Indians of North Central California.", Amer. Anthr., N. S., Vol. 28, pp. 467-493, 1926.

The second myth recorded by Loeb can hardly be considered a creation myth in the true sense of the term, though it does account for the origin of seals and other forms of sea life. It is in reality a variant of the myth which we have recorded under the title of *"Thunder Kills Coyote and Creates all Forms of Sea Life"* which is our myth No. 41.

Loeb's third creation myth is from an Eastern Pomo source and gives in some detail the creation of the earth above mentioned by him from gum from the armpits of Kuksu, and with the aid of a pipe possessed by Marumda. This whole conception is, however, so foreign to Pomo thought in general that it may be doubted that it represents a really aboriginal Pomo concept, especially when the source of the information is taken into account.

This same conception in even more elaborate detail is given by de Angulo and Benson.[4d] where we find it combined with a very long series of creations, destructions and other events which are, to say the least, most unusual and which introduce many concepts and details which were never mentioned by the older informants with whom we dealt in the earlier part of this century. The whole tale, or series of tales, is such a fantastic fabrication that it must be accepted with the utmost reservation.

MADUMDA

Madū'mda is in appearance quite human though little is known concerning his abode or his dress. He has the power of transmutation, as has Coyote, but never uses his power since he has no occasion to practice deception. It is said that Madū'mda lives directly above in the first upper world where he has a radiant, white assembly-house which can be seen from a great distance on account of its brilliant light. He never goes about, even in his own domain, nor does he ever descend to the earth. No one knows just what he does or just what he wears or eats.

He has six servants who do his every bidding and carry all his messages. These are: Ya'-tca (Wind-man), who is also the chief of these servants, Kaba'-tca (Cloud-man), Pō't-tca (Fog-man), Yū'-tca (Snow-man), Ema'-tca (Frost-man) and Gī'lak. These servants all reside in Gī'lak's house which is at the eastern extremity of the first upper world.

This Upper World is an absolutely level plain without trees, rocks,

---

[4d]Op. Cit. pp. 261-274 and 779-795, 1932.

streams or bodies of water of any kind, but completely covered with brush and grasses and beautiful flowering plants, all of which are perpetually in bloom. There are no mammals, insects or reptiles, and the only birds present are the vulture, the eagle, the hawk and the buzzard.[5]

Here again we find considerable divergence of opinion concerning this first upper world. One informant maintains that the Upper World is very much like our own country here. It is like a big, pleasant valley surrounded by hills and mountains and most beautifully situated. There are lakes, rivers, and all kinds of game, such as deer, bear and elk. The waters are filled with fish; the whole country is covered with grass, and flowers of all kinds are blooming continually. Every conceivable kind of the best foods is to be found here.

There are, however, no snakes or other frightful things of that sort anywhere in the whole Upper World.

There are people living in the Upper World though there are no specific tribes mentioned. These people have houses, sweat-houses and all of the buildings, etc., that we have down here on the earth.

Amid all this beauty and all these ideal conditions lives Gīʼlak, a large, bird-like individual said to fly about and capture people whom he takes up to his house in the Upper World and devours.

THE ZENITH GATE

Informants are quite well agreed that the Upper World is reached only by means of the Zenith Gate. This is a very small door with two teeth on either side which interlock when the gate is closed. It is made of rock quite like that found upon the earth. It operates horizontally and, according to some informants, is guarded by a cordon of rattlesnakes who prevent the entry of anyone who does not belong in the Upper World or who has not been sent for by Madūʼmda. The gate is in charge of Spider who opens it for anyone whom it is proper to admit.

The ascent to the Zenith Gate is always made through the instrumentality of Spider who takes the passenger into his hunting sack and carries him up there. In most cases we are led to infer at least, that the Spider who takes up the passenger is the actual gate-keeper. One

---

[5]According to some informants, nothing was known aboriginally concerning the upper worlds except that these two dieties Madūʼmda and Tsīkoʼlkol resided there. The specific statements concerning the appearance of these two upper worlds are said by them to be due to ingrafted ideas, derived from the missionaries, concerning the beauties of heaven which has been pictured to them as a land of perpetual flowers and plenty.

myth, however, specifically states that this is not the gate-keeper, but that the Spider who takes Coyote up calls to his grandfather, who is another spider, to open the gate. He does so and lets Spider and his passenger, Coyote, through and then lets them go back to earth again later on.

In most instances we are specifically told that Spider descends from and ascends to the Upper World by means of his own web, but in one myth we see Spider coming down to rescue Coyote and his children from the great world fire. He does not descend by means of his own web but by means of a feather rope (yū'lūk). On the way up four stops are made. Upon each occasion Spider spins a web to enable Coyote and his children to do some specific thing, such as to drink water, eat some food and the like.

In another instance we are told that Spider, the Zenith Gate-keeper, has a very big, protruding belly in which he has coiled a great length of rope (yū'lūk). Whenever Coyote wishes to ascend to the upper world he calls out to Madū'mda who sends Spider down to earth upon this rope which he uncoils from his own belly.

TSIKOLKOL

Tsīko'lkol is of ordinary human form and size. He is attired in a feather suit (cīyō' ptakal), a pair of bone ear plugs (cma' kasak), a head net (kala'i), a large skewer (kanō'), a single falcon feather, a bead belt (cbū), a bead neck-band (na'mūle), and bead wrist-bands with pendants (talē'ya kūtsī).

The second heaven or upper world in which he lives is an extremely ethereal abode and is likened by informants to a summer haze. They maintain that there is earth here but that it is invisible as are all other things connected with this highest of the three worlds. It is here that Tsīko'lkol lives without any fixed abode and entirely unattended by servants or messengers. He never concerns himself with the activities of the human world or with those of his elder brother, Madū'mda. In fact, his entire existence appears to be of negative importance.

COYOTE

As already stated, Coyote was the first being in existence and we find him first floating about on a cloud and later actively regulating the affairs of earth as culture hero, and, according to some informants, actually creating the world.

He is usually depicted as in human form though he has the power of instantly transforming himself into any desired shape, animate or inanimate. Most frequently he takes the form of the mammal coyote, or as he is called "iwī'" or "diwī'" in the Pomo dialects. As the diety he is called "Iwī' Madūmda". He is without question the most important single character in all Pomo mythology and is found playing the role of culture hero and transformer on the one hand, and of trickster on the other, in a large body of myths.

He travels about the earth with supernatural rapidity working some beneficent miracle in one place or in another, next performing some malevolent deed, and interspersing these with tricky incidents.

SUPERNATURAL BEINGS

The Pomo world was originally peopled with many supernatural beings, most of which were malevolent. Some were great major beings, like Gī'lak, who endangered the ancients at every step, others were minor localized ones, like the Bagil of Blue Lakes, which rendered some particular locality dangerous to man.

Most of these major supernatural beings have been destroyed by Coyote and others. The contests between them and the culture heroes forms a large and very interesting body of myths.

Most of the local spirits, on the other hand, still survive and continue to menace man.

These supernatural beings, great and small, and their special features and attributes are here set forth in order to bring together all that we know concerning them for comparison. Many of these facts are drawn from the details given in myths while others are secured through careful questioning of informants for additional data concerning the appearance, habits, or abodes of certain of these beings.

THE SUN-PEOPLE

The Sun-people were quite numerous and were presided over by a principal sun deity called Sun-man[6] (Da'-tca). He lived originally in the Sun-house at the extreme eastern margin of the world.[7] It is pre-

---

[6] According to one informant, Sun-man is said to be the most important of the Sun-people and perhaps the most important of all supernatural beings. He is the one who regulates everything and who assigns the various other supernatural beings to their proper places.

[7] The house of Sun-man is of the usual underground Pomo dance-house type, with a tunnel and door said to be guarded by rattlesnakes, or according to one informant the fangs of rattlesnakes. The roof of this house and the area immediately surrounding the building are covered with the bleached bones of Sun-man's human victims so that the building appears from a distance to be a glistening white structure. Descriptions of it are quite the same as those of the abode of Gī'lak.

sumed that he still resides there though, since the sun was stolen from his people and placed in the heavens, little is known of him and his activities. The Sun-people are, in general, much to be feared, particularly on account of their cannibalistic habits. Ordinarily they live and eat as do human beings and resemble human beings in most every way; but they do, upon occasion, devour people.

This principal sun deity is described as being about the size of a man and as having, in general, human attributes. He is said, however, to have a very wide, immense mouth which will allow him to swallow a human being whole. He has a very big belly, a bald head and very large eyes. Stiff, hard whiskers cover his entire face.

The sun itself is supposed to be a luminous disc. There are a number of fairly elaborate myths concerning its theft from the Sun-people and its placement in the sky. The sun was suspended by a grape-vine loop passing around its periphery, a loop at its top edge serving as a holder for the grape-vine rope which passed around the neck of the Sun-man who wore the sun upon his breast.

The four Sun-messengers or Da'-tcatc, were human in form. Each wore a brightly-shining, white, feather suit which covered him from head to foot and was provided with strong wings and powerful talons. These messengers flew about over the world at the behest of their chief, Da'-tca, but whenever they returned to the Sun-house, they usually removed their suits and took on their ordinary human form.

The Sun-prophet or Sun-dreamer, Da'-matū, also had the power of flight through a suit similar to that of the Da'-tcatc but he rarely had occasion to fly. He received his information concerning the world at large from the Da'-tcatc whose special province it was to act as messengers. It was through the agencies of Da'-matū that dreams came to people. By a simple process of his will he could cause a person to have any dream he desired.

According to another informant, when the sun was stolen and the world was given light, Da'-matū took up the task of travelling with the sun and carrying it through the heavens to shed light upon its course, being attended upon his journey by the four messengers of the sun.

Another division of the sun deities was the Da'tcma, or what may be termed the Sun-executioners. They received their instructions from the Messengers whose special duty it was to fly about over the world and discover wicked individuals who should be punished. The Da'-tcma were then sent with their shining arrows to shoot such an individual with this invisible weapon and cause his death which might be either sudden or lingering. The presence of this invisible arrow or "pain" was invariably fatal unless proper treatment was administered by a medicine-man. These executioners were in readiness to receive the spirit (kū'ya) as it left the body. It appeared always as a shadow in the daytime and as a bright light at night. This they took to the Abode of the Dead at the southern extremity of the world.

The term "kū'ya" refers specifically to the spirit or soul while in the body and directly after it leaves it. As soon as it begins its life as an independent spirit or ghost it is called "tca' dūwel". According to some informants, this ghost wanders about in the woods, in the mountains and at will over the earth. According to others, at least some, and probably most of these ghosts are taken by the Sun-executioners to the Abode of the Dead which is called "tca' dūwel ma", located at the southern extremity of the world. Here is a large sweat-house presided over by Gū'ksū and called "tca' dūwel canē", "kū'ya canē" and "ho' canē", literally, ghost sweat-house, spirit sweat-house, and fire sweat-house, respectively. Here, according to some informants, these ghosts are consigned to the perpetual flames within this fire sweat-house.[8]

In cases of unconsciousness, the Pomo maintain that the spirit of the person afflicted has been taken by the Sun-executioners to the abode of the dead in the south. If Da'matū so decrees it is kept there and the patient never recovers; if not, the spirit is returned to the body and the person recovers.

Gū'ksū is always on the lookout for the arrival of new ghosts and invariably comes out to meet the Sun-executioners when they bring new spirits to his domain. He meets the Sun-executioners at the line between the human world and his own supernatural territory, and here receives the spirits and takes them to the fire sweat-house where they provide fuel for his eternal fire. According to one informant, this line between our world and that of Gū'ksū is marked by a large number of bleaching human bones strewn irregularly over the ground.

The spirits of good people are taken by certain other deities such

---

[8]According to one informant the fire burning perpetually in this sweat-house is the burning body of Hŏ'matū (Fire-prophet). The aboriginality of this conception seems doubtful.

as Danō'-matū (Mountain-prophet or Mountain-dreamer), and others, and become residents of the mountains, forests, etc.[9]

It will be seen, therefore, that the relationship existing between Gūksū and Sun-prophet is not entirely clear. Gū'ksū is the one who governs the Abode of the Dead in the south and who actually receives the spirits of the departed at the border of his domain and consigns them to their new abode.

There is no indication of a conception of division of governing power over the Abode of the Dead, but Sun-dreamer or Sun-prophet exercises a kind of judicial function down there. In case he does not approve of the coming of a spirit to this southern abode he simply sends it back and the human to whom the spirit belongs regains consciousness. Thus he might properly be considered the judge of the afterworld, for apparently each departed spirit which appears there must meet the approval of this official before he can remain. Apparently here his function ends, so far as the dead are concerned.

The only other function of Sun-prophet which was mentioned by informants was that of causing people to dream.

The remaining class of sun deities is the Da'-mata or Sun-girls. These maidens are quite numerous and seem to serve no other purpose in Pomo mythology than to ensnare young men. They are wont to appear about bodies of water, particularly lakes. They are endowed with extreme beauty and are especially attractive to hunters and others whose occupations take them into lonely places. These maidens, who are to all appearances human in every respect, are supposed to lead a man to make love to them and to finally kill him by means of their pubes which are furnished with live rattlesnakes.

Many very circumstantial accounts are given of visits by Coyote and others to the abode of the Sun-people over at the eastern edge of the world. In most of these accounts no mention is made of any one except Sun-man himself, or else the Sun-people as a group are referred to without particularization. The incidents in some of these myths are so parallel to those in the Gī'lak myths that it would seem that there

[9]There seems to be at present a conflict of ideas regarding the destiny of the spirits of the dead. It would seem likely, however, that the most truly Pomo belief is that the spirits of the good people continue to reside here on earth, in the mountains and elsewhere. The spirits of evil-doers go to this fire sweat-house in the south where they must keep Gū'ksū's perpetual fire supplied with fuel. It seems highly probable that the idea that these souls are condemned to eternal burning is purely an adaption of the missionary teachings concerning punishment.

was probably at one time an identity of these two in the Pomo mind. In one myth, in fact, we find the definite statement that "the Gī'laks owned the sun." In no other instance is the identity of the Gī'laks and the Sun-people so clearly stated, though the implication is everywhere very strong. At present, however, the two are sufficiently distinct so that they should be considered as quite separate beings. In fact one informant specifically states that they are separate beings but that the two live together in the same house.

In one of the myths we find a carefully detailed account of a visit by Falcon to the abode of Sun-man, which this time is localized within a prominent rocky peak just north of Witter Springs in Lake County. The description of the house, with its snake-guarded door, and all the incidents attendant upon the visit of Falcon are duplicates of the Gī'lak story. The localization of Sun-man's house, or of the abodes of any of the other major supernatural beings, within the confines of actual Pomo territory is most unusual. Another interesting feature of this particular account is the rationalization of the placement of this abode here. The account particularly states that Sun-man is a cannibal but that he never molests anyone living in his immediate neighborhood. He secures his food from distant parts of the world, and is on most friendly terms with his immediate neighbors so that when he and Falcon contest all the people of the region are invited to witness their exhibition of skill.

THE GILAKS

Next in importance to the Sun-people come the Gī'laks or Kī'laks, as they are called in some dialects. They are bird-like beings who soar about over the earth and carry off human beings whom they use as food. Many of the stories and exploits which deal with the Gī'laks are duplicated in the incidents relating to the Sun-people and there are some similarities found in myths relating to Thunder. These latter are almost wholly confined, for some reason or other, to the people of the immediate coastline of the ocean. Thunder as a mythological character is very rarely mentioned by those living farther inland. Why this should be it is difficult to see, for there is no particular prevalence of actual thunder heard along the coast. In fact thunder is heard only upon rare occasions anywhere in the Pomo country. It is an interesting fact also that lightning which we are wont to associate so very closely in our own minds with thunder, receives hardly passing mention in Pomo mythology.

The abode of the Gī'laks is variously placed, but its location at the far eastern margin of this earth, or in the first of the Upper Worlds at a point far to the east of the Zenith Gate, seems to be fairly well established.

The Gī'laks are cannibals and subsist entirely on human beings. Sometimes one only is mentioned, but the best accounts speak of six, an aged father and mother who live always at the Gī'lak home and four young men. The home of the Gī'laks is known to be an extremely dangerous place. It is glistening white, due to the fact that the top of the large dance-house in which they live and the area immediately surrounding it are completely covered with the bleached bones of human beings whom they have used as food.

It appears that this assembly-house which is the abode of the Gī'laks, is a large building of the usual underground dance-house type, but with four smoke-holes, one in each of the cardinal directions.

In addition to the old Gī'lak father and mother, above mentioned, there are four sons. One is assigned to each of the cardinal directions. It is his business to search about over the earth in his particular direction and to capture humans for food. Each one has his own smoke-hole, which serves him as a door. When he returns with a victim he throws it through his particular smoke-hole where it is properly disposed of by the attendant, Bottle-fly, and after he has thrown the body out, again through the smoke-hole, then Gī'lak enters.

These Gī'laks have human forms and attributes except when flying about. To accomplish this flight the Gī'lak puts on a feather suit. He can then fly about like any bird of prey. His victims are carried in his great talons, or in a hunting sack according to other informants.

One variant of this flight notion was encountered in a myth which showed Gī'lak as residing at the northern edge of the world. His suit was said to be red and to be in reality a flame blanket or blanket of fire (hō'-bata N). With this he is able to fly about at will. He flies by flapping his wings, not by sailing through the air, and when he flaps them lightning flashes.

When Gī'lak has finished his hunting for the day and starts to fly home his house trembles and creaks as a token indicating the fact and giving warning to those in the house. The sound that it makes is said to be: "tsitīt, tsitīt, tsitīt."

Upon his arrival, Gī'lak circles the house four times in each direction before lighting at his particular smoke-hole through which he then throws his live victim to the floor below.

As for the food of the Gī'laks, all agree that they live entirely on human beings. Some informants maintain that they devour all but the bones. These they throw out on top of their house. Hence the glistening whiteness of its roof and the ground surrounding it, due to the bleaching bones. One informant likened Gī'lak's house to a snow-capped mountain. Others maintain that it is the blood only, and possibly the marrow, which is used as food. According to one informant their food consists solely of human flesh and blood. If anyone succeeds in visiting them he is offered, in accordance with good Pomo custom, food as soon as he arrives. However, this food is very dangerous. The mush and bread consist of human blood. The meat offered them is human flesh. The fish offered them consists of the meat of rattlesnakes and bull-snakes.

BOTTLE-FLY

The Gī'laks keep as a slave and servant Bottle-fly or Blue-fly, (bita'-tsamō C or bita'ka-tsamō C, literally "bear-fly"). By some Blue-fly is said to be a one-eyed old woman. By others she is said to be very lame. One informant stated that she hangs from the roof of the house by means of a grape-vine binder which holds her prisoner. Others make no mention of this but simply state that she is a slave of the Gī'laks.

When a human being is brought in, it is the duty of Blue-fly to break, with a pestle, the bones, particularly those of the shins; and then to extract the blood from the body and the marrow from the bones. She then throws this maimed individual back out through the smoke-hole, where he dies a lingering death on the roof. It is only after the work of Blue-fly has been finished that Gī'lak enters.

The Zenith Gate is the only means of entering or leaving the Upper World. Spider, who is the guard at this gate permits Gī'lak to pass at any time he likes. Spider is very much afraid of Gī'lak.

In addition to the four smoke-holes in Gī'lak's home there is a door. It is located on the south side, as is customary in Pomo assembly-houses, and has the usual tunnel. At this door there is a trap which means death to any unwary visitor. According to some accounts this is some kind of a spring-trap or snare which catches the victim and throws him over against the rear wall of the house. There is a second, similar mechanism a little farther in, so that if the intended victim should escape the first device he will be caught by the second. The more prevalent idea concerning this trap is that it is not a mechanical device but a large number of rattlesnakes in the tunnel and about the door. One myth states that this trap consists of rattlesnake fangs instead of the actual snakes themselves.

The only possibility of entering the house of Gī'lak is to first spring this trap, and many stories are told of those who have gone to contest with Gī'lak, who did this. The hero would carry a large bead grinding-stone which he would insert in the door. It would be caught by the trap and thrown far back into the house, or the mother whom the hero had come to rescue would throw a pestle into the tunnel. The rattle-snakes would strike at it, dislodge themselves from the door-frame and tunnel walls and fight among themselves until they were all killed. In either case the visitor could enter with safety.

Various accounts exist of people who have gone to Gī'lak's house but practically none save Coyote, or someone directly under his patron-age, ever did so and remained normal after his return to earth. Even though he had been rescued from Gī'lak's house intact such a person died after his return or enroute home.

THUNDER

Relatively few myths concerning Thunder appear in our present series and these are confined to sources on the coast. In fact the attri-butes of Thunder and his abode are so similar to those more frequently mentioned for Gī'lak that there seems considerable probability that there is a close relationship between, if not indeed an actual identity of, the two.

Thunder's house is quite like that of Gī'lak, its door being guarded by a trap.

In one myth the abode of Thunder is said to be located across the ocean and at the western edge of the world. His house is filled with all sorts of snakes.

Another description, which is quite detailed, places the abode of Thunder at Big River on the coast of Mendocino County.

A very extraordinary conception of Thunder is given in one myth. There is a reef just north of Point Arena on the Mendocino coast where the water is constantly agitated and where there is always more or less white foam. Directly below here is the abode of Thunder.

He lives in a very large crystal-clear house in which, though the interior is said to be absolutely dry, there are imprisoned myriads of fish of different species. He has a door to this house which is operated by a tremendous lever. When he opens this door, even slightly, great numbers of fish escape and run up the rivers to spawn. The Garcia River flows directly to this building and the salmon go up this stream in vast numbers.

In his house, Thunder has some kind of a reflector which shows him everything that everyone is doing. When he moves, even slightly, a loud clap of thunder is heard. It is said that whenever it thunders the sound always starts from this spot. Under his armpit, Thunder has a square piece of crystalline substance. When he takes this out and moves it about, lightning flashes as the result. If he were to hold this device out from under his arm for any considerable time, everyone would go blind and the world would burn up.

It is said that relatively little is known about Thunder and his abode for the reason that this is such a dangerous place that no one dares venture near it. Not even the most powerful medicine-man would venture so much.

Loeb[9a] says that in his investigation he gathered that Thunder was an important personage among Pomo deities, and fairly full descriptions of him were obtained. One informant stated that he had a white skin and long hair, that he had a buzzard feather suit which he donned when he wished to fly about. The rapid flapping of his wings caused the sound of thunder. Lightning was caused by something bright under his wings. According to another conception the sound of thunder was produced when this deity shook his abalone-shell coat. His eyes were made of abalone shell and when he winked the lightning flashed.

GUKSU

As has been previously stated, Gū′ksū or Kū′ksū[10] is a supernatural being who lives at the southern extremity of the world. His special

---

[9a]Op. cit., p. 301, 1926A.
[10]The term "kū′ksū" (C) is also applied to an insect called locally the "gallinipper".

function is that of doctoring the sick. Various accounts are given of his being called to doctor Coyote for instance. He, it seems, is permanently dressed in the regulation Gū′ksū "big-head" head-dress and in the other elaborate doctoring paraphernalia. Other mythical characters sometimes attire themselves in similar outfits and try to perform cures but they always fail. Finally the real Gū′ksū himself appears and performs the cure. In impersonation of this supernatural shaman, human doctors attire themselves and perform cures.

It is said that there is a close connection between Gū′ksū and Fireman (hō-tca), who has the ability to transform himself at will into a gū′ksū.

Gū′ksū has the ability to travel at great speed. As one informant put it, "Gū′ksū travels everywhere just as the clouds do."

Another conception of Gū′ksū is that he is the ruler of the Abode of the Dead which is located at the southern extremity of the world. He receives the souls of the departed who are brought there by the Sun-executioners.

Around this class of supernatural beings centers a rather elaborate ceremonial system in which Gū′ksū is impersonated and an elaborate series of dances and dramatizations are performed by members of a secret organization. This whole subject has been elsewhere treated at length.[11] Dr. Kroeber[12] has further discussed the Guksu Cult as it is found throughout Central California; two recent papers[13] treat of the Kuksu Cult in great detail throughout this North Central California region from the high Sierra Maidu on the east through to the Coastal Pomo and others on the west.

Associated with the several impersonators of Gū′ksū in the Pomo ceremony is a single actor impersonating Ca′lnis who is presumably identical with the creator Madū′mda.

OBSIDIAN-MAN

There seems to be a close connection between the supernatural being, Obsidian-man, (Katca-tca C, E) and the Gray Squirrel. No very full description has been given of Obsidian-man's physique, but

[11]Barrett, S. A., Ceremonies of the Pomo Indians, Univ. Calif. Publ., Arch. Ethn., Vol 12, pp. 397-441, 1917.
[12]Kroeber, A. L., Handbook of the Indians of California, Bur. Amer. Ethn., Bull. 78, 1925.
[13]Loeb, E. M., The Western Kuksu Cult and The Eastern Kuksu Cult, Univ. Calif. Publ., Amer. Arch. Ethn., Vol. 33, pp. 1-232, 1933.

we know that he originated from an obsidian arrowpoint which was shot into the body of Coyote when Coyote was found stealing the fish from basketry traps in a fish dam.

This miraculous boy was not received too kindly by the other people of the village, and it was only through Coyote's careful teaching that he was instructed so that he could preserve his own life. He won all the various contests that he was subjected to during his youth; and developed into a man who was extremely rapid in his movements, a wonderful dodger of arrows, and who had the very special gift of being able to chop down brush or even large trees with a single stroke. Whenever he goes out to get wood for the sweat-house he jumps into an area of brush and cuts the bushes down almost instantly. When he gets into a contest with Mountain-man he demonstrates his ability at cutting, by felling with a single stroke of his hand a tree of almost any diameter. It is said that he can cut with either right or left hand, or right or left foot, with equal ease.

In the myth relating to the contest between Mountain-man and Obsidian-man, it is related that when Obsidian-man returned to Mt. Kanaktai, he got caught in some brush and that his body broke into many pieces. For this reason there is a very large area, several square miles in extent, on the southern slope of Mt. Kanaktai that is now covered with blocks and pieces of obsidian of all sizes.

This seems a very strange explanation of the presence of obsidian here when we read in a number of other places, including the same myth, where Obsidian-man was able to cut down great trees or cut up large areas of brush with the utmost ease, due to the fact that his body had the cutting qualities of obsidian.

According to another myth the presence of this obsidian on the south slope of Mt. Kanaktai is accounted for by the fact that Obsidian-man in descending the mountain heard a noise toward the north and, in turning around to see what this noise was, his long hair became entangled in the brush. He jerked so hard to free himself that he fell over and his body broke into pieces.

According to another myth Obsidian-man still lives in a big sulphur spring near Calistoga.

ROCK-WOMAN

At a point very far to the south there lives Rock-woman (Kabē-mata) in her "Rock-woman's house" (Kabē-mata tca). This supernatural being is a woman made out of stone but who looks entirely human. Anyone who ever enters this house never returns alive. Just beyond, to the south of this little house in which Kabe-mata lives, there is a great rock wall. The rocks are vertical and they extend clear up to the sky. There is but one narrow opening here through which one may pass. Just beyond this rock wall there is a great valley. This opening in the rock wall closes suddenly and crushes anyone who attempts passage beyond the rock wall unless he has the proper magic to enable him to pass.

MOUNTAIN-MAN

Mountain-man (Danō'-tca) is said by one informant to be next in power to Sun-man. He is said to have control of the Water-people and everyone else on "top" of the ground: the valleys, the deer, the brush, water and everything above ground.

One informant states that Mountain-man has various shapes, and that he is sometimes as much as a hundred feet in height, and that he varies from this down to the stature of a man. By this he means, of course, that there are many of these beings and that they vary in size as above indicated. Mountain-man wears no clothing at all, and he is of the consistency of smoke or of a shadow.

This description of Mountain-man does not agree with some of the other descriptions which give him a very material body consisting of rock covered with trees, brush, grass, etc.

Mountain-man is quite fully described in one of the myths as a giant, about forty to fifty feet in diameter and about twenty feet in height, who in certain respects resembles a turtle, particularly in his bodily form. He has arms, legs, a mouth and other members and items like a human being, but he has no skin. His body is completely covered with grass and low bushes, (about two feet in height). He has a very high-keyed voice and has prodigious weight and strength. So great is his power that he can, by running against a huge tree, knock it over; or he can knock down a great pile of stones by running against it. The contest between Obsidian-man and Mountain-man is a very interesting myth.

Ya'koda is a creek, now called Elk Creek, about two miles south of Greenwood. In the creek at this point, there is a very deep pool. In fact there is a cave which runs back under the mountain here and this makes the water very deep and blue. It is in this cave that the spirit of Mountain-man still dwells. It is a very dangerous place to visit; many people have been drowned here, because when they go into this deep pool the spirit of Mountain-man drags them down and puts them to death.

Along the edge of this pool, there is a considerable area of quick-sand; and if a stranger passes this way he is sure to go down in this soft material and lose his life. This sand is not always soft. It is sometimes hard, so that one never can tell whether it is safe to journey this way or not. It is made soft this way by the spirit of Mountain-man to serve as a trap for people.

BRUSH-MAN

Brush-man (Seē-tca) is a supernatural being, similar in some respects to Mountain-man. Perhaps our best conception of him may be obtained from the following account.

A certain man by the name of Cache Creek Albert went hunting one day up on Mt. Kanaktai, despite the fact that his father-in-law had told him never to go hunting there because it was a very dangerous place. Furthermore it happened that Albert's wife was at this time passing through a menstrual period, when it is strictly forbidden any man to go hunting.

Presently he saw something on this mountain which looked strange. Its body was covered with feathers, brush and hair. He walked up to it and hit it with a rock. Then he returned home and soon both he and his wife were very sick. His father-in-law knew then that he had been out on Mt. Kanaktai hunting.

In four or five days Albert's wife died. Then they took Albert back over to his old home on Cache Creek and there he told his mother about what he had seen and told her that he could not drive the vision away. He had seen Brush-man, and Brush-man had told him that he was going to have him, and that he would let him know very shortly when he was to die. Albert was sick for quite a long time and before he died he had sprouted feathers and brush and hair all over his body and when he did die his abdomen was very greatly distended. After he died leaves and feathers and such things ran out of his abdomen.

Another thing that Brush-man had told Albert was that when he died it would snow and on that very day it snowed very hard indeed.[14]

FIRE-MAN

Fire-man (Hō'tca) is an individual concerning whom relatively little is known. The accepted conception of him seems to be that he is an indestructible, unextinguishable fire, which looks very much like an ordinary wood-fire. One myth recounts how one character who was making an extended journey met Fire-man and upon being refused a request he took a club and beat the fire all out thus killing Fire-man. As soon as he had passed on, however, Fire-man came to life again and went right on burning as lively as ever.

No account has thus far been found which shows Fire-man as having human form, though he has the power of speech and other human attributes.

One informant stated that he has the ability to, at will, transform himself into Gū'ksū.

By some it is said that the abode of Fire-man is the fire sweat-house at the southern extremity of the world, and in the land to which the spirits of the departed are consigned and where they are received by Gū'ksū who presides over this Abode of the Dead.

PUTRID-MAN

Putrid-man (Pa-tca) is an individual of human form, but composed of a very soft and putrid smelling material. He has all the usual human attributes of speech and the like but is indestructible. By most he is supposed to be a net-maker, constantly weaving nets of various kinds. One informant mentioned him as an arrow-maker. This Pomo term "pa" refers to any putrid material with a fetid odor, especially to excrement.

WIND-MAN

The descriptions given of Wind-man (Ya'-tca) are quite meager. He is said to have four legs, very long ears, and a body covered with

---

[14]Informants says that it is very dangerous for anyone to hunt on the north and east slopes of Mt. Kanaktai, but that it is possible to hunt on the south and west sides of the mountain without danger. The fact of the matter is that Mt. Kanaktai is part of an extinct volcano. The north and east sides of this mountain are very precipitous and are formed by the crater wall of the old volcano. The south and west sides have a relatively moderate slope.

dark yellow hair. He causes the wind to blow so violently whenever he desires that he can blow people around at will. The wind is always blowing to such an extent where he is that no grass can grow near him.

According to one myth he resides far to the south, at a place called "Nemehī napō."

Another informant localizes Wind-man in Potter Valley at a place called "Ya mō", near the head of the valley. His house is under the ground. He makes a noise early in the morning which you can hear if you are near this locality, but you can never see him. Obviously this is a place where it is considered to be dangerous for humans to linger and if a person has occasion to pass this way he does so as expeditiously as possible.

SHADE-MAN

No particular importance seems to be attached to Shade-man. He is a being, human in form, size and all other respects. His only special characteristic is his black color.

WATER-MAN

Water-man has the form of a human being, but is very much larger. He has very big eyes which protrude like those of a snail, and a big, protruding belly. His hair is very long. You always see him sitting in the water, "holding his arms." His hair floats down with the current. Fish play around his body and through the strands of his hair. In fact it is Water-man who has control of all fish, frogs, water-snakes and other water-life, and is in control of springs, ponds, lakes and rivers. He is the one who is responsible for the movement of the water. He controls the waves and ripples in lakes and rivers.

He sometimes comes out and sits on logs or on rocks, but if he sees a human being coming toward him he immediately goes under the water again. He particularly keeps in the deep pools, far back under the bank of a stream or the shore of a lake. In fact, there is one of these super-natural people to be found in every deep pool in a river or lake. When he comes out on land it is always in some swampy place.

Informants say that they never have heard of his doing anything tricky or doing any damage to human beings. He can change his form; he may become a fish or any of the water mammals. He may become either a woman or a man. When he is in his normal form, however, his body is all water.

It is said that he does not show himself to everyone. He is particularly likely to show himself to someone who has done wrong. If a person sees him, it is very likely that that person may become scared. Seeing such a Water-man may on the other hand give a person good luck.

He is particularly likely to be seen by fishermen, especially those who dive into the water to drive the fish toward a net or toward a fish dam, because such men dive down into the deep pools and feel around among the rocks and roots of the trees to drive the fish out. If such a man does see one of these supernatural beings, he is very likely to dream that night when he goes home and he will be told just what to do by this Water-man. If he does not do what he is told in his dream he will certainly have bad luck. If he follows instructions he will have good luck.

In case a man does have bad luck in connection with fishing, he always goes out to gather medicine roots at some point in the valley near a river, just as he would gather roots to give him good luck in gambling. If such roots are properly used they will give good luck in fishing and will remove any bad luck caused by Water-man.

SHARP HEEL

This is a malevolent woman who kills people while they sleep by stabbing them with her heel which she keeps very sharp. This may be the same person referred to by one informant as Whittled-leg-widow.

HUK

The Hūk is said to be a large bird similar to a wild turkey in size and general form. It has, however, the foot of a deer and looks just like a deer from the knees down. It has a bare, red head like that of a turkey. Its beak is straight and broad. Its feathers are peculiar in that each quill is partly filled with a reddish liquid which always runs up hill no matter how you hold it. The feathers are not all of one kind, in fact there are many different kinds of feathers on its body, also the hair of different mammals and the leaves of various bushes and trees.

This being lives down in springs and at various places under the water. That is to say, it does not live in the water but lives in the ground under the water. Anyone seeing this bird may do so without special danger, provided the bird does not call to him. If a person is unfortunate enough to hear it cry "hūk" he is doomed. He will live as many years as this being cries "hūk" at him.

There is only one way to prevent death from this source. If a person is properly doctored by a medicine-man who knows the correct ritual to prevent the "hūk death" he may be cured.

If anyone kills one of these birds he will himself die immediately and every person living in his village will become insane.

It is said by some that the Hūk has something to do with the rainbow. Just what it is could not be learned.

SPRING-MAN

Spring-man (Kapa'-tca) is a dwarf with very large round eyes, who lives in springs. He is not especially dangerous but is looked upon with some fear. It is said that there is still another Spring-man quite like this one, but who has no face at all.

SPRING-BABY

This being, called "Kapa'-kū", is a baby which is sometimes found near a spring. It apparently looks like a normal child which has been abandoned by some mother at this spring. Finding such a baby will make the finder sick.

PCE-DAM

Pcē'-dam is a white deer. It is always considered to bode ill to see a white deer.

PCE-STU

This is a very diminutive deer with large horns. Pcē'-stū is supposed to possess great power and often a medicine man invokes its aid in curing disease. This is, of course, done by songs.

DAKO-TCUWAK

This individual has human form, with the peculiarity that in one ear he wears a stone pestle in place of an ear-plug. The other ear carries a large and elaborately decorated bone ear-plug. Dakō'-tcūwak can walk about on top of a white oak tree just as anyone else would walk on the ground.

IWE-TCA

One informant mentioned also the Iwē-tca, a spirit who lives in the mountains but concerning which little other information could be given.

CAKA-TCA

Another being, Caka'-tca, was also mentioned. No detailed information concerning him was given.

BAGIL

This particular kind of supernatural being seems to be quite numerous and to be located in many places. The descriptions vary considerably concerning them. One which was caught in a rabbit snare is described as a lizard-like animal, six to eight feet long, with a tail like that of a salmon and a body striped like that of a watersnake. This one lived in a hole in the ground.

Another description shows the Bagil to be a great serpent living in Blue Lakes in Lake County. On his head he wears inverted a red-feathered basket (what is commonly spoken of as a "sun basket"). Across his forehead passes a yellow-hammer-feather band, and on the sides of his head is a large pair of deer horns. His eyes are made of abalone shell and they glint in the sunlight. Another description adds a network covering for the body, this net being ornamented with abalone shells. Also a bead belt about his middle and a bead necklace. Several myths in the following pages give further interesting information concerning the Bagil. (See myths 43-45.)

One myth recounts that this whole class of monsters originated through the transformation by the culture hero of the Sun-people into Bagils.

It is not at all uncommon to find among aboriginal myths in many localities tales of great water-serpents. The origin of this concept is sometimes hard to fathom. In this particular case, however, it may be a rationalization of a purely natural phenomenon. There is in Blue Lakes a small species of fish, which, at spawning time moves in a great shoal perhaps a hundred feet in length by several feet in width, up and down the lake. When this is seen from a considerable elevation it looks not unlike a great serpent moving through the water. This is possibly what has given rise to the belief by the Pomo that the three Blue Lakes are the abode of one of these great serpent monsters. To see such aggregations of fish from a considerable elevation here at Blue Lakes may be very easy indeed, for the hills surrounding these lakes rise very abruptly.

A rather different conception of the Bagil idea is given by Loeb[14a] where we find that there is a single Bagil only, a female water monster who can take at will any desired form, particularly that of a serpent. She is the sister of Gï'lak, with whom she goes about at times to frighten people who have violated taboos.

DATALALI

A minor being in human form whose habit is to steal babies, and to entice older people away and cause them to become mentally unbalanced, or at least a little queer, is the class of spirits called "Data'lalī" (C).

A fairly clear indication of the behavior of these spirits is shown by the account given by one Central Pomo informant, which is as follows:

At a place called "Bo'tcimat", located on the McNab Ranch south of Hopland and a short distance south of the ranch house, there formerly lived a man and woman who had a baby boy. The woman was making pinole. They were not at the village at this time but had gone to a place called "Kabē bot" a little farther to the south.

The man was out hunting and a Data'lalī came and took the baby away from the woman. When the Data'lalī appeared, the woman was very much afraid and did not talk to him. In fact she did not even look up at all. He carried the boy away, the woman following along, crying after him.

The Data'lalī took the child into his house, which is inside of the rocks not far from this spot. The woman followed along to the entrance and looked in. Then she became afraid and returned home.

When her husband returned to the camp he found his wife crying and asked why. She told him that the Data'lalī had carried the baby away. He took his bow and arrows and the woman showed him the entrance to the house of the Data'lalī. Upon entering they saw a great many of the Data'lalī in the house and they were taking turns carrying the baby around and as they did so they were all repeating over and over again "data'lalī, data'lalī, data'lalī."[15]

[14a]Op. Cit., p. 303, 1926A.

[15]The term "data'lalī" could not be exactly translated, but it was learned that when a person is holding something very loosely and drops it, someone will always say "data'lalī kamabem."

Finally the man jumped into the center of the house and took the baby away from them, but as he did so the Data'lalī said that the baby would die before morning and that is exactly what happened. As a result no one ever camps close to this place now.

The informant stated that his own grandmother, not more than a year previous to the time he was giving this information, got lost one day and she was led around by some supernatural being in this same vicinity. The informant thinks that it was one of the Data'lalī. Always after that he was very much afraid that the old lady would wander off again and be led away by some one of these supernatural beings so that he used to chain her in camp to prevent this occurrence.

He also knew of another case where a woman was led away two or three times by some supernatural beings out in that same neighborhood. Finally they found her dead there one day.

MUYAMUYA

Mū'yamūya was a giant about nine or ten feet in height and very heavy who was said to be indestructible. He was much disliked by the people. Many attempts were made to kill him but without success, until finally it was discovered that under the nail of the great toe on his right foot there was a tiny hard kernel. This was his heart and when this toe was cut off he died. Myths numbers 52 and 53 give the details of this incident.

THUNDER-FISH

The Thunder-fish (makē'la-ca) is said by one informant to be a small fish, about five or six inches in length, which looks something like a trout, but is slightly different in appearance. When these fish are taken out of the creek it always commences to thunder. The creek where they live is a short distance south of Bridgeport on the coast and is called "Makē'la pda". The water in this creek never runs into the ocean. It always remains just as you see it. There are no dangerous mammals in this immediate vicinity. This is obviously a very dangerous place for human beings to visit.

In addition to the above, each of which is specifically described, we may add several other spirits which were included in a list secured from informants who provided the detailed information concerning Pomo

Bear doctors.[15a] These are Night-man, Valley-man, Disease-man, Insanity-man, Whitled-Leg-Widow, Dream-man, Pond-man, Blind-man, and Deer-man. There are also Flower-man and Tco'dok.

MAGIC PLACES

Many spots are invested by the Pomo with magic attributes. Springs, rocks, caves, hills, mountains; in fact any spot which has some real or fancied peculiarity may serve as the abode of one or more spirits. Some of these are benevolent spirits but most of them are malevolent ones. Hence, as a rule, such magic places are fraught with danger to the unwary visitor who finds himself in that vicinity.

Many tales are told of the dangers attendant upon seeing Waterman, Bagil or others of the same class of spirits. Likewise hearing the cry of Hūk in an ill omen. Certain places, like the precipitous northern and eastern sides of Mt. Kanaktai, must be shunned by hunters.

Mention was also made by informants of several localities and spots where danger lurks:

1. Red Mountain (Ma'kīsil) is said to be a very bad place for people to visit. When the great World-fire came this was the only place that did not burn. It got so hot, however, that the top of the mountain turned red and that is why it is called Red Mountain.

2. A place called "Kabē' bot", south of the McNab Ranch, is known as a magic place and is a spot particularly known to hunters.

3. Another place west of the McNab ranch, and called "Cma'kapa", is a magic spot where the wind never stops blowing.

4. A place on the McNab Ranch, and called "Kō'm ka", is a magic spot which always gives off a bad odor. It is said that in olden times people used to steal clothing, basketry, hair and any other personal articles that could be found and put these on Kō'm ka. While informants did not specifically say so, it is to be presumed that the placing of these objects here was an act of magic which would do some sort of damage to the owner.

5. An old man had for a long time had poor luck in hunting. One day he went out hunting as usual and was taken by Deer to his home which was located inside of a mountain.

When he did not return to the village the people hunted for him everywhere but could not find him and finally they mourned him as dead

---

[15a]Barrett, 1917a, pp. 459, 460.

for they thought he had been stolen by Gī'lak or that he had been killed by bears.

The deer showed the old man why it was that he had no luck in hunting any more. He made a big fire in his house and made the old man go round and round the fire and made him sweat profusely. He killed all the vermin on the old man and cleansed him thoroughly. He also cleansed his bow and his arrows. Then the deer taught him the proper song to bring him good luck in deer hunting. He told him that if he wanted to have good hunting luck he must have nothing to do with the women of his village and he must never go hunting during his wife's menstruation.

He then gave the old man a deer-head mask and gave him a very fine bow and fine arrows and instructed him that under no consideration was he to let anyone know where he had obtained these things and he must not take them home, but must keep them hidden away from any contact with women or children.

After that the old man had excellent hunting luck and could kill deer at any time.

The mountain in which this deer's house was located was called "Haiū kalel" (tree white) and the deer's house is called "Pcē cenē" (deer sweat-house).

6. At the mouth of Elk Creek "Ya'kōda pda" (E) there is a dangerous spot and this is a place where many people have lost their lives by sinking down into it.

METHODS OF STORY TELLING

It is customary among the Pomo to tell stories and recount myths only at night and among the older informants there were those who declined to recount the stories during the daytime, even to a white man, on the ground that it was strictly against custom.

The reason for this custom is that if this rule is disobeyed the one who recounts the myth will become hunchbacked and also the telling of a story in the daytime makes night come quickly.

Another rule is that the listeners may not sit erect during the recounting of a myth. If they do they will become hunchbacked.

The term "xaē'lī" (E) signifies a story I have heard, that is to say, a quotation from someone else, the authenticity of which is not guaranteed. It is something that the narrator never saw or experienced and therefore cannot prove in case of doubt.

The expression "min xaē'lī dok" (E) signifies, "Once upon a time there was." This expression is used as a beginning of a fairy tale or story and is frequently used by narrators in this sense.

In contradistinction to this "īhība" or "mīnba īhība" (E) signifies something that the narrator saw with his own eyes. It is equivalent to, "I saw it myself."

The term "marū'" (E) is practically synonymous with the term "xaē'lī" (E) but there seems to be some fine distinction between the two which was not made clear.

In the Central dialect the term for myth is "matū'", while the telling of a myth or story is referred to as "matū'matū". The term for myth in the eastern dialect is "marū'".

There is a set ritualistic ending for myths which must always be employed. In the Eastern dialect this is cōhla*t* bōhla*t* in we'lai xaian maiaūwa'lala welai xaa'pī xataiinhimai. (From the east and from the west may the Mallard girls hurry and bring the morning).

In the Central dialect this formula is slightly different. It is as follows: yō'l   hwat,   tūla'l   hwat,   bō'   hwat,   cō'   hwat,

   cō-mī   ka-a   kai-yan   yan   cīl-ckan   ka   na-hī   boli
ītsesē   dūtc-kam-men   īhīmī   hlan   kaa' cbak-tcī   kam.

This ending is supposed to make the daylight come quickly. The "Kaa'-kaiyan" (literally "Daylight-duck") is a very bright, shiny, white duck which precedes the dawn. Every time this bird moves it produces a little light. These birds come only at certain seasons and very few people have ever seen them. The above ending is a prayer that these Daylight-ducks may come quickly and bring the daylight very soon.

THE POMO MYTHOLOGICAL SYSTEM

As is the case with practically all mythological systems, that of the Pomo is based upon the assumption that there was a time when everything was the opposite of what it is now. All these conditions were changed to those of the present. Such changes must be accounted for. Myths concerning these changes have arisen. Some concern great and important matters, some relate to very minor ones, but all are important in the system and together they form a rather complex religion.

Many of these myths relate to one or another of the supernatural beings already mentioned, but there is a very large series of stories which deal with those people who formerly inhabited the earth but who were later transformed in one way or another into the birds, mammals and other forms of life which we now have about us. These first people are commonly referred to as the "Bird-people".

We will now proceed to the recounting of this body of myths, after which we will take up a further discussion and comparison of their important features and indicate similarities between the myths of the Pomo and those of adjacent tribes.

MYTHS OF CREATION AND TRANSFORMATION OF HUMAN BEINGS

1—FALCON BRINGS FOOD FROM ACROSS THE OCEAN[16]

INCIDENTS AND CHARACTERS

I. *Falcon kills geese with a magic sling.*
    1. *Coyote*, 2. *Falcon (grandson of Coyote)*, 3. *Magic sling.*

II. *Falcon secures food from across the ocean.*
    1. *Falcon*, 2. *Magic canoe*, 3. *Four tokens*, 4. *Thrasher brothers*, 5. *Condor*, 6. *Fish Hawk*, 7. *Blue Jay brothers*, 8. *Red-headed-woodpecker brothers*, 9. *Cloud*, 10. *Coyote.*

III. *Coyote creates people from feathers.*
    1. *Coyote*, 2. *Falcon*, 3. *Mole*, 4. *Gopher*, 5. *Ground Squirrel*, 6. *Woodrat*, 7. *Blue Jay*, 8. *Panther*, 9. *Wildcat.*

IV. *Putrid-man and Falcon gamble.*
    1. *Putrid-man*, 2. *Falcon*, 3. *Blue Jay.*

V. *Falcon transforms himself into an elk and goes to Kī'lak's house.*
    1. *Falcon*, 2. *Elk*, 3. *Kī'laks.*

VI. *The ancients are transformed into birds and mammals.*
    1. *Falcon*, 2. *Blue Jay.*

I

(Falcon Kills Geese with a Magic Sling)

Coyote and Falcon lived together in one house in a village called Kō'mtil, on the headwaters of Big River (Bū'lpda). They were the only people in this village. Coyote was Falcon's grandfather. They were both very hungry. Falcon went out and found some geese sitting in a field. He came back and told Coyote what he had seen and asked how he could kill them. Coyote gave Falcon a sling and a round stone and told him how to use these. Falcon went out and shot this stone at the geese and it went around from one to the other until it had killed every goose in the flock. Then Falcon held up his hand and the stone flew back into it. The next morning he went to the same place and did the same way. He did this way for four days.

---

[16]The Pomo title of this myth is, "Cĕ'mĭ iwi-ya katsa'mtiū de tata-ya ka-bo-wal maa' ba dakal duman nun ke matu de", in olden times Coyote . . , Falcon across the ocean steals food, it is said.
Informant: Bob Pot, Garcia River, Northern dialect, 1906.

II

(Falcon Secures Food from across the Ocean)

On the night following the fourth day, Coyote dreamed. He jumped up out of a sound sleep.

Falcon asked him, "What is the matter? What did you dream? Did you dream about women or the grass game or what?"

Coyote said, "Well, I dreamed I saw food and acorns which grew over across the ocean and I dreamed you went over after these."

Falcon then asked Coyote for arrows and a bow, a quiver, beads and clothes to wear. Coyote got the things together, putting the beads in a little fawn-skin bag.

Falcon then told his grandfather, "I am going away in the morning. There will be no one here to pack wood for you or build a fire for you."

He then started west and finally arrived at the ocean. He stopped on the shore and wished that a canoe might come along; and very soon, a green canoe came up to the shore. This canoe was long like a water trough. It had two paddles and a rope made of grass. Falcon took a head-skewer or hair-pin made of mountain mahogany and, tying some feathers on one end, he stuck it into the bank on the shore. He told this skewer to shout and make a big noise for him when he came back, in order that he might know the way to return. He did not, however, tell it just what to say. He then went down and stepped into the canoe. The canoe started off toward the west and traveled on until they had gone about half their journey. Falcon then took another skewer, this time made of oak, and having tied a top-knot of owl feathers (makū'gū kaaitcil, owl top-knot) to it, stuck this down into the water for this was a very shallow place so that the skewer was fast in the ground. He told this token to say "hu-hu huhu hu-hu-hu ku ku ku ku ku ku ku ku," (the last being in a sort of heavy whistle), just the same sort of a sound an owl would make. He went on some distance farther and put down another skewer, this time made of the wood called "cta-hai". To this one he tied a top-knot of blue-jay feathers and it kept crying "tsai tsai tsai tsai tsai tsai." Some distance farther on, he took five arrows and stuck those down in the water. They were feathered with fish-hawk feathers and they made a noise like the call of that bird, a sort of whistling sound.

After a while, he came near land over on the west side of the ocean and approached a sandy shore, edged with tule. A little way offshore, he put another arrow down in the water and told it, "Now, when I am ready to come back, you must tell me 'Come on, come on; come this way. Come on, come on; come this way.'" Falcon's quiver was made of coyote skin and this barked like a coyote. Whenever he swung it, it would say, "ma' ma." As Falcon approached the shore, his quiver barked and the people on shore, hearing this strange noise, said among themselves, "Hear that noise. Something is going to happen. We must be going to have a war."

The chief of the village then addressed the people. He appointed two brothers, Thrasher (wocwoc), to stand watch over the village. He said, "You brothers are always awake to watch around. You had better go down and watch now."

So these two went out to a tree over the trail and sat there and frequently gave their cry. They thought by this means that Falcon would believe everybody in the village awake. Falcon waited for quite a while, but finally he concluded that the people must be trying to fool him and decided that he would go up anyhow.

The chiefs, Condor (Sūl) and Fish Hawk (Batcal), told the Blue Jay brothers, "You two are always bragging how wide awake you are and how you never sleep. Now is your time to show it. You go up by the door to watch there and see that no one comes in." They also told the Red-headed-woodpecker brothers, "You two fellows are never sleepy. You had better go up on the center pole and watch there to see who is coming."

So the Woodpeckers went up on the center pole to watch and the Blue Jays took their posts near the door. They had their bows and arrows all ready to shoot if somebody should come by; but all of these guards went to sleep, just as everybody else did.

Falcon finally came to the sweat-house and found everybody asleep, so he went in and began to braid their hair. He braided the hair of the Blue Jays first and then went right around the house, braiding the hair of each person to that of the two people lying next to him. He then went out and visited each one of the houses of the village, braiding the hair of everyone in each house in the same manner. From each house, he removed all the acorns, all the baskets of bread and everything good to eat. He had some hunting sacks into which he put all these good things. Then he broke open the houses. He took all of the food and went back to the shore, passing under the tree where the Thrasher men were still singing.

He then got into his canoe and started back across the ocean, guided by the tokens which he had left on his way over. He pulled up each token as he came to it. If he had not done this, the tokens would have made a great deal of noise after he had passed, for many people were pursuing him. He finally arrived at the point on the coast where he had left the first one of the tokens. He made this return journey very quickly because he wished all the way that he should get to land soon. After he had landed, he wished that the canoe would go away and it did. Then he said, "I want to get home before dark and when I get there I will find my grandfather singing."

One man, Cloud, was pursuing Falcon but he could not catch him.

Falcon went on toward home and, as he approached the house, he found Coyote singing.

Coyote asked, "Is that you coming?"

Falcon said, "Yes, it is I."

Coyote then asked, "How are you getting along? Did those people see you or hurt you?"

Falcon said, "O, I am getting along all right. Nobody hurt me and I got back all right. I think I can beat at anything people try to do against me. You better get outside, old man, and see my empty sacks and see what is there."

Coyote then went outside and found the sacks so full that he could not lift one, to say nothing of carrying it. He took out some bread and ate it and went again into the house.

Falcon stopped and picked up the sacks with his fingers and brought them in, saying, "Why, what is the matter, grandfather? There is nothing in those sacks."

III

(Coyote Creates People from Feathers)

Coyote again dreamed and Falcon asked him what he had dreamed about.

Coyote said, "I dreamed about building a sweat-house." There were no people at this village, but Coyote dreamed about building a sweat-house anyway.

Falcon said, "We will do what you dream. I do not know much about building a sweat-house or where we will get people but we will do what you dream, anyway."

Coyote talked a long time that evening. He talked just as a chief does when he addresses the people of his village. He said, "Now you fellows must get up early in the morning and we will build a sweat-house." He then appointed Mole(wūn), Gopher(lam), Ground Squirrel(mke), and Woodrat(baiyok) to dig the pit. He said, "Twenty people must go and get the poles to make the rafters, twenty others must get the material to make the matting, and twenty others must get the grass."

These last two materials were to make the covering for the roof. These people finally finished building the sweat-house.

Coyote was absent when the people finished building the sweat-house. No one, not even Falcon knew where he had gone. He had gone off somewhere and was getting a lot of bird feathers. While he was gone, he wished that the people would make a great number of dwelling-houses, which they did. Finally, he came back with the feathers, which he distributed in the different houses. There were baskets filled with this food which Falcon had brought from over in the west, in each house for these people to eat. On the morning of the fourth day after this, Coyote heard people in these houses; and then everybody came out of the houses and he addressed them. He told them that twenty people from each side of the fire must get wood. The people on the north side of the fire got wood first, then everybody sweated and, when they had finished, Coyote addressed the people again, saying that they would have a dance. Blue Jay was to be fire-tender.

Falcon came out for the first time since the people had been created. He commenced shooting and throwing sticks. There were two sisters, Panther and Wildcat, who were standing near each other. They wished that one of the sticks which Falcon was throwing would pass between them. This happened and they caught it and each was trying to take it from the other when Falcon came up.

He said, "Here, here, don't break that. That is my throwing stick (mlū'i)."

They said, "All right," and then added, "We were thinking about going to your house to visit you."

So Falcon took them both home. That night they all slept together.

IV

(Putrid-man and Falcon Gamble)

Next day, while everyone was eating and sweating in the sweat-house, Putrid-man (Pa-tca) came to the village and they gave him a place in the sweat-house, just in front of the center pole. Falcon was chief in this village, because he had provided all the food and other things for the people. Pa-tca said to Falcon that he had made a head-net for him and that he would bring it there in four days. Falcon said, "All right," and Pa-tca immediately went away. The people who lived in this village were all good people, never growled at one another and never fought with their neighbors.

In four days after this, Pa-tca returned. They saw him approaching the village and called him into the sweat-house. As he entered, Blue Jay told him to sit down close beside Falcon because he, Falcon, never talked very much. Falcon was lying down at the time and payed no attention whatever to Pa-tca for a long time. Finally Falcon said to him, "When you and I gamble, I will win all you have; so I do not need to give you anything for this net, because I might just as well keep that now as to win it after a while."

Pa-tca answered, "Well, that is not the regular way. You should always give your friend a present, when he gives you one."

Then Blue Jay spoke up, saying, "Well, I think I am going to join in this. I am going to be 'medze' (the man who holds stakes and acts in a general way as a go-between in gambling)."

They both said, "All right, you seem to always know what is to be done. Now you go out and get the sticks to gamble with. We will play witcili." So Blue Jay went out and got some wormwood (kaa′pūlū) sticks for the game.

Falcon then said, "Blue Jay, go and get my beads. I would like to gamble."

So Blue Jay rolled into the sweat-house a very large basket filled with beads. They played witcili until Pa-tca had won all that Falcon had. Then he said, "I am going to quit now for a while."

At this Falcon fell over backwards but his people remonstrated with him, "You better get up and play. What is the matter with you? A young man like you never should mind such a small thing as losing a game. We are going to make a fire pretty soon and sweat."

V

(Falcon Transforms Himself into an Elk and Goes to Kilak's House)

Falcon lay there for a long time but finally arose and went outside the house and stretched himself. He had still left a few beads, a few hair-skewers and a few Cī skins. He started over toward the east, dropping a few beads at almost every step. As he went, he kept dropping beads in this way until they were all gone. Then he took to dropping Cī hides. He travelled on in this manner until he had reached as far as Kelseyville. He then took his hair-skewers and dropped them along the trail as he went.

By and by it grew late and he sat down near the base of Mt. Kanaktai, on the west side. He had nothing to use for bedding or to cover himself with, except a few of the hair-skewers. He, therefore, collected a lot of grass, dug for himself a hole and covered up in it. He had still left two elk horn hair-skewers (kasizi-kano). He stuck these into his hair, one on each side of his head. When he arose in the morning, he was transformed into an elk and he went off into the mountains and stood under an oak tree. Shortly after arriving at this place, he heard a noise. It was

"kilak kilak kilak kilak
kilak kilak kilak kilak
kilak kilak kilak kilak
kilak kilak kilak kilak"

Presently, Kī'lak arrived and sat down on the south side of Elk, saying that he was glad to find Elk and that he had never seen such an animal before although he had been all over and into every sort of a place. He said he hoped that the animal would give him good luck.

Kī'lak had two human beings in his hunting sack. He offered Elk every different kind of food but he declined all. Elk and Kī'lak then gambled. Elk won from Kī'lak. When Kī'lak took off the beads he was wearing, and handed them over to Elk, Elk proceeded immediately to eat them.

Kī'lak then fed Elk more beads, dropping just a few at a time along in the trail as he walked to his own house. Thus Elk was tolled along toward Kī'lak's house. Kī'lak had, however, only a few beads and these were soon exhausted. Then Elk stopped.

Presently, they heard another sound such as Elk had heard when the first Kī'lak came, and Kī'lak's brother came up with them. He had some magnesite beads and these were fed to Elk in the same manner; but by this means, they were only able to toll Elk about half-way home. Then the brothers went on ahead to get a big sack full of large shell beads (winamuli). When Kī'lak arrived at the house, he told his mother what they were doing.

She said, "That is good. I should like to have such an animal as that. We have plenty of beads here to feed it."

They then took a sack of beads and went back after Elk. With this sack, they were only able to get a short distance. Kī'lak then made other trips home for beads until he had made four trips and they finally arrived at the house. He then told his mother to make a place for Elk to defecate because elk's excrement would be beads, it could be nothing else. Elk defecated but his excrement was not beads. The Kī'laks examined the excrement but could not see the reason for the fact that it was not like the food eaten.

The two boys then went to bed and left their mother to watch Elk because they were afraid someone would steal him. This way they kept Elk until he had eaten all their beads. Then one morning, Elk heard Kī'lak cry, again coming from the north, and presently Kī'lak flew down and struck him on the head and killed him.

VI

(The Ancients are Transformed into Birds and Mammals)

The people of the village missed Falcon and hunted all around for him. Finally, one day, Blue Jay came into the house and found Falcon there.

Blue Jay said, "Well, where did you come from?"

Falcon answered, "Oh, I have been here all the time."

Then Blue Jay said, "Well you better get up and go to the sweat-house."

When they arrived at the sweat-house, Blue Jay said, "You better play again."

But the people in the sweat-house remarked, "How is he going to play? He lost everything he had before, you know that."

Blue Jay then said, "Well, I am chief here. I know as much as you fellows and more, too. I lead you people. I like to see you people have dances and have good times but you have told me at two different times that I do not know what I am talking about so I am going to leave." Blue Jay and his brother then gave their usual cry, "tsai tsai tsai tsai tsai tsai."

The rest of the people then decided, each for himself, what they wanted to be and all ran out.

2—HAWK STEALS FOOD FROM THE MINKS AND COYOTE CREATES PEOPLE[17]

INCIDENTS AND CHARACTERS

I. *Hawk steals food from the Mink-people.*
    1. *Coyote,* 2. *Black Hawk (Coyote's son),* 3. *Magic raft,* 4. *Token of Coyote skin quiver,* 5. *Token of hair-skewer,* 6. *Mink-people,* 7. *Mink.*

II. *Coyote creates people from feathers.*
    1. *Coyote,* 2. *Black Hawk,* 3. *Mole,* 4. *Magic flute.*

III. *Coyote creates fish.*
    1. *Black Hawk,* 2. *Coyote,* 3. *Magic flute.*

IV. *Coyote places people.*
    1. *Black Hawk,* 2. *Coyote.*

V. *Coyote creates vegetal foods.*
    1. *Coyote,* 2. *Magic flute.*

I

(Hawk Steals Food from the Mink-people)

At a place called "Kabē tsaka wanī", signifying "solid blue rock", which is located about six or seven miles north of Rock Pile lived Coyote and his son, Kabē u katc (Black Hawk). Food was very scarce and Coyote lay sick and starving by the fire. Finally Black Hawk said that he was going away for a few days to see what he could find. He started off toward the south going past Rock Pile and arriving at a place called "Kū'ba hmū'ī bida". Here he took a trail which leads on the south side of the creek down to the ocean and he stopped at the

---

[17]The Pomo name of this myth is: Cĕ'mi īwī-ya tca dōtc ke maa badakal, ancient Coyote people make food steal.
Informant: Bill James, Garcia River, Central dialect, 1906.

mouth of this creek where it emptied into the Gualala River. He crossed the river and went up onto the ridge toward the west, then down the opposite side of the ridge and came to a level stretch which he crossed and then descended to the beach at a place called "Tca't batē", which is located about two miles south of the mouth of Gualala River. Here he stood, looking at the water, and not knowing what to do. He was carrying, at the time, a large hunting sack (mako yet). From this he took a rope of milkweed fibre, then he rolled some logs down to the water and tied them together and made a raft.

He again reached into his hunting sack and took out a long string of beads. He broke the string and threw the beads, loose, into the water and said, "Now I want you to float well on this water." Then he pushed the raft down to the water and tied it to the shore, but presently the breakers rolled in and parted his lashing and scattered the logs of his raft on the waves.

He again collected logs and tied them very securely and made a good solid raft.

He then took out more beads, this time taking out four lengths instead of two as he had done before. He broke these strings and threw these beads into the water as a sacrifice, saying, "I want you to float well this time." He then pushed the raft down into the water, but again the waves broke it up.

Again he took this rope and rebound the logs and this time he made a little larger sacrifice. He took four lengths of ordinary heads and two lengths of the thick, heavy beads, broke these strings and threw these into the water and pronounced the same wish as before.

For the third time his raft was broken up as formerly. He was quite discouraged, but could not see what was to be done about the matter; so he collected the logs again and again bound them into a raft.

This time he took from his sack four lengths of common beads and he took from his neck the beads that he was wearing. These were large and very fine beads and he took four lengths of these and threw all these beads into the water. As he did so, he said, "Now I want you to float on the water and to go swiftly across the water to the island."

He then pushed the raft out in the water and climbed aboard. It floated like a cork. Then he came ashore, took his hunting sack and his bow and arrows, but before he went aboard the raft again he took a

Coyote-skin quiver (īwī ka*t*). He hung it on a bush and said to it, "If I come back this way you must shout as loudly as you can so that I may know where I am coming to." The quiver made no reply.

Then he went aboard the raft and started away, directly out across the water toward the west. He himself did nothing. This magic raft propelled itself. When he had reached about the middle of the ocean he took a hair-skewer (cna' ganō) and stuck it down into the water just as if it was a shallow place, although the fact of the matter was that the water was extremely deep here. The skewer stuck there and he said to it, "If I come back this way you must shout and make a loud noise so that I shall know where I am."

Then he went on and when he came near to the village (of the Mink-people) on the western shore of the ocean he made the following wish, "When I come near the village I want it to get dark so that I can arrive unseen by the inhabitants." Presently it began to grow dim and the farther he traveled the darker it became until finally he could see only a little fog along this western shore. Finally it became very dark as he came close to the village where he could look and see what was going on.

This village was Maa' napō, literally "food village". This was really not located on the western shore of the ocean but was on a great island. The people were making fires in all parts of this village to bake bread. Some had their fires up on the hill, others down by the shore. The chief of the village was delivering a speech. He said, "I want all of you people to come to the dance-house tonight and we will have a celebration."

Finally when everyone had finished with his cooking and baking all went to the dance-house. Black Hawk could hear this although it was so dark that he could not see. He could hear them dancing. As soon as he saw that everyone was busy in the village he pushed his raft quietly through the tule which edged the island and tied his raft securely to the shore. Then he took his sack and his bow and arrows and went stealthily up to the village.

He went on top of the dance-house and looked through the smoke-hole. Some dirt fell down and the fire-tender became suspicious and said, "Some dirt is coming down from the roof. There must be some stranger up there."

Hearing this Black Hawk ran down from the roof and went as fast as he could to the shore, pushed off in his raft and stayed out in the water for some time where he could listen.

The people ran out of the dance-house and looked all around but could see no one. Some said, "There is no one out here. The dance-house is just settling a little bit and that is why the earth dropped down from the roof." Then they returned and continued their dance. They danced and danced for a long time and Black Hawk wished that all of them would fall asleep.

Finally when everything was quiet ashore he knew that his wish had come true and that everyone in the house was fast asleep. Again he went ashore stealthily and listened. He heard them all snoring so he went on past the dance-house and to the dwellings in the village. From these he took all the acorns, every one from each house, and put them into his sack. Then he went to the places where the bread was being made. He opened them, took out all of the bread and put this also into his sack. Then he collected all the seeds he could find and so he went on, emptying all of the foods of every description that he could find, into his hunting sack.

Then he went back to his raft and put all of this food onto the raft, after which he returned to the village. This time he went to the dance-house. He found it almost completely dark within. There were just a few embers left and these gave a little light, so he walked in. He stirred up the fire so that he could see what he was doing, and then he began to braid the hair of each person to that of his neighbor. He began at the door and took first the hair of the fire-tender and braided that onto the hair of the man lying next to him and so he went on completely around the house and braided the hair of each person to that of his neighbor. This made a continuous braid, running all around the house.

He next stirred up the fire still more so that he could see to better advantage and then he went out and tied the door securely with a rope so that nobody could run out quickly. Then he went up on the roof and looked down through the smoke-hole and shot the man who was lying directly in front of the center pole. As the arrow entered this man's body, he shouted most lustily and woke all the others.

Black Hawk then ran down to his raft and pushed off a short dis-

tance. Then he stopped to listen and heard the people making a terrific noise trying to liberate themselves.

Finally they did free themselves and they looked all over the island
trying to find him. He listened to this tumult for a time and then went
away. As he traveled back toward the east he said, "When I come
near my hair-skewer daylight will break.

He traveled on eastward for a long time and finally, just at daybreak, he heard something calling directly ahead of him; and he went
straight to the point from which the noise came. There he found his
hair-skewer and picked it up. He kept on going and could hear, by and
by, another call. That was the call of the quiver which he had left as
a token to guide him on the shore. He landed, pulled his raft ashore
and took off his sack and then untied the raft and set it adrift.

When he started westward he had hung his quiver on a purple lupine
(ka'tsa). He now started to pick it up. Now, one of his pursuers,
Mink (Sīli'l), from the island where he had stolen the food, had by
some means been able to reach shore before Hawk did and had concealed himself in a bush near the lupine upon which the quiver token
was hanging. As Hawk reached to take his quiver, Mink shot at him,
but Hawk dodged and the arrow missed him. Then Hawk shot at Mink
and killed him.

Hawk then took his quiver and put his arrows back into it, took his
sack of food and started eastward back toward his own home. He came
to the river at the mouth of Kūbahmūi bida where the trail crossed at
this point. Here he sat down and rested for he was weary. He had
not eaten any of the food he had taken from the island.

Then he went on up the hill and down again to Kūba' hmūi bida
where he crossed the stream and then went on over on the trail running
west of Rock Pile and finally he arrived home.

About a quarter of a mile away from his home he left his bag, with
all of the food, on a log. He took a small piece of common, ordinary
white-oak bread, which is not a good kind at all, and went to the house
where he found his father lying covered with ashes as if asleep.

Hawk found this bread very hard and he had to break it across his
knee. It made a loud cracking noise and this woke Coyote up. He
said, "Well, what is that?"

Hawk replied, "Oh nothing. I just brought some bread for you."

Coyote replied, "That is good, now I can come to life again. I am glad you got that for me." He then ate all of this bread and both he and Hawk fell asleep.

II

(Coyote Creates People from Feathers)

When they woke up, Coyote asked, "Where have you been?"

Hawk told his father where he had been and that he got a little food from there, and asked if they should eat it alone or call some of the other people (as a matter of fact, there were no other people except those on the island, from whom he had taken this food).

Coyote replied, "If you want to have people in your village I will make you some people, if you have food to feed them."

Hawk replied, "Yes, I want to have people around here. I like to see them. I like it when they are happy and have a good time." Then Hawk gave Coyote the remainder of the piece of bread from which he had broken the first piece and Coyote ate it all up.

This bread made Coyote strong again and when he had finished this second feast, he said to Hawk, "I will go out now for a while." He then took down his hunting sack, put on his dancing-feathers and started southward. He went a mile or so and there found an open place. He then took off all of his clothing and placed it at the edge of the brush. He then lay down and took a flint knife and cut himself wide open, from his neck down to below his umbilicus, and spread his body open and let his viscera protrude. He had been there only a very few minutes when the buzzards began to fly around him. In fact all kinds of birds arrived, and as they came down he caught them, and pulled their feathers out, and threw their bodies to one side.

In this way he got feathers from all different kinds of birds and when he had collected all that he wanted he arose, put his entrails back into his body, and immediately his wound healed. Then he assorted these feathers and made bundles of each different kind and put them into his hunting sack. Then he put on his clothes and started home.

He went into the house and told his son, "Now I want you to go out and stake out the place for each of the houses in the village. Mark where each house should be, and wherever you want two fires in one house mark them and mark the places for the beds near these fires.

Dig small holes for the beds. Mark out just as many houses as you want and be sure that you make plenty. Put them in lines extending from north to south, a line for each size of house and alternately place lines of large and small houses in this way."

Hawk then placed these houses according to instructions, putting two feathers in each one of the pits he had marked as beds.

Coyote did not participate in the placement of these feathers but he remained in his own bark house. When Hawk had finished placing these feathers he came in and reported to Coyote that everything was in readiness and that he had placed the feathers two and two at every point as indicated.

Then Coyote took his flute (wo'lwol) and began to play. He played on the flute twice and then he said, "Mole, I want you to fix these beds." Then he told his son to go out and see that everything was in proper shape.

Presently Hawk came back and reported that the beds were all made, but the houses were not yet quite finished.

Coyote played his flute once more and sent his son out to see what progress had been made and received the report that the houses were then completely finished.

Hawk said, "Next I want a sweat-house so that these people can dance and have ceremonies to enjoy themselves."

Coyote said, "All right go out and mark out the place where you want the sweat-house and then come in again."

Hawk did this and came in and reported to Coyote who again played his flute twice and sent Hawk out to see what progress had been made. He returned and reported that the pit was dug but that none of the posts were yet in place. Then Coyote played his flute again and when Hawk went out this time he found that the poles were set up.

Then Coyote told Hawk, "If I play this flute twice more you will see everything set up and finished."

Then Coyote said, "Now I want my son to sleep," and immediately Hawk fell asleep though he was not aware of it.

Then Coyote played his flute twice and immediately he heard a noise and heard someone delivering an oration calling the people to the dance-house to have a celebration.

All this happened during a single night and daylight was now coming. As the dawn came the one who was delivering this speech told the people to go and bring wood and that all should join in having a sweat.

Then Coyote woke Hawk and said, "Now go out and see what you can find."

III

(Coyote Creates Fish)

Hawk did this and saw the dance-house and all the people in the village. Then he returned and said to Coyote, "Now, I want some fish and some deer for these people to eat with their acorns and their acorn bread. I also want some wild potatoes and some clover to grow, also some berries and buckeyes and acorns of all kinds."

Coyote replied, "You go out and get some dry brush of all kinds and break each piece you get up into four pieces and then come back to me."

Hawk did this, and when he returned Coyote said, "Now I want you to go down to the river and throw all these sticks into the riffles above the falls (there is a fall at this point about twenty feet wide and eight or nine feet in height) and when you have done this come back again."

Hawk did as he was told and then came back and reported to Coyote who again played his flute. He played his flute four times and then told Hawk to go down to the river and see what had happened. Upon doing so Hawk found that the river was literally filled with fish of all kinds.

IV

(Coyote Places People)

When Hawk came back this time he said, "How is this? Do you think that it is good for all these people to stay here together? They all speak different languages."

Coyote thought about this and on the fourth day he assigned each of the different kinds of people to their respective places. As he named each place he sent a man and a woman to live there. Toward the east he sent people to Pda'teyama (Boonville), Yō'kaia-ma (Ukiah valley), Côka (Clear Lake region), Sĕ'napō (East of Cache Creek), Sagara mentik-kēya (Sacramento Valley), Dagō tca kēmīge (where the sun rises).

Then he appointed places to the north and assigned the people to live there. These were Pda-ha'ū-kēya (Garcia village), Bō'ya (Cliff Ridge), Bū'l-pda (Big River), Baka'mōla (very far to the north), Yū'danō (Snow mountain) (still farther to the north), Tcūlama' ham napō (north end of the world).

Toward the south he appointed the following places and assigned the people to them: Kū'ba hmūi, Kaca'yama (Stewart's Point), Kahwalalīkē (the mouth of Russian River), Xam *tara* (Bodega Bay), Yōma hamke (the south end of the world).

As he named each place in each one of these three directions he designated what kind of trees and what kinds of food would be found there.

He did not name any places toward the west because this all happened on the coast and the ocean is to the west.

As he named each place he sent a man and a woman there and that is why we have so many different languages and so many different kinds of people in all these different places. There were many people left at the village, however, and this was a large village always after that.

Coyote, then said, "Those fish that we have created will go down to the ocean and up all the different rivers and salmon will come up once in the spring and will go back in the summer."

V
(Coyote Creates Vegetal Foods)

Coyote then created the different kinds of berries: blackberries (tītō-nōō) strawberries (ma'mūl), salal-berries (tōltōl), wild currants (kō'tō), raspberries (ba'c-kōt), salmon-berries (da'wai), huckleberries (ka'kai). He also created clover and all of the various kinds of plants and he designated where each would grow and ordered everything about them. As he created each one he, of course, played his magic flute which caused everything to come as he directed.

3—WOLF AND COYOTE CREATE PEOPLE[18]
INCIDENTS

I. Wolf catches deer in a magic wier.
II. Wolf and Coyote create people from willow sticks.

---

[18]Informant: Bill Coon, Yokaia, Central dialect, 1904.

I

(Wolf Catches Deer in a Magic Weir)

Coyote and his uncle, Wolf (smē'wa), lived together on the west bank of Scott's Creek at the old village of Kuca-dano-yo, which was situated at the foot of a small hill called by the same name, about a mile and a half southwest of the town of Upper Lake. They were the only people living here and occupied the same house. They had a fish dam down on the creek.

During the night, Wolf was taken ill. He said to Coyote, "I feel badly. I have a toothache."

Next morning, Coyote went down to Big Valley, on the southern margin of Clear Lake to dig some Indian potatoes. He stayed there all day and when he returned to the house at night, he brought some potatoes, some gophers (lami), some gray squirrels (saka lalai), some ground squirrels (gumar) and some jackrabbits (mohya).

He found Wolf still feeling badly, so he cooked some of the potatoes and roasted some of the gray squirrels and rabbits for him. Then he said, "Well, my uncle, would you not like to eat something?"

But Wolf answered, "No, I can not eat. yu—— yu—— yu——," and thus he wailed all the time. He wailed so loudly that you could hear him way off for a mile. Then he said, "No, Coyote, I can not eat. I do not feel like eating, I ache so badly." So he ate nothing and he did not sleep but he kept on wailing all the time.

Next morning, Coyote went again to Big Valley and killed some game. When he returned and had cooked the food, he said, "Well, my uncle, can you not eat something?"

Wolf answered, "No, I can not eat anything. I ache all the time. I can not eat."

That evening, Coyote put a couple of rocks on the fire and put some water in a basket. In the middle of the night, when the rocks were hot, Coyote got up and put them into the water. He said to Wolf, "Well, my uncle, you had better put your mouth over here. Maybe it will make you feel a little better."

But Wolf said, "No, I can not stand it. That is too hot."

With this, Coyote began to think that Wolf was playing a trick on him and he became a little angry. Next morning, he arose and told Wolf, "Well, my uncle, let me feel of the place that hurts you so. Let me suck it and draw the blood out."

Wolf had a big swelling on the side of his face. It was as big as your two fists. But Wolf answered, "No, I can not"; so Coyote went out and went down to Kilem, just south of Rocky point, to get some tule.

As soon as Coyote was out of sight, Wolf arose and went down to the dam at the creek. Now this dam was built just like a fish dam but it was not for fish at all. It caught deer and each one of the deer that it caught, had a basket on its neck that was filled with acorn mush and bread. Sometimes, of course, the dam would catch foxes or other animals but it was made particularly to catch deer. Wolf sat down by the dam and waited, until finally, he saw a deer being washed along down the stream. He had a big rock in his hand and when the deer came close he hit it. Then he took out the deer with its basket of mush and took it up to the house, where he skinned and cooked it.

Coyote, meanwhile, had come back near enough to the house so that he could see all that Wolf was doing. It made him very angry and he went away, but about noon he returned with some soft tule. When he arrived at the house, he found Wolf again groaning and pretending to feel very badly.

Whenever Wolf thought that Coyote was near, he had a small pestle (daka-batal), which he placed in his mouth, so that it made one cheek swell way out, just as if he had a bad toothache. This pestle was the same one with which he killed the deer. He acted this way when Coyote returned this time, so Coyote prepared the soft green tule and offered it to him, because it was something soft which he might eat. But Wolf said, "No, I am afraid I can not eat that either. I can not stand it." So Coyote ate it himself.

When night came, they both retired but Coyote listened during the night. About midnight he heard Wolf breaking acorn bread (karo), and said, "That sounds like someone breaking acorn bread."

But Wolf answered, "No, there is no one around here at all. There is nobody here to break any bread."

Then Coyote said, "Well, how do you stand it when nobody takes care of you when you are sick? Most people have someone to care for them when they are sick. I want to care for you but you will not let me." Wolf then commenced to wail and Coyote said, "This looks as if you were trying to fool me." In the morning, Coyote rose, had his breakfast and then told Wolf, "I think I am going to Big Valley." So he went away.

Southeast of the house, the hill, Kuca-dano-yo, rose with the trail leading to Big Valley passing around its base. Coyote took this trail and when he had passed around the hill out of sight, he ascended to the top and there watched to see what Wolf would do. He could hear Wolf still groaning down in the house but presently, as soon as he thought Coyote out of hearing, he stopped. He then stepped out of the house and looked all around, in every direction, to see that no one was coming. Then he pulled the pestle out of his mouth and went down to the dam. After sitting there for a few minutes, a big deer came down the stream. As it passed through the dam, Wolf reached down and took off the basket of mush and then hit the deer with the pestle and killed it. He then took the deer to the house, skinned and cooked it. He placed the skin on top of the house and covered it up well with tule, so that no one would be able to see it. Then he went into the house and commenced to eat venison and mush.

Now, Coyote had watched all the time and had seen everything that Wolf had done, so he ran down the hill just as Wolf commenced to eat. As he arrived at the house, he said, "Now, uncle, I know you have been fooling me, because people always have somebody to take care of them when they are sick. You did not do that way, so I see what you have been doing. You are very stingy with your food and have been playing a trick on me. Now, I guess you had better leave. I am angry now with such things and I think you had better leave here."

Wolf wept all day, but along in the afternoon, he moved away. He tore down the house, in order to get the deer hides, and Coyote saw that there were thousands and thousands of hides hidden in under the thatch of the house. Wolf moved to Maiyi, just across the creek, about a half mile.

Coyote remained there at Kuca-dano-yo all alone and built for himself a good new house. When Wolf left, he said, "I hope there will be no deer in that dam. I hope there will be only fawns and foxes and snakes, but no big deer."

II

(Wolf and Coyote Create People from Willow Sticks)

Wolf made a good tule house at Maiyi and lived there. He commenced to study about the building of a sweat-house and after four days, he determined to build one. So, on the fifth day, he went out into the hills and procured the fir poles and posts and the center pole. On the sixth day, he dug the pit for the sweat-house. On the seventh day, he set the center pole and the posts and put on the rafters; and on the eighth day, he covered the sweat-house with brush and dirt and finished it completely. When he had finished this sweat-house, he went over to Tule Lake and gathered a quantity of green tule which he cut up into pieces about fifteen or eighteen inches long. These he took into the sweat-house and stuck close together into the floor in four rows near the wall. Then he said, "I wish that in four days this tule would turn into human beings." He made a big fire that same evening in the sweat-house but when it got good and hot, all the tule wilted, and at the end of four days, he had no people.

Wolf studied about his failure to create people, and next morning, he went out and got four bundles of willow poles. He selected good solid heavy ones. These he brought home and split up into sticks about the size and shape of women's gambling staves (kadaika). He made a great many of these sticks, so that he had a large pile of them when he had finished. Then he painted each one of them in four places, painting a black band with charcoal around in each place and finally, he placed these as he had done the tule, in rows in the floor of the sweat-house near the wall; but this time, he made eight rows instead of four. Then he built a big fire as before, and this time they did not wilt. When he saw that everything was going properly, he said, "I wish people would be here in this house in four days. I want to find people here on the morning of the fourth day."

He slept just behind the center pole in the sweat-house and at about daybreak on the morning of the fourth day, he awoke and found that the house was completely filled with people. He said to them, "How are my people? How are all my relatives? How are my children?";

and then he shook hands with all of them. Everyone then went outside and laughed, talked, shouted and enjoyed themselves greatly.

That evening, while Coyote was in his house over at Kuca-dano-yo, he thought he heard something strange. He ran out of the house and listened but heard nothing, so he returned. Presently, he heard the sound again but when he ran out he heard nothing. He heard this sound and ran out four different times but he went to bed that evening and along toward morning, he was awakened by a similar sound. This time he ran out and there he saw a large number of people over at Maiyi. He returned to the house and ate a little breakfast, meanwhile thinking about the people that he had seen, for he knew where they and Wolf lived. After breakfast, he took a sack full of beads and started off toward Maiyi, as he wished to be friendly again with his uncle, now that his uncle had so many people with him. When he came to Maiyi, he found there a great number of people all of the same kind and color. He found Wolf also, and presented him with the sack of beads, saying, "Here now let us be friends. Let us divide these people. You take one-half and I will take the other half."

But Wolf said, "No, I do not care to divide these people. They are mine. You had better take your beads back home with you."

Coyote said, "Well, my uncle, can you not at least tell me where you were able to get these people? How did you get them anyway?"

Wolf said, "No, I can not tell you. You drove me away from your house, so I can not tell you where I got these people."

Coyote finally said, "Well, my uncle, I will come over here. I will live with you."

To which Wolf replied, "That is all right for this time but if you come over here, you can not live with me. You may live over there, a little way back from the village and from my people."

So Coyote returned to Kuca-dano-yo, moved over everything he had and built a tule house for himself near the village.

After a time, Coyote went to Wolf again and said, "Now, my uncle, I want you to tell me how you made those people."

Wolf said, "Well, all right. You build a sweat-house first. You must cut the timber for it and next morning, you must dig the pit."

On the following morning Coyote went out and cut the timber for his new sweat-house. Next morning, he dug the pit. Next day, he set the posts and built the frame and on the fourth day, covered the house and completed it. He made a good sweat-house just as Wolf had done.

That same evening, he went to Wolf and told him about the sweat-house and asked him what he ought to do next, saying, "Well, my uncle, now tell me how you made those people."

Wolf then told him, "You go out to the lake and get tule. You go and get all you can carry and bring it home. Get enough so that when you cut it up into pieces about a foot long, you will have enough pieces to make four rows in the floor near the wall. Then make a fire after you have finished. That is all I can tell you."

Coyote returned to his house and on the following morning, went to the lake and brought tule as Wolf had directed. He cut this tule up into pieces and placed them in the sweat-house. That evening he made a big fire but all the tule wilted as it had done for Wolf.

On the following morning, he again went to his uncle and said, "My uncle, that doesn't look good. All that tule has wilted. That will never make human beings."

Wolf replied, "Well, all right, this time I will tell you the correct way to make human beings. You go down to the river and get willows. Get four bundles of willow poles. Bring all you can carry." And then Wolf described to him in detail just how to create people from these willow sticks.

Coyote brought a large number of willow poles and split them up, so that he had a great quantity of sticks. Coyote was always doing this sort of thing, trying to get more than he really should. He always wanted too much of anything. He painted the sticks in four places and placed them in eight rows about the wall of the sweat-house. Then he wished that people might come into existence there in four days. On the morning of the fourth day, he was awakened by a sound and upon arising, he found that the sweat-house was completely filled with his people. Everybody was up and they all talked, laughed, shouted and played games. They commenced to play shinney (pīkō'taik).

III

(Wolf and Coyote Create Grizzlies and Rattlesnakes)

Presently, Coyote's and Wolf's people began to play against one another. Two of Coyote's people were good players and won constantly from Wolf's people. They played this way for four days. They would play all day long and sleep at night and then be ready to play again just as soon as the sun came up again in the morning. But Coyote's people had the best of the game always. This made Wolf and his people jealous and Wolf studied about it for some time. Finally, he said to himself, "I think I am going to kill those two fellows."

So he made two grizzly bears[19] and put them in the brush near the line at which the Coyote people always won the game. On the fifth day, therefore, when they again played shinney, and the Coyote people won, the two bears killed these two of Coyote's people. Then others of the Coyote people took their places but they were also killed by the bears. In this way, the bears killed several of Coyote's people.

That same day, Coyote studied over this for some time and finally said to himself, "Well, I think I am going to make something to kill those other people. He made those bears, I know, so I am going to make something now."

During the night, therefore, Coyote went and cut two pieces of deer hide about three or four inches wide and two feet long. He took some kind of brown color and painted these pieces of deer hide with spots like those on the rattlesnake. Then he took some thorns (lum) from a gooseberry bush (lum-maai) and made fangs of these. He placed these two rattlesnakes near the goal of the Wolf people and on the following morning, when they had another game of shinney the Wolf people won and the rattlesnakes bit them. They kept on playing this way for four days, until the bears and the rattlesnakes had killed off all the people whom Wolf and Coyote had created.

IV

(Coyote Goes to Live in the Mountains)

After all the people had thus been killed, Coyote said to Wolf, "Well, I think I am going to leave you. I shall no longer be a relative of yours. I shall go to the mountains. I shall not come back here any more. I shall live under the rocks anywhere. I shall never come back here again and people shall call me Coyote (diwī)." We call all kinds of crazy people diwī.

---

[19]One northern Pomo informant stated that Wolf created bears out of buckeye root, using sharp points of mountain mahogany wood (macū'm) as teeth for the animals.

4—CREATION OF PEOPLE BY WOLF AND COYOTE[20]

INCIDENTS AND CHARACTERS

I. *Wolf catches food in a magic wier.*
    1. Coyote, 2. Wolf.
II. *Wolf and Coyote create people from maple sticks.*
    1. Coyote, 2. Pestle (son of Coyote), 3. Wolf.
III. *Wolf and Coyote create grizzlies and rattlesnakes.*
    1. Wolf, 2. Coyote, 3. Grizzlies, 4. Rattlesnakes.
IV. *The Coyote boys are killed by the Sun-people.*
    1. Coyote boys, 2. Wolf boys, 3. Coyote, 4. Wolf, 5. Sun-people.
V. *Coyote steals the sun.*
    1. Coyote, 2, Sun-children, 3. Sun-people, 4. Mice (2), 5. Fire-tender,
    6. Red-headed-woodpecker, 7. Fog, 8. Rabbit, 9. Crow, 10. Humming-
    bird, 11. Falcon, 12. Pigeon, 13. Robin, 14. Buzzard.

I

(Wolf Catches Food in a Magic Weir)

Coyote and Wolf lived together in a place over east of Graveley Valley. Coyote had a small pestle (dako). Wolf made a fish dam near the head of Eel River and set in it a fish basket. He wished that bread would run down the stream. In doing this, Wolf hid everything from Coyote. He even hid the river away.

He fooled Coyote and told him that he had the toothache, and put a kamilat (the nub at the base of the deer horn) in his mouth and showed Coyote that he had a big swelling. Coyote asked him if he was ill and Wolf replied that he had toothache and that he could not sleep. Coyote asked if Wolf wanted anything to eat but Wolf said he did not. Then Coyote asked, "What sort of food is good for toothache?" Wolf replied that all he wanted was some gopher (lamo) meat. Then Coyote went to sleep but Wolf cried all night.

Next morning, Coyote arose and told Wolf to take care of himself because there was no one to care for him. He told Wolf that he was going over into the Sacramento Valley. Coyote went out with his cane (macu) and his carrying sack (maatc).

About an hour after Coyote had left, Wolf arose and after looking out of the smoke-hole (tcabuma) of the house, in order to see that no one was about, he went out and washed himself and then went to his

---

[20]Informant: Jim McCalluck, Potter Valley, Northern dialect, 1904.

dam. He found his basket trap filled with everything, ready cooked. He had white bread (kasīlasoi), deer meat, fish and so on, all cooked and ready to eat. He took out the best food and took it home and the rest he let go down the river. He ate what he wanted and had a good time. When he had finished eating, he dug a big hole and put everything left into it. Then he covered this with a big flat slab (kol) of pine. He then made his bed over this and lay down, replacing the nub of deer horn in his mouth, to produce the swelling due to his pretended toothache.

When Coyote returned in the late afternoon, he asked Wolf how he was feeling, at the same time laying his hunting sack with gophers beside Wolf's bed. After feeling of Wolf's swelled jaw, Coyote came to the conclusion that Wolf was growing worse instead of better. He then skinned three of the gophers, placed them on a flat rock, pounded them up finely, and cooked them. Then he told Wolf that he had the gophers cooked and asked him if he cared for a drink of water. Wolf replied by a nod of his head. Then Coyote asked him if he wanted to eat, to which he also replied with a nod. Coyote brought the gophers and Wolf put a piece of the soft, minced meat into his mouth and held it there a while and then swallowed it. He pretended his mouth was so sore he was unable to chew.

Coyote felt very sorry for Wolf and commented, "It is pretty hard when a man has toothache. You should be very careful not to bite on the tooth."

Wolf slowly ate the three gophers in this manner. Coyote then cooked the rest of the gophers and ate them himself, and that night, he slept only a little, for he cried nearly all night, he felt so sorry for Wolf. He would wake up from time to time and say, "Oh, my brother!" and then cry for a long time.

Finally, morning came and after examining Wolf, Coyote concluded that he was growing worse. He said, "Oh, my poor brother! I know you can not eat anything. I feel very sorry because you can not eat anything. I will go and hunt for gophers again. Take care of yourself because there is no one here to take care of you." He again went over to the Sacramento Valley.

As Coyote started off, Wolf slipped around to where he could watch him and after Coyote had departed over the hill, he took the nub of deer horn out of his mouth and laid it at the head of his bed. Then he went out and washed his face and again went down to the dam, which he found full as usual. He took out the basket of food and placed it in the hole which he had dug under his bed. In fact, the stream itself flowed under the ground under his bed and all he had to do with anything which he had left over from his meal, was to open up the hole, which was near the foot of the bed, and drop it in. The stream would wash it away. Having finished his meal, he replaced the nub of deer horn in his mouth and again lay down.

Upon Coyote's return, he laid down his hunting sack filled with gophers and inquired how Wolf had fared since he had been gone. He examined the swelling on Wolf's jaw and after pressing it with his finger, said that Wolf was certainly going to get better as the pus had begun to run from the jaw. He then asked Wolf if he cared to eat and said that he was afraid that his strength would not hold out if he did not eat more. He again prepared the gophers and fed Wolf as before, but Wolf was able to eat only a very small piece. Coyote wanted to bathe Wolf all over with hot water as a cure for his illness. Coyote really wanted to ascertain what the trouble was but Wolf did not allow Coyote to even put his hand on his jaw after that.

That evening, when they went to bed, Coyote lay with his mouth toward the door and wanted to dream something, but after lying in this position for some time and not dreaming, he shifted his position so that he lay over against the wall. This, however, was of no avail and he turned with his feet toward the door but again he was unable to dream and was obliged to shift his position for the third time. This time he placed his head toward the fire and lay crosswise of the house and while he was in this position, the dream came to him. After he had dreamed he said to himself, "Nobody can cheat me."

Early next morning, he awoke and told Wolf, "I am going away again. Be careful of yourself. I can not help going but I cry for you because you are ill and have nobody to watch over you." So Coyote went out again and started over the same trail by which he had gone to the Sacramento Valley on the previous mornings. He went over the hill out of sight as usual, but then instead of going to Sacramento Valley, he went around until he came to a tree which overlooked his house. He climbed this tree and watched to see what Wolf did.

Again Wolf watched Coyote until he had gone out of sight over the hill and then he removed the nub of deer horn from his mouth, washed himself and went out to the dam. As soon as Coyote saw this, he ran to the house and got his bow and arrows. Then he went down by the river and hid to see what Wolf was doing. Having seen Wolf's method of getting food, he ran back to Wolf's house and took up the board and found a great quantity of good food there which Wolf had thrown away. He also found the nub of deer horn which Wolf had been using. All these things made him very angry and he went around until he came to the place where he could watch Wolf to the best advantage and see everything that he did.

After seeing all that Wolf had been doing, Coyote was so angered that he shot at Wolf with his bow and arrow. The arrow passed between Wolf's legs and did him no harm other than to frighten him; but this it did, so that he yelled with fright and ran away. Coyote gave chase, crying to him all the time to return. Coyote did not shoot at him with a regular flint-tipped arrow, he used only a wooden-pointed arrow such as would scare him much more than harm him if it should strike, but Wolf was so frightened that he did not return. Coyote then put Wolf's dam in shape to catch food as Wolf had done.

Wolf, however, said, "Things will not go as they did when I had the dam. Everything that comes there will be bad food. There will be poor deer, fawns, etc."

Coyote tended the dam and took everything up to the house but he did not know how to take care of such a great quantity of food. He left it lying around until it became mouldy and decayed. The odor of the putrid meat attracted eagles, buzzards, vultures and all scavenger birds, until finally, things became so bad that Coyote was obliged to abandon the house and the whole site.

II

(Wolf and Coyote Create People from Maple Sticks)

When he left, Coyote took with him the small Pestle (Dako) which was his son. He presently became angry and said, "Look here, you are making too much noise;" and then he kicked the Pestle around. Also when he went to bed that night he took the Pestle with him but presently pushed it over on the other side of the fire because it was making too much noise. Then he said, "Where did my brother go? Where did my brother go? I did not shoot at him meaning it."

Wolf lived at a place called Minawel, far in the north, near the north end of the world (djuhula-ma-ye). Here he got some acemaika-tite (maple?) wood which he split into small sticks, marking (with human features) the fronts of them. These sticks he carried out into the mountains, placing them under straight trees all about the region. Having finished placing the sticks, he said, "These sticks which I have placed under the straight trees must become human beings. They will be men and women, and will speak the same language that I use. They will all be my children." That night, Wolf heard a noise. The sticks had all become human beings and they had danced down from the mountains and had all come together in one place, near Wolf's sweat-house.

Wolf then rose and went out onto the roof of the sweat-house where he could see the people. He then wished that there should be houses all around and immediately many houses appeared, so that there were enough for all the people. He then said, "Every kind of food that we eat shall be here for my children," and immediately all sorts of food appeared in these houses and were there ready for use when the people finally entered them. Presently Wolf heard the people again playing, shouting and laughing. They were now coming near his sweat-house and all had on fine new dancing feathers. As they came near, Wolf called out to them, "All right, my children, come right in this way. I created you, my children, and you people shall all be married." They then entered the sweat-house to dance. There were so many people that they completely filled the sweat-house. All danced and had a good time, after which Wolf told them to go out and to enter the houses which he had created, each pair having a separate house, which they found furnished with all kinds of food. After this, they played shinney (kapiyem).

Coyote spoke to the small Pestle which he had for his son, "Now you are big enough to know something. You are big enough to hear something. You are big enough not to make a noise." Then Coyote slept and tried to dream. As in the case of his dream to discover Wolf's deception, he slept in four different positions before the vision came to him. After he had succeeded, he said, "I always see everything." Then he said to his boy, "Tomorrow morning, I am going away. Don't you run around too much. I have a great many things here and you must stay at home to watch them."

When morning came, Coyote took his hunting sack and started on his journey. He succeeded in finding the way Wolf had gone and followed his tracks. He finally arrived at Wolf's sweat-house and entered. He said to Wolf, "Half of these people shall be yours and half shall be mine," but the people refused to have anything to do with Coyote and would not own him as their father.

Then Coyote said to Wolf, "Now see here, partner, how did you create these people?"

Wolf replied, "Well, I do not know how I did create those people."

Coyote said, "You must tell me how you created these people. I will pay you well for it," and he pulled a long string of beads out of his hunting sack and gave it to Wolf.

So Wolf said, "Well, all right then, if you want to know, I will tell you. It is not very hard work to create people; you just go down to some wet place and get some tule, cut this up into short pieces and stick it all around in the sweat-house. Then build a big fire."

Coyote then went home to try it. He procured some tule on the way home, and, after cutting it up into short pieces, placed it in the sweat-house and built a big fire as Wolf had directed. Of course the tule soon wilted and shrivelled from the heat and no people were created.

Coyote dreamed again that night after the usual four attempts and on the following morning, returned to Wolf's sweat-house in the north. He entered the sweat-house and took his seat in the same place as he had upon the former occasion. Then he said to Wolf, "Now, I want you to tell me correctly this time about creating people. I will pay you well and will give you the finest beads I have."

Wolf agreed and said to Coyote, "You must go out and get all the most crooked sticks you can find and put these out in the open field."

Coyote followed this new advice but of course his efforts at creation were fruitless. After his new failure, he again went to bed and vented his wrath on the small Pestle, his son. "Why do you make so much noise? I tell you not to leave the house. There are many things here. Someone is sure to steal these things if you go away while I am gone." In the morning, Coyote returned to Wolf's sweat-house. On the way, he said to himself, "Everything nice and good shall be in this hunting sack. All good beads and other things shall be here." So when he stood in front of the door of Wolf's sweat-house, his hunting sack contained all kinds of good things.

As he entered the sweat-house, he said to Wolf, "This is the last time I shall come. These are the last things I have. These are all I have. Now you must tell me the truth this time. Brothers sometimes become angry with each other but they never remain angry all the time. You must tell me the truth about the creating of people this time."

Wolf replied, "All right, you must be a good man. We will be good friends after I tell you this. It is not very hard work to create people. I got some acemaikatite (maple?) wood and split it up into small straight sticks. Then I marked (human features) on the fronts of these sticks and put them under straight trees out in the mountains. Then I said, 'These sticks that I have placed here must become human things.' After that, I willed that houses should appear all around and then that there should be food in the houses. Then I told the people to dance and have a good time."

Coyote then ran home as fast as he could go and said to his boy, "Now you be a good boy. You lie down and sleep well tonight. You must be a good boy this time." Coyote did not sleep at all, he was so happy. Coyote was in a great hurry to see the outcome of this trial. He said to the boy, "Listen, listen, keep quiet. I hear a noise. I do not think it can be human beings. It sounds like bees buzzing on the buckeyes and manzanitas." Then he heard people's voices and said, "O, my people, this is good. I am glad, my people. There shall be many houses here and all kinds of food." Then he went out on top of the sweat-house and made a speech and called to the people to come into the sweat-house. All entered and danced for a long time, after which Coyote placed sticks in the wall and the roof of the sweat-house as pegs upon which to hang the dancing feathers. Then he took the people out and gave them their houses and told them, "Here you people must live and be happy. You shall play shinney and grass game (coka)."

III

(Wolf and Coyote Create Grizzlies and Rattlesnakes)

Wolf came over to Coyote's village and challenged the Coyote people to a game of shinney, to which Coyote replied, "This is good. We will play." Coyote's people won the first game, and then the second, and so on. In fact, Coyote's people were lucky all the time.

Wolf's people began to ask him, "Why is it that we always lose?"

Wolf said, "Well, I do not know, but I shall know it yet. I have not thought very much about it but I shall find some way for us to win."

Wolf then made two grizzly bears and placed them near the two goal posts where the Coyote people would pass when they won the next game. As the Coyote men ran between the posts at the end of the next game, the bears caught and killed two of them.

The Coyote people then enquired of him, "Well Coyote, what are we going to do? You act smart and claim that you know what happens all over the world."

Coyote was then sitting on a deer skin and he cut off two long strips. In one end of each strip, he made a mouth in which he set some gooseberry briars for teeth. Then he made large spots on each piece and placed on the tail end of each, a rattle made of the leaves of the maple.

He then placed these two strips of hide in holes near the goal posts which the Wolf people would pass if they won the next game, saying, "Anything that I have made never has refused to do what I have said. You two will become rattlesnakes."

The Wolf people won the next game and as they passed between the goal posts, the snakes bit and killed two of them. Thus the two sides played on and on with constantly decreasing numbers until there were but two people left on each side.

IV

(The Coyote Boys are Killed by the Sun-people)

These four played together not the regular game of shinney but by throwing the ball around with their hands. The two Coyote boys were quite small and the Wolf boys kept the ball away from them most of the time so that the Coyote boys came crying to their father because they wished to have something nice to play with. They said, "Father, we want to play with something nice and you are smart enough to give us something."

Coyote leaned back and rolled his head around from side to side and finally spat out two pieces of abalone shell which had come up from his stomach. He said, "Here, boys, play with these."

The Coyote boys threw these up in the air and as the sun light fell upon them, they looked very pretty.

The Wolf boys saw them and wanted to have these also. They spoke to their father about it and Wolf said, "I wish these things would not come back to their hands when they throw them up but would fly along in front of them away back east to the big sweat-house there."

This they did, and the Coyote boys followed them over to the east and finally, as the pieces of abalone shell flew into the sweat-house, they themselves entered.

The people there were all kinds of birds and they immediately caught the two Coyote boys and killed them. They skinned the two Coyote boys and made a sack out of the skins. They filled this sack with light and after tying it up securely, hung it up in the sweat-house. And by means of this light, the people there were able to go hunting for food.

V

(Coyote Steals the Sun)

Coyote missed his children and began to track them, finally arriving at the big sweat-house in the east. He found only two children in the sweat-house. As Coyote was travelling along, he was a middle-aged man but just as he started to enter the sweat-house, he transformed himself into a very old man with abalone shell ear-rings tied into his ears. When he found the two Sun-children near the sweat-house, he asked them, "What is that, my children, that is hanging up in the sweat-house?" But the children refused to tell him.

Coyote asked again and finally the children said, "If you will give us those pretty things you have tied in your ears, we will be able to tell you."

Coyote gave them his abalone shell ear-rings and they informed him that the skins from which the bag was made were once Coyote's sons.

Coyote began to cry and the children made fun of him because of it, but Coyote told them he was not really crying, but the tears were running because he was such a very old man. He then went to the inner door of the tunnel of the sweat-house and lay down across it, where if anyone entered or left the sweat-house, they would step on him. Toward evening, the Sun-people began to return and as they entered all agreed that they had better have a dance that evening. Consequently, a large fire was built, in order to have a good light by which to dance.

As the dance commenced, Coyote sat up and watched it for a long time, finally saying to them, "Well, is that the way you fellows dance? I do not call that dancing. I am going to take a place after you fellows get through dancing."

They all laughed and said, "Let the old man dance. I should like to see him dance, he brags so much about his good dancing. Give the old man the best dancing stuff you fellows have."

Then Coyote commenced to dance. He told the people, "You fellows may dance if you feel like it but if you feel sleepy, you must lie down so that all of you who have long hair will have your heads in one direction but all of you who have short hair will have your heads in the opposite direction."

Now, Coyote had brought with him his hunting sack (maatc) and in this hunting sack he had secreted two mice. As he commenced to dance, he grew younger and younger and the Sun-people grew more and more sleepy. He then liberated the mice who went up the center pole and began to gnaw on the lash which held the light-sack to the rafters. Finally, all except the fire-tender were in a sound sleep.

The fire-tender said to Coyote, "There is something flying around up there where the sack is."

But Coyote said, "Oh, no, that is only my shadow."

Finally the fire-tender became so drowsy that he too fell asleep.

When he saw that every one in the house was sound asleep, Coyote said to the mice, "How is it up there? Are you almost ready?"

The mice replied, "Yes, it is nearly ready now. The lashes are almost cut."

Coyote then began to tie the hair of the long-haired people together. Upon the heads of those who had short hair, he placed pitch and string, thus tying their heads together. This done, he gave a great leap, seized the light-sack and ran from the sweat-house with it.

The commotion, however, aroused the fire-tender who shouted to the people that someone was running away with the sack and at the same time, Red-headed-woodpecker, who was the watchman outside the sweat-house, ran in and cut the people loose with his obsidian knife (bat) and everyone pursued Coyote.

Coyote ran as rapidly as possible back toward the west over the same trail by which he had come but Fog caught up with Coyote. Coyote, however, had a sling and shot Fog, so that the Fog was entirely dissipated and he was able to proceed a little farther but the rest of the Sun-people kept gaining on him and were almost up with him when Rabbit appeared. He was fresh and took the sack and ran on again. He ran for a long ways but Fog finally almost caught him. The fog this time was so thick that you could hardly see through it, at all. As Fog was almost ready to catch Rabbit, he came to two big rocks, between which his trail lay, and he hit the light-sack upon these rocks and broke it open, and we have had light ever since.

Soon Coyote and all his pursuers arrived at these rocks and they then began to discuss what should be done.

Coyote said, "Some of you smart fellows who are long-winded must take this sun up into the sky." Then he created a lake there for the people to fall into when they came back from the sky, after trying to put the sun up. This place is far in the east and the lake is there still, although none of the present race of people has been there to see it. The first person to try to take the sun up was Hummingbird (Tsūdūyūn). He, however, failed and, as he fell back to the earth, jumped into the lake. Then Falcon (Tata), Pigeon (Tcaba'tbat) and Robin (Tsito'ktok) each in turn tried to put it up but each failed. Robin had a reputation for being the greatest traveler of any of the birds and therefore they expected he would be able to place the sun in the sky. Next Buzzard (Kawena) tried but he also failed.

Finally, Crow (Kaai) said, "I could put that sun up there and fly down again easily."

So they told Crow to try it. He did and succeeded in hanging the sun up in the sky. As he was flying down to earth again, he said, "A———— a———— a———— a———— a———— a————   .   .   . " and fell into the pond.

Coyote said, "You are certainly the best man I have found. That is good for the world. Now I am going to quit. This is the last thing I am going to do."

5—COYOTE CREATES MAN BUT LIZARD GIVES HIM PROPER HANDS[21]

Characters: 1. Coyote, 2. Lizard.

There was no one here originally but Coyote. Finally he tired of living alone and determined that he would create people. He made them just as we are now except that he made their hands like his own.

Lizard said to Coyote, "If they have hands like that they cannot do anything. They should have hands like mine. Then they could do something. They could use baskets and implements."

Coyote was on the east bank of the creek. He shouted across the creek to one of these newly created men who did not understand him at all, because the water was making so much noise as it ran down the creek.

Then Lizard became angry and said, "We will all have a different language after this and will not be able to understand one another."

So they all picked out their different places of abode and lived there always after that.

6—WATERDOG AND LIZARD CREATE HUMAN BEINGS AND GIVE THEM HANDS[22]

Characters: 1. Coyote, 2. Lizard, 3. Waterdog.

There were three people, Coyote, Lizard and Waterdog, who were contesting with each other to see who could create human beings first. Waterdog and Lizard, who lived together way across the water in the north where it is very cold, each endeavored to create human beings for himself. Waterdog, however, was unable to do so; Lizard succeeded in making human beings, all except their hands. He made the nose, ears, eyes, arms and all parts except the hands. To make the hair, he took grizzly's and black bear's hair and put this inside of the head. Then he put a covering over this and the hair grew out through it. The eyebrows grew out in the same way.

When Coyote made his people, he endeavored to make them with hands like his own, so that people would be unable to work or do anything, but Lizard asked him what human beings could do with such hands as he had and Coyote said nothing.

---

[21]Informant: Will Snow, Eastern dialect.
[22]Informant: Sam Haskett, Pinoleville, Northern dialect. This is a very fragmentary myth.

7—PEOPLE ARE TRANSFORMED INTO ANIMALS

Characters: 1. Panther, 2. Eagle, 3. Buzzard, 4. Crow, 5. Vulture, 6. Jackrabbit, 7. Thunder, 8. Coyote, 9. Spider, 10. The Bird-people.

At a village called "Maa'i tūnī" or "Masū't napōl",[24] there was a large dance-house. Panther was the Chief here at this village and he delivered a long oration, telling the people what to do and what they must not do. To his admonitions they all agreed as they sat about listening to him.

The hunters had brought him twenty deer as food. When the Chief had finished his oration they skinned the animals, cut up the meat and divided it among the people.

Then Panther again arose, standing near the center pole, and announced that a month from that date they would all assemble in the dance-house and have another celebration. Consequently at the appointed time fifteen or sixteen of the men went out with their bows and arrows and set deer snares all around the base of Capa'lawel. They set about sixty snares. Then several of the men went into the brush to frighten the deer out and make them run into the snares. One of these men was Panther himself. They threw up their hands and shouted loudly to scare the deer out and they were very successful for they caught about forty deer.

They were all so interested in the deer that they had taken and in getting their game home to the village that no one noticed for the moment that the Chief himself was missing. When they arrived at the village, however, he was not there. No one knew what had become of him. He did not return during the whole day and the following night. Then everybody in the village went out to look for the Chief. They hunted everywhere but he was not to be found.

Eagle, Buzzard, Crow and Vulture all had exceptionally good senses of smell. They tried to smell out the Chief and find where he had gone, but they were unable to do so. Then they got Jackrabbit to hunt for him. He hunted all around in the south, the east, the north and the west but Panther was nowhere in any of these directions. Finally Jackrabbit looked up and there he saw Panther, for Thunder had taken him up with him into the Upper World.

---

[23]Informant: Charlie Brown, Northern dialect.
[24]This village was located about two and a half miles north of the town of Calpella.

Neither Jackrabbit nor any of the rest of the people could reach Panther and everyone mourned his loss for a long time.

Finally along came Coyote. Now Coyote was a very wise man. He could look right through anything. He could look through a hill or a rock or anything solid like that and see what was on the other side. He found the people mourning for their lost Chief and said that perhaps he might be able to get him down out of the Upper World. At least he was going to try to do so, but even Coyote with all of his power was not able to reach the Upper World. Finally Spider came along and they told him their troubles. Spider went up to the Upper World, fastened his web there and then came down and took Coyote up with him, carrying Coyote in his hunting sack (maa'tc).

When Coyote reached the Upper World he found there a big sweat-house in which the three Thunders lived. When he arrived at the door he saw Panther inside so he went in, took him by the right hand and led him out and over to the sky door where Spider had remained. Spider then took Coyote and Panther into his sack and took them down to earth again.

Everybody was exceedingly glad to have their Chief back again and he announced that they would have a celebration for four days. This they did. They danced and feasted for four days and then Panther announced that thereafter when anyone died they would lie in the ground for four days and then they would go up into the sky.[25]

They celebrated for another four days, dancing and feasting and having a grand celebration and on the fourth day Panther announced that he had had a dream the night before. He had dreamed that the people were going to be scattered out in the mountains and elsewhere and that that was the last day upon which they would be able to talk to each other. He said that on the following morning he would call all the people together again and that then they would disperse.

On the following morning he arose at daybreak and called the people out of the dance-house into the open. He was the only one left who could talk. He spoke to each one and told him what he would be, deer, bear, coyote, rabbit, birds of various kinds, yellowjackets, snakes, lizards and so on. As he called off and designated each one in this way he at

---

[25]Panther did not mean that they would die in the ground in the sense that they would be buried but according to ancient Pomo customs a dead body was cremated in a shallow pit and the ashes were then covered with earth.

once took the form indicated and ran or flew away into his proper place. When everyone else was gone the Chief said, "I myself will be Panther."

8—PEOPLE ARE TRANSFORMED INTO BIRDS BY FOX[26]

Characters: 1. Coyote, 2. Fox, 3. The Bird-people.

Coyote made a sweat-house at a place called *T*am nōyō.[27] When he had finished the house he procured a great many feathers and placed them in the house. He then willed that they should become people and soon there were a great many people there. There were so many people in fact that they divided up and inhabited three different villages.

When these people went out hunting they used to bring in their food and eat in the sweat-house.

Nothing grew around these villages for two years. People spent most of their time in the sweat-house dancing. Finally they all turned into Bird-people. Some were older and some younger. The youngest of them all was a boy, Fox, who was so young that he could not fly. He went around and gathered up all of the dancing paraphernalia that he could find and placed these in the sweat-house. There were so many dancing suits that they completely filled the sweat-house.

Then he told the people to pick out the kind of feathers that they preferred and that when they did this each would be transformed into the particular kind of bird corresponding to the feathers he had picked out. Each one did this and immediately he touched a particular feather he was transformed at once into that kind of a bird and flew out of the house.

Fox alone was unable to fly. He tried for two days. He placed all kinds of feathers around on his arm but was unable to fly until the third day.

Now, there were four Fox brothers; three of them took Mallard duck feathers and were able to fly but Fox himself could not. The rest of these birds as they flew out of the house, circled four times around the house and around the hill and then they flew off down the river.

Fox followed along on the ground crying, and singing a song, "kīdē kīdē katsīlō katsīō", over and over again.

<hr>

[26]Informant: Kūmala, Central dialect.
[27]This place is located on what is known as Duncan's Sheep Ranch, about a mile east of the present Indian village at Hopland.

Finally all of the birds alighted at Pieta and waited for Fox. When he caught up with them they again started on flying slowly, but when they saw that Fox could not keep up with them by the time they had reached Echo, they all went on and did not wait for him any more. They flew down to Tomales Bay and alighted on the water and from there they went everywhere over the world.

MYTHS OF MISCELLANEOUS CREATIONS AND REGULATIONS

9—COYOTE GIVES PEOPLE IMPLEMENTS AND FOODS[28]

Characters:. 1. Coyote, 2. Wolf, 3. Wolf's son, 4. Wolf-boy's mother.

After Coyote had created people he gave them everything. He gave them bows (ha'i cim) and arrows (tsū) to shoot with. He gave them string snares (ta'slēma) with which to catch birds, and rope (badī'uk) to catch deer, and fish nets. He told people what kinds of foods they should eat. Of the plants which grew above the ground, he told them that they should eat teca', kala'kū, tcawai'yū, ho'mtca, kacai'yū, kala', tala', naka' and bamū'. Of the foods which grew under the ground, he told them they should eat cbū, batū'm, baba', mtīt, kakō'-bū, tala'-bū, cka'le, hō'-bū, and pūtī'. Of the foods which grew upon the trees, he told them they should eat tsapa (white oak), dūtsī' (live oak), wjū (a large species of post oak), kakū'l (a small species of post oak), ūcī' (mush oak?), ūtce'c (tan oak), bahe' (pepper-wood), bōca' (buckeye), bakai' (manzanita), dūcī' (hazel), kahe' (a long nut which grows in the mountains).

He told them that they should eat the following animals, pcē (deer), īge' (ground squirrel), tcūma't (gray squirrel), lam (gopher), cakō't (mouse), makī'ū (cottontail), maga'la (jackrabbit), mpē (skunk), baiyō'k (woodrat), yamō't (mountain-lion), dalō'm (wildcat) and kaū (fox). He told them that they should eat the following birds caka'ka (valley quail), tsū'wa (mountain robin), tsai (valley blue jay). He told them that when they were very hungry, almost starving, they might eat cai (eagle) and djucī'l (meadowlark), but never to eat buzzard (tūtcī'?), sūl (vulture) or makū'kū (night owl). He said that very old people might eat night owl when they wished to. He also told them

---

[28]Informant: John Beatty, Yokaia, Central dialect, 1904.

that there were certain other things which they must not eat.　They were tala'k (flying squirrel), all the snakes except one kind, bōwa'l (eel), which he told them he was going to put into the river, īwī' (coyote) and smē'wa (wolf).　Coyote also made bears and told them to kill some of these people.

Coyote then told the people, "Go out and hunt but do not go near the brush, because that is a dangerous place.　I have put bears in there close to the edge of the brush and they will bite you people so you must look out for them.　You must also be careful not to go near holes in the rocks, I put rattlesnakes (makō'ya) in there and they will bite you people.　I also made spiders (mtca) which will bite and kill you people."

He told the people all about these things which he had created to kill them, but he also told them that he would show them medicine to cure these bites.　He said, "I am going to show you another thing.　When you get hurt, when you get sick, you must sing.　One of you must be a doctor and must sing over those who are ill.　One of you, only, must be a doctor for the whole people."　Coyote then made the dancers and doctors feathers and other paraphernalia.

He then told the people, "I am going to put one chief over you people to direct you when you go out to hunt.　This man shall be Wolf.　He shall tell you how many you may kill.　He shall tell you that you shall kill two or three or four deer and if you do not kill that many, you will see something wrong, something bad."

When Coyote made Wolf chief for the hunting, he gave him something with which to kill deer.　Wolf did not take this home but hid it out in the mountains.　After that, every time the people went out, Wolf would tell them how many deer they should kill and everybody always killed the number he designated.

By and by the people began to grumble at Wolf and some of them said, "Why do you not bring that stuff which Coyote gave you for luck home?　Why do you always keep it out in the mountains?"

Wolf replied, "If I were to bring that home, then you fellows would see all about how it was done."　These people talked this way for a long time and finally, Wolf became angry and said, "I am going to get that stuff and bring it home."　So he went out to the mountains to get it.

While he was absent, the people were transformed into birds, each claiming his separate place. One would say, "This is my bushy place", and then he would go there to live. Another would say, "This is my canyon" and then he would go to that place to live.

After all the rest of the people had been transformed into deer and the like and had departed, the chief's son alone remained, but later, he too was transformed into a deer. At length, his father returned, saying to his son, "I don't think that you believe what I tell you. If you do believe what I tell you, you will be turned back into a human being again." His son believed what his father had said and was immediately returned to human form.

When his father went out to hunt, the boy would cry, because he was lonesome. After that, he got to taking the boy along with him but he told the boy, "Now when I find a deer, I will go up toward it in order to shoot it but you must look down. You must lie still right here. Don't you look at me, because if you do, I shall be transformed into a deer and you will be transformed into a deer also." After a while, they saw a deer in the shade of a tree. The father went up toward the deer but the boy looked at him and both were immediately transformed into deer.

The boy then started out to hunt for his mother. He went all over in search of her and all the time he sang; sang about his mother, his uncles, his aunts, his grandparents, his sisters, his brothers and all his other relatives. The song was as follows:

(A)

helema tcu ho helema tcu ho helema tcu ho helema
    tcu ho (Repeat four times)
hau wan tauk ke mi mu nai ke ku ne
helema tcu ho helema tcu ho helema tcu ho helema
    tcu ho (Repeat four times)
hau wan tauk ke mi mu nai ke ku ne
helema tcu ho helema tcu ho helema tcu ho helema
    tcu ho (Repeat four times)
hau wan tauk ke mi mu nai ke ku ne
mul bice bo pilau kau ya

(B)

Repeat *A*, ending with
hau wa tai ka he ke tce ma tca ha nai

(C)

Repeat *B*.

tcadai tedai he tana hune
tcedai tedai he tana hune
tcedai tedai he tana hune
tcadai tedai he tana hune

(Note: Here follow four involved changes in this song, which were unobtainable in detail from the informant.)

The boy sang to his mother in this way, saying, "My mother, I want you to tell me where you stay, upon what mountain you stay, in what canyon you stay, in what valley you stay, in what timber you stay, my mother, tell me." He went along singing this way, for a long time, and finally his mother answered him and said, "I stay here in this place they call 'bana' (a large canyon on the mountain over east of Boonville)." Then the boy went over there and stayed with his mother.

10—COYOTE'S CREATIONS[29]
INCIDENTS

   I. *Coyote creates sickness.*
  II. *Coyote creates Grizzly Bear.*
 III. *Coyote institutes cremation.*
 IV. *Coyote creates the rattlesnake.*
   V. *Coyote creates the elk.*
 VI. *Coyote creates "Indian Potatoes".*
VII. *Coyote institutes divorce.*
     Character: Coyote throughout.

I

(Coyote Creates Sickness)

After Coyote had created people he walked around all over and finally he came to the eastern end of the world.[30] Here lived a people[31] whom Coyote had created and sent over to this place. Coyote married one of the women of this place and settled down here to live. These people were all quite rich but Coyote was very poor. He had nothing. He thought over the matter and finally decided that he would have to make some of the people sick so that he could doctor them, for he was a great medicine-man.

---

[29]Informant: William James, Garcia River, Central dialect.
[30]cô'ma hamda.
[31]cô'ma hamda ke tca.

Pretty soon the Chief's wife fell ill and the people came to Coyote and told him that they did not know what was the matter with her. She lay there sick for four days. Finally Coyote told his wife that he knew what was the trouble and that he could cure her. "Yes", said Coyote finally, "I will cure that woman for four strings of beads.[32]" The Chief agreed to this so Coyote went out and collected eight of the large cocoons such as are used in making the cocoon rattle. These he took from the hazel, the blue blossom, and from one other shrub called "tsū'kale". He first removed the pupa from each of these and then hung them up to dry. Next he secured certain feathers, some of which were to put the cocoons on while other, finer feathers were to be used as trimmings around the edges of the rattle and as a sort of a top-knot on it. He also found some fine gravel to use in the cocoons. Then he very carefully made a fine rattle. Next he procured some obsidian. Finally he dressed in a full medicine-man's costume and then he went to doctor the woman.

He came into the Chief's house singing and shaking his rattle, and there he found the woman lying on the floor with her head toward the east. At her head they had placed a pole about five feet in height and on it hung the beads. He sat beside her bed and sang for quite a long time. Then he went out. This he did each morning and each evening for four days. On the last day he took her down to the river and made her sit down on the bank. Then he dipped his top-knot into the water and sprinkled her all over with it four times. Then she was completely cured.

No one had ever been sick before. This is the way Coyote created sickness.

II

(Coyote Creates Grizzly Bear)

Coyote decided that, since some of the others were well off, he would make something else to do them harm, so he created grizzly bear and sent him out into the brush. After a time the hunters went out and set their snares for deer. They set many snares and then they went into the brush and made a great noise in order to drive the deer out and into

---

[32]These were the small discoidal shell heads much made and used by the Pomo. Such beads were measured in "strings". A string was measured on the outstretched right arm from the thumb nail to the tip of the chin, and such a "string" was supposed to contain approximately four hundred beads. As a matter of fact it was customary to count off the beads and mention the number instead of calling for so many strings.

the runways where the snares were placed.	They caught several deer but when they came near one of the snares they saw the grizzly who acted as though he had been caught in it.	Of course the hunters did not know what the bear was, for there never had been any such animals until Coyote created them.	They came up close to the snare thinking to kill the grizzly but when he had them near enough to do so he attacked them and killed one of their number.	The rest ran away until the bear had gone.	Then they went back, made a stretcher,[33] and four of the men carried his body back to the village.	The whole village wailed and mourned his death.

III

(Coyote Institutes Cremation)

They mourned over the body of this man for a time, but no one knew what to do with it.	Finally they asked Coyote what he would advise.

He said, "Well, my friends, I will tell you what to do.	If you bury that fellow in the ground by and by the flesh will decay and make a very bad smell.	So you had better dig a shallow place about a span deep, as long as a man, and about half as wide.	Then build a big fire and place the body in it and let it burn.	When it has burned until only the shape of the bones can be seen among the ashes you must throw dirt over it and cover it up completely.	Then it can not harm anyone and there will be no smell."

They did this just as Coyote directed and people have cremated their dead ever since.

IV

(Coyote Creates the Rattlesnake)

Coyote saw that the women of the village went out to gather seeds to make meal, so he created Rattlesnake and told him to go out and hide in the grass.	He instructed Rattlesnake, "Now, whenever a woman comes out there to harvest seeds during her menstrual period you must bite her."	Soon such a woman went out with her basket and her seed-beater to gather wild sunflower seed and Rattlesnake bit her as Coyote had told him to do.

---

[33]Informants state that in olden times a very good stretcher was constructed out of poles and brush.	It was especially used to carry the wounded, sick, or dead back to the village in any such a case as the one here mentioned.

They brought the woman home and got Coyote to doctor her. This he did for a fee of the usual four strings of beads. He doctored her only one day and then he told her relatives to take out four baskets of seed-meal and have everyone eat some of it at a feast in honor of this woman. Then the woman got well.

Ever since this women know that they must not go out to harvest foods during their menstrual periods.

V

(Coyote Creates the Elk)

The people had always hunted deer but Coyote decided to make a larger animal for them so he created elk. The hunters went out one day and saw some of these elk.

One of the hunters said to Coyote, "What kind of a big deer is that over there?"

Coyote replied, "They call that the elk."

Then the hunters killed two of these big animals and everyone in the village had some of the meat there was so much of it, much more than on a deer.

VI

(Coyote Creates "Indian Potatoes")

After this Coyote created "Indian potatoes"[34] and caused them to grow all over in different places. One day the women went out and saw these plants. They asked Coyote what kind of new plants these were. Then Coyote showed them how to dig the "Indian potatoes" with a digging stick and how to cook them in the ashes and then sift the ashes away from the potatoes by means of an open-work sifting basket.

VII

(Coyote Institutes Divorce)

Coyote created all these things and told the people all about them and how to use them. Then he left these people and left his wife and went away. He came back over here toward the west where we now

[34]The term "Indian potato" is applied to almost any kind of bulb, tuber, or corm found in the region, which is exceptionally rich in different species of brodeas, calachortis, and many other similar plants.

live. That is why we now have these various things and why we do as we do now. That is why a man among us will sometimes leave his wife. It is because Coyote did that way for the first time and showed us how to do.

11—COYOTE CREATES THE OCEAN[35]

Character: Coyote.

Coyote wished that the ocean would come into existence and roll up against the shore furiously. Before this there was no ocean and the land was even all along its edge. At once, after Coyote had made this wish, the great water appeared and came rolling in, in great waves against the shore. It came so hard that it tore away a lot of the land and made the present rough shoreline.

When Coyote saw how rough it was and how it tore the land away he became afraid and made the water roll in more gently and be more calm so that anyone could walk out in it and get mussels, abalones, seaweeds, and all the different kinds of sea foods that we now eat.

12—COYOTE INSTITUTES DEATH[36]

Characters: 1. Coyote, 2. Rattlesnake, 3. Chief, 4. Chief's daughter, 5. Coyote's daughter.

This all happened at Mee'ū which is only a short distance from the old village of Latcū'pda, on the North Fork of the Gualala river. Mee'ū was never inhabited by any of the present day Indian peoples but was a home of some of the race of "Bird-people" who formerly lived here before the Indians were created.

One of these people was Coyote. He went out to gather wood for his wife who was going to make acorn bread. As he went along under a large buckeye tree in the midst of a patch of wild sunflowers, he saw a rattlesnake run into a hole and then stick its head out so that he could watch the people in the village which was very near at hand. Coyote stopped and danced around the rattlesnake, meanwhile calling to his wife and telling her to get all the rest of the people of the village to come out and watch him dance. The people gathered around and asked Coyote what he saw and what he was dancing for.

---

[35]Informant: Tom Mitchell, Eastern dialect, 1902.
[36]Informant: William James, Central dialect.

He said, "I see a very fine kind of a bird in that hole there. You have to dance around for a time before you can see it and pick it up." He then told the Chief and his daughter to dance right up close to the grass where the snake was hidden, and finally he told the girl to dance up still closer.   She did so and the snake finally slid out of the grass and bit her on the leg.   She sat right down there and said, "Something bit me here on the leg."   The snake went back into his hole at once.

Coyote said, "You people do not dance correctly.   That is why you got hurt."

They picked the girl up and carried her back to the village where she died in a few hours.

Then the Chief came to Coyote and said, "Well, Coyote, we want to have the people come to life again."

But Coyote replied, "No, that will not do.   Pretty soon we would have too many people in the world and there would not be enough food to go around."

To this the Chief agreed so they made a hole in the ground, built a big fire and soon cremated the girl, after dressing her up very nicely with a great many beads.

The Chief knew that Coyote was to blame for all this and in a couple of days he poisoned Coyote's daughter and she died.

Everyone mourned, and Coyote went to the Chief and said, "Well, Chief, my daughter is dead.   I want to bring her to life again."

The Chief replied, "I think that would not do.   We wanted to do that once but you said that that would not do.   I think we will have to let her remain dead and burn her up as we did my daughter.   There would be too many people here in the world if we were to bring them all back to life again and then we would not have enough to eat."

Coyote mourned and wailed for a long time, but finally he said, "Well, we will have to let it go that way and let people die after this."

So it is that people now-a-days die as the Bird-people did then.   If Coyote had not done and said these things people would not die at present.

13—CREATION OF SALMON[37]

Up at John Day's on Eel River in olden times someone took a piece of wood and carved it, in every respect, in the form of a fish.   He tied

---

[37]Informant: George Dashields, Northern dialect.

a string to this wooden fish and placed it in the river and held onto the string. This wooden image immediately turned into a real fish and there have been many salmon in that river ever since.

14—COYOTE CREATES THE SUN, MOON AND STARS AND PEOPLES THE EARTH[38]

Characters: 1. Coyote, 2. Moon, 3. Sun.

Coyote took four sticks of a pine called "cīya'kale". He peeled the bark off from each of these four sticks and carefully prepared them. To the upper end of each of these sticks he fastened the feathers of vulture, eagle and buzzard. These feathers, together with eagle down, he attached to the sticks with milkweed string.

He then placed himself in four different positions. He first stood upon his head, then he laid upon his belly, next he laid upon his back and finally he sat up erect. He then took a dipper and dipped up water and threw it up into the sky. As this water sprinkled back down to earth the sky became a little cloudy. These clouds formed in the north and in the south and gradually increased and spread until they came together over in the east where the sun rises and then they traveled toward the west until they had completely covered the sky. It took four days for these clouds to travel from the east to the west in this way.

Coyote next took an oak ball and cut it with an obsidian knife so that it had five corners. This he threw up into the sky and it immediately became the Sun.

Sun then said to the Moon,[39] "I will make you my mother. You know who made all of us."

"Yes, replied the Moon, "I do, I will tell you. He made the sky also. It was Diwí tca'kale."

The Sun then remarked, "Mother, I will tell you what Coyote wants to do for us."

"What is it my son?" said the Moon.

"He ought to make a good hot fire and then he should take four good live coals and throw them up into the sky so that they will stick there. Those will be stars. He ought also to take a good hot coal and throw

[38]Informant: Charley Brown, Northern dialect.
[39]The moon created by Coyote in this myth was made out of blue mud, that is blue clay (maca'la).
The Indians in olden times used to make dolls out of this same blue clay.

it over toward the east. That will be the morning star."

Then Coyote added, "Mother, how can we make it dark?"

Moon replied, "Well, we will make a big fire and we will then take a willow club and strike it and make it go out. That will make it dark."

Coyote did that and that is what made night. Then Coyote said, "Mother, you will not come out for two or three nights sometimes and then you will come out and grow again." To this Moon agreed.

The Sun, however, said, "I will not go out myself. I will rise every morning regularly. Now we shall have to separate but how shall we make the earth shake?"

To this Moon replied, "Well, when I shake my head the earth will shake and this will be the earthquake."

Coyote then said, "Now I will commence creating things."

Then he made the Sun and the Moon go away to their respective places in the sky.

Coyote then created the various birds, mammals, plants and all kinds of food. He created all these and told them just what they were to do; how some would live in the mountains, some were to live in the water and so on.

Then he said, "I will live in the mountains myself and I will always be there, even if they kill me, I will still be there." All these things that he had created required two days and two nights. Then he proceeded to create supernatural beings. These required two days and two nights more. Thus eight days all told were required for the creation of everything by Coyote, four days for the creation of the sun, moon and stars and four days for the creation of mammals, birds, food and supernatural beings.

Having finished his creations Coyote said, "Now I am done and I shall go home and the rest of you shall live here as you like. My son, my father and my mother will be here also."

Then he said to rattlesnakes and to grizzly bears, "You shall bite people if they do not behave themselves and if they are bad."

Then he made it very foggy. People crowded around him but he disappeared. No one saw which way he went, but he just went away.

Coyote's mother and all the rest of the people cried when Coyote left them. Then all went away to live in their respective places as Coyote had designated.

MYTHS OF DESTRUCTION. THE BURNING OF THE WORLD

15—THE BURNING OF THE WORLD AND THE CREATION OF CLEAR LAKE[40]

INCIDENTS AND CHARACTERS

I. *The birth of Coyote's children.*
>   1. *Coyote, 2. Wood-duck sisters (two), 3. Grandmother of the Wood-duck sisters, 4. Coyote's children (two).*

II. *Coyote burns the world.*
>   1. *Coyote, 2. Coyote's children (two), 3. Spider, 4. Creator (Madū'mda).*

III. *The Creation of Clear Lake.*
>   1. *Coyote, 2. Kū'ksū.*

IV. *Coyote creates people from feathers.*
>   1. *Coyote, 2. The Bird-people, 3. Falcon, 4. Blue Jay, 5. Bluebird, 6. Gray Squirrel, Obsidian-man, 7. Red-headed-woodpecker, 8. Crow, 9. Hummingbird, 10. Kingbird, 11. Thrasher, 12. Eagle, 13. Panther, 14. Wolf, 15. Wood-duck, 16. Makō, 17. Kakaū'.*

V. *The theft of the Sun.*
>   1. *Coyote, 2. Mice (four), 3. Cmaï'kadōkadō, 4. Condor, 5. A species of hawk (tcitcī), 6. A small species of hawk (dakát), 7. Loon, 8. A species of hawk (tcīyá), 9. Sun-man, 10. Sun-messenger, 11. Red-headed-woodpecker, 12. Hummingbird, 13. Eagle, 14. Ce'tata, 15. Crow, 16. Blue Jay, 17. Gray Squirrel, 18. Sleep charm, 19. Sun-people, 20. Falcon.*

VI. *Coyote transforms people into animals.*
>   1. *Coyote, 2. Deer, 3. Wolf, 4. Bear, 5. Panther, 6. Loon, 7. Coot, 8. Duck, 9. Dīkū'būhū, 10. Crow, 11. Red-headed-woodpecker, 12. Sapsucker, 13. Kingbird, 14. Daka't, 15. Night-hawk, 16. Great-horned owl, 17. Cmaï'kodōkadō, 18. Falcon.*

I.

(The Birth of Coyote's Children)

There was a large village at Nō-napō-tī and here there lived two Wood-duck sisters who always kept apart from the rest of the inhabitants of the village, and, although there were many of the men of the village who admired them, the sisters persistently refused to have anything to do with them. One of their admirers was Coyote, who tried various means to induce one of them to become his wife, but all without

---

[40]This myth was printed in "A Composite Myth of the Pomo Indians," Jour. Amer. Folk-Lore, XIX, 37-51, 1906.
Central dialect, 1904.

success, so that he finally determined to resort to trickery. It being then the food-gathering season, he proposed that all of the women of the village should go on a buckeye gathering excursion into the neighboring mountains while the men were busy hunting and fishing, or were engaged in making implements at the village.

The Wood-duck sisters had a very old and partly blind grandmother who had gone out camping with another party, although they did not know this. When they went to get her to go with them, they found an old woman there who was covered with a rabbitskin blanket and looked exactly like her, but who was really Coyote. The Wood-ducks led this blind old woman along out to the camp and made a bed for her, for she was very tired.

That evening when the food had been prepared, the Wood-ducks gave some to the old woman, but she said, "My daughters, I cannot eat. I cannot raise myself up. I want to sit up and eat." The elder of the two sisters sat at the old woman's back to hold her up, but Coyote said, "I cannot sit up when only one of you holds me up. One of you must sit in front of me." Eventually they became aware of the deception which Coyote had played upon them. Then the two sister began to fight Coyote and were soon joined by others of the women of the camp, who brought clubs and stones, for every one now knew that Coyote had been playing another of his tricks. There were born immediately four children. The first two Coyote rescued, placing them in his hunting sack. The other two were killed by the enraged women. Coyote immediately ran back to the village and the women followed soon after.

II

(Coyote Burns the World)

Coyote continued to live at Nō-napō-tī with his two children, but he had no one to care for them while he was away hunting and fishing, and the people of the village treated them very badly whenever he was gone. They threw rocks and sticks at the children, called them bad names, and even threw coals of fire on them. When the children were old enough to get around by themselves, Coyote determined to revenge himself and his children for the abuse they had suffered. He accordingly went east to the end of the world and there dug a huge tunnel which he filled with fir bark. He disappeared regularly every morning for four days, and no one could think what he was doing, for he went about it very secretly. Some of the people asked what he was doing while he was gone all day, but he replied that he was only hunting food for his children.

After a long time Coyote put all kinds of food, water, clothing, a fire drill and other implements, and also his two children, into his hunting sack, and after sundown went on the roof of the dance-house, where he watched toward the east for some time. Finally he called out, "I do not know what can be the matter; it looks as if something is wrong. Come out and see." Soon there was a great noise like thunder, and smoke and fire appeared all over the east as far as they could see from north to south. Every one knew that Coyote had something to do with it, and all began to ask him to save them, calling him father and other terms of relationship; but Coyote replied, "I shall not be saved either. I do not know what has happened. I shall burn up too, I suppose; my body is no rock or water." But the people all cried to him to save them as the fire came nearer and nearer, until at last it completely surrounded them and left but a very small space about the village unburned.

Coyote now shouted, "ē——", with his hand uplifted (all finger tips pointing upward), four times, and presently there came down out of the sky a feather rope (yúlūk) on the end of which Spider (tó-cbū) hung with his back downward. Coyote jumped on to Spider's belly and the feather rope immediately started to ascend. After a short time Coyote wished to stop, so Spider stopped the ascent and instantly spun a web large enough for Coyote to walk around on and look at the burning world beneath, which was by that time entirely on fire. They then went on upward for a time, whereupon Spider stopped and spun another web so that Coyote might give his children some food. A third stop was made and a web spun so that Coyote might give the children water, and a fourth and last stop was made and a web spun so that all might rest and take a last look at the burning world. At last they arrived at the gate[41] leading into the sky and entered.

Spider, who was its keeper, remained at the gate, but Coyote and his children, who now got out of the hunting sack, went eastward toward the house of Madū'mda,[42] which they saw immediately upon entering

_____

[41] The gate, an opening through the sky, is guarded by snakes who allow only those who reside in the heavens, or persons for whom Madū'mda has sent, to enter.

[42] Madū'mda, who is the chief deity in Pomo mythology, is the elder brother of Coyote and lives in a large sweat-house in the sky, where, to a great extent, the conditions are the same as on earth except that there is nothing disagreeable.

the gate. Their road lay over a plain covered with grass and sweet-smelling flowers. There were, however, no people to be seen. On the way Coyote and the children stopped and rested four times, but at last arrived at the house, where Coyote knocked on the door.

Madū'mda came and invited them into the house; saying, "He hé, sīnwa nō balma; what have you come here for? I know you have been doing something. That is why you come here in this manner. Why do you want to do something bad always? Why do you want to treat your children (all people) that way? Why are you not sorry for your children? Now, go back and live as you did before and do not act that way."

Coyote said he would go back on the following day, and Madū'mda then instructed him as to what he should do when he went to the earth and how he should act toward people in order that he might be on friendly terms with them.

III

(The Creation of Clear Lake)

Coyote returned to the gate and Spider then took him back to the earth in the same manner as he had come; but the earth was much changed. Formerly the mountains were high, but now they were much lower, the tops having been burned off. The trees, rocks, and streams were all gone, and the appearance of the whole country was different. He found all things which had lived on earth lying around roasted, and he commenced to eat everything he found, deer, birds, fish, snakes, and so on, until he grew very hot and thirsty. He then began to look for water, running about from place to place where there had formerly been springs and streams, but all were dry, and he nearly gave up the search. Finally, however, he wandered toward the west and found water in the ocean. He drank copiously four times. Having completely satisfied his thirst, he started homeward, but had not gone far when he began to feel sick. He grew steadily worse as he raced on, endeavoring to reach his home before he should die, and was only able to reach Kabái-danō (Wild Onion Mountain), a bald hill on the western shore of Clear Lake, where he fell upon his back groaning.

Kabái-danō was really Kúksū's[43] sudatory, and when he heard Coyote groaning on the roof he came out much surprised. "O——, who's there? I did not know there was anybody here."

Coyote replied, "Yes, it is I. I have been eating fish and meat, and I got hot and thirsty, and there was nobody around, so I went west and found water. I took a drink, but I took too much and am sick. I did not know that there was any one here. I wish you would doctor me in any way you know."

Kúksū soon prepared to doctor Coyote, and returned with his body painted black, and wearing a very large headdress. He had a large whistle in his mouth and carried a long black medicine-wand in his hand. As Kúksū came out of the sudatory he ran in a counter-clockwise direction four times around it, then in a clockwise direction four times around it. He then ran four times around Coyote, then ran up to him from the south, and returned backwards to the point of starting, where he turned his head as far as possible to the left. Again running around his patient four times, he approached him from the east and completed the same cycle, following it by the same cycle from the north and then from the west. He then ran four times around his patient in a counter-clockwise direction, after which he turned his head to the left; then four times in a clockwise direction, again turning his head to the left. He then told Coyote that he would cry, "ē—— " four times, and jump on his belly. He then ran around the sick man in a counter-clockwise direction and cried "ē—— " four times; then ran up to him blowing his whistle and pointing his medicine-wand at his belly four times, and at the end of the fourth time he turned his head to the left. He then repeated the complete cycle of four runs and the turn of the head to the left. He then cried "ē—— " once, ran, and jumped on Coyote's belly, which burst with a sound like that of a great explosion. The water which Coyote had drunk at the ocean ran down in every direction even to as far as Tule Lake and Scott's Valley, and the rivers com-

---

[43]Kúksū is an important character in Pomo mythology and in certain ceremonials. He is a person of characteristic Pomo physique, but possesses great power as a medicine-man or doctor. He always appears painted entirely black, wearing on his head a very large head-dress, called "big head", or "Kúksū-kaiya", and with a tuft of shredded tule fibre attached to the small of his back. He carries a black cane or wand (cakoik), and, while doctoring, blows constantly a large whistle made of elderberry wood.

According to Dr. Dixon (Maidu Myths, p. 42) Kúksū is found also among the Maidu, there being the first man created by Earth-initiate. His appearance is, however, quite different, he being depicted as a person of pure white complexion, with pink eyes, black hair, and shining teeth, and withal very handsome. He possessed great knowledge and played an important part in the final disposition and distribution of the people created by Earth-initiate.

menced running, so that the water collected in the lowest places and formed Clear Lake,[44] and in the water there were fish, snakes, turtles, and all kinds of water-birds.

As Kúksū jumped upon his belly, Coyote said, "There will be much water and plenty of fish, snakes, frogs, turtles, and water-birds. They will all come from my belly alive, and by and by there will be people in this country to eat them."

Coyote then arose and walked a short distance. Then he turned and said to Kúksū, "I will make a dance-house and make a big dance and feast and will call you. I will let you know when everything is ready."

Kúksū said, "All right, that is good."

IV

(Coyote Creates People from Feathers)

Coyote went northward to Yŏ-būtūi (near Upper Lake) and there built a small tule house for himself. He then went all around the lake and talked with all the different birds about the coming dance, and secured the services of two young men from every species of bird to assist in building the dance-house. These all came at the appointed time, and there were so many of them that they were able to dig the pit and complete the house in a very short time. Meanwhile Coyote made many tule houses and had a large village prepared. After finishing the dance-house the birds all left, Coyote promising to notify them when all things were ready for the dance.

While the birds were at work, Coyote took from them without their knowledge two feathers each, and in each one of the tule houses he placed a pair of feathers, except in the best house, where he placed a single falcon feather. He then went to bed in his own house, and lay there talking to himself all night. He said that the feathers should turn into people,[45] and that there should be people there before daybreak on the following morning, a man and a woman in each house; that Falcon should be the Chief of all and should be the last one to leave the house; that Blue Jay (Tsai) should be a doctor and poison-man (wizard); that Bluebird (Tsápū) should be a poison-man also; that

---

[44]The fact that there are at times waves of considerable height on Clear Lake is explained by some of the Indians as a necessary condition, since the water originally came from the ocean, where there are waves at all times.
[45]According to other versions people were created from sticks instead of feathers.

Gray Squirrel should be Obsidian-man (Katcá-tca) and that he should
be a quick fighter and dodger, a high jumper and able to run up trees;
that Red-headed-woodpecker (Katák) should be a slow man but able to
see farther than any one else; that Crow (Kaái) should be a slow man
but very long-winded and able to fly higher than any one else; that
Hummingbird (Tsúdīyūn) should be able to fly faster than any one
else and should be a doctor with the power to carry away disease
by pulling hair out of a patient's body and carrying it out where the
wind might blow it away; but that before doctoring in this manner he
should dance; that Hummingbird should also have the power to fly up in
the air and cause thunder and lightning; that Kingbird (Kapintadátadaū)
should always be the first awake in the morning and should wake the
rest of the village; and that Thrasher (Wócwoc) should watch over the
people of the village and wake every one at intervals throughout the
night so as to prevent some one from poisoning them; it would be particularly his duty to keep a close watch on Blue Jay, who was a poison-man.

Coyote had just finished designating the duties and powers ot each
individual when he heard Kingbird say, "Wē wé, it is daylight now,
wake up, wake up." He went out but saw no one astir. He went into
the dance-house, but there was no one there. Soon however he heard
some one cough outside the house. He then went up on the roof of
the dance-house to a point near the smoke-hole, from where he commenced to speak to the people: "Now, my children, you young men go
out and get wood for the dance-house. You young women make mush,
pinole, and bread, and when you have finished preparing the food, bring
it into the dance-house so that we may all eat. After we have all eaten
I will tell you what to do next, my children."

As the young men started to get wood, the old people told them
that the first man to return would be considered the best man. Then
Gray Squirrel ran swiftly up the hill until he came to a large dry
manzanita bush which he cut down and into short lengths with his feet
very quickly. He bound the wood in a bundle with a withe of white
oak and ran back to the village, arriving there long before any of the
others. As he threw the wood into the smoke-hole it struck the floor
with a loud noise and those within cried, "He hé, be careful there.
Don't make so much noise up there. You will break down the dance-
house." Finally, after all the young men had returned with wood,

Coyote directed the fire-tender (láimōc) to kindle the fire and then to begin the fanning. This was done and the men fanned one after another until all the wood was burned and all the men were very warm, after which they ran to the creek and bathed for a short time.

When all had returned to the dance-house, Coyote spoke again from the roof, and directed that all the food should be brought into the house, where every one might enjoy the feast. This was done, and every one feasted for a long time. Then Coyote rose from his place between the fire and the centerpole and again spoke to the people, finishing with these words, "Eagle and Gray Squirrel will be your Chiefs (tcá-kalik). They shall be of equal rank, and each will care for his own people." Then speaking to the two captains, he said, "You shall be captains. You shall talk to your people and shall instruct them in all that is just and right. Henceforth I shall be an old man and shall have nothing to do but eat."

The two Chiefs then consulted and decided to appoint Panther (Damót) and Wolf (Sméwa) chief huntsmen, Makō and Kakaū' chief fishermen, and Wood-duck female Chief. Others were appointed fire-tenders (láimōc), head singer (kéūya), and drummer (tsīlo'tca). Eagle then announced[46] the appointments of the two huntsmen and two fishermen, one each for each division of the village, and of Wood-duck as the female Chief of the entire village, also of the dance-house officials for the entire village. In conclusion he said, "Now you hunters and fishermen must tell us how we can all live together and get along well together. We have finished speaking now."

The huntsmen and fishermen consulted, but finally said, "We know very little. We can only hunt and fish for the people, and must follow the instructions of our Chiefs."

Then they asked Wood-duck what she would have them do. She replied, "I do not think we are living now as we should. We should have one head Chief (tcá-yedūl-bate) to govern us all, and Falcon (táta) is the proper one for that office. Coyote created us all, and I think we should make Falcon head chief, as his grandfather (Coyote) was before him."

As Coyote had willed it, Falcon had not yet left his house; so the

[46]In speaking to the people Eagle always spoke in a loud voice, repeating *verbatim* what Gray Squirrel said to him in a low tone.

fire-tenders were sent to bring him to the dance-house. A large black-bear-skin blanket was spread immediately in front of the centerpole in the dance-house, and when Falcon had seated himself on it saying, "Yes, this is good," Coyote asked him to tell the people what should be done. Falcon replied that the best thing that could be done would be to hold a big dance to which all of the neighboring people should be invited; meaning all the people who had assisted Coyote in the building of the dance-house.

A great dance was then celebrated for four days and nights, after which a feast was spread on the dancing ground in the dance-house, and Eagle told Falcon to address the people. This he did and finally called the two chiefs, the two huntsmen, the two fishermen, and the two fire-tenders to come and divide the food among the people so that all might eat and enjoy themselves. Those appointed divided the food, giving the best food to the head singer, next to the chorus singers, and so on until every one had had an abundance of food. This feast ended the celebration and all the visitors departed. The people whom Coyote had created out of the feathers continued to live at this village for a long time.

V

(The Theft of the Sun)

At this time the sun did not move across the heavens as it does now. It only rose a short distance above the eastern horizon and then sank again. Coyote finally determined to see why the sun behaved in this peculiar manner. He collected and placed in his hunting sack food, dancing paraphernalia, a sleep-producing tuft of feathers (sma-kaáitcil), and four mice. With these, and accompanied by singers and dancers he started eastward, in which direction they travelled for four days. Coyote took with him as his head singer Cmai-kadōkadō. Among his dancers were Sūl (condor), Tcitcī' (a species of hawk), Dakát (a small species of hawk), Kok (loon), and Tcīyá (a species of hawk). These were all very strong people and were taken not only because of their ability to dance, but also in order that there might be strong men who were able to carry the sun back to the village. At the end of the second day all of the party dressed themselves in their dancing paraphernalia and finished the rest of the journey dancing and singing.

Near evening of the fourth day the party arrived at a big dance-house, the home of the Sun-people,[47] around which they danced in a counter-clockwise direction four times, then in a clockwise direction four times. They then entered the house and danced in the same manner around the fire, then around the centerpole, and finally around the fire and pole together, at last halting and seating themselves in front of the centerpole.

Sun-man saw Coyote and his people entering the Sun-house and sent one of his messengers to welcome them. As the visitors seated themselves the messenger said, "It is good, friends, that you have come here."

Coyote replied, "My people wished to come and have a little dance with you tonight."

The messenger replied, "Yes, that is good, we will dance."

By and by the rest of the Sun-people came home, Sun-man, as was his custom, hanging the sun by the grapevine withe to one of the rafters of the dance-house. Wood was finally brought and all things were in readiness for the dance, the first of which Coyote proposed should be the fire-dance (hó-ke), a dance in which all might join.

As the dance began Coyote liberated the four mice which he had secreted in his hunting sack and told them to run up the centerpole and along the rafters to where the sun was tied, and gnaw the withe that bound it to the roof. Presently one of the mice fell from the roof into the fire, but sprang out and attempted to escape. He was caught by one of the Sun-messengers, who was about to throw him back into the fire when Coyote called to him, "Here, here, do not throw that away. I eat those. Give it to me." The messenger gave Coyote the mouse and Coyote pretended to eat it, crunching a piece of charcoal to give the sound of breaking bones, while the mouse ran down his arm into the hunting sack. From here he was soon able to again run up the center-

---

[47]Informants differ somewhat in their opinions of the Sun-people, but according to one informant they are: the Sun-prophet (dá-matü), who has the power, by means of visions, of seeing and knowing everything that transpires upon the earth, and directs all the movements and conduct of the other Sun people; the Sun-man (dá-tcatc) who carries the sun, a large shining disc, in his hand or suspended from his neck by means of a grapevine withe; two Sun-women (dá-mata), the daughters of Sun-man; and four Sun-messengers (dá-tcma), who always accompany Sun-man and do his bidding. As Sun-man soars in the heavens with the sun, he sees everything done by the people on the earth and, when some misdeed is committed, he sends one of the Sun-messengers to the earth to shoot the offender with an invisible arrow and carry away his spirit to the Abode of the Dead beyond the southern end of the world, where, if Dá-matü approves of the death, the spirit remains. Otherwise the messenger returns the spirit to its body and the victim recovers consciousness.

pole and renew his gnawing on the withe that held the sun. During this dance all four of the mice fell one at a time from the roof and were rescued by Coyote and returned to their work in like manner. The fire-dance was finally finished after four intermissions, and the usual plunge and short swim followed. Then came a war-dance (tcmá-ke), which was followed by still another dance; the three dances lasting until nearly midnight.

By that time all of the Sun-people were very tired and Coyote commenced to dance the fourth dance alone. He placed the sleep-producing tuft of feathers which he had brought in his hunting sack on the end of a stick, making a wand which he waved over the people as he danced, with the result that after a time all of the Sun-people were sound asleep; but Coyote's people were not affected by the wand. By this time the mice had succeeded in gnawing in two the withe which held the sun and bringing it down to the floor.

Coyote's people then caught hold of the edge of the sun and all danced out of the house in exactly the reverse order in which they had entered. They danced around the center pole and fire together, first four times in a clockwise direction, then four times in a counter-clockwise direction, following this by the same cycle with the center pole as a center, with the fire as a center, and with the dance-house itself as a center, after which they started westward toward their home. Coyote now willed that the earth should contract so that they might return home quickly, and they found that they were soon near their village.

Red-headed-woodpecker, the far-sighted man, first saw the party as it returned, and called every one in the village out to see the new light. The sun was laid on the ground in the village and its final disposition was discussed, with the result that Coyote told the people that it must be hung up in the middle of the sky. Falcon accordingly called forth two brothers of each species of bird, and instructed them to try to take the sun up into the heavens and hang it there according as Coyote had directed. Those who successively attempted the feat were Hummingbird, Dakát, Eagle, Loon, Cé-tata, and many others. All except the Crow brothers had tried and failed, and when they came forward to try every one laughed at them and remarked upon their slowness of flight and their physical weakness; but one of them grasped the sun by its edge while the other flew under it so that it rested on his back. Thus they flew higher and higher, interchanging their respective positions frequently in order to rest each other. As the Crows flew they cried, "a——, a——, a——," until to the great surprise of the watchers below they reached such a height that they could no longer be heard; and then such a height that they were lost to view to all save Red-headed-woodpecker, who was able to see much farther than any one else. He announced from time to time the progress of the Crows: "They are a long way up now. They are getting near the spot where the sun must hang. They are flying very slowly. They seem very tired. They have stopped now to take a rest. They are only a very short distance from the place now. Now they have reached it. There, they have hung it up. Now they are coming back down."

After a long time the Crows reached the earth again, having travelled downward like bullets. The people of the village rejoiced greatly that they had the sun and had it hung up in the proper place so that it could give them light. They brought out all kinds of beads, baskets, blankets, and food as presents to the Crows for the service they had rendered.

Presently some one cried, "ē——," and Blue Jay told everyone to assemble in front of the dance-house. Here they found Coyote and Falcon standing on the roof; they announced their decision that a dance should be held to celebrate the occasion. The first dance was the fire dance in which every one joined, dancing until all were very warm and then, as usual, taking a swim.

When they returned to the dance-house Coyote noticed that Gray Squirrel was not among then and said, "There is one man who is gone but none of you have noticed it."

They all asked, "Who?"

"It is Gray Squirrel who is not here. He has gone away and left us because he does not like the way we do things; but we need not worry or try to hunt for him, for he does not seem to like any one."

So all returned to the dance-house and resumed the celebration.

VI

(Coyote transforms people into animals)

Not long after this Coyote became provoked at the actions of the people and said, "You people do not try to do as I tell you to. You do not seem to care to do the proper things and try to be somebody.

You might as well be animals and go and do the way you like best."
So he proceeded to turn them all into animals and birds and to desig-
nate the habitat and characteristics of each:

"*You* shall always live in the mountains. You shall be afraid and
will be shot for meat. Your name shall be Deer (Pcé).

"*You* shall live in the woods and shall hunt for deer. Once in a
while you shall kill a man. Your name shall be Wolf (Sméwa).

"*You* shall always live in the mountains and in the woods. You
shall hunt for deer and shall sometimes kill me. Your name shall be
Bear (Bitá).

"*You* shall live in the woods and in the mountains. You shall hunt
for deer and shall sometimes kill people. Your name shall be Panther
(Damōt).

"*You* shall live around Clear Lake. You shall live in the trees, make
your nest there, and defecate upon them. You shall eat raw fish. Your
name shall be Loon (Kok).

"*You* shall swim around Clear Lake and eat bugs and grass. Your
name shall be Coot (Kátsiya).

"*You* shall also swim around in Clear Lake and eat bugs and grass.
Your name shall be Duck (Kaiyán).

"*You* shall stand around in the lake and whenever there are big
schools of fish coming out of the lake into the creeks you shall cry,
'íts dīkūbūhū'. Your name shall be Dīkúbūhū.

"*You* shall fly around in the air and catch bugs and eat them. You
shall hunt around in places where there are many bugs and grasshoppers
and shall eat them raw. Your name shall be Crow.

"*You* shall fly around in the trees, gather acorns, make holes in the
trees, put the acorns in there for winter time, and then eat them. Your
name shall be Red-headed-woodpecker.

"*You* shall live among the trees. You shall peck holes in them and
shall eat the sap. Your name shall be Sapsucker.

"*You* shall fly around in the open country where there is plenty of
room and fresh air and shall fly down and catch bugs and grasshoppers
and eat them raw. Your name shall be Kingbird.

"*You* shall fly up very high in the air and then fly very swiftly down
to the ground and catch mice or birds, or any kind of food. Your name
shall be Dakát (a species of hawk).

"*You* shall live out in the woods in a hollow tree. You cannot see in the daytime. During the night is the only time you will be able to see. Then you shall catch mice and eat them. Your name shall be Nighthawk (?) (Natótō).

"*You* shall live out in a hollow tree during the day for you cannot see except at night. Then you shall catch mice and eat them and you shall sing at night also. Your name shall be Owl.

"*You* shall live out in the woods during the day for you cannot see during the daytime. You can only see at night. You shall hunt and sing at night. Your name shall be Cmáikadōkadō."

When Coyote finally finished designating the attributes of each different animal and bird he said, "I shall go by the name of Coyote (īwí). Falcon here shall be called Táta. He shall be a flying bird and shall live where there are no other birds around. All you birds and mammals shall raise children, and their children shall raise children, and all shall be called by the names I have given you. I shall be Coyote and I shall be able to smell as far as any of you can see. I shall be able to smell very far and tell who or what is there. I shall sneak around and steal things. Sometimes I shall even run after human beings and kill and eat them.

"Now you all stand up and get ready; when I cry four times we must all run off to our respective places:" All rose and Coyote cried, "ē————ī————ye! ē————ī————ye! ē————ī————ye! "ē————ī————ye! yū——he! wē wē!" All were immediately transformed into the birds and animals Coyote had indicated and went to the various places he had designated. Coyote went away last.

ABSTRACT

(1) The licentiousness of Coyote prompts trickery. Coyote saves two of his miraculously-born children and cares for them unaided.

(2) The people of the village abuse the children in his absence. Coyote revenges himself and his children by setting fire to the world. The three escape to the sky by means of Spider, the gate-keeper of the sky, and a feather rope. They visit Madúmda. He is displeased with the conduct of Coyote and sends him back to the earth with instructions as to his future actions.

(3) Upon returning to the earth Coyote finds the tops of the mountains burned off, the streams dried up, and all kinds of food roasted by

the great world-fire. He eats a prodigious quantity of the roasted meat, becomes thirsty, and searches for water which he finally finds in the ocean. He drinks four times, becomes very sick, and succeeds in reaching Kabái-danō, where he is doctored by Kŭksū with the result that the water he drank forms Clear Lake, and the roasted meat eaten turns into the water fauna of the region.

(4) At the northern end of Clear Lake, Coyote causes the construction by the Bird-people of a large dance-house. He, meanwhile, erects many dwelling-houses and secures two feathers from each of the birds. These he places in the houses and thus creates human beings. Officials are appointed, and a dance and feast are celebrated.

(5) The sun did not formerly rise. Coyote and party journey eastward to the home of the Sun-people and dance with them. Coyote sends up four mice from his hunting sack to gnaw off the withe with which the sun is hung to the roof of the dance-house while he dances and induces sleep among the Sun-people by means of a magic wand. The sun is finally secured and all escape and return to the village at Clear Lake. The Bird-people are called together, and all try to carry the sun up and hang it in the middle of the sky, which feat is finally accomplished by the wisdom of the two Crow brothers. Thus the world has proper light.

(6) Coyote soon becomes provoked at the actions of his people and transforms them into animals and birds, assigning the attributes and habitat of each.

16—COYOTE DESTROYS THE WORLD BY FIRE[48]
INCIDENTS AND CHARACTERS
I. The World-fire.
    1. Coyote, 2. Coyote's sons (two), 3. Magic rope.
II. The creation of Clear Lake.
    1. Coyote, 2. Frog, 3. Ocean.
III. Coyote creates people from feathers.
    1. Coyote, 2. Duck, 3. People, 4. Magic rope.

I

(The World-fire)

Coyote and his two little boys lived at Nǒnapōtī. He dug a big tunnel into the side of a mountain and filled it with dry wood, pitch and

---

[48]Informant: John Beatty, Yakaia, Central dialect, 1904.

rotten wood, and set fire to it. At this time the people were having a big dance at Nŏ́napōtī and when Coyote returned to the village, smoke could be seen rising from the hills. He called the attention of the people to this and they all talked about it. Coyote was the first to see the smoke and to call attention to it because he was the one who built the fire. He told the people that he thought that the world was going to burn up and then they all knew that it was Coyote who was doing this, and they knew that he would have some way of going up into the Upper World. They begged him to save them but he said he could not. Even when some pretty girls came and asked Coyote to take them up with him, he insisted that he could not do it for he must save himself or he too would burn up. As the fire came closer the people became frantic and ran about as if insane, but still Coyote refused to save them. At last when the fire was very close a rope dropped down from the sky. Coyote placed his two children in his hunting sack and ascended by means of this rope to the Upper World where he remained for four days.

II

(The Creation of Clear Lake)

At the end of this period of four days Coyote descended to the earth and remodelled it, giving it its present form, and created the present race of people, entirely different from the former Bird-people who had been destroyed by the World-fire. After this Coyote traveled all around the region where Clear Lake now is. As he went he found all kinds of animals roasted by the World-fire and, being hungry, he ate his fill of deer, bear, bird, snake and other kinds of meat.

Finally he became thirsty and started off in search of water, but where there had formerly been an abundance there was now none and he traveled on and on in his search, passing along an old Indian trail which led near where the Blue Lakes now are, until he finally arrived at a place called Kūbúkbul which is situated just north of the town of Ukiah. There is here a large spring and at this time Frog was living there. Coyote asked Frog for a drink but Frog had seated himself over the spring in such a manner as to nearly or quite hide the water in it and replied that he had no water to spare. Coyote therefore had to go on without a drink and finally arrived at the ocean.

Having drunk a great deal of the water, for at this time the water of the ocean was not salty, he started to return to the lake region. When he had gone a short distance from the shore he looked back and saw that the ocean lay perfectly still. He did not like the looks of the water lying so quietly so he went back to the shore and told the water not to lie so still but to jump around. It did. In fact it jumped around so much that it nearly covered Coyote up before he could get out of the way. It jumped around so hard that it nearly covered up the hills so Coyote went back and said, "You must not do this way. You must not jump around so hard. You must come up only so high." And then he drew the shore-line and the waves have never come up above that since.

Then Coyote started again toward the Clear Lake region. On the way he began to feel sick and when he reached the Ukiah Valley he wanted to vomit but the people there would not allow him to because the valley was not wide enough. He went on over past Blue Lakes and finally came to the old village of Yōbūʇūi, just southwest of the present town of Upper Lake. This old village had been inhabited by the people who lived on the earth before the great World-fire and was now occupied by some of the people whom Coyote had created after the fire. He asked these people if he might vomit there and they said that they thought that the place was large enough and that he might. He then vomited all of the water that he had drunk at the ocean and this made Clear Lake. With the water came all the meat he had eaten and this was transformed into all the different species of fish which are now found in Clear Lake.

There were, however, no streams flowing into the lake, and in which these fish might spawn. Coyote then made creeks. He made a large one, Middle Creek, at Upper Lake and also a large one, Cache Creek, at Lower Lake, as well as the numerous smaller creeks all about Clear Lake. This was at a time of year when there were heavy rains and there was much water in these creeks and the fish were anxious to run up them. They ran up the creeks just as they do now.

III

(Coyote Creates People from Feathers)

Coyote made his home at Yōbūʇūī and remained there right along He came out every morning and every evening and made speeches like a chief does to his people, but there were no people there. Coyote lived alone. He finally decided to build a dance-house, so he went out and found Duck (Tana), and made a man out of him and took him home to help do the building. Every time Coyote went out to work on the dance-house he would call out, "Come on everybody. Let us go out and work." He talked just as though there were many men to work on this house, but there was only Duck and himself. They would go out and work at it, dig and place timbers, and in this way they finally finished it.

When the house was finished Coyote called out, "Let us go to the dance-house and sweat." There was no one there but he said that just the same. Duck went out and got some wood and he and Coyote went in and built a fire and sweated. After they had sweated they came out and went to lie down to sleep. Before they lay down Coyote said to Duck, "There will be many houses around here. Before morning we will see a great many." A great many houses sprang up around the dance-house as Coyote had said, and when Coyote saw them he and Duck went into the dance-house.

He then sent Duck out with instructions to bring all of the buzzard, eagle and other feathers he could find. Duck succeeded in finding a large number and Coyote stuck them in rows into the floor of the dance-house. He told Duck, "Tomorrow this dance-house will be filled with people." He then scattered some kind of grass seed all around among the feathers in order that there might be fleas and lice when the people should come into being. Coyote and Duck then went to their house for the night. During the night Coyote awoke and heard the people talking. He jumped up and danced around in his joy. When morning came he said to Duck, "I think there are people in the dance-house. I heard them laughing and singing. Let us go and see who is there." This they did and found a great number of people, so many in fact that there was no room for them to move around in this large dance-house.[49]

Coyote took up a position near the center pole of the dance-house, the position usually occupied by the chief when delivering a speech, and spoke to the people. He told them all about how things were going to be, how they were going to live and what they were going to do. When he had finished all this he said "Now, let us have some fun; let us have a dance. We will have a feather dance." They, of course, had never had a dance before and were glad to hear him say this. They all shouted

---

[49]These people formed the present race of Indians.

and made a great noise to show how glad they were. Then Coyote danced to show them how to do it.

He then taught them how to catch fish, kill deer, and otherwise to provide for themselves. Then he said, "Now, you people are going to do all this yourselves. I am going to quit. Do not forget all that I have told you. I am going home."

Then he started to ascend to the Upper World by means of the rope, in the same manner in which he escaped from the World-fire. As he went he said, "Good bye. This world is going to be burned four times and after that it will continue forever."

17—COYOTE BURNS THE WORLD IN REVENGE FOR THE ILL TREATMENT OF HIS CHILDREN[50]

INCIDENTS AND CHARACTERS

I. *Coyote burns the world.*
> 1. *Coyote,* 2. *Wood-duck,* 3. *Louse (Coyote's son),* 4. *Abalone-shell-small-piece* [hwil-biyūmen] *(Coyote's daughter),* 5. *Feather rope.*

II. *Coyote regulates the ocean.*
> 1. *Coyote,* 2. *Ocean.*

III. *Coyote creates Clear Lake.*
> 1. *Coyote,* 2. *Frog,* 3. *Girl (doctor),* 4. *Obsidian-man.*

I

(Coyote Burns the World)

Coyote lived at Maiyi, a large village a short distance west of the town of Upper Lake. Coyote's wife was Wood-duck (Wadawada). She became jealous of Coyote and left him and their two children, a boy and a girl. The boy was Louse (Peréc) and the girl was Abalone-shell-small-piece (Hwil-biyūmen). When Coyote's wife left him he was obliged to care for the children who were very small, and in order to provide food for them, it was necessary for him to spend the greater part of the day out hunting gophers, gray squirrels and other game. While he was away, the children would go about the village and would visit different houses.

Now, the people of this village disliked Coyote very much and consequently were as mean as possible to his children. They would hold out some food toward the children as if intending to give it to them

---

[50]Informant: Bill Coon, Yokaia, Central dialect, 1904.

but when the children reached for it they would jerk it away and then laugh at them. They would also whip the children every day, would poke them with fire-brands, and would abuse them in every way possible.

When Coyote came home every evening, the children would recount to him the happenings during his absence and how all the people of the village had abused them. This made Coyote very angry but he did nothing for a long time. However, when the people of the village continued to abuse his children he determined to take revenge. Therefore, he secretly left the village and went away toward the east, no one but his children knowing of his plans. He dug a big hole, a sort of tunnel, at the foot of a mountain. He was gone eight days and during this time his children kept saying, "Our father has gone east to put pitch in the ground." When he returned after having completed the tunnel he brought food for the children. Next day he returned to the tunnel and gathered dry wood, rotten wood, dry grass, and all kinds of combustible material. All these he mixed together, covering everything with pitch, so that all would burn easily. This took him four days, during all of which time, his children at the village kept saying, "Our father is over east and is filling up the tunnel." Finally he succeeded in filling his tunnel up completely, poking combustible material in so that it was tight all around. He then set fire to it and returned to the village, arriving there at about sunrise on the morning of the fifth day. As he ran around the village, he called out: "Over east it looks as if something was wrong;" and when the people looked, they saw smoke and the red glare of the fire coming up from the mountain.

Coyote's children were very happy and ran around the village with their father, dancing and laughing, for they knew that the people who had abused them were now to be punished. The people knew that Coyote was to blame for this fire because his children were so happy; and as the fire came closer their fear increased and they ran to Coyote, begging him to save them, each one saying: "I will give you something to eat. I will give you beads if you will save me."

But Coyote replied: "You didn't give my children something to eat when I was away. You made fun of me and abused my children. You are too late now. You have abused my children and I can not save you."

Coyote's wife came and begged him to save her, saying: "Save me, my husband. I want my children. I want to go with you."

Coyote said: "How do you know I am going somewhere else?" The fire was then very close to the village, so Coyote took his two children and placed them in his hunting sack.

When the fire began to burn the village a feather rope (yúlŭk) came down from the sky and hung just above the center of the village. Coyote, meanwhile, ran round and round, with the people pursuing him; and as the fire came very near, he ran under the rope, gave a jump and caught it. The rope took him up, far out of sight, into the sky, into the Upper World. As he ascended, he laughed at the people and said: "You people are the ones who didn't give my children anything to eat."

The village and the rest of the world burned, all save Red Mountain (má-kesil). This mountain was the only place in the world which was not burned up, but it was heated so much as to make it red.

II

(Coyote Regulates the Ocean)

When Coyote came down from the upper world, he became thirsty and looked for water, but all the water had been burned up except that in the ocean. So he went by way of an old Indian trail which led to Cow Mountain over Pine Ridge, and through Low Gap[51] to the coast which he reached at a place called Dáidŭl, near the town of Greenwood. He went out in the edge of the ocean and drank his fill.

The water, which was fresh, lay perfectly still, there being not even ripples. When coyote had satisfied his thirst, he started back toward home, but after he had gone a short distance, he looked back and noticed how still the water lay and thought this did not look good. He returned and went again into the water. After looking around for a while, he said: "Well, this doesn't look good. You stay too still. You ought to move around. You ought to do this way" (waves his hands up and down). "That would look better." Then he came out of the water and started home again. The water began to move and moved so vigorously that it washed way up into the timber. When Coyote saw this, he ran

---

[51]Cow Mountain is just south of the confluence of Cold Creek with the east fork of Russian River. Pine Ridge is a high ridge separating the Russian River and Big River drainages at a point due west of the town of Ukiah. It is heavily timbered with pine and Douglas spruce, which accounts for its name. Low Gap is a depression in the summit of one of the higher of the ridges to the west of Pine Ridge and on the headwaters of Big River.

back and said: "Don't do that way. Just come up as far as you can. You come up to here." He drew a line on the ground to show how far the water was to come. He then stood on this line, which is now the shoreline and looked at the water for a little while. Then he said: "People will be coming here to get something to eat. Don't scare them. Just make things a little salty so they will like it but don't scare anybody."

III

(Coyote Creates Clear Lake)

Coyote came back by a different trail than that by which he had gone to the coast. This trail led by Philo. As he approached Philo he saw water ahead of him and thought that now he would have a drink of good water. There was a single grass-house here and when Coyote entered, he found an old lady, Frog, making a basket. Coyote said to her: "Where is the water? Have you any water here?"

She said: "No, I have no water here, no water at all." The fact is, Frog had made a large flat basket of tule just large enough to cover up the spring from which the water came. She sat upon this basket and thereby completely hid the spring. Coyote knew that there was water here but he went on up the hill, on the other side of the valley. When he got up the hill he looked back and again saw the water, so he ran and picked the old lady up and threw her off the basket. When he took the basket from the spring, he found the water and drank it all.

He then returned to the vicinity of Clear Lake and went to the old village of Kabái, about two miles north of the town of Lakeport. He lay down here at Kabái and remained for a long time. Presently a girl came there. She very quietly slipped up close to where Coyote lay and jabbed him just below the floating ribs with a sort of cane which she carried. All the water which Coyote had drunk ran out of his belly and made what is now Clear Lake. Coyote lay perfectly still until all this water had run out.

He then pulled from the hole in his side the snakes which he had eaten on his way back from the coast, after he had drunk the water. As he pulled each one out, he transformed it into a particular kind of fish and designated where it should live, what it should eat, and all about its existence. In this way, he made perch (ditá), blackfish (cakál), hard-mouths (kōnōtōnōtō), suckers (kōm), whitefish (?) (tsūLītsūLīū), silversides (miyá), flatfish (tsawál), pike (capál), stīlíc, hītc, and many other kinds.

Coyote then started to make Middle Creek but the fish were so anxious to run up this creek that they followed right along after him as he was making it. Coyote did not like this and said: "Don't come too fast. Give me time to make the little creeks. You must stay a little way back. When the time comes, you may come up this creek." This made the fish angry and they went back into the lake and would not go back into the creek. In fact, they never go up this creek even now.

Coyote took Obsidian-man (katcá-tcatc) and placed him at the mouth of Kelsey Creek to run up the creek ahead of the fish called "hītc". Obsidian-man was dressed with various ornaments about his head and presented a frightful appearance. When he reached Kelsey-ville, where the old village of Nónapōtī stood, the people came out and there was a big fight in which Obsidian-man succeeds in killing all of the people. He then went down to Calistoga (Lál-napō, "goose village") and has since lived in the big sulphur spring near that place.

18—COYOTE CREATES PEOPLE, BURNS THE WORLD AND MAKES CLEAR LAKE[52]

INCIDENTS AND CHARACTERS

I. *The sons of Wolf and Coyote contest.*
    1. Wolf, 2. Coyote, 3. Coyote's son, 4. Wolf's son, 5. Bear.
II. *Coyote creates people from feathers.*
    1. Coyote, 2. Duck.
III. *Coyote burns the world.*
    1. Coyote, 2. Coyote's children (four), 3. Creator.
IV. *Creation of Clear Lake.*
    1. Creator, 2. Coyote, 3. Frog, 4. Salamander, 5. Kū'ksū.

I

(The Sons of Wolf and Coyote contest)

Wolf and Coyote lived near the shore of Clear Lake. They were the only people at this place but they lived, each in a separate house. They had no wives. They were very lonesome and talked about it and finally decided they ought to have some children. Each one wanted a boy. So Coyote scraped up some dirt and molded it into the form of a boy.

---

[52]Informant: Jocie Kylark, Yokaia, Central dialect, 1904.

He then told the form to get up and be a boy. He made two boys in this way, one for himself and one for Wolf. Coyote showed the boys how to play a shinney game. The two boys played together but Coyote's son won all the games. After they had played this way for a long time, Wolf's son became angry because he could never win and the two boys fought with the result that Wolf's son killed Coyote's. He killed him right by the goal, on the ground where they played shinney. This made Coyote feel very badly. He and Wolf burned the boy's body as was the custom in those days, and then Coyote went to bed to mourn, he felt so badly.

After a while, Coyote went out hunting. He wanted to catch some moles (lam). Wolf went down to the river with a seine to catch some fish. Coyote, however, did not allow him to catch fish but arranged matters so that he caught ducks with his seine. After this, Coyote, with Wolf and Wolf's boy, went out into the mountains, deer hunting. Coyote carried a round stone with him and when he came to a favorable place, he threw this stone into the brush and told it to become a grizzly, and when Wolf's son came along, to kill him. When the bear had killed Wolf's boy, they carried the body back to their village and burned the body near where Coyote's boy had been burned. Coyote wailed and made every pretense of the deepest grief. He even attempted to jump into the fire as a token of his deep feeling; and in this way he made Wolf think that he felt very badly.

Four days later, Wolf told Coyote, "We better make our boys come back to life, after having been dead four days;" but Coyote said, "No, that can not be done. They can't come back to life again because by and by there will be Indians here and they will have to die and be burned. They can't all come back to life again in such a way."

Then Wolf told Coyote that he was going out into the mountains to kill deer and feel sorry over his boy who was dead; and inquired of Coyote what he intended to do. Coyote said that he was going to stay right there in the one place; so Wolf went away while Coyote stayed alone in the village.

II

(Coyote Creates People from Feathers)

There were no people at this village but Coyote went out and made a speech just as any chief would do. He said he was going to be good.

Everybody must be good and everybody must be happy and he announced that they were going to have a big dance. He then commenced to dig a pit to make a dance-house but before he had dug far he found in the ground *Taná* (a small species of duck). He took this little man out of the hole and commenced to talk with him and told him that he must help in the building of this dance-house. They must work hard for they must finish it that same day; so they went out in the hills and got timbers and brush for the roof and succeeded in covering the roof and finishing it all in one day. Coyote then created many houses all around this dance-house. These he did not have to build as he did the dance-house. He simply said, "There will be many houses around here", and they came. These houses were created all in the same day also, and then Coyote went out to procure all kinds of feathers. He brought home a great number of feathers and stuck them all around in the dance-house: in the floor, in the side walls, and all around. He also placed feathers in the houses.

He then took milkweed bark (macá) and shelled off the dry outer covering, just as is done when procuring the fiber used in string-making. This made a lot of very fine bits and these Coyote scattered all around in the dance-house, and in among the feathers which he had placed there. These he scattered here in order that they might become fleas, so that people could have fleas to bite them when they were created.

Coyote then lay down on top of the dance-house. He lay down on his back with his arms outstretched and told the feathers to become people. He told them four times and then he heard the feathers talking, "málakata, málakata, málakata." The people talked this way because the fleas were biting them.

One of the houses in this village belonged to Coyote and the feathers in that house became Coyote's father, mother and two wives. After a while, each one of Coyote's wives gave birth to twins and because of this, his father, mother and wives believed that he was not an ordinary human being like themselves and so they left him and the four children.

III

(Coyote Burns the World)

Coyote went over east and while he was gone the rest of the people of the village made fun of and abused his children. They would even

poke them with fire-brands. The children kept on saying, "Our father
has gone over east to do something", but the people did not believe it.
Coyote, meanwhile, went around the world and set it on fire. The people
at this village were the only people in the world and by and by the fire
came up close to the village. Then Coyote came home and his father
and mother tried to induce him to save them, but he refused, saying
that he was going to live down here alone. Then the people of the
village got together a great quantity of beads and other valuable articles
and tried to induce him to stop the fire. He, however, refused to have
anything to do with them and took his four children, put them in his
hunting sack and went up on Red Mountain.

From the summit of this mountain he shouted up toward the sky.
Presently, a spider-web (tó-cbu) was let down from the sky and Coyote
went to the Upper World and thus escaped the fire which burned the
whole of this world.

He found Madúmda up there. Madúmda said, "Well, how are you
getting along, making people? What do you come up here for, anyway?"

Coyote said, "I made people. I made my father and my mother and
two wives; but when these wives gave birth to twin boys, the people
did not like that and that is the reason I burned up the world."

IV

(Creation of Clear Lake)

Madúmda then told Coyote to return to the earth and look around
and see what he could find. Coyote looked all around over the world and
he found much roasted meat so that he ate a lot of snakes, deer, bear
and other meat, all that he could find nicely cooked.

He became very thirsty and started out to look for water. He went
on until he came to a place where he found Frog (Kawó) and Salamander (CákawōLo) making baskets. He could get no water here, however, and was obliged to go on over to the ocean.

When he had satisfied his thirst, he went back to Red Mountain and
lay down here with his head to the north. Presently Kúksū came along
with a big skewer such as is used for pinning on a head-dress. He
stabbed Coyote in the belly with this. All the water which he had drunk

at the ocean ran out and down the mountain to form Clear Lake. Then Madúmda told Coyote, "You go down into the ground", and he went down into the ground and is now called "Coyote-fire-man" (īwí-hō-tcatc).

19—COYOTE BURNS THE WORLD AND CREATES CLEAR LAKE[53]
INCIDENTS AND CHARACTERS

I. Creation of the fire-drill
    1. Coyote.
II. Coyote burns the world.
    1. Coyote, 2. Coyote's two sons.
III. Coyote creates Clear Lake.
    1. Coyote, 2. Coyote's two sons, 3. Frog.

I
(Creation of the Fire-drill)

There used to be no fire around in this part of the world where the Indian people lived. All the fire that there was, was away over at the east end of the world. Coyote said one day that he knew how to make fire, so he got an elderberry limb, two or three inches in diameter and two feet in length, and made an elder drill-stick. He drilled for a long time on this stick and finally succeeded in make fire.

II
(Coyote Burns the World)

By and by Coyote became angry because the people would not do as he thought they should and said he was going to destroy the world with fire. The people told him that he could not do it but he told them that the fire would be there very soon and burn up the whole world; burn up everybody. Coyote had two sons and when the fire came he and his sons went off toward the west with the rest of the people. The fire burned up the mountains as well as all living things.

Finally, when the fire came very close to where the people were, Coyote took his two sons in his hunting sack and gave a big jump and jumped over the fire so that he came down behind it, where the fire had passed and left everything burned.

[53]Informant: Charley Brown, Northern dialect, 1904.

III

(Coyote Creates Clear Lake)

Coyote and his boys found here all kinds of roasted meat and they ate whatever they wanted. By and by the boys said, "We are thirsty. We are nearly dead for the want of water", so Coyote took the boys in his sack and started out to hunt for water. When they got on the top of the divide between Eel River Valley (Tcidiu) and Potter Valley (Balō-kai), they saw some water running in Potter Valley at a place called "Kŏtata", on what is known as the Grover ranch. Coyote ran down to this place and there they found a big frog sitting on top of the water, so that he could get none of it. Then Coyote heard water running, over in Eel River and ran back that way. When he reached Eel River Valley, there was no water to be seen. He then started back toward Potter Valley but when he reached the top of the ridge, one of his boys died. He buried the boy on top of the ridge, right in the low gap where the trail goes over the summit of the ridge and piled rocks on top of the body. He then ran toward Clear Lake, but when he reached a place call "Sūlūmōī" near Upper Lake the second boy died. Coyote piled brush and rocks over the body. He then ran on down what is now the west shore of the lake, past some water which was at Lakeport, and finally came to Big Valley. Here he drank a great quantity of water. He went back toward the north and finally reached the old village of Maiyi, about three-quarters of a mile west of the town of Upper Lake. He became very ill here. He tried to lie down but he could neither lie down nor sit up.

He finally succeeded in lying down on his back. He had an awl and with this he stabbed himself in the umbilicus; and from this opening all the water he had drunk ran out and with it came fish. This water formed Clear Lake. Then Coyote put pitch over the cut and healed it up so that there was no wound left. Then he said, "People will take their nets and catch fish, and when people are bad the bones of the fish will stick in their throats when they eat them."

20—COYOTE BURNS THE WORLD[54]

Characters: 1. Coyote, 2. Coyote's children, 3. Magic rope, 4. Frog.

Coyote had two little boys. The people used to abuse them very badly. Coyote was out travelling around, visiting, and there was no one to take care of his children. The children, meanwhile, kept saying, that their father was out putting pitch in the ground. The people did no know what they meant by this but they kept right on saying it just the same.

By and by, the people saw a fire burning up in the north. Then, presently, they saw a fire over in the east, then another in the south, and finally one in the west. There was fire all around them. The people then ran to Coyote and talked to him. One and then another would say, "I think something is going to happen. I think the world is going to come to an end." The fire burned with a very great noise. It sounded like thunder. It burned up everything, the water and all. The people saw that the world was going to burn up and there was no chance for them to be saved, so they ran around wildly, in every direction, the fire had come so close.

About this time, something came down from the sky like a rope. Coyote had two hunting sacks and he put the boys in these. Then he and the boys went up to the sky by means of this rope. The fire burned up all the people.

Coyote returned to the earth and found one place, at Djómī in Anderson Valley on Navarro River, where there was water. He found Frog-woman here but she refused to give him any water. She told him that there was no water in this place and that she had to use saliva to wet the sticks of the basket she was weaving. Coyote then said he was going south. He went over into Ukiah Valley on Russian River and then on over to Clear Lake.

One of the boys took some sticks such as are used for basket material and threw them into the water. Coyote then told his son to get this kind of sticks. He went for them but came back without them and told his father that something was growing in the water where he had thrown the sticks and that he had better go and see about it. The boy had found nothing but snakes in the place where he went to look for the sticks.

[54]Informant: Bob Pot, Garcia River, Northern dialect, 1906.

Coyote had vomited and thus had produced these snakes. The boy had become frightened and had gone home to get his father.

After a while, people found fish in Clear Lake. They did not know what kind of fish they were but an old lady tasted of them to see whether they were good for food. She found that it was a good food and after that the people ate fish. The snakes which Coyote had vomited had turned into fish.

21—COYOTE CREATES CLEAR LAKE[55]
INCIDENTS AND CHARACTERS

I. The World-fire and Coyote's search for water.
    1. Coyote, 2. Frog, 3. Waterdog, 4. Magic basket.
II. Clear Lake is created.
    1. Coyote, 2. Frog, 3. Waterdog, 4. Kū'ksū.

I
(The World-fire and Coyotes Search for Water)

The world was burned up, all save a place over near Philo on the headwaters of Navarro River. Frog and Waterdog were the only people not destroyed by the great World-fire. They were making baskets. Coyote went around the world eating all the roasted meat which had been cooked by the World-fire. He then started out to hunt for water.

Coyote came to this place and asked for water but Frog said that they had none. The fact is she was sitting over the water all the time. She said, "We have not found any water yet so we have to spit upon the basket material to make it soft enough to use", and she went through the motions to show Coyote how they did. They used pine root to make their baskets. The first basket they made was a simple-twined basket. The next one was a very finely finished burden basket with arrow-head designs and ornamented with quail plumes and beads. When this basket was about half finished they threw it into Blue Lake. When a menstruating woman passes near these lakes she is very likely to see this basket and to be made ill by it.

II
(Clear Lake is Created)

Coyote passed on after Frog and Waterdog refused him water. He went to the coast and drank a great deal of water. He then returned to

---

[55]Informant: Jocie Kylark, Yokaia, Central dialect, 1904.

the Clear Lake region, but he became so tired that he lay down on his back as if dead. Kúksū came along and cut his belly open with a skewer such as is used to pin on a feather head-dress in a dance. All the water ran from Coyote's belly and formed Clear Lake. This water came from the ocean originally where the water always shakes around more or less and this is why the water in Clear Lake always shakes all of the time.

22—THE BURNING OF THE WORLD AND THE CREATION OF CLEAR LAKE[56]

INCIDENTS AND CHARACTERS

I. *The World-fire.*
    1. *Coyote, 2. Blacksnake.*
II. *Creation of Clear Lake.*
    1. *Coyote, 2. Bullfrog, 3. Hisīndata, 4. Coyote's Children (4).*
III. *Creation of people.*
    1. *Coyote, 2. Wolf.*
IV. *Contest between Coyote's people and Wolf's people.*
    1. *Coyote's people, 2. Wolf's people.*
V. *Coyote creates various things.*
    1. *Coyote.*

I

(The World-fire)

Coyote lived in Round Valley. He caused a great world fire which burned everything, including all the snakes and lizards (then follows a long list of these by name). He spared only Blacksnake (mīca'kala), because he was a very good man.

II

(The Creation of Clear Lake)

Coyote then went about the world gorging himself on the roasted snakes and lizards. He became very thirsty, and went in search of water. He journeyed south from Round Valley, across Snow Mountain. Here he encountered Bullfrog and his friend Hisīndata, who hid all the water from Coyote. He journeyed on to Potter Valley but found no water.

He then started for Upper Lake, but on the way two of his children died. He had with him on this journey two boys and two girls, all of whom were walking along with Coyote. He and the two remaining children journeyed on to Lakeport and to Big Valley.

---

[56]Informant: Captain Bill, Northern dialect.

Here Bullfrog had a large supply of water and Coyote drank every
bit of it. Coyote became ill and lay there sick for four days. Finally
Bullfrog doctored Coyote, and cut his swollen belly open with an
obsidian knife. This water filled the entire valley and Clear Lake is
the result.

Coyote made all kinds of fish out of the snakes and lizards he had
eaten.

III

(Creation of People)

Coyote then went to Upper Lake, built a fish wier there and lived
near it. Thereafter Coyote's son, Wolf, remained in Big Valley and
built a big sweat-house there as he was instructed to do by Coyote.
Then Coyote created people by placing four rows of sticks around the
sweat-house. He then blew four times upon them and they came to life.

IV

(Contest between Coyote's People and Wolf's People)

The people then played games (contested), until Wolf's people had
killed all Coyote's people. Coyote had created bears and Wolf had
created rattlesnakes.

V

(Coyote Creates Various Things)

Coyote then created and placed on the hills, trees, brush and grass.
Then Coyote went away.

MYTHS OF DESTRUCTION. DELUGE

23—THE DELUGE AND THE ESCAPE OF FALCON[57]
INCIDENTS AND CHARACTERS

I. The Deluge and the building of Mt. Kanaktai.
   *1. Coyote, 2. Falcon, 3. The various swimming and diving birds, 4. Duck
   (Tsū't kil), 5. Wood-duck (Wara'wara), 6. Xa'gūnūla, 7. Loon.*
II. Falcon hunts with a magic sling.
   1. Falcon, 2. The magic sling.

---

[57]Informant: Mary Louie, Upper Lake, Eastern dialect, 1906.

I

(The Deluge and the Building of Mt. Kanaktai)

Coyote and Falcon lived at Bidámīwīna on the west bank of Kelsey Creek. It rained a long time and Clear Lake commenced to rise. Falcon gathered a lot of dry grass. He mashed this up fine and made a bundle of it, which he tied on top of his head. He tied his hair over the grass and covered all with a head-net. He then pinned a dance head-dress over this. As it rained, the water rose higher and higher until all the land in the world except a very small area at the top of Mt. Kanaktai, which was then much lower than it is now, was covered. People tried to escape when the water rose but they were unable to find any place where they could keep dry. Even Coyote was drowned.

When the water rose to where Falcon was, he flew up and flew round and round over the water. He flew around this way for four days and finally became so tired that he was about to fall into the water and drown with the rest but he saw the little piece of dry land at the summit of Mt. Kanaktai and flew there. He was the only person not drowned except the swimming birds. They had been able to swim around on top of the water and had not drowned. These swimming birds were all Falcon's uncles and grandfathers.

These birds all came to him on the summit of Kanaktai and he sent them to dive in the water for some material from which to make land. Some brought up weeds, others, a kind of moss (xásibū) which floats around in the lake; others tules which have become waterlogged and have sunk to the bottom of the lake, and still others brought up bor, a bluish mud, which settles to the bottom of the lake. This mud they mixed with the various plant stuffs and placed the mixture on top of the mountain. As the water kept on rising, they kept diving and building. Falcon sat on top of this piece of newly made land all of the time.

Finally, the water stopped rising. The birds had then built Mt. Kanaktai much higher than it was before, and had a good large place upon which Falcon might remain and to which they might go when tired of swimming. They needed some fire up here and to two ducks (Tsútkil and Waráwara) dove down to their house which was at the bottom of the water and undertook to bring fire back with them. They wrapped the fire-brand up in something and swam back to the mountain with it. When they unwrapped it, it immediately gave a flash and went out. They dove again to their house, this time taking with them the hollow stem of a waterlily (kūLá). They took some lake mud and plugged up one end of the tube, then put in a piece of bark which was afire and plugged up the other end of the tube with mud. When they swam back to the mountain, and opened this tube, the bark only smoldered and they were able to start their fire. Falcon then pulled out the hair-pin or skewer which held his head-dress and took from his hair the bundle of dry grass which he had placed there before the flood came. He threw this down by the fire and when it struck it made a big noise and was just like a big load of wood. He gathered this up and made a hot fire and all his uncles and grandfathers came up around it.

While they were all gathered by the fire, one of the birds, Xa-gúnūla, said, "You fellows better go out and look for fish."

One of the small ducks, Tsūʈkil, said, "I will go and look for fish", but Xa-gūnúla said, "Oh no! You always catch little fish. Whoever goes out for fish, must catch big fish, must catch blackfish." Finally two birds, Loon (Kok) and Warawara, started out, each in a tule boat, to fish with dip-nets. While they were gone, Tsúʈkil and Xá-gūnūla dove down to their house under the water and brought up some acorn mush and some acorn black bread. When the birds returned with the fish they had caught, they commenced to cook them over the coals. The first fish cooked Falcon ate and he continued to eat until he had all he wanted. Then the rest of the people ate until everybody had satisfied his hunger.

Two days later they could see the tops of some of the higher mountains sticking up out of the water, and on the next day there were many mountain peaks to be seen all around them. The water kept on going down farther and farther for a long time until it got so low that they could see the floors of the valleys around the mountain. The whole land was just like a swamp, soft and wet. When the land got dry enough to walk around on they all moved down from the top of the mountain to their old home on Kelsey Creek.

II

(Falcon Hunts with a Magic Sling)

Falcon had a boat and used to go out hunting ducks and mud-hens. He made an adobe ball and dried it in the sun. When dry, this ball was very bright and shone whenever the sunlight struck it. He used to keep this ball tied up in his hair with a head-net tied over his head. He went out hunting and would throw this ball into a flock of ducks or mud-hens with his sling. The ball would go from one to another of the birds until it had killed the whole flock and then it would fly back to him in the boat. He would then wipe it off with a bunch of shredded tule which he carried for the purpose and would again wrap it up in his hair. He would then paddle about and gather up the ducks and mud-hens and put them in the boat.

He did this way all the time but he never caught fish. When he returned to the shore he would have a boat full of ducks and mud-hens. These he would place in a head-net which he wore and he would then tie this back on top of his head. As he did this, he would say, "This will be a light load" and then he would start off toward his house singing. He always went home singing and that made his heavy load light so that he could carry a great burden easily. Falcon lived here all the time but Coyote never came back.

24—COYOTE CAUSES A DELUGE TO DESTROY THE WORLD[58]

INCIDENTS AND CHARACTERS

   I. Coyote causes a deluge.
      1. Coyote.
  II. The creation of mountains.
      1. Coyote, 2. Mole.
 III. Creation of people.
      1. Coyote.
IV. Creation of mammals, birds, etc.
      1. Coyote.

I

(Coyote Causes a Deluge)

Coyote dreamed that water was going to cover up the world but no one believed him. At that time there were no mountains or hills. Coyote told the people, "There is going to be water all over the world. It will come tonight and tomorrow. Tomorrow the water will be over the world." Still the people did not believe him. Next morning, however,

---

[58]Informant: Charley Brown, Pinoleville, Northern dialect, 1904.

it was raining and presently the water began to rise. The people got on whatever little elevations there were on the land and climbed trees because there were no mountains up which they might go to escape. Coyote took a tree and broken it so that he had a large log. He, with a number of people, climbed on this log and floated around. The log did not move or try to roll over and the people were able to sit upon it easily. Coyote said to those with him, "Don't be afraid. The water will go down by and by."

II

(The Creation of Mountains)

At the time, Coyote was trying to create some mountains but he could not. He, therefore, hired Mole to create mountains. Mole went down under the water and made the hills and mountains, and the water went down. This took him several days but when he had finished his work Coyote rewarded him by giving him a large storage basket full of magnesite beads.

III

(Creation of People)

When the mountains were created so that the water went down, grass and flowers soon grew, so that the whole world was nice and new. Coyote then thought that he had better create some more people to inhabit this new world in place of those who had been drowned by the flood. He, therefore, made a big dance-house. It had a center pole and eight side posts. He went into the house and built a big fire and remained there during the day. In the evening, he went out and shouted four times while he faced toward the south. Then he went back into the house and slept. When daylight came, he procured some willow and some elder wood. He split these into small sticks. He did this way for four days, and for four evenings, he shouted this way toward the south. The last evening when he shouted this way, he said, "hw———— e———— ū———— he————."

Then he heard people laugh and talk and shout inside the dance-house. He called the people whom he had created from these sticks to come out of the dance-house and divided them up into groups of five and six and ten and different numbers, and told each group where to live and what to do and what its name should be. He then told the

people that all must be good and act properly and if they were not, they
would perhaps fall from a tree and break their limbs or a bear would
bite them or some other ill would befall them.

IV

(Creation of Mammals, Birds, etc.)

Then he created all kinds of animals: bears, deer, elk, panthers,
wildcats, buzzards, eagles, owls, ducks, etc. He made the bear out of
a burnt log, and the deer out of a human rib. He transformed an old
man into the wolf; and to make the big horns of the elk he used a
buckeye limb. In fact, Coyote created everything that we now have on
the earth. This took him four days after he had completed the creation
of people in the dance-house. Then he said, "I will quit. I will be
Coyote."

25—THE THUNDER CHILDREN ESCAPE THE DELUGE AND FLY TO THE SKY[59]

INCIDENTS AND CHARACTERS

I.   *The Thunder-people are transformed into deer.*
    1. The Thunder-people, 2. The miraculous trout.
II. *The Deluge.*
    1. The Thunder children (three), 2. An old man (Coyote)
III. *Creation of angleworms*
    1. Old man (Coyote), 2. Thunder-girl.
IV. *The three Thunder children.*
    1. Elder Thunder-boy, 2. Thunder-girl, 3. Younger Thunder-boy.

I

(The Thunder people are Transformed into Deer)

The people of this village were Thunder-people. They all went
into the mountains north of Potter Valley to a very large spring there
and remained for some time, gathering acorns and buckeyes and other
foods for winter. This spring flowed such a large stream that the water
boiled and bubbled up very energetically from the bottom of it.

The women had their acorn leaches near the spring and used to dip
water for leaching from it. One day, many large trout appeared in the

---

[59]Informant: George Dashields, Potter Valley, Northern dialect, 1904.

spring. The women in dipping for water, dipped these up repeatedly but each time threw them back into the water, because they felt afraid of them.

After several days the people were short of meat and fell to discussing what they should eat with their mush. One man made a speech in which he advocated catching and eating the big trout in the spring. Another man, however, spoke against this, saying that it was not safe to eat these fish and that although the trout in the river were good meat it was very dangerous to eat "spring-trout" such as these because they must have come into the spring by some miraculous means. However, his words were not heeded and the people gathered by the spring and caught and cooked these fish, and had a great feast of trout and acorn soup that evening.

Among the people, however, there was an old woman who lay in her bed during the feast. She called her three grandchildren, two boys and a girl, to her and asked them if they had eaten any of the fish, and, upon being told that they had not she said: "Don't you eat that. You mind what I tell you. That isn't fish; that is something else. Don't you eat it." The children ate none of the meat.

Presently everyone went to bed as usual but when the children awoke next morning, no one was astir in the camp. The children looked around and saw everyone lying about as if dead; but presently, in the door of a house near by, they saw a deer. The deer looked about for a moment and then walked slowly up a chemese ridge near by. The children watched him and knew not what to make of it, that a deer should walk about unmolested through the camp. Before long, from another house, two or three deer ran out and off into the hills; and this continued until everyone in the village who had eaten the trout the evening before, had been transformed into a deer.

II

(The Deluge)

The children went away toward the north. They wanted to find a very high mountain upon which they might live and finally they did. It soon began to rain very hard and it continued for many days. The elder of the two boys determined that he must do something so he went away every day for a number of days, always, however, returning toward evening. On the last day he returned long after nightfall. The water had been gradually rising during the rain until the uncovered portion of their mountain was a piece of ground only a few feet square. The children did not know what to do next, the water had come so high, so they finally built a fire and sat there waiting for something to happen. Theirs was the only bit of dry land on earth. It stopped raining and as far as they could see there was water.

On the fourth day after the rain stopped, an old man came. The children did not know where he came from but he came and sat by their fire. Finally the elder boy said: "Grandfather, can't you do something about this water?"

The old man replied: "I don't know, my son, I can't do anything about it. I don't know what to do."

When night came, they fixed their beds and all lay down. The children went to sleep. The old man, however, commenced to dig down into the ground right there. He did not tell the children what he was going to do, but he dug in the ground all night. In the morning he came home and wakened the children by saying: "Wake up, children, open the door and come outside and see how things are."

The elder boy opened the door a little so that he could see outside and he found that all the water had disappeared and the whole country was covered with green grass and clover. He said: "My grandfather, I am glad to see this. This is a beautiful place." Then they all went outside to play on the grass and eat clover.

III

(Creation of Angleworms)

The old man took some sinew and shredded it into fine bits. He placed this on a bunch of green grass and put something that looked like salt upon it. This made the sinew change into angleworms. This is the way the old man made angleworms.

By and by the girl said to the old man: "Now what am I going to do?"

The old man said: "You get a sharp stick, and stick it into the ground close to that bunch of grass and wiggle it back and forth this

way, and pretty soon angleworms will come up. Then you can pick
them up and eat them." She did this. Then the old man went away.

IV

(The Three Thunder Children)

The elder of the brothers was working now every day fixing something. He made a belt and a head-dress and other things to wear.
When he had these finished he told his sister: "When I wear this belt
and these other things you watch that big rock standing over there."
When the sunlight struck these things that he wore, it made them shine.
The light from these struck the rock and much water came out of it.
There was also a big pine tree standing on the mountain and when the
light that shone from his suit struck this, fire blazed up and the tree was
burned. This light that shone from the boy's suit was the lightning.

Next morning, he went up to the top of the mountain and when the
fog came in from the ocean, it lifted him up and he got half way up to
the sky but fell back again. He did this way three times, then he told
his sister that the next time he was going way up north. He went up
north and then it snowed and rained and was very cold where his sister
and brother were. When he returned it was all clear again and the sun
shone. The snow had all melted and the air was warm. He said to
his brother and sister: "How are you getting along here?"

They replied: "We have been freezing to death. We can not provide for ourselves here because there is so much snow and wood is so
scarce. Don't do that way so long. Next time, only do that way for
a little while. We have no way to get wood down here. Food and
everything is very scarce."

The younger brother asked, "When you went up north, did you see
anything up there? Was there any kind of a place up there?"

The elder brother said, "Yes, there is a place up there."

Then the younger brother said, "Well I guess we must all go up
there some day."

The elder brother then made a suit of the same kind for his younger
brother and the morning after it was finished, the two of them went up
on to the same high mountain. The elder said to the younger, "Now
you stand by me and hold your arms out just as I do. Hold them out
this way." He did this and the fog carried them up. When he got

about half way up, he fell back just as his elder brother had done but finally he succeeded in rising and flying away. The elder brother said, "Now you go south and I will go north." When they did this, the whole world shook, because the two of them were working together. While they were gone, it snowed very hard and was very cold.

That evening they came home and made a suit of the same kind for their sister. Then the three of them went up on to the same mountain and after the same sort of trial and failure, the sister succeeded in flying as her brothers had done. Then the elder brother said: "This time, you, my brother, go north. I shall go south; and you, my sister, shall go east." They did this and have always remained there.

26—GOPHER SECURES FIRE AFTER THE DELUGE[60]

During the Deluge everyone except Gopher was killed. He saved himself by climbing to the top of Mt. Kanaktai. As the water rose he climbed higher and higher, and just as the water was about to wash him off the top of the mountain it began to recede and finally left Gopher high and dry on the top of the mountain.

Gopher was, of course, without fire and he had no neighbors from whom to borrow fire as was the custom in the olden times, so he began to dig down from the top of the mountain. He dug on and on down into the mountain until he finally found fire inside of it. In this way he got fire again for the world.

MYTHS OF THE SUN
27—THE THEFT OF THE SUN[61]

Characters: 1. Falcon, 2. Lizard, 3. Blue Jay, 4. Dove, 5. Gi'lak, 6. Buzzard, 7. Crow, 8. Mice (4), 9. Sun-people.

There used to be a village in Scott's Valley in Lake County. At that time, the sun did not shine and everything was dark. When the people hunted, they had to carry torches. The chief said, "My people, you will have to be very careful because you can not tell what is going to happen." He addressed his people sometimes during the day, sometimes at night, because it was dark all the time and he could not tell which was day and which was night.

---

[60]Informant: Tom Mitchell, Eastern dialect, 1902.
[61]The Pomo title of this myth is "cĕ'mi, da ma kôyau mŭn i ma wi makoyau mŭn matŭ dike."
Informant: Bob Pot, Garcia River, Northern dialect, 1906.

There was one man, Lizard (mtulu), who was always hunting with a torch. When he went hunting, he always went toward the east; and when he returned, he would come crying along because he felt so badly on account of the fact that there was no light. As he hunted each day, he would go a little farther toward the east than he had gone the day before. In this way, he would be away all day long. Some of the people asked him, "What is the matter with you? You keep away from the village all day. You go farther and farther away every day. Have you lost your mind or what is the matter with you?" Lizard said nothing but kept on hunting, just the same.

After a long time, he thought he saw a little light over in the east. He then went on toward this light, going until he could see where it came from. There he saw that the houses were all white. Then he turned and went crying back toward his own village. When he arrived there, he entered the sweat-house and said, "Well, my people, I don't know whether it is so or not but I dreamed that I found daylight."

The people said, "Now you are lying to us. We do not believe that."

Blue Jay was the bravest and the meanest man in the village and the people said to him, "You are the bravest and the meanest man here. You take your brother (another Blue Jay) and go over and see if this fellow is telling the truth." The Blue Jays went and when they returned, reported that Lizard's story was untrue. The people then assembled from all the villages round about and selected the bravest men and sent them out to investigate; but none of them were brave enough to go over to where Lizard had made his camp-fires. They were not even brave enough to go over to where Lizard had made his first or nearest camp-fire. After that, they sent Dove (mayū'). They said, "Now, Dove, you are a brave man. You and your brother go over and see if you can find the fire." So the Doves blackened their faces with charcoal and went over with their bows and arrows to find the fire. When they returned, they said, "It is true. We went out and found all the fires that Lizard had made and we found the light over in the east also." Then the one who was speaking, added, "No, I do not expect we will live here. You people think about what you will do to get this light."

The people then discussed the matter and decided that they would go over east and war with the people over there. So they made bows and arrows, torches and other necessary implements and started out. After travelling a very great distance, they finally arrived at the last fire which Lizard had made. Lizard only, remained at home. The people stopped at this place where Lizard had made the last fire, while a few of the bravest went over to see what the Sun-village looked like. The Gi'laks owned the Sun. Finally, the people all went over to the Sun-village. They came to a very large sweat-house but it was too small to hold all the visitors.

At the top of the center pole in this sweat-house, there were four large bags. One of these contained snow, one wind, one rain and one the sun. Gi'lak and Falcon gambled at the grass game with the result that Gi'lak was killed. Then four mice climbed up the center pole and gnawed off the string which tied the Sun up there. Then they threw this sack out through the smoke-hole and it rolled down the roof and to the ground. Buzzard was the only man who was able to break open this sack which was sewed up very tightly.

The people then started to roll the Sun along toward their village but the Sun-people pursued and fought with them, with the result that arrows were shot in all directions and fell everywhere. That is the reason why you can find arrow-heads scattered all over the country now. They all came from this war.

When they had taken the Sun about half way home, they tried to put it up in the sky. All of the different kinds of birds tried this. Dove tried first, then others. Finally, the Crow brothers succeeded in hanging it up and it stayed there. The Crows were able to hang the Sun up in the sky, because they were able to go without water for a longer time than any of the other birds.

28—COYOTE STEALS THE SUN[62]
INCIDENTS AND CHARACTERS

I. *The theft of the Sun.*
 1. Lizard, 2. Coyote, 3. Mice, 4. Sun-people, 5. Short-haired-man, 6. Bird-people, 7. Sleep wand.
II. *Placing the Sun in the sky.*
 1. Coyote, 2. Red-headed-woodpecker, 3. Crows.
III. *The Blue Lakes monsters.*
 1. Coyote, 2. Crows.

---

[62]Informant: John Beatty, Yokaia, Central dialect, 1904.

I

(The Theft of the Sun)

There was no sun at all and everything was dark. There was one
man among the "Bird-people" who was an especially good hunter. This
was Lizard (ce'm*t*ūlū). He went up to the summit of Mt. Kanaktai
(cakál-gūnal) and here, after looking all around, he finally saw light
way over in the east. He never had seen a light before and could not
think what it could be. He thought that some of his relatives had died
and he commenced to cry. He then went home and told Coyote about
it. Then the people asked Coyote what he was going to do about it.
Coyote said he was going to have a dance and good time over it. He
then caught some mice and put them into his hunting sack and started
over toward the east.

When he arrived at the village of the Sun-people, over in the east,
he told them, "You must all lie down with your heads toward the fire,
when you go to sleep. You must all have your heads close together."
In the night, Coyote braided the hair of these people together all around
this circle, at the same time waving a wand tipped with feathers over
them and repeating a ritual, which made them sleep soundly. One of
the people had very short hair which he was unable to braid and he laid
this man out to one side of the circle.

While Coyote danced around, he let loose the mice which he had
brought and they climbed up the center pole and gnawed off the string
which tied to the rafters the elk-hide bag containing the sun. They
would come down from time to time to rest and tell Coyote how they
were progressing. At last they told Coyote, "Now, you get all ready.
We are about ready to finish cutting off the string which holds the sun.
If you are all ready, we will go and take that Sun away with us."

Then they took the bag and started away but the short-haired-man
saw them go and saw that Coyote was stealing the sun. He cried out,
"Coyote is stealing our sun." And with this, the people who were thus
aroused, endeavored to pursue Coyote.

II

(Placing the Sun in the Sky)

Coyote ran as rapidly as he could and carried the sun home to his
own people. Then he said, "Let us put this sun up in the sky." And

everybody said, "Yes, that is good. We will try it." Coyote told them to appoint one man to keep watch and announce the progress that was being made, so Red-headed-woodpecker sat down and watched, while the others tried to place the sun in the sky. Everybody tried it and as they would fly up, Red-headed-woodpecker would tell the people how close they were getting. In this way, he kept watch of the sun all the time they were trying to put it up; and because he looked at the sun for such a long time, his eyes are now shiny, just like glass.

Finally, the two Crow brothers decided to try to put the sun up, and Red-headed-woodpecker told the people how the Crows were getting along. At last, he announced, "The Crows are getting very near now. Now they are going to put the sun on. Now they have put it on and it is going to stay there. Now they are coming down. You people go and get something to pay them with. Get a big lot to pay them. Get baskets, beads, arrows, blankets, all kinds of things we use."

III

(The Blue Lakes Monsters)

Then Coyote took the Crows and put them into Blue Lakes, saying, "Now you fellows stay there and when Indians come around close to look at you, you scare them and make them ill." They did this and succeeded in killing everybody who came near where they were. Then Coyote went back and told them, "Now you fellows must not do that way. You must kill only one, now and then." The Crows wanted to break through a mountain on the northwest side of Blue Lakes but Coyote told them, "No, don't you do that. You must let that mountain side stay right where it is." So the Crows did that and have lived there ever since.

29—THE STEALING OF THE SUN SACK[63]

INCIDENTS AND CHARACTERS

I. *Coyote steals the sun.*
   1. *Lizard, 2. Coyote, 3. Crane, 4. Sun-children, 5. Salmon-trout, 6. Mice (eight), 7. Sun-people.*
II. *Placing the sun in the sky.*
   1. *Hummingbird, 2. Dove, 3. Red-headed-woodpecker, 4. Robin-red-breast, 5. Crow brothers, 6. Coyote.*

---

[63]Informant: Kumula, Hopland, Central dialect. 1904.

III. The sun is regulated and Crow is rewarded.
        1. Coyote, 2. Sun, 3. Crow.
IV. Origin of the Bagils.
        1. Coyote, 2. Bagils.

I

(Coyote Steals the Sun)

There was formerly no light. It was dark all the time. Lizard used to hunt and finally, while out hunting one day, he saw a light over in the east. He came home and told the people and Coyote about this. Then Coyote went up on the summit of Mt. Kanaktai to see what it might be. He found that the light was really there and when he returned to the village, he went directly to the sweat-house and told the men that he intended to go over east and see that light.

Crane took Coyote across the lake and by and by, Coyote arrived at the village where the sun was kept. These people had the sun in a bag made of four thicknesses of elk hide and it was tied up to the roof of the sweat-house with four cords or ropes.

When he arrived at the village, he found no one there except some very small children, who were unable to talk. He asked the children where all the people had gone but they were unable to talk and therefore could not tell him. Coyote had four birds in his hunting sack. He had also, a long string of shells (pci) and he gave the birds and these shells to the two children. These children watched the sun sack continually.

They had not only the sun sack (da-hola) in the sweat-house but they had also the rain sack (tce-hola), the snow sack (yu-hola), the cloud sack (kaba-hola), the cold sack (kasi-hola), the fog sack (pot-hola), the wind sack (ya-hola) and the frost sack (ema-hola). When he had given the children the birds, and this string of shells, he asked them what kind of sack the largest one was. But the children replied that all their uncles, brothers and other relatives had warned them never to tell anything about this sack. But Coyote told them, "I gave you those shells. They are worth a great deal, so you certainly ought to tell me. I am not going to do anything. I just want to know about it." Then the eldest boy said, "All right, I will tell you. The sun is in that sack. If you were a young man, I would not tell you anything about it but as you are a very old man and unable to do anything, I will tell you." Coyote then told the boys that he was going to return to his village and bring over all his people, in order that they might have a dance and he asked them to tell their people about it.

Coyote, therefore, returned to his village and reported that the people over in the east had the sun there, that they kept the sun in a sack and that there were two holes in the sack, through which, the light of the sun could shine. He also told them that they must all go over to that village and have a dance. Accordingly, every one started for the east.[64] When they arrived there, all danced until far into the night when all of the Sun-people fell asleep. In the dance house, there was a small pond in which Salmon-trout lived. He was the only one of the people living over there who did not go to sleep. Coyote had brought with him in his hunting sack, eight mice. These mice went up and gnawed off the string holding the sack which contained the sun, so that it fell to the floor. Trout warned his people that some one was trying to steal something. When the sun sack fell to the floor, the people tried to pick it up but it was so hot that they were unable to do so. They poured water over it but were unable to cool it sufficiently, so finally, they tied a rope around it and started to drag it home.

II

(Placing the Sun in the Sky)

Coyote told Hummingbird (Tsuidun) to take the sun and place it up in the sky. He provided a red-feathered basket filled with water for him to drink on the way. Dove (Mayu) went along to carry this basket of water for him. They appointed Red-headed-woodpecker (Katak) to watch and announce the progress that they made in placing the sun in the sky. Woodpecker finally announced that Hummingbird had given out and was coming down. They had, meanwhile, dug a large pit and filled it with water so that if he fell, he would land in this pit.

Dove next tried to take the sun up, but he also failed and fell back

[64]According to one informant of the Central dialect it appears that when Coyote desired to start east to liberate and steal the sun he first called together all of the poison-doctors. These were Kalĕ'cakcak, Sapsucker (Kalĕ'tsat), Bluebird (Tsapŭ), Kabĕ'djicĭl, Baka'ka, Great-horned Owl (Makŭ'gŭ), Cma'i kadōkadō, Hummingbird (Tsŭ'duyŭn).

Coyote consulted with these medicine men on methods to be pursued and tricks to be played in his attempt to steal the sun. Each made his particular poison-medicine and each medicine was tried. That of Kalĕ'cakcak was found to be the strongest of them all, so this poison was rubbed onto the bows and arrows, pipes, dancing paraphernalia and other objects which Coyote and his assistants took with them. His assistants were, according to this informant, Falcon and Eagle and four mice.

This is the only mention of the fact that Falcon and Eagle accompanied Coyote on his sun-stealing expedition.

into the pond.   Next Robin (Tsatoto) endeavored to place the sun in the sky but he also failed; as did many others who tried after him, although each succeeded in flying a little higher than his predecessor.

The two Crow brothers were lousy, uncouth fellows, whom the rest of the people would never allow to come near them.   They always kept apart and were at this time sitting a little distance away from the rest. But when all the other birds had failed, then Coyote called the Crows and asked them to come up and eat with the rest of the people.   Then they tried to take the sun up, that is, the elder of the brothers took the sun and the other just went along.   Coyote asked Woodpecker how Crow was getting along with the sun.   Woodpecker said, "All right. He is keeping up the flight as well as when he started out."   He kept on announcing from time to time the progress which Crow was making, until finally, he announced, "Now, he has put the sun up all right." Then the elder of the Crows came down while the younger remained up in the sky with the sun.

III

(The Sun Is Regulated and Crow Is Rewarded)

Coyote then told the sun to go over toward the west, so that it would be dark, then to go around the world and not to stay in one place.   He told him to do this so that everybody might have light.   When the Crows hung the sun up in the sky, the people rewarded them by cleaning the lice off them.   That is all the pay they received.   To do this, they dug another pond and filled it with hot water.   Then they took Crow and dipped him in this and it killed all the lice.

IV

(Origin of the Bagils)

The people who had kept the sun over in the east were the Bā'kil-people.   When Coyote and his people stole the sun, the Bā'kils went all around the world and lay in the water.   The first water they went into, was McGough's slough (Ka-pohol, just west of the St. Turbius' mission in Big Valley).   From there, they went out into Clear Lake.   Coyote sent men down to see what the Bā'kil were doing at Clear Lake.   They were lying right in plain sight at the surface of the water.   The men became so frightened that they died immediately.   Finally, Coyote him-

self went down. He found the Bā'kils there and told them, "I did not
tell you to scare people that way." But the Bā'kils said, "The water is
not deep enough here." So Coyote took them out of the water, hit them
upon the ground and then took them over to the ocean and threw them
in. Now there are Bā'kils all around, in all the springs, rivers, lakes,
and wherever there is water.

30—COYOTE STEALS THE DAYLIGHT SACK AND LIBERATES THE SUN[65]

INCIDENTS AND CHARACTERS

I. *The Coyote boys are killed by the Sun-people.*
   1. *Coyote, 2. Coyote boys, 3. Bear boys, 4. Sun-people.*
II. *Coyote steals the sun.*
   1. *Lizard, 2. Coyote, 3. Mice (two), 4. Sun-people, 5. One-eyed-old-woman, 6. Dove, 7. Robin, 8. Turtle, 9. Frog, 10. Mudhen.*

I

(The Coyote Boys Are Killed by the Sun-people)

Coyote lived at Maiyi. It was formerly always night there.
Coyote's two nephews and two Grizzly-bear boys used to play shinney
(pīkō'taina). The ground upon which they played, lay east and west.
Near the west goal there were bears and, when the children won behind
the east goal, rattlesnakes would bite them. Finally, the ball with which
the boys were playing went behind the goal post on the east and the two
Coyote boys ran after it. The ball continued to go on toward the east
and they followed it. Finally, they came into another country far in
the east where there were other people and they were killed. These
people skinned them and made a sack out of their skins. Old Coyote
was the uncle of these boys and when he heard that they had been killed,
he mourned. He even went and put his head into the fire and thus cut
his hair off short very quickly.

II

(Coyote Steals the Sun)

At that time, it was always night here. Lizard used to go deer hunting. He went up onto a very high mountain and there he was able to
see a light over in the east. He came home and told Coyote about the

[65]Informant: Dave Thompson, Upper Lake, Eastern dialect, 1904.

daylight and that it always stayed over in the east and never came west. Coyote went himself to look. He had a hunting sack (tcūlū') and in this, he put two mice. When he had come near the village where the sun was kept, he stopped and studied a while as to what he had better do. He was uncertain as to whether he had better become old or young or a woman or how he had better transform himself. He finally, however, decided that he would become an old man with a cane. He did this. He was such an old man that he could hardly walk. He went on toward the village and finally arrived, just at evening.

He found the people all dancing and having a good time. As he came to the dance-house, the people saw that he was a very old man and they told the boys to show him a place where he could lie down near the fire but Coyote said, "No, I cannot lie there. I might lie somewhere else. If I were to lie down there, the dancers might step on me." So the people gave him a place farther back and he lay down. Presently, while looking around, he saw the skins of his two nephews, which had been made into the daylight sack to hold the sun. He asked some of the children, "What is that, boys?" But the boys said, "My mother and my father told me that you must give me some beads before I could tell you that." Coyote then went and lay down near the center pole.

He turned loose the mice which he had brought with him and they climbed up the center pole when every one was dancing. They climbed out to where the daylight sack was but by and by, one of them fell right down in the center of the floor. Some of the people caught it and they were about to throw it into the fire but Coyote said, "Hold on, there! I eat that kind. I am the only fellow who eats that kind. Give it to me." So they gave the mouse to Coyote who put it in his mouth. He put in with it a piece of charcoal and chewed that so that it would make a sound as if he were chewing the mouse.

After a while, Coyote said, "That is a funny way you fellows sing that song. I never heard that kind of a dancing song before."

Then the people said, "Look, that old man is going to dance now."

But Coyote said, "I cannot stand that. How can I dance? How can I stand it to dance when I am so old?"

Presently, however, he went out of the dance-house and studied what he was going to do. He finally decided that he would dress himself for the dance out there and that he had better turn young again, and then he said, "I wish I had some dancing paraphernalia", and immediately a whole suit of feather and other dancing paraphernalia came to him. He dressed himself and then went inside. He danced, and sang for himself.

Finally, he said, "When I dance, you people must all lie down with your heads toward the fire so that your heads will all be on one side." He continued to dance until every one had fallen asleep. He then braided their hair together, that of each man being braided to the one on either side of him. He did this in order that the people would be unable to run.

By this time, the mice had gnawed the ropes which tied the daylight sack, so that Coyote was easily able to pull the sack down. This he did and put the mice back in his hunting sack. He then ran out with the daylight sack. He ran home with the sack.

One old woman, who had but one eye, was the only person in the village who was not in the dance-house. She saw Coyote running away with the daylight sack and ran to the dance-house crying, "Coyote has stolen our daylight sack." This awakened every one and they endeavored to pursue Coyote but as each man tried to rise, he felt the man nearest him pulling his hair and said, "Let me alone. What do you hold me here for?" After a while, the old woman came with a flint knife and cut their hair apart.

By this time, however, Coyote had gone a long way toward home. He was going very rapidly but many people were pursuing him. The Dove brothers were following him but were unable to catch him; so also the Robin brothers and the Mud-hen (Katsiya) brothers. Turtle also followed him but was unable to catch him. Fog and his brother finally got ready and pursued him but they were unable to overtake him until he had reached the mountain just east of Clear Lake. Here, they ran around to head him off and were about to catch him but Coyote saw that Fog was about to catch him, so he broke open the daylight sack and liberated the sun. Then he went home and told the people, "I know that those people over there fooled and cheated us. That is the reason why I did that."

Lizard asked him, "Did you succeed in getting over there?"

Coyote said, "Yes, I got over there all right." Then everybody celebrated because they had daylight.

31—COYOTE STEALS THE MORNING SACK, CONTAINING THE SUN, MOON AND PLEIADES[66]

INCIDENTS AND CHARACTERS

I. Coyote steals the morning sack.
>   *1. Black Lizard, 2. Coyote, 3. Turtle, 4. Sun-children, 5. Mice (four),*
>   *6. Blue Jay, 7. Dove, 8. Fog, 9. Sun-people.*

II. The sun is placed in the sky.
>   *1. Crow brothers (two).*

I

(Coyote Steals the Morning Sack)

In old times at the village near Sleepers Ranch-house, they say everything was dark. Black Lizard (xa' du'nu tal) went out hunting deer. He hunted toward the east for some time and finally found light. He then returned to the sweat-house and told the others that he had found daylight far to the east.

Black Lizard, Coyote and Turtle started out to go to find the light. Coyote could change himself at will into any form, young or old. They went on and on to the east and finally arrived about evening at a village.

They found two boys in the sweat-house. He asked them what that was hanging up in the sweat-house. The boys said that they could not tell as their fathers, mothers, grandfathers, grandmothers, aunts and uncles had told them never to tell what was up there. But Coyote presented them with some periwinkle-shell ear-rings and they finally told him that it was a small sack made of Coyote skins. Coyote began to cry, just to blind them and fool them. He knew of course what it was before. Coyote then went out.

At night a large crowd assembled in the sweat-house where a fire had been built and they were fanning each other. Presently Coyote, who had changed himself into a very old man and walked with a stick, came in and asked if he might lie down by the center pole close to the fire. They assented, being sorry for him on account of his crippled condition. He lay down close to the center pole, curling himself around the pole as if to sleep.

They danced on till midnight, when all the dancers fell sound asleep. The mouse which Coyote had concealed in his hunting bag then ran up the center pole. Someone spied him and said, "Look out! Look out!

---

[66]Informant: Tom Mitchell, Eastern dialect, 1902.

something is running up the center pole." Another said, "Kill it." Coyote said, "No, bring it here, I eat that kind. Give it to me." Coyote then stuffed the mouse in his mouth and made a noise as if eating him.

They all danced again until very tired and then Coyote said, "I will dance alone." Then three mice ran up the center pole and gnawed the string which tied the bag. Coyote danced and danced until nearly daylight, no one assenting to a stop. The mice came down and told Coyote that the bag could be easily pulled off now. Still dancing he put them away in his hunting bag again. Blue Jay lay by the door. Coyote stationed Turtle at the door. Then he made himself a young man again. He then leaped up and pulled off the sack and ran outside. As he ran out the door, he stepped on Blue Jay's leg. Blue Jay yelled "yi———— Coyote has stolen the morning sack, Coyote has stolen the morning sack."

The people sent after him their swiftest racers, Dove and Fog. Fog ran around and headed off Coyote while Dove came after him. Turtle stayed in the doorway and the people shot arrows at him (hence the streaks across his shell).

Coyote finally broke the sack on a stone and suddenly the day appeared and the sun shone. Then the fog disappeared. He carried the sun home, also the Pleiades and the moon.

II

(The Sun is Placed in the Sky)

All the people gathered there and contested in trying to take the sun up into the sky. Finally the two Crow brothers succeeded in taking the sun up and hanging it there.

Crow said "A—a—You fellows cannot take the sun up." Then they took up the moon and the Pleiades and hung them up also. They then came down and lived there, and everybody knew that the Crows took up the sun.

32—THE HUMMINGBIRD BROTHERS RESCUE PEOPLE HELD IN THE SUN VILLAGE[67]

INCIDENTS AND CHARACTERS

I. *Men are killed by the Sun-people.*
  1. Falcon, 2. Blue Jay, 3. Woodpecker, 4 Tala'k, 5. Crow, 6. Kaba'ltū, 7. Bluebird, 8. Sun-people, 9. Bird-people, 10. Sun-man.

II. *The Hummingbird brothers are instructed by their grandmother Turtle.*
  1. Turtle, 2. Hummingbird brothers.

III. *The Hummingbird brothers win contests by means of their Yellowjackets.*
  1. Turtle, 2. Hummingbird brothers, 3. Mink, 4. Sun-man, 5. Yellowjackets, 6. Sun-boys, 7. Bird-people.

I

(Men Are Killed by the Sun-people)

At Mayī' there was a large village and here lived all the various kinds of Bird-people who lived in the vicinity of Clear Lake. Their Chief was Falcon.

Falcon made a speech to the people and he told them that the acorn crop was a complete failure and that messengers must be sent in all directions to discover where acorns could be found. He then appointed Blue Jay to search toward the east, Woodpecker toward the west, Tala'k toward the north and Crow toward the south.

In due time Woodpecker came back from the west and reported that no acorns were to be found in that direction, that he had visited every place where they usually grew but that there was not a solitary one to be found. Presently Tala'k returned from the north and reported that there were no acorns there, not even one on a tree. Crow, coming from the south likewise reported that none were to be found in that direction. Finally, however, Blue Jay returned from the east and brought a single white-oak acorn with him. He said that there were just a few to' be found over there, one or two only on a tree. He said that they were located very far toward the east and that it would take a very long journey to secure them.

After discussing the matter the people decided that they must go over there to harvest these acorns, even though there were few, in order that they might have some acorn food to use in the feast connected with their dance.

---

[67]Informant: Jim McCalluck, Northern dialect.

The Chief instructed everyone to prepare for the journey toward the east to harvest acorns and told them to take along baskets and other useful items to transport the crop home.

This was a very large number of people who went on this expedition and they traveled a very great distance.[68]

After they had traveled a long time they came to a village and as they approached in such large numbers, the people of this village thought that they were coming as a war party, but the Chief of the village, Kaba'ltū, came out to meet them and to inquire, "What do you want?" To this query Falcon replied that they were in search of acorns but Kaba'ltū told him that there was not an acorn to be found in that part of the country. They therefore passed on toward the east.

After they had traveled another considerable distance they came to another village. Here Bluebird (Tcō'tcō) was the Chief and when he saw the people approaching he came out and welcomed them and invited them to the village saying that he felt very sorry for them and asking where they were moving to. He assumed that they were moving to a new region to make their residence there permanently.

However, Falcon informed him that they were not moving but were merely going out in search of acorns. Bluebird then informed them that very, very far over toward the east there was a land where a few acorns were to be found.

After they had traveled still farther toward the east, very far indeed, they came to the place where Sun-people lived and to what is known as the Fire sweat-house. Here Sun-man who was the Chief, welcomed them and said, "I feel very sorry for you people who have come so very far to get acorns." Then he ordered all the women to leave the sweat-house because they then wanted to have a sweating contest. Then he fanned the fire and fanned against all of the men who had come as visitors. He fanned and made a heat so great that it killed every man. He then threw their bodies into another sweat-house of his and covered them all up.

It is because of this that people are always afraid of the Sun, Moon, Morning, Night and the Stars.

When he had finished this he then selected two of the women as his own wives and allotted the remainder to the men of his village. These men were all his slaves and it was a large village.

---

[68]The expression indicating a very long journey toward the east is cō co pilĭdjai cō pilĭdjai

II

(The Hummingbird Brothers Are Instructed by their Grandmother, Turtle)

When the people left Mayī to make the journey over toward the east there remained at this village only one old grandmother, Kawīna (Turtle-woman) and two very tiny babies, the Hummingbird (Tsū'-diyūn) brothers.

When the people left the babies were very tiny, just able to crawl and toddle about, but they grew rapidly for the old woman gathered clover and wild potatoes and other foods for them and fed them well. By and by they were about half grown and then they began to wonder, for they saw their grandmother crying a great deal of the time. They asked her what she was crying about and she told them, "I am crying for your father, mother and other relatives. A long time ago they went way back over toward the east in search of acorns but they never returned. I know that they have been killed there."

The children played about as children always do and they gathered some willow branches. Then they asked their grandmother what they should do with them. She told them that they could make bows and arrows out of them and this they did. They played with these bows and arrows and day by day they wandered farther and farther away from home, playing about out in the woods and in the brush. One day they came upon a gray squirrel as they were playing about and they were very much scared so they ran home and told Turtle what they had seen and described this animal with the great bushy tail and she, of course, knew just what it was and told them all about it, saying, "You must go back out into the woods where you saw that animal and kill it with your bows and arrows. It is good food. Do not touch it while it is still alive because it might bite you." This they did and when they brought the gray squirrel home the old lady pounded it up and cooked it on hot rocks and gave it to them.

The next morning they went out to play again. Then they saw a strange animal lying down in the brush. It was gray in color, had long ears, and a very short tail. They ran back and told Turtle about this and she told them that they had seen a rabbit. She told them, "You must go back and hunt for that animal. Approach it as close as you can and shoot it. It will make a great noise but it will not hurt you."

Presently they returned with the rabbit which they had shot and their grandmother pounded this up and cooked it for them to eat also.

Next they went out to play and this time they went way out in the mountains. Soon they saw something standing in among the manzanita bushes. When they got where they could get a good look they saw that there were two animals. They ran back and told their grandmother that they had seen two large animals. There were very long, had very small legs with forked feet and fingernails on these feet. These animals carried brush around on their heads and they had short, white tails.

"That," said the grandmother, "is the finest food of all. What you saw was deer. That is the food which really makes our home."

Then they went back and shot the two deer and left them where they had fallen. They returned to their home and told their grandmother about it. She immediately went out with them because she wanted to bring the deer in to their camp. She made a pack and carried the two deer at once. As she started to lift this heavy load she said, "This load must be as light as a feather until I carry it home."[69] When they had returned home the deer were cooked and eaten.

Presently when the children were out playing again they saw something hanging from a tree and again they ran home and told their grandmother about this, saying, "We saw something hanging from a tree over there. It is white and looks as if it was made of buckskin. It is round, but has a very small hole near the bottom of it and from this hole some kind of an insect flies in and out."

The grandmother told them, "That also is good for us to eat but it is very dangerous. When you want to secure that you must take fire on the end of a long pole and hold it against this thing which hangs from the tree and make it burn. When the outside burns off it will fall to the ground. Then you can pick it up and bring it in. We call this 'cīta" (hornet)." They then returned to the place where they had seen this nest and did as their grandmother had told them, brought it back and all ate of it.

The next time the children went out to play they were playing around in the grass. They saw something that hopped about in this

---

[69] This is a sort of formal invocation which was used by the Bird-people because, when it was used, it always came true. The load became very light and they could carry it off with ease. It is still used to this day by the Indians for the reason that the Bird-people used it in ancient times.

grass. They went home and told their grandmother, "We saw something out there in the grass, that hops around, sits on the grass and is always running about in it. This thing has long legs but does not fly. It only hops about."

"That," said the grandmother, "is also a good food. That is grasshopper (cako'). When you want to get that you must take out many firebrands in a bunch. Then you set the grass afire in a large circle. As the fire burns in toward the center it will roast these creatures and when the fire is burned out you can go over the ground and pick up the roasted insects and they are all ready to eat."

When they were next out to play they were in a large field and presently they noticed something entering and leaving a small hole in the ground. They took a good look at it and went home and told their grandmother, "We saw something which was a little yellow. It flew humming in and out of a small hole in the grass." "That," said the grandmother, "is what we call the yellowjacket (tcoo). It is good food but very dangerous and when you get it you must go out and take some of the dried tops of the soaproot (a'm sūla). This you place in the hole where the insects are flying in and out and set it on fire. Then you blow the smoke into the hole. Do this about three times and all the insects will be dead. Then you can dig up the ground there and bring home the comb that you find. It is a very good food."

The next time the children went out to play they wandered down near the river and as they were playing along the bank they saw something swimming around in the water. They took a very good look at these very strange creatures and went home and told their grandmother, "We saw something very strange down in the water in the river. There are many of these, some large and some small. They are long and slender, have short heads and are different from anything we have ever seen before. Their eyes are on the sides of their heads and their heads all point in one direction, toward where the water comes from."

"Those," said the grandmother, "are fish and we are very fond of them. They are an excellent food. When you get them you put in a dam down below them and put in a basket and leave it there. Then the next morning you go back and you will find that these fish have been caught in this basket."

When the children returned to this place again to play they found such a dam as their grandmother had described and there were baskets placed in it. They marveled at this but remembered what their grandmother had told them and on the following morning they went back to this same spot and found these baskets literally filled with fish which had been caught here during the night. All the fish that they had seen in the water were in these baskets.

They ran home and told their grandmother what had happened and she said, "I shall go with you boys to carry the fish home. You shall bring the fish out of the water and pour them on the ground and I will carry them home." As soon as she had carried the fish home she procured some wood and built a fire outside of the house and when she had a fine bed of coals she cooked the fish and let the children eat them while she cooked.

Next these children went out to a hill to the west of the village where they found angelica (batco'a). They gathered some of the tender young shoots and ate them and found that they were very good. As they were doing this they found a large hole in the ground and when they looked in they heard something grunting in there and ran away for they were frightened and then something came to the entrance and looked out of the hole and finally it came out completely and sat by the hole and finally stood right up on its hind feet. It was black.

The boys ran home to their grandmother and told her what they had seen. They said, "This peculiar animal has a small head and a long sharp nose and small eyes, a big hand and long claws."

"That," said the grandmother, "is what we call the bear. He is very bad. He kills people. You must never meddle with him. Whenever you see a bear go on the upwind side of him and do not let him smell you."

To this the boys replied, "That is nothing for us. We can handle him."

They went back to the place where they had seen this strange animal and as they approached the hole in the ground the bear smelled them and darted out. They ran away as fast as they could go. Then the bear came out and looked toward the east. They crawled up very close to the bear unobserved, in fact they came so close that they could actually touch the animal and could feel around in the bear's hair over his body and even his face. The bear became very sleepy and eventually laid down and died. They had killed the bear with their magic.

Then they went home and told their grandmother what they had done, that they had actually killed this bear.

III

(The Hummingbird Brothers Win Contests by means of their Yellowjackets)

They then asked their grandmother again where their father and mother and other relatives were. Their grandmother replied, "I told you that they are away over toward the east, that they were killed over there."

The boys then asked, "What should be done about that? We are big enough to know something now and to do something. We can shoot and as for meeting anyone we feel that we are pretty good warriors. We want to get some bows and arrows, some quivers, some paint, some nets and feathers for our heads and anything else that is necessary to enable us to travel properly."

Their grandmother replied, "I cannot do that for you boys but your grandfather Mink (Sili*l*), who lives up toward the north has plenty of bows and arrows and other things of that kind and I will go and get some for you."

When she had secured all these things that were needful for the boys and given them to them the younger brother said, "I must now follow the tracks of my father and mother. Who can beat me at the game of war? I believe that I can fight better than anybody. They cannot outdo me in a fight. I claim to be smart, although I am small and young. Tomorrow morning I shall build a big fire in the sweathouse and when it is all burned down I will use that to paint myself."

The elder brother sat very quietly and did nothing while his younger brother was making this boast, but presently he said, "Grandmother, you must now take a rest for a while."

On the following morning the boys built a big fire in the sweathouse and from it they obtained a lot of charcoal which they mashed up into a fine powder and painted themselves all over with it. They then put on their head net (sūlě') and their war feathers (tsūka'). When they were all ready and fully dressed for war they stood up and looked each other over carefully.

The younger one said, "You must go out first and I will follow you."

The elder said, "How do I look when I am dressed for war?"

"Very well," replied his brother, "how do I look when I am dressed for war?"

"You look well indeed," said the elder. Then they went out and stood in front of the sweat-house for a while and the elder brother took the lead.

The younger said, "Run way out from me and we will see how we can do when we have to go to war. I feel pretty well this morning and I feel like fighting and I want to see how we will do when we are in battle." He then jumped around and put the quiver under his arm. Suddenly he stopped and while his elder brother ran and dodged he took aim and shot at his elder brother, the arrow passing directly between his legs. As he did so he said, "pū——".[70] To this the elder replied "yē——".[71]

The younger brother then ran over to where the elder was standing and the elder told him to go off a certain distance and do his dodging, "I want to see how an old man can shoot. You know I am much older than you are." After he had placed the quiver under his arm the elder brother took his shot and the feathers of the arrow just struck the side of his brother who had dodged properly. As these feathers struck the elder brother cried, "pū——" and the younger brother replied, "yē——".

Then they came together and the elder brother said, "Now we are doing very well. We will fight with these good actions all day for we must see what our people are doing. We must see how many sackfuls or housefuls of acorns they have been able to gather. It may be that the load is too heavy for them to carry and that that is the reason why they have not come home."

With this they started out toward the east, arriving at the first of the villages which their own people had seen. Here they inquired if their people had passed this way.

They said, "No, they did not pass this way." But the boys said, "Here are their tracks. We will follow them nevertheless."

Presently they came to a second village. These people inquired of them what they were doing and were told by the boys that they were

[70]This is a sound made with the lips vibrating and with a short note of descending inflection and signifies in this game, "I shot you."
[71]This is an expression made in a manner quite similar to the above and signifies, "No, you did not."

going to visit their father and mother. These people offered them food but they refused, saying that they would prefer to pass on and reach their destination as quickly as possible.

So they ran on and finally arrived at the village of the Sun-people. Here they found a large acorn cache (maa'cūwit). They stood in the shadow of this acorn cache and watched to see what they might discover. Presently two boys came out of the house and began to play the throwing-sticks game (tsū'dūyen). Finally one of the throwing sticks flew over near the acorn cache, and one of the boys ran after it. He saw the two Hummingbird brothers and put his hands over his eyes so that he could get a good look at them. Then he went home and said to his mother, "I saw some people out there that look like my brothers, that you used to tell me about."

Their mother replied, "What do you want to tell me such a thing as that for? How can they get here? Do you suppose that they came up through the ground?"

The boys went out again and came back. "Yes, mother, those are the same boys you used to tell us about."

Then their mother went out and found the two Hummingbird brothers and cried over them saying, "I have no appetite because I cry for you all the time and I stay here as a slave constantly."

She then took the Hummingbird brothers into the house and covered them up and hid them from her husband so he could not even smell them. Sun-man, however, could smell from a very great distance and immediately he returned home he knew that these boys were present.

In the meantime, however, they had asked their mother to go out to the acorn cache and bring in their bows and arrows which she had done.

As soon as Sun-man arrived he said to his own son, "You must get my stepsons and bring them into the sweat-house so that they may eat with us." But when these boys came for the Hummingbird brothers their mother refused to let them go because, as she said, "Sun-man always kills the people who come here. These are a different kind of people." Sun-man, however, sent the boys back and insisted that the Hummingbird brothers should come over to the sweat-house.

The elder of the Hummingbird brothers said, "I must go and see what is going to happen." He then followed the boys back to the sweat-house and went in.

As soon as he arrived Sun-man came over, took him by the arm and led him to the very center of the building where he seated him. He then went out and brought in a large oak limb which he split in two and he then stood the boy up by the center pole and bound him very securely at the knees and the shoulders. He then told his slave to build a big fire so that everyone could have a fine sweat.

They built the fire close to the elder Hummingbird boy and it became so hot that he could not possibly stand it. He wriggled about and tried to liberate himself but could not and finally he died from the heat, his head rolling over on one side and his tongue lolling out.

All of the men then went out of the sweat-house and went down to the river to swim and while they were gone this boy came to life again. He wriggled about and broke his bonds and went down to the river and plunged in just below the rest of the men.

Upon seeing him there Sun-man said, "What kind of a man is this that comes to life again after I have killed him? I thought I had killed him certainly."

When the young man returned from the river he did not return to the sweat-house but went to his mother's house and upon seeing him she embraced him and said, "My son, how does it come that you are alive now? I know they tried to kill you. How did it happen?"

Soon Sun-man sent another messenger to the house and invited the boys to come over to the sweat-house, saying that everything was in readiness for the feast.

Again the elder brother went to the sweat-house and, to be sure, here was the whole feast set out. The boy had an elderberry tube (kitĕ'catŏlo) which he placed up to his mouth with the opposite end running down into the ground. He did this in such a way that Sun-man did not see it. As he ate the food he did not swallow it but it simply passed down this tube and disappeared. They served him great quantities of food, so much that if he had actually eaten it, it would have killed him from the mere quantity of it. When he had finished eating he went home in a perfectly normal condition.

Sun-man marvelled at this and said, "What kind of a person is this? He beats me at everything when I try to kill him." Presently he sent a messenger to ask both of the Hummingbird boys to come over to the sweat-house, this time saying, "You are to get both of those brave men and bring them here. Our people are going out to hunt rabbits and we want them to accompany us. They will eat the rabbits out there in the woods."

Both boys went over this time and they joined the crowd of hunters. Sun-man told one of the boys to take these two Hummingbird brothers up to a certain place toward the north where there was a large open space with manzanita bushes in its center and where there were a great many rabbits and that there they were to set their traps and hunt their rabbits.

The rest of the hunters went off toward the east.

As soon as they had reached this open space designated by Sun-man, the boy who was guiding the Hummingbird brothers said to them, "Now my brothers, be very careful and look out for yourselves." In this meadow there was a considerable clump of manzanita bushes. The boys set many snares around these. Then they went into the brush to scare the rabbits out. Almost immediately they encountered two large bears which attacked them. Immediately the boys transformed themselves into hummingbirds and flew up and made their escape. As they flew about above the bears they shook their quivers and out of these came a swarm of yellowjackets which stung the bears to death.

The oldest boy then said, "I should like to know who can excel me in doing anything. I am the best fighter there is." Then he said to his younger brother, "Let us go and visit the other hunters and see what success they have had."

The younger brother said, "That is the right idea. The old man will not like it if we are late."

They immediately again transformed themselves, taking human form, and went over to where the other hunters had returned to the village and found them just finishing their meal of rabbit, but there was still a large pile of game left.

Now the boys knew that this food was unsafe for them to eat and each had one of the hollow elderberry tubes and each ate prodigiously of this food, passing it, of course, down the tube and actually not eating a single mouthful of it.

This made the Sun-people very angry. The Hummingbird boys had again defeated them in their attempt to kill them. The Sun-people therefore determined that they would have to attack them directly and shoot them to death, but as they attempted to do this the two boys again transformed themselves into hummingbirds. They flew so very fast that none of the people could hit them with their arrows. After they had flown in this way for some time they again liberated their yellowjackets from their quivers and killed all the people including Sun-man, save the one little boy who had served as messenger and who had taken them out to the place where they had been attacked by the bear and who had warned them there.

This little boy ran back to his mother's house and told her to assemble all of the people who had come from the west, to get them all together in a single house because the Hummingbird brothers were killing all of the Sun-people and that the only safety for the people who had originally come from the west was to separate themselves from the Sun-people.

Almost immediately the Hummingbird boys came flying in to the house, for they were flying about now as hummingbirds and not walking in human form. As they flew back toward the house where their mother lived they shook their quivers over the houses of the village and the yellowjackets descended and killed all of the Sun-people but did not attack any of those who came from the west.

They then assembled all of these people who had come from the west and ordered them to collect everything owned by the Sun-people and to start on a return journey, assuring them all that they were going to return to their original homes and saying also, "These heavy things that you are going to carry shall be light and shall be very easy to carry until you finally reach your old home. We will follow behind you and protect you as you travel."

Finally they reached the second of the two villages which they had passed on the way toward the east and found that they could pass here without difficulty. But when they reached the first one of the villages they had encountered, all the people were out ready for war so the people ran back a short distance until they met the Hummingbird brothers.

The Hummingbird brothers reassured them, however, and told them not to be alarmed and promised that they would kill all enemies. Consequently they again transformed themselves into hummingbirds, flew up and over the warriors. Here they shook their quivers and the yellowjackets stung the warriors to death. Then they went on to the village itself and in the same way succeeded in killing everyone in that village.

These were yellowjackets which flew out at the bidding of the Hummingbirds and when they had accomplished their mission, always returned to their respective places in the quivers.

Then they continued their journey and finally returned to their old home at Mayī.

While the Hummingbird brothers had been away, Turtle-woman had brought together all kinds of vegetable foods and all kinds of meat so that she had a fine feast for everyone when they arrived. This food was distributed and there was great rejoicing over their return.

These people lived at Mayī always.

33—THE SUN PEOPLE ARE KILLED BY YELLOWJACKETS[72]

Characters: 1. Hummingbird brothers (?), 2. Grandmother of these boys, 3. Crane, 4. Meadowlark-people, 5. Bluebird-people, 6. Duck-people, 7. Buzzard-people, 8. Vulture-people, 9. Yellowjackets, 10. Beaver, 11. Bird-people, 12. Sun-man.

Near Upper Lake there was a village, Ta'-napō, Bird-village. This was a village of the Bird-people, and the Sun-people lived far to the east. Nothing ever grew around this village of the Bird-people and they started toward the east to try and obtain food from the Sun-people. Everyone went except one old woman and her two little grandsons. After the people had gone, the little boys started down to the creek. It commenced to sprinkle as the boys went out but they went on down to the creek which they found full of fish. They immediately ran back to the house and asked their grandmother if those fish were good food, and then they all ate fish.

When evening came, they asked their grandmother, "What makes all those houses empty? Where are our father and mother? Where did all the people who used to live here, go to?"

The old lady replied, "Your father and mother, your brothers and sisters were all killed. The Sun-people killed them."

The boys then asked their grandmother for bows and arrows and quivers. They said, "Now grandmother, you give us all these things and we will go out and set fire to the grass and catch yellowjackets to fill up these skins."

[72]The Pomo name of this myth is "cĕmī tc owī tca tcotcka dūman ke mū matū de," in olden times Yellowjackets killed people, my story.
Informant: Bill James, Garcia River, Northern dialect, 1906.

She gave the boys what they asked for and they started off on their journey. They went southward, along the shore of the lake and passed by Lakeport and Kelseyville, following the tracks of their people.

They finally came to Lower Lake, the southernmost arm of Clear Lake. Here they found Crane (Mako), to whom they said, "Where is the trail by which our people passed this way?"

Crane said, "Here is the trail by which your people went. Take this trail to the east and you will come at first to the Meadowlark (Djicil) village." The boys went by this trail and finally arrived at the Meadowlark village.

The Lark people offered them food but the younger brother said, "We do not care for anything to eat. We just came by this way on the trail. Tell us which way the trail leads from here." The Lark people showed the boys the trail and they went on toward the east, finally coming to the Bluebird (Madjō'djō) village.

The Bluebird-people offered the boys food but the younger brother again said, "We do not care for food. If you will only show us the trail by which our mother and father and the other people went over east, we will then go on." The Bluebird-people then showed the boys the trail and they continued their journey, finally arriving at a Duck (many different species) village.

The people here were dancing and having a good time. They offered the boys food but again the younger brother said, "We do not care for food. Only show us the trail toward the east. That is all we want."

They went on from here and finally came to the Buzzard (Kīwē'na) village. Some of the Buzzard people saw the boys coming and told the chief of the village, who came forth and invited the two boys to come to the sweat-house and enjoy themselves with the rest, for all were dancing and having a good time. Again the younger brother declined food and every hospitality and asked for the trail toward the east, saying, "We want to find the trail toward the east. We want to find our mother, father and sisters. This is what we came here for and what we want to find."

The Buzzard chief said, "You boys better return to your own home. That is a dangerous place. There are many dangers over there in the east and you had better return."

The boys said, "No, we must find our people and we must go on."

Next they came to the village of the Vulture (Sul) or Condor people, where they were again offered food which they refused, the younger brother saying, "We are looking for our people and crying for them. We want no food. We want to find our people."

The Condor people then said, "Here is the trail. You are pretty close now. Do you see that mountain over there? The Sun village is just on the other side of it. That is the place where your people now live. That is the place you are looking for."

They went on and came to the top of the mountain and saw, in the valley on the other side, a large village, in the center of which there was a large white house. This was the dangerous house of which they had been warned. The younger brother went down to see what kind of people were at this village, because the older brother was afraid to go down. The younger soon came back and they both started on. When they had gone about half way down the mountainside, the elder again became afraid and the younger went down to the first little house at the edge of the village. He hid behind a basket of acorns and presently a little girl came out of the house. She looked all around and finally saw him. She then went into the house and told her mother, "There is a boy out there who looks like my brother." The younger brother. meanwhile returned and both boys came down to the village. The little girl's mother came out in front of her house and watched the boys as they approached the village. When they had come to where she was, she said to them, "You boys better return to your home. This is a dangerous place. This is not a good place to live. It is very dangerous."

They went inside the house and the elder brother buried the younger in the floor and then sat down beside his mother; for this woman was the mother of the two boys although she was now the wife of Sun-man.

Along toward evening, the woman said, "My husband is coming home now. What will you do?" The boy, however, made no reply. Presently Sun-man came into the house and asked his wife, "Why did you not tell me that some one was coming to visit us, that my children were coming here?" He saw the elder brother there in the house and told the other people, "Now, my people, you will have to get some wood and we will all go into the sweat-house and have a good time." The people then took the elder brother to the sweat-house and tied him securely to the center pole, and built a fire near him. They stood around and watched him burn up until there was nothing but bones left and then the chief told them to go outside and bathe. All went down to the river to bathe and while they were gone the boy whom they had burned, came to life again and joined them at the river, saying, "Well boys, it is pretty hot in that sweat-house."

Sun-man then said, "Well, that is the first time I ever saw anybody who could beat me at anything." Then he continued, "Now, you people must go to bed and in the early morning you must get up and go hunting on the other side of that ridge."

Everybody had gone to the sweat-house to see them burn this boy except his mother, who remained at home and taught the younger brother, who was buried in the floor of the house, what to do to save himself and his brother.

Next morning, all the men of the village including the two brothers, started out to hunt. Sun-man told the two boys where the deer were always to be found, in the very thick brush. The boys went into the very thick brush, according to Sun-man's direction, and found there many grizzly bears. The brush was full of bears. The younger brother then said to the elder, "Now wait a little. You stand on the west side of me." The boys had with them two black-bear skins filled with yellowjackets. They opened these bags and the yellowjackets flew at the bears and killed them all.

Then the boys returned to the village and told the people, "We killed one little deer over there. You people better go over and get it." Sun-man then began to cry. He mourned because they had killed all his pets, the bears. He knew what had happened. The younger brother noticed that the hunters were all whispering among themselves. He said to his brother, "Now we must be careful or they will kill us. If you see anything move, watch it carefully." After a while, they opened their bags and turned the yellowjackets loose again. This time they attacked the hunters and killed them all.

After they had killed all the hunters, they went back to the village alone and burned up everything; and all the people that Sun-man had killed in past times returned to life. Then they started to return home and all the baskets of food which had belonged to the Sun-people rolled along in front of them, without any effort on their part.

Upon their return journey, they found that all of the Bird-people from the various villages they had passed, had gathered into the first, the Meadowlark village. They determined to kill all these Bird-people and finally did so, notwithstanding the protests from them.

They then went on and came to Cache Creek, the outlet of Clear Lake. Here they found Crane (Makó), whom they asked how they might cross the creek. Crane said he would put a bridge across, so he lay down and stretched his neck over to the other side.

Beaver (Kage) then asked these people, "Which way are you people travelling?" They, however, did not answer her but went right along until they came to their old village near Upper Lake. Their grandmother was sitting there when they arrived, with all the people they had brought home with them. They had a very large village and the two boys were chiefs. They had a big dance here and all the people assembled at this village.

During this dance, the people all became ill and died and their bodies, along with the houses, food, implements and everything about the village turned into water and ran into the lake. This did not make Clear Lake, however for there was a lake there before this time.

MYTHS OF SUPERNATURAL BEINGS
34—FALCON KILLS THE KILAK FAMILY[73]
INCIDENTS AND CHARACTERS

I. *Coyote creates human beings.*
  1. *Coyote, 2. Coyote's mother, 3. Duck.*
II. *Coyote's mother is killed.*
  1. *Coyote's mother, 2. Coyote, 3. Coyote's wife, 4. Young men.*
III. *Coyote burns the dance-house.*
  1. *Coyote, 2. Sleep charm, 3. Bird-people.*
IV. *Coyote's mother is resurrected.*
  1. *Coyote, 2. Frog-woman, 3. Turtle, 4. Coyote's mother, 5. Falcon.*
V. *Falcon kills the Kǐ'laks.*
  1. *Falcon, 2. Kǐ'laks (6), 3. Coyote, 4. Buzzard, 5. Animal-people, 6. Crane, 7. Crow-people, 8. Falcon's wife, 9. Magic flute.*

I

(Coyote Creates Human Beings)

Coyote lived at Katsa'mūkal, an old village about two miles north of Lakeport. No one lived with Coyote except his old mother and he grew very lonesome. He decided, therefore, to build a large dance-house.

He arose the next morning and went out into the village and delivered a speech saying: that everyone should assemble for the building of this dance-house; that, first of all, they would dig the pit, and that then the young people would go out to gather the poles, brush, grapevines, and other materials required for finishing the building. He announced that it would be completed in four days. As a matter of fact no one lived in this village except Coyote and his mother, but Coyote talked as if the people were already there.

Then he went back to his house for breakfast, after which he again came out. He marked out the place where the pit was to be and began digging. He had not dug very far when he found Tana' (chub duck). He set Duck out on the bank and danced around in great glee, saying that he would be Duck's grandfather and that he would make him the Chief of the village. Then Coyote plucked from Duck a considerable number of feathers which he put away carefully.

He then told Duck that he must get up very early in the morning and talk to these feathers and tell them what to do, and particularly he must send them all out to get the posts and other materials required to build the dance-house.[74]

The short feathers became women, the very small feathers became children, and the big feathers from the body became young men, while the big wing feathers became middle-aged men. At last, on the fourth day, Coyote put all of these feathers around the pit, laying them down flat on the ground. Those which he placed near the middle of the pit became good singers and dancers. He then talked to these feathers and to Duck and told them what each would be.

Then Coyote went home and told his mother what he had done and she said that it was very good.

Coyote next built a small house for Duck where he could live entirely alone and apart from the others.

That evening Coyote went out and again orated saying: "Early in the morning before the sun is up the young people will go out and

---

[74]This duck (tana') carried all these posts and the other heavy loads of material required in building the dance-house. He was a very strong man and did very hard work. He carried so much in fact that his neck became sore and that is why when you skin one of these birds at the present time you always find a great deal of blood around the neck.

gather the poles and brush, and we will finish the dance-house before sunrise. You older people will help put on the roof. Some of you old women will carry the dirt for the roof while others carry the water and still others will be busy cooking, but we will not eat anything until we have completely finished the dance-house."

Coyote did not sleep that night and toward daylight he heard a noise, as if somebody were laughing and talking and whistling. He went out to where he had placed the feathers but saw nothing. He returned home and just at daybreak he heard someone coughing, and again heard someone singing and laughing.

Then Duck went out and addressed these newly created people and told them what to do just as Coyote had instructed him. They all agreed to help finish the dance-house. All went out and returned very quickly and they worked so rapidly that by sunrise the dance-house was completely finished. Then they built a big fire in it and had a fire-fanning contest, everyone enjoying himself greatly. After this they went out to swim and finally they had their feast.

Then Duck, who was now the Chief of the village, announced that they were all going to have a big ceremony, a dance which would last four days and nights. Everybody rejoiced and joined in the dance with a will. They all danced four days and four nights and then they had another big feast.

II

(Coyote's Mother Is Killed)

For some time after this no ceremonies were held and there was nothing in the life of the village which was out of the ordinary. Coyote's mother still lived there, but Coyote used to stay in the dance-house at night with the younger men. However, he presently decided that he wanted to marry one of the girls. He slipped away from the dance-house four different nights to see this girl but it was not until the fourth that she would have anything to do with him. The next morning he returned to the dance-house with his face badly scratched. Then the other young men knew that this scratching was a sign of the girl's affection for Coyote and they made fun of him, but they did not like it that Coyote had married one of their number and they decided to retaliate by killing Coyote's mother.

They therefore heated a white rock (kawin tsala). Part of the young men took this heated rock and went out to where Coyote's mother lived. The rest of the young men remained in the house and kept Coyote talking and all laughed and made a great noise so that Coyote could not hear any outcry of his mother.

Those who had gone out to kill Coyote's mother, did so by choking her with this hot rock. Then they covered her up with a blanket just as if she were alive and sleeping. Finally they all returned to the dance-house, built a good fire, took a sweat and went swimming.

When Coyote went home for breakfast along with the rest of the young men he found his mother dead. Then everybody heard Coyote cry. They all knew what he was crying for and they watched to see what he would do. He wrapped his mother up very carefully in a blanket made of weeds and in a deer hide, and bound this bundle with grape-vines. He then took the body out and buried[75] it.

III

(Coyote Burns the Dance-house)

Before doing this, however, Coyote cut open the breast of his mother and took out her heart. He took a stick and removed the bark and with the blood from his mother's heart he made four red bands around it. Just below each band he tied some down. Then he put a top-knot of falcon feathers at the upper end of this wand. To this upper end he attached also a streamer made by tying many white feathers to a single string, at the lower end of which he suspended the heart of his mother. This made what is called a "yū'lūk." Thus Coyote made a sleep-producing wand (sma'kaaitcīl).

Coyote then went out into the village and commenced to dance and make a great noise. He made as much noise as a great many people coming to the village for a "surprise" dance.[76]

At first no one paid any attention to Coyote but finally someone heard him and came out to see what was going on. Then someone ran to the Chief of the village and told him what was happening and he went to the top of the dance-house and told everyone to come in, which they all did, except the Chief himself.

Coyote then approached, dancing, singing and waving his wand.

---

[75] It was customary in ancient times to burn a body but Coyote buried his mother.
[76] The informant states that it was quite customary for the people of one village to go unannounced to a friendly village and suddenly appear there dancing and singing.

He danced four times around the dance-house, before he entered. After Coyote had entered the Chief also came in. Coyote continued to dance around in the dance-house for some time, waving his wand as before and presently everyone felt sleepy and eventually all went to sleep.

Coyote then tied the wand to the center pole of the dance-house, placing it so that the heart was toward the fire. Then he went out, tied the dance-house door securely, and closed and fastened tightly the smoke-hole. Then he set fire to the house and burned everyone in it. All these people, of course, were "Bird-people" and they were thoroughly roasted in this great fire.

Coyote then commenced eating some of the roasted meat. When he had satisfied his hunger he thought that he would dry some of the meat and put it away for winter. He next brought to the village four loads of white-oak limbs. He then went out and brought in four lots of grape-vines. When he brought in the last lot and threw it down, some of the ducks, mud-hens and other birds and also some of the ground squirrels and other mammals jumped up from among the dead people. They had returned to life, but they were no longer human beings. They had turned into these different species of birds and mammals.

Very much astonished to see this, Coyote jumped back crying, "What is the matter here?"

IV

(Coyote's Mother Is Resurrected)

Now, there was no water at this place and Coyote became very thirsty, so he started out in search of water to drink. He first went into the hills, but could find no water there. Then he went on into a field where there was some wet grass. Old Frog-woman was sitting there.

Coyote said, "Do you know where there is any water?"

Frog replied, "No, I have no water. I wish I could find some, too. I am very thirsty. I am so thirsty that I cannot produce any saliva." She attempted to expectorate to show Coyote how very thirsty she was. "Go over there toward the southwest and you might find some water over there."

Coyote went over in the direction indicated, to a place where there is now a pond. There he found old Turtle. He asked Turtle if he knew where there was any water. "No," said Turtle, "I have no water here. I am extremely thirsty myself."

Turtle told Coyote to go over toward the southwest and that he might find some water there. (There is in fact another pond over in that direction.) Coyote went over there to the place indicated and found another old Turtle. Of Turtle he made the same inquiry. But Turtle replied that he had no water at all and he was very thirsty himself. He advised Coyote to return to the place whence he came.

"But," said Coyote, "I have just been there and Frog tells me that she has no water at all."

Turtle said, "She is lying to you. She has water. You go over there and ask for it again and if she refuses you then push her away from the place where she is sitting and you will find that she has water under her."

Coyote followed these instructions and when he arrived he found that the old Frog-woman was making a basket. She had no water about so she had to expectorate upon the basket to make the material moist enough to enable her to weave it.

Frog said, "Didn't you find anybody over there?"

"Yes," said Coyote, "I did, and he told me that he had no water, but that you have water and advised me to come back here."

The old Frog-woman sat and said nothing for quite a long time. But finally Coyote said, "If you do not show me where this water is I shall have to kill you."

Frog-woman replied, "I have no water. Don't you see I'm making a basket and have to use my own spittle to keep the material soft?"

"Well then, " replied Coyote, "get up and let me look under you."

Frog replied, "I cannot get up. I am very old and lame. That is why I have no water. I cannot walk about to get it."

Again Coyote threatened to kill Frog if she did not show him the water and once more she denied having any and insisted that she was so lame that she could not even stand up, nor could she lie down when she tried to sleep. She insisted that she was so lame that she could not move and had to sleep and work and do everything that she did right where she was sitting.

Coyote became vexed with this parley so he took a bow and fitted an arrow to the string and pointed it at Frog's heart. Then he told her that if she did not show him the water at once he would shoot. At this Frog finally moved and there indeed was fine cool water directly under her.

Coyote drank some of that water and then returned where his mother was buried and there he cried and mourned her loss. He remained at the grave four days and four nights and then he commanded her to come back to life again and to become a young woman and sure enough on the following morning, there she was, a beautiful young woman.

Coyote and his mother lived there together for a long time. Now, Coyote had a falcon feather over which he performed a ceremony in order that it might become his grandson.[77] Next morning the feather had become a young man. This was Falcon and Coyote made him the chief.

V

(Falcon Kills the Kĭ'laks)

Falcon wanted to go over to the east to gamble with Kĭ'lak. Now Kĭ'lak was a man-eater of a peculiar supernatural power which enabled him to hold people seated in his house until his return. It made no difference whether he was present or not. If anyone entered his house he would never be able to leave it due to this supernatural power.

At first Coyote told his grandson that the place was too dangerous for him to go, but upon Falcon's insistence that he was going to start over toward the east on the following morning, Coyote insisted upon accompanying him.

After they had traveled a very great distance they met Buzzard who immediately recognized them and said, "Well, here indeed comes the Chief." They asked Buzzard to direct them to the home of Kĭ'lak. He told them that they must journey toward the southeast, whereas as a matter of fact they were then going due east.

They journeyed on until they met a large number of the Animal-people holding a foot-race. They stopped and asked their way to the home of Kilak. Now, these people told them that it was a very dangerous place and warned them against going on any further.

However they continued their journey and finally came to a river

---

[77] The exact relationship here is said to be that of maba'ts, that is to say, "father's father". Coyote became maba'ts to this newly created man.

with a very deep, swift current which it was impossible for them to cross. Here they found Crane standing on the bank and asked him if there was anywhere that they could find a foot-log bridging the stream.

Crane said, "No, this is a very hard place to get across. Nobody ever crosses here."

Falcon said, "Is there not some way that you can take us across? We must reach the other side of this stream."

To this Crane said, "Yes, I might take you over, where are you going?"

Falcon replied, "We are going over to Kī'lak's house to play a grass game."

Crane warned them that that was a very dangerous place to go because Kī'lak is a great cannibal and eats people alive. He warned them that there was a trap right by the door and that as soon as an unwary visitor set a foot inside the door the trap would catch him and he would be thrown back there and held until Kī'lak arrived and devoured him. He also said that they would see the bones of dead people all around the home of Kī'lak and on top of the house, in fact, Kilak had killed and eaten so many people there that you could distinguish this place because it was snow white, due to the bones on top of the house and all around it.

"All right," said they, "we will beat him playing the grass game anyway."

So Crane came close to the bank and stretched his neck over and they crossed the water.

They went on and met some of the Crow-people. They were eating bugs and worms in the high grass of a valley. They saw Falcon and Coyote coming and, of course, knew them as soon as they saw them. They asked these two where they were going and were told that they were going to Kī'lak's to play the grass game.

The Crows said, "That is a dangerous place to go. Kī'lak is looking all over the earth for people because he eats nothing but human flesh and he robs people of their beads and other valuable things that they have. Everybody is afraid of him."

Falcon said, "Have no fear. I will win when I play with Kī'lak."

To this Crow replied, "I will tell you my friend, before you go in you must be very careful. He has a trap inside the door. He catches people in this trap and eats them alive. There are a great many bones all around the house too. You will smell nothing but blood. You must be very careful when he gives you something to eat. The mush and bread he gives you will be made of blood. The meat he gives you will be human flesh. The fish he gives you will be the meat of the rattle-snake and the bullsnake."

However, Falcon and Coyote continued their journey, and went on and on until finally they saw the house where Kī'lak lived.

Now Coyote was a very smart man. He really knew everything, but he pretended to know nothing. He really had a hunting sack in which he had anything that a person might want. He had in this bag a bead polisher (tūwī'u kabe).

Coyote said to Falcon, "Now my son, let us stop here. I want to tell you everything you do not know about these matters, but especially I want you to know that when you commence playing the grass game with Kī'lak, you must watch very closely when he shoots at you and particularly watch how he holds his bow.[78] The first time he shoots at you, you must dodge under his arrow. His second shot you must dodge by going above the arrow. The third shot you must dodge to the left of it and the fourth shot you must dodge to the right of it. Coyote knew exactly how Kī'lak gambled and exactly what to expect when he went to Kī'lak's house so he gave Falcon still further instructions as follows:

"When he gives us food, I will tell him that you do not know how to eat."

Now Coyote had a flute (wo'lwol) in his hunting sack and he was going to pour the food from the basket served by Kī'lak, into this and it would run down into his magic hunting sack and disappear there.

Coyote further instructed Falcon as follows: "When we arrive at the house you must not go in first. I will do that. If he gives you a bow and arrows I will tell him that you never gamble with another man's grass-game bones (cōka')."

Then he showed Falcon the magic bow and arrows which he carried

[78]This was not in reality a grass game, although it is mentioned as such by the informant. It was a game in which the contestants shot at each other with bows and arrows. If the player shot four times and missed, his opponent was considered the winner. In this game the person doing the shooting was seated near the fire, while his opponent, who was the target, flew about the roof of the dance-house in the vicinity of the smoke-hole. This sort of a shooting and dancing game is mentioned in several of the myths as being played by the Bird-people.

in his hunting sack. Thus he told Falcon all about how everything
would be and just what he might expect when he arrived at Kī'lak's
house.

They first went on top of the house and then they went to the door.
Coyote drew out the bead polisher from his hunting sack and placed it
in the door. Then they heard a great noise like the booming of a drum.
The stone had been thrown by the trap at the door far back to the rear
of the house.

Now there were in the house the old Kī'lak man and woman and
when they heard this noise they said, "ai—— (inspiration) who is
there?"

Coyote replied, "It is I. I came to see you folks. My son here wants
to have some fun with your boy. He wants to play a grass game with
him."

Kī'lak replied, "Yes, that is good. He will be home very soon."

Almost immediately they heard a noise overhead, "Kī'lak, kī'lak,
kī'lak, ..." The noise was coming from the north. That is the kind
of noise that Kī'lak always makes when he is traveling. Kī'lak arrived
and ran four times around the dance-house and then alighted at the
smoke-hole and said, "He—— somebody must be here. Who is here?"
Then he flew down inside the house and went immediately to the rear
and took off his feather suit, after which he looked just like any human
being.

Then Kī'lak said, "Yes, it is good that you came to gamble with me."

Pretty soon another of the Kī'laks came, this time from the west,
making the same kind of noise as his predecessor. He went around the
dance-house four times and alighted at the smoke-hole and said, "U——
something smells here." He came in, and took off his feather suit the
same as the first Kī'lak had done. Then he said, "It is good that you
came to gamble with us."

Presently another Kī'lak came from the east and did exactly as his
predecessors had done. He said "Hu—— what is smelling in here?"
When he had taken off his feather suit he also said, "It is good that
you came to gamble with us."

Finally a fourth Kī'lak came, this time from the south, making the
same noise and as he came close to the house they heard the voice of a
woman crying. This was the prey he had brought back from his hunt-

ing. He then went four times around the dance-house in a counter-clockwise direction and four times in a clockwise direction, after which he alighted at the smoke-hole and said, "Hu—— I smell something bad in here. There must be some strangers here." Then he came in, re-moved his suit and said, "I know that this is my friend who came to see me and came to gamble with me."

Coyote then said, "You know that a gambler, when he wants to come to see you and to play with you, does not say very much. My son wants to play a game with you but he does not talk much. He is all ready to play whenever you are ready, so get ready as soon as possible."

Now this last Kï'lak who had arrived from the south had a woman in his talons. She was groaning as he flew in and placed her on the floor.

Coyote and Falcon were seated on the west side of the fire.

Kï'lak said, "I did not get much meat, this is all I could get. You have come to visit us but we have very little meat."

Then Falcon spoke for the first time. "Is that what you call meat? I call that a human being."

Then the last Kï'lak who had arrived took off his feather suit and told the one who had arrived from the north to give the visitor some-thing to eat. He brought out four baskets full of mush and four big baskets full of meat and said, "That is all I have here to eat now. After you have eaten this food we will place our bets. We have very little, but will bet something anyway so as to keep the game going."

Coyote took his flute and said, "This boy never eats at all. He does nothing but gamble all the time." Coyote then poured the eight baskets of food down into the flute and they all disappeared. Then the bets were made.

Now the Kï'laks had four storage baskets (*tït*) full of beads. Each basket was about two feet in diameter. Coyote on the other hand had only three or four hundred beads in his hunting sack but he pulled and pulled and kept on pulling out string after string of beads until he had enough from his magic hunting sack to "top" the bet made by the Kï'laks and still he had beads left.

Then they commenced playing. First they made a very hot fire. The Kï'lak who had arrived from the south was the owner of this house and the Chief of the Kilaks. Then Coyote said, "You commence playing."[79]

Kī'lak flew round and round above the fire. Falcon took his bow and arrows and got ready to shoot. He took his time and was very slow about making his first "guess" (taking his first shot). Finally Falcon said, "Hold on there, this is pretty hard to guess. Are you ready?"

Kī'lak replied, "Yes, I am ready." Falcon shot and Kīlak fell directly into the fire. He rolled out of the fire and as he did so he said "O——. It looks as though this is the first time I have ever been beaten in this game. I am sweating (as he wiped the blood from his mouth)." And then he dropped over dead.

Now this was the first Kī'lak who had arrived. The one that had come in from the north.

A second bet was made, this time a bet of about twice as many beads as had been wagered in the first instance.

Then the Kī'lak who had arrived from the west flew up and around the smoke-hole above the fire.

Again Falcon took very careful and deliberate aim and his shot felled this one of the Kī'lak brothers, who as he rolled out of the fire made the same statement as his predecessor had done and then fell dead.

The Kī'lak from the east next laid his wager and Coyote "topped" his bet. The result was the same as before. Falcon's arrow passed directly through Kī'lak's heart and he also fell into the fire making the same statement as his brothers had made.

Finally the southern Kī'lak bet and said, "If you beat me you can take everything I have in my house."

Then Kī'lak said to Falcon, "It seems that you win every time. Why do you not lead in the playing this time?" So Falcon agreed. Coyote commenced singing a magic song and Falcon commenced flying around above the fire which by this time was very hot. Then Kilak brought out a big pipe and put into the bowl four double handfuls of tobacco, forced the tobacco down very hard and put on a live coal and smoked. He took his time and put more wood onto the fire so as to make it even hotter. The house became red hot. Kī'lak smoked all the tobacco out of the pipe, cleaned it and put it away with his sack of tobacco. Then he brought out a bow and put on the string very tightly. He then took his bow and arrows and took a great deal of time in preparation for his first shot. Finally he asked Falcon, "Are you ready now?" Falcon replied, "Yes I am ready whenever you are." Kī'lak aimed very deliberately at Falcon and shot, but missed him. He did this three times. Then he poked up the fire to make it a little hotter. He said, "Well, well, you are a pretty good player. You are the only one I ever saw who knows how to play." He again stirred up the fire deliberately and then rested a while. Then he got up and took his fourth shot at Falcon but missed him again. Falcon flew down and said, "You play too fast my friend. If you would only take your time when you are gambling you could play much better. Now you fly up and I will shoot."

So Kī'lak flew up and flew around as the others had done but as soon as Falcon picked up his bow and arrows Kī'lak tried to fly out through the smoke-hole. Falcon saw this and shot so as to hit the frame of the smoke-hole. This scared Kī'lak so that he flew back. He told Kī'lak not to try to cheat in that way and then let him fly round and round the house until Kī'lak became very tired. Then Falcon shot and killed Kī'lak and threw him into the fire.

Then Coyote and Falcon took the father and mother of the Kī'lak brothers and threw them into the fire also, so that all six of the Kī'laks were dead.

Now the woman that the southern Kī'lak had brought in as food was still alive so Coyote and Falcon took this woman and they collected all the beads and clothing and other things that the Kī'laks had, which had all been stolen from the people. When they had taken all of these out of the house they set fire to it and started back toward their home in the north.

When they had gone a short distance Coyote told Falcon that he and the woman whom they had rescued should be married. Falcon then said that he was going on toward the east and that he and his wife would live there and that Coyote should return to their old home so they went to their places and there they have lived ever since.

35—FALCON IS TAKEN BY KILAK[80]

INCIDENTS AND CHARACTERS

I. *Falcon is taken by Kï'lak.*
   1. *Falcon, 2. Quail (Falcon's wife), 3. Kï'lak, 4. Vulture, 5. Coyote (Grandfather of Falcon), 6. Spider (the Messenger), 7. Spider (the keeper of the Zenith Gate), 8. Blue-fly (Kï'lak's slave).*
II. *Owl marries Wind-man.*
   1. *Night-owl girls, 2. Night Owl (Father of Night-owl girls), 3. Wind-man.*
III. *Wind-man creates people.*
   1. *Wind-man, 2. Coyote, 3. Blue Jay, 4. Screech Owl.*
IV. *Coyote transforms People.*
   1. *Coyote, 2. Bird-people.*

I

(Falcon Is Taken by Kï'lak)

Falcon and his wife, Quail, lived at Tō'mkai.[81] Falcon had a deer-head mask with which he used to hunt. One day he went off toward the north, hunting, and presently he saw two deer. He stalked them and as he came close to them Kï'lak came and picked him up and carried him off to his house in the far north. Kï'lak wears a red suit and his house is as white as snow. His red suit is really a blanket of fire without which he is entirely unable to fly.

Falcon's wife missed him, of course, and she watched for him to return, but when he did not come back she went to Vulture and asked him where Falcon had gone. "You can smell anything, from a great distance. You can tell where there is anything dead. Go out and smell around and see if you cannot find my husband."

So Vulture went out on top of the sweat-house and faced toward the south. He smelled in that direction carefully but could find nothing. Then he turned toward the west and smelled in that direction with the same result. Then toward the north and toward the east and finally he smelled downward. From all these five directions he got no odor at all. Finally he smelled upward and there he discovered where Falcon had gone, because it smelled as if there was something dead up there.

Coyote came along and asked Vulture what had become of his grand-

---

[80]The Pomo title of this myth is "tata yatcŏl kï'lak ya pï," Falcon Kï'lak took. Informant: Jim McCalluck, Northern dialect.
[81]This is an old village site on the west side of the creek about two or three miles below Traveler's Home.

son, Falcon, and Vulture replied, "They took your grandson up into the Upper world."

Coyote was so distressed at this news that he jumped into the fire and burned his hair off.

Then Coyote hunted up Spider and asked him to take him up into the Upper World so Spider put him into his hunting sack and carried him up on his web and when he reached the Zenith Gate he called to his grandfather to open up the gate and let them in.

When they came out into the Upper World they saw Kī'lak's house standing there just like a snow-covered mountain. It was white from the bones of people whom Kī'lak had already eaten and had thrown the bones out there on top of the house.

Spider and Coyote went to the house and there saw the body of Falcon lying outside. They went in and sat down to await Kī'lak's return. Presently he came in, this time bringing a man from the east. Blue-fly, a one-eyed fellow who was the slave of Kī'lak, was there in the house. When Kī'lak approached the house he carried the man he had brought four times around it and then threw the body inside. Then he asked Blue-fly, "What kind of people is it that are sitting in my clean sweat-house?"

Now when Coyote and Spider arrived at Kī'lak's house Coyote immediately dug a hole in which Spider could conceal himself. Then he went about and placed arrow-heads in different parts of the house to make a trap for Kī'lak. Then he went over and sat down in another place.

Finally Kī'lak flew through the door and ran to attack Coyote. Coyote dodged and Kī'lak ran against some of the arrow-heads, cutting himself badly. He pursued Coyote round and round inside the sweat-house and Coyote again and again dodged whenever Kī'lak sprang at him, and each time he dodged Kī'lak struck some of the arrow-heads which Coyote had placed for this purpose. Finally Kī'lak died because he was simply cut to pieces by the arrow-heads.

Spider then came out of his hiding place and Coyote went outside and took the body of Falcon and placed it in his hunting sack. Then he told Blue-fly to go home where he belonged and Blue-fly did. Then Coyote took all of the things that Kī'lak had taken from the many people whom he had killed and eaten, he put these all in his hunting sack and then he burned the house in which Kï'lak lived. Then he and Spider went back to the Zenith Gate and Spider said to his grandfather, "Open up the gates, we are going home again." He put Coyote in his own hunting sack and they went down the spider-web to the earth.

When they arrived at their home Coyote took a large basket and partly filled it with water. Then he placed Falcon in it and inverted another large basket over it. Around this he tied a rope and fastened the rope to his arm. Then Coyote lay down to sleep. In the middle of the night he felt the rope move so he arose and looked into the basket but Falcon had not yet returned to life. Toward morning Coyote felt another pull on the rope and when he looked in this time, there was Falcon, alive. He took him out and Quail bathed and cleansed him thoroughly and he was again able to walk and move about just as he had done before.

Falcon then announced to the people that they should assemble and have a dance, which they did.

II

(Owl Marries Wind-man)

Now, Night Owl had two daughters. They were very noisy. Their mother scolded them and one of the girls ran away. She went over the mountain toward the south and came to the house of Wind-man and married him.

A long time after that her father came to visit them. Wind-man said, "I heard a Night Owl out there."

His wife replied, "That is my father," so she went out and invited him to come in.

She gave him food and Night Owl said, "I came over for a little visit. I am only going to stay a short time. I am going home tomorrow."

That night Wind-man went hunting. He killed some geese and gave them to Night Owl to take home.

III

(Wind-man Creates People)

Now, Wind-man took some vulture feathers and placed them in the sweat-house and from them he created people. Coyote came there and asked Wind-man how he was able to do that. He told Coyote just exactly how he did it, and he said, "You must take some red paint and

stripe your body with it. Then you must lie out on the mountainside
where the vultures can see you. They will come to you and then you
will get the feathers."

Coyote went home and did this, but instead of striping his body as
he had been told, he simply took a large basket covered with red feathers
and crawled in under it. Presently the vultures came, a large flock of
them, and they put their bills through the basket and picked the meat
all off his bones.

Now, Wind-man had done this same sort of thing but he had taken
a very large basket, one so large that the vultures could not reach him.
Coyote, however, had made this basket just the size of his own body
and therefore the vultures could reach him and they ate him up.

His bones lay there on the mountainside all mouldy and two men,
Blue Jay and Screech Owl, came along to doctor him. They ran four
times around his remains in a counter-clockwise direction and then four
times in a clockwise direction. Then Coyote woke up, growling as he
always does, "I do not want anyone to bother me when I am trying to
sleep."

IV

(Coyote transforms People)

Then Coyote went back to the village very much disgusted and he
said to the people, "Whatever I try to do never seems to come right.
I am going to stop trying to do things. You people who are living here
can do whatever you like and you can turn into whatever kind of animal
you wish."

Then the people turned into birds of various kinds and into all kinds
of animals and they all left the village.

36—FALCON AND EAGLE JOURNEY TO GILAK'S HOME[82]

Characters: 1. Falcon, 2. Eagle, 3. Gi'lak, 4. Magic rock, 5. Magic sling.

Falcon used to hunt deer over on Mount Kanaktai. He did this until
one morning he saw a woman over on the eastern shore of Clear Lake.
She was going toward the north when he looked down from the top of
the mountain and he decided to follow her. He went down to the lake
shore and took a tule boat and crossed the lake so that he might intercept

---

[82]Informant: Dave Thompson, Eastern dialect.

her on her journey. He hid near the trail but as she came along he was ashamed to show himself and let her know that he was there. He let her pass by and then he made a wide circuit and again came back to the trail, but this time, instead of hiding, he went out into a wide, open glade through which the trail led.

Finally this woman came into the glade and he called to her to stop. When she had done so he asked her where she was going. She told him that she was going very far to the north and that he must not try to follow but that he must go back to the place whence he had come.

Falcon replied, "No, I will go with you." So he accompanied her and by and by they arrived at Maiyī'.

Now the trail here led through a hole in a large rock and there was no other way of passing. This was a magic place and if a person came here from the south and attempted to pass through this hole it would shut up and cut his head off completely. If a man approached it from the north and tried to pass through this opening to go toward the south he met the same fate.

The woman knew all about this trail and knew how to pass through this hole without danger. She could fly just exactly like a bird so she sailed along and shot rapidly through the hole and it closed instantly but not until after she had passed through.

Falcon watched her and then he prepared himself and flew as the woman had done and succeeded in passing through the hole. When the woman saw this she said, "You are a good medicine-man and have succeeded in this difficult trial. You may accompany me and you shall become my husband."

They continued their journey until they arrived at the point in the hills opposite what is now called Bachelor Valley. Then they went on down into Potter Valley where they remained over night in their first camp. From there they started northward. They traveled a long time, but toward evening they saw a large white house in the distance, toward the north. They could see this house a long way off.

Finally they arrived at this house, which is the home of Gī'lak, a supernatural being who eats humans. The whiteness of his house and his surroundings is due to the bones of the people Gī'lak has eaten and thrown out of the house. No one who enters the house of Gī'lak ever comes out alive.

As they approached Gī'lak's house the woman, who was as a matter of fact, Eagle, told Falcon, "You must stay here by yourself. I will go in and kill Gī'lak. I am doing this because he killed my brother."

She then went into the house, leaving Falcon outside. Gī'lak welcomed her and gave her a place on the east side of the house. That night Gī'lak came over to the eastern side of the house so that he might sleep near Eagle. Now Eagle had fingernails which were very sharp like knives and she watched her chance and about midnight she attacked Gī'lak and cut him in two.

She then collected all of the beads and other things which Gī'lak had taken from the people and took them outside the house. Then she and Falcon burned the house and started back toward home. By morning they had arrived at Potter Valley.

Continuing their journey they again came to the rock with the hole which closes and Falcon said to Eagle, "Now you must close your eyes for I am going to try my power on that rock. You must close your eyes very tightly so that you will not see what I am doing." Falcon had a sling and he intended to shoot with the sling at this rock. This, of course, was a magic sling and Falcon hit the rock fairly and broke it into many pieces so that they were able to pass through here without further danger.

They finally arrived at the village of Maiyī' and Falcon said, "I am going home now and we must separate here and you must go to your home." Falcon lived at Nō'napōtī and Eagle lived down at Sulphur Bank (Kawĕ'na). Thus Eagle had to travel down the eastern shore of Clear Lake while Falcon had to travel down the western shore.

Of course, Falcon had a wife at home and he had been gone a long time. The people of his village missed him and they thought that a bear had killed and eaten him. They looked everywhere in their vicinity for him but did not find him.

To their surprise he returned and the people asked him where he had been. He said that he had been very far to the north.

37—QUAIL DESERTS HER HUSBAND AND GOES TO GILAK'S[83]

Characters: 1. Black Chicken-hawk, 2. Quail, 3. Kūsū't, 4. Gī'lak, 5. Hawk's brother, 6. Fisher, 7. Bat, 8. Blue Jay, 9. Red-headed-woodpecker, 10. Hummingbird, 11. Bottle-fly.

Black Chicken-hawk lived with his wife, Quail, at a big village. Quail became angry and left her husband. She went down by the beach and walked along the coast out on the breakers, so that no one could follow her tracks. She went along for a great distance but finally came to a big river, which she could not cross. She stood there a long time, thinking what to do but finally she wished that the water would dry up. It did and she walked across. After a while, she came to another river and caused it to dry up in the same way, so that she was able to pass over. Then she passed through a big field and by and by, saw smoke rising way off in the distance. She went toward the smoke, and, finally, from the top of a little hill, she saw a big sweat-house. This house was pure white all over. This whiteness was due to the bleached human bones which covered the sweat-house. This was Gī'lak's house and on the top of it stood Kūsū't, whose business was, to announce to Gī'lak the approach of strangers. Kūsū't saw Quail coming and told Gī'lak about it. He told Gī'lak who it was and who her husband was. They did not harm Quail when she came to the house but admitted her and gave her a place over by the fire.

Hawk, finally, after about three days, found out where his wife had gone and determined to follow her. His brother determined to go also. Hawk said, "All right, if you are man enough, you may go. When I go, I never expect to return." So they started out and followed Quail's tracks down to the ocean, then turned south and followed her tracks over the breakers, crossing the river in the same manner she had. They came finally, to the knoll near Gī'lak's house. They stopped at this knoll, where nobody could see them. The elder brother combed his hair out and then said to the younger, "I do not expect to come back from here alive, so I will put you in my own hair, in order that they may not know that you are here." He did this and tied his hair up so that his brother was covered completely. Pretty soon the lookout, Kūsū't, called out to

---

[83]The Pomo name of this myth is "cēmī cakakaiya mata ma baiyel kaū dūmman matū," "Quail her husband left long ago story."
Informant: Bill James, Garcia River, Central dialect, 1906.

Gī'lak that someone was coming and told him to get ready with his sharp-est arrow. Hawk approached the sweat-house and, without ceremony, entered. As he entered, Gī'lak shot him right in the throat. He then laid the body near the fire but, after a moment, concluded that it would be better to put the body outside the house and let Hawk die before trying to cook him.

As soon as the body had been laid outside, the younger brother crawled out from the elder's hair, and, taking the body upon his back, started to return home. He crossed the first river with the body but left it between the two rivers and ran on rapidly toward the village. He called loudly as he approached the village and the people heard him from a great distance and they knew what had happened. They called out to one another and said, "Now one of those brothers is killed. We had better run out and see what is the matter." So some of the swiftest runners started out to see what had happened. Fisher (Slil)[84] was the first to arrive. He came back and made a big fire and sweated. He then bathed and returned to the house and they all discussed what they ought to do. Fisher said, "Now you all make arrows and get ready to go over there tomorrow." All agreed to this and set to work to make arrows.

Now, Bat (Hō cmatala) was the best arrow-maker. They gave him a big piece of obsidian. He put this in his mouth and chewed it up and swallowed it; and then he vomited a great quantity of arrow-heads. The rest of the people prepared shafts, foreshafts and feathers for the arrows. It was very warm in the sweat-house where they were at work and the arrows dried quickly. Blue Jay and Red-headed-woodpecker were poison-men. They made a poison for these arrows, which was so strong that when they put a little of it on a tree to try it, the tree dried and shriveled up immediately.

Everything having been prepared, the party left early the next morn-ing. They came to the first river and caused it to dry up as had been done before in order that they might pass. By and by, they came to the dead body of Hawk. Hummingbird (Tele) who was a medicine-man, decided to try to bring Hawk to life again. He entered Hawk's mouth and passed entirely through his alimentary canal, thus removing the poison which had killed him and purifying his body completely. Hawk immediately returned to life. They told Hawk to stay where he was until they returned.

---

[84]There is some doubt as to whether this animal was Fisher or Mink.

They then went on and finally arrived at the little knoll, a short distance from Gï'lak's house.

Kūsū't called out to Gï'lak, "Some people are coming. Fix up good now. A lot of people are coming."

When they came near the house, Blue Jay and Red-headed-woodpecker placed some of the poison on the end of a long pole and poked this pole in at the door. Immediately the poison was inside the house, the string of Gï'lak's bow broke and then everything in the house broke. Then the two Gï'lak brothers invited these people to come in. They could not help themselves. They had nothing now with which to defend themselves.

They invited the people to sit at one side of the fire and then served them with food. This food was human blood and flesh. One of the people had with him an elderberry stick with the pith out, he poured all this great quantity of food into this elderberry stick, and it looked as if the people had eaten it. Some of the people proposed that they play a grass game.[85] The people had two crane sacks (mako-yet) full of beads with which to bet. The Gï'laks matched this and they proceeded to play. Fisher and his brother started the game. The younger brother wanted to play first but the elder Fisher objected, saying, "No, you cannot dodge quickly enough. They would kill you." So they finally arranged that the elder should play first. The elder Fisher, therefore, commenced to play. He dodged, jumped up, lay down, and in every way possible endeavored to escape Gï'lak's arrow. Bottle-fly (Pcē'-tsamō, deer-fly) who was one of the inmates of Gilak's house, though an unwilling one, whispered to Fisher and said, "You must always dodge down, never dodge up; if you do, he will shoot you right in the heart." Gilak finally shot but missed Fisher, for Fisher dodged down so that he lay flat on the ground. Gï'lak then began to jump around and dodge so that Fisher might shoot at him. Bottle-fly told Fisher, "You must shoot him right in the top of the head."

Fisher finally shot and hit Gï'lak squarely in the top of the head, so that he fell down dead. Everyone there yelled and rejoiced because one

---

[85]The playing of a grass game with the Gï'laks or with some other powerful mythical character is frequently mentioned in Pomo myths but the ordinary grass or hand game, a form of guessing contest played by four people, is not meant. . . . The game played in such instances is always spoken of by the Indians as the grass game and is given the same Indian name as the regular grass or hand game but the contest really is one of life and death, in which the contestants shoot at one another, usually with arrows, with the result, of course, that one or other of the contesting players is killed.

of the Gī'laks was dead. There was now but one of the Gī'laks left, so the same bet was made and Fisher played first again. Gī'lak shot and missed him, then Gī'lak played and was, like his brother, killed by Fisher.

The people then took the Gī'laks and mashed their bodies completely. They took Quail and Bottle-fly out and then set fire to the sweat-house, burning everything in it. They started back toward their village and found Hawk where they had left him.

He said, "I cannot stay with you people any longer, because I have been dead and I smell too badly. I must die again." They returned to their village and brought his wife to him but he said, "She must not come near me because I smell too badly." Then he flew away and all the people flew away from that place because he did.

38—GAMBLING LUCK IS GIVEN BY GILAK[86]

Characters: 1. A gambler, 2. Blue Jay, 3. Deer, 4. Gī'lak.

A long time ago, there was a village in which the people used to play wi'tclī.[87] Blue Jay was the medze.[88] There were two men who played a great deal but one of them kept winning all the time. The loser played until he had lost almost everything he had and then he took his deer mask, consisting of a deer head and hide, and went away into the mountains. Finally, he came to an open place in the timber and dressed himself up in his deer mask, so that he looked exactly like a large buck. He stood here in this open place all day. Toward evening, he heard a noise and presently, a very large being, with large wings and covered with feathers and having sharp claws, but otherwise like a human being flew down beside him. This was Gī'lak and as he approached he sang: "gilak, gilak, gilak, gilak, gilak."

Gī'lak tried to talk to this deer but the deer would not speak. He then brought green grass and tried to induce the deer to eat but he would not. He then brought dry grass, pepperwood boughs and all kinds of green stuff but the deer would eat nothing. Gī'lak tried stones, and as a last resort, beads. He placed some beads on his hand and held these out to the deer, who then began to eat for this was the only kind of food that the deer would eat.

---

[86]The Pomo title of this myth is "cĕmī kabatclĕ'yaŭda tsaiya medze itcaŭ i dūmal mentseba tī'tŏ ptĕmak tsība kamaletcba *ta*'ba ĭdetc."
[87]A game in which the number of small sticks held in one hand is guessed at.
[88]Stake holder in a game.

Gī'lak then grasped this deer by the back with his talons and flew off up into the sky with him. He took the deer to his house for a pet. He had a great quantity of beads for the deer to eat and plenty of water, so he placed the deer in a sort of yard near his house. He fed the deer all the beads he would eat for four months, until finally, his supply of beads became entirely exhausted. The deer had eaten up all his beads. He then tried to get some more, but could not furnish enough to satisfy the deer. He commenced to wonder what he should do. He did not want to kill the deer, so he decided to return him to the place where he had found him. He did this and left the deer in the same opening in the woods where he had first seen him.

The man who changed himself into the deer this way, had relatives at home who mourned and nearly killed themselves because of their grief, when he disappeared, for they thought he had been killed. When Gī'lak returned the deer to the opening in the woods, he immediately stripped off the deer mask and again became a man. He put on the clothing which he had discarded for the deer mask and returned to his house. He arrived at the village in the evening, as Blue Jay was making his daily address to the people. Blue Jay said, "Here this man has at last come back and we will have to have a game in the morning. You must get wood and make a big fire. Have a good sweat and then swim." The men all did this in the morning and when they returned from their bath, they commenced to play. They played four nights and four days and this man who had been away won all the time from the man who had formerly beaten him at this same game.

On the morning of the fifth day, Blue Jay, in his daily address to the people, said, "We must all have a big time at gambling. Everybody must play even up."

Some of the people growled at him and said, "You are always talking and telling us how we should do. We can't be making beads every day and all the time."

This made Blue Jay angry and he said, "You people are always growling at me because I am the chief here and make the living for all of you. I am the only man who can talk loud enough and who understands everything. Now you people who are always growling at me shall all be transformed into birds. This is the last day you shall be human beings. You shall all follow me out of that hole (pointing to

the smoke-hole of the sweat-house) and shall be transformed into birds."
He then flew out of the smoke hole, crying, as he did so, "tsai, tsai, tsai,
tsai, tsai, tsai."

Then all the rest of the people followed him, saying, "I am going to
be (naming a species of bird and giving the call of that particular bird)."

39—THE ABODE OF THUNDER UNDER THE OCEAN[89]

*Characters: 1. Thunder, 2. Thunder's sister, 3. Thunder's brother-in-law, 4.
Thunder's son, 5. Thunder's wife.*

A brother and his sister lived in the same village. The brother had
one son. The sister had no children at all. Her husband had a dam and
caught all the fish they wanted. Her brother went out hunting and tried
to get food for his little boy. The little boy went to his aunt to beg for
fish but his aunt refused to give him any. This made the little boy and
his mother cry.

Finally, after they had been doing this way for four days the man
found out what was the matter, because he came home then and found
his wife crying. He asked her what was the matter and she told him.
She said, "I am crying about my baby. He tried to get fish to eat and
your sister will not give it to him. That made me feel badly and I have
been crying for four days now."

Next morning the man went to his sister's house. Her husband came
with a lot of fish and she cooked some in the ashes. Her brother stayed
there for a long time but they did not take the fish out. After he had
stayed nearly a half day, he became angry and asked, "When are you
going to take those fish out of the fire?" Then he stood up and stepped
on the fish where they were buried in the ashes.

After this, he went to his house and took down his dance paraphernalia and beads. He went out and dressed up in the dance costume,
taking with him his bow and arrows. He told his wife he was going
away because his sister would not give fish either to himself or his child,
so he went off toward the east.

He went on till he came to the ridge north of Brush Creek. He
stopped on this ridge at the site of the old village of Kodalau. He
rested here for a little while, then went down across Brush Creek, past

---

[89]The Pomo title of this myth is, "Cemī madekī yedjol ca pkelman hi koldjatc hī bōka kai
yoya i dumal ke matū de," "Old time sister her fishing go away ocean water go in been my
story."

Informant: Bill James, Garcia River. Central dialect, 1906.

the old village of Pda'haū. From here he went westward, passing
along the south side of a big lagoon just west of the town of Man-
chester to a small lagoon west of this, near the shore of the ocean. He
stood here for quite a while. His sister, his wife and his son came
crying to him and begged him to remain but he walked out into the
water.

He walked on and on, all the time getting shorter to those on shore,
until only the tops of the feathers of the plume-sticks which he wore in
his hair were visible and finally even these disappeared.

This place where he went out of sight is the point farthest north of
the Point Arena light-house, where you can see breakers and white
foam now at all times. Before he went out there, there never were any
breakers at this place and no white foam. It was always smooth before that. Whenever you hear thunder, it always starts from that place
and some people think that Thunder was the man who went down there.

This man has a big house at this point. It is made of a sort of glass-
like substance. You can see right through the side of this house and
see everything that is going on inside. There are many fish in here and
they jump and strike against the walls in their endeavor to get out.
The inside of the house is, however, perfectly dry, notwithstanding the
fact that it is submerged in the ocean.

The Garcia River flows directly to this house and he is the one who
sends the fish up the river. He has a big lever, as large as a redwood
tree, which, when he pulls it down only a very little, lets millions of
salmon out, so that they may run up the river. They always run directly
up Garcia River, because the river flows right to them.

Inside the house, Thunder has something which acts as a kind of
reflector and shows him what the whole world is doing. It shows him
all the people and he can see what is going on all over and what everyone is doing. Nobody knows just what he eats but he lives there all
alone.

Whenever he moves any part of his body, even when he rolls over it
makes a great noise. Under his left arm, he keeps a square piece of a
glass-like material and when he takes this out and moves it around, it
flashes and makes the lightning. If he were to hold this out for any
considerable time, everyone would go blind and the whole world would
burn up. On the plate which supports the rafters over the door, he

keeps four split-stick rattles. These, he just keeps here but nobody knows what he uses them for. No one dares to go out near this place where Thunder lives, not even a shaman may venture so much.

40—FLOWER-MAN KILLS THUNDER[90]

Characters: 1. Flower-man, 2. Bullsnake (wife of Flower-man), 3. Coyote (Grandfather of Flower-man), 4. Ducks (two) (wives of Flower-man), 5. Magic rock, 6. Magic sling, 7. Thunder (father of Ducks), 8. Turtle, 9. Magic swing.

Flower-man (Tcīdō'-tca) was travelling from the south toward the north. At every river he came to, he made a fish dam but was always unable to catch any fish. His wife, Bullsnake (Kakō'ī) was with him. They camped at Big River (Bul-pda) and he made a fish dam here also. He made a basketry fish-trap out of all kinds of snakes and set it in the dam. In the morning, he found it full of all kinds of big ocean fish, such as whales, sharks, etc. He said to his grandfather, Coyote, who lived there at Big River, "I wish you would go down there and look at my dam. I am getting hungry." Coyote went down, but when he saw what was there he became ill. Next day, Flower-man went down to the river to look after his dam.

While he was gone, Coyote and Bullsnake went out to get some wood. When Flower-man returned to the house, he commenced digging a big hole to cook his fish. As he did so, Coyote asked him to make the hole a little larger, so that he could put his fish in also. Flower-man did this and when he had finished, he put Coyote into the hole and and cooked him, because he had had marital relations with his wife. Having cooked Coyote, he whipped his wife and kicked her off the bluff into the ocean. When he returned to his house, he found that Coyote had again come to life. Flower-man then returned to the ocean to see what had become of Bullsnake, whom he had kicked off into the ocean. He found that the woman had crawled up on a rock out in the water and had given birth to a child.

He tried for four days to induce Bullsnake to return home but at last he gave it up. He spread his skin blankets and lay down and commenced to sing of women. Presently, various women came to him and finally his wife returned. He tried to induce her to let him hold the

---

[90]The Pomo title of this myth is "Cĕmī tcīdō tca yi ya makĕla jadjōl ma anyôhī hī kū'mayaŭ mŭn ke matu de," "In olden times Flower-man Thunder kills story."
Informant: Bob Pot, Garcia River, Northern dialect, 1906.

baby but she would not trust him with it and finally went back to the rock where she had been. Flower-man finally married two Ducks (Badabada).

Then he started off out into the ocean toward the west. One Duck grasped him by one elbow, the other by the other elbow and thus they were able to lead and assist him through the water to their home at the other side of the ocean.

When they finally landed on the other side of the ocean, they continued on by land toward the west till they reached a very high rock. This rock was so high that it reached up to the sky and there was but one opening in it through which any one might pass. This opening was like the jaws of a vise and these jaws opened and shut at intervals. The Ducks went through here easily but Flower-man was afraid to venture. Finally after a long time, he got up courage and jumped through at one of the times when the jaws were apart. He then took his sling and shot a stone at this rock, causing the great death-trap to collapse.

They then went on until they arrived at the home of his wives. Thunder was their father and he had nothing but snakes of all kinds all around him. He had rattlesnakes, bullsnakes, watersnakes, milksnakes, snakes of all kinds all over the inside of the house.

While they were sitting in the house, Thunder came and told his son-in-law, "I want you to go out and catch some fish. I am hungry for fish." Flower-man went out to the river and, after a time, saw some salmon, of which he killed all he wanted. Then he went home and told his father-in-law, "I have caught the fish. Now you go down and get them." So Thunder went down to get the fish but when he had brought them back to the house, he said these were not the sort of fish he ate, because these fish were too small, but put them into the fire and cooked them. When they were cooked, he took them out and commenced to eat them, taking two salmon at a bite.

He told his son-in-law, "These are not the right sort of fish for me. They are too small. Now you will have to go and get some wood. It is going to be cold. We are out of wood and you must get some. We can not sleep without wood." There was a big redwood tree standing near the house. Flower-man took his sling and, standing on the east side of the tree, threw a stone at it. When he hit the tree, it fell on to the house and crushed it into pieces, but it did not hurt any one. As Thunder crawled out of the demolished house, you could hear a great noise like thunder. He lifted the house right up into the air in order to endeavor to frighten Flower-man but Flower-man was not at all alarmed.

Thunder soon made the house anew and they all went in and went to sleep. In the morning, Thunder told Flower-man to go out and get some wood, from which to make arrow shafts. The grove of timber in which this kind of wood grew, was filled with rattlesnakes. Flower-man was just about to enter the grove when Turtle came along and said to him, "Hold on there. I will go and get that wood for you." He did this and Flower-man took the wood home.

Thunder then sent his son-in-law to get pitch for arrow-making. There was one tree where this pitch might be had and on each side of this tree, there stood two grizzly bears. Flower-man was making his way toward the tree when a small bird, Kalē'-tata, came to him and said, "See here. That is a dangerous place. You must not go there. Give me your sack and I will get the pitch for you." When he had procured the pitch, in this manner, Flower-man, again went home.

That night, they all went to bed again and the next morning, Thunder and Flower-man went out to have a game. Thunder made Flower-man fly up and then he tried to shoot him but Flower-man knew how to dodge, so that Thunder was unable to injure him. Then Thunder flew up and Flower-man shot and killed him. Flower-man returned to the house and that night went to bed as usual.

Thunder, however, came to life and returned to the house early next morning and said to his son-in-law, "Well, we will have to go out and have a swing. I will show you what a good swing I have." They came to the swing and found that the ground all around and under the swing was full of spears. Thunder told his son-in-law to get in the swing. Of course Flower-man was afraid, but Thunder forced him to get in. As the swing started up, however, Flower-man said to the spears, "You are all my people. You are my friends. I want you all to dodge down when I fall." Thunder twisted the swing round and round. Finally, Flower-man told Thunder that he had had enough but still Thunder twisted and finally let the swing fly. Flower-man jumped far out over the spears and thus escaped death.

He then made Thunder get into the swing. Thunder was afraid to do so but could not help himself. Flower-man twisted and twisted the swing and Thunder said to him, "Now, my son-in-law, you will kill me. Do let me go." But Flower-man kept right on twisting and told the spears, "Now, when I get ready to let this fellow go, you will spear him." So, when Flower-man let go the swing, Thunder was thrown out onto the spears and killed. Flower-man said, "Well now, this is the way to kill people when they bother you." He then went home and took possession of everything that Thunder had and lived there all the time after that.

Thunder used to kill a great many people but when he finally died, the bones of all these people, which were strewn about the place, came to life again, and they returned to their former homes. Flower-man, however, lived at this place always.

41—THUNDER KILLS COYOTE AND CREATES ALL FORMS OF SEA LIFE[91]

Characters: 1. Coyote, 2. Thunder (son of Coyote), 3. Thunder's wife, 4. Seal, 5. Skunk, 6. Buzzard, 7. Mallard, 8. Magic flute.

Coyote and Thunder lived together at Ft. Bragg, right where the town now stands. Thunder was married. Coyote was his father. Thunder made a fish dam and tied it up with nothing but snakes. He made a net entirely of snakes also. When he had set these in the river, he came home and went to sleep. Next morning, he arose and went to the river where he saw whales (kate) in his net. He brought these home and made a big hole at the fireplace and cooked a whole whale at once. Next morning, he arose and went out again to look at his net.

Thunder's wife went out to get some wood in her basket. Coyote slipped out and watched to see where she got the wood. Coyote was all the time pretending that he was ill and so he slipped back to the house and lay down again before Thunder or his wife returned. After a while, Thunder returned and cooked his fish as he had done the day before. It took half a day to cook it. On the following morning, Thunder again went to the dam and his wife started out for wood. Coyote, however, slipped out and, by a circuitous route, reached the place where the woman obtained wood before she arrived. He dug a hole and got

[91]The Pomo title of this myth is "Cemí makela mael hone'm dü'mman matü," "In olden times Thunder cooked Coyote story."
Informant: Bill James, Garcia River, Central dialect, 1906.

down in it and covered himself up, leaving only a very small hole where the woman would set the basket down. When she came up, she set the basket down at this place and filled it with wood. Then she tried to pick it up but could not. She threw out about half of the wood and again tried to pick it up. Then she threw out still more but found that she was unable even yet to raise it from the ground. Then she turned the basket over and found Coyote there. Coyote then jumped up and played with the woman.

When Thunder returned from his dam, he found his wife weeping and he knew immediately what was the trouble. He sent Coyote out to look at the fish dam but Coyote became frightened at so many snakes and fell down very ill. Thunder then came out and picked him up and took him to the house. He then told Coyote that he must dig a big hole to cook fish on the following day, which was the fourth day after they had commenced to get fish from this dam. Coyote agreed and, on the following morning, dug a big hole. Then Thunder put Coyote in the hole and cooked him.

Thunder then asked his wife why she cried so much but she did not answer. He repeated his question again and again but received no reply. Finally, he became so angry that he kicked her out of the house and then kicked the house down. Then he continued to kick her until she rolled off into the ocean at the bluff. She begged him to spare her but he paid no attention to her pleading. She climbed up on a rock way out at sea. She gave birth to a child that same day.

When Thunder saw this, he called out to her, "You better bring that child back here," but she refused. He then removed his clothing and swam out after her, but as he reached the rock, the woman slipped off on the other side and dove. Thunder then swam back to the shore and went to his house and got all the beads, necklaces and other valuable articles he had, and tried with these to induce her to return to him but she persistently refused.

Thunder then flew into a rage and threw sticks and stones into the water, calling out as he threw each what it should be. Thus he made abalones, mussels, fish, etc. At the same time he said to the woman, "You will be a seal. When you see a person approaching, you will crawl off of your rock and dive into the water."

Thunder then went home and made a flute. He played this flute four times and another woman, Skunk, came and wanted to marry him. Thunder had provided a basket of fish as food for the women who might come. Presently, other women also came but all were bashful and did not venture to eat until finally Buzzard said, "I will commence to eat," and did so. Thunder finally chose as his wife, Mallard duck. They say that the Mallards were the best looking of all the Bird-people.

42—TCO'DOK KILLS GU'KSU[92]

INCIDENTS AND CHARACTERS

I. Tco'dok kills Gū'ksū.
>   1. Eagle sisters (two), 2. Gū'ksū (husband of the Eagle Sisters), 3. Eagle (father of the Eagle sisters), 4. Tco'dok, 5. Diver, 6. Kalē'kol, 7. Sleep charm.

II. Gū'ksū is brought back to life.
>   1. Gū'ksū's sons, 2. Gū'ksū, 3. Tco'dok, 4. Loon, 5. Crane, 6. Mink, 7. Otter, 8. Beaver, 9. Diver, 10. Coyote, 11. Eagle, 12. Hawk, 13. Buzzard.

I

(Tco'dok Kills Gū'ksū)

At Maiyī' there lived two sisters (cai, bald eagle). The Eagle sisters always kept off by themselves and refused to marry anyone or have anything to do with other people. No one knew it, but they were the wives of Gū'ksū. Eventually each of the Eagle sisters had a son and this so provoked the old Eagle himself, who was Chief of the village, that he decided to contest with Gū'ksū by challenging him to a fire-fanning contest.[93] In this contest Gū'ksū proved his superior power and killed Eagle. Then Gū'ksū went home across the southern ocean where he regularly lived.

There was one man, however (Tco'dok), who followed Gū'ksū. He followed the trail of Gū'ksū down through Napa Valley and so on southward until he came to the northern shore of San Francisco Bay. Here he saw his uncle, Diver (Tcūɾkil), and asked him how a person

---

[92]The Pomo name of this myth is "Tco'dūk kalaiūbuk marū." The term "tco'dok" is said to be somewhat of a general one, the specific name of the particular person in this myth is "Būra'kal būkaiūkke."

Informant: Dave Thompson, Eastern dialect.

[93]Such a fire-fanning contest is often mentioned in myths as a means of settling disputes or of determining who is the better and more powerful medicine-man. Fire-fanning was quite common among the Pomo Indians in aboriginal times. A special fire-fan was used and the contestants alternately fanned each other, driving as much of the heat and smoke from the fire in the center of the sweat-house across to the opponent as possible. The one who gave up from the heat first, was considered the vanquished.

could cross that big body of water. Diver gave him a tule boat and he crossed easily and landed on the southern shore of the bay. Now Tco'dok was carrying with him a very powerful medicine and as he passed through Napa Valley he met Kalē'kol (a species of worm). To him he said, "My friend you must go over onto the sunny side."

Worm replied, "You have nothing. Let me see what you have?" So Tco'dok showed him the medicine that he carried. Worm looked at it and it made him crazy and finally killed him.

So Tco'dok continued his journey on toward the southern end of the world and finally came to the ocean which is just this side of this southern end of the world but which is only knee-deep. He had no trouble in wading across the ocean here and finally he came to the sweat-house in which Gū'ksū lived.

Gū'ksū welcomed Tco'dok and invited him to have a seat on the west side of the house. That evening they built a big fire and were going to have another fire-fanning contest. Now Tco'dok carried a sleep-producing poison (sīma'koo). Tco'dok used this medicine and very soon after the contest began, Gū'ksū was sound asleep so that Tco'dok was able to kill him with the fire.

On the following morning Tco'dok returned home and when the people of the village learned what he had done they wanted to pay him well for it. They wanted to give him all of the beads in the village. However, Tco'dok would not have this. He said that he was the greatest Chief in the village and that, as such, he had killed Gū'ksū because it was his duty to do so.

II

(Gū'ksū Is Brought Back to Life)

When the boys found out what had happened and learned that their father had been killed, they started out to find his body. They crossed the southern ocean and finally found their father whom they attempted to doctor in the usual way. Finally they threw his body into the deep water. Then they doctored him after he had sunk in this deep water and finally he came to life again.

Then they told their father never to come back to the village again because if he did and anything happened to him they could not come out to doctor him any more. If they did this bears would bite them or snakes would bite them or somebody would kill them. Then the boys went back to the village.

Upon their arrival they found everyone in the village dancing and rejoicing over the fact that Tco'dok had killed Gū'ksū. This celebration lasted four days, at the end of which there was a big feast to which all contributed. Loon, Crane, Mink, Otter, Beaver and Diver each contributed fish. Coyote contributed deer, Eagle contributed rabbits, Hawk contributed squirrels, and so on, each one according to the food which he liked best. Even Buzzard contributed some putrid meat, which is what he liked best, but the people would not eat it.

The people lived there at this place always after that.

43—BAKI'L[94] IS CREATED AND PLACED IN BLUE LAKES[95]

Characters: 1. A young woman, 2. Her brother, 3. Tsaa't, 4.Baki'l, 5. Unfinished burden basket, 6. Madumda.

In olden times there was a village just below Blue Lakes.[96] Here there lived a young woman who occupied a house by herself. Her brother lived in an adjoining house. Finally she began to make a burden basket of the type called "ptcī." She needed many feathers to ornament this basket so her brother went out and caught quail and red-headed wood-

---

[94]This serpent-like, supernatural being lives in lakes and other bodies of water and is said to be extremely dangerous. If one sees the head of this animal he is absolutely sure to die. The informant in this case maintains that she saw the head of one of these at a point on Russian River one time and, as she looked at it, it produced thunder and lightning. The tail was somewhat like that of a salmon but much more forked. These supernatural beings are found in many different places, including springs, deep holes in rivers and particularly in lakes. The main Baki'l lives in Blue Lakes. This is an extremely large one, so large that it is said that he could not get into the Blue Lakes as they originally were.

The body is said to be striped and the head looks as though it had on it a red-feathered basket (ta'sitōl). It is also said that before this animal was changed to his present form he was a tsaa't (a supernatural baby).

[95]Informant: Jocie Kylark, Central dialect.

[96]Blue Lakes, as pointed out in speaking of *The Ethnogeography of the Pomo Indians* (Univ. Calif. Publ., Am. Arch. Ethn., VI, pp. 130, 131) are three small, but very deep, lakes, situated in a narrow, steep-walled canyon extending northwestward from the main canyon of Scott's Creek, and draining into that stream. The lowest of the three lakes is called by the whites "Wambold's Lake," and the upper two, which are connected by a comparatively broad channel, have received the name "Twin Lakes." The Indians, however, name each separately, as follows:

Wambold's Lake is called "xa'silī'ō" or "xala'-xatū" (clam lake); the lower of the Twin Lakes is called "dilē'-xa" (middle water), and the upper has received the name "xa'-cinǎl," (water head), which is a term applied with equal propriety to the head of any lake, as Upper Lake, which is regarded as the head of Clear Lake.

Mention is here made of the rise of the waters due to Baki'l's song to such an extent that they were about to pour over the pass onto Cold Creek, had he not been stopped by Madū'mda. It is an interesting fact to note that according to the findings of Professor R. S. Holway (Science, n.s., XXVI, 382, 1907) the water from these lakes did actually formerly drain into Russian River by way of Cold Creek but that they were, in comparatively recent prehistoric times, diverted to the Clear Lake drainage by a landslide which formed the ridge here mentioned as the pass or notch and which now stands about one hundred sixty feet above the level of the lakes themselves.

peckers for this purpose. He also made many beads, which he gave her to place upon the basket to make it beautiful. After this had gone on for a long time he grew weary of providing these things for her and one day he said, "How long is it going to take to make this basket? How big are you going to make it? I am getting tired of getting feathers and making beads for you all of the time."[97] This made the sister feel very badly indeed, but he went right on getting red feathers and quail plumes and making beads for her just the same.

By and by he thought he heard the cry of a baby but he did not know where it was. He did not know that his sister had this baby boy in the house. This baby cried all the time. It would not eat and it cried all night. She sat up with it and tried in every way to quiet it and to make it feel right, but it was impossible. Finally the young man found where this baby was and came over to his sister's house with a bow and arrow, saying that he did not believe that this was a real human baby and that he thought he had better kill it.

The baby immediately spoke up, saying, "You are right, my uncle, I am not a human baby. I am Tsaa't. You must not kill me. You must take me up to the spring. There you must put on my head a 'sun basket' (ta'sitōl). You must put a feather belt[98] running from my head clear down to the tip of my tail. You must put around my middle a bead belt and about my neck you must hang ornaments made of big, thick, white beads (na'mūlī). You and my mother must take me up to where that spring is and place me in it. Then, next morning, you must come up and see how I am lying there."

Then the boy gave his uncle a song[99] and admonished him, "When

---

[97]As a matter of fact it was not customary for any kind of feathers or beads to be used in ornamenting a burden basket.

[98]This belt is called "hwil stīt," literally "abalone shell blanket." It is not actually a blanket, nor is it a belt, but it is apparently a network, decorated with abalone shells, which covers the entire body of this supernatural being.

[99]When the boy was thrown into the spring by his uncle, he was singing a special song called "kainē'au ke."
    The boy gave his uncle also, five songs which were to protect them from the danger of seeing the Baki'l and also to enable them to cure anyone who was made sick through this cause. These five songs were:
    1. kaiyōmitītci, a song relating to Baki'l's lying down in the water.
    2. badadon ma'tcī, the song for creating the creek.
    3. bida batai matcī, the song for enlarging the lake (the underlying idea of this song is that he will break or push the mountains aside and spread the place for the water out wider),
    4. Tōto'teē matcī, the song used for creating the living quarters and bed down in the water where Baki'l is to reside,
    5. A song, the name for which was not given, but which tells just what he is to have placed on him as he is thrown into the spring. This, of course, includes all of the items, such as the red-feathered basket and all of the other special ceremonial items which he ordered to be placed upon him before he was put into the spring.

you come up there to see me you must not be frightened. All you need to do is to sing this song and you will be cured. This is the song which will cure anyone who is badly frightened."

They did as they had been directed by the baby and on the following morning they went out to see him. There was no spring there now at all but there was in its place a large body of water, Blue Lakes, which the baby had made in order that it should be big enough for him to live in. The baby was changed. He was no baby at all. He had changed and become Baki'l.

His uncle threw four arrows at him so that he would be good. They then threw into the lake the unfinished burden basket (ptci). This was in accordance with the instructions which they had received from the boy before they placed him in the spring. Further, he had told them that when they went away they must never look back, else it would make them very sick. When they returned home they did not look back and therefore were able to get away safely.

Now, of course, at this time, Baki'l was lying in the water in plain sight and could be seen by anyone who might pass that way. Creator[100] (Madū'mda) came here and saw Baki'l. He said, "It will not do for you to lie here in this way because everyone who comes and sees you will immediately die." He then showed Baki'l how to sing a song which would make the lakes bigger so that he could hide himself down in their depths where people would not see him all the time. Baki'l sang the song and the waters very greatly increased in size and depth. Then he came back and told Madū'mda that he had found a very fine place in which to live, where there were many fish and much food upon which he could subsist. But Baki'l went right on singing these songs and the water rose higher and higher until it nearly overflowed the pass or notch at the north end of Blue Lakes which leads over into Cold Creek.

Madū'mda came back again and stopped Baki'l and told him that he must make the lake deeper and not cause the water to run over here in this way. Baki'l therefore, made the upper of the three lakes very much deeper and made himself a good dwelling place down in its depths among the roots.

---

[100] It is very unusual to find the Creator changing anything on the earth. It is very probable that the informant here really means Coyote, who is sometimes referred to as Coyote Creator.

He then gave instructions that people must never go about in these lakes and must never eat fish from them. Particularly must they be careful to keep away from the upper of these lakes and if it was necessary for a person to pass that way at any time he must not look at this lake but keep his head turned always away from it.[101]

It was particularly necessary for women to be careful in passing this lake. The only thing that was permitted to be taken from these lakes was clams which could be taken from the shores of the lower of the three lakes (Wambolds Lake).

44—THE MONSTER OF BLUE LAKES[102]

Characters: 1. Crow brothers (two), 2. Bagil.

Crow placed his brother in North Lake and then told him to lengthen out his entire body. This he did until he had become so large that his beak rested on the northern shore of North Lake, his body stretched down through the narrows, and his tail rested on the southern shore of Middle Lake. Thus he stretched from end to end of the Twin Lakes. Crow then placed a large red-feathered basket on the monsters head, a great yellowhammer-feather band on his forehead, and a pair of large

---

[101]It is considered extremely dangerous for a woman, particularly during menstruation (ka'l tciu) to venture near Blue Lakes. While the Baki'l, who resides in the upper of these lakes might, under normal circumstances not come up toward the surface and into view, if a woman in this condition passes he is sure to come up and this, of course, results in her becoming very ill. It also causes the illness of anyone who may see this monster. One informant, a woman of the Central dialect, claims that upon one occasion she passed the upper of the three Blue Lakes while in that condition and that the Baki'l actually came up and took her down under the water where he gave her special instructions, that she must never again at such a time venture near any of the springs or other bodies of water and that she must be very careful not to expose herself to these dangers. After a long illness following this experience she finally recovered through proper doctoring.

It appears that a woman in this condition may also see other dangerous things about Blue Lake. There is also here a very large fish with green algæ growing all over its body. In fact, it is said, that the fish in general in these lakes have this kind of moss, called "ka'kasû", growing on their bodies. This particularly dangerous big fish is said to have these green "whiskers" growing all over its body and if it is seen by a woman in this condition, it is very dangerous for her.

Another dangerous thing which she may see here is the partly finished burden basket which was thrown into these lakes at the time that Baki'l was placed here. And still another very dangerous thing is what is called "water cat" (kaia' mot).

Approximately the same restrictions are placed upon hunters as upon menstruating women. They must not go near any of these bodies of water where these dangerous things are to be found. It will ruin their hunting luck as well as make them seriously ill.

Gamblers also must be very careful, but some there are who know the proper songs to be sung in connection with such places; they can go to them, even in fact, to Blue Lakes, which is probably the most dangerous of them all, and can actually swim across the upper of these lakes. If he sings his songs properly and bathes in this water and swims across, this will give him extremely good luck.

If a gambler wants to assure himself that he will win every hand he plays he can go to the middle of the three Blue Lakes, scarify his arms and wash off the blood in the water. This is sure to bring good luck, provided the one who undertakes this knows the songs and uses them properly. If he makes even the slightest mistake, however, he is bound to die.

[102]Informant: Tom Mitchell, Eastern dialect, 1902.

deer horns on the sides of his head. He also gave him some eyes of abalone shell which would shine brightly with the glint of the sun. Thus he made of his brother a Bagil, or monster, and told him to remain there in the water so that he could scare everyone who came along that way.

Then he himself went off a little way in order to get a better look at the Bagil, and became so frightened that he was made ill almost immediately. Then he changed his mind and told the Bagil not to stay out there all the time but to hide himself and to only appear to a woman who came that way during her menstrual period or to a man should he come there while his wife was in that condition.

Accordingly the Bagil went out on the eastern shore of Middle Lake and crawled into the mountainside there, and after he had disappeared a great spring gushed forth. That spring is still flowing, but some day the Bagil will tire of staying there inside of that mountain and will come out. Then the spring will dry up just as the one did down on Dry Creek in the Ukiah Valley after the Bagil which inhabited it came out and went away a long time ago.

As long as this Bagil remains here at Blue Lakes it is very dangerous to go near them for it is said that at times even now he comes out into the water where he may be seen by people. While it is especially dangerous for a menstruating woman or her husband to see this monster it is not at all safe for an ordinary person to look at him. That is why no one ever goes past the Blue Lakes if he can avoid it, and when he does have to pass there he always looks away from the lake.

45—A BAGIL IS CAUGHT IN A RABBIT SNARE[103]

Characters: 1. Two brothers, 2. Bagil.

There used to be a large village called "Pdahau" at the north end of the wagon bridge across Garcia River at Bridgeville, just north of Point Arena. Two brothers lived here, of whom the elder snared cottontails (makiu). He used to set snares in twenty to forty places at once and catch a great many cottontails. Once, during his wife's menstrual period, he snared rabbits this way but instead of catching the rabbits, he caught a Bakil, a lizard-like animal which is six or eight feet long,

---

[103]The Pomo title of this myth is "cemī tamnamda bakil tcaū dūmman mūn ke matū de," "In olden times Bagil snared story."
Informant: Captain Charley, Garcia River, Central dialect, 1906.

has a tail like a salmon and is striped like a watersnake. The Bakil pulled down the poles to which the snare was attached and turned his head toward the hole in which he lived.

When the man saw the Bakil, he became frightened and ran home and told his brother about it. He said, "You better come and see what kind of an animal I have caught." So he took his brother to where he had caught the Bakil and showed it to him.

The younger brother said, "This is something very bad which you have caught."

He had caught the Bagil down on the shore of a slough on the north side of the river, so his brother told him that he was going to take him off to a good place and doctor him. He then walked eight times around the Bakil, leading his brother by one hand and singing constantly

kidī	kidī	kīnō	pūyemlī	pūyemlī
brother	brother	anything never before seen and which will give good luck	looking around	looking around

Then he turned his brother around four times, then he walked around in the opposite direction eight times and again whirled his brother around eight times. Then the younger brother untied the Bakil. The elder brother became well again and everything went nicely.

46—COYOTE CREATES OBSIDIAN-MAN FROM AN ARROW POINT[104]

INCIDENTS AND CHARACTERS

I. *Coyote Creates Obsidian-man.*
> 1. *Coyote,* 2. *Frog (wife of Coyote),* 3. *Bullsnake,* 4. *Buzzard,* 5. *Obsidian-man.*

II. *Obsidian-man wins in the contests.*
> 1. *Obsidian-man,* 2. *Coyote,* 3. *Frog,* 4. *Eagle.*

III. *Obsidian-man places Coyote and Frog.*
> 1. *Obsidian-man,* 2. *Coyote,* 3. *Frog.*

I

(Coyote Creates Obsidian-man)

In olden times there was a large village at Hla'l napō, near Calistoga. Coyote and his wife, Frog (Mitsa'karai), lived here, not in the village

---

[104]Informant: Bill Coon, Eastern dialect.

itself, but in an underground house about a quarter of a mile distant from it. At this time there were no people in this village at all. Coyote and his wife lived alone. Coyote went fishing. He went to a creek called "Tcai′ bidame," about five or six miles from Kelseyville. Coyote started very early in the morning from Calistoga and presently he met Bullsnake (Kabaoyel). Coyote said, "Well, Bullsnake, you are a good man. You are a chief and an honest man. Tell me, how are the fish over there? Have the fish come up the creek yet?"

Bullsnake made no reply but simply lay where he was. Coyote then went on until he met Buzzard to whom he said, "Well, Buzzard, you are an honest man, tell me, how are the fish running down there in the valley?"

Buzzard answered, "cī ——————" (which was his way of saying that there were a great many fish running in the stream).

Coyote then procured enough white willow withes to make a burden basket in which he could carry home the fish that he expected to catch. He finally arrived just about dusk at the creek and made a fire. He sat down beside this fire and wove the basket which he then took down to the bank of the creek. Someone had made a fish dam here and had placed basketry traps in this dam. These Coyote found filled with fish. He emptied these into his burden basket and went back to the fire where he cooked and ate as many as he wanted.

Then Coyote started home and traveled all night, arriving just before daylight. He told his wife that the people where he had been had given him enough fish to fill his basket and that they had invited him to come again. He did not want to tell his wife that he had stolen these fish.

Early the next morning Coyote started back again but this time he met no one on his journey. About dusk he arrived at the same place where he had built his fire the evening before and here he again made another basket and finally went down to the creek to fill it with fish.

Meanwhile, however, the people who owned this fish dam had found that someone had stolen their catch and ten or twelve of them, armed with bows and arrows, were watching the dam this time. Just as he raised the first basketry trap to pour the fish into his burden basket one of the watchers shot him with an arrow which entered Coyote's body just above the short ribs. This arrow passed very near Coyote's heart and the point almost came out on the opposite side of his body. Coyote immediately pulled out the arrow shaft but the arrow-head itself still remained in his body. Of course, he ran away as rapidly as possible but became very ill. He then stopped and tied up the wound with his belt. He finally arrived at home about daylight the following morning.

Coyote told his wife, "I am very sick. I did not carry the fish home this time, I was so sick. I have no idea how I became ill, but I am very ill indeed."

He lay in the house all day long and all the following night. For three days and nights he lay here, growing more and more ill and with his body swelling bigger and bigger. Finally on the fourth day this swelling began to head up and Coyote placed a hot rock here in order to stop the pain. After a time this point opened up and Coyote pulled the arrow-head out of his body.

Coyote then rose and procured a very beautifully feathered basket (ta' sītōl). He then took a common basket (stū'p tci) into which he poured some water and he very carefully washed his arrow-head, which was made of obsidian. When he had thoroughly cleaned the arrow-head, he threw out the water and placed the arrow-head in the same basket. Then he set this basket away, placing the beautifully feathered basket immediately beside it. He left these here for four days and just as daylight came on the fourth day he said, "I want you to become a very nice boy." All this time Coyote had continued to be very ill. After he made this wish he went back to bed just as ill as before but that evening he got up and found that he was entirely well. He sat beside the fire in the dance-house all night long and he constantly watched the basket in which he had placed the arrow-head for fear that his wife might touch it. Thus he sat and watched four days and nights, but on the fourth night, just before dawn, he slept for a very short time.

When Coyote finally awoke at daybreak he found, sitting beside the fire, a young man. He immediately jumped up and took the young man on his knee. After pouring out the water in the basket and refilling it with fresh water, he very carefully washed the young man, after which he gave him a rabbit-skin blanket. All this was done just at dawn and before the sun actually came up. This young man was Obsidian-man (katca'tca), who had been created from the arrow-head which had been shot into Coyote's body. Thus, as the sun came up, the young man went out and sat on the top of the dance-house.

II

(Obsidian-man Wins in the Contests)

When the people of the village saw him they wondered where he had come from because they knew that Coyote had no young people in his house. Some of them went over to see him and get acquainted. They talked to him for a time and finally some one suggested that they should all go and eat clover. The young man then went in to tell his father and mother about this invitation but Coyote said, "No, do not go. You might be killed."

Coyote's wife began to cry because she thought that the people intended to kill the young man.

However, Coyote gave Obsidian-man a bow and some arrows and all went out into an open glade where there was much clover to eat. They sat down and all were eating clover when they noticed that the space around where Obsidian-man sat was evenly mowed off just as if it had been cut with a knife. They then knew what kind of a person Obsidian-man was, so they decided that they would kill him.

One of the men slipped up and shot Obsidian-man squarely in the back but the arrow did not enter his body or hurt him in the least. They then saw that he was really a supernatural being and decided to do nothing more at the time.

They all started home and finally someone said, "Let us go and get some wood for the sweat-house."

When Obsidian-man gathered his wood he was able to gather a very large bundle of it, almost instantly. This further proved to the people that he was a very powerful medicine-man.

When they arrived at the village they said to Obsidian-man, "Now you better come over and have a sweat with us." To this Obsidian-man agreed and he went home to prepare for the sweating. He took off his rabbit-skin blanket and got all ready. He did not, of course, know anything about the sweat-lodge or what to do, but Coyote gave him instructions and provided him with everything that was necessary for the sweating. While they were waiting for Obsidian-man, the others agreed upon the way Obsidian-man should be dealt with when he came to sweat. As he entered the sweat-house, Eagle, who was the head chief of the village, caught him and the others tied him to the center pole of the sweat-house with grape-vine. Then they tied his hands by means of vines passing across to the sides of the house. Then they piled on all the wood they had and made a very big fire. Finally, as the fire roared on, Obsidian-man's head drooped and everyone thought him dead, and they left him there because they did not know what to do with his body. No sooner had they gone out of the sweat-house, however, than Obsidian-man cut himself loose and stepped out of the sweat-house. The people were very greatly surprised and all cried, "Look! Look! What kind of a person is this whom it is so hard to kill?"

Then Obsidian-man went down to swim and finally returned to Coyote's house.

The following morning after breakfast Obsidian-man went as usual onto the top of the house and sat there. Again a number of the people came and invited him to go with them. Now, Obsidian-man had not told Coyote about the attempt of the people to kill him but Coyote knew all about it just the same. When he was invited to join the other young men upon this occasion he cheerfully went and when they were many miles from the village they played at various games and finally some-one said, "Let us play at war. Let us have a war with this Obsidian-man. We will all fight against him." To this he agreed. He was an extremely good bow shot and never missed. Soon he had killed six of the young men and this made the others very angry so that they pursued him as he ran toward home until finally he said, "Well boys, we had better quit this game or I shall kill all of you."

When they arrived home they told all the people how Obsidian-man had killed six of the boys that day. Then they went out and collected these bodies and burned them that same evening as was the custom in the old days.

Then the chief set a watch on Coyote's house to make sure that Obsidian-man would not go away during the night and they all planned to attack him during the following day. At sunrise on the following morning the people began to growl at Obsidian-man and Coyote. Eagle, the Chief, started by saying to Coyote, "We are going to pull you out of your house because we are going to kill you today and we do not want to kill you inside the house."

Coyote said, "That is all right." Obsidian-man asked if everyone was ready outside.

Eagle answered, "Yes, you cannot go out of the house because if you go we will surely kill you."

Coyote then made a large head-dress (kūtcū'n) of buzzard feathers for Obsidian-man to wear in his battle and Coyote wanted to go out and help him but Obsidian-man said, "No, my father, you will be killed if you go out there." Then Obsidian-man put his head out of the door and everyone shot at him but it did no harm at all because the arrows passed through the head-dress and did not touch him. When he finally got outside he knelt down and commenced to shoot. He shot so rapidly and so accurately that almost immediately he killed about one-half of the men who were attacking him. The others ran away and he followed them, shooting as he ran and presently he had killed them all. Then he went over to the village and killed all the women and children. He killed everyone.

III

(Obsidian-man Places Coyote and Frog)

Then Obsidian-man went back to Coyote's house, removed his head-dress and put it away and put away also his bow and arrows. Then he swam and washed himself thoroughly. After this he returned to the house and sat studying for a long time. Finally he said, "Father, I feel very sorry for those people. I feel sorry for what I did. It was not my fault, it was their fault, but I cannot stay here alone. I think I am going away this evening."

To this Coyote replied, "Well, my son, I have here a great deal for you, bows and arrows, beads, blankets and everything that a young man likes. So you must not feel that way. You must not go away."

But Obsidian-man insisted that he must go and finally Coyote said, "Well, all right. If you are going to go away, we are going with you."

To this Obsidian-man agreed. They started off and travelled to a place called "Katsi'l gago."[105] Here they found a spring and Obsidian-man said, "I think you might as well stay here and live at this fine spring."

Now Coyote's wife was Frog and this place suited her very nicely so that she was anxious to remain here. Coyote said, "Well, all right,

[105]This is said to be a place called "Cold Creek" about seven miles from Kelsey Creek on the Lower Lake road.

I think I will stay here with my wife while you travel on." Then Obsidian-man picked up his mother and placed her in the water.[106]

Then Obsidian-man said to Coyote, "My father, if you are going to stay here also, I want you to stay in this big mountain. I do not want you to stay in the water."

Then Obsidian-man went on to a place two miles west of Lower Lake, which is called Tsiya'gago.[107] He looked this place over and decided that the water was good here and that he would remain here all the time. He said, "I am going to stay right here and I am not going to kill people any more."

47—THE STORY OF ARROWPOINT YOUNG MAN[108]

Characters: 1. Coyote, 2. Arrowpoint-young-man.

Coyote lived at Yō'butūi.[109] A short distance south of this place is located the old fish camp, Kūca' danō yō, on Duck Creek. There was a very large fish dam at this place and Coyote was stealing fish out of the basketry traps that were set in this dam. After Coyote had been stealing fish in this way for a long time the people became very tired of constantly missing part of their catch so they determined to lay in wait for the thief, which they did. The next time Coyote visited this fish dam and attempted to remove the fish, they shot him. One of the arrows entered Coyote's body and the arrow-head remained there. Coyote ran home immediately and lay sick for quite a time. Finally he succeeded in extracting the arrow-head from his body and found that it had turned into a young man. He washed the young man carefully and wrapped him up.[110]

When he was a very small boy he went around with Coyote all the time and when he grew bigger he then started to go about with other people as well. When this young man went out to eat clover the place from which he gathered the clover looked as if it had been cut with a

[106]This spring is said to be an extremely dangerous place for people to visit. If anyone goes near it they are almost sure to die very quickly. Several people have been killed by going near this spring already.
[107]This is probably a small, wet-weather lake just north of the road and up on the side of the mountain near a place called "Cūta'nnomanok".
[108]The Pomo name of this myth is "Gūnū'la xagᶜa cēla xawī."
Informant: Tom Mitchell, Eastern dialect.
[109]This place is located at a point about three-quarters of a mile south of the present town of Upper Lake and about half a mile south of Kūca' danō yō.
[110]The name of this young man was Xagᶜa' cēla, signifying "arrowpoint-young-man".

sharp instrument. This was because this young man had sprung from an arrow-head.

Whenever this young man went out to play at the game of throwing sticks with the rest of the boys as he was growing up, he always won. When he went to cut these throwing sticks he could cut them off very easily and always got a large number whereas the rest of the boys had great difficulty in getting theirs. Whatever this young man did was always done in the finest possible way and with the greatest success.

Finally he grew to be a man. Then he went out to gather wood for the sweat-house. This he did very quickly, just the same as he did everything else with great speed. In fact, he was so successful with everything he did that the rest of the men became jealous and hated him for it. He did not know this because he was a stranger there, but the other men wanted to shoot him because he was so successful. In fact they did shoot at him with arrows but they glanced off. No one could penetrate his body.

He got his wood very quickly, brought it back quickly and always got home before anyone else arrived. All he had to do was simply to throw himself into the brush and cut it off with his body.

When he reached home the other men tied him to the center pole of the sweat-house with grape-vine. They tied these vines about his feet, his knees, his waist and his neck but they never could keep him tied because he could cut with any part of his body any grape-vine or other tie that they could use. They built a great fire when they thought they had him tied in this way, but when it began to get hot he simply cut the bonds and liberated himself.

They tried four times to kill him in this manner but were unsuccessful and gave it up.

By and by they told him to go out and get some more wood. He paid no attention to their endeavors to kill him and sometimes they paid no attention to him and did not harm him in any way.

They went out hunting and tried again to kill him by shooting him but he paid no attention to that. Once they caught him and tied him up to a tree out in the woods and thought to leave him there but as soon as they were gone he cut himself loose and returned home, arriving long before they did.

Finally he grew tired of their constant endeavors to do away with him and decided to have a fight with all of the men. [The informant was not certain of the details of this myth from this point on.]

48—OBSIDIAN-MAN KILLS THE FOUR THUNDER BROTHERS[111]

INCIDENTS AND CHARACTERS

I. *Coyote creates Obsidian-man.*
>   *1. Coyote, 2. Frog (wife of Coyote), 3. Obsidian-man, 4. Blue Jay.*

II. *Obsidian-man kills the Thunder brothers.*
>   *1. Obsidian-man, 2. Thunder brothers, 3. Coyote, 4. Grizzly Bear, 5. Mountain Lion, 6. Black Bear, 7. Another mountain lion, 8. Magic polishing stone, 9. Magic snare, 10. Ice garment, 11. Fog tube, 12. Thunder's daughter, 13. Snake dam, 14. Kawolwol, 15. Gray Squirrel, 16. Magic tree, 17. Lizard, 18. Green Lizard, 19. Fire, 20. Blue-fly.*

I

(Coyote Creates Obsidian-man)

Coyote and Frog, his wife, lived at Mt. Kanaktai. Some people had a fish dam near the mouth of Kelsey Creek, some miles distant, and Coyote went over there to steal fish but one of the fish-dam owners was on watch and shot Coyote as he was about to take the fish from the dam. The obsidian arrow-head stuck inside of Coyote's body and caused almost immediate death.

Coyote's body lay there for many days until the maggots had nearly devoured it all, but one day Blue Jay came along and doctored Coyote who immediately jumped up, alive again. As he saw Blue Jay, he said, "What did you wake me up for? I was having a good sleep here. What did you wake me up for, anyway?"

Then Coyote went home, took the obsidian arrow-head out of his body and placed it in that of his wife, saying, "That arrow-head will become a boy before morning and by the time I get up, the boy will be washing his face here before the fire." Coyote awoke at day-break the next morning and there he saw the boy sitting before the fire. He then said to his wife, "See here, we have a boy, as fine a looking boy as you ever saw." Then they both went to the child and bathed and cleansed him.

---

[111]The Pomo name of this myth is "Makela matu," Thunder story.
Informant: Charley Pinto, Yokaia, Central dialect.

II

(Obsidian-man Kills the Thunder Brothers)

Obsidian-man very quickly grew into a young man. The home of
the Thunder brothers, of whom Obsidian-man had heard much, was
over on the coast in the edge of the redwoods, on the north bank of
the Big River and just east of the present town of Mendocino. It is
said that there are even yet to be seen the old poles and pit of the
Thunder's sweat-house there. Obsidian-man had heard a great deal
about what fine players the Thunder brothers were and he very much
wanted to go and contest with them. So Coyote took Obsidian-man
and another boy and, after putting some things in his hunting sack
(among them a large, flat stone upon which beads are polished), started
off toward the west to visit the Thunders. As they started out on their
journey, Obsidian-man said to Coyote, "Father, you had better let me
go on ahead, because we might meet something bad on the way."

Everything went well until they reached Eight Mile Valley. Here
they came upon a big grizzly bear. Bear told Obsidian-man to get out
of his way and let him have the trail but Obsidian-man refused. So
Bear jumped about and bit a tree to show Obsidian-man how he would
serve him next, if he did not obey. The outer edges of Obsidian-man's
arms were sharp and serrated, thus giving him very great cutting power.
So powerful was Obsidian-man with these saw-like arms that he could
swing one of them through the air and cut off trees as though they had
been so many stems of tule. Obsidian-man, in his turn, jumped about
and slashed down a large tree with his arm, in order to show Bear what
would happen to him if he persisted in demanding full rights on the
trail. Bear, however, did not get out of the way, so Obsidian-man immediately cut him to pieces with his saw-like arms, as he had done the
trees.

They then went on toward the west, crossing the Ukiah Valley, at a
point three miles or so south of Ukiah, thence up Robertson Creek to a
point near the old village of Bodono. Here they met Mountain Lion,
who advised them not to go any farther, as it was a very dangerous
country over where the Thunders lived. They, however did not heed
him but continued their journey. In Anderson Valley, they met Black
Bear who advised them to go no farther, warning them that if they con-

tinued, they would never return. Again they paid no attention to the warning but proceeded on their journey. Finally, when they had come near the coast, they met another Mountain Lion who warned them to go no farther, saying, "The Thunders will surely kill you if you go on. They do that way with everyone who goes there." But Obsidian-man was determined to visit the Thunders.

Finally, they came to a point about half a mile south of Big River and here they saw the smoke rising from a house on the edge of the bay. Here they found a man who asked Obsidian-man where they were going, and upon being told, advised them very strongly to go no farther. "You see those white bones on top of the sweat-house there, those are all human bones. When the Thunders eat people, they throw the bones out there on top of the sweat-house." In fact, the sweat-house and the ground around looked like snow, there were so many bleached human bones strewn about. This warning, however, did not deter Obsidian-man and Coyote.

They went on up the river in the hope of finding a place where they might cross. Finally Coyote pulled a large polishing stone out of his hunting sack and hit the water in the river with it. This immediately dried the water up and they passed through the bed of the river and started up the hill toward the Thunders' house.

As they went on the bears became so numerous that the whole party was nearly devoured. Finally, however, Obsidian-man told his father and the other boy to stay down by the river, while he went up and disposed of the bears. This he did with his saw-like arms and when he had cut his way through and arrived near the Thunders' sweat-house, he called to them to follow.

When they had all arrived at the Thunders' sweat-house, Obsidian-man asked his father, "Well, what are you going to do now?" In reply, Coyote drew out the big polishing stone and slipped it into the door of the sweat-house. Immediately it sprang a great snare which caught the rock and jerked it clear to the rear of the sweat-house. Then they entered, Obsidian-man leading the way and calling out to Thunder, "Hello, good player."

Thunder replied, "The good player who comes here never goes back. I always keep him."

Then Thunder brought out bread and pinole and mush which were all made from human blood. These, Coyote ate alone, that is, he pretended to eat them, putting something into his mouth, so that the blood ran out and it was unnecessary to swallow it. He told Thunder that his boy Obsidian-man never ate, that playing was all that he ever did. To play a game was as good as a hearty meal for him.

Then Thunder told Obsidian-man, "Let us go down and get some wood to make a sweating fire." Obsidian-man spoke to his father about it and was told that it would be safe to go. Thunder went out of the sweat-house before Obsidian-man and, as the latter appeared in the door, shot at him but Obsidian-man caught the arrow on his saw-like arm and split it.

Thunder then told Obsidian-man, "You go down there," pointing to a timbered place, "where there is much good wood which is easy to obtain. I will go up this way." Obsidian-man followed Thunder's suggestion but when he had reached the designated spot, he found that the bears were so numerous that it was almost impossible for him to get through. He succeeded in killing a large number of the bears and then cut down a dry mazanita bush, and hurried back to the sweat-house, in order to get there before Thunder should return. This he succeeded in doing.

Thunder then told Obsidian-man to make a fire. This he did but the fire flew up, struck the sweat-house and fell back upon him. Coyote, however, had given Obsidian-man a garment made of ice and he had run a tube up from the ocean, so that the fog might come to his assistance if it became too hot.

Presently, when the fire was burning nicely, Thunder said to Obsidian-man, "Now, get ready, I am going to guess (as in playing the grass game)." He took a basketry seed-beater and scooped up a large quantity of red hot coals, which he placed upon Obsidian-man. They did not injure him in the least. He set the seed-beater near the center pole of the sweat-house. Obsidian-man then said, "Now, Thunder, you get ready. I am going to shoot this time." He got the seed-beater and poured on fire until Thunder cried out with pain, which was the sign to stop. Thunder then poured more coals upon Obsidian-man without injury to him. In turn, Obsidian-man poured coals upon Thunder with the same result as before. Thus they continued to pour coals alternately upon each other, until Thunder endeavored four times to burn Obsidian-man. Then Obsidian-man said to him, "I thought you were a good player, but you are no good at playing. Now, I am going to show you how I really can play." He heated up his saw-like arms until they were very hot, then heaped a quantity of red-hot coals upon Thunder, and held his heated arms very close, finally killing him. While he was thus engaged, he derided Thunder. "I thought you were the best player in the world, but I can see that you are no good at playing at all."

It was nearly night now and one of the three remaining Thunder brothers told Obsidian-man, "Now you are my son-in-law. When you are ready to go to bed, that is where my daughter's bed is located." Obsidian-man told his father what Thunder had said to him, and Coyote said, "That will be all right. I will fix that. I will go there first and when I tell you, you may come." Coyote went where the woman was and as soon as he had come near her, rattlesnakes tried to bite him but he had a kind of weed (cmaya) with which to kill them. He killed the rattlesnakes which were all over the girl's body. She had many snakes lying about, so that if anyone came near her, he would surely be killed. Then Coyote called to Obsidian-man to come into the house. As Obsidian-man started, Thunder called to him. "Hold on, I want to tell you something. When you get up in the morning, go down there and get some fish."

Next morning, Obsidian-man arose and went down to the fish dam. At the dam he found all kinds of snakes. In fact, the very dam itself was made out of snakes, they having been woven and twisted together, instead of boughs which we now use. He did not know what to do at first but after thinking the matter over, he began to hit the snakes with the polishing stone which his father had brought from home, and killed them all. He then took the fish out of the dam and also piled the snakes which he had killed, up near the dam. Then he returned to the house and told Thunder, "My hands were cold so that I did not bring the fish back. That kind we never eat. That kind kills us. If you want those fish, you will have to go down and get them yourself." So Thunder took a basket and went down to the dam for the fish. When he saw all the snakes had been killed he cried, because he had created all those snakes and they were just like so many children to him. Thunder got together a lot of wood which he piled over the bodies of the snakes and cremated them all.

When night came Obsidian-man again went to sleep with Thunder's daughter but as he was about to go, Thunder said, "Now, my son-in-law, I want to tell you something. Tomorrow morning when you get up, you must go out and get some wood from which to make bows and arrows," and he then told Obsidian-man just where to find the right kind of wood. Obsidian-man told his father, who said, "Well, that is all right, while I am here, they cannot hurt you. When I am dead they can kill you." In the morning Obsidian-man did as Thunder had directed and when he arrived at the place designated he found there some very large snakes, kawolwol (a very large snake with a body six inches or more in diameter, sixteen or eighteen feet in length). When he saw these snakes he did not know just what to do but decided to shoot them with his bow and arrows. He sat down to think a little while as to just where he had better shoot them, whether in the head or somewhere in the body. Then he decided that he would shoot them in the middle of the body. This he did and killed them all. He then went into the brush and procured the wood which Thunder wanted for making the bows and arrows. Thunder did not like it at all that Obsidian-man was always able to procure whatever he sent him for and was never killed, as was the case with former visitors.

Again night came and Obsidian-man went to sleep with Thunder's daughter. As he was going Thunder called to him and said, "Tomorrow you must go and get some obsidian for making arrow-heads and get some pitch with which to fasten the arrow-heads to the shafts." Obsidian-man told his father what Thunder had said to him and Coyote replied, "Well, that cannot hurt you while I am here. Your grandfather lives there, close to where that obsidian is and will see you there and will get it for you."

In the morning he went out as Thunder had directed but when he came to the tree from which the pitch was to be obtained he found it so slim and so slick that no one could climb it. He studied there for a little while, thinking what could be done when he heard someone coming.

It was Gray Squirrel. Gray Squirrel said to him, "Well, sonny, what are you going to do?"

Obsidian-man replied, "I came out here to get some pitch."

Gray Squirrel replied, "You cannot get pitch there. I will get it for you." So he climbed up the tree. As he started up the tree, it began to grow and it grew taller and taller until it looked as though it was going to grow clear up through the sky. The wind began to blow very hard but Gray Squirrel was used to climbing in trees and held on very tightly until he was able to fill the bag with pitch. Then he came down and gave it to Obsidian-man.

Obsidian-man then went to find the obsidian and here again he was assisted by Lizard (Haūbala) who procured the obsidian for him. There were so many rattlesnakes where the obsidian was to be found that no one could go near the place. Obsidian-man then took both the pitch and the obsidian home to Thunder.

When night came Thunder told Obsidian-man, "Now, I want you to go out tonight and kill deer. I will show you where there is a good tree by the trail. You can climb up in this tree and watch. I will give you the arrows and quiver." Obsidian-man told his father about this and Coyote told him that this too would be all right, assuring him that he had relatives all about him who would assist in protecting him. Obsidian-man went and found the tree which Thunder had indicated but saw no deer tracks near it. There was nothing but dust all around the tree, such as there is where bears are in the habit of playing.

He thought a while as to whether he had better go home or not but pretty soon Green Lizard (Bice-ui-saale) came and asked him, "Well, sonny, what are you doing here?"

Obsidian-man replied, "Thunder told me to come up here to kill deer, that there were many deer coming here to feed on the grass around this tree."

Lizard answered, "Bears come here all the time. No deer ever come here at all. I will take you up into the tree where I live. From there you can shoot."

They went up into the hole where Lizard lived. The bears soon came. First two appeared and Obsidian-man killed these, and presently four more came. He killed these also. Then eight appeared which he also shot. After this the bears came in groups of eight for a long time but Obsidian-man killed them all. As the bears attempted to climb up the tree, he would shoot them, until about day-break the ground all around was completely covered with their dead bodies.

Obsidian-man did not know just how he should get down out of this tree but finally daylight came. It, was however, a queer looking day-light. It looked red like fire and when it became lighter he saw that was no daylight at all but was really fire. Lizard, however, said "I will tell you where to shoot. This fire is a sort of supernatural being and there is but one place that you can hit him so that it will kill him. I will raise the shell ornament on his throat and then you shoot him right there." When Fire came near Lizard raised the shell ornament on his throat and Obsidian-man shot the spot directly under it. Then Fire fell dead, just as the bears had done. Then Obsidian-man went home and told Thunder that he had killed the deer but that his hands were so cold that he did not try to bring it in. Thunder went out to get the deer but when he found that Obsidian-man had killed so many of his bears, he cried a long time and finally piled wood over their bodies and cremated them.

Night came and, as Obsidian-man was about to start for bed, Thun-der stopped him and said, "Now, son-in-law, I am getting old. I am going to show you all that I have. Tomorrow we will go down in the flat and I will show you what kind of fire I have. Then you can have it when I am dead."

Obsidian-man told his father of this but Coyote replied as usual, "No one can hurt you while I am here."

That night, Thunder's daughter said to Obsidian-man, "You never are hurt by anything. Why do you not kill my father. I do not like to stay here with him. I wish you would kill him and my uncles."

In the morning Obsidian-man and the three Thunder brothers started to get wood for a fire in the sweat-house. The three Thunder brothers left the house first. As Obsidian-man appeared in the door, they shot at him but, of course, were unable to injure him, as he split the arrows with his arm each time.

When they had returned with the wood they made a fire and com-menced to play again in the same manner as they did when Obsidian-man had killed the first of the Thunders. Coyote provided Obsidian-man with a garment of ice and the same sort of a tube for fog. Before they commenced playing Obsidian-man told them, "I am going to shoot differently this time. I thought that you fellows were good players." He intended, of course, to kill at the first shot.

They built up a big fire and one of the Thunders said, "Are you ready? I am going to shoot now."

"Yes," said Obsidian-man, "I am ready."

Thunder took a seed-beater and sprinkled red-hot coals all over Obsidian-man. This, however, had no effect upon Obsidian-man as the ice and fog completely surrounded his body. Obsidian-man then took his position and said, "Now it is my time to shoot. You get ready." He took the coals in the seed-beater and heated his obsidian saws as before. Thunder commenced to kick and thrash about, but Obsidian-man said, "Do not do that way. We haven't begun to play yet." When he was all ready he sprinkled a large quantity of coals on Thunder, at the same time holding his red hot arms near him, with the result that this one of the Thunders was killed.

Then another one of Thunder brothers said, "Now it is my time to shoot. Are you ready?" When Obsidian-man replied that he was ready, Thunder sprinkled coals upon him but as before, without any effect.

Then Obsidian-man said, "Now it is my time to shoot. I told you that I was going to shoot differently this time." He then heaped the hot coals upon Thunder who kicked and thrashed about and cried aloud but Obsidian-man told him, "Do not do that way. We have only just commenced to play," and he continued to heap on coals until this one of the Thunders was dead.

Obsidian-man then told the one remaining Thunder brother that he was going to quit playing the game and that he did not care to kill them all. Thunder replied, "That is right. That is the way good gamblers always do. A good gambler never tries to win everything." Then Obsidian-man told Thunder to go outside the sweat-house and said that he was going to return home now. When they came outside Thunder said, "Now we will go out in the field here and I will show you all my magic so that you can have it after I die." Thunder then flew up into the air and it soon became foggy and then it began to rain. The rain continued to come down until it seemed as if the water was being poured out of a basket, it came so thick and fast.

Thunder said to Obsidian-man, "Well, how do you like it?"

Obsidian-man replied, "O, this is great magic."

Obsidian-man said to Thunder, "Now I am going to show you my kind of magic." With this he flew up into the air and made it very hot. Thunder, however, liked this very well.

Thunder then said, "Now I am going to show you my good magic."
Obsidian-man replied, "That is good. That is what I came here for."
Thunder then went up into the sky and it began to become cloudy.
Then hail-stones (yū'ksū) began to fall. Obsidian-man like this sort of
magic very much.

Obsidian-man next flew up into the air and made it very hot and
caused little stones to fall all around. Many of these hit Thunder and
Obsidian-man kept this up until Thunder was nearly dead from the
effect of it. Thunder, however, professed to like it.

Thunder next told Obsidian-man that he was going to show him
some good and beautiful magic. Obsidian-man replied that he would
be very pleased to see it, for that was what he came to visit the Thunders
for. Thunder then went up into the air and caused it to snow but when
the snow had reached the height of Obsidian-man's head, Thunder
stopped it.

Obsidian-man then told Thunder, "Now I am going to show you
my good magic." He went up in the air and caused it be become very
warm. Then he caused a shower of fire and coals to fall all around.
These burned Thunder's body and singed his hair until Thunder cried
to the boy that he had had enough. Then Obsidian-man stopped the
shower.

Thunder then told Obsidian-man, "Now I am going to show you my
very best magic." With this, he flew up into the air and caused it to
become foggy and to rain very hard. The water came down so hard
and fast, in fact, that it nearly washed Obsidian-man away. Finally,
however, Thunder stopped the rain.

Obsidian-man then asked Thunder, "Are these all the kinds of magic
you know?"

Thunder replied, "Yes, these are all. These are good magic."

Then Obsidian-man said, "Now I am going to show you my best
kind of magic and that will finish you. Then we will quit." Thunder
began to cry, for he knew that he would be killed but Obsidian-man
flew up into the air and again made it hot and this time caused a shower
of great stones to come down. Some of these stones hit Thunder,
knocking him down and mashing his body completely. Obsidian-man
then said, "Now I have won everything. I will quit."

Returning to the sweat-house, Obsidian-man gathered together a great lot of manzanita wood, some of which he put inside the sweat-house and the rest he piled about it on the outside.

He then went in to see Thunder's daughter. She begged him to take her with him when he went home, saying, "I wish you would take me with you. I am glad to see that you have killed my father. He was my father but I did not like him. I want you to take me home with you."

But Obsidian-man replied, "No, I cannot do that. I came over here to gamble. I did not come to get a woman."

He then set fire to the wood and burned the sweat-house and its occupants. In the sweat-house was an old woman, Bita-tsamo (bear fly), Bluebottle-fly, and when the house began to burn, this old woman commenced to wail. So loud was her wailing, in fact, that you could hear her for hundreds of miles. Obsidian-man, however, paid no attention to her or to Thunder's daughter but started for home alone.

On his way home he met many people and everyone rejoiced greatly at his success in killing the Thunder brothers. As he recounted his experiences to them each would shout and jump for joy to know that the Thunder brothers were at last killed. Obsidian-man finally arrived at his home at Mt. Kanaktai.

49—OBSIDIAN-MAN CONTESTS WITH THE KILAKS[112]
INCIDENTS AND CHARACTERS

  I. *Coyote creates Obsidian-man.*
      1. Coyote, 2. Blue Jay, 3. Frog, 4. Bird-people.
  II. *Obsidian-man wins contests with people.*
      1. Obsidian-man, 2. Coyote, 3. Frog, 4. Magic arrow.
  III. *Obsidian-man kills the Kī'laks.*
      1. Obsidian-man, 2. Coyote, 3. Frog, 4. Bear, 5. Magic arrow, 6. Kī'laks
        (six), 7. Magic flute, 8. Magic hunting sack, 9. Bottle-fly.
  IV. *Obsidian-man assigns homes to his father and mother.*
      1. Obsidian-man, 2. Coyote, 3. Frog, 4. Tsatī'.

I

(Coyote Creates Obsidian-man)

At Nō'napōtī lived all kinds of Bird-people. They had here a large fish dam with basketry traps in which they caught their fish. They left this dam at night and Coyote found out about it and every night he

---

[112]Informant: Sally Burke, Central dialect.

visited the dam and stole as many fish as he wanted from the trap. The people missed their catch of fish day after day. In the morning when they came to the dam they would find the trap empty so they decided to place a watch on the dam and see what happened for they suspected that Coyote was doing this stealing. These watchers dug a pit near the fish dam such as was often used by hunters in watching for deer. In due time they saw Coyote coming down to the dam and one of them shot him, the arrow entering his belly.

When Coyote came over here to steal the fish he always brought with him two large baskets which he filled. He would then stop on the bank of the creek, build a fire and cook and eat as many fish as he wanted which was always one whole basket. In fact he was so ravenous that he would not even wait for these fish to be completely cooked, but would eat them in a half-cooked condition.

When Coyote was shot he fell over into the creek and there he lay for four days. Finally Blue Jay flew over him and gave his characteristic cry "tsai, tsai, tsai, tsai," whereupon Coyote jumped up out of the water and scolded Blue Jay, "You are always making a great noise when I want to sleep."

As soon as Coyote sprang up out of the water the arrow-head came out of his body. He picked it up and carried it in his hand as he went home to his wife, Frog. He put the arrow-head into her mouth and she swallowed it.

That night, before they went to sleep, Coyote said, "Before daylight that arrow-head will turn into a young man and he will be sitting here on the other side of the fire combing his hair when we wake up in the morning." Sure enough, on the following morning there the young man sat on the opposite side of the fire combing his hair just as Coyote had willed it.

II

(Obsidian-man Wins Contests with People)

Now the people of the village had not been told that this young man had arrived, but everybody knew it just the same. They all went to the sweat-house and built a big fire and then they went over and invited Obsidian-man to come over to the sweat-house, but asked him to come alone.

Before he arrived the people cut a considerable number of grape-vines and got them ready to use for binding purposes. When the young man arrived they took him to the center pole and bound him there, tying his arms around behind him on the opposite side of the pole. Then they put on more wood until they themselves could not stand the heat in the house. They ran out and went down to the creek for a plunge in the water and, when they came back, Obsidian-man had broken all of his bonds and met them on the way. He went on down to the creek and had a swim also.

As Obsidian-man went down to the creek a number of the young women of the village followed him and tried to talk with him but he paid no attention to them. When he came out of the water he walked back to Coyote's house where Coyote and Frog had remained all this time.

He then took feathers, obsidian, and other materials and made arrows.

Then the people of the village made another fire in the sweat-house and made more binding material. This time they used ctïn and when Obsidian-man came into the house they bound him very securely to the center pole. Again they made such a very hot fire that none of them could stand it and all went out to swim. Again Obsidian-man broke his bonds and went to swim also.

Twice more they attempted to kill Obsidian-man in this way. Then they suggested that they should have a war in which he would fight against all of the other men. To this he agreed and all prepared for this contest. Everyone was arranged against Obsidian-man except Coyote and his wife. They helped him in every way they could. Coyote fought on his side, using his sling and using rocks as projectiles.

At first Obsidian-man did not shoot with arrows but spent all his time dodging the arrows of each band of men as it attacked him. He was an extremely agile fellow and a good dodger and was able to dodge all of the arrows. Finally he began to shoot at them. His first arrow, which was a magic one, killed the entire band, striking first one of his enemies and then another.

The same thing happened when the second batch of men came up to fight with him.

The men came in four bands all told and he killed each band with a single arrow. He used only four arrows to kill all of these men, but the battle lasted for four days. In this way he killed everyone in the village. One band of fighters each day.

III

(Obsidian-man Kills the Kï'laks)

Then Obsidian-man decided that he would take his father and mother and go away toward the north. On the journey he met Bear. He told Bear to get out of the way and let them pass but Bear refused and told Obsidian-man to leave the trail so that he might pass and, to prove his ferocity, he snapped at the grass and bit it off easily saying, "That is the way I will do with you if you do not get out of my way."

Obsidian-man countered by shooting a tree with one of his magic arrows and cutting it down and by saying, "That is the way I will do with you if you do not get out of my way." Bear saw that Obsidian-man had greater power than he and left the trail.

Then Obsidian-man, Coyote and Frog continued their journey northward until they met another bear who blocked the trail. He and this bear engaged in the same kind of exhibition of power and the same kind of threats until the bear left the trail. Then they continued their journey until they met two other bears and the same thing happened each time.

Obsidian-man was going to the home of Kï'lak in the north and took his father and mother, Coyote and Frog, with him. Finally they reached their destination and arrived at Kï'lak's house. When they reached the door Coyote took from his hunting sack a bead grinding stone (tcūwï'u kabē) and threw it into the trap which was located just inside the door. Then they entered and took the same bead grinder and threw it into a second trap located a little farther in.

Immediately after they entered, one of the Kï'laks jumped up, grabbed Frog and dragged her away into a rear room of the house.

Coyote paid no attention to this, simply seated himself and remained there for quite a long time. Presently they heard one of the Kï'laks coming. He made a loud noise, "kīla, kīla, kīla, kīla." Then they heard someone groaning. This Kï'lak had captured a human being and was bringing him in for food. When he arrived at the house this Kï'lak ran four times around it in a counter-clockwise direction before ascending the roof where he dropped his victim through the smoke-hole which is located on the northern slope of the roof (in Kĭ'lak's house there are four smoke-holes—one for each of the cardinal points).

Then this Kĭ'lak entered the house, but before coming in he remarked, "It must be that someone has come to visit us." He then dropped down through the smoke-hole, walked behind the center pole, and hung up the feather suit which he wore. Then he brought food for his visitors. This food was human flesh and blood. Coyote had a flute in his hunting sack and poured the food into this flute and it disappeared. Presently they heard another noise. The Kĭ'lak from the south was coming. He alighted at the southern smoke-hole and threw his prey into the house. This was a young man, very well dressed, with a feather belt (cbū) about his waist. As this Kĭ'lak dropped in through the smoke-hole he made the same remark as his predecessor, hung up his feather suit and also brought food for the visitors which Coyote disposed of in the same manner.

Later the two remaining Kĭ'laks arrived from their respective directions and did the same as their predecessors.

When the visitors reached the house there were already two of the Kĭ'laks present. Thus when all had arrived, there were six Kĭ'laks in the house.

They went to gather sweat-house wood and clover and took their visitors with them. They showed their visitors just where to go to get the best clover and they told Obsidian-man to go over to a certain spot entirely by himself. Whenever Obsidian-man went out to get clover it was observed that wherever he ate everything was cleaned off as if it had been mowed and also everything dried up.

When they returned to the house each one took a big manzanita bush as wood for the sweat-house fire.

Before they even started the fire, however, they made their bets. All of the Kĭ'laks bet against Obsidian-man alone, but from Coyote's magic hunting sack he was able to produce beads enough to "top" any bet they made.

Then they made the fire and the Kĭ'laks told Obsidian-man to fly up above the fire near the roof. One of the Kĭ'laks stood near the center pole armed with an ĭ'plŭk.[113] Presently Kĭ'lak shot at Obsidian-man with his bow and arrow but missed him.

Kĭ'lak then flew up and Obsidian-man by and by shot at him. He hit him directly in the throat and he dropped into the fire.

Coyote rejoiced and said, "I am glad. That is the way this fellow always guesses. He guesses right the first time in any game. The next time he plays I presume he may miss."

The Kĭ'lak that Obsidian-man killed was the one who first came home, the one who flew in from the north. Now the second Kĭ'lak made his bet and it was again met by the visitors.

Then they put more fuel on the fire and made a very hot fire indeed. This time Obsidian-man flew up first as he had done before. Coyote had in his sack some buckeye, and was able to produce a very dense smoke so that they could hardly see Obsidian-man as he flew about above them.

The Kĭ'lak who was now contesting with Obsidian-man also had an ĭ'plŭk the same as his predecessor. This he used most vigorously, fanning it around, striking at Obsidian-man with it and knocking him about against the wall until Obsidian-man was extremely tired. When Kĭ'lak thought that he had tired Obsidian-man sufficiently so that he could not dodge properly he shot at him; but he missed his mark. Then Obsidian-man flew down and Kĭ'lak flew up. Obsidian-man kept Kĭ'lak flying for a long time, until he finally became quite tired. At intervals Obsidian-man would strike at Kĭ'lak as though he was going to shoot, but he did not shoot until Kĭ'lak was very tired indeed. Then he hit him directly in the heart and this Kĭ'lak dropped into the fire.

The same cycle of events followed with the other two Kĭ'laks who had flown in from the other two directions. When Obsidian-man had killed all four of these Kĭ'laks he took Coyote and Frog out of the house.

Now there was an old woman, Bottle-fly, who lived here in this house. She was lame. She was so lame that she could not walk at all. In fact she was hung up by means of a grape-vine binder. She lived here in the home of the Kĭ'laks all the time and assisted them in eating the dead human beings. Obsidian-man did not take her out of the house but left her there when he set fire to it.

---

[113] An ĭ'plŭk is a stick about the size of a skewer, to one end of which is fastened a large bird-wing. It is said that such an instrument was used in ancient times to make a big dust and to fan smoke onto an opponent in order to blind him in a contest.

After the fire had burned Kï'lak's house, Obsidian-man, Coyote and Frog started southward again. They found the same four bears along the route barring their way as they had done upon the northward journey, and in the same manner Obsidian-man scared these bears away.

IV

(Obsidian-man Assigns Homes to His Father and Mother)

Finally when they had reached a point a short distance from Upper Lake, they stopped and Obsidian-man told his father, "You will hereafter be Coyote. You will stay in the mountains and you will say 'wū wū awū awū ——'." Then he said to his mother, "You will be Frog. You will live in the lake here and you will say 'wa'tak, wa'tak, wa'tak'."

Then he left them and went on down south and climbed to the summit of Mt. Kanaktai. He then started down the south side of this mountain and as he traveled along he heard someone shout very loudly, four times. The sound came from very far toward the north. It was a Tsatï' yelling at him. He looked back to see if he could see anything and in doing so his long hair became entangled in the bushes. He jerked very hard to free himself and in doing so he fell and his body broke into pieces. That is why there are so many pieces of obsidian on the south side of the mountain. These all came from the body of Obsidian-man.

50—THE CONTEST BETWEEN OBSIDIAN-MAN AND MOUNTAIN-MAN[114]

INCIDENTS AND CHARACTERS

I. The foot-race of the Bird-people.
　　1. Crane, 2. Loon, 3. Mud-hen, 4. Bird-people.
II. The Contest between Obsidian-man and Mountain-man.
　　1. Obsidian-man, 2. Coyote, 3. Mountain-man, 4. Bird-people.

I

(The Foot-race of the Bird-people)

At Upper Lake lived the Bird-people of ancient times.

The Bird-people had a big dance and then were going to have a

---

[114]The Pomo name of this myth was given by the informant as "ta' matū", signifying "bird story". The word "ta" applies to all kinds of birds.
Informant: Lee Peters, Central dialect.

foot-race. The race-course was the shore of the lake and they were to run completely around Clear Lake including, of course, Upper Lake, Lower Lake and East Lake. All the best runners among the young men of different species of birds came up and joined in this race. They ran four times around the lake.

Crane sat on the top of Mount Kanaktai to watch this race and announce its progress to the rest of the people.

The racers ran three times around the lake and started on the fourth lap, but about half way around on this last lap almost everyone became exhausted and could go no farther. Crane announced this fact to the people.

There was but one representative of each kind of bird in this race. One after another they became exhausted and dropped out of the race until only Loon (kok) and Mud-hen (katsīya) were left. The race between these two contestants was very close indeed. They kept up almost neck and neck in this race until they reached a point about a mile from the finishing line at Upper Lake. Then Loon gave out and Mud-hen finally won the race.

There was great rejoicing in the village and a big fire was made in the sweat-house and everybody participated in a good sweat-bath, after which they jumped into the water and then came back into the sweat-house again. Everybody was having a very joyful time, particularly making fun of the losers in the race and praising Mud-hen for his endurance and speed.

II

(The Contest Between Obsidian-man and Mountain-man)

They made a big dance in celebration of this event, but they told Obsidian-man nothing about it. This angered him very much because he considered that he should have been invited to this celebration, so he decided to go away from that place entirely.[115] Coyote went with him. They traveled down through Big Valley and way on beyond Lower Lake, far into the mountains in that direction until finally they met Mountain-man (Danō'-tca).

---

[115] The term "bagō'l-tca" (C) signifies a man who is sad, made so particularly by the fact that his relatives and friends do not treat him properly. The term particularly applies to a man who goes away from the village or from his relatives and friends with the intention of dying because he feels so badly about the way they treat him.

Mountain-man is a giant with legs, arms and other parts of human form, but his body is flat and shaped somewhat like that of a turtle. He always lies flat on the ground like a turtle and has no skin. His body is covered with all kinds of grass and short brush (about two feet long). He is about forty or fifty feet long in each direction and about twenty feet in height. Mountain-man asked Obsidian-man where he was going.

"I am going off to see a man," was the reply.

"Well, I am the man you want to see. I am a man for anybody (signifying that he was ready to fight with anyone)."

"Who are you then?" said Obsidian-man.

"I am Mountain-man."

Of course, Coyote knew as he always did just what was going to happen and whom they were going to meet so, before they met Mountain-man, Coyote was instructing Obsidian-man in the methods he should follow when contesting with Mountain-man. "You tell him to raise his body when you fight with him, and whenever he raises his body you must try to get him under the left arm. That is his softest spot and it is the place where his heart is located."

Consequently when they finally met Mountain-man and he gave Obsidian-man the challenge, Obsidian-man replied, "What do you do when you want to kill anybody. Let me see what you can do."

To this Mountain-man replied, "I am not the man that wanted to see anybody. You were the one who was looking for someone. Let us see what you can do. Let us see what you do when you dodge an arrow that is shot at you."

Obsidian-man thereupon ran up a tree and sprang from it to another tree and then jumped down to the ground saying as he did so, that he could jump where no one else could possibly follow. Then he said to Mountain-man, "Now let us see what you can do when you are fighting with anyone."

Mountain-man then ran up to a small tree and knocked it over.

Seeing this Obsidian-man said, "O! that is nothing. I can do that myself." He thereupon ran up to a tree somewhat larger than the one that had just been knocked over by Mountain-man and with a single stroke of his hand he chopped the tree completely in two. In chopping this tree down he had used his left hand but he could cut off a tree with a single stroke no matter what one of his hands or feet he used. He was very powerful in this way.

Next Mountain-man knocked over a still larger tree and Obsidian-man immediately followed by chopping off one even larger yet. The tree which Mountain-man had broken down was a good four feet in diameter and the one that Obsidian-man had cut in two was even larger than that.

Finally Obsidian-man became disgusted with this contest of strength and told Mountain-man to get out of his way because he wanted to continue on his journey. To this Mountain-man replied, "No, this is my trail, this is my place to travel, you cannot pass."

Obsidian-man then took a shot at him and Mountain-man rushed up toward Obsidian-man with the intention of jumping upon him and mashing him completely. Obsidian-man, however, was very very quick at dodging and when Mountain-man jumped at him, Obsidian-man dodged under him. Then Obsidian-man took another shot at Mountain-man.

Thus did Obsidian-man and Mountain-man contest for a long time, running round and round and fighting with each other until finally Obsidian-man ran up a tree. Thereupon Mountain-man ran against this tree and knocked it down. Obsidian-man jumped to another tree which again Mountain-man knocked down. And so they contested in this way, Mountain-man knocking down each tree to which Obsidian-man jumped, until finally all the trees in the neighborhood had been laid low. And then Obsidian-man started to run across country toward the coast.

He ran up onto a big rock pile finally and Mountain-man, in hot pursuit, broke this rock pile down as he had broken down the trees.

Finally they came way down onto the coast to a place called "Kaū'ca" where there is a very large redwood tree. Obsidian-man climbed up into this tree and Mountain-man endeavored to break it down, but was absolutely unable to damage it. Mountain-man then lay about under the tree trying to think of some way in which he could get the best of Obsidian-man. He finally decided to collect wood and build a fire around this tree and set it on fire. He did this, gathering many logs and trees and all sorts of firewood. He started a very big fire but the redwood absolutely would not burn.[116] As a matter of fact, when the other Bird-people saw the danger in which Obsidian-man then found himself, they all came and brought water and poured onto this tree so as to keep it from catching fire. All the bird-people helped in this and saved Obsidian-man in this way.

The tree stands there yet, up about four or five miles east of Greenwood on the top of a ridge at the eastern edge of an opening. The tree is about half rotted away now because it eventually died but there is water still coming out of the place where Obsidian-man stayed in this tree, about thirty feet up from the ground. It is a little seeping spring that comes out of the tree at this point and there are weeds and grass and ferns growing here. In the winter and early spring the water runs down from this point in a regular stream, but later in the summer this becomes a little seepage and it behaves just the same as other springs do. This spring high up in the tree stump is a favorite place for birds to go to drink even now.

So it was that Mountain-man was unable to burn this tree, no matter how big a fire be built about its base. In time he grew very tired and when night came he lay down near this fire at the base of the tree and went to sleep. Obsidian-man listened until he heard Mountain-man snoring and was thus sure that he was sleeping soundly. Then Obsidian-man came down out of the tree and looked Mountain-man over very carefully.

Now Mountain-man had suspended from his neck a large abalone shell. He kept it hanging here to protect and hide his heart which was located immediately under it.

Obsidian-man gently pulled the abalone shell away and plunged his spear into the soft spot and pierced the heart of Mountain-man and killed him instantly.

Mountain-man's body broke up with a great crushing noise like thunder. His body turned into rocks and broke up and the boulders rolled down into the ocean.

The spirit of Mountain Man went away to Ya'kōda, a creek, (now called Elk Creek), about two miles south of Greenwood. In the creek

---

[116]The well known indestructibility of redwoods by fire is here recognized. Another incident of an entirely different sort states that "Meadowlark came over from the east and told the people that the world was burning up. Presently the world was on fire and it burned up completely except for that portion along the immediate coastline which is covered with redwood forests. The redwoods did not burn."

at this point there is a very deep pool. In fact there is a cave which runs back under the mountain here and this makes the water very deep and blue. It is in this cave that the spirit of Mountain-man still dwells. It is a very dangerous place to visit and many people have been drowned here because when they go into this deep pool the spirit of Mountain-man drags them down and puts them to death.

Along the edge of this pool there is a considerable area of quicksand and if a stranger passes this way he is sure to go down in this soft quicksand and lose his life. This sand is not always soft. It is sometimes hard, so that one never can tell whether it is safe to journey this way or not. At times, however, it is made soft this way by the spirit of Mountain-man to serve as a trap for people.

After Obsidian-man has disposed of his adversary in this way he started back to his home on Mount Kanaktai. When he finally reached Mt. Kanaktai he got caught in some brush and his body broke up into a great many pieces. That is why you see such a great amount of obsidian in pieces, in all kinds of blocks and pieces around on the southern slope of this mountain.

51—THE CONTEST BETWEEN ROCK-MAN AND GRAY SQUIRREL[117]

Characters: 1. Rock-man, 2. Gray squirrel.

Rock-man and Gray Squirrel met out in the mountains. Rock-man said, "Let me try your bow." Rock-man was very strong indeed and could break anything he wanted to. However, when he tried Gray Squirrel's bow he bent it completely double, but did not succeed in breaking it.

Then Gray Squirrel tried Rock-man's bow. He pulled it back and broke the bow in two. Rock-man then pursued Gray Squirrel but Gray Squirrel was very swift and was a good dodger. He ran down the hill with Rock-man close after him. Rock-man was rolling right along and had almost caught up with Gray Squirrel when the latter went up a tree. Rock-man, however, cut the tree down. Gray Squirrel then ran to another tree and scurried up it but Rock-man cut this tree off and so

---

[117]The Pomo name of this myth is "Xabē xaūk sakalalai cūmū'i", Rock-man and Gray Squirrel pull bow string.
Informant: Tom Mitchell, Eastern dialect.

on they went in this contest, Rock-man cutting down every tree that Gray Squirrel tried to take refuge in.

Thus they ran on and on toward the west until they arrived at the sea-coast close to where Greenwood now stands. Southeast of this place there is a "cliff ridge" upon which stands a redwood tree. It is there yet. It is a very big tree. Gray Squirrel ran up this tree and Rock-man tried his best to cut it down just as he had the other trees, which were much smaller. But this tree proved to be too much for Rock-man to cut. He therefore determined to set fire to it and burn it down and kill Gray Squirrel.

Gray Squirrel, however, was a very powerful medicine-man and he made a wish, "I wish that this tree would not burn. I wish that a spring would start from where I am now sitting and run down to the base of the tree so that it can not burn." Immediately the tree became very wet and refused to burn. The tree stands there yet and the spring still runs from the spot where Gray Squirrel sat and there are ferns growing on the trunk of the tree at the present time.

52—THE DEATH OF MU'YAMUYA[118]

Characters: 1. Mū'yamūya, 2. Grizzly Bear.

Mū'yamūya is a giant. He was very heavy and was nine or ten feet tall. He behaved very strangely all the time. Whenever anyone came in sight of his house he always proposed that they gamble and would go through the motions of gambling, but people would pass by without stopping. Everyone hated this giant and desired to do away with him. They discussed how they might kill him but he warned them never to try to kill him because if they did they would all be turned into birds and mammals.

One day he was caught by Grizzly Bear and was bitten and chewed up into fine pieces but he immediately came to life again and returned home. Finally the people had a big celebration and invited Mū'yamūya to attend. They seized him and beat him to pieces and threw out the dead body but the next day he returned to life and laughed at them and invited them all to gamble with him.

He lived by himself out in the brush, about a quarter of a mile south of the old village of Lē'ma. The people of this village tried many times

---

[118]Informant: Rosie Peters, Central dialect.

to kill Mū'yamūya but he always returned to life no matter what they did to him. He told them that they must never kill him because if they did they would be transformed into birds and mammals, but still they kept right on trying to do away with him. Finally they took him down to a big rock east of their village and started to pound him up as they would a rabbit but he told them that they must not put him into the fire because the smoke would descend upon them and kill them all.

He told them that if they wanted to really do away with him they should dress him up in the finest of clothing and put rocks around him and throw him into a deep pool in the river, that this was the only way that he could be exterminated. They, however, paid no attention to his admonition and proceeded to pound him up bit by bit.

Finally they came to the nail of the big toe of his right foot. Here they found a hard lump like a rock under the nail and decided that this must be his heart. They opened it, looked in and there, indeed, was Mū'yamūya's heart. They cut the toe off and rolled the rest of the body down over the cliff and rolled many large rocks down on top of it. That is why there are so many boulders at the base of this cliff and down in the river immediately adjacent to this point. He was never able to get up again because they had taken his heart away from him. They hung his big toe on a stick and danced back with it to the village. Here they held a great dance around it and presently all were turned into birds and mammals just as Mū'yamūya had warned them.

53—MU'YAMUYA[119]

Characters: 1. Mū'yamūya, 2. Grizzly Bear.

A supernatural being called Mū'yamūya was very troublesome. He would take anything he wanted away from the people and they used to try to kill him. Even Grizzly Bear ate him but nothing succeeded in killing him.

Finally his mother was bitten by a snake and died. The people sent a messenger to inform him of this fact and to ask him to come home to her funeral. He, however, paid no attention to this messenger but merely asked when the messenger started to return home what he had been saying.

---

[119]Informant: Jocie Kylark, Central dialect.

They burned his mother's body and gave her proper funeral rites.

Finally when they were next able to catch Mū′yamūya they laid him down on a big rock and pounded him to bits. This time they were very careful to pound every part of his body and finally they pounded up a small hard kernel under the toe-nail of his big toe. This was, as a matter of fact, his heart, so this time they succeeded in killing him. He never came to life again.

54—HUK TRANSFORMS PEOPLE INTO DEER[120]

Characters: 1. Sister, 2. Brother, 3. Hūk, 4. Grandmother, 5. Coyote.

At the foot of a ridge on the west side of Little Lake Valley there stood in olden times a large village. There lived at this village a young woman and her little brother.

The little brother became very thirsty and besought his sister, "Oh, Sister, I am very thirsty (dead for water). Let us go and get water."

His sister replied, "Yes, my brother, I pity you for you are so very thirsty. We will go for water at once."

They then went down the trail, the girl carrying a basket in her hand with which to bring water back after they had drunk at the spring.

As they came near this spring the little boy cried, "Oh my sister, what is that with its head caught in that trap?" For, sure enough, near the spring there was a snare in which a large deer was caught.

Now the fact of the matter was that this animal looked exactly like a deer but in reality it was not a deer at all, it was a Hūk which had transformed itself into a deer and had placed itself as if caught in the trap so as to fool people.

When his sister saw this deer caught in the snare she said to her brother, "Come, let us run home and get our people to come back and cut up this deer." The little boy then ran home as fast as he could and called the people of the village and told them what he and his sister had discovered.

The people of the village came down to the spring with their burden baskets and commenced to cut up this animal and when they had partly finished suddenly there appeared on the animal's head, antlers with four prongs each. Then the boy knew that this was a magic animal and he immediately began to sing.

[120]Informant, Charley Brown, Northern dialect, 1902.

However, the rest of the people paid no attention to this manifestation of the supernatural and disregarded the warning given them by the
boy. The meat was apportioned among the people and they all returned
to the village.

When all had returned to the village the boy said, "I will not eat
this meat of the 'Hūk deer'. Neither will my sister or my grandmother
eat any of it. We three are afraid of this deer. I will sit here by the
door and sing. I shall not sleep tonight. I shall not lie down. I will sit
up and keep my eyes open and watch you people for you will all be transformed into deer, but we three will not. We will live on as before."

Presently Coyote came and sang to the boy.

Then the boy asked Coyote to save him, his sister, and his grandmother. Coyote made a heavy fog roll in and as it passed, he and the
other three disappeared with it.[121]

55—BAGIL TRANSFORMS PEOPLE INTO DEER[122]

Characters: 1. Boy, 2. Elder sister, 3. Bagil, 4 Blue Jay.

There was in olden times a village some distance north of the present
village at Upper Lake (about eight miles). In the summer (grass-
hopper-burning time) a boy in this village became very sick. He and
his elder sister started for water at a spring. As they neared this spring,
however, his sister became frightened and was very much afraid to go
near the place, and turned back.

The boy went on and found near the spring a strange looking spot
where the ground was all slick and smooth as if some animal had been
there. He set a trap here in hopes of catching this animal.

On the following morning he went back to this spot and found that
he had caught something very strange looking and frightful. It had
somewhat the form of a deer. Immediately he saw it he began to sing
a song which was intended to keep away the evil of this animal from
himself. After he had finished his ritual he went back and told his
mother and the rest of the people of the village that he had caught
something strange in a snare.

[121]The informant here gave some statement to the effect that this fog carried these four
up into the Upper World. This, however, seemed to be very much of a modernization and is
so absolutely contrary to all truly Pomo conceptions of such matters that it can only be considered as a borrowing from missionary teaching.
[122]Informant: Tom Mitchell, Eastern dialect, 1902.

His uncle, Blue Jay, addressed the people and said that all would go down to the spring and see what the boy had caught. Immediately the entire population of the village started out and the boy knew that when they arrived they would undoubtedly eat this strange animal so he began to sing and wail because he knew that it would do them great harm. "Oh my poor people, Oh my poor uncle, Oh my poor grandfather, Oh my poor grandmother. I did not say that this animal that I have caught is good for food. It is like a deer but it is really a dangerous animal. It is Bagi'l bicē. Oh my poor father, Oh my poor sister. That is another kind of deer. Oh my poor people."

The boy continued this lamentation during the entire journey to the spring.

Upon arriving at the spring Blue Jay again addressed the people. Some of them began to build fires. Others took the animal from the trap and cut it up. The meat was put on the fire and all ate of it, that is all except the boy, who did not participate in any way, but who simply sat there and sang his magic protective song.

Presently a baby began to snort like a deer and soon hair began to grow on its ears and back, and it stamped upon the ground like a deer. The boy still continued to sing his magic protective song. Soon this baby had turned completely into a deer. Then the older people became deer and all ran away to the mountains.

The boy himself was left entirely alone and he went home. There were now but three people, his sister, his grandmother and himself.

Next day he went out hunting but could find no deer at all. He came back to the village. On the following day he did the same thing, this time going father toward the north. He sang constantly and carried with him a pair of deer horns. Finally he went far enough so that he came to the deer village. Here he saw a large deer, shot it and carried it home. His sister, his grandmother and himself ate it with no bad effects. They always lived in that same village after that.

56—THE WATER SPIRIT IN BLUE LAKES[123]

Characters: 1. Water-man, 2. Vulture, 3. Coyote.

Water-man (Ka-tca) lives under the water at Blue Lakes. He eats nothing but fish. He has a large assembly-house under the water on

---

[123]Informant: Charlie Brown, Northern dialect, 1902.

the west side of the lake. He went into the assembly-house and there he found his friend Vulture of whom he asked what he ate. Vulture replied that he ate abalones, mussels, and all kinds of shell-fish which grow in the water. Water-man then said, "I am never sick because I always eat fish and you, because you also eat things which are found in the water, are never sick either. Because I live under the water I was saved at the time of the great fire which came from the east and cremated every living thing. I alone was spared. That great fire burned over the world, destroyed all of the old and bad things on the earth and made it over into a new world.

"Then Coyote came and took all of the snakes of every description and cast them into the lake and made fish of them. These fish went everywhere that there was water: the lakes, streams and all over the world.

"Now I live here under the water, as I did before, where everything is good and if people want fish they can come to this lake and perform the regular ceremony, singing their songs four times, and I will always give them what they want."

57—FALCON IS STOLEN BY KILAK[124]
INCIDENTS AND CHARACTERS

I. *Falcon is stolen by Gï'lak, and later rescued.*
  1. *Falcon, 2. Blackbird, 3. Coyote, 4. Swan-people, 5. Goose-people.*
II. *Falcon's children avenge his death.*
  1. *Bear brothers, 2. Elk-people, 3. Kï'lak.*

I

(Falcon Is Stolen by Gï'lak and Later Rescued)

In olden times Falcon lived in Long Valley. It was his custom to hunt geese. He would bring home enough geese each time for the entire village. He hunted over toward the east but one day he did not return at nightfall as was his custom. After four days he had not returned and his wife, Blackbird, started out to hunt for him.

Falcon's father, Coyote, was so grief-stricken at the loss of Falcon that he put his head in the fire and burned off his hair as a token of his feelings.

---

[124]Informant: Tom Mitchell, Eastern dialect, 1902.

Blackbird walked eastward following the footprints of her husband and crying continuously in indication of her sorrow. She finally arrived at the place where he had last hunted but found nothing of him there and could not see that his tracks went any farther. She then returned homeward.

On the following morning she started out in company with Coyote to hunt for him again. They went back to the same place where she had been on the previous day but could find no tracks going anywhere. Finally she found his bow and arrows hanging on a small tree. These she took and returned to the village crying.

She told her father-in-law that she was going away farther than anyone had ever gone before and in the morning started out and walked, crying all the way, a very great distance toward the east. She went until she finally came in sight of the smoke from the village of the Swan-people. She asked them if they had seen anything of her husband. They replied that they had not so she remained here for the night and on the following morning again went on eastward, crying as before.

Finally she arrived at the village of the Goose-people where she again asked if they had seen anything of her husband and again received a negative reply.

On the following morning she took a course leading to the south and went crying and chanting along until she saw a smoke in that direction. She went toward it and finally arrived at a brush-house. Of these people she inquired if they had seen anything of her husband and they replied that they did not know but that he might be "over there", indicating a place a short distance away. Upon visiting it she found many human bodies and some people still alive. The search here did not find Falcon so she went over and entered the sweat-house which stood near by, where there were many more dead people. Here she commenced her search on one side of the door and she looked at all the faces as she passed round the house. When she was at a point about opposite the door she found Falcon. She wrapped up his body and started to carry it back home. Coyote, of course, accompanied her, both wailing continuously.

Blackbird's song was as follows:

"Gūnūla kedīle, gūnūla kedīle, gūnūla kedīle," (repeated).

Coyote's song was "Laiwē, laiwē, laiwē, laiwē, laiwē, waies," (repeated).

Finally they arrived on the side of the creek opposite their own village and Coyote said to Blackbird, "My daughter-in-law, you go home first." She went ahead and entered the village crying.

Now, when Coyote was left alone with Falcon he set about doctoring him. He put him down into the water and told him, "After four days you will come to life and come home. You will go to the house of your grandfather and ask him to open the door and you will say to him, 'I am very cold.' "

Coyote then went home and entered the sweat-house. He and Blackbird continued to sing and wail for four days but at midnight on the last night they ceased their wailing.

Shortly after that they heard a voice outside of the house calling, "My grandfather, my grandfather. Open the door. I am very cold." Coyote then opened the door and Falcon entered and sat by the fire. When the people saw him some of them gave a startled cry which caused all to stop their wailing and to look about and sure enough, there sat Falcon.

Coyote then addressed the people, telling them to go out and gather sweat-house wood early in the morning because Falcon had returned home. This the people did. Many people brought in wood. A big fire was built and that day everyone danced.

II

(Falcon's Children Avenge His Death)

When Falcon's children were grown they went away into the mountains and transformed themselves into bears. They entered a small opening in the chemese and there the elder of the two began to sing. He sang for a long time and they practiced bear movements and manners. The elder of the two brothers dug a hole in the ground with a stick. He rolled about on the ground and hair began to grow on his shoulders. Finally he became a real bear.

His younger brother then did the same thing and became a bear also.

The elder brother then tried to run and jump like a bear and succeeded. Immediately the younger brother did likewise.

Finally when both had perfected themselves in the ways of the bear, they ran very far to the east, finally arriving at a village. When they neared it they rested and transformed themselves back into human beings, then they went to the village.

The people of this village inquired where they were going. They replied that they were hunting food. These men knew how hungry they had been when travelling far away so they gave them food, mush and pinole and meat. The people were really afraid of these two for they thought that they were poison-men.

Toward morning they ran back to where their bear suits were and transformed themselves again into bears by putting these on.

They then ran east again for a long distance and finally came near to a village but did not go to it. Here they turned southward toward the village of the Elk-people. They passed this village and kept on toward the south until they saw a straight column of smoke ascending from a village. When they arrived at this village they threw into the sweat-house a large amount of wood and burned up the entire house.

Then they ran up onto the mountainside nearby and sat down and watched their fire and wished that Kī'lak might come and endeavor to rescue the things in his burning house.

Presently Kī'lak did come. He ran into the sweat-house and was immediately burned up.

Then the two boys started back toward their home. They ran for a long time toward the north and then for a long time toward the west until they finally arrived at a point just east of their village. Here they stopped and transformed themselves from bears back into human beings.

58—THE ORIGIN OF THUNDER[125]

Characters: 1. Coyote, 2. Thunder.

Coyote, the Creator, went from Mount Kanaktai to Sanhedrim Mountain (Batsom-dano, Black Oak Mountain) and from there he went across to Redwood Mountain (Capalawel-dano).

On this high mountain he created Thunder and sent him from there to the coast to Big River where he now lives in a house under the water.

Thunder always comes from the west to the east and returns. This is the origin of the sound we call thunder which emanates from this house at Big River and always returns to the same place.

---

[125]Informant: Charlie Brown, Northern dialect, 1902.

TRICKSTER STORIES

59—COYOTE TRICKS HIS MOTHER-IN-LAW[126]

Characters: 1. Coyote, 2. Coyote's mother-in-law, 3. Coyote children (four).

Coyote told his mother-in-law that everyone in the village was going out to gather buckeyes. They were going to establish a camp out in the mountains for that purpose. She believed what he said and started off with him for the camp. When they had gone some distance the old woman observed that she had seen no tracks of the others and that they must have gone by some other trail. They went on, however, and after a while Coyote made a wish that it would rain very hard.

Soon a pouring rain commenced. They stopped and Coyote built a small lean-to shelter. Coyote crawled under the shelter but at first the old woman staid out in the rain. Finally Coyote said to her, "You better come over here and sleep where it is dry. If you are afraid of me we can lie with our heads in opposite directions and even place a piece of bark between us." She agreed to this and soon went to sleep. Of course Coyote could make any thing happen as he wished, so during the night he willed that the old woman should sleep very soundly.

When she awoke in the morning there were four little Coyote children there with her. All started home in the morning, but Coyote went a different way from that taken by the old woman and the children. He arrived long before she did. He sat around waiting for her for a while and then he observed to the others, "Well, I guess my mother-in-law must have taken the 'children's trail.'[127] That is the reason that she does not come home." He said this because he wanted to throw the blame for the children onto the woman.

As she finally approached the village, Coyote said, "There she comes and she has four children with her. I knew that she had traveled the 'children's trail'." As soon as she reached the village the people killed the children.

---

[126]The Pomo name of this myth is "Gūnūla la macal baca' mikerk tcadi", "Coyote mother-in-law hunt took away."
Informant: Tom Mitchell, Eastern dialect.
[127]The "children's trail" is a mythical trail formerly believed in by the Pomo. It was thought that if a woman traveled this trail she would automatically conceive and bear children.

60—COYOTE KILLS HIS SISTER-IN-LAW, SKUNK[128]
INCIDENTS AND CHARACTERS

I. *Coyote kills his sister-in-law.*
    1. *Skunk sisters (two),* 2. *Coyote,* 3. *Eagle.*
II. *Coyote is killed by Skunk's scent.*
    1. *Skunk,* 2. *Coyote,* 3. *Blue Jay.*

I

(Coyote Kills His Sister-in-law)

There were two Skunk sisters. The elder was Coyote's wife. The younger had a large and very painful swelling on the sole of one of her feet. Coyote said to his wife, "I am going to doctor my sister-in-law." Accordingly he took her a long way off out into the hills where no one could see what he was doing and built a good fire. Then he held the sore foot up close to the fire, saying that he intended to cook it. This he literally did, even though she cried loudly with the pain. In fact he held Skunk's foot in the fire until he killed her and then he broiled her until the skin was all cracked open and until the grease ran out. This he had intended to do from the first. That is why he had brought her so far from the village, where no one could interfere.

Coyote then sat down under a large tree to eat Skunk. Soon Eagle flew down and lighted on the top of the tree. Coyote looked up and said to Eagle, "It looks as though we were going to eat some nice fat meat doesn't it? Well, you are not going to get any of this. It is all mine." Soon Coyote went away a short distance and Eagle swooped down and took the meat up to the top of the tree and proceeded to eat it. When Coyote came back and found Eagle eating his meat he said to Eagle, "Please give me a little piece anyway. Anything will do. Any little piece you have left."

Eagle replied, "Wait a little while. I am saving the nicest, fattest piece for you." Coyote waited around for a while and finally Eagle said to him, "Now get ready, I am going to throw down a fine piece to you. Come right up under me and keep your eyes shut and your mouth open so that I can throw this piece into your mouth." Coyote did as he was told and Eagle threw all the offal, including the gall bladder, right

[128]The Pomo name of this tale is "Gūnū'la mahal cak nūper daiyaūwal", "Coyote sister-in-law skunk girl (grown)."
Informant: Tom Mitchell, Eastern dialect.

into Coyote's mouth. The gall bladder broke and Coyote choked. He cried out and started running toward home, crying as he went:

wīmaha ōī ōī ōī

wīmaha ē ē ē

(Repeat indefinitely)

He was crying over the death of his sister-in-law. He was saying, "I am awfully sorry about my sister-in-law. I feel very badly about it. I can never forget about it." So loudly did he wail that even those in the house heard him.

They said, "There comes old Coyote with another big lie. Look at him crying for his sister-in-law. I'll bet that he killed her himself. That is the reason he is crying so hard."

II

(Coyote Is Killed by Skunk's Scent)

Coyote's wife, who was Skunk's elder sister, fixed herself up and played that she was sick. Coyote came in and told his wife about her sister's death, but she pretended to be so sick that she was not interested. She moaned constantly and asked Coyote to try to doctor her at once. She said that she had a very bad pain in her buttocks. Coyote was a great doctor and could cure people either by singing over them or by sucking the cause of the pain from the affected part. She urged him to suck out the pain. Coyote still continued to wail over the death of his sister-in-law for some time, but finally his wife persuaded him to doctor her. She said, "The pain is right down there (indicating the spot), it is nearly killing me, do suck it out." Coyote put his mouth down near the painful part and, just as he had his mouth open ready to begin sucking out the pain, Skunk shot her scent into his mouth. Coyote fell over, choked to death by the scent. Skunk then took a stone and mashed Coyote's body to a jelly and threw it outside.

Presently along came Blue Jay. He flew over Coyote's body and cried, "tsai, tsai, tsai". Coyote sprang up and said, "he, he, Can't you ever let a fellow alone when he wants to sleep. You are always waking me up."

61—COYOTE TRICKS SOME GIRLS[129]

Characters: 1. Coyote, 2. Several girls.

The women of Pine Ridge went over to The Devil's Elbow[130] to gather buckeyes. No men went with them. There were at the village two very pretty girls whom Coyote, who was an old man, strongly advised to go on this excursion. Accordingly they went and were later surprised to see a very old woman come into the camp at The Devil's Elbow. She carried an old burden basket and appeared to be very feeble. This was really Coyote, whose magic power had enabled him to take this form in order to trick these girls.

Presently Coyote said to the girls, "It looks like rain. I am going to make a good shelter. Then you girls can sleep there and keep dry too." After much labor the old woman completed a shelter just large enough for three.

Then one of the girls came along and said, "Well, grandfather, you got it built."

Coyote again warned her of the coming storm but she said that she did not believe it would rain that night. A third girl overheard this reference to Coyote as grandfather and said to this girl, "Why do you say 'grandfather'? That is my grandmother; can't you see that?" Then to Coyote she said, "That is a pretty small house, grandmother, why do you not build a larger one?"

Coyote replied, "I can't get enough grass to make it bigger. I think that this one is large enough. It will shelter us from the rain."

About sundown another girl came and said to Coyote, "My grandmother says that the buckeye soup is nearly ready to eat. You must come and eat with us pretty soon."

Coyote replied, "I am not able to walk way down there to eat. I will stay here and see if I can find some old, rotten wood for a fire to keep us warm tonight."

At sundown the women all came from the place where they had been cooking and preparing the buckeyes and for a long time they laughed and played around in the camp near the shelter Coyote had built.

Coyote meanwhile slipped out of the camp and went some distance

---

[129]Informant: Jo Beatty, Central dialect, 1904.
[130]This village of Bō'ano, at Pine Ridge, was located somewhere east of The Devil's Elbow, Pō'kal, which in turn is about one mile down on the southern slope of the "red-topped" mountain south of Doolan Canyon, near Ukiah, Mendocino County.

away. There he said, "Now, I wish it would rain very hard all night."
Then he returned, still in the form of the old woman, and went to bed
in the little house. Presently it began to rain torrents and the women,
none of whom had provided against bad weather, all sought shelter with
Coyote. "Ah," said he, "you would not believe me when I said that it
would storm. You see that I was right. Now come and stay here, as
many of you as can." Thus, several of the young women crept into the
shelter and presently fell asleep, with the "old woman" in the middle.

Presently Coyote said to himself, "I wish they would all sleep very
soundly." Of course, Coyote was able, by his magic, to make any wish
come true. The girls all slept soundly. Coyote then transformed himself
into a young man. Later he again took the form of the old woman.

Finally one of the girls awoke feeling strangely. She woke the
others and all felt the same way. Then they knew that the old woman
had fooled them in some way. They woke the old woman, who protested
that she had been sound asleep all the time and had not moved except
as she became tired of sleeping on her side and had changed position.

In the morning the old woman said, "Well, I guess I shall go away.
I shall not go home for I have no home. I do not know where I am
going. I am just going away like a deer or some other animal." Then
she went away and all the girls left also. None of them went home
either. They were all Bird-people and went away like birds.

Coyote was always tricking people like this.

62—COYOTE TRICKS TWO GIRLS[131]

Characters: 1. Coyote, 2. Two girls, 3. Coyote children (ten).

One day in summer Coyote transformed himself into a dead fish[132]
and floated about on the surface of Clear Lake over near the eastern
shore. Coyote had transformed himself into a perch which is one of
the fish that the people used to like very much. By and by he floated
down near the old village of Cī'gōm.[133] Some of the people on shore

---

[131]The Pomo name of this tale is "gūnū'la cakanas padîle marū", "Coyote cakanas padîle
story."
Informant: Tom Mitchell, Eastern dialect.
[132]This story is based upon the fact that in olden times the Pomo, at least those in the
Clear Lake region, ate dead fish, especially those of certain species such as the perch and the
trout. No reason could be learned for this custom and it is difficult to see why they should
have eaten these half putrid fish in a region where there was such an abundance of fresh fish
at all times.
[133]This was one of the old villages on the northeastern shore of Clear Lake at a point
now called Morrison's Landing, and about two miles southeast of the present Bank Ranch
village. Univ. Calif. Publ. Amer. Arch. Eth., VI, 190, 1906.

saw this dead perch floating on the crests of the small waves. Two girls, twins, went out in a canoe to try to get it. As they approached, however, it floated farther out into the lake. They followed it nearly out to the middle of the lake before they got close enough to attempt to pick it up with the paddle. Each time they missed it until finally it suddenly jumped out of the water and into the canoe, at the same time turning back into Coyote. Straightway each of the girls gave birth to five children. Then Coyote jumped back into the water and disappeared.

The girls were very much ashamed, but finally went back to the village, taking the ten coyote children with them. When they reached the shore the people saw that they had these children and decided that they must die. The mother of the girls accordingly went into the canoe and killed the ten children by hitting each with the canoe paddle.

63—COYOTE IS TRICKED BY GROUND SQUIRRELS[134]
INCIDENTS AND CHARACTERS

I.   Coyote rescues Duck.
    1. Duck, 2. Kabadatetes, 3. Diver, 4. Magic wand, 5. Coyote.
II. Coyote catches Ground Squirrels by magic.
    1. Coyote, 2. Chicken Hawk, 3. Chub Duck, 4. The Ground-squirrel-people, 5. Meadowlark, 6. Blue Jay, 7. Bullfrog-women, 8. Sleep charm.
III. Coyote regulates death.
    1. Bullfrog-woman, 2. Meadowlark, 3. Blue Jay, 4. Coyote.
IV. Coyote builds Kelsey Creek and establishes fishing customs.
    1. Coyote.

I

(Coyote Rescues Duck)

At the old village of Nō'napōtī[135] lived Duck.[136] He was a boy and was playing around near the village. At Xabe'l[137] lived Kabada*te'tes*. He went down and stole Duck. The people missed the boy and hunted all around in the neighborhood of the village for him. Diver[138] used to make journeys between these two villages and he told the people of Nō'napōti that the boy was at Xabe'l.

---

[134]Informant: Dave Thompson, Upper Lake, Eastern dialect, 1904.
[135]Near Kelseyville, Lake County, See U. C., Publ. Amer. Arch. Ethn., VI, 197, 198, and map, 1908.
[136]A species called "baca'badalat."
[137]At "Rock Point" on the northwestern shore of Clear Lake. See Univ. Calif., Publ. Amer. Arch. Ethn., VI, 157, and map, 1908.
[138]A species called "tcū'tkil".

Coyote got together the strong, young men and instructed them to go to Xabe'l, but they wanted to know how they were to travel thither. Coyote said, "You must go by water." Accordingly they prepared to swim. They attired themselves in costumes like those worn by medicine-men, with feathers on their heads, and pepperwood boughs about their foreheads. When all were ready to start Coyote said, "When you get there, you must land and pass around the house four times (in a counter-clockwise direction)."

They reached the house, which was a semi-subterranean dance-house, and followed Coyote's instructions. Then Kabada*te'te*s came out and said, "Why do you men come here? The boy is all right. He will be back at Nō'napōtī in four days." The ten medicine-men had with them a special wand[139] which possessed magic powers. When they finished their ceremony Kabada*te'te*s went to sleep. They then took Duck out of the house and burned the structure with Kabada*te'te*s in it.

Duck was much changed, owing to the magic of Kabada*te'te*s for he now had a human head while the rest of his body had its original bird form. However, they took him back to Nō'napōtī and turned him over to Coyote.

When Coyote saw the boy he did not know just what to do with him. He wanted to change his name but decided that that would not do.

II

(Coyote Catches Ground Squirrels by Magic)

Coyote went over to see Chicken Hawk (I'lil), who was famous as a hunter. He wanted to fool Hawk. He asked Hawk, "How do you do when you hunt squirrels. I should like to hunt just the same as you do." Hawk would not tell him so Coyote went away.

Coyote changed his form and became a fine-looking young woman. Then he came back and also immediately Hawk fell in love with Coyote and they married. That night Coyote again asked Hawk how he suc-ceeded in killing so many squirrels. Hawk now told Coyote all about it and showed him all the tricks he used. Then Hawk discovered that Coyote was really a man and not the fine young woman he had thought.

---

[139]Called "sima'koo".

Coyote went out and placed an abalone-shell ornament[140] on each finger. Then in accordance with Hawk's instructions, he put his arm, full length, down in a ground-squirrel hole. The squirrels got hold of these ornaments and Coyote was able to pull them out. Thus he captured many squirrels.

Coyote was, however, not satisfied with catching what squirrels he really needed as food. He went right on catching more and more all the time, this method was so easy. Finally the squirrels became angry and pulled Coyote's arm off.

Coyote returned home very sick. He went to bed and put an old, dry, mush-oak limb (pa'lo) in place of his arm. It immediately became a real arm.

Coyote told the people to get together and have a dance at Maiyï' to celebrate his recovery. Another chief[141] there said "Yes, that is good. We have ordered a dance, but we must first have a dance-house. We will all turn in and build a dance-house. First we will dig the pit." So all started to dig, the chief himself assisting.

After a while he dug up a Chub duck (tana') The chief picked up the duck and sat it on the bank. He wondered how it came to be down there in the ground and observed that it was a very beautiful bird.

Next the poles and other materials for the roof were brought. Then the chief called the women to help put the earth cover on the roof.

Then he told Duck to go out and get the wood for the dance-house. Duck went off over to Cow mountain.[142] Here he gathered all the manzanita that grew on the entire mountain and carried it down in one load. That is the reason why there is now no manzanita growing on this mountain. In fact there is just one bush. This grew from a stick which Duck lost from his load as he came down the mountainside. When Duck got back to the village he had so much wood that it covered the entire dance-house completely.

All the people[143] were already inside and ready for the dance. Coyote was the chief and directed the ceremony. He called the people to the dance-house and supervised the whole thing.

---

[140]From Haliotis or abalone shells are made ornaments of various shapes which are especially used as pendants at the ends of strings of beads. They are used in certain ornaments of the person but more especially on fine basketry. These ornaments ar called "hwil".
[141]Also called "Coyote".
[142]This mountain, called "Ca'kabē", is located a short distance from Upper Lake.
[143]All were Ground Squirrels except Coyote, Meadowlark, Blue Jay and Duck.

The Ground Squirrels (Xōma′r) were the first to dance. They danced the war dance, after which a feast was served to all the peole. Then Coyote danced. He said, "When I dance past you must all turn your heads toward the fire." Coyote had a magic wand (simako′o) with which he put all the Ground Squirrels to sleep. Then he tied their hair together, each to that of his neighbor's. Then he set fire to the house.

Meadowlark flew out and lighted in a field. Blue Jay lighted in a tree, and Duck in the lake. Coyote also ran out and saved himself. There were only Ground Squirrels left in the dance-house.

When the fire had died down all the Ground Squirrels were cooked. Coyote gathered them up and gave one each to the many old Bullfrog-women who sat constantly in their houses weaving baskets of tule. There were many roasted squirrels left. These he told the Bullfrog-women to watch for him while he was gone. He told them that they must not take any because he could see them even if he was far away and would know everything they did.

Now, in those times there was no brush to be found nearer than Scotts' Valley, so Coyote went there to get some willow poles to build a house in which to store these squirrels. When he returned he threw down his load of poles near the pile of cooked squirrels. As he made this great noise the squirrels jumped up and ran away.

Then Coyote upbraided the Bullfrog-women, saying, "I told you to pick out the best ones and put them away. Why did you not do as I told you?"

III

(Coyote Regulates Death)

The fact is that some of the women had eaten heartily of the squirrels. One had eaten so many that she presently died. They burned her body, but she came back to life in four days.

Meadowlark and Blue Jay were present when Bullfrog returned. Lark sniffed the air and asked, "What is it that smells so badly around here?" Blue Jay had in his hand just then a wooden implement (xa′ibahlaū). Meadowlark's question made him mad and he shoveled hot coals onto Meadowlark, saying "That will do, now, you had better keep quiet."

Coyote then stated that thereafter he intended to make all people

return to life after four days. Lark, however, objected that this was not
wise because those returning from the dead had such a foul odor. That
is the real reason why Coyote arranged it so that people do not return
after death.

Besides, if he had arranged matters so that the dead would return
there would be too many people in the world. There would be the same
old ones here all the time and finally the world would get so full that
there would be no room for newcomers. Hence no more children would
be born.

IV

(Coyote Builds Kelsey Creek and Establishes Fishing Customs)

Coyote went down to Nō'napōti and commenced to make what is
now Kelsey Creek. He finished it all in one day. As fast as he dug it
out the fish followed him up from the lake. A particular kind of fish,
hī'tc, followed him so closely that he finally had to tell them not to
come so rapidly. Then they stayed back a little distance. He built the
creek way up into the mountains and did it all in one day. At first the
fish did not go up into the headwaters of Kelsey Creek but they do now.

Next Coyote made a conical fish-trap (ca'mītce). He did not cut
the brush and weave the trap as we do now. He simply wove the trap
on a bush just as it was standing. He did not take the trap off the bush.
However, he went right on making these traps, two for each person he
invited to come here to fish.

He sent out invitations to come fishing, in his new stream, to the
people in all the neighboring villages, even as far over as the Russian
River settlements. Everyone who came brought beads as presents.
These were divided among the people of the village at Kelseyville. In
return they received great quantities of the special fish. This was the
start of the custom which the people of Big Valley have ever since followed, that of sending out invitations for fishing whenever it is the
season for the run of this special fish.

Then Coyote said, "Well I guess I will go to Upper Lake and see
what they are doing up there." Another Coyote was chief of that village.
"Let us all go up there and see what they are going to do. This is the
last good time we can have here until the fish run next year."

So they all went to Upper Lake.[144]

---

[144]The entire Upper Lake region was called "ka'kaiyaū".

64—GROUND-SQUIRRELS STEAL COYOTE'S ARM TO MAKE A RATTLE[145]

INCIDENTS AND CHARACTERS

I. *Coyote loses his arm.*
   1. *Coyote, 2. The Crow-women (two), 3. Falcon.*
II. *Coyote builds a dance-house.*
   1. *Coyote, 2. The Crow-women (two), 3. Chub Duck.*
III. *Coyote burns the Ground-squirrel-people.*
   1. *The Ground-squirrel-people, 2. Coyote, 3. Chub Duck.*
IV. *The Ground-squirrel-people come to life.*
   1. *Coyote, 2. The Crow-women, 3. The Ground-squirrel-people.*

I

(Coyote Loses His Arm)

At the old village of Maiyï'[146] lived Coyote. He lived alone except for a couple of Crow-women who were blind and who lived at some little distance from Coyote's house. Coyote had the power to transform himself into any thing he wished, so he became a very beautiful maiden and took up a place beside the trail along which he knew that Falcon was going to come. Falcon, who was a famous hunter, presently came along and as soon as he had seen this fine-looking girl he fell in love with her and took her home as his wife. During the evening the girl asked Falcon how he managed to catch so many ground squirrels. Falcon replied, "I first place on my hands some bright bits of abalone shell; then I go out and find a ground-squirrel hole and put my hand as far as possible into the hole. When the squirrels see the pieces of shell they come onto my hand. Then I draw my hand out very carefully and kill the squirrels. No matter how many squirrels I kill in this way there are just as many left in the hole." This was all that Coyote wanted to know, so during the night he became himself again and when Falcon awoke in the morning he found that his new wife was gone.

Coyote, now in his old form, returned home and soon he went out to try the new method of catching squirrels. The first time he put his hand down into the hole he got several squirrels. He tried it two or three times more with good success. Finally, however, the squirrels

---

[145]The Pomo title of this myth is "gûnûla lal gᶜûmar hûla bagᶜal pûdïagᶜï 'mïhya' tïhlim tïhlim'" "Coyote Ground-squirrel shoulder 'your bone rattle rattle'".
Informant: Tom Mitchell, Eastern dialect, 1902.
[146]Univ. Calif., Publ., Amer. Arch. Ethn., VI, 155, 1908.

became suspicious of the hand that was being put down into their hole. It did not look just like the one they were accustomed to when Falcon was hunting. They carefully inspected the hand and found that it was not the one they liked so they concluded to catch and hold it there in the hole. Accordingly all took a good hold and in spite of all the pulling that Coyote could do he could not get his hand out. Finally he pulled so hard that he tore the arm off at the shoulder.

The wound bled a great deal, so Coyote found some pendant moss on a tree and plugged up the wound with it. Then he found an elder-berry stick which he put in place of his arm. Then he went home.

II

(Coyote Builds a Dance-house)

A long time passed and finally Coyote went out in the place where he lived and delivered a long speech just as a chief of a large village would do. Of course, there were no people here except the two blind Crows, so when Coyote called upon all the people to come and help him build a big dance-house no one responded, and Coyote set about building it alone. First he started to dig the pit. He had not dug far when he dug up Chub duck (*T*ana). Duck was a good worker and the two soon had the whole dance-house completed and everything prepared for the dance.

III

(Coyote Burns the Ground-squirrel-people)

When the Ground-squirrel-people saw that the dance-house was finished they decided to go over and take possession of it and have a good dance. Accordingly they prepared dancing suits and everything else that we now use at such times. The only thing that was very differ-ent from our present way was that they made the bangles on their head-dresses out of the bones of Coyote's arm which they had cut up into small bits. They also made some banner-like poles which they decorated with the pieces of the bones of Coyote's arm. These they carried along when they went over to Coyote's village. They rattled these purposely as they went along just so as to tantalize Coyote. They also sang a song about them: "mīhya′, mīhya′, tīli′m tīli′m: your bone, your bone, rattle rattle." This especially infuriated Coyote.

There were so many of the Ground-squirrel-people, however, that Coyote decided to take his revenge by fooling them. Accordingly he welcomed them all as if nothing had happened to anger him. They all danced for a long time and finally, in the middle of the night, they began to get sleepy. Coyote announced that it was the custom in his village that those with the longest hair should always sleep with their feet nearest the fire, thus forming the inner circle. Those with shorter hair were to sleep in an outer circle, placing their feet between the heads of the ones in the inner circle. The Ground-squirrel-people all went to sleep in that way. When all were sleeping soundly Coyote went about and tied the hair of each to the feet of the one nearest, thus connecting all the Squirrel-people together.

Meantime Coyote had sent Duck up onto Cow Mountain to get wood. Duck pulled up by the roots every manzanita bush on the mountain. That is the reason that there are no manzanita bushes to be found on that entire mountain today. Duck was very powerful and was able to carry this entire load of brush home at a single trip. He reached the dance-house about the time that Coyote had finished tying the hair of the Ground-squirrel-people and the two piled the brush on top of the dance-house, in the door and in the smoke-hole. Then Coyote set fire to it.

As soon as it began to get hot in the dance-house the Ground Squirrels roused up and tried to escape, but each one found that he was held fast either by his hair or by his feet. So they fell to fighting among themselves because each thought that his neighbor was holding him purposely. So it was that all these Squirrel-people were killed and roasted.

IV

(The Ground-squirrel-people Come to Life)

Now, Coyote fell to thinking how he might save this great lot of meat which was so nicely roasted. So he went out to get some coarse grass.[147] On the way he met the two blind Crow-women making their way toward the sweat-house. He told them, "You must not go there and take any of that meat. I have counted all of those squirrels and shall know it if you touch any of them. I want them all for myself. If you

---

[147]This is a coarse grass, called "mūtī'p", which is much used for drying fish. It is spread upon the ground and keeps the fish out of the sand or dirt while it is drying.

take any of them I shall surely kill you." Nevertheless the old women did take quite a number of the squirrels and carried them home.

Presently Coyote returned with a great load of the grass. When he threw it down near the dance-house all the Squirrels came to life, jumped up and ran away.

Then Coyote went over to where the old Crow-women lived and ate some of the offal from the few squirrels which they had taken. He was very angry and asked, "Why did you not take a whole lot of those squirrels? I told you to take as many as you wanted."

The old women replied, "No you did not. You told us that if we took any of them you would kill us."

Coyote then said, "No, I did not say that. I told you to take a lot. You should have taken more."

65—COYOTE IS TRICKED BY THE SKUNK BROTHERS[148]

Characters: 1. Skunk brothers (two), 2. Coyote, 3. Parents of the Skunk boys, 4. Blue Jay, 5. Crow brothers (two), 6. Kingfisher brothers (two), 7. Buzzard brothers (two), 8. Vulture brothers (two), 9. Kabaʹnasiksik brothers (two), 10. Kūʹksūs (two).

The two Skunk brothers lived on the east side of Bloody Island, which is at the northern end of Upper Lake. One day they decided to go out hunting grasshoppers. Each took his hunting sack and they started off northeastward from the big rock which was really their house. They went by way of a big canyon and finally reached a large open place, called "Kabaʹi gagō" (buckeye field), which was a very good place in which to hunt grasshoppers. They caught a great many of these insects here. They caught them by hand, one at a time, and threw them into their bags.

Presently they saw Coyote coming over the hill. He was coming from Cīʹwa. As he came up to where the boys were he held out his hand and said, "Give me some of those. I should like to try them." The younger of the Skunks gave him one grasshopper which he ate at once. Then he asked for some more. The elder of the boys gave him one and the younger gave him two. These he ate and called for more. Again they each gave him two grasshoppers. Then Coyote said, "If you boys will give me a handful at a time I will soon eat what I want, and then

---

[148]Informant: Mary Louie, Eastern dialect.

I will take you both out hunting with me." They agreed and each gave
him a handful. This they repeated four times. He ate all these and
there was only a few grasshoppers left in the sack of the younger
brother. The boy gave him the sack so that he could pour the rest into
his mouth. But Coyote ate sack and all. The boy tried to stop him, but
Coyote said, "That is all right, you will get your sack back. You will
find it in my excrement." Then he asked the elder of the Skunk brothers
for his sack and ate that also.

Then Coyote took the Skunk boys up the mountain to a chemese
ridge. Here he took his station ready to shoot any deer that came over
the ridge. He sent the Skunk boys down into the canyons on either
side of the ridge to drive out the deer. One deer came along presently.
Coyote shot it and hid it away before the Skunks came back. He then
went to a spring farther up the ridge where he leaned his bow and
arrows up against a tree and sat down to rest.

When the boys came up they noticed that one of the arrows had
some blood on it. One of them said, "How is this, uncle, your arrow
has blood on it."

Coyote replied, "O, I killed a snake, that is snake's blood."

Shortly one of the boys again asked what kind of blood was on the
arrow. Coyote answered that it was frog's blood. The third time the
question was repeated he said it was the blood of a waterdog that he
had killed. The fourth time, however, he replied truthfully that it was
the blood of a deer. Then he went and got the deer from where he had
hidden it. He spread some brush upon which to place the meat as he
cut up the deer. He put all the good meat on one side and the offal on
the other side. Next he built a big fire and cooked the liver and the entrails, telling the boys to eat all they could. This they did for they were
very hungry.

Coyote then sent the boys out to get some white-oak withes with
which to tie up the meat so that they might take it home. While they
were gone Coyote cut up and cooked the best parts of the meat. Any
that were burned he threw to one side. The rest he ate. When the boys
returned Coyote told them that they had brought the wrong kind of
material, even though they had secured some very fine, long withes of
white oak for him. He then gave them some of the burned pieces of
meat and sent them off again to look for the right kind of withes. As

soon as they were gone he cooked more of the choice parts of the meat and ate them. This time the Skunk boys brought grape-vines, but Coyote told them that they had made another mistake and sent them out again. So they went time after time until they had brought all the different kinds of trees, bushes, tules, etc.[149] Finally they brought a material called "bō'dehase." Coyote said, "Yes, yes cousins that is what I want." Coyote had kept the Skunk boys going so long that they were nearly tired out. Meanwhile he himself had eaten nearly all the deer. In fact there was nothing left except the head, hide, and bones. These Coyote fixed up to look like a good big pack of meat and they all started for home.

At first Coyote carried the pack while the little boys followed him. Finally they came past a place called "Ganō'sai" and over to an open country. Here Coyote laid down the pack and went over to a place a little off the trail. The boys looked the pack over and the younger tried to lift it. Then the elder tried it. Finally both succeeded in carrying it.

As they went down the trail Coyote saw them and said to himself, "That is good that my cousins are carrying the deer off. I have already eaten the best parts."

The Skunk boys knew that Coyote had tricked them and they wanted to steal the deer meat and get even with him. As they looked back and saw Coyote sitting there they pronounced a curse upon him. They said, "A grape-vine will grow up into your body. This will hold you where you are until we get home. After we reach home you will be able to pull the grape-vine out of your body and stuff up the hole with some grass."

It happened as they willed and they reached home safely. Finally Coyote succeeded in getting the grape-vine out of his body. He stuffed some grass into the opening and finally arrived home.

When Coyote got to his house he sat down and commenced to cry. His mother said to him, "What is the matter with you anyway. Can you never beat anyone at anything you try." She then offered him food but he said that he was not hungry and refused the food. Before Coyote had left the house that morning he had been making some bows and arrows. Presently he resumed this work. He had a fire in the center of the house and as he finished the arrows he stood them up around the

---

[149]The following were specifically named by the informant: bagō', tsīwi'c, tsū'baha, kūca'l, kūhū'm, gūca'l, and bō'dehase.

fire to dry. He was using a large obsidian knife in shaping the arrows. He was also chewing some deer sinew in order to get it soft and pliable for binding the arrow-heads onto the ends of the shafts. This he did while he was chipping the heads out of obsidian.[150] He worked thus all night and finally finished his full set of arrows, and finished a fine bow with a good bow-string.

Next morning he took his bow and arrows and went outside of the house and shouted for everyone to come and join him. Of course he knew that there was no one else there except his father who was so old that he could not work or hunt or anything of that kind. Then Coyote ran down south for some distance. Here he stopped and called as loudly as he could, "Cīwa hītōnō ————, tcetamalil kabōtca mēka."[151]

No one answered his call, so he ran on toward the south again until he reached a certain point called "Tōtsawa'laka," a little to the southeast of Bloody Island. Here he stopped and shouted as before, with the same result. He ran on southward to a point, called "Cūhnī'la" (bow sun), half a mile or so south of the last, and again called, but without result. About half a mile farther on he again stopped and called, but, hearing no reply, he ran down to a place called "Xōdee'lim," on the eastern shore of the lake. Here stood a large rock so Coyote climbed up on top of it and again called as before. He heard no reply, but when he looked around he noticed smoke rising from beneath his feet, in fact it was coming right up between his toes. Coyote moved his foot and saw the smoke curling up from a very small crack in the rock. He shot first one arrow and then another into this crack but all broke into splinters. Then he took his bow and tried to pry the crack open. Of course he only broke the bow.

During the previous night the Skunk boys had eaten all of the remaining meat and had filled the skin with grass, earth, and all kinds of other refuse. Now they called out to Coyote, "Uncle, uncle, the whole meat is here yet." Coyote then caught hold of the head which they thrust out of the crack in the rock and began to pull on it. The Skunk boys told him to shut his eyes and pull as hard as he could. The Skunk boys and their father and mother pulled against Coyote. So Coyote

---

[150]The informant stated that this chipping was done with another stone which was very much harder and bluish in color.
[151]A call freely translated by the informant as "where do you fellows stay".

pulled and pulled for a long time without success, and until he was very tired. Then the Skunk boys said to Coyote, "Now shut your eyes very tightly and pull as hard as you possibly can." As he did this all four of the Skunks let go and Coyote fell over backward, striking against a rock that was down behind him. As he struck the rock he said, "ai————." His back was broken.

Then all the Skunks came out of the rock, which was really their house, and the old folks pounded Coyote up like rabbit-meat and threw him down in the tule. As they did so, the old woman said, "Yes, yes, that is the way to do it when dealing with a bad man. You made my boys give out. The poor fellows went out to gather grasshoppers and you took away all they caught. Then you took them out to hunt and you ate all the best parts of the meat and gave them only hard work."

Coyote lay there for a long time but finally Blue Jay flew over him and cried, "tasi, tsai, tsai, tsai," as usual. He did this four times and upon each occasion he perched for a time on a nearby bush. Then Coyote said, "I smell the nice blooming fields, but I haven't heard anything. I have just been lying around here for my health. I am not hurt anywhere." Then he saw Blue Jay and said to him, "You are an ugly looking fellow. Your legs are all cracked. You are a bony fellow and your eyes are all sunken." Then he yelled, "tcīyūhe'——————." This he repeated four times.

The people way off in a village toward the south heard the cry that Coyote gave. Here there lived two brothers, Crows. The chief called them and said to them, "I think I hear some trouble over there somewhere. You two must dress up in full costume and go over there to see what it is all about." They put on the different parts of their suits in the following order: head-net, down, trembler plumes, yellowhammer-feather forehead-band, feather tuft, feather skirt, and whistle.[152] When they were fully dressed they started off northward to see what was the trouble, constantly blowing their whistles as they ran. They went directly to the spot where Coyote lay and proceeded to doctor him. First they ran four times around him in a clockwise direction as he lay on his back with his head toward the north. Then they halted at Coyote's feet.

---

[152]The native names of these articles are: bŏ'lmakĭ, te, kaṭa's, tsō'lŏpa, biṭe'rk, xaicī'gĭ, and lĭbū' respectively.

He said, "Ya————————, you are not the fellows that I sent for. You are lousy and full of nits. You are ugly looking fellows."

The Crows went over under a tree a short distance away.

Again Coyote gave the same four long cries that he used in giving his first call. Again the chief of this same village heard the call. This time he sent the two Kingfisher brothers, dressed the same as their predecessors, to visit Coyote. When they reached the place where Coyote lay they did just as the others had done. When they stopped Coyote said, "He————————, you are not the fellows I called. You are ugly looking fellows. You eat nothing but fish." Then they went over with the Crows and sat down there.

For a third time Coyote called. This time two Buzzards came and tried to doctor Coyote. But Coyote told them, "You are not the ones I want. You are ugly fellows with bald, wrinkley heads." They too, went over and sat under the tree with the others.

The fourth time he called, Vultures came, but Coyote told them, "I didn't call you fellows. You are dirty fellows. You eat rotten meat and fish. You are always looking for some rotten stuff to eat." The Vultures then went over under the trees with the others.

So Coyote went on calling, time after time, and each time the chief sent a different kind of bird to doctor him until nearly every kind of bird had come. Coyote, however, turned each one of them away in the same manner. The last one to come was a small bird called "Kaba'-nasiksik." Then Coyote said, "I do not want any of you fellows. I want a real doctor. None of you knows how to cure anyone."

The Coyote called for the last time. This time he called for Kū'ksū. It was the first time that he had said just whom he wanted to doctor him. The two Kū'ksūs dressed up as the others had done but put on a big-head head-dress and a skirt of shredded tule. They fastened the head-dresses on with very long skewers. Each brought his special wand[153] which he used for doctoring. When they arrived Coyote laughed and was very pleased for they were the ones he had wanted all the time. With their wands they pried at Coyote's mangled body from all sides, and then they rolled the wands over him in various ways. Presently Coyote's body came together and the Kū'ksūs took hold of his wrists

---

[153]The informant said this was a black stick an inch or so in diameter and about four feet in length. It was called "kalū'l".

and pulled. This brought Coyote to his feet. As soon as the Kū'ksūs began to doctor Coyote the others who had tried to cure him started away and by the time he was well all were gone.

66—THE SKUNK BROTHERS TRICK COYOTE[154]

Characters: 1. Coyote, 2. Skunk brothers.

Coyote hunted with a deer mask. The Skunk brothers were watching him one day and saw him kill something. They went up to him and asked what he had killed. He showed them a deer that he had killed and told them to take its entrails out and get it ready to carry back to the village. They set about this work and told Coyote to find some kind of a good rope with which to carry it. He brought first one kind of thing and then another but none suited the purpose so he finally decided to go over to the ocean to hunt for something.

While he was gone they made a tie out of hazel and carried the deer over to their house which was a large rock at Kabe'ndōlaū, just north of a prominent rocky mountain, known as Rock-pile and located on the North Fork of the Gualala River at a point about twelve miles from the coast.

Coyote tracked the two Skunk brothers to their house. After he had called repeatedly to them to come out, he saw a small hole in the top of the rock. He climbed up on top of the rock and thrust his spear through the hole several times. Finally the Skunk boys put some blood on the spear and when Coyote saw this he thought that he had killed the Skunk boys.

By and by they called out to Coyote and told him that they had the whole deer in there and that they would give it to him if he would pull it out of the hole. They had filled the skin with grass and made it look as if it were a real deer. When he pulled it out and found how they had fooled him he was very angry.

Then the Skunk brothers came out on the other side of the rock and laughed at Coyote. He said, "Well, you fellows fooled me all right, now we better have a game. Let us have a shooting contest. You go over there on the other side of the gulch, lie down there, shut your eyes and open your mouth." Coyote shot at one of them and missed. Then

---

[154]The Pomo title of this myth is "Mpē' kawī matū", "Skunk boys' story."
Informant: William James, Central dialect.

Coyote lay down and one of the Skunk boys shot and hit him in the mouth. Then the Skunk brothers went home.

After a while the younger of the Skunk brothers went out to look for Coyote but he was not there. He had come to life and gone away.

67—COYOTE IS TRICKED AND KILLED BY SKUNK BROTHERS[155]

Characters: 1. Coyote, 2. Skunk brothers (nephews of Coyote), 3. Blue Jay.

Coyote lived at Maiyī'.[156] With him lived his two nephews, the Skunk brothers. One day he went out and spent the whole day setting snares over on Hma'r danō.[157] The next morning he said to his nephews, "Come, boys, let us go over and see our snares now." They went from one to another until they found one which had caught a large four-pronged buck.

Coyote said, "Now, boys, get something with which to make a net to carry this meat. Get some tule (bō'dĭhase)." The boys did not know what this was but they started off to hunt for it. Presently they returned with some grape-vine.

Coyote said, "Why, boys, this is no bō'dĭhase. Go a little farther out when you look for it."

Next they brought him hemp, but Coyote said, "That is not bō'dĭhase. Go still farther out. You are now very close to it."

Then they brought him successively, nettle, and wire-grass, and finally the tule for which he had asked. Coyote was much pleased and wove a carrying net from it.

They started for home, Coyote carrying the carcass for a long distance. Finally he became tired and laid down his burden to rest. He said to the boys, "I am going aside here for a little while. Will you not try to carry the load for a short distance?"

The smaller of the Skunk boys said, "Now, brother, let me try to carry it." But the elder insisted that he should make the attempt. He found that he could rise with the load but could not take a step. Then the smaller brother tried. He found that he could carry it quite easily. When they had gone a short distance, they said, "We wish that the old

---

[155]Informant: Dave Thompson, Upper Lake, Eastern dialect, 1904.
[156]This is an old village-site at the foot-hills on the extreme western side of Upper Lake Valley, Lake County. See Univ. Calif. Publ., Amer. Arch. Ethn., VI, p. 155, and map.
[157]This is a mountain about one and one-half miles east of the present town of Upper Lake.

man would 'stick fast' where he is now." Coyote found that he could not rise.

Meanwhile the boys journeyed on along the eastern shore of Clear Lake to Bicē gauk kedī,[158] where there was a rock house.

Finally Coyote became desperate, and pulled out all his intestines. He then filled the cavity with tree moss (xalē' sībū). He started on the trail. When he had gone a short distance he stopped and called for the boys. So he went on and on calling at short intervals. The fourth time he called he had just crossed a small slough and had climbed up on a big rock. As he stood here he could see smoke issuing from just between his toes.

The Skunk boys said, "Here we are Uncle, here we are. We haven't done anything with that deer yet. He is just the same."

The fact is that the boys had eaten the whole of the deer except the head. This they stuck partially out of the small door of the house, and then they said, "Uncle, you just take hold of the head and pull the deer out. Pull as hard as you can."

Coyote did so, but the boys pulled against him. Now, there was a large rock just behind Coyote, so that when the boys suddenly let go Coyote fell over against it and was stunned. Then the Skunk brothers went out and beat Coyote to death.

As Coyote's body lay there, Blue Jay came along and flew over it, talking very loudly. Coyote said, "See here, Blue Jay, don't talk so loudly when a person wants to sleep. I was feeling happy and was just taking a fine rest when you woke me up."

Then Coyote went back to Maiyī'.

68—COYOTE IS TRICKED BY THE SKUNK BROTHERS AND AGAIN BY SMALL BIRDS[159]
INCIDENTS AND CHARACTERS

I. *Coyote is tricked by the Skunk brothers.*
    1. *Coyote, 2. Skunk brothers (two), 3. Blue Jay.*
II. *Coyote is tricked by small birds.*
    1. *Coyote, 2. Small birds, 3. Tree, 4. Blue Jay.*

---

[158]This place is located about one-half mile south of Bloody Island which is in the northern part of Clear Lake.
[159]Informant: Lee Peters, Yokaia, Central dialect, 1914.

I

(Coyote Is Tricked by the Skunk Brothers)

Coyote lived alone at Xaba'i.[160] While out hunting he found two little Skunks. They were just big enough to run around. Coyote said to them, "Come on, boys, let us go hunting. We will kill deer and take them to my house. I will give you the best parts of the meat to eat if you will help me to carry the game home." The Skunk boys agreed and followed Coyote. Finally they saw a deer and Coyote told the boys to remain a little way behind while he shot the deer.

When the deer was killed Coyote told the Skunks to go and get a long kelp.[161] They did not know what that was but started off in search of it anyway. Presently they returned with some pepperwood boughs. Coyote told them that that was not what he wanted and again sent them out. Each time they returned with some new kind of a branch or vine Coyote told them that it was not what he wanted and again sent them off.

Meanwhile Coyote had skinned the deer and he finally said to the boys, "It is of no use for you to look for the kelp. You cannot find it. I shall go for it. You two stay here and watch this meat while I am gone. Do not go away or I shall follow you and kill you with my bow and arrows. Do you understand?"

The Skunks replied, "Yes, we understand. We will stay right here and will not allow anyone to touch the meat while you are away."

So, after a while, Coyote returned with the kelp, but the boys were gone and there remained only a pile of brush where the deer had been. When Coyote kicked over the pile of brush and found nothing, he exclaimed, "ai!"[162] He began to look for the Skunks' tracks and after a long time he found them. He began tracking them toward the south. He would run a short distance, stop, listen, and then call to the boys: "hū————tsa kawiku-laiya." He did this four times as he ran along. Then he stopped running and walked on. He was tired, angry and very hot.

Finally he thought he heard something. It sounded like boys laughing, so he put his ear to the ground and listened, then to a tree to see

---

[160]This is an old camp-site located on the west shore of Clear Lake, Lake County. See Univ. Calif. Publ., Amer. Arch. Ethn., VI. 158, Map, 1908.
[161]The term for "kelp" is "ka'ce", but the term used in this instance is "bō'na ka'ce", a ceremonial designation.
[162]Made by a short, quick inhalation.

if they were up in the tree. But he could hear nothing, so he started on.

Presently he came to an opening in which stood a big boulder. He climbed up on this and again gave his call as before. He heard a very faint answer, as if from afar or as if from deep down in the ground. He jumped down and ran around the rock and again listened. He could hear nothing so he travelled on until he came to another similar boulder. Here he repeated his shouting and listening. Again he heard an answering call, but this time it seemed nearer. A little farther on he came to a third such boulder. This time the answer was quite plain.

Finally he came to a big rock at the mouth of a canyon. Here he shouted, as before, four times. Then he heard the answer very plainly. He looked all around and finally he looked under his foot. From a small crevice in the rock there issued a tiny curl of smoke. Then he called to the Skunks and told them to come out of there. This rock was in reality their house.

The Skunk brothers only laughed at Coyote, and told him that there was a door on the south side of the rock. Coyote ran around until he found the door, which was a circular hole not more than six inches across, and through which, of course, Coyote could not enter.

Then Coyote said, "You boys come out of there. What have you done with my meat?"

They replied, "Your meat is here. We thought we would bring it home for you till you returned. It is all here. We have taken nothing out. We will stick the legs out so you can pull the deer out." Coyote agreed and they put the hind feet of the deer through the small opening.

They asked, "Do you see the legs now?"

Coyote replied, "Yes."

Then they said, "Catch hold of them and pull hard. It is very heavy, since we did not take off any of the meat. The hole is so small that you must pull very hard.

Coyote was meantime anxiously pulling, and he said, "That is all right. I have pulled it about half out already." He thought he heard the boys laughing as they told him, "We will say 'pull' four times and each time you must pull very hard so that we can push from the inside here and help you. That is the only way you can ever get it out of here."

Coyote did pull very hard each time the Skunks gave the word, and the last time it came out with a great jerk which threw him over back-

wards, deer and all, down into the bottom of the canyon. This broke
every bone in his body and killed him.

The Skunk brothers came out and saw Coyote's body lying there in
the canyon and laughed for a long time over the joke they had played
on him.

Coyote lay there dead until the next spring. In fact only his bones
were left by that time. Finally Blue Jay saw Coyote's bones lying here
and he flew around them repeatedly, crying, "tsai, tsai, tsai, tsai." This
attracted all the other birds who gathered around and watched Blue Jay.
After a time Coyote sat up, rubbed his eyes, and said, "Ha—— ha——,
you are always making a big noise whenever a fellow wants to sleep.
I have been sleeping here where I could breathe the fresh, sweet air as
it blows off from that field."

II

(Coyote Is Tricked by Small Birds)

Coyote then arose and walked toward the south. He came to an open
place where there were many small birds. They saw him and flew into
the bushes. When Coyote came to where the birds had disappeared he
stopped and peered into the bushes. He saw one of the birds and asked,
"Why do you do that? Why do you fly up that way into the thick
brush?"

The bird replied, "We do that because we are happy."

Coyote said, "You are happy when you fly into the bushes that way?"

The bird said, "Yes."

Then Coyote asked, "But how do you do it? How can you fly that
way?"

The bird replied, "Well you go back quite a ways in the clearing
there so that we can do so and we will come out and show you how we
do it. Now you go back to the other side of that bush and do not look
this way until I come over there and tell you to."

Then all the birds made many sharp sticks and set them in the edge
of the brush. They were set so that Coyote could not miss them when he
ran into the brush. Then the birds went over to Coyote and showed him
where to run into the brush. They told him to sit around where he then
was until he saw someone coming and then to run hard into the brush.
He agreed to this but asked how he was to fly. The birds agreed to give

him a feather apiece. So each bird contributed a feather and they placed these all over Coyote's body. Then the birds all went away.

Coyote sat around in the opening for some time, just as he had seen the birds doing. Finally he saw someone coming. He ran and flew into the brush as the birds had done. In doing so, however, one of the sticks the birds had placed put one of Coyote's eyes out. This was very painful. Coyote yelled and cried around, begging everyone for another eye.

Finally he went to Tree, and Tree gave him some moss, which Coyote placed in the eye-socket.

Presently Blue Jay came along and sang over Coyote and doctored him and caused his eye to return. Then Blue Jay said, "I will tell you what is the matter with you, and why you have such bad luck. You are a good hunter, but you never give a feast. You must remember that next time."

Then Coyote went home.[163]

69—COYOTE IS TRICKED BY SAPSUCKER[164]

INCIDENTS AND CHARACTERS

I. Sapsucker tricks Coyote in hair-dressing.
    1. Sapsucker, 2. Coyote, 3. Frog (wife of Coyote).
II. Sapsucker tricks Coyote in getting wood.
    1. Coyote, 2. Sapsucker, 3. Frog.
III. Coyote and Frog dance for food.
    1. Oak Ball, 2. Blue Jay (chief of the village), 3. Coyote, 4. Frog.
IV. Falcon kills Kï'lak and Sun-man.
    1. Fish Hawk, 2. Falcon, 3. Sun-man, 4. Coyote-old-man, 5. Kï'lak, 6. Putrid-old-man.
V. Barn Owl gambles.
    1. Barn Owl, 2. Falcon.
VI. The Wanderings of Fox.
    1. Fox, 2. Wildcat (wife of Fox), 3. Fox (son of Wildcat), 4. Blue Jay, 5. Ground-squirrel-people, 6. Wasp, 7. Panther, 8. Crane, 9. Crane's wife, 10. Frog, 11. Mosquito-people, 12. Water-bird-people, 13. Sea-lion-people.

---

[163]The Informant could not recall just what happened on Coyote's homeward journey, but said that he had other experiences.
[164]Informant: Mary Louie, Eastern dialect.

I

(Sapsucker Tricks Coyote in Hair-dressing)

At Kūca'danō yō near Upper Lake lived all kinds of birds and mammals in the old days.

Sapsucker (kana'bati'ltil) was always making head-nets (bō'lmaki).

Coyote asked him how he made the string and how he wove the head-nets and added, "I know, of course, that you never tell me the truth, but I really want you to answer me truthfully and tell me this time because I want to make one of those head-nets and fix myself up in a nice manner the way you do."

"All right," said Sapsucker, "I will tell you the truth. I go and get my material for making the string from the kō'lōlō. I scrape the outer part and handle it just as they do in making string from milkweed fibre (maca'). When I get it mashed up in good shape I put it by the fire in order to get it very dry. Then I twist and splice it together until I have four long pieces, each about ten or fifteen times as long as a man's arm. Then I make the head-net. When the net is finished I comb my hair this way. I wet it a little and tie it up securely and I fasten it all up with a hair-skewer (kanō)."

Coyote did not believe what he was told and said to Sapsucker, "Oh now do tell me the truth." Sapsucker then repeated the same instructions but still Coyote refused to believe him.

Then Sapsucker said to Coyote, "I will tell you how it is done. I go out into the woods and look around until I find a pine tree that has a fine lot of soft gum (gō'te kalē kahwē). I take a large piece of bark and put in all the bark will hold. Then I take a hair-skewer and mix into this pitch as much dry dust as it will take, just as we do when we are making a fire in the sweat-house."

"All right," said Coyote, "I will try that." Accordingly on the following morning Coyote went out, found such a tree and made up the mixture and applied it to his head, after carefully combing his hair and tying it up at the back of his head. He mixed the pitch and dust thoroughly, worked it into his hair in good shape and found that it held his hair firmly. He then rubbed his hands thoroughly with some of the dust to remove the pitch which had stuck to them. Then he came home, put on a rabbit-skin blanket and laid down in the sweat-house.

The people noticed how Coyote had primped himself up and said, "I think Coyote has been out with those daughters of Sapsucker. That's why he has fixed himself up so finely."

The fire-tender made a good fire in the sweat-house and got it very warm. Then they said to Coyote, "Why do you not come in and join in the fanning contest. Come in from the east side and since you are feeling so fine today we will let you be the first in the contest."

Coyote was flattered and agreed to this. He went in and they on the opposite side fanned him. He was able to stand it for some minutes but finally he became very hot and he went and lay down again in his old place. Then those on the opposite side ran after him and fanned him still more.

Then Coyote jumped up, ran after them, and fanned them and they in turn again fanned Coyote. They did this back and forth for three times each and the fourth time when he came back from fanning then he cried, "hō tō tō tō tō tō ——." Then he slapped his shoulder. Then the other side followed him up, saying, "This is not good mush (fire). Old woman make this kind. It tastes sour."

Coyote again cried "hō tō tō tō tō tō ——," jumped up and ran out, his head ablaze.

The children were playing out in the village when Coyote came out of the sweat-house and they all cried, "Oh! Coyote-old-Man is burning up" (ē gūnū'la būtsike maLa'ka). He jumped into the water and his whole scalp came off. The boys followed him down to the river to watch him and they made fun of him and yelled at him as before, "Oh! Coyote-old-Man is burning up."

Some of the people of the village came down to see what had happened to Coyote. Coyote's wife, Frog, said, "You are always thinking of something else so that you are constantly getting into trouble."

Some of the other women came out and said, "How is it that Coyote is the one who gets burned and no one else ever gets into such trouble?"

Frog, said, "He put pitch all over his head in order to hold his hair down. That's why he got burned up. Who did you ever see putting pitch on his hair like that?" Frog was very much disgusted with the actions of Coyote but she took him by the arm and took him home and put him into bed and he lay there groaning "tcīai, tcī'ē, tcīoi, tcī'ī."

II

(Sapsucker Tricks Coyote in Getting Wood)

Finally Coyote recovered somewhat and he decided to go out and get some wood. He had to carry it by passing the burden-band of his basket across his chest. His head was too tender to bear the weight of the net.

Again he met Sapsucker to whom he said, "You always get the very best wood of anyone. How do you manage that? It is always good, dry wood and it looks as if you did not pick it up off of the ground. How do you get it?"

To this Sapsucker replied, "I go out into the timber and look for dry limbs up in the trees. I make a wood-hook (baka'r), with which to pull down these dry limbs. If such a dry limb does not come down easily I just let it go and try another one. When I pull on a limb and see that it is going to break and fall I jump out from under just before it breaks off and run out of the way so that it will not hit me when it comes down. Then I go back, pick up the limb and hit it against a log or a tree to break it up until I get it just right to carry and then I go home."

Coyote said, "You never do tell me the truth and I do not see why I always ask you. You ought to tell me the truth some times."

"All right," said Sapsucker, "I always tell you what I do. I tell you again that I take the wood-hook, hook it over one of these dry limbs and pull it off. This is the way I get my good wood. I always tell you the truth."

Coyote did not believe him and asked again, in all three times.

Finally, when Coyote asked him the fourth time, he said, "Very well, I will tell you really how I manage this time. I go out and take a rope with me. I take a long pole and when I see a good dry limb I stand the pole up against the tree and climb up the pole. I rest on the limb a while, then I stand on the limb and jump up and down and when the limb breaks off I jump to one side and catch another limb, and then climb down and get the wood and take it home."

Coyote was very glad to get this information because he felt that he had finally learned the truth about the best method of collecting good dry wood.

Coyote tried this plan and succeeded on the first trial so he came down from the tree loaded up the wood and put a bundle of grass on his forehead to take off the strain of the cord.

Coyote continued to get wood successfully in the same way for three days, each day climbing up and jumping on a dead limb and breaking it off and swinging himself with great agility off this limb before it actually fell. On the fourth day, however, when the limb broke Coyote went down with it and struck the ground very hard and bruised himself very badly. He made a great outcry and he was in great pain. The people came running to see what had happened and said "Coyote has been all bruised up. He fell from a tree and is nearly dead." They cried over him because they felt so badly for him.

Then they made a stretcher (xaitsa'k) and they carried Coyote home to the village. He made a great noise and complained of his injury. When he arrived at the village he asked them to dig a hole in the middle of his house. He instructed them not to dig it too deep but to so place it that when he was laid in it, his head would be toward the place occupied by his wife near the fire.

They did this and then all went out of the house leaving only Coyote's wife to attend him. She sat by the fire crying bitterly. The burden of her song was, "My husband is very poor. He is always starving. He never finds anything. He always has bad luck."

As soon as she began to sing this doleful song Coyote laughed and told her, "Do not sing like that. You must say 'My husband is a rich man. He has plenty of everything, beads and riches of all kinds. He is a very rich man. He is great and has everything.' "

[From this point on Coyote and his wife are entirely lost in this story and the scene changes quickly.]

III

(Coyote and Frog Dance for Food)

Night came and one of the men of the village heard a noise far off. He said, "Hush, children, be quiet. You children always make so much noise. You must keep very quiet and listen to me. I hear some trouble coming far off, making a noise." He heard a song "neū naū, neū neū, naū naū, etc.," and as he listened the song came nearer and nearer, constantly approaching the village. Someone was coming in a canoe across the lake and the burden of his song was, "Where is your village rich man? Where is the chief of this wealthy village?"

Everyone came out and listened but no one could understand this song or surmise what it meant.

Finally they called out a very old woman Oak Ball (Patō'l). She was said to be the smartest woman in the world and had the sharpest eyes and ears. She went down to the shore of the lake and looked off down the lake and then she announced, "That is Coyote-old-man (Gūnū'la-būtsike) and his wife who are coming up here. They are going to dance and have something to eat. They are starving. That is the way they always do when they are starving."

The chief of this village then made an announcement to the people telling him what Oak Ball said and that Coyote and his wife were coming to their village to dance. He instructed the fire-tender to prepare the dance-house and get everything ready for the arrival of Coyote.

Finally when Coyote and his wife, Frog, arrived they were attired in dance costumes made of all kinds of flowers, leaves and branches. They had flowers of all kinds around their heads and in place of a feather cloak and other kinds of costume they wore weeds around their waists. It was springtime and the dance in this case was not held in the regular dance-house but in a large brush house made for the purpose and called "se' hmarak."

When Coyote's canoe came near enough to shore the chief of this village went down to welcome Coyote and his wife and said, "Come right this way. Look down where you step. Be careful that you do not stumble. A person is always bashful when he goes to a different village."

Coyote and Frog came ashore (these were not the same couple with which the early part of this narrative concerns itself but an entirely different Coyote and Frog) and to the dancing place and there they danced four times. They had come from Kabē'napō. When Coyote and his wife had finished with their four dances Blue Jay, who was chief of this village made a speech and told the people to bring such food as they had: mush, pinole, fish and the like, to feed the dancers and make them welcome. The people brought out a great deal of food, basket after basket, and Coyote and his wife began to eat. Coyote took a whole fish and put it into his mouth at once. Then he took a whole basket of soup and poured it into his mouth just like water. His wife ate relatively little but Coyote ate prodigiously.

Then Blue Jay sent some of the people out to gather more wood in order that they might have a dance at night.

[From this point on this second couple, Coyote and Frog, are lost in this narrative.]

IV

(Falcon Kills Ki'lak and Sun-man)

Fish Hawk's (Kīca) husband was Falcon (Tata), but she discovered that he was not true to her for she caught him making love to her own sister. This made Fish Hawk very angry and she went away from their home which was at Taa'ya xa, which was only a short distance south of Tsawa'l xabē and Cīgom, near Kītsī'danō.

She came along a trail which formerly ran south of the town of Upper Lake and went down toward Kūca'danōyō.

As she approached Kūca'danōyō dawn came and it began to grow a little lighter. The chief of the village announced that a stranger was approaching the village and that it was his opinion that this traveler had had some trouble, possibly her father or mother had run away but she had had some trouble in any event. A big dance was in progress at Kūca'danōyō and when Fish Hawk arrived she was invited to remain and join the others in their festivities.

She did remain there all day and on the following day she started off toward the north passing along the north side of Tule Lake, and finally arriving at a rock pile in the canyon north of Witter Springs.

This big rock pile was in reality a house. It belonged to Sun-man (La'gaūk). This house and its immediate surroundings were all white due to the presence of the bleached bones of people who had been eaten. Their bones had been then thrown out of the house.

As soon as Fish Hawk entered this house she saw a finely-dressed young man. He came over immediately and took her by the hand and said, "Ha! My wife. You are my wife. You belong to me." She looked about and saw that the door which was on the south side of the house just as any ordinary sweat-house door is, was guarded by many rattlesnakes.

Falcon started out to follow his wife. That night he arrived at Kūca'danōyō and there he learned that his wife had turned northward that very morning so he tracked her toward the house of Sun-man.

Sun-man saw Falcon approaching and as soon as he arrived in front of the door of Sun-man's house the snakes began to rattle and were ready to bite him.

Now, before Falcon had left home he had consulted with his grandfather, Coyote-old-man, who had told him all of the tricks about this house and had told him where his wife had gone.

When Falcon heard these snakes he threw a bead-grinding stone (catane gūwĭ kabē), in at the door and the snakes bit at it. That knocked all of the snakes off the door-frame for these snakes were arranged all around the door-frame and when they had been removed in this way Falcon entered the house without any trouble. Falcon entered and went directly back and sat down beside his wife. When she looked up and saw Falcon she upbraided the snakes, saying, "What are you fellows doing out there, you ugly brutes. Before this no one could get in here without being bitten."

It seems that Sun-man and Kĭ'lak lived together here in this house which is near the top of a ridge, called "Tsīya' kabē," at a point about two miles north of Witter Springs. Kĭ'lak challenged Falcon to a game which, of course, was a game of shooting at each other with bows and arrows. The arrows used in this contest were provided with hardened manzanita points about three or four inches in length. The fire-tender was Putrid-old-man (Pa'būtsīke) and he made a rousing fire and prepared everything for the contest. Kĭ'lak commenced the contest and when he was ready the fire blazed up and actually touched the roof where they were to fly around and dodge and show their cunning.

A great many people had assembled to see this contest because Sun-man, while he was a cannibal, did not bother anyone in his immediate neighborhood, only taking people from a distance. He was on friendly terms with his neighbors and they all came to visit him whenever they wished.

As Kĭ'lak played he sang his special song which was "wēwē gīla" (repeated over and over again).

Now, when Falcon had started out to make this journey he had placed the large bead-grinding stone in a bag and suspended this around his neck so that it rested on his breast. It was this same bead-grinding stone that he had thrown into the entrance and that the snakes had struck at and dislodged themselves, so that it made it possible for him to enter the house in the first place. He still carried this bead-grinding stone on his breast as he played against Kĭ'lak. As Kĭ'lak flew about Falcon shot at him the required four different times and each time he missed his mark. Every one yelled and made fun of Falcon because he had missed him this way.

It was then Falcon's turn to fly and let Kĭ'lak try his luck at shooting him. This was done and Kĭ'lak took four shots in the usual way but missed his mark every time.

Sun-man then said to Kĭ'lak, "What is the matter with you? Are you dying? Are your fingers breaking off or what is the matter?"

It then became Kĭ'lak's turn to fly and this time Falcon shot him in the belly with the first shot and Kĭ'lak fell to the floor. Sun-man was very much disgusted with Kĭ'lak and after growling about his failure to play a good game he began to mourn Kĭ'lak's loss.

They then quit the game for the day and the visitors went home. The people in the Sun-house went to bed but Sun-man announced that they would have another game the next evening.

During the night Sun-man called out to Falcon every little while, "How is it are you asleep yet?"

"No, I am still awake," Falcon would reply.

Finally along toward morning Sun-man got no answer to his question so he went over and laid down beside Fish Hawk and put his arm around her. She immediately scratched him on both sides of the face with her long, sharp claws. In fact she scratched him very severely and he bled profusely from his wounds. Finally he left and went back to his own place on the other side of the house.

On the following evening they made another fire and commenced another game of the same sort and this time Falcon flew up first and Sun-man made a fair hit the first time he shot at Falcon. He hit him squarely in the belly and would, of course, have killed him but for the fact that Falcon was wearing the big grinding-stone. The arrow struck this and broke its point squarely off. Out of his four shots Sun-man hit Falcon twice but neither shot did him any harm on account of the protection of the big grinding-stone.

Then Sun-man flew up and Falcon missed his first shot entirely. Whenever either one missed a shot the people made great sport of them for their bad marksmanship and had a great deal of fun at their expense.

Then Falcon watched Sun-man for a long time, got all of his movements and waited until Sun-man had flown about until he was quite tired. Then Falcon took careful aim and shot and hit Sun-man directly in the heart. When he fell he came down directly on the drum.

Now they had a pestle as the tsï'lō. Falcon took this pestle and broke the leg-bones of Sun-man and threw him out through the smoke-hole just as he had been throwing out people after their legs had been broken in the same way.

Everyone rejoiced and was glad that Sun-man was dead because they were afraid of him and they all said, "That is just the right way to do. That is the way he does to human beings when he gets them."

Now since Falcon had succeeded in killing Sun-man he took all of Sun-man's possessions. He ordered the fire-tender to throw out all of the bones and other bad things around the house, to clean it all up in good shape and a few days later he invited the people to come over for a grass game.

V

(Barn Owl Gambles)

Barn Owl gambled for a long time and he had very bad luck. He bet everything he had and at last he bet his own head. He lost that to Falcon and Falcon caught Barn Owl's head and tried to pull it off. He pulled and pulled as hard as he could. He pulled until Barn Owl's neck popped but he was utterly unable to pull the head off. Finally when he let go of Barn Owl's head he was pulling so hard that the head flew back way down in Barn Owl's shoulders. That is why he has such a short neck and has his head way down in his shoulders now.

[From this point on we lose Falcon and the others of the Sun-house in this narrative.]

VI

(The Wanderings of Fox)

While this game was going on there were two people who did not come, Fox and his wife, Wildcat.

Fox remained at home while his wife went out to hunt deer and she was always successful. She always brought in a deer each day. Her good luck in hunting aroused Fox's curiosity and he wanted to know just how she was able to get this game every day as she did, so he determined to follow her and see what happened. Accordingly on the following day he followed Wildcat out to a pond in the hills, called "Xō'maxa," which was a special drinking place for deer. Wildcat then removed her clothing and went and lay down at the edge of the pond, keeping her bow and arrows near by. Presently many deer came there and approached very close to her. She shot the fattest and biggest one, then she arose, broke the deer's neck and put on her clothing, tied up the deer's feet and carried it home.

When Fox had seen all that happened at the pond, he went back. He arrived home ahead of his wife. He was very much angered by his wife's actions so he lay down back of the fire and covered himself up with a blanket and there he remained. Now, before that, whenever he had seen his wife coming home with her game, he had always jumped up and helped her bring it in and helped her skin the animal and cut up the meat and start it cooking. This time, however, Wildcat brought the deer in alone and she sat down for a while without any comment. She wondered at his strange actions but said nothing and shortly went out of the house and brought the deer in and put it cooking. Then she brought out mush and other food and got everything all ready. Then she said to him, "Old Man, everything is ready to eat. You better get up now and have your meal." He, however, made no reply and did not stir so Wildcat and her son (Fox) commenced to eat.

Night came and Fox did not move. On the following morning, however, he got up and dressed himself in his best clothing. Then he brought out the sack containing their store of beads and pulled out a long string and broke it in two, thus dividing their wealth between them. He then told her that the one-half was her part and that she also could have one-half of everything else. Then he said, "You live entirely on meat anyway so you may as well stay here alone and take care of yourself. You do just as you have been doing. Strip yourself naked and catch your game by that method. I do not like to see that. That is why I am going away."

Fox then made up a bundle of his possessions and prepared to start off. This made Wildcat very angry and she said to their little boy, "I

do not want you. Go with your father." So Fox took the little boy
and put him on top of his pack and they went over to Danō' xa.

The chief of this village was Blue Jay and he announced that someone was coming and called upon his people to come out and welcome
the stranger. Said he, "Put on your best blankets and other good clothes
and be friendly with this man. You must welcome him. You must
never look any other way than friendly when a stranger comes to our
village."

The people did this and brought food and he and the little boy had
a good meal.

When they had finished he put out a long string of beads, on a
blanket and said to the chief, "You must watch me when I leave here
but you must not tell my wife where I have gone. I am leaving her and
do not want her to follow me." Fox remained in that village that night
and left the next morning.

He went through Cī'gōm, which was a village inhabited by the
Ground-squirrel-people. The chief of this village told the people to come
out and welcome the stranger and to give him and his little boy food.

Here Fox spent the night and when he and his little boy started off
on the following morning he told the people of this village the same as
he had those at the other village, that he did not want them to let his
wife know where he had gone.

He then went on, this time toward the east and ascended the mountain until he came to a little valley near the top of a mountain (ga'c
gag°ōi). There was absolutely nothing here in this valley but as he
looked about he saw smoke issuing from a small hole in the ground.
He went over to it and there he found Wasp (Tara). Wasp was burning off the weeds in order to fell them for wood.

Fox asked Wasp, "What are you doing that for?"

Wasp replied, "That is the way I get wood. I cannot get wood any
other way. I have to have wood in my house and have no other way to
get it."

Fox put down his pack and went over to where the weeds were very
abundant and broke off a large armful and brought them over to Wasp.

This made Wasp very happy and he said, "Oh, Oh, you must be my
son, that is why you do this kindness for me."

Fox then inquired if Wasp knew where there was a village anywhere in that vicinity.

Wasp told him that there was a village over in Long Valley (Na'wek) so Fox continued his journey and finally arrived at this village which was inhabited by all sorts of people who live in the mountains, Rabbits, Deer and many others. Panther was the chief of this village.

Fox remained at this village that night and made the same request of these people as he had of those with whom he had formerly stopped, namely that they should not inform his wife where he had gone.

Next he journeyed toward the southeast for a great distance and came over to a point on the Sacramento River where there was a village, called "Po'lpol," in the language of the people themselves who lived there. These people were all sorts of birds and the like who live in this great valley. Their chief was Crane (Makō').

Fox remained there that night and just as he was ready to start away on the following morning the chief of the village came to him and asked him to wait a moment saying that his wife, Crane, wanted to see him. Presently Crane's wife came along with a būgū full of beads. She put this down in front of Fox and said, "I have no children, no relatives at all. I am alone and am getting old and have no one to take care of me. I have brought you this little lot of beads and would like to buy this little boy from you. I want to raise this boy so that he can take care of me."

Fox said, "All right, that is very good, I have no home, I have no way to take care of the boy. You will be my relative now. If I take him with me and something should happen and I have to get killed, I do not know what would become of him. You must take good care of him. Do not whip him or scold him. I do not know where or how far I am going but will keep right on going until I die."

Everyone was gathered around by this time and listening to this discussion. Crane told Fox that he should not travel any farther but should remain there in their village and live with them. The rest of the people agreed that this was right and assured him that he would not have any worry so far as food was concerned, that they always had plenty.

Fox then inquired if there were any other villages farther toward the south and they told him that there were many villages toward the south so he continued on his journey southward. By and by he came to a place where he found Frog sitting by a spring. He asked her what she was doing there. She told him that this was her house and he again inquired if she knew whether there were any villages farther to the south. She assured him that there were many, so on southward he went.

Finally he came to a large village way out in the plains. This was a village inhabited by the Mosquito-people (Dūla'dūlaū). Here he remained over night and on the following day he turned toward the west. He crossed the Napa Valley and went by Santa Rosa and Sebastopol and finally he came to Bodega Bay (Lakō' ka wīna) and here he found a large village of Water-birds. This was a village inhabited by all kinds of Water-birds. Here he remained over night again, but by this time practically all of the beads which he had brought along were gone for he had given a present to the people in each village where he had stopped.

On the following day he went north along the coast to a high point just south of Point Arena. Here he stopped and rested for a while and studied, trying to figure out just what he should do. As he looked out over the ocean from this high point he saw some people traveling westward in a canoe. He watched them for a long time, saw them come to a small island and disembark. He determined to make himself a canoe and travel out over the ocean in that same way so he went down to the shore and picked up some kelp which he wove into a tight fabric like a tule basket. This he tied up in the shape of a canoe, tying it all securely with dry kelp. Then he made a stout paddle out of white oak. The blade was of white oak and the handle which was bound to it was made of pine. Then he started out in his boat and traveled rapidly across to this island which he found was inhabited by the Sea-lion-people. He found that this island was one great house with doors leading out of it in various directions. He was made welcome by the Sea-lion-people and he remained there over night and he gave them the last of his beads.

They made a big hot fire the following morning and had a fanning contest and this despite the fact that there is no wood on this island. They had to bring all the wood that they used from the mainland by canoe. They fanned and fanned in this contest until everything got red-hot. It became so extremely hot that the house took fire but each one of the Sea Lions had a hole in the floor down into which he could disappear and get away from the smoke and the heat. Fox had no such hole in the floor and he was burned and killed.

70—OSPREY AND MINK FOOL COYOTE[165]
INCIDENTS AND CHARACTERS

I. *Osprey tricks Coyote.*
      1. Osprey, 2. Coyote.
II. *Mink tricks Coyote.*
      1. Coyote, 2. Mink.

I

(Osprey Tricks Coyote)

Osprey sat down by the river making a fish-spear. Coyote came along and asked him how he got such a fine piece of bone from which to make the spear he was at work on.

Osprey replied, "Well, old fellow, it is a pretty hard thing to do, but I will tell you how to do it anyway. You take a good big stone, lay your legs across another big one and let it fall. This breaks the bone in your leg and you can get a fine piece."

Coyote accordingly went down near the river and found a suitable stone. He commenced hitting his leg with it. He hit very easily at first but found that it hurt and cried out with the pain.

Osprey said, "No, no, that is not the way to do it. You must hold the rock up high, shut your eyes, and let it fall hard. That is the way to knock a big piece of the bone, and it will not hurt."

Coyote replied, "I do not know whether I want to do that or not, it hurts pretty badly even when I hit it just a little bit."

Finally, however, he did let the rock fall. Of course, it broke his leg and hurt him terribly. He rolled around on the ground and cried with the pain.

Osprey laughed at him for being so foolish as to do as he was told. He said, "What is the matter with you? You did not do it as you should."

After a time Coyote got up and made his leg heal up quickly. Then he said to Osprey, "Well you fooled me in good shape. I guess I will leave you now."

---

[165]The Pomo title of this myth is "Iwī′ ya dzŏl ma bana′waiyŏl matū", "Coyote him try fooling story".
Informant: William James, Central dialect.

II

(Mink Tricks Coyote)

Coyote then went down the river for a way. Here he found Mink who, he observed, had very fine, long, black hair. He said to Mink, "My friend, how does it come that you have such fine, long, black hair?"

Mink replied, "It is pretty hard to do but I will tell you how I do it anyway. I do not know whether you can do it or not. First you go and find a pine tree which has a big lot of thick gum. Set this on fire and while it is burning at best you run into the fire and let it burn all the hair off of you."

Coyote went out and took a firebrand with him. He found a good pine tree and set it on fire, but it blazed up so fiercely that he was afraid to go into it. He said to Mink, "I am afraid of that fire."

Mink replied, "You want to shut your eyes and run right in there so that it can not hurt you."

Coyote tried to do this but stopped because he was afraid. Then he tried again and finally did run into it and his hair was all burned off. He cried with the pain of his burns for a long time, but Mink only laughed at him and made fun of his pain. Then Mink went home.

After a time Coyote made himself well and then he went over to Mink's house and said to him, "Two of you fellows have fooled me now so I think I shall leave this place."

Then Coyote went away.

71—OAK-BALL, HAWK AND OWL TRICK COYOTE[166]

INCIDENTS AND CHARACTERS

  I. Oak-ball tricks Coyote.
      1. Oak-ball, 2. Coyote, 3. Blue Jay.
  II. Hawk tricks Coyote.
      1. Coyote, 2. Hawk, 3. Blue Jay.
III. Owl tricks Coyote.
      1. Coyote, 2. Owl. 3. Tree, 4. Red-headed-woodpecker, 5. Blue Jay.

---

[166]The Pomo title of this myth is "palŏ'cai ye īwī ya djŏl mabana'wan", "Oak-ball Coyote him try fool".
Informant: William James, Central dialect.

I

(Oak-ball Tricks Coyote)

This happened at a place called "Ka't matcū pda." Oak-ball[167] was floating lightly down-stream in a freshet. Coyote came along and asked Oak-ball how it was that he was able to float so easily on the water.

"Well," said Oak-ball, "that is easy enough. You climb up on that tree there and get out over the water. Then you let go and drop down into the water and you will bob up and float along as I do."

Coyote said, "That is very easy. I shall try it. It looks good to see you fellows float."

When Coyote got up on the tree and out over the water he was afraid to jump. He said, "I do not know about jumping down there. I am afraid of the water."

Oak-ball said, "Do not be afraid, jump right off into the water. When you strike the bottom you will bob up again just like that." Just then one of the Oak-balls fell into the water and floated away down the stream easily.

Coyote finally got up his courage and jumped off, but he did not come up as the Oak-balls did. Instead he was carried down the swift current for quite a distance, finally coming to the surface in an eddy. He was drowned and the Oak-ball-people pulled him out onto the bank. There he lay for some time.

Finally Blue Jay came along and flew over him, crying, "tsai, tsai, tsai," as usual.

Coyote complained, "Why do you make such a loud noise? I was sound asleep." Then Coyote told Oak-ball, "You fellows fooled me. I am not light enough to float as you do. I am going away."

II

(Hawk Tricks Coyote)

Then Coyote went off up into the mountains. Here he met Hawk[168] who was eating ground squirrels. He came to Hawk's house and found that he had a great many squirrels stored away in the house.

Coyote remarked to Hawk, "Say, you have a lot of ground squirrels here."

---

[167]A kind of very light gall on oak trees.
[168]This was the Western Red-tail Hawk, commonly spoken of as the Chicken Hawk.

Hawk replied, "Yes, I always catch a great many so that I can have plenty of meat on hand all the time."

Then Coyote said, "Tell me how you catch them. I never can catch any."

Hawk replied, "All you have to do is to watch and see where the ground squirrels run into their holes. Then run your arm down into the hole up to your shoulder. When the squirrels bite your hand simply pull it out and take them off."

Coyote thought that the was easy enough so he went out and tried it, but a rattlesnake bit him and he died at once. He lay there until his body had decayed, but one day Blue Jay came along and cried, "tsai, tsai, tsai." Then Coyote came to life and, as usual, he growled at Blue Jay for waking him up.

II

(Owl Tricks Coyote)

Coyote went farther up into the mountains and there he met Owl[169] who was famous for his ability to sing at night.

Coyote said to him, "How do you make that nice noise of yours at night?"

Owl replied, "I go up and crawl into a hole in a tree and then stick my head out. Then I am able to make that noise."

Coyote tried it, but when he had crawled inside the tree closed up on him so that he could not get out. He died there and after a long time his body dried up.

Finally Red-headed-woodpecker came along and commenced pecking on the tree. At last he succeeded in pecking a hole into it and there he found Coyote's bones which he threw out onto the ground. Soon Blue Jay came along and made his usual noise which brought Coyote back to life again. Coyote growled at Blue Jay, saying, "You are always in the way when I am trying to sleep."

Then Coyote went away.

72—COYOTE FALLS FROM A TREE[170]

Characters: 1. Coyote, 2. Woodcock, 3. Frog (wife of Coyote), 4. Lizard.

Coyote lived at the old village of Elem[171] on Sulphur Bank Island. Woodcock, who also lived there, brought in a great deal of dry wood

---

[169]This was the Great Horned Owl, called "Makū'kū".
[170]Informant: Mary Louie, Central dialect.
[171]See Univ. Calif. Publ., Amer. Arch. Ethn., VI, p. 208, 1908.

on his back. This was a special kind of dry wood, called "xar,"[171a] which was found only high up in the trees. Woodcock secured this wood by pulling it down with a special hook on the end of a long pole, called "baxa'r." Coyote asked Woodcock how he succeeded in getting so much wood. Woodcock replied that he took his hook with him, hooked it over a piece of the dry wood, pulled it down and broke it up.

Coyote said, "He, he, why do you not tell me the truth? I do not want you to lie to me. I am asking you this question because I really want to know how you do it."

Woodcock replied, "Well, that is the way I do it. I take the hook and try to pull down a dead limb. If it is too hard I have to leave it and try another one which comes more easily. When I get this wood down I break it up and carry it home. That is what you asked me for and I have told you the truth about it."

Coyote still believed that Woodcock was not telling him the truth and he said so. Then Woodcock said, "But this is the way I get the finest and best of my wood. I go out and hunt up a good, long pole which I carry with me everywhere. I then hunt up a tree where there are some good, dry limbs high up in the tree. Then I climb up the pole to a dead limb and look it over carefully to see just where I can jump on it and break it off. Before I jump on it I take hold of the limb above so that when the dead limb breaks off I can hold fast to this limb above and not fall. As the dead limb strikes the ground it breaks in pieces. Then I climb down the tree trunk or down the pole."

Coyote went out and tried it. He came back with a good load of wood. Next day he did the same thing and came back with a good lot of wood. On the third day he went out as before but, as he was jumping up and down on a dead limb to break it off, he lost his hold on the limb above and went down with the dead one and smashed up badly as he struck the ground. It did not kill him, however, and he called for help. Someone was over in that vicinity and heard Coyote's outcries. He came back to the village and reported that he had heard Coyote's cries and thought that he was hurt. Some of the men of the village then went out and brought him home.

[171a] The term "xar" is applied only to the dry limbs in which the woodpeckers have placed acorns. This is commonly done by the Red-headed-woodpecker. These birds drill holes in dry limbs and in the bark of the trunk of a tree and place the acorns here in order that they may become infested with worms which are then eaten by the birds.

Frog was Coyote's wife. As soon as she saw Coyote she began to wail and to sing a mourning song. The burden of this song was that Coyote was a poor, starving man who never had anything and who was always getting hurt. Coyote told her not to sing like that, but to always sing of a rich man who was always lucky, who always got everything he wanted and was a great chief.

Pretty soon Lizard came along and said to Frog, "Why do you cry for that ugly fellow? You and I will make love together."

Coyote heard something and asked his wife, "Say, old woman, who is that talking to you?"

Lizard and Frog sat and talked together for a long time, and every now and then Coyote repeated his question to Frog.

After a long time Coyote got well again and went about as before.

73—GRAY SQUIRREL TEACHES COYOTE HOW TO RUN UP A TREE[172]

Characters: 1. Crane, 2. Gray Squirrel, 3. Coyote.

Crane and his wife, Gray Squirrel, lived in a big sweat-house. One day Coyote came along and asked Gray Squirrel how she could run up a tall tree to the very tip-top point and then clap her hands there and then run down head-first and jump across from one tree to the other and clap her hands again,[173] and he asked her how many magnesite beads she wanted to show him just how this was accomplished.

After watching the demonstration by Gray Squirrel, Coyote himself tried to leap from one tree to another but, of course, he was unable to do it and fell to the ground and was killed.

74—COYOTE IS TRICKED BY LITTLE BIRDS[174]

Characters: 1. Coyote, 2. Small birds, 3. Buzzard, 4. Blue Jay, 5. Crow, 6. Gī'lak, 7. Kū'ksū.

Coyote was traveling along one hot day near the shore of a partly dried, wet-weather lake, or sink-hole. He saw some small birds.[175] These were a kind of bird with dark brown and light gray stripes on

[172]Informant: Charlie Brown, Northern dialect, 1902.
[173]By the clapping of the hands is meant the chattering which a squirrel commonly does.
[174]The Pomo title of this myth is "Tsĭtū'm pahē marū."
Informant: Tom Mitchell, Eastern dialect, 1904.
[175]The general term for small birds is "tsĭt."

their heads. They were sitting on willow branches and jumping into the water.

Coyote said, "What makes you fellows do that way?"

The birds replied, "We do that so that we may grow rapidly. Our old people told us to do that way in order that we may be happy."

Coyote watched the birds for a time and then he said, "Well, I guess I had better do that too."

Accordingly Coyote climbed up into a tree and out on a limb over the water. Now the birds wished, "We hope that when he jumps the water will disappear and there will be nothing but mud there." Accordingly, just as Coyote jumped down, the water suddenly went away and left only soft mud. Into this Coyote sank so that only his hind legs were visible.

Coyote could by his magic call from where his head was down there in the mud, though he was unable to extricate himself. He shouted, "tsītū'm pahē ———, tcīhū'i hū'ūyū ———, tsīhūī hūūyū."[176] Coyote was calling Kū'ksū to come and doctor him so that he might get out.

Buzzard said to his children, "Listen, I hear something. There, I hear someone calling me." So he got out his medicine sack and took from it a feather stick.[177] This was the only part of his paraphernalia that he had ready. He had to make all the rest of his "big-head" head-dress.[178]

When it was finished he reached into his sack and took from it successively, a single whistle (lībū) of elderberry, some charcoal paint,[179] a diaper (kato'lī) of shredded tule which he used as a tail, his head-net (bō'l makī), and finally his staff (cakō'ik). He first painted himself properly, put on the head-net, the head-dress, the tail, took the whistle in his mouth, the staff in his hand, and started northward to where Coyote was.

Meantime Coyote had yelled four times. Buzzard worked very rapidly in order that he might arrive before someone died. When Coyote

---

[176]This expression is said to be meaningless. It is the regular call for Kū'ksū in ceremonies. The term tsītūmpa, however, is one said to have been used by Coyote to refer to any one with magic power. It is even yet used jokingly by people in a similar sense.

[177]It is called "gī", and is the special stick of the "big-head" head-dress. It is a stick wrapped with feathers and tipped with down. It is inserted in the front of the head-dress so as to protrude at an angle of about forty-five degrees with the horizontal. The head-louse is also called "gī".

[178]Kū'ksū kaiya.

[179]Called here puī, which term signifies fat of any kind. The proper term for charcoal is "masik".

called the fourth time Buzzard was ready to go and answered him. Coyote kept right on calling even after that.

Buzzard traveled very rapidly and soon reached Coyote. He immediately began to doctor him. He went four times in a clockwise direction, then four times in a counter-clockwise direction around Coyote, the while constantly blowing his whistle in alternate short and long notes. Finally Buzzard stopped at Coyote's back.

Then Coyote said "Hehe',[180] you are not the doctor. I did not call for you. You do not know anything. You are hungry. You are starving. You have a bald head. You eat what other people throw away."

Then Buzzard went away into the shade of a nearby tree.

Coyote again gave his call for Kū'ksū. Blue Jay heard the call and dressed, as had Buzzard, and rushed off to doctor Coyote. He performed the same kind of a ceremony.

Then Coyote said, "Hehe', you are no doctor. You are Blue Jay. You have a big head. You have dry legs. You have a big nose. Your legs are so dry that they are cracked. You are ugly looking and full of lice. I did not call you."

So Blue Jay went over to where Buzzard was and sat down with him.

Coyote again called, as before. This time Crow dressed as Kū'ksū and went to doctor Coyote as the other two had done.

When he had finished Coyote derided him also. "Hehe, you are Crow. You have a black nose. You are black all over. You are full of lice. What do you know? You do not know anything about doctoring."

Crow felt ashamed and joined Buzzard and Blue Jay under the tree.

Again and again Coyote repeated his call and always with the same result. Each time some one of the birds fixed up like Kū'ksū and came to doctor him. Each time Coyote knew the deception and derided the impostor.[181]

Finally he called very loudly and Gī'lak heard him. Kūksū did not have to fix up at all, he was naturally that way, so he started from his home down at the south end of the world and came up. He danced and whistled just as the others had and at the end drove his staff down into

---

[180]An ejaculation of disgust.
[181]This collective paragraph is said by the informant to be typical of the method followed by the raconteurs in olden times. After recounting specific details of a few they would then lump the rest in such a collective statement.

the mud and pried Coyote up. He had the necessary power and he alone could save Coyote.

All the others who had tried and failed were sitting around and saw Kū'ksū succeed.

75—COYOTE IMITATES THE WILLOW[182]

Characters: 1. Coyote, 2. Willow, 3. Blue Jay.

Coyote came along a stream one day and saw Willow[183] standing out in the water and noticed that the twigs and leaves constantly shook.

Coyote said, "Why do you stand out there in the swift current and shake all the time?"

Willow replied, "O! I do that just because it tickles me and makes me feel so good."

Coyote decided to try it for himself so he got out onto a big riffle and stood in the center of it. The water was low just then and consequently the current was not very strong. Presently, however, the water rose and the swift current washed Coyote down stream and soon he was drowned.

His body presently drifted ashore. Soon Blue Jay flew over Coyote and gave his characteristic cry, "tsai, tsai, tsai." Coyote woke up and grumbled, "He', he', can you never let a fellow alone and let him sleep?" Thus Coyote came back to life.

76—BLUE JAY KILLS COYOTE'S MOTHER WITH A HOT ROCK[184]

Characters: 1. Coyote, 2. Blue Jay, 3. Coyote's mother, 4. Blue Jay's mother.

Coyote invited Blue Jay to visit him. They went to the sweat-house to take the usual sweat-bath. Blue Jay did not want to remain there as long as Coyote did so he said that he would go on ahead and that Coyote need not hurry. Coyote told him not to fasten the door when he went to bed. On the way Blue Jay picked up a small flat stone and, when he reached the house, he placed it in the fire to heat. Presently Coyote's mother felt the burning of this rock as Blue Jay applied it.

---

[182]Informant: Tom Mitchell, Eastern dialect.
[183]This was the "basket willow" as the Indians call it. Its native name is "tsūba'ha".
[184]The native name of this tale is, "tsai ūla gūnūla ye ha mīte dīmot kōlō hōle xahwo xabē xa gaūbanēle," "Blue Jay ūla Coyote his mother dīmot kōlō hōle xahwo rock hot place within."
Informant: Tom Mitchell, Eastern dialect.

She asked Blue Jay what he was doing, and he assured her that there was nothing wrong but that she felt the burning sensation because of his ardent regard for her. He did this in order to kill her.

When Coyote came home he found his mother dead and asked Blue Jay how he had killed her. Blue Jay said that he did it with a flat, hot stone but he wrongly informed Coyote as to just how he had used the stone. Coyote determined to get even with Blue Jay, so he visited the latter's house in order to kill Blue Jay's mother. He did just as Blue Jay had told him. He heated the rock very hot, but did not apply it properly. The rock began to burn Coyote and he began to cry, "hō tō tō tō tō tō tōī."[185] Coyote danced about in great pain from his burn and finally died. Blue Jay's mother then threw his body out of the house and pounded it up with a stone.

Presently Blue Jay came along and found Coyote's body. He said, "tsai tsai tsai" over it and Coyote woke up. Of course he growled at Blue Jay for waking him up, just as he always does.

77—COYOTE GETS MAGIC BLACK BREAD FROM THE SUN[186]
INCIDENTS AND CHARACTERS

I. *A small bird tricks Coyote.*
  1. *Būra'kal bakaiūkke,* 2. *Coyote.*
II. *Coyote obtains black bread from the Sun.*
  1. *Coyote,* 2. *Sun,* 3. *Bird-people,* 4. *Turtle brothers (two),* 5. *Blue Jay.*
III. *The Bird-people trick Coyote.*
  1. *Coyote,* 2. *Bird-people,* 3. *Hawk.*

I

(A Small Bird Tricks Coyote)

Būra'kal bakaiūkke[187] was always snaring birds. Coyote came along, called him by name and inquired how he was able to catch so many birds. At first Būra'kal bakaiūkke refused to tell Coyote but finally he said, "I first burn out a valley and then set my snares."

Coyote was much pleased and set about preparing snares and getting ready poles with which to set them. By the next morning, however, he had forgotten the details so he returned and again inquired. Būra'kal

---

[185]This exclamation, "hō tōī," is the usual one used to indicate pain caused by a burn.
[186]Informant: Dave Thompson, Upper Lake, Eastern dialect, 1904.
[187]This is a small species of bird with a top-knot. He is frequently mentioned in myths. The Indian title given for this myth was "Būra'kal bakaiūkke marū."

bakaiūkke again told him and he started off to try it. Before he had gone far, however, he had forgotten just what to do. He thus forgot and returned for the information several times. Finally Būra'kal bakaiūkke became tired of all this so he told Coyote, "First set your snares and then burn out all the grass and brush in the valley." Coyote followed these directions, set a great many snares all over the valley and then set fire to the grass. He then sat down on the mountainside nearby to see how many birds he would catch.

As the fire passed along a great many birds flew ahead of it. As each bird flew up Coyote said, "Ah! there I caught another." So he went on counting them as each bird flew ahead of the fire until he had counted a great many and he was much pleased that he should have such fine luck in hunting this new way.

After the fire had burned out, Coyote went over into the valley. He found that all his traps had burned save one which was in a spot which escaped the fire. In it he found one bird which he plucked and proceeded to roast.

II

(Coyote Obtains Black Bread From the Sun)

Now, Sun had some black bread, and Coyote asked him for some of it. Sun said that he had none; but Coyote begged hard for any old dry piece, so Sun finally admitted that he did have just a little bit, and threw down a small piece of it.

As he did so there was a great noise and Coyote ran to hide, seeking shelter under any rock or tree that would give him protection, for he was afraid the bread might hit him as it fell. When the bread finally struck the ground Coyote went to pick it up. As he reached for it the bread moved. This happened again and again. Finally Coyote got a net with which to capture it but the net could not hold it. The net he had was made of sinew, but the bread always went through it. Then he went and got some tule and made a tule net for this was the only kind of a net that would hold this bread. He set this net and drove the bread into it and finally captured it.

Coyote tasted this bread and let the Bird-people taste of it. They all agreed that it tasted very nasty. One of the birds picked it up and threw it into the water.

The bird-people then went home, but Coyote slipped away, went around in the opposite direction and came back to where the bread had been thrown in. He dived repeatedly to try to get it. Some children came along and saw Coyote so they called the older people and told them what he was doing. They were very angry and finally they killed Coyote.

Then they told Turtle and his brother to take care of the bread. Accordingly the two dived down with a hunting sack which they filled with bread and hid under the water for themselves. They brought to the surface only a small piece.

Their theft angered the people, who decided to kill them. Someone suggested, "Let us make a fire and throw the Turtle brothers into it."

Turtle said, "No, if you burn us it will make a big smoke which will kill all the people."

Then someone said, "Let us throw them into the water and drown them."

"All right," said Turtle, "we will then be gone for good and can never come back any more."

Just as the people were ready to throw the Turtles into the water they said, "Hold on, hold on, I want to catch my breath again." As they were ready the second time the Turtles said the same thing and obtained another respite. Finally they threw in the Turtles with a great splash, and they called back a farewell to the people on shore.

Coyote lay beside the creek, dead and all flyblown. Blue Jay flew over him several times and talked very loudly. Finally Coyote said, "Blue Jay, why do you talk so loudly when a person is asleep? You ought to know better than to yell around over a fellow when he is having a good time and taking it easy this way."

III

(The Bird-people Trick Coyote)

Coyote then smelled around where they had had the bread. As he walked along by the bushes the birds were all scared and ran away into the brush, but Coyote said, "What is the use of your being scared and running into the brush all the time? Now, come boys, will you not each give me a feather?" Then the birds came out and played with Coyote in the open. Each gave him a feather and he stuck these around all over his body. Presently along came Hawk. Everyone was frightened; all except Coyote flew away; Coyote couldn't fly. When Hawk had passed, the birds came out and resumed their play with Coyote. Soon they got scared again. Coyote had been trying to learn to fly. This time he tried to fly away with the birds. He succeeded pretty well but when he lighted in a bush he put one eye out. Then he begged the birds for an eye but they said that it was impossible for them to spare one, as each had only two eyes. Coyote then made himself an eye out of a shell bead. He then left that country and went off somewhere.

78—TULE BOY[188]

Characters: 1. Tsīko'lkol, 2. Tule-boy (Coyote), 3. Tsīdī'mal girls, 4. Frog (wife of Coyote).

In the village of Maiyī[189] lived all kinds of Bird-people. Tsīkolkol lived here. He was making string out of kotohlo. He was making it just as we make milkweed string now-a-days.

Tule-boy (Coyote) came along one day and said to him, "What are you doing? You are always making this kind of stuff."

Tsikolkol replied, "I am going to make a head-net."

Tule-boy said, "You are trying to fool me. Why do you not tell me the truth?"

Tsīkolkol held one of these strings up and said, "Here is one. I am going to make a head-net out of this."

Tule boy repeated his question four times, and finally Tsīkolkol said, "I will tell you better than that. I am making that to keep my hair nice."

But Tule boy said, "That is an ugly-looking thing and no good."

"Well," said Tsīkolkol, "I will tell you another way I keep my hair nice. I go out here in the woods and find a good pine tree with a lot of pitch on it. Then I take a lot of pitch on a skewer[190] and rub it into the hair all over my head."

Tule boy decided to try this, so he went out and found such a tree. Then he combed his hair nicely and rubbed a lot of pitch into it, doubling his long hair up so that it looked nice and thick on the back of his neck.

---

[188]The Pomo title of this myth is "Gūnūla būtsīge tibe cēla," "Coyote old man tule boy." Informant: Mary Louie, Eastern dialect.
[189]An old village-site near Upper Lake. See Univ. Calif. Publ., Amer. Arch. Ethn., VI, p. 155, 1908.
[190]Called "kabe'kkī kanō." This is a nicely-shaped stick about the size of a lead pencil, used to fasten feathers and other ornaments onto the head.

Then he took dirt and rubbed it on his hands in order to get rid of the remaining pitch. Then he went back to the village.

The people said, "It is well that you have come. We are going to make a fire in the sweat-house. We know that you have made up your mind to do something nice. That is why you have dressed up your hair in such a fine way. You are going to make love to the Tsīdī'mal (nobles) girls." These were some girls who never went out anywhere or had anything to do with the men in any way.

Everyone went into the sweat-house and they built a big fire. When it was very hot they began to fan with the big deer-skin fans to increase the heat and make everyone perspire profusely as was customary in sweating. Coyote had come in last and they told him to sit down on the east side of the fire because the opposite side was full. He was the only one on the east side. They began to fan from the west side. Next Tule-boy fanned those on the west side. So they fanned back and forth and on the third time his head became very hot.

When they fanned for the fourth time the pitch began to melt and run down all over his body and then it took fire. Tule-boy then jumped up and tried to brush off the burning pitch. Then he ran out of the house and it made a great blaze. The little boys who were playing around laughed at him and said that Tule-boy was burning up. He ran to the river and jumped into the water, and commenced rubbing himself. As soon as he rubbed his hair it all came off and went floating down the river. Then the boys said that Tule-boy's head had burned off and was floating down the river.

Frog was Tule-boy's wife. The boy's called her to see what had happened to her husband. She ran down to where Tule-boy was and took him home. There she wrapped one of her buckskin dresses about his head and doctored him. He was sick for quite a while but finally he got well and again went about as usual.

79—COYOTE BRAGS OF HIS WEALTH[191]

Characters: 1. Coyote, 2. Kalkalma'ptseū.

Coyote and Kalkalmáptseū were bragging about wealthy people. Coyote said to Kalkalmáptseū, "You say you are a wealthy man. Let us do something to show our wealth."

---

[191]Informant: Capt. Charlie, Garcia River, Central dialect, 1906.

In answer, Kalkalmáptseū said, "All right, let us see how you can make beads."

Coyote said, "All right," and he went out to defecate. His excrement consisted of pcī (a small shell something like a periwinkle).

When Kalkalmáptseū defecated his excrement consisted of nothing but beads. Then he made fun of Coyote and said, "You are not a rich man. I am the rich man."

80—WOODRAT, THE TRICKSTER[192]
INCIDENTS AND CHARACTERS

I. *Woodrat is refused food by his sister.*
   1. *Woodrat, 2. Woodpecker, 3. Pine-nut-man.*

II. *Woodrat tricks Pine-nut-man.*
   1. *Woodrat, 2. Pine-nut-man, 3. Dummy token, 4. Blue Jay, 5. Gray Squirrel.*

III. *Woodrat at the Crow village.*
   1. *Woodrat, 2. Crow-people, 3. Toad.*

IV. *Woodrat and the growing-tree.*
   1. *Woodrat, 2. Woman and boy, 3. The growing-tree.*

V. *Woodrat and the magic swing.*
   1. *Woodrat, 2. The Kaba'ltū sisters (two), 3. Magic swing.*

VI. *Woodrat kills Fire-man.*
   1. *Woodrat, 2. Fire-man.*

VII. *Woodrat and the Basket-people.*
   1. *Woodrat, 2. Basket-people.*

VIII. *Woodrat and Putrid-man.*
   1. *Woodrat, 2. Putrid-man.*

IX. *Woodrat and Spider-woman.*
   1. *Woodrat, 2. Spider-woman.*

X. *Woodrat and Sharp-heel.*
   1. *Woodrat, 2. Sharp-heel.*

XI. *Woodrat and Mouse kill Bear.*
   1. *Woodrat, 2. Mouse, 3. Bear, 4. Dummies (two), 5. Bear Girls (2).*

XII. *A woman kills deer with her magic pestle.*
   1. *Woodrat, 2. Mouse, 3. Woman, 4. Bice-taba-dawente girls (two), 5. Magic pestle.*

XIII. *Woodrat and Mouse are transformed.*
   1. *Woodrat, 2. Mouse.*

[192]The Pomo name of this myth is "Dakalak tcakale *tat*," "Woodrat chief bad man." Informant: Jim McCalleck, Northern dialect.

I

(Woodrat Is Refused Food by His Sister)

Woodrat lived over on Snow Mountain. His sister was Woodpecker. She lived some distance away from him and he decided to go over to visit her. When he arrived she was cooking acorn mush.

Now it is customary when a visitor arrives, no matter who he may be, to offer him food as a sign of welcome, but Woodpecker did not do this. She gave Woodrat no food at all. She was afraid to do so because she was afraid of her husband Kūtītcūlīya.[193] Woodpecker told her brother that her husband did not want him to come visiting and that she did not dare give him any of the food because it belonged to Pine-nut-man entirely. She said that she was very sorry for her brother and did not want to see him hungry but that she dared not give him any of the food nevertheless.

II

(Woodrat Tricks Pine-nut-man)

Woodrat then went out and tracked Pine-nut-man to the place where he was gathering pine-nuts and asked him to gather all the pine-nuts possible.

Pine-nut-man replied, "Who are you anyway? I heard someone talking."

Pine-nut-man was up in a tree gathering the pine cones. One of them had dropped and was lying on the ground under the tree and Woodrat picked it up and commenced getting the pine-nuts out of it. He said to Pine-nut-man, "These are very good pine-nuts my brother-in-law." Meanwhile Pine-nut-man went right on gathering the pine cones and presently when he had picked all the pine cones off from the tree and had them packed away in his carrying sack he came down. He paid no attention to Woodrat at all but sat down a little way off and commenced to crack open the pine cones.

Finally Woodrat said to him, "My brother-in-law, if you do not want me around then you must dig a big hole in the ground. Dig it very deep and throw me into it. That is the way they always do when they do not want me." To this Pine-nut-man agreed. He then took a digging

---

[193]The term "kūtī" signifies "pine-nut" and the term "tcūlīya" signifies "man" or "young man," hence the term "pine-nut-young-man" or "pine-nut-man" is given to this small mammal because he never eats anything except pine nuts.

stick and commenced to dig the hole as suggested by Woodrat. He dug this hole way down into the ground, throwing the earth up with his hands. Finally he asked Woodrat if he was still up there at the surface. Woodrat said that he was and Pine-nut-man then inquired if Woodrat could hear him plainly. "Yes," said Woodrat, "But you must not ask me any more questions. You must dig there for quite a long time before you ask me another question."

Then Woodrat took some rotten wood and wrapped it up in his rabbit-skin blanket and put with it a bow, some arrows, and a spear, and he said to this bundle, "You must answer that fellow when he asks questions. You must answer him just the same as I did."

Then he ran away across country, over rocks and logs and everything until he came to the Sacramento Valley and there he went into a big sweat-house.

After a long time the bundle which Woodrat had left said to Pine-nut-man, "Come out of that hole now and throw me in and break my neck." So Pine-nut-man came up, picked up the bundle and threw it into the hole with all his might. When the bundle struck the bottom of the pit the rotten wood broke up and Pine-nut-man then found that he had been deceived and that this was not Woodrat he had thrown into this hole at all. He was very much chagrined but said, "That is all right. If anyone is smart enough to cheat me let him do so. But who is there that can fool me? I can see through anything. I can see through a mountain or can see under the ground. I can track anybody, even if he is very small and if he walks on the rocks or runs along on logs." Then Pine-nut-man started out to track Woodrat.

Now Blue Jay was the chief of the village to which Woodrat had gone. Blue Jay was standing on top of the sweat-house and announced, "I see someone coming toward our village from the west. Something must have happened over there."

Woodrat said, "That is a fellow who hates me. He did not want me around. You must shut the door to the sweat-house and shut up all the holes except one and let him come down through that."

They did shut up the sweat-house completely. They made a small hole at the very apex, right by the center pole.

Pine-nut-man finally arrived and called out, "Where is my brother-in-law? I want to see him. I am very fond of him. Let me in."

Woodrat replied, "Do you see that hole at the top of the house? Come right in there. Even if it is small for you, please do it anyway. That is the way I always come in."

So he started in through this small opening. Woodrat stood directly below it with a sharp pointed stick and as soon as Pine-nut-man had partly entered Woodrat prodded him and poked a hole into his abdomen. A small quantity of pine-nuts ran out. Then Woodrat prodded him still more and more pine-nuts ran out of Pine-nut-man until there was nothing left of him except his hands, feet, head and skin. This man had no bones at all. His whole body was filled with pine-nuts. When he finally fell to the floor the people picked up what remained of him and threw it out of the house.

Blue Jay then inspected the great pile of pine-nuts on the floor and asked if there was anyone there who knew what this food was and how it was used but there was no one present who knew anything about it.

Then they sent a messenger over to another village and asked Gray Squirrel to come over.

When Gray Squirrel arrived they brought him into the house and gave him a seat. Then the chief said, "Do you know what this is?"

"No," said Gray Squirrel, "I do not know this kind of food, but I will taste it." When he did so he recognized it at once and told them that it was the best food in the world and that it was the very kind of food that he ate all the time.

Then he filled his hunting sack full of the pine-nuts and told the chief to distribute the rest among the people. At this everyone made a rush for this new food. They fought over it and stole it from each other. They even cut open the hunting sack that Gray Squirrel had filled with these pine nuts and took all that he had so that he went home without any.

III

(Woodrat at the Crow Village)

This did not suit Woodrat at all, so without a word he left and went up north. After he had traveled quite a long distance he came to the Crow village. These people were all blind, but despite that fact they were hunting deer at the time. They had built a brush fence and had set their snares and were out driving the deer in the usual way. Woodrat stopped here with them for a time. Woodrat went out with the Crow-people to hunt and he slipped back and went into the brush and rolled a large boulder down the hillside through the brush. When the Crows heard this sound they thought it was a deer running toward their fence and were sure that it would be caught.

Now with the Crows lived Toad, a one-eyed, old woman. She was the only one in the village who could see at all. It was her special business to keep watch and see that everything went right. When she saw Woodrat she said to the chief of the Crow-people that they must be very careful because he was the one who always fooled people.

Then Woodrat slipped away and started toward home. He went down the river for a short distance to where some of the Crow women were leaching acorn meal. He remained there for some time and ate much of their food because they were unable to see. Finally, however, Toad arrived and spied him and warned the Crow women that Woodrat was there fooling them and eating their acorns and their acorn soup.

From there Woodrat returned to the Crow village and entered the sweat-house. Presently the Crows came back and went into the house to have a sweating contest. Woodrat began to fan the fire violently as was the custom in such a contest, but the Crows told him that he was not the only one who was good at fanning. They did not know, as a matter of fact, that Woodrat was there. They thought that the fanning was being done by one of their own people.

Presently Toad came in and, again seeing Woodrat, she warned the Crow-people that Woodrat was there and was trying to kill them by making the air so hot.

As soon as they had finished with their sweating they went, as was customary, down to the stream to swim and then returned to the sweat-house. The chief of the Crows then announced that they would have a feast and told the attendants to bring in the food which was already prepared for this feast. Accordingly many baskets of acorn soup, deer meat, bread and various foods were brought into the sweat-house and the chief proceeded to distribute this food among all the people present. He distributed it very equally so that no one should be missed and be without his proper portion of the food. As the baskets were carried over to each individual, Woodrat jumped in and took the baskets in each case and put them all in one place for himself.

Again Toad arrived on the scene just in time, and when she saw what had happened she said, "Now, why do you give Woodrat all the food you have? You ought to know that he has been fooling you right along. He has fooled you many times so why should you give him all the food at this time?"

The chief then announced that the feast was over and that all must prepare to sleep. As a matter of fact the Crows only simulated slumber and about midnight when they felt certain that Woodrat was sound asleep they held a council and decided that they must kill Woodrat because he had been tricking them all and had done it so frequently.

As a matter of fact Woodrat was not asleep at all and he overheard their plans so he watched his chance and when the Crows finally fell asleep he picked up the chief of the Crows and carried him over and placed him where he had himself been lying. The chief was so sound asleep that he did not know what had happened and did not realize that he had been moved. Then Woodrat ran up on the inside of the house and concealed himself among the rafters near the center pole where he could watch and see what happened.

A number of the Crow-people next went out of the house and presently came back with knives and gathered around the spot where they presumed Woodrat was asleep. Then suddenly they all sprang upon the chief and began to cut him to pieces with their knives. He shouted most lustily and told them that they were killing their own chief, but they said among themselves, "That is Woodrat again just trying to fool us. He is saying that so that we will not kill him." Then they proceeded to cut the chief's body up with their knives and killed him.

Shortly after this Toad arrived at the sweat-house and said, "Why do you people kill your own chief? Of course you think that you have killed Woodrat but he is up there on top looking down to see what you are doing."

As soon as they realized what they had done they became still more determined to do away with Woodrat. They determined to surround the sweat-house and captured him as he attempted to escape. This plan amused Woodrat because he knew how totally blind they all were so he went up on top of the sweat-house and when they had made a circle around it he rolled down some clods of earth. They, of course, assumed that the noise made by these clods was the noise made by Woodrat in his attempt to escape so they struck wildly where they thought he was, striking the ground and hitting each other. While they were doing this Woodrat ran outside the circle and made his escape.

IV

(Woodrat and the Growing Tree)

As soon as he got away he immediately started toward the west and presently he came to a place where there lived a woman and a boy. She was pounding acorns and making acorn meal.

Directly in front of the house there was a sugar-pine tree with long cones hanging from its branches. These were only a few feet off the ground.

Woodrat asked the woman, "Where is your husband? Do you live here by yourself with this small boy?" When the woman said that she did, the boy began to cry and the woman told him that the boy was crying for pine-nuts. Woodrat tried to reach some of these pine cones for him but the woman told him that he could have to climb up into the tree in order to get them. This he did and when he had climbed nearly to the top of the tree he saw what was going to happen, for the tree began to sway. This was a magic tree which threw people way over into the ocean and killed them. Woodrat quickly sprang from this tree into the branches of an adjacent tree.

As the old woman saw the tree begin to sway she said, "That is the way I make my living. That is the way I treat people here."

But presently Woodrat came back into the house and the old woman was very much surprised. Woodrat said, "I am very cold. I am freezing. I must build a big fire." He sat around this fire until it had burned down so that there was nothing but a large bed of very hot coals. Then he picked up the old woman and the boy and threw them into the fire and held them there with a big stick. They cried loudly and begged for mercy, but he held them there until he had killed them.

The place where this happened was on a mountain east of Big River and close to the ocean.

V

(Woodrat and the Magic Swing)

Woodrat then traveled on farther westward and finally he came to a place where there were two girls swinging on a grape-vine hung from a tree.

These girls were Kaba′ltū (a small species of bird). As Woodrat approached they said, "This is the way we play. It is fine sport. If you want to swing you can come right in here and use our swing."

Woodrat replied, "I will gladly swing but when I do you must sit on my lap."

This they did and after a while they wanted Woodrat to sit in the swing alone. He did this and they twisted the swing up until only Woodrat's neck and head were visible and then they pulled the swing back and let it go. This was a magic swing and when they had it set properly in this way it flew up and threw Woodrat and the seat of the swing far out toward the ocean, but Woodrat was able to jump on the way through the air in such a manner that he lit in a tree and the swing went on into the ocean without him.

After some time the swing came back and the girls rejoiced saying, "That is the way we play. That is the way we kill people."

Then Woodrat came back and insisted that if that was their special plaything that they thought so much of that they must get in and he would swing them. Finally one of the girls did get into the swing and he twisted it up in the same manner and let it go and it threw the girl far out into the ocean and killed her. In due time the swing itself came back. This all happened at a place called "Ya′katapopo."

VI

(Woodrat Kills Fire-man)

Woodrat then left the other girl there and went away toward the north. Finally he arrived at a place called "Hō′napō" where he found a hot fire burning. There was no one there. The fire itself was human. This was, in reality, Fire-man. When Woodrat arrived he said, "This is my fire. I will sit down here and get warm."

Now, Fire did not want him around there so it increased in intensity tremendously and endeavored to kill him so he took a stick and poked it until it was all out and thus he killed it.

VII

(Woodrat and the Basket-people)

Next Woodrat turned toward the east and traveled a long distance until he came to where the Basket-people lived. There were none like ordinary human beings there but all kinds of baskets and they were human. Woodrat said, "This is fine. I have found my baskets at last. These are all my good baskets. I will have my soup and mush in these baskets." But the baskets did not want him and they jumped all around and would not remain where he placed them. Finally he became very angry and kicked them about and broke them all up. This happened at Pīka'napō.

VIII

(Woodrat and Putrid-man)

Woodrat then journeyed still farther east until he arrived at a place called "Pa'napō" where Pa'-tca (Putrid-man) lived. He found Pa'-tca making arrows and arrow-heads. In fact this is all he ever does.

Woodrat said to Pa'-tca, "You are making some very fine arrows there. I would like to have some of those so that I can kill game as I travel along."

However, the old man refused his request and Woodrat killed him, but he did not take any of the arrows when he left.

IX

(Woodrat and Spider-woman)

Woodrat traveled still farther and came to the home of Spider (Mīca'). The old Spider-woman said, "It is good that you have come. I want someone to marry my daughter. I wish you would marry my daughter and live right here with us."

In due time Woodrat retired and when the old Spider-woman thought that he was sound asleep she came towards him. Woodrat was, as a matter of fact, not asleep, for he had his suspicions and when he saw the old woman approaching him he jumped up quickly and killed her.

X

(Woodrat and Sharp-heel)

Then Woodrat traveled still farther east until he came to a house standing all alone. Here lived Kama-silī-dūketya (Sharp-heel) and her daughter. Again Woodrat was invited to marry this daughter and to live with Sharp-heel.

That night while Woodrat appeared to be asleep he saw Sharp-heel first whetting her foot, then coming toward him, and finally standing over him just ready to spear him through the heart with this sharp heel of hers. He quickly caught the foot and succeeded in sawing off this sharp point on her heel and throwing it away. That, of course, killed the old woman.

XI

(Woodrat and Mouse Kill Bear)

Woodrat next journeyed toward the south. As he went along he saw someone following him. He looked back and found that it was none other than his own brother, Mouse. He waited until Mouse caught up with him and then the two journeyed on together toward the south until they came to Bita'-pōpō where lived the old Bear-woman and her two daughters.

Bear said, "It is good that you have come here. I should like to have both of you for my sons-in-law and should like to have you remain here to hunt for us. Tomorrow we will go out on that mountain over there and you will stand on this side while I go around and drive the deer over toward you."

Accordingly on the following morning they went onto this mountain which lay westward from the village. She stationed the two men on the south side of the mountain telling them that there was a certain tree there with the trail passing under it and that she would go around the mountain and drive the deer along this trail.

They suspected that Bear intended to do them some harm so they took some dead wood and put blankets on it and put a bow and arrows with one of these dummies and a spear with the other. Then they climbed up in the tree above the dummies and prepared to kill Bear when she should attack the dummies.

Presently they heard Bear calling to them, "Look out now, the deer are coming. Here they come, look out for yourselves." So she came running along and jumped on one of the dummies and Woodrat immediately shot her and Mouse speared her. So they killed her there on the trail.

Then they went home and told the two Bear girls what had happened and asked them why their mother had not tried to kill them in the house. Then the two Bear girls wept because they knew that their mother was dead.

XII

(A Woman Kills Deer with Her Magic Pestle)

Next Woodrat and Mouse started back toward the north and they traveled until they came to a house where a woman and two girls were living. These two girls were called "Bicē-*t*aba-dawente."

The old woman made the two young men welcome and gave them nicely cooked venison and bread and acorn mush.

When it came time to retire they gave Mouse a deerskin blanket and wanted him to sleep way over near the wall but he objected to this and said that he could hardly breathe with that kind of a blanket so they gave him a rabbit-skin blanket and let him sleep out toward the front.

Now this old woman had a magic pestle (bicē-dakō). She would stand in front of the house and by the magic of this pestle would cause many deer to come right up to her. She would then pick out the best of them and kill them by striking them on the head with the pestle and would then throw their bodies into the house. Mouse watched this performance for some time and it seemed to him a very ludicrous procedure. He finally laughed outright. As soon as he did this the pestle broke squarely in two in the old woman's hand.

Woodrat became angry with his brother at this and ran out of the house; Mouse followed him.

As he went out the door the old woman struck at him and just touched his ear. Mouse followed along after Woodrat crying and calling to him, "My brother, do not leave me. My ear hurts where the old woman hit me with the pestle." Woodrat, however, paid no attention to him and went right along as if his brother were not calling to him. Mouse followed along crying away and presently his ear began to swell. It swelled up just as if he had a big blister on it.

XIII

(Woodrat and Mouse Are Transformed)

Then Woodrat waited for him because he saw that his ear was so badly swelled that he could hardly walk. When Mouse came up to Woodrat, the latter said, "I do not want you. You are doing wrong. I do not want you any more. You shall be Mouse from now on and you shall be bothering people all the time, stealing their things, running around

behind baskets and other things in the house and they shall call you
Mouse. You shall live under logs or any place you can find. I shall
turn into Woodrat now and shall live in my house in the woods. I will
build my own house in the woods. This shall be the last of us."

81—WOODRAT KILLS MORNING-STAR WITH A MAGIC SWING[194]

*Characters: 1. Morning-star, 2. Woodrat, 3. Morning-star's daughters (two),
4. Magic swing.*

Morning-star (Kaa'-toltol) used to catch people in his swing which
he set on Mt. Kanaktai. He set this swing in one place in the fence
which was on the rocky ridge running north and south on the summit of
the mountain. He drove people every day over from the east toward
the mountain. The younger and more nimble people were able to climb
over but he always caught one of the older or the lame people.

He had two daughters who lived in a house quite a distance away
but they were unable to get husbands because Morning-star was jealous
of all the young men and watched his daughters so very close that no
one dared venture to court them. Finally, however, Woodrat went to
the house and courted these girls. He courted them for a long time and
endeavored to get one of them to marry him.

Finally, the elder of the two girls said, "Well, Woodrat, if you like
me, all right, I will marry you, but you must know that my father has
protected me with thorns."

Rat married the girl and then took a stone and broke off all these
thorns.

When Morning-star came home, and found Woodrat, he said, "Well,
my son-in-law, we will have to have a little fun. We will have to play."
So the two went over west to Mt. Kanaktai, where they were to have their
game. Morning-star had a large swing which swung out over the cliffs
on the east side of Mt. Kanaktai and away out over Little Borax Lake.
This swing was made of grape-vines. When they arrived here, they argued
for a long time, each one endeavoring to coax the other to swing first.
Finally Woodrat yielded and got into the swing. Morning-star then
swung Woodrat out over the cliff for some time, but finally stopped
the swing and twisted it round and round, till the grape-vines had

---

[194]The Pomo title of this myth is "Cemī kaa'tōltōl yetca kawan kemūn matū de," Old time
Morning-star-people eat my story.
Informant: Bill James, Garcia River, Central dialect, 1906.

wound around each other so that they bound down into Woodrat's neck and doubled him up in the swing. Morning-star then let the swing go and it unwound with terrific force; but Woodrat came off unharmed.

He then told his father-in-law to get into the swing and he swung it out over the lake and then twisted it just as his father-in-law had done. He twisted and twisted the swing until the ropes came down and caught Morning-star and still he twisted until Morning-star's body was mashed and the bones stuck through the flesh. When Woodrat saw this, he let go the swing and it untwisted with great force and threw Morning-star far out over the bluff. Then Woodrat went home to where his wife was and lived there.

82—SKUNK KILLS DEER WITH HER SCENT[195]

Characters: 1. Skunk-woman, 2. Skunk boys (two), 3. Deer-people, 4. Deer (Grandfather of Skunk boys).

Old Skunk-woman had two boys but no husband. She wanted to kill a deer, so she pretended she was ill and told her boys to go to a certain place and get a doctor. The boys, accordingly, took their bows and arrows and started off toward the east, the elder singing as they went along about how his mother had been taken ill, and that he was going for a doctor, going to get his grandfather, the big Deer. The boys went on until they came to a big mountain, in the side of which there was a hole. This mountain was the sweat-house where the Deer-people lived and the hole was the entrance. The Deer-people invited the boys to come in and sit down. They told the Deer-people what they wished and that they had come to get their grandfather to doctor their mother, who was ill. So the biggest deer came out from his place in the sweat-house near the drum. He always stayed far back in the house this way.

The three then started back toward Skunk's home. As they returned, the elder of the two brothers sang the same song and finally, their mother heard them singing and knew that they were returning. When they came in, she asked Deer to sit down. She told him she was ill, that she felt badly in her buttocks. Now Deer was what is known as a sucking doctor and when he commenced to doctor her, she shot him

---

[195]Informant: Bill James, Garcia River, Central dialect, 1906.

right in the mouth with her scent and killed him. The boys immediately skinned the deer and they cooked and ate it that night.

The next morning, they again went out and got another doctor. They did this way four times but the fourth time they whispered to each other and Deer heard them, became suspicious and ran back to his house. The boys then went home and told their mother that their grandfather would not come with them but that he had returned to his home. Then their mother returned with them to the Deer sweat-house. She shot into the sweat-house with her scent and killed all of the deer there. She left these dead deer in the sweat-house and they went home.

MYTHS OF MAGIC DEVICES

83—THE GROWING ROCK[196]
INCIDENTS AND CHARACTERS

I. *The rescue from Growing Rock by Measuring Worm.*
    1. *Bluebird brothers (two), 2. Crow, 3. Bluebird, 4. Buzzard, 5. Crane, 6. Eagle, 7. Chicken Hawk, 8. Cīna'-batcōdok, 9. Vulture, 10. Green Measuring Worm, 11. Growing Rock.*

II. *The theft of fire by Jackrabbit.*
    1. *Measuring Worm, 2. Bat, 3. Oak-ball, 4. Crane, 5. Eagle, 6. Buzzard, 7. Vulture, 8. Duck, 9. Jackrabbit, 10. Fire-man.*

III. *The Adventures of the Bluebird brothers.*
    1. *Bluebird-woman, 2. Measuring Worm, 3. Bluebird brothers (two), 4. Blue Jay, 5. Crow, 6. Mink, 7. Chicken Hawk, 8. Wind-man, 9. Stone-woman, 10. Magic basket, 11. Magic pestle, 12. Magic stone wall, 13. Arrow-man, 14. Menelĭ people.*

I

(The Rescue from Growing Rock by Measuring Worm)

At Kōwa'nnō[197] there were two Bluebird brothers who went down to the river for a swim. They found a flat rock near the river and sat there for a time and finally fell asleep, it was so warm.

Presently along came Crow (Kaa'i) who had come down to the river to get water and when Crow saw these two children sleeping here

---

[196]The Pomo name of this myth is "kūtcīya ka kōma kabē tōl kōtc matū."
Informant: Bill James, Central dialect.
[197]This place is said to be located east of Rock Pile, and somewhere between Cloverdale and Yorkville.

he made a wish, "I wish that rock would grow tall and reach clear into the sky with those children still on it."

Immediately this rock began to grow. It grew and grew, very tall indeed. By and by their mother missed them and looked all over the village for them. She finally hunted down by the river and eventually saw this tall rock on top of which were her children clear up in the sky. She immediately began to cry for the children. Then she went back to her house and collected all of her valuables, all her beads, her belts, baskets and other valuable things and brought them down to the river and placed them in a circle around the base of this tall rock and she said that whoever was able to rescue the children and bring them down to her could have everything that she had placed there.

First Buzzard tried to climb up to the top of this rock. He climbed and climbed but by the time that he had reached half-way to its top he was very tired and very thirsty and finally gave it up and slid back down to the ground. Then Crane made an attempt to reach the top but he only succeeded in climbing a little higher than Buzzard had gone. Then Eagle, Chicken Hawk (Tcīya'), Cīna'-batcōdok, Vulture and many others made the attempt, but all without success.

Finally the mother appealed to Green Measuring Worm (mtca'-tsīmūl). She said, "I want you to try to get my children up there in the sky. If you succeed I will give you all the things I have placed around that high rock."

Now Measuring Worm lived in a house by himself and was very old. He replied, "I am a very old man but I will try. I will see what I can do."

Measuring Worm then went home and dressed himself properly. He put on a top-knot of feathers, painted himself with red paint, striped with black his face and covered his face with grease so it would look shiny. Not only did this improve his looks but it made him very strong. He also put two strands of beads about his neck and put on his hunting sack. Then he walked over to the magic rock with the aid of his cane.

Soon he began to climb just as any measuring worm would climb, length by length, and he went on and on and on, higher and higher, up the sheer precipitous side of the rock and the people as they watched him began to feel very much elated because they knew that he would make the top of the rock and bring the children down.

Now, the very top of this rock flared out, somewhat like a mushroom, and when he came up near the top he stopped and rested. Then he turned around and started up this last flaring section backwards. Finally when he came to the very edge he flipped over it head first onto the very top of the rock. The children were extremely glad to see him and jumped about with glee but he warned them that they must be very careful and not jump about too much or they might fall off the top of this rock and be killed.

After the old man had rested for a time he put the children into his hunting sack and descended the rock quite rapidly. This descent was very easy because, whereas he had had to "measure" his way up, he could now simply slide down.

Old Bluebird was at the bottom of the rock to welcome the children and all the people praised Measuring Worm for what he had done. They picked him up and put him into a large basket, gave him a bath, and gave him water to drink out of another basket. The basket in which they bathed him was a very large flaring basket of the type called "stūptcī." The one from which they gave him the drinking water was a very beautifully made, small basket, decorated with quail plumes and red-headed-woodpecker feathers about its edge.

Finally he collected all of the gifts that were his reward for having rescued the children and went home.

II

(The Theft of Fire by Jackrabbit)

Now, everyone in the village was extremely interested in this rescue by Measuring Worm. They all collected around the rock and watched him as he slowly made his way to the top and as he brought the children down and they were so intent upon this that they forgot all about their fires and every fire in the village went out so that everyone was cold. The trouble was that no one knew how to make fire in those days.

Bat (Hō'smatalak) had very small eyes and could not see at all well.

Bat insisted that he could see fire only a short distance away but the people were very much provoked with him and said, "You have such small eyes that you can hardly see at all. Why do you want to tell us something like that, when we are all freezing?" They would not believe Bat at all.

They called Oak-ball, who had very good eyes and could see a long distance, and he climbed up a tree and looked around. Then he asked Bat where the fire was.

Bat replied, "Right over there."

Finally Oak Ball saw it and said, "Yes, I see that fire. It is right over there. They have a big fire and there are people around it."

They wanted someone then to go and get some of this fire and various of the Bird-people tried it. First Crane (Klē′yaka) volunteered saying, "I am a good runner, I will go and get that fire." He tried to but failed. Then Eagle, Buzzard, Vulture, Duck (Cna″-batcū′dŭk), and many of the other Bird-people tried to get this fire but they all failed. Finally Jackrabbit (Maka′la) was the only one who had not tried and the people said to him, "We want you to try and see what you can do. We need that fire very much and you must try to get it."

He agreed to see what he could do and started off toward the east. Oak-ball watched him on the journey for he was the one who could see farther than anyone else. Finally he announced that Jackrabbit had nearly reached the place where the fire was located. Finally he arrived at this village and stopped and looked the ground over to see just what he could do. Finally when he heard the man who kept the fire snoring so that he was sure that he was sound asleep Rabbit slipped in and stole a piece of bark which was on fire and ran as fast as he could down to the valley but when this man woke up he pursued him and finally caught him and took the fire away and put it back. He again went to sleep and Rabbit slipped in and stole another firebrand. He was pursued again with the same result.

Then Rabbit studied to see just how he could hide the fire. At first he thought of putting it under his arm but it was too hot so he ran off with it in his hand again. Again Fire-man caught up with him, this time just as he had reached the edge of some brush. So Rabbit sat down on the fire and covered it completely. The man felt around all over him but could not find it. Of course Rabbit fidgeted around all the time because the fire was burning him as he sat there but he was able to hold out until Fire-man gave up in disgust and returned home.

Then Rabbit picked up his brand and came on to the village with it in his hand. They then made a big fire and everyone got warm.

Because Jackrabbit sat on this firebrand and concealed it in this way he now has a large area on his rump which looks as if it had been burned.

III

(The Adventures of the Bluebird Brothers)

A few days after this old Bluebird-woman fell to thinking about the fine things that she had given to Measuring Worm for rescuing her two little boys. It made her feel very badly that she had given away so much and now was so poor and had so very little so she left the two boys and started off toward the south.

The smaller of these boys was a mere baby and presently he became hungry and cried for his mother. The elder of the two looked about the village for her and inquired of the people if they knew where she had gone. To this they replied that she had gone toward the south, so he took his little brother and started out, following the mother's tracks. Finally they came in sight of her and he called to her saying that the baby was hungry. The mother, however, did not look back at all or pay any attention to him, so the boys followed on and on until she went behind a hill and they lost track of her.

Finally they came to a place where they found an old man, Blue Jay, and his wife. The old man said, "How does it come that you two children travel this way?"

The elder of the two boys replied, "Our mother left us and we have to follow her. We would like to know if you saw her go by."

Blue Jay said, "Yes, she went this way two or three hours ago but she did not come here."

Blue Jay and his wife took the little boys in and gave them some food. The baby had grown very rapidly since they started on this journey and was now large enough so that he could walk.

After they had eaten they journeyed on, still following their mother's tracks. They went farther and farther. They saw various kinds of game but they did not know what it was.

Finally they came to another house where Crow and his wife were living. Crow asked, "Well, my boy, how does it come that you come here?"

The elder boy replied, "Mother left us and we are in search of her. Did she go this way?"

"Yes," said Crow, "She went by here but did not look at me."

Crow gave them food and after they had eaten the elder of the two children said, "Grandpa, I want a bow and some arrows, and I want also a bow and some arrows for my little brother who is now growing very rapidly and getting bigger." Crow gave them bows, arrows and quivers and they journeyed on still farther to the south.

By and by they saw a deer lying at the edge of some brush and the little brother asked, "My brother, what is that there near the edge of the brush? It looks like an old log."

"That is what they call an elk. It is good food."

The younger brother said, "I am going to kill that animal." Whereupon he slipped up and killed him. They took some of the skin and made a quiver but did not eat any of the meat.

Then they went on and came to another house. This was the place where Mink and his wife lived. When they saw this house the younger brother said to his elder brother, "Let us go up to that house and see if we can get some arrows."

They did go to Mink's house and were received there, given food and they remained over night there also. When they had breakfasted in the morning they told Mink that they would like to get more arrows. He filled up their quivers and they started on.

After they had gone for some time the younger brother wanted to know if the elder had ever engaged in a war. Upon being told that he had not this younger brother said, "Well, let us try and see what we can do. Can you shoot an arrow swiftly and straight? You go over on the other side of that tree and we will shoot at each other."

They practiced this shooting for quite a long time until they had used up almost all of their arrows and then they concluded that they had had enough practice so that they could take care of themselves in a battle.

Then they went on their way and finally they came to another house. This was the house of Chicken Hawk (Kabē kat) who lived here with his wife. Again they asked for arrows and their quivers were filled. Besides these, Chicken Hawk gave them a bundle of arrows neatly tied up. They were also given food and then they went on their way.

Presently the younger brother saw something on a sugar pine tree biting off the cones. He said to his elder brother, "What is that biting off those limbs over there?"

The elder brother replied, "That is a grizzly bear. He will eat people."

The younger brother then said, "I am going to kill him."

"No," said the elder brother, "He will eat you."

To this the younger brother replied, "No, he will not eat me. I am raw, I am not cooked. I will kill him."

So he went up to the tree and scratched with an arrow on the tree. The bear came down and grabbed him but he fought with the bear until it was tired and gave out and then he killed him. They skinned this bear and made another quiver out of the skin.

The younger brother told his elder brother to give him the deerskin quiver as it was the most ordinary and insisted that the elder brother take the bearskin sack or quiver which was the better of the two.

They went on south again and saw something there in an open place.

The younger brother asked, "What is that long-eared thing over there?"

"That," said the elder brother, "is Wind-man (Ya-tca). He is a very dangerous being. He makes the wind blow. He could blow you completely away."

"I am going to kill that fellow," said the younger brother.

"No," said the elder brother, "you must not do that. He will blow you away."

"No," said the younger brother, "he cannot do that, I am no feather." So he went down there and took an arrow and played with this peculiar being's ear. Finally Ya-tca woke up and seeing the boy, blew at him and blew him way back to where his brother was.

Then the elder brother said, "Did I not tell you he would blow you away? He can blow anything away. He can blow trees down if he wants to."

This encounter had scared the younger brother so he made no further attempt to kill Ya-tca, but passed on.

The boys went on still farther to the south until they came to a small house standing near a very high, vertical, stone wall, a wall which reached clear to the sky and which had only one narrow opening through which it was possible to pass. On the opposite side of this wall there was a valley. This little house was Kabē-mata-tca, the residence of Stone-woman (Kabe-mata), a woman made entirely of stone but in human form. Anyone who ever enters this house never returns alive.

When they arrived at the house of Kabe mata there they saw their mother. When she saw the boys she said, "My poor children. How does it come that you are here? Did you see me coming here?" The younger brother was behind the elder and when he saw his mother he took an arrow and shot her. The arrow entered just below the umbilicus and she fell over dead into the fire and burned.

Stone-woman then threw a basket at them. It was a flat basket and it had an edge like that of a saw. This basket chased these boys around and wherever the basket hit anything it cut it in two. She also had a pestle that followed them along on the ground so that if in dodging the basket they dodged downward and lay flat to get away from it, the pestle would catch them. As the basket and the pestle chased the boys Stone-woman followed after them. They succeeded, however, in escaping the two miraculous objects and finally ran up to the stone wall. As they did so a place opened up in the wall and the one who controlled this place called to them to come through and they did. Stone-woman tried to go through also but, as she did, the opening closed suddenly and caught and killed her.

When the boys had passed through this stone wall they saw Arrow-man (Tsū′-tca). He was the one who made all the arrows for the Menelī village. He had, in fact, a whole houseful of arrows there. His arrow straightener was a small stick with holes in it.

When the younger brother saw the great quantities of arrows that he had, he said, "Well Arrow-man, you make many arrows. Are you a good shot?"

"Yes," said Arrow-man, "I can shoot pretty well."

"Well then," said the younger brother, "let us have a shooting contest. Let us shoot through the hole in your arrow straightener. If I shoot through the hole I win and if you shoot through it, you win."

"All right," said Arrow-man, "And if I shoot through the hole in the stick I will kill you and if you shoot through the hole in the stick you will kill me."

To this the younger brother agreed. The elder brother then put up the stick as a target and Arrow-man took the first shot. He missed the hole. He hit it just on the edge but his arrow did not go through it.

"Why," said the younger brother, "I thought you could shoot better than that. Now I will shoot. I will show you how to shoot." Whereupon he shot and his arrow passed directly through the small hole in the stick and then killed Arrow-man.

Then the whole Meneli village descended upon them and began to shoot at them. They stepped to one side, dodged properly to escape the arrows of their antagonists, and began to shoot back. In the course of a short time they had killed every member of the village. Then the boys went back to their homes whence they had come.

84—QUAIL ASCENDS INTO THE SKY ON A MAGIC CANE[198]

Characters: 1. Quail, 2. Magic cane, 3. Meadowlark brothers (Sons of Quail), 4. Coyote, 5. Magic stone tower, 6. Kï'lak, 7. Blue-fly, 8. Token at Kï'lak's house.

Quail was an old woman. She had two boys, one about five years old and the other about twelve. She went out to hunt clover.

As she was picking clover she heard a noise above her and looking up she saw a cane (walking-stick) coming down from the heavens. It struck the ground and stuck there near her. She took hold of this cane and it took her up into the heavens (Xalï' wïnaūna).

When the old woman did not return to the village the people missed her and began hunting for her. They followed her tracks out to where she had been gathering clover and they finally found the basket that she had taken out there. Then they found her tracks over to a point where they suddenly stopped. This was where she had taken hold of the magic cane when it had taken her up into the sky. They looked up and they saw blood-red line going straight up into the heavens.

Her two boys were Meadowlarks. These boys remained at home alone all the time. The elder said to the younger, "I hope you will grow up very quickly and that we will both become men very soon." They were all the time practicing at flying and trying to see how high they could fly. They wished for a round, hollow, rock tower and it came. They wished that this wall should be about eight feet in diameter and that at first it should be about twenty feet in height and it was. They

---

[198]The Pomo title of this myth is "Dok dagara yeek kal so babï'le idaixa cakoik kaiyū'ï giwa gaiyek dïgïle," "A long time ago old woman (kind) clover go after at that time cane fall."

wanted this rock tower so that they could practice their flying without permitting anyone to see what they were doing. They flew round and round in their tower all the time until they were able to fly up easily to the top of it.

Then they wished that the tower would grow still higher. Immediately it did so and they practiced flying to the top of this. Then they wished that it might grow still more and then still more and the wall always grew in accordance with their wishes, higher and higher all the time until finally the rock tower grew so that it actually touched the sky.

They, of course, did not know this but really Coyote was doing this for them and was causing this magic tower to grow as they wished. They had to have this tower so that the wind could not blow them away as they flew upward. Coyote caused this tower to grow up to the very spot where the gate to the Upper World is located and through this the boys entered into the Upper World and out onto the top of the sky. It had taken them many days to perfect themselves in flying this way and to get this tower high enough to reach the sky but all this time they had not eaten a thing nor had they taken any water.

When they reached the Upper World they journeyed over toward the east from the gate and there they found the house of Kī'lak and they found that the door to this house was on the south side. No one ever dared to go to the house of Kī'lak, he was such a dangerous man. But the boys had come up here to fight with him and to avenge the taking of their mother. Kī'lak was out hunting at the time. He is hunting a great deal of the time. He takes people and eats nothing but human blood.

The boys went to the door and saw their mother inside. The younger of the brothers said, "See, there is our mother in there."

But the elder replied, "Do not say that. We did not come here to see our mother. She is gone. She is now a ghost (xa hlūī xak)."

Kī'lak had, just inside the door of his house, a trap made of rattlesnakes. Quail saw her two sons and before they attempted to enter she threw into the trap a short pestle. This trap was located in the tunnel at the doorway, which was six or eight feet long. As the pestle struck the ground the rattlesnakes bit at it and bit at one another and killed one another. Then the boys entered the house with safety.

When they entered the house their mother asked them to sit down.

Then she said, "My sons, I am nobody. What makes you come to me? I am your mother no longer. They killed me and took me up here."

Blue-fly ("bura'gal-tsa'mal" or "tsa'mal") lived in the house here with Kī'lak. His special business is to break the shin-bones of people whom Kī'lak brings to the house as food. These people are then allowed to lie there with their shin-bones broken in this way and suffer for a long time before they finally die. Blue-fly takes the marrow out of their bones and sucks their blood. When Kī'lak brings a victim home it is always alive. He lights at the smoke-hole in the roof and throws his victim into the house. Blue-fly drags the victim over behind the center pole and breaks his shin-bones with a pestle. He then extracts the blood and the marrow, and then throws the victim out through the smoke-hole again. Not until then does Kī'lak enter the house.

Quail dug a hole in the floor of the house, under one of the acorn storage baskets (ditīr) and hid the two boys in it.

Then Kī'lak came home. When Kī'lak is out hunting and is ready to start home, his house always shakes and creaks, thus giving the sign to the occupants that Kī'lak is on his way. When the old woman heard this sign she told the boys that Kī'lak was coming and that they must hide and keep very quiet. The boys, however, did not care about Kī'lak's coming because they had come there to contest with him and to kill him.

Every time Kī'lak reaches home he first flies around his house four times in each direction before entering it. He did this, of course, this time and then he alighted at the smoke-hole and threw his prey in through the smoke-hole. He had to stand there at the smoke-hole until Blue-fly had broken the legs of the victim, which in this case was a woman, and had sucked the marrow out of the bones before he could enter.

Upon this occasion Blue-fly did not break the bones immediately. He was afraid to do so because there were strangers present and he was afraid that if the boys saw what he was doing they might kill him. Kī'lak became impatient and called down to Blue-fly to know what was the matter and why he did not proceed with his work. Finally Blue-fly broke the shins of this victim, sucked out the marrow and threw the victim back where it belonged. Then Kī'lak entered. He asked Quail-woman what she had done with the boys who came to visit him and told her to make them come out of their hiding place. This Quail did and the boys came out and talked with Kī′lak.

Kī′lak asked them, "How did it happen that you boys thought about your father?" They made no reply to this question. That evening he said to the boys, "Tomorrow we will have a game. I would like to contest with somebody but no one ever comes here to play with me."

On the following morning they had a "grass game". This was not a grass game such as we now play, but a game in which the opponents shot with bows and arrows.

Now, before the boys had started up, on this visit to Kī′lak, Coyote had given them some instructions and told them what they must do when they met Kī′lak. Coyote told them that they must make Kī′lak take the lead in this game because it was his custom to make a visitor take the lead and he always won when he played with anyone else on that account.

Before they began to play Kī′lak and the boys argued for a long time as to which should "take out"[199] first. Finally they induced Kī′lak to do so. The younger of the two boys wanted to shoot at Kī′lak first, but the elder insisted that he should first because he considered himself to be more sure of his aim and knew that Kī′lak would dodge downward to avoid the arrow. His shot was successful and he struck Kī′lak in the throat. Kī′lak fell down dead and simultaneously everything in his house fell down from the wall.

When Blue-fly saw that Kī′lak was dead he rejoiced and told the boys how very sorry he was that he had been obliged to break the bones of so many people and suck out their marrow and blood. Outside of Kī′lak's house there were all kinds of dry bleached bones, of young and old people who had been long dead; some who had died very recently; some who were just alive and about ready to die; other people who were suffering from the way they had been maimed. Blue-fly asked the boys not to burn the house because he wanted to continue to live there.

Finally the boys took a tump line (kōkō) which they had brought with them. They tied this around their mother, Quail, and started back home. They carried her in this manner all the way back home where they lived a long time after that.

---

[199]The term that is used in playing the grass game is "take out" or "come out." This signifies that the person holding the bones in the game and arranging them in his hand behind his back, brings his hand around in front of him so that his opponent may guess in which hand the marked or unmarked bone is located.

85—A MAGIC TREE KILLS FALCON[200]

Characters: 1. Falcon, 2. Quail (Falcon's wife), 3. Coyote, 4. Cē'tata, 5. Magic sling, 6. Doves, 7. Magic tree, 8. Meadowlark, 9. Blue Jay.

At a village over on the shore of Clear Lake, Falcon lived with the Quail sisters, one of whom was his wife. In this same house lived Cē'tata, who was a "noble" (tsī dī man).[201] With them also lived Coyote.

Falcon used to go hunting over toward the east. He went way out into the plains (kagō'mōrī).[202]

Cē'tata had a bed made of poles raised off the ground such as is used only by a dignitary and which is called "xai'dasōtī." Upon this he was accustomed to recline all the time without doing any work and without ever hunting. His brother Falcon did all the hunting. He had a magic sling and a magic rock. When he threw this rock it would strike a goose or other target and then would come back to him. He would catch it with his hand. He hunted geese regularly and with this sling he could take as many as he wanted at any time. He would pick them up and put them in his hair to carry them home. He wore his hair tied up directly over his head so as to make a tall, pointed, cap-like arrangement and into this he would put, sometimes as many as twenty geese at a time. Now, this nobleman, Cē'tata, and Coyote lived together in a large sweat-house but Falcon, his wife, and his sister-in-law, lived in an ordinary house nearby.

When Falcon came home with his load of geese he gave some of them to his brother, Cē'tata, and Coyote, and took some home to his wife and his sister-in-law. He did this every day. Finally, however, Cē'tata became provoked with his brother Falcon and told him, "If you have any regard for me you will go over to that tree (indicating a tree about a mile or so west of the village) and get me those young doves out of

---

[200]Informant: Tom Mitchell, Eastern dialect.

[201]The term "tsī dī man," which is here translated as noble or nobleman, was said by informants to indicate a person who is of the very highest rank, one who is so important and so wealthy that he does not have to do any work at all, but lives in the utmost ease. He has a special kind of chair and has a bed made of poles set up off the ground. He lives in a very fine house, wears the finest of clothing and never has to exert himself in any way. He has a servant to bring him his food and even to bring him water when he is thirsty.

[202]The term "kagō'mōrī" signifies any very large valley with waving fields of tall grass. The term "mōrī" signifies a waving field of grain as it appears with a gentle breeze blowing over it, or a similarly waving field of tall grass. The term "kagō'" means "valley," hence this term literally means "valley waving." The waving of a field of grain or grass is quite distinct from the water wave or from the heat waves that are seen on the ground.

the nest there." Cĕ'tata knew that if his brother went to this tree it would kill him.

Falcon replied, "Those birds are pretty hard to catch." However because it was his brother who had made this request and it had been his habit to take care of his brother in every way, he went. The tree was a short one, perhaps twice as high as a man, and he could touch the limbs from the ground. It was on one of these limbs that the dove's nest was located.

Now, before Falcon started out, Coyote had endeavored to warn him against this venture saying, "That nest is very bad." These were as a matter of fact, magic birds.

When Falcon arrived at the tree he found that he could reach the nest from the ground quite easily so he put his hand into the nest but the birds jumped out and ran a little way up and Falcon jumped up after them. But as he jumped the birds climbed still higher in the tree. He jumped repeatedly but the birds evaded him and went higher and higher in the tree. Finally he climbed up into the tree and chased the birds all around in its branches.

All this time Falcon was so intent upon catching the doves that he looked only at them. He never looked down and did not see that the tree was growing all the time. The tree reached a prodigious height and Falcon did not notice it at all. Meanwhile Falcon's wife had followed him and she sat beneath the tree crying for him because she knew that he was going to be killed. When the tree reached a great height a mighty wind came and blew Falcon out of the tree and as he tumbled down through the air he was blown all to pieces. There was nothing left of him at all.

When Falcon's wife and his sister-in-law saw that he was killed they both cried for him for a long time.[203]

---

[203]The wailing song used by Falcon's wife was the following:
> wa'lila matŏ'ya ha'nŏse
> wa'lila matŏ'ya ha'nŏse
> wa'lila matŏ'ya ha'nŏse
> hŏ'kĕya hŏ'kĕya hŏ'mala
> hatŏ'ya hanŏ'se
> hatŏ'ya hanŏ'se
> (Repeat above indefinitely)

The song sung by his sister-in-law was as follows:
> hŏ'pŏ hŏnĭ'sĕ hŏ'pŏ honĭ'se
> (Repeat indefinitely)

This latter song was in the nature of a burden to the main song which was sung by Falcon's wife. The informant said that neither of these were used by a present day people as dirges, but that these were the special songs sung by the two Quails on this particular occasion.

Finally the Quail sisters went home. On the following morning they went out to this same place and they found that the tree had come down again to its former normal size and height. They looked all around to try to find some part of Falcon's remains, even a fragment of bone or anything of the kind. Falcon's wife finally found a little of his hair and brought this home.

When she brought this home Coyote told her to put it into some water in a cooking basket and then to invert a burden basket over this in order to cover it and to place it in the house. When this had been done Coyote came and curled his body around this basket and slept there.[204] The two women continued their mourning, crying and singing in the same manner as they had before. They continued their mourning during all the time that Coyote slept, coiled about this basket, which was four days and four nights.

On the fourth night he heard something in the basket. It sounded like fish swimming about in the water and jumping up out of it. Then he heard a voice calling "ma'tīle, ma'tīle."[205]

Coyote then jumped up and lifted the burden basket and behold there was Falcon brushing and drying his hair.

Falcon came out and next morning they prepared to have a celebration, a Maai kako bako.[206] They also built a big fire in the sweat-house and all sweated and swam as is customary at such times and then they returned to the sweat-house.

Now Falcon was formerly chief of this village and he alone did not participate in this feast and celebration, but after they had all returned to the sweat-house he decided that he would go over there and see the people. He entered the sweat-house and sat down on the west side of the fire. Everyone was talking and rejoicing over the recovery of Falcon when Meadowlark entered. Meadowlark was a very morose and testy fellow and was given to speaking out without ever stopping to think what he was saying. He entered the sweat-house and sniffed the air. Then he said, "hūⁿ————, it seems as though I smell something.

---

[204]This curling around or wrapping around anything is called "parītkī." It actually refers to coiling after the manner of the coiling of a snake or the coiling of a hop-vine about a pole. It does not, however, refer to the ordinary curling up of an animal like a cat or a dog as it sleeps. Coyote was said to "coil" himself around this basket.

[205]The term "ma'tīle" signifies "paternal grandfather."

[206]The term "maai kako bako" signifies a feast held by friends outside the family to celebrate the recovery of someone who has been dangerously ill.

hūⁿ————, what is that that smells as though it had been burned? What have you people been putting into the fire?"

No one answered him. Everyone disliked him. Finally Blue Jay cursed him and picked up a stick of firewood and struck at him. Meadowlark dodged and started to run out of the sweat-house. As he dodged the blow aimed at him, the stick missed his body but it struck his tail and cut off about one-half of it. That is why the tail of the meadowlark is so short even now.

The rest of the Bird-people had said nothing about the odor because they felt sorry for Falcon and were really glad that he had returned to life but when Meadowlark spoke out the way he did Falcon realized that he still bore the odor of the dead and that he was not a fit person to associate with living people so he went away.

Meadowlark is always foolish and is constantly doing such crazy things. If Meadowlark had not said what he did at this time people would come back to life four days after they die.

86—SWAN FISHES IN HER STONE CANOE[207]

Characters: 1. Swan, 2. Magic stone canoe, 3. Bear, 4. Swan's daughters (two), 5. Falcon, 6. Fog bridge.

Swan lived down at the lower end of these lakes, down in the vicinity of Sulphur Bank. She had a canoe which was made entirely of stone. No one knows how she built it or where she got it. She used to go out fishing in this stone canoe and she would always start at the north end of the lake and fish as she traveled toward home. She had an immense fish-net and when she put this into the water it reached completely across the lake from the east to the west shores so that no fish could possibly get past it. She would put this net in, up at the extreme upper end of Clear Lake, and continue to fish with the net set this way and would not lift it until she had reached a point opposite Bald Hill (Kitsī danoyo). Here she would lift her net, take the fish out of it and place them in her boat and then she would go on home.

Now, Bear was Swan's husband and she had two Swan daughters.

As she unloaded her canoe and placed the fish in her burden basket

---

[207]The Pomo title of this myth is "Koᵣ daxaraiyeek xabe onnai ca hip dūlī," "Swan old woman rock boat fish hunting."
Informant: Tom Mitchell, Eastern dialect.

to take them home, she would put a dry manzanita bush on top of the basket. In the evening she would cook these fish with hot rocks in an underground oven. Swan-woman fished in this way regularly every day.

Falcon went out hunting on the slopes of Mt. Kanaktai. He went out very early in the morning and went to the very top of this high mountain. From this point of vantage he saw a smoke arising from across the lake at a point near Sulphur Bank and he decided to go over and visit the people who lived there. He, therefore, caused a bridge of fog to cross from the top of Mt. Kanaktai to the top of Bald Hill. He crossed over on this bridge and then went from there down toward Sulphur Bank.

It was a bright morning and the two Swan girls were sitting out on the sunny side of the hill near their house when they saw Falcon coming.

The younger of the girls said, "There is my husband coming toward the house."

But the elder one replied, "Where is the man? I do not see him."

The younger one replied, "I did not find that man for you anyway. That is my husband."

"No," said the elder, "He is mine. You are too young to have a husband."

To this the younger one replied, "That makes no difference. He is mine for I saw him first."

Thus the two girls argued about the matter and finally the elder one said, "Let us not argue about the matter. We will have him as our husband together." To which the younger Swan girl agreed.

As a matter of fact these girls did not know who this man was, nor did they know anything about whether he intended to remain there.

Finally Falcon arrived, sat down close to the girls and inquired, "What are you girls doing here? Where is your home?" They were ashamed to answer and sat without making reply. Then Falcon continued, "I am talking to you two girls. Where is your home? Where are my mother-in-law and my father-in-law?"

To this they replied, "You are not our husband. What makes you ask for your mother-in-law and your father-in-law?"

Well," replied Falcon, "I should like to go over to see them."

The girls were really very bashful and it was with great reluctance that they took him to their home but they finally did so and he remained there.

The next morning the old Swan-woman took her magic stone canoe and went out fishing as usual. She was gone all day long. The others remained at home. She went to the upper end of the lake and as usual fished down toward Sulphur Bank. When she arrived at Bald Hill she pulled up her net and took out the fish. She always had to do this because the passage from Clear Lake into East and Lower Lakes is so narrow that she could not pass it with her big net. She came home with a canoe full of fish. When Swan returned to the house, she, as usual, brought in a basketful of fish, with a large, dry manzanita bush on top of her basket. She then cleaned out the baking pit, heated it and the rocks needed for the baking and then put in the fish, protecting them with the tule bark as above mentioned.

Swan did this day after day for several days while Falcon remained at home with Bear and the two Swan girls. Finally Bear said, "My son-in-law, there are good ripe manzanita berries now, without seeds. I like them very much. I hope you will go out in the morning and get me some of them."

Falcon said, he would do so and Bear told him just where to go. He went out early in the morning and followed Bear's instructions. When Falcon reached up to get some of the manzanita berries a bear jumped upon him and bit at him but Falcon was very agile. He sprang to one side and avoided the bear's rush, whirled and shot and killed the bear on the spot. He then gathered some of the berries and returned home, arriving at about noon. He gave some of the berries to the girls.

Falcon's father-in-law was there. He said nothing but went out to see what had happened. Then he came back and said, "What is the matter here? This seems strange to me." It did seem very strange to Bear that Falcon was able to go into such a dangerous place and escape with his life.

Falcon leaned over and whispered to his wife, "I killed a bear over there. He was near the manzanita bush and jumped at me and I killed him." Now the bear that he had killed was a relative of his father-in-law.

Bear then took a firebrand and went out to the place where the body of this bear lay and mourned for his relative and burned his body.

Then he fixed up a tree at a deer-lick, that is he made an artificial deer-lick at this tree. Bear returned home after that and they noticed that his eyes were all swollen because he had been crying so much over his dead relative.

That night he told Falcon that he had found a deer trail where deer came in large numbers from both directions, and said, "I wish you would go over there and kill me some deer. I feel as though I should like some venison to eat. I haven't had any for a long time."

In the morning Falcon went out to the point where Bear had directed him and climbed up into the tree, finally climbing out near the end of one of the limbs. Presently he heard a big noise coming toward him from the east and soon a big bear came running up the trail and jumped up into the tree trying to bear him down with its weight and the weight of the branches. Falcon, however, was a clever dodger and succeeded in thrusting an arrow down the throat of this bear as he rushed at him with his mouth open.

In a very few minutes another came from the east and did the same thing with the same result.

In this same way he killed four bears. Then he decided that this was no place to hunt deer so he climbed down out of the tree and went home without any venison. He had been gone almost all day.

Of course, Bear knew exactly what had happened, although he was not present. He said nothing at all when Falcon returned without venison but Falcon's wife noticed that he was scratched up and asked him what had happened. "Oh," said Falcon, "That is nothing. I was just scratched as I came through the brush." Then she whispered to him an inquiry as to whether he had killed any bears and he replied that he had.

Then Bear inquired, "Did you see anything at all out there where you went?"

"Yes," said Falcon, "I saw something out there. It was very ugly. There were four of them and I killed them all and piled them up. If you want to see what I did you can go out there and look for yourself."

This made Bear very angry. He took a firebrand and went out again and remained there all day.

Now, the old Swan-woman knew what was happening and knew

that Bear was trying to kill his son-in-law. This made her angry and she scolded Bear.

Bear went away and was gone for quite a long time, during which he prepared another tree as a trap for Falcon. That evening he said, "Tomorrow, my son-in-law, I want you to go out again. I found a very fine tree and an excellent place where there are many deer tracks all around. Deer come from the north and from the south to that place and you can surely get venison there."

Swan scolded her husband terribly for what he was doing and accused him of trying to kill their son-in-law in this way. Bear made no reply to his wife.

In the morning Falcon said to the girls, "Do not look for me. I see what Bear is doing. He is trying to kill me. I may come back or I may not." With this he went out. Bear had told him where to go and he went out early in the morning and went to the tree that Bear had indicated this time. About half-way up this tree there was a very thick lot of branches. There were no limbs above or below. He started to climb up this tree frog fashion but found it very slippery. Before he could reach these thick branches a bear came and started to attack him but Falcon was near enough so that he could reach the lowest of the branches which he grasped and by it he swung himself up. As he did so one of his arrows dropped to the ground but he still had three arrows left. He immediately killed this bear, in fact he killed six bears at this spot, one after another.

Then he came down out of the tree and pondered for a long time as to what he had better do, whether he should go home or whether he should run away. He was becoming very weary of these traps that Bear was always setting to try to kill him. He climbed a nearby hill and sat there thinking for a long time, but finally he decided to go home.

Again Bear went out with a firebrand and wept over the relatives whom Falcon had killed. He then built a big fire and cremated the bodies of these bears.

Before Bear returned to the house Falcon said that he was going back home where he had come from. His real home was at Kūhla'napō and his people had missed him and were worried because he did not return.

Accordingly Falcon went back to Bald Hill and here he wished for the fog bridge again and it carried him across the lake as it had before but Falcon died before he reached home.

MYTHS OF THE DEER AND BEAR CHILDREN

87—BEAR KILLS HER OWN DAUGHTER-IN-LAW, DEER[208]

INCIDENTS AND CHARACTERS

I. *Bear kills Deer.*
> 1. Falcon, 2. Deer, 3. Deer boys (two), 4. Bear, 5. Bear boys (two), 6. Tree, 7. Basket token, 8. Meadowlark.

II. *The Deer boys kill the Bear boys.*
> 1. Deer boys, 2. Bear boys, 3. Bear, 4. Old Net-maker, 5. Log, 6. Small birds, 7. Crane.

III. *The Deer boys kill Sun-man.*
> 1. Deer boys, 2. Magic bow, 3. Poison-man, 4. Loon-people, 5. Mother of the Deer boys, 6. Rattlesnake-tooth trap, 7. Sun-man, 8. Blue-fly.

IV. *The Deer boys attempt to bring their mother home.*
> 1. Deer boys, 2. The mother of the Deer boys.

I

(Bear Kills Deer)

In Coyote valley in olden times, they say, there lived Falcon, his wife, Deer, and their two little boys, together with his mother, Grizzly Bear, and her two little boys, Falcon's younger brothers.

Falcon snared many birds and brought them home, always giving his mother the birds with rank tasting meat, such as pigeons, while for his own family he kept the sweet-meated birds, rabbits, etc.

This state of affairs was satisfactory to all concerned till one day the Deer boys were outside of the house eating some jackrabbit meat and the Bear boys persuaded them to let them try some of it. They found it nice and sweet and finally took some of it home to their mother to try.

When Bear saw what nice meat her son's family was living on and what poor meat he was giving her it made her very angry and she vowed that she would kill her son. Very early (before sunrise) the next morning she went out to lie in wait for her son. She ran and ran, follow-

---

[208]The Pomo title of this myth is "Būragal yeek tata yeek al cak hibax cela." Informant: Tom Mitchell, Eastern dialect, 1902.

ing the trail along which her son had set his snares, till she came to the end where there was a snare which had caught a cottontail. Close by here she dug a hole and sat down in it to await the coming of Falcon.

Meanwhile Falcon had gone out on the trail of his snares, he took off a great many birds and rabbits from the snares and carried them along on his shoulders. Finally, arriving at the last snare very tired, he sat down on the ground to rest. Bear jumped out at him but he dodged and Bear pursued him. He ran to a tree and round and round it, Bear in hot pursuit.

Now this tree was his grandfather and he called out to it to open up and rescue him. This Tree did, splitting its trunk sufficiently to admit him and then closing after him again.

Bear scratched furiously at the tree trunk but to no avail, so she ran home and, finding her daughter-in-law there alone, said, "My daughter-in-law, let us go and pick clover," to which she assented.

Bear then said, "We will run a race up to Ma-tu'-xal (near the Hopper Ranch on Cold Creek). You run around Cow Mountain (Ca' xabe, fish rock) and I will run up the creek-bed; if you arrive there first wait for me."

Before they started out from home, Deer had made a big basket and set it up on the center pole and told her boys, "I think that your grandmother will kill me. If she does, this basket will fall towards the fire by which sign you will know that I am dead."

They started on their race, Deer running along the mountainside and arriving in advance of Bear. After a while Bear arrived and, sitting down close beside her daughter-in-law, asked her to look for lice in the hair of her head.

Now, Bear had stopped down at the creek and caught some snakes and put them in her hair, tying her hair as usual, thus keeping them from escaping. As Deer parted the hair she saw rattlesnakes and bullsnakes. These she threw away. She was very much frightened.

Bear said, "What are you doing?" (taking it as an affront that Deer did not eat the lice as is customary).

Deer answered, "Nothing."

Finally, having had her head cleaned, Bear told Deer to sit down and have the lice cleaned from her head. Deer, being very scared, dared not refuse. Bear, instead of commencing in the hair of the head, seized

Deer and commenced to tear off the flesh from her neck with her fingers. Finally, there being but a very little left, Bear shook Deer, whereupon her head fell off.

At this instant the basket which Deer had left in the house with her boys fell and they knew that their mother was dead.

Bear took Deer's body and head home, dug a hole and prepared everything for baking. Then she put in Deer and allowed the meat to bake all night. In the morning she uncovered the meat and gave the Deer boys some from the shoulder which they took and ate as they played around out of doors.

At that time Meadowlark was flying over. He said to the boys, "You are eating your own mother's shoulder."

Then one of the Deer boys said, "Grandmother, we need some water. I will get some water. I want to take mother's big basket to bring it in."

Bear gave it to him and he dragged it down to the brink of the stream, when out of sight of his grandmother, he threw it into the water.

He then ran back to his grandmother crying that the basket had escaped and was floating down the river. Thereupon Bear ran down below the basket and tried to catch it as it floated by but failed. This she tried again and again, going farther and farther away from the village.

The boys said, "I hope that basket will float down to the ocean."

II

(The Deer Boys Kill the Bear Boys)

The two Deer boys then built up a big fire in the sweat-house and all four boys, the Deer and the Bear boys, engaged in a fanning contest which ended in the Bear boys being killed by the heat. The heat was so intense they say, that the mountain was scorched (hence the red spot at present).

The Deer boys took the Bear boys and placed them so that they would, to all appearances, be looking out of the smoke-hole.

Bear, after having chased the basket for a number of miles (nearly to Hopland) gave it up and returned in a very ugly humor only to find her two children apparently laughing at her through the smoke-hole of the sweat-house.

In a rage she cuffed one of them, whereupon the skin peeled from the side of his head. Then she knew that the Deer boys had killed her sons and she immediately started in pursuit of them.

Meanwhile the Deer boys had made good their escape toward the east.

The one, being the elder, was much stronger and larger, so he carried his younger brother on his shoulder in such a way that he could be facing to the rear and could watch to see if Bear was coming in pursuit.

First they came to the abode of old Net-maker living nearby and hurriedly explained the situation to him and requested him not to say which way they had gone. Next they came to Log and asked him to keep secret their direction. Next they came to a flock of small birds playing with throwing-sticks in an opening and requested them similarly.

Bear took the trail of the Deer boys and came first upon the Net-maker whom she asked, "Did you see anything of my poor children, Net-maker?"

"What children?" asked the Net-maker.

Bear said, "I will mash you." She proceeded to do so but no sooner was she gone than the old man came together again and went back to work at his nets.

Bear went on east till she came to Log whom she asked about the children but Log being blind could only tell her that he had seen no one. He felt some one step over him.

Bear finally came to the small birds whom she asked concerning the children and finally, since she could get no knowledge from them, she tried to crush them with her mouth but could not since the birds could run out between her teeth.

Finally as the boys were coming up the divide between Cold Creek and Blue Lakes the younger saw that Bear was pursuing them and told his elder brother to hurry. This the brother did, but too late, for Bear gained on them steadily till finally, having reached the valley on the east of the divide, the elder brother saw that something must be done so he spat upon the ground, expressing at the same time a wish that the earth there should become muddy and that a body of water should appear which would cause Bear some delay in swimming. This happened.

When the boys had gone but a little way south, however, Bear had passed through this and was again in pursuit. The younger brother told the elder to run faster as Bear was after them. The elder brother again spat upon the ground and the same thing happened as before. The boys then passed eastward for some distance before Bear came in sight again. The elder brother spat upon the ground again and this time wished that his grandmother should float around a long time. This happened.

They then turned southward and finally arrived at Rocky Point. Their grandfather, Crane, lived upon the opposite side of the lake and the elder brother called to him to put a bridge across so that they might pass over. This he did by stretching his neck across and the boys crossed over onto the east shore.

The boys told their grandfather that Bear was chasing them and they then heated a stone. When Bear came up and called for a bridge Crane furnished it by means of his neck as before. Bear started across but when she had reached the middle of the bridge, Crane, by a sudden turn of the neck, dropped Bear off and she "bounced around" in the water. Crane called out to her to shut her eyes and open her mouth wide. When she did this they dropped the hot stone into her throat and she sank to the bottom.

III

(The Deer Boys Kill Sun-man)

The younger boy heard behind them a sound like that of his mother's voice, but his elder brother did not believe it.

Their grandfather made for them two stone bows. These they tried by pointing them at objects which immediately began to smoke like a fire before blazing.

They then started to travel eastward toward the place where the younger brother had heard his mother's voice. They started southward and traveled on the west side of the lake to Big Valley. Here they turned eastward near the water and passed by Mt. Kanaktai, where they met a poison-man who spoke to them and advised them to pass on the sunny side. The boys did not go on the sunny side as they knew the man. He then dried up a tree with his poison and told them that his people would do the same way to them. The boys pointed their bows at the man and burned him up.

They then went south and then east a very great distance till they finally came to the water. Here they found their grandfathers (all fish-eating birds were the paternal grandfathers of the boys) in a fishing camp by the shore. These were the Loon-people. The boys asked them to take them across the water. Loon said that he was sorry that they were determined to go across as there was something frightful there, but since they wished it he took them into a tule boat (a special kind of tule, "xa ci," something like carex) and took them over to an island where he left them in charge of another Loon and went back.

The boys again asked their grandfather to take them across the water. He said there was something frightful there but agreed to take them over. They traveled very far to the east and finally landed at night upon another island where Loon said their grandfathers lived. He then returned. Again, after warning them of the frightful beings to the east, another of their grandfathers took them far to the east, leaving them in charge of their grandfathers on another island, who, after weeping and warning them of the dangers, took them far to the east again.

This time they went very far and at last espied something shiny and bright, which was the landing place of the sun. They paddled toward this and after traveling a long time arrived there and landed, their grandfather returning.

They saw the house of the sun and went up to it. The younger brother kept watch of the house and finally saw someone who looked like their mother. He told his brother who asked him not to say such a thing. The younger insisted, however, that the woman looked like their mother, except for the fact that she had but one eye.

The old woman looked out and saw the boys. There were many rattlesnake teeth by the door. The old woman threw out a pestle and the rattlesnake teeth bit each other. Then the boys came into the house and sat down. Human beings were never to be found here and the old woman was afraid for the safety of the boys so she dug a hole under the big acorn granary and hid the boys in it.

Sun-man went hunting every morning and returned at night. This was the time for him to start home. The house shook whenever he started home. He came, running a long time, toward the sweat-house.

He at last arrived at the house and after circling around it four times in each direction he entered and went over by the smoke-hole. He asked his wife what it was that he smelled, it smelled like human beings. "Are you hiding my people from me?" Then she made the boys come out and sit down. Sun-man said to them, "You fellows thought of me." (A form of salutation equivalent to "Well you fellows have come to see me, how did you come to think of me?") "I am your father and I am sorry for you, you stay here and we will have fun today, we will run a race."

The boys said, "All right."

Then after a while they all went out and the three stood facing the east on the race-track at the eastern end of which stood a rock. Sun-man said, "The one who first arrives at the rock wins the race. Now you fellows start first."

But the boys said "No, you know the road. You start first."

Sun-man said "No, that is not good, this is not my way, you fellows start first."

The boys refused and they argued this way until nearly nightfall. Finally Sun-man agreed and the three stood up ready for the start. Sun-man started and the boys ran behind. They ran and ran and ran, and finally Sun-man arrived at the rock and jumped over it and waited for the boys to do the same but they turned back and went the other way.

Then Sun-man asked them "Why did you fellows turn back?"

The boys said, "You left us and we could not help it."

The boys then followed Sun-man back to the house and as it was night they all went to the sweat-house to sleep. The boys, however, did not sleep. The time went on very slowly till morning.

They finally came out and Sun-man said, "We will run a race again."

The boys said, "All right," and agreed between themselves to kill Sun-man this time.

Again Sun-man wanted them to run first but they again protested that they did not know the road whereupon Sun-man became angry and said, "All right, I will run first again."

They then got ready as on the previous day and started. As Sun-man got some distance ahead the boys pointed their bows at him and killed him.

The boys returned to the house and their mother was very glad as was also Bear-fly (Blue-fly) the servant of Sun-man.

IV

(The Deer Boys Attempt to Bring Their Mother Home)

Their mother said that she was no longer a human being and commenced to cry. The boys told her that they were going to carry her back to this world. She agreed but said that if they rested her on the ground before they got home she would disappear.

They made a packer of grape-vines similar to the wood-carriers and took turns in carrying her. They traveled a very long distance and finally arrived at the lake shore east of Upper Lake, but one of them forgot the condition and allowed his mother to touch the ground whereupon she disappeared. They cried because they had brought their mother so near home and had then lost her.

Two grape-vines grow at this place now.

The boys then went back past Blue Lakes and past Cold Creek and finally arrived home.

Co hlat bo hlat in welai xaian maiaūwa'lūla xaa'x me. (From the east and from the west may the Mallard girls hurry and bring the morning.)

88—THE DEER AND BEAR CHILDREN[209]

Characters: 1. Bear, 2. Deer (son of Bear), 3. Wildcat (wife of Deer), 4. The Deer boys (two), 5. The Bear girls (two), 6. Blue Jay (Bear's husband), 7. Putrid-man (grandfather of Bear girls), 8. Pestle (token), 9. Meadowlark boys, 10. Magic basket, 11. Owl, 12. Sticks (tokens), 13. Crane, 14, Grandmother Flea (bērc'mal liha"mile).

At the old village of Hlal'napō near Calistoga lived Bear. She had two young daughters. Her son Deer was married to Wildcat and they had two sons.

Deer went out and set snares all along the edge of the brush and he caught many jackrabbits, cottontails, and birds of all kinds. Every time he went out to visit his snares he always brought home a great deal of game and he always brought home wild pigeons for his mother.

His own children were all the time playing about and they always had quail breasts to eat. One day one of the boys went over to Bear's

---

[209]Informant: Mary Louie, Eastern dialect.

house, despite the fact that his brother warned him that their father had told them never to go there.

When the boy went into the house Bear said, "Let us see what you have there?"

The boy gave her a quail breast that he was eating and she tasted it. This made her angry because it was much better meat than her son had given her.

The next time Deer went out to set his snares Bear followed him and took from the snares the best meat she could find and put it into the sack she was carrying, leaving in the snares only the poorer kinds of meat which Deer had been giving to her up to this time.

After a while Deer came home and brought her a lot of pigeons which he threw in at the door. Now when she had visited the snares she had counted the number of birds that she had left in the snares so that she knew when Deer brought her these pigeons that he had been fooling her.

Then Bear and her husband cooked and ate the bulk of the meat that she had brought and they talked about the way Deer had been fooling them. She was very angry and said to her husband, "What did we raise that young man for anyway? Our son ought to treat us right. He ought to bring us good meat, not the poor meat that he has been giving us."

Now, Bear and her family lived in one house, Deer and his family in another house, and the grandfather, Putrid-man, in a third.

The next morning when Deer went out to look at his snares he found that some of them had been sprung and had not caught anything. These he reset. He took the birds and other game out of those that had caught meat and reset these. All of this game he put into his hunting sack and then he went on somewhat farther and sat down for a while.

By and by Bear went out again and found that more game had been caught in the snares so she took out the best meat and left the pigeons. These snares were set all around a big thicket of brush. The more Bear thought about the situation the more vexed she became and she said to herself, "What did I raise these children for anyway? My own son deceives me. He gives me nothing but the poorest meat, never gives me anything really good. I raised him to do right by me. I had to work hard to raise him. He ought to do the same by me and he ought to give me good meat. That woman that he lives with there is not his mother. He certainly ought to treat me as well as he does his wife."

By and by when Deer came home again he gave his mother a lot of pigeons and took some over to Putrid-man.

On the following day when Deer went out to visit his snares he took his wife with him and he showed her where the snares were and just where he always went and where he sat down to rest.

Bear went out again and visited the snares and again she took out the best meat and left the pigeons.

Again Deer went over the snares and sat down to rest and remained there until evening. Then he was going to look over the line of snares again as he went home.

His wife, Wildcat, meantime had returned to the house after she had been out with her husband and had seen just where the snares were located. She took with her a lot of the game that he had caught and, as she approached the house, Bear saw her coming in with this game.

Finally in the evening Deer came home rather early and he brought with him, as he always did, some pigeons for his mother.

Then Bear went out to a point near the first of the snares. There, near a tree, she dug a deep hole so that as she crouched down in it she could just see over to the first snare. Then she came home and found that her husband had the evening meal cooked and they ate their meat together with bread and acorn mush.

Next morning, before daylight, Bear went out and hid herself in the hole that she had dug by the trail. Presently Deer went out to look at his snares and he found that the first one had been sprung but there was nothing in it. When he stooped over to reset this snare Bear jumped at him and tore him all to pieces and as she did so she said, "This is what I will do with you. I am no longer your mother. You have deceived me and this is the best punishment that I can give you." Then she went along the line of snares and found all kinds of birds and small game. She brought back to the house a big load of game and she took a large number of these birds and mammals and gave them to Putrid-man. She gave him all he could possibly eat.

After sundown Wildcat knew that her husband had been killed because he did not come home and she commenced to mourn his loss.

When she reached the first snare she found the remains of her husband. Nothing was left of him except the bones. She returned home
and told Putrid-man that Bear had killed her husband and that she had
found nothing but his bones left. She asked him to go out and help
her bring home his remains.

They went out and Putrid-man told her to go and collect all the
snares that had been set by Deer and that they would throw them into
the hole which Bear had dug and that they would throw Deer's bones
in there also and then cover them up. Then he said, "Do not cry that
way because if you do Bear will kill us also." When they threw in the
bones of Deer, his wife put in beads, bead belts and the very best things
that she possessed as a sign of her grief and mourning at the loss of
her husband.

Then they all lived at the same place for quite a long time but by
and by Bear came to Wildcat and told her that she thought that they
had better go out and get some greens (pabō). Of course Wildcat was
afraid but she had to go. She knew what would happen before she
started out. So she set up against the center pole of her house a pestle
(bata'l) and she told her children that if that pestle fell over and broke
into pieces that they would then know that she had been killed and that
Bear was the one who had killed her. She also told them that if this
happened they must take out all of her possessions and burn them as a
sign of mourning. Then she said to the elder brother, "After you have
burned up all of my possessions tell your little brother to cry for water,
to cry for two or three days until Bear gives you that big basket to get
water in. Then you tell him to take it down to the river and let it float
away."

So Bear and Wildcat went out to gather their greens and when they
had filled their burden baskets they set them down and leaned them
against a tree and went a short distance away to eat a little clover before they returned home. After they had eaten clover for a while they
sat down to rest.

Bear said, "Daughter-in-law, I wish you would look over my head
for vermin."

Now, Bear did not have the ordinary kind of vermin at all and when
Wildcat began to look for vermin she found first a lizard (Katūnutal).

This she threw behind her but Bear said, "Ai! you better eat that. That is what I asked you to hunt for."

Next Wildcat found Kaṯū lūṯūdūk (a species of snake). This also she threw behind her. Then Bear said, "You had better stop. You do not eat the vermin you find in my head the way you should. I will show you how to catch vermin. I will look for them on your head."

Wildcat sat down and Bear began to look for vermin on her head and she ate each of the lice as she took them off. She kept right on eating this way for a long time and then she commenced to scratch deeply into Wildcat's scalp and Wildcat cried out with pain. Bear told her to keep still but Wildcat could not stand the scratching and again she screamed. Then Bear pulled her hair and told her to keep still. Wildcat then commenced to cry and Bear snapped her head off and threw it away.

At this very moment the pestle, which Wildcat had left in the house as a token for the children, fell over and broke and the children began to cry and mourn. Their Grandfather came over to the house to see what the noise was all about and whether the children were frightened or just what had happened. They told him that their mother had been killed and that they knew it because the pestle had fallen over and broken. He then took the two boys out with him to where he was weaving a net and tried to comfort them. By and by they stopped crying and began to play around in the usual way.

After Bear had killed Wildcat she dumped the contents of her basket into that of Wildcat and put it inside her own so that it would look when she came back to the house as though she was carrying simply her own basket full of greens. She then skinned the body of Wildcat and took the meat home to eat. Then she dug a hole and put the skin of Wildcat into this hole and covered it up with rocks. She put weeds on top of the body of Wildcat so as to cover it up so that no one would suspect what she was carrying when she came back to the house.

When she arrived there she cooked the body of Wildcat and when she had the meal prepared she called in the Putrid-man and her husband and all four of the children to eat.

Now, on the other side of the creek from where they lived there was another village and the Meadowlark boys were playing on the opposite bank of the creek. When the children came out of the house eating some of this meat the Meadowlark boys chided them and made fun of them and told them they were eating their own mother.

When the Wildcat boys told their grandmother what the Meadowlark boys had said and that they were eating their own mother's flesh, Bear said that she would go over there and see about it. She then gave them some of the greens to eat and gave some of these also to Putrid-man.

Then one of the boys asked her for water. He said that he was very thirsty and wanted to go down to the river to get some water. He cried very hard because he was so thirsty. Bear offered him a small basket but he refused it and continued crying. He cried so long that he finally fell asleep and Bear took a rabbit-skin blanket and covered him. Then she began to cry. She really felt sorry for these children who now had no parents at all.

Then her husband Blue Jay said, "If you feel that way about it why did you kill their father and mother? You killed both of them, they did not die of any sickness," but Bear threatened that if Blue Jay did not stop talking about the matter she would kill him too. She would stab him with a bone awl.

Now the elder of the two boys slept that night with Blue Jay and the younger of the two boys with Bear. The next morning the younger again asked for a basket. He said he wanted a big one, a very fine basket, but she offered him a small basket and he threw it away and continued to cry. He rolled around and cried violently. He tried to kill himself in his fit of crying so finally, to pacify the little fellow, Bear gave him the big basket that he wanted and he went down to the creek.

Bear told him, however, when he started out that he must not go out where the water was swift. He dragged this basket along toward the creek and of course Putrid-man and the elder brother knew what he was going to do with it. He went down to the creek and dipped the basket in a number of times and finally he let it go and it floated swiftly down the stream. As it disappeared he cried out to Bear who came running down to the creek and ran as fast as she could in order to try to rescue the basket. She followed this basket clear down to the mouth of Napa River.

While Bear was pursuing this basket the boys ran back to the house and told their grandfather, Putrid-man, to get some sweat-house wood as they wanted to have a contest with the Bear girls. The grandfather kept a hot fire going and when the boys got hot and tired in their fanning he poured water over them to keep them cool.

The girls also grew tired and they wanted to quit the contest but the grandfather told them that they must keep on. They fanned and fanned and finally the younger of the two girls became exhausted and had to give up. The elder girl, however, kept right on fanning until finally both of the girls were killed from the heat which the Bear boys fanned across to them.

Then Putrid-man took the two boys down to the creek, gave them a good bath and took them to his house. They then said to him, "Grandfather, we think that we had better leave. We think that we had better go away on a long journey."

Putrid-man said, "I think that if you remain here Bear will kill you when she returns and finds out what you have done." He then asked the boys which way they thought they would go and they told him that they thought they would make a journey around and visit their grandfathers.

First the boys went toward the north and it turned red wherever they walked. After a while they came back and then they journeyed over toward the east. They came back again and journeyed toward the south and finally toward the west.

Finally Owl came over from the other village and said to Putrid-man, "Why is it that those boys want to run away?"

He replied that Bear had killed the father and mother of those two boys and that they wanted to get away from that place because he was afraid that when Bear returned she might find them.

"Well," said Owl, "I will give you some good medicine that will protect them." Then he reached under his left arm and took from there a feather, which he gave to them.

The boys knew that when Bear returned she would search for them. She knew precisely where they played and so they went out there and placed two sticks toward the north of that place, two toward the east, two toward the south and two toward the west, and told these sticks that they were to answer when Bear called to them.

Then their grandfather put the two boys each on a feather and blew them up toward the sky. They sailed very far toward the south and finally landed and then they walked on from there. As they were walking along they said, "It will be a very long day. The sun will not go down for a very long time." And it was that way. The day was very long so that they could make a long journey.

When Bear finally came back there was no one at home. Her husband, Blue Jay, was always going off somewhere anyway. He was never around when he was wanted. She went to the house of Deer in search of the boys, but there was no one there. Then she went to the house of the grandfather and asked him where the children were. He said, "I heard them playing around here a minute ago. They are just outside somewhere."

She went into the sweat-house and there were her two girls lying there and she said to them, "What are you two pretty little children sleeping here for?" Then she commenced to sing to them. She loved these two little girls very much and as she saw them lying there apparently asleep she sat down and began to sing to them. "You are very pretty children, you have limbs like oak trees (meaning that they were plump)." Then she sat down and started to rub and pat the face of one of the children but the skin rubbed right off. They had been burned. Then Bear knew what had happened and she jumped up and ran to Putrid-man and asked, "Where are those two boys?"

He said, "I do not know, I presume they are over there playing where they always play."

Bear said to him, "I will crush you with my teeth."

He replied, "That will do you no good. I will be sitting right there after you have crushed me."

Then Bear ran out to the playground and called, "cīṭó'm ōkōdō cīṭó'm ōkōdō."[210] The two sticks which the boys had placed toward the east to answer for them said, "pū pū'," and she ran over toward the east but did not find the boys. Then she repeated her call and the sticks toward the west answered in the same way. She ran thither, but did not find the boys. Then she repeated her call and the sticks toward the north and finally the sticks toward the south answered her in the same way, but of course the boys could not be found anywhere.

Bear ran back to the grandfather and said, "Which way did those

[210]This is not in the Pomo language but in a language spoken in an adjacent valley (Alexander Valley). This old Bear-woman could speak two different languages.

boys go? I will kill you if you do not tell me. I will mash you with my feet."

To this the grandfather replied, "That will not hurt me. If you do that I will sit here just the same."

Bear thought to herself, now it is most likely that those children went over there to their grandfather so she ran down Napa Creek.

There was a steep bank and a soft place just across the creek from Crane's house which was on the west side of the creek.

When the Deer boys saw Bear coming, they had reached this point and they called out to Crane and he helped them across the creek.

Presently Bear came to this same place and she called to Crane four times and asked him to send her a boat so that she could cross over the stream. Bear said, "I am coming crying for those two children I lost. They came down this way somewhere. I do not know just where they went. Do take me over the stream in some way so that I can find them."

Now, the boys had already told Crane all about what Bear had done, how she had killed their father and their mother. Crane walked up to the bank and stretched his neck across the stream, stuck his beak into the ground and flattened out his neck so that it became about two feet wide, so that Bear might cross. She started across the bridge and when she was a short distance from the shore Crane moved his neck a little bit. Bear was very much frightened and told him that if he would not throw her into the water she would pay him a whole basketful of beads. When she reached about midway of the stream Crane again moved his neck and Bear promised him another basketful of beads if he would not let her fall.

Finally, however, when Bear had reached the opposite end of the bridge, not more than a step from the land, Crane jerked his head and Bear went down in the water and was never seen again.

Crane came back to the village after this and someone came out and called to Bēre'mal līha"mīle (Grandmother Flea) and asked her to come out and sing. He called four times but she did not come out because she did not like the way he had called.

She told them that she would not come out and would not come to the dance house unless they called her by her right name. When they did this she answered them and said, "Before I come to the dance-house you must make a small hole for me to sit in, just in front of the center pole."

When they had done this she came and sang for them while they danced.[211] All the older people were dancing in the dance-house but the Deer boys were playing outside. Finally the younger of the two brothers heard something way over in the east over where the Sun-man lived. He said to his brother, "It sounds like our mother's voice crying over there just a little way toward the east. Let us go over." Then the boys went and told their grandfather here at this village that they were going over toward the east a little ways to see if their mother was there. Their grandfather counselled against it.

He said, "No, you must not go. It is a very dangerous place over there. You will probably never be able to get there, and if you do, you never will be able to come back, and you certainly never can bring your mother back."[212]

However, the boys started off toward the east and as they began their journey they said, "The sun must not go down until we arrive at that place to which we are going." They arrived at that house that very night. When they looked in, there sat their mother. She had no head but still she could talk so they went in and sat down beside her. She said, "My sons, you must not stay here over night. I am not a person any longer. I am a ghost."

The boys replied, "But mother, we came to take you, we will take you anyway."

She replied, "Well if you care to take me you will have to carry me and you must not let me down onto the ground and you must not look back. If you ever let me down you will never see me again."

The boys started back toward the west and carried her in turn. The elder of the boys carried her for a very long time until he became very tired and then the younger boy took up the burden and went on. So they alternately carried her and rested each other until finally the elder of the two boys wanted to step aside from the trail for a minute. He

---

[211]The song that Flea sang was

    mīlīnai
    mī———————lī————nai
    tcōtcōno
    tcō————————tcō————nai

The dance that they were dancing at this time was the Mako'make or Crane Dance.

[212]The grandfathers of these boys who were here at this village were Mako' (Crane), Kala'k (White Crane), Dīkū'būhū, Nanhwa', Ka'nakaūkaū, Wara'wara (Wood Duck), Kok (Loon), Dūka'r, Tsū'tkilbek (Diver), Xagū'nūbek.

was carrying his mother at the time so he set her down on the ground telling his brother to keep good watch over her while he was gone, but no sooner had their mother touched the ground than she was gone.

Then the boys came crying back to the Crane village and their grandfather again took them in and comforted and finally brought them back to their own home and they lived there always.

89—THE THUNDER AND BEAR CHILDREN[213]
INCIDENTS AND CHARACTERS

I. The Thunder and Bear children.
    1. Thunder, 2. Bear (mother of Thunder), 3. Thunder children (son and daughter), 4. Bear children (daughters), 5. Deer (wife of Thunder), 6. Bow-string token, 7. Deer's token, 8. Blue Heron, 9. Sun-man.
II. Placing the Sun in the sky.
    1. Crows (two), 2. Blue Heron, 3. Deer.

I

(The Thunder and Bear Children)

Thunder made traps for the purpose of catching rabbits, squirrels and other small game. He arose very early every morning, in fact he was up before daylight, to look after his traps.

Thunder selected the least desirable meat and gave this to his mother, Bear.

Now, Thunder had two children, a son and a daughter, and his mother also had two young daughters. The four children went down to the spring to get water and took along some of this meat to eat on the way. The elder of Thunder's sisters said to Thunder's daughter, "Let me taste your meat?" It was very, very good meat, much better than that the Bear girls were accustomed to.

This elder Bear girl took a piece of this same meat home and gave it to her mother and said, "Mother, our relatives over there at Thunder's house use this kind of meat and they give us only the bad parts."

Bear tasted the meat and when she found how excellent it was in comparison to the meat that Thunder was giving her and his two little sisters, she became very angry and said, "I will show him that he cannot treat us that way."

---

[213]Informant: Geo. Dashields, Northern dialect.

That night Thunder had a dream. He dreamed that his mother had killed him. The next morning Thunder was much troubled about this dream and he told one of his children, "Last night I dreamed that your grandmother killed me. You had better run over to her house and see whether she is there and see what you can find out." The child did so and upon arriving at Bear's house peeped in and saw Bear lying in the house. She then came back and told her father that Bear was still lying there and had not yet gone out.

The fact of the matter is that Bear had left a dummy, a bear-skin stuffed so as to resemble herself, lying there so as to make it appear that she had not gone away. The old Bear had really gone very early to the place where her son had his traps set. She arrived there before he came and she took from the traps all of the squirrels, rabbits and other game and hid it. She left in the trap only one wildcat. Then Bear went and concealed herself by the trail and when Thunder came along she caught him. He struggled and finally succeeded in breaking away from Bear, who then pursued him. He first ran into a hollow tree and then into a hollow rock and then all around with Bear close upon his heels. She finally caught and killed him and then only did she return to her house.

Thunder's wife, Deer, and the two Thunder children only, were left now. Deer did not feel well that morning because she felt that there was something wrong. She felt that her husband was in grave danger. She knew that something bad had happened to him because as she and the children were sitting by the fire, she looked at Thunder's bow and arrows and just at that moment the bow-string broke. Then she knew that Thunder had been killed.

Two days later Bear came over to Deer's house and said to her daughter-in-law, "It looks as though it is going to be a fine day. We had better go out and gather clover this morning."

Before Deer left home she told her son, "You need not expect me to return tonight. I shall not come home at all. I know that Bear is going to kill me as she did your father."

Deer set off for the appointed place and arrived there first. She was weary so she sat down in the shade to rest. Presently Bear arrived. She said to Deer, "I do not know what makes my head itch. You had better look and see if there is something there."

When Deer had finished, Bear said, "Now I will look you over, too."

As she was looking for vermin in Deer's hair, she pulled her hair very hard and it hurt badly so that Deer made an outcry. Bear said, "What makes you cry that way? If you do that I shall break your neck." Then she killed Deer. She took out both of Deer's eyes and took them home. The rest of the body she left where it was.

Bear then returned home and found all four children playing together at her own house. She then built a small fire and proceeded with her cooking. As she did so the Thunder boy noticed what she was doing and said to his sister, "There is something wrong here. That meat that grandmother is cooking looks like our mother's eyes." In fact Bear cooked and ate them right before the Deer children.

When it was getting late that evening and Deer did not come home, the boy said to his sister, "I feel sure that grandmother killed our mother today." The little girl cried because her mother did not return, but finally the two children went to bed without her. During the night some object that belonged to Deer made a noise and then the children knew that their mother was dead. The following morning Bear was busy grinding acorn meal and sent the four children off to gather ma sï'l. They went out and took baskets with them to bring back what they gathered.

After they had returned the boy told his sister to go down and bring some water. He told her to go into the house and get a certain basket which their mother had made. He said, "You get that good basket of our mother's. You tell grandmother you want that particular basket and if she gives you another one you cry and say you want that one and do not take any other."

Accordingly the little Thunder girl went into the house and said, "Grandma, I want that basket that mother made, over there."

Bear said, "You must be very careful of that basket."

The little girl took it down to the creek just as her brother had told her and she placed it in the middle of the creek where the water runs very swiftly because her brother had instructed her just what to do with it. Then the boy told her, "You wait until you think that the basket has floated way down the creek and has arrived close to the ocean.

Then you cry and run up to the house and let our grandmother know what happened to it."

The little girl did as her brother told her and when the basket floated away down the stream and after it had gone for a long time, she ran up to the house crying to her grandmother, "Grandma, the water took away the basket." The old Bear woman went down the creek and followed the basket all the way down. She followed it all along the creek and followed it as it floated down the river and it was not until it had reached the mouth of the river and was just floating out into the ocean that she caught up with it so that she could see it float away.

Now the Thunder children ran away while the old Bear woman was gone and they went down to the coast to visit their grandfather, Blue Heron (Kala'k).

When they found their grandfather the boy said, "Grandpa, can you not help us to get across the ocean?"

The old man replied, "Yes, I will put something across so that you can get over."[214] The boy knew that Bear would follow them and presently she did. When she reached the coast she found Blue Heron and asked him if he had seen her grandchildren and where they had gone.

Blue Heron replied, "They have gone over onto the other side of the ocean."

"How did they get across?"

"I will put the bridge across so that you can go over there too if you want to see your grandchildren."

He then put the bridge across and Bear started to go over to the western side of the ocean. Now Blue Heron knew that Bear had killed Thunder and Deer, so when Bear reached about the middle of bridge he caused it to shake and turn.

This made Bear angry and she said to Blue Heron, "If you do not stop that I shall break your neck."

Blue Heron said, "All right," and then he pulled the bridge back and let Bear fall into the water where she drowned.

Now the children could see what was going on all the time and as the old Bear approached the coast the little boy said to his sister,"There is our grandmother following us." They saw just what happened to

[214]This myth does not specifically state what it was that Blue Heron put across so that the children might use it for a bridge, but other myths state that it was his own neck. This is undoubtedly what is implied here.

her and when they saw that she was drowned and could do them no more harm they called across to their grandfather, Blue Heron, and told him that they wanted to come back across the ocean to see him. He again helped them across and they remained there with him for quite a long time.

The little girl was always listening for something, particularly just before sunrise every morning. From time to time she heard a sound which came from far over toward the east. It sounded just like the voice of her mother. She would tell people, "It sounds like our mother crying way over in the east somewhere. That is the way our mother used to cry." She bothered her brother a great deal, mourning for the loss of her mother and she was constantly asking him to take her back toward the east. So one morning he told his grandfather, "I am going to take my sister way over there toward the east. She hears our mother crying over there. We know that she was killed over toward the east."

They traveled and traveled day after day for many days and the farther they traveled toward the east the more plainly the little girl could hear her mother cry. Finally one day they met a man in a big valley, far to the east. The boy asked him "How far is it over there to where somebody is crying?" This man could make no reply, He had no mouth and could not talk. He could only make motions, but with his hands he indicated that it was a long way still to the place they sought.

Finally they reached a village and from one of the houses they heard this noise which the little girl had been hearing all the time. The boy sat down outside of the house but the little girl went around and found the door to the house closed. She peeped in and finally opened the door and there she saw her mother plainly. Her mother told her to come in and welcomed her. When she got inside so that she could see plainly she was very much frightened because it is true that her mother was there, but her mother had no head. Her head had been shaken off by Bear. She immediately ran out to her brother and told him what she had seen, and the boy went in with her. He also saw that his mother had no head, but he was not frightened.

He sat down beside his mother and she told him, "I have a very bad husband. One time I was killed. My head was shaken off. That is the reason I have no head now." She then told the children all about her busband who is Sun-man and she warned the children, particularly the boy, that they must be very, very careful when her husband came home. "He is a very dangerous man. When he shuts his month there is no light and when he has his mouth open the light shines. When he comes home he walks four time around the house before he enters."

The boy then put some rocks into the fire in the house before Sun-man arrived. The boy had a snowball in a hunting sack which he carried on his left side.

Finally he heard Sun-man coming. He flew down near the house, and walked four times around it. When he started to enter the house the boy was all ready for him and as he appeared in the door Sun-man opened his mouth very wide. The boy immediately threw one of the hot rocks into his mouth and followed this by another. They burned Sun-man and he fell over dead outside. The rocks were so hot that they set fire to Sun-man's body and it burned for a long time. It burned until there was very little left of it, only a piece about the size of a new moon. Then someone came along with water and put the fire out.

II

(Placing the Sun in the Sky)

Presently all the people gathered around to see what was going on and the chief of the village said, "What are you going to do about this? Can you not put this sun up in the sky?" They discussed this matter for quite a long time and finally two men, one on either side, took what was left of the sun and tried to place it back in the sky. They, however, were unsuccessful. Then two others tried, and so on. A great many pairs of the people tried to put the sun up where it belonged, but all were unsuccessful. Finally two Crows took it up and put it back again and it remained there.

Finally the boy wanted to return to the ocean where his grandfather Blue Heron lived. His mother said to him, "My son, you must take me back there to your grandfather with you. You must carry me all the way. It is a long distance but you must not put me down until you arrive at your grandfather's house."

They started out toward the west and the boy carried his mother for a very long time, but finally he became very weary indeed. He became so tired that he could go no farther with his burden and set it down. His mother immediately turned into a great rock.

90—GRIZZLY BEAR KILLS HER DAUGHTER-IN-LAW[215]

Characters: 1. Grizzly bear, 2. Deer (son of Bear), 3. Deer-woman (wife of Deer), 4. Deer children (two), 5. Meadowlark, 6. Wasp, 7. Crane, 8. Yellowhammer, 9. Tsatī'.

At a place called "Tīhēma pda" lived Grizzly Bear, an old woman who was the mother of Deer. Her son's family consisted of his wife (also Deer) and their two children.

Deer used to snare a great many birds and he provided his mother, as well as his own family, with game. He used to give his mother the pigeons that he caught which were considered to be inferior meat but he kept the good meat for himself and his own family. Deer did this for three days.

Finally one of the Deer boys was passing his grandmother's house and she called him in and said, "Lie down here. I want to see your teeth." He laid down on his grandmother's lap and she picked his teeth and got out quite a number of bits of meat. She tasted this meat and found that it was very sweet and delicious and asked the boy, "Is that the kind of meat you eat?" To which he replied that it was. "Then," said Grizzly, "why did your father give me the strong, bad meat?" The little fellow confessed that he did not know anything about it.

The more Grizzly thought about this matter the more angry she became and finally she went out and found one of her son's snares with a grouse caught in it. This was a spring snare and the bird was suspended in the air. Grizzly dug a hole directly under it and crawled in here and covered herself completely with leaves so that she was entirely hidden and nobody could possibly know that she was there. She then bit a hole in one of the leaves and put it right over her eye so that she could see out when Deer came.

Presently Deer came along and sat down beside the snare and in order to take the grouse out of it. It was then that Grizzly caught and killed him. She then skinned Deer and put the skin in the bottom of her basket. She cut up the meat and put it in on top of the skin and then she went to gather clover and put that in as the last layer. She took her load home and cooked and ate the meat of Deer.

Deer's wife missed her husband and told her little boys to go over and ask their grandmother if she had seen their father. They did so and

---

[215]The Indian title of this myth is "Ptakai ya maodil pcē kūm," "Grizzly daughter-in-law deer kill."
Informant: Bill James, Central dialect.

she told them she had not seen him anywhere. She then gave them some of the meat, in fact a whole shoulder of venison.

As the children started home eating this meat they met Meadow-lark who said, "You are gnawing your father's bones." Grizzly over-heard this remark and she became very angry and tried to kill Meadow-lark but Lark dodged and she only reached the tip of his tail and cut that off. That is why Mealowlark now has such a short tail.

When the boys came home and Deer's wife saw what they were eating she then knew that her husband had been killed and she wept bitterly.

Grizzly came out and called to Deer-woman and said, "Come on out, and let me clean the vermin out of your hair." When Deer had come out Bear said, "Now sit right down here and I will clean your hair for you."

Bear then began to pick the vermin out of Deer's head and she picked so hard that she took bits of the flesh off and Deer finally noticed that the blood was running down her neck and she said, "What is the reason that the blood runs here on my neck?"

Bear replied, "Oh, my claws are a little sharp and I guess I scratched your head." She kept right on scratching and picking in the same way, however, until Deer's head was nearly off. Then she told Deer to shake her head. When Deer did this her head fell off completely.

The head lay there on the ground by itself and cursed Bear, saying, "Lok nis an baset (you are certainly ugly looking)." Then Bear be-came more enraged and mashed the head into the ground.

When the two boys learned what had happened to their mother they cried for a long time but finally they went down to the creek to play. Meadowlark came down here and told them, "You have already lost your father and your mother. You had better leave here now while there is a chance for you to save yourselves. If you do not do some-thing to Bear she will kill you also. I will tell you what you had better do. One of you must go to the house and call for that "sun" basket (ta'sītōl). It is the finest, most beautiful basket there. It hangs up at the end of the house and is all tied up and is never used. Do not call it by its true name but when you ask for it call it 'pa'tolka'." This was as a matter of fact a name which no one had ever heard before and was a name which was invented by Meadowlark for this occasion.

Accordingly the youngest brother went home and asked Bear for this basket. Bear did not know what the boy was talking about and so she got down everything that there was in the house and the last thing of all was this basket. The boy was very glad to see this when it was unwrapped and danced around in great glee. So Bear gave it to him and he went back to the river. He rolled it down the hill and over the bank into the water.

Then both boys ran up to Bear's house and told her that the basket was adrift and she ran out after it. She jumped into the water and tried to catch the basket but it drifted right under her. She followed it in this way clear down to the ocean.

When Bear started on her quest of this basket the two boys ran away and journeyed toward the north. The first important place that they came to on this journey was the mouth of Russian River (Kahwa'-latī). As they passed on beyond this place they saw Wasp (Ma'n kitsī) cutting down a tree with an elk-horn wedge (p!ŏ'ma). He was striking this wedge with a stone hammer which had no handle. When he saw the boys he asked them where they were going and they replied that they were running away from their grandmother who had already killed their father and their mother.

Then they journeyed on northward and by and by they came to a place where a man was burning a log in two for the center pole of a sweat-house. He also inquired where the boys were going. They replied, "Our father and mother were killed so we are going away."

They journeyed still farther toward the north until finally they came to a place where the sky comes down and meets the earth. Here there was a big river. Crane (Kalē yagaū) lived here, and when the boys approached him, he asked them where they were going. They replied that their father and mother had been killed so they were running away and going as far up north as they could. Then they asked Crane if they could cross that river.

Crane replied, "There is no way to cross that river."

"Well," said the boys, "You ought to manage to put us across some way."

"All right," said Crane, "I will manage it for you." He then sat down and commenced to stretch his neck and it grew and grew until he stretched it clear across this great river. He made it flat on top so they could cross.

The boys started across this bridge and they found that the water was extremely muddy and very swift. It was an extremely dangerous river but they crossed successfully and when they arrived on the opposite side they found Yellowhammer (Katsī'yō).

By the time the children had reached the opposite side of this great northern river, Grizzly Bear had returned from her quest of the basket, which, of course, she was not able to recover. She looked for the children but could not find them. Then she knew that they had run away. She said, "Well, you will be the first ones that I could not track. I will certainly be able to track you. I know where you have gone." So she started out to track the boys. She came to the Russian River and swam across. Then went on north along the coast until she found Wasp to whom she said, "Did you see any boys go along here? I lost my children."

"No," said Wasp, "I did not see anyone go this way."

Bear said, "I know now that you are lying." So she killed Wasp and went on northward. When she had left, Wasp came to life again. Presently she came to where Tsatī was burning the log in two and asked him, "Did you see any boys go by here?"

But Tsatī said, "No, I saw no one."

Bear said to him, "Now I know you are lying," so she killed him by mashing him all up, but as soon as she had passed he came to life again.

Finally she came to the place where Crane stayed, on this side of the great northern river, and to him she said, "Did you see any boys go by here?"

"No," said Crane, "I did not see anyone."

To this Bear said, "I saw them go by here myself. I know where they went."

Crane replied, "I did not see anyone."

"Well," said Bear, "You had better put a bridge across anyway for me." To this Crane agreed.

He stretched his neck across as he had done for the boys, but he made it round so that it was very hard for her to walk. Then Crane told Bear, "You must open your mouth wide and shut your eyes when you go across this bridge."

Yellowhammer, who lived on the opposite side of this great river heated a rock until it was white hot, then he wrapped it up and put it under his arm so that Bear could see nothing that looked red or fiery.

But Bear asked Crane, "What is that over there that looks like fire?"

Crane replied, "That is only the spot under Yellowhammer's arm. Now open your mouth and shut your eyes tight, otherwise you will fall off the bridge if you look while you are going across."

Bear did as she was told and nearly reached the other side before anything happened. Then Yellowhammer threw his hot rock right into Bears' mouth and she rolled off into the water and was killed.

The boys remained on the other side of the river.

MISCELLANEOUS ANIMAL TALES

91—THE RACE BETWEEN MUD-HEN AND OTHER BIRDS[216]

Characters: 1. Butterball, 2. Bird-people, 3. Mud-hen, 4. Blue Heron.

Butterball was recognized as the swiftest runner among the Bird-people. Mud-hen was a very clumsy fellow and was very slow in a race. The Bird-people decided to have a race. Two of each different kind of bird entered.

They placed Blue Heron (Makō) at the eastern foot of Mt. Kanaktai along the base of which the race was to be run.

The race started on the west shore of Clear Lake at a point near what is known as Upper Lake Landing (Dīsa'hwai) and they ran south along the shore of the lake. They ran on past Pūlī'ts-ūwī, Xalaxak, Kaiyē'bīdas, Kabél, Kalelis.

By the time they had reached this point the two Mud-hens had been left far behind in the race. As the race progressed Blue Heron announced its progress loudly from his station at Mt. Kanaktai. And as he made these announcements the rocks on the precipitous eastern side of Mt. Kanaktai slid down in great numbers and piled up at the base of the cliff.

They raced on, passing Da'tsim, Kō'batap, Xabai, Katsamūkal, Bōa'malī successively to Lakeport. Here they turned and traveled toward the southeast and east, through Big Valley, Soda Bay and thence on the south side of the lake until they reached Lower Lake. By this

---

[216]The Indian name of this myth is "Xatsīya yeek welba xaiuga xaēlī." Informant: Tom Mitchell, Eastern dialect.

time the Mud-hens had begun to gain on the other racers. They raced on passing around the end of Sulphur Bank or East Lake and on up the eastern shore of Clear Lake, passing Kītsī'danoyo and finally, by the time they had reached Cī'gōm, the Mud-hens had passed the rest of the racers and were leading.

Then Blue Heron announced in a very loud voice, "The Mud-hens are going to win the race." Every time he made one of these announcements in this way, large boulders rolled down from the eastern side of Mt. Kanaktai and piled themselves up in greater and greater numbers at the foot of the cliff.

The racers ran on and on toward the north, past Matī'l and Badō'nbaten, and finally when the race was ended the Mud-hens were far in the lead and had won.

It was at this time that the whole eastern side of Mt. Kanaktai slid off in boulders and rolled down to the shore of the lake. It was caused by the jar produced by Blue Heron's loud announcements of this race.

92—THE RACE BETWEEN DEER AND MUD-HEN[217]

Characters: 1. Deer, 2. Mud-hen, 3. Goose (Koto'c).

At a village over near the mouth of Kelsey Creek the Bird-people had assembled for a great celebration and dance.

Deer announced that he was the best runner present and that he could beat anyone in a foot-race. At first no one answered him, but after he had made his boast, about his racing ability, a number of times, Mud-hen finally said, "I am the one who can outrun you. I will run a race with you."

They posted Goose (Koto'c) on the top of Mt. Kanaktai to watch the race and make announcements to the people as it progressed. The race-course was around the entire shore of Clear Lake and its associated lakes.

When everything was in readiness Goose started the race by counting "one, two, three, four" (ta'tō, ko, sī'bō, dū'ōka). The two racers started off and in no time Deer had outdistanced Mud-hen by several miles. Goose announced this fact to the people and stated that Deer was so far ahead that it would be quite impossible for Mud-hen to overtake him.

---

[217]Informant: Charlie Pinto, Central dialect.

However, by the time the racers had reached Lower Lake, Mud-hen began to gain on Deer who was sweating and showing signs of fatigue.

Goose announced to the people that Mud-hen was gaining and expressed the opinion that he would at least catch up with Deer so that the race would be a close one. By the time the racers had reached Bald Hill, Mud-hen had gained on Deer so far that they were running neck and neck. By the time they had reached Upper Lake, Mud-hen was about three steps ahead of Deer. Goose announced this to the people.

As the race went on, Mud-hen gained more and more, and by the time they had reached Lakeport, Mud-hen was about a mile and a half ahead of Deer. At this point Goose announced to the people that undoubtedly Mud-hen would win the race. This brought a great cheer from the people and they began to make fun of Deer because he had made his brag that he was the fastest runner of them all.

Finally when the race was ended Mud-hen was far in the lead. He was several miles ahead of Deer. Deer was so chagrined that a slow-mover like Mud-hen should be able to beat him in a foot-race that he wanted to give Mud-hen his horns and his hide, but Mud-hen refused them. Mud-hen was a very generous man and did not want to kill anyone.

93—WOLF KILLS DEER BY MAGIC[218]

Characters: 1. Wolf, 2. Chicken Hawk (husband of Wolf), 3. Oak-ball, 4. Naka'ca kaiyan.

At Gōnhō-yō lived Wolf and her husband, Chicken Hawk (Kabē'-katc). There was a famine in the country and they had no food. Chicken Hawk was extremely hungry, in fact he was starved to such an extent that he could not move about.[219]

Wolf had somewhat more strength than her husband and she told him one day that she was going to go out and try and procure some wood for the fire and asked him to watch the baby if he had sufficient strength. This he agreed to do and she took her basket and walked on toward the east for some considerable distance. She went over toward the east until she came to a soda spring and deer-lick.

[218]The Pomo name of this myth is "Smewa pcē īlen matū'. The scene of the story is at a place called "Gônhō yō," signifying literally "Chemese under."
Informant, Bill James, Central dialect.
[219]There is a special Pomo term indicating this condition. It is "katsa'm tiu" and signifies a person lying by the fire so weak and emaciated from starvation that he cannot go about to get food.

Here she divested herself of her clothing and lay down near the deer-lick and began to sing the regular Wolf song for taking deer. Presently many deer came as the result of the magic of this song. The largest of them was a tremendous buck who had horns like an elk. He approached Wolf and at an opportune moment Wolf choked him and killed him. She then loaded the meat into her basket and started home. When she had gone about half-way she added some wood on top of the load of meat in order that she might have something with which to cook this food when she arrived.

Upon her arrival her husband remarked that it was very strange that in these days of famine she was able to go out and bring in such a fine deer and asked her how it was possible for her to do so. She replied that she found it dead and had brought it in anyway. Chicken Hawk then observed that if he could have food like that he would be able to get well again and that it might save his life. Wolf then proceeded to cook this deer and Chicken Hawk ate almost all of it. He began by eating the entrails first and then he ate right on through until he had consumed almost the entire deer, leaving only a very small part.

On the follow day Wolf again went out saying that she was going to get wood. She went to the same deer-lick and succeeded, in the same manner, in taking another animal. She brought this home and cooked it for her husband in the same way.

Three times on successive days did she do this and Chicken Hawk grew quite strong but on the third day he noticed something peculiar about the taste of the meat and said to his wife, "What is the matter with this deer meat, it tastes so strange?"

Wolf replied, "I guess it is because I find the deer dead and that they have lain too long before being opened up."

Chicken Hawk, however, became suspicious and thought that there was something irregular about the way his wife was obtaining their meat so he determined to follow and watch while she did her hunting the next day. He saw her go down by the soda spring and saw what she did there and how she lured the deer to her by her nudity and then killed them, selecting always the largest one of the herd of bucks that came.

This made him very angry and he went home, gathered together all of the beads and dancing paraphernalia and other valuables he had and

left home. He journeyed over toward the east and by noon he arrived at
Mt. Kanaktai. When he reached the top of the mountain he stopped
there for a while to look around.

Toward the east he saw a big smoke so he started out toward it
and when he arrived at that place, the chief of the village invited him
into the dance-house and gave him food. When he had finished eating
his meal and had been made welcome by these people, the lookout Oak-
ball (Poto'ce), who was stationed on the top of the house to keep watch,
announced that very far away a woman was approaching. Oak-ball had
the strongest eyes of anyone and could see farther than anyone else.
Soon he announced that it was Wolf who was approaching.

Finally Wolf arrived and the chief of the village invited her in. She
had on a large belt, had strings of beads about her neck, and carried also
a fine basket. With these she hoped to induce her husband to return
to her. Upon entering she placed them on his lap and begged him to
return but he paid no attention to them, simply let them remain there
where she had placed them for a minute and then pushed them away
saying that he would have nothing to do with them in any way and
telling her to take them back and to return home.

On the following morning he started back toward Mt. Kanaktai
but from a distance he saw his wife approaching so he took the trail on
the south side of the mountain, while she passed on the north side,
purposely so that he might avoid her.

He then went on to his own house. He took his carrying sack (yet)
made of a single skin of bōka'pcūt, a small animal said to resemble a
mouse in size and color but to live under the ground and to travel entirely at night.

He filled this bag with beads and started northward. He traveled a
very long distance until he reached a great valley called "Kasi'lmnē."
As he approached this valley he saw rising a great smoke like a fog, it
was such a large village. He therefore dressed himself up in full dance
costume with all of his paraphernalia and came dancing into the village.
It was an ancient custom that when a man or group of men came dancing into a village in this way the residents of that village were expected
to make presents to the dancers, particularly presents of beads. Consequently the chief of this village told his people that they must go and
bring valuable presents of beads to be given to Chicken Hawk. In fact

they brought him so many beads that they nearly filled the sweat-house.

He danced for quite a long time and then he took out his tiny little bag in which he carried his beads and put in handful after handful of the beads that they had given him, but he was never able to fill the bag. In fact with all this vast quantity of beads that they had brought they little more than filled one hind leg of this bag, for this was a magic bag and when he placed beads in here they passed right on through it and immediately went back to his house and accumulated there.

By and by the Royal Maiden of the village Naka′ca kaiyan, brought him food.

After a while someone looked out and saw a stranger coming. Oak-ball again went up on top of the sweat-house to see who it was and soon reported that it was Wolf.

Wolf again came and this time she brought twice as much in the way of presents to Chicken Hawk as she had before but he refused them all and she returned to her home crying because he would not come back to her.

Chicken Hawk then journeyed on farther toward the north along the coast until he came to another large village at a place called "Kabē hō" where he again dressed himself in full dance costume and went dancing into the village, dancing as usual four times around the sweat-house in each direction before entering.

Again the people brought great quantities of beads, so many that they made a great pile around the center pole. Again he placed the beads in his magic bag and again someone announced that a stranger was approaching. Oak-ball called out that it was Wolf and presently she arrived.

This time she brought a large number of valuable presents. She brought a very fine bow, one of the finest that could be made, called "manam kī." She brought also beautifully decorated, bone ear-plugs, called "kē′ya-cma″-tcakle." She also brought four bead belts and three very fine "sun" baskets (ta sītōl) and three beautiful, bead neck-ornaments (kē′ya cbū). All of these valuable things, however, he refused and insisted that he would not return home with her and ordered her to take them back.

On the following morning he journeyed still farther north until he finally came to a place called "Baka′m alaū," which signifies "chemese pointed down." He dressed and danced into the village as before and was presented with great quantities of beads which he again put into his magic sack and caused to disappear in the same way as in the other instances.

Presently Oak-ball announced that Wolf was again coming. This time she brought a very fine *talē'ya kalai* (a fine head-net made of human hair, interwoven with beads, and considered to be very, very select). She also brought bead belts, neck ornaments and various other things as presents to him. When she placed these new presents on his lap he accepted them and she told him, "I want you to come back with me. Why do you leave your child?" He agreed to return home with her and they went back together and they lived there a long time.

Chicken Hawk finally recovered from the effects of the famine, grew stout and strong and was able to hunt and provide food for his family in the regular way.

94—PANTHER'S WIFE KILLS DEER BY MAGIC[220]

Characters: 1. Panthers, 2. Panther's son.

There were two Panthers, husband and wife. The wife told her husband to make some bows and arrows so that he could go hunting. He worked at this arrow-making for two days, making bows and arrows out of manzanita. These two Panthers had a small boy.   .

One day the Panther-woman went out hunting with a bow and some arrows and when she arrived at a place where she knew deer were abundant she divested herself of her clothing and lay down as if going to sleep. She was lying on her back, singing, as a matter of fact, a magic song that would bring the deer. These animals heard this song and many came toward her. Finally a very large and fine buck came directly up to her. At the first opportunity she shot this animal in the throat with an arrow, immediately springing to her feet and holding the deer down so that it died almost immediately. She then put on her clothing and made the deer up into a pack and carried it home.

When she arrived she found that her husband had already pro-

---

[220]The Pomo title of this story is "Wīk!a' marū," in other words, "Panther old time." The term "wīk!a'" which is here translated "Panther" is somewhat doubtful. It is said to be an animal larger than a wildcat and similar in color. It may possibly be the lynx, but one informant said it was really the panther or mountain lion. The term for "mountain lion" in the Central Dialect is "yamō't."
Informant: Mary Louie, Eastern dialect.

cured a goodly amount of dry wood to cook with, and when he saw
her coming he started a fire, and they took the deer to where he had
spread branches upon which to cut up the meat, as was customary.
When the meat was piled up ready for broiling, the fire had reduced
itself to a fine bed of coals and they cooked this meat and all, including
the small boy, ate their fill. They ate the entire deer that day.

Early the next morning the Panther-woman went out to hunt again
and once more succeeded in killing a deer through her magic as she had
done on the first day.

All that her husband did was to watch the fire and to get wood and
water. This went on day after day, Panther-woman going out before
breakfast in the morning and divesting herself of her garments which
consisted of a two piece dress, spreading the skirt on the ground and
lying upon that and using the upper part of the dress as a pillow. Thus
she would lie and sing her magic song to bring the deer and her magic
was always successful.

By and by her husband became curious at the wonderful success
that she had in killing deer and began to wonder how she proceeded in
her hunting, so he followed her and watched to see just what she was
doing. When he saw this he was greatly angered and immediately
returned home, arriving there before his wife.

As she approached the house on this occasion he did not come out
as was his custom to help her bring in the deer. He merely sat there in
the house and sulked and his wife knew therefore that he was angry.

Finally, however, he told her what he had seen and that he was very
much displeased with her methods of hunting. He then went and took
their bead-bag[221] and divided their wealth. These beads were in a long
string. He pulled out this string and doubled it over and divided the
beads equally, tying the two ends of the string as he cut it to make the
division. One half of these beads he put back into the sack and the
other half he placed in his own sack.

When his wife saw what he was doing she knew that he intended
to leave her and she cried bitterly, but when he had finally prepared to
leave he told her that he was going and enjoined her to take good care of
their boy.

She refused to do this and told him that she did not want the boy

___
[221]It was customary to keep beads in a fawn skin bag in ancient times.

at all and that he could take the boy with him. He therefore placed his bag of beads on his shoulder and perched the boy on top of this bag and started off toward the east.

At some distance to the eastward there was a large village of the Bird-people. As he approached this village its chief came out to meet them, telling his people meanwhile to bring out food to the visitors and to make them welcome. After they had eaten, Panther divided his beads in half and gave one-half of them to the chief of this village.

They remained here for the night and early the following morning they started out toward the east again and in due time they came to another large village. Here the chief of the village welcomed them and they were given food. Here again Panther divided his beads and gave one-half of them to the chief.

Again they remained over night and they became well acquainted with some of its people. These people inquired just why they were journeying toward the east, wondering whether or not they had been run out of their own village or whether they had left of their own volition. Here, at this second village, also one of the women gave Panther a considerable number of beads among which were some of magnesite. Then she asked him to give her the boy for she never had had any children of her own and she wanted this little boy.

Panther returned the beads which she had given to him because he would not sell his boy but he gave the boy to her.

He then asked the people if there were any villages toward the south but was told that they had never heard of any in that direction so he started off toward the southeast. He traveled for a long time in that direction, then changed his course toward the south and finally toward the southwest, coming back to the coast at a point south of his old village.

Here he found an island on which was located a village and he wanted to reach this village but could not do so on account of the wide expanse of water. He therefore decided to make a canoe. This he did, using kacī' as the material for it.

The people of this village saw Panther approaching with his canoe and they immediately procured wood and prepared to welcome him in the sweat-house. Upon his arrival there he dumped his sack of beads and completely emptied it.

This was a small island and one which was occupied almost exclusively by the village. There was room enough around the sweat-house for forty or fifty dwellings but there was no wood on this island. It was necessary for the people to go to the mainland for their wood and to bring it across in canoes.

When everything was in readiness a fire was built in the sweat-house and more and more wood was added and it became extremely hot. In fact it became so hot that the house itself was set on fire. The beads which Panther had poured out on the sweat-house floor were still lying there when this happened. No one had handled them as yet.

This fire burned and burned, until it had consumed the entire village and burned everyone up.

95—BLACK HAWK LEAVES HOME BUT IS INDUCED TO RETURN[222]

Characters: 1. Black Hawk, 2. Panther (wife of Black Hawk), 3. Son of Black Hawk and Panther, 4. Oak-ball, 5. Kū'sūt, 6. Mallard-duck girls.

Black Hawk (Kabékatc) and Panther (Yamót), his wife, lived far over in the east. They had a little boy. Their food supply was very short. Black Hawk was nearly starved to death. He was so thin that he had hardly any flesh at all. Panther and their little boy had no food either but they did not grow so thin as Black Hawk.

Finally, one day, Panther told him to watch the baby and take good care of him for she was going out to get some wood. She went over east onto a mountain. Then she went away up on this mountain to a small stream where there was a soda spring and deer-lick. Here she found deer trails coming from every direction toward the spring. She removed all her clothing and left that with her burden basket behind the spring, while she lay down beside one of the trails with her head toward the east.

As she lay here, she sang
nū nū hūkūmkū hûn a tsī (Repeated)
She then raised her head and looked up the trail toward the north but saw nothing, so she sang the song again, the same as before. Again she raised her head and looked toward the north but saw nothing, so she

---
[222]Informant: Captain Charley, Garcia River, Central dialect, 1906.

sang the song again, raising her head a third time and looking toward the north but again seeing nothing.

After singing the song four times, she looked toward the north as before and she saw many deer coming along the trail. Then she continued to sing this song until the band of deer had approached very near to her. Then she stopped. The deer who approached her was a spike with whom she refused to have anything to do. Then one after another approached but she refused each one in turn, until, finally, the largest deer, who was in the center of the drove approached her. She showed this deer signs of affection, putting her arm about its neck and squeezing it hard. She did this until the opportunity came and then she bit its throat and killed it. Then she let go the deer and ran down to the spring for her clothing and the burden basket. She put the deer in the basket and started toward home. She also got some wood and piled it on top of her load.

When she arrived at the house, she laid her basket down in front of the door, took the load out of it and threw the deer inside the house.

When Black Hawk saw the deer, he said, "That is good that you bring that deer. How did you find it?" But she made no answer.

She took a flake of flint and cut the deer open and skinned it. Then she cooked one flank and gave it to her husband. She continued to cook this meat until they had eaten the whole deer, on that same day.

Next morning, she arose, washed her face and again told her husband to take care of the baby. She took her basket and went out to the same place and did exactly as on the previous day, singing the same song the same number of times and in every way acting as before. Again the deer came and she succeeded in killing the largest one of the band. She then dressed herself, put this deer into the basket, gathered some wood and went home.

As she took this deer in, her husband said, "It is good that you have this deer. Now I will 'come alive' again because you have this deer and we have food." She again cooked the hams for her husband and continued cooking the other parts during the day, even mashing up the bones with stones. She cooked every bit of the deer and they ate it all that day.

Next morning, Panther arose and did exactly as on the previous days and again, after singing as before, she succeeded in killing the biggest deer in the drove that came to her. She dressed and carried this deer home and again Black Hawk asked her how she came to get the deer but she made no reply. She skinned and cooked the deer as before and gave her husband the first meat cooked, which was the ham.

Black Hawk was getting stronger every day and after they had eaten three deer, he was well again. He now remembered that there was a bitter taste about these hams, and by this taste, he knew that something wrong was going on.

On the morning of the fourth day, his wife asked him again to watch the baby while she went for wood. She said, "Don't let the baby fall into the fire, while I am gone for wood." She went out to the deer-lick and did the same as she had done on the three previous days, singing for the deer and finally bringing a large drove.

Her husband, who had become suspicious that everything was not going as it should, followed his wife on this morning and when he saw her remove her clothing and lie down by the trail, he slipped up behind the nearby bushes and lay down to see what would happen. When the drove of deer came, the largest deer came and lay down with the woman and presently, she bit its throat and killed it. Black Hawk had never seen anything like this before and could not understand just what was taking place and as the woman started home with the deer in her basket, he said, "Well, that is the way my woman has been killing deer?"

Black Hawk did not return home, but instead he went off toward the east, because he felt badly about his wife's actions and was jealous. Panther went home and found her husband gone, so she took the baby and started out to hunt for him. She followed his tracks toward the east. She finally found the place where her husband first sat down to rest. She also sat down and rested. This place was only about half-way over to where she was going.

Finally Black Hawk arrived at a village, Kaūnakī-napō, situated in a little valley about a mile east of Sulphur Bank. The people who lived here welcomed him and invited him into the sweat-house. Then they brought all kinds of foods: mush, pinole, fish, meat, etc. for him to eat.

All this time, however, his wife was following him. Finally, she came near the village. She had brought with her a feather belt, a bead belt and various other valuable articles, by the aid of which, she hoped to be able to induce her husband to return home. As she approached the village, she inquired of the people, "Have you seen my husband? Did he come to this village?"

They told her, "Yes, he has just gone to that big house in the center of the village."

She then entered the sweat-house and took a seat on the left hand side of the house. She offered her husband all she had brought, if he would only return home. He refused these things and kicked them all out of the sweat-house. She recovered these articles and then went to her village and returned to this place with double the amount; but this he also refused. She then went home and returned with three times the amount but he declined this also. But finally, after she had made a fourth trip and brought four times as much as at first, he accepted her offer and they started home. On the way, they stopped to rest at the same resting place above mentioned. Finally, they arrived at their house.

Very soon, Black Hawk took down his dancing paraphernalia and prepared to go off visiting and dancing. He had, among other things, a small purse made of an animal skin (bólkapcūt, a very small mouse-like animal) which he tied up with a string. He took his dancing paraphernalia and this purse and started over west toward the ocean. When he came to the ocean, he turned northward. He travelled on toward the north until he finally came in sight of a cloud of heavy smoke which looked very much like fog. This was the biggest village in existence. When he came near the village, he stopped out in the brush and dressed and painted himself for the dance. As he approached the village, he sang the song—

    n n hōwû
    hōwû hōwû hōwû hōwû
    cō mīna cō mīna tca tcu ha
    n n hōwû
    hōwû hōwû hōwû hōwû
    cō mīna cō mīna tca tcu ha

As usual, Oakball and Kū'sūt were on the lookout, on the roof of the dance-house and, while he was some distance away, they announced, "There is something coming from somewhere way off." As he came nearer to the village, he sang as before.

When he arrived at the dance-house, he ran in the usual manner around it four times in a clockwise direction, then four times around it in a counter-clockwise direction and, having entered the dance-house, he ran around the fire, likewise four times in each direction and then he commenced to dance.

The chief of the village told the people to go home and get some beads to pay for this dance. They all brought beads and threw them on the floor. There were so many people that they could not all get into the dance-house and those who could not, climbed up on the roof and tore holes in it in order that they might look through and see Black Hawk dance. He kept right on singing and dancing for a long time.

He had this little purse made of bol-kapcūt skin and into this he put all the beads which the people had brought as presents to him for the dance. However, notwithstanding the great number of beads that they brought, when he placed them in this little purse, they hardly filled up one leg of it. They did not even fill up to the body.

There were two Mallard-duck girls who took a fancy to Black Hawk and wanted him for a husband. While he was sacking up the beads they sat one on either side of him.

About this time, Kūsūt and Oak-ball, who were lookouts on top of the dance-house, announced that someone was coming and presently, Black Hawk's wife arrived. As before, she brought one each of the various kinds of head ornaments and valuable things that she thought Black Hawk might care for. He, however, refused to have anything to do with them and threw them outside the dance-house.

The next morning, the chief of the village gave him food and he went on toward the north. Here he found another village and dressed for the dance. He went singing into the village. Kūsūt and Oak-ball saw him coming and announced it to the people. He entered the dance-house in the same manner as before, and after his dance the people gave him a large quantity of beads. These beads filled up his small purse a little more. Here also, two Mallard-duck girls made love to Black Hawk.

Soon Oak-ball and Kūsūt announced that Panther was coming. This time, she brought two each of the various head ornaments and valuable things but Black Hawk refused these and threw them away as he had done at the other village.

Next morning, he journeyed on toward the north, and came again to a village, where he sang and danced as before, his coming having been announced, of course, by the lookouts. When he had finished the dance, the chief of the village told his people, "It is rather dangerous when a man goes around dancing for a living. It is dangerous and you must all pay him well." So everyone brought beads and scattered them about on the floor. These beads filled the little purse up nearly to the breast of the skin. At this village also, there were two Mallard-duck girls who made love to Black Hawk.

Again Panther came but this time with three each of the various valuable articles which she had brought before. These, however, he refused as he had done those before and on the following morning, he went still farther north, where he found another village at which he danced. As he approached this village, he sang, as before.

The chief called all the people to come to the dance-house and when they came, the ground shook, there were so many of them. Black Hawk danced for a long time and he continued to dance even when the beads were thrown in by the people. Then he sang again as before.

Finally, he sat down and commenced to sack up the beads in his little purse which was, by this time, nearly full. Again the lookouts announced that Panther was coming. This time she brought four of a kind of each one of the valuable articles before mentioned and these Black Hawk accepted, and they returned to their home. They lived there always.

96—THE PEOPLE ARE UNABLE TO KILL TURTLE[223]

Characters: 1. Turtle, 2. Chief of the village.

Turtle started out to visit a village over in the east. Someone saw him approaching and called the chief out of the sweat-house. When the chief saw Turtle, he told the men about him, "You people better kill that fellow, Turtle." The people then caught Turtle.

The chief then asked, "Which do you think is best, to club him to death or to burn him?"

Someone said, "I think we had better take him into the sweat-house and burn him."

Then Turtle spoke up and said, "No, do not put me into the fire. If you do, lots of steam will rise and the odor which will come from my body will kill everybody." They believed Turtle and, instead of burning

---

[223]Informant: Captain Charley, Garcia River, Central dialect, 1906.

him, they took him out and commenced to shoot him with arrows and this is what makes the marks which we now see on Turtle's back. The arrows glanced off from Turtle's shell and they were unable to kill him this way.

So someone said, "We cannot kill him in this way. Let us take him down and throw him into the water and drown him quickly." Then they took Turtle down and threw him into the deepest pool they could find.

Turtle presently came to the surface and said, "I just thought I would fool you people. This is the way I fool children." Then some of the people ran home to get dip nets and bows and arrows and everybody hunted for Turtle but they were unable to find him, for he crawled in under the sand. Later he crawled out upon a riffle, then swam ashore and went home.

97—TURTLE TRICKS THE PEOPLE[224]

Character: 1. Turtle.

Turtle stationed himself just inside the outer door of the tunnel to the house, where no one could see him, and he succeeded in shooting many of the people. He shot them one at a time very stealthily, but finally one man, who was watching to see where the arrows came from, espied him. He caught Turtle and pulled him out of the tunnel and shouted for the rest of the people of the village to come.

The people wondered just what they would do with Turtle to punish him. Someone suggested that they make a big fire and throw Turtle into it, but Turtle said, "If you do that the smoke will poison all of you." Another one suggested that they should mash Turtle up completely with big rocks, but Turtle told them then that if they did that his blood would spatter all around in the village and would poison everyone.

Someone else suggested that they should tie a big rock onto Turtle and throw him into the water. Turtle said, "There, now you have made a wise suggestion. There is a man who has real sense and who knows how to kill me without doing damage to others. You tie me up in good shape with a big stone. Then tie a bead belt on top of the other binding. Then catch hold of my arms and legs and stretch them out as far as you can. Then everybody should yell four times and heave me out as far into the water as you possibly can."

---

[224]Informant: Mary Louie, Eastern dialect.

The people did this and threw Turtle way out into the water yelling as loudly as they could. They saw bubbles coming up for a long time from the place where Turtle had gone down. Finally these bubbles stopped rising and they were sure that Turtle was dead.

Presently Turtle rose to the top of the water just like a dead fish. He came to the surface belly up with his legs stretched out. Then he held his head up and stuck out his tongue at the people as a snake does. Then he slapped the water with his feet and made a sound "bap, pip, bolop[225], etc." Then Turtle dove under the water and everybody dove in after him, carrying arrows and sharp sticks with which to kill him. They looked everywhere, in the water and in the rushes along the bank but could not find Turtle anywhere. He had tricked them completely.

98—FALCON DIES AND RETURNS TO LIFE[226]

Characters: 1. Pelican, 2. Falcon, 3. Meadowlark.

In olden times Pelican (Kalai) was chief, but the people deposed him and put Falcon in as chief in his place. This made Pelican angry and he made up his mind that some day when Falcon went out hunting he would waylay him and kill him. Pelican knew just where Falcon was in the habit of hunting so he went out and lay in wait by the trail and watched for Falcon.

Now Pelican was a bear doctor so he put on his bear-doctor[227] suit and when Falcon came along the trail Pelican sprang upon him and bit and clawed him, as a bear would do, and killed him.

Pelican then put away his bear-doctor suit and went home. Some of the other hunters found Falcon and brought his body back to the village. They mourned the death of Falcon and finally cremated him, in the usual way. They dug a pit about the length of the body and about two feet deep. In this they built a great fire and laid Falcon's body upon this pyre with his face down. They threw many offerings into this fire, beads, baskets, nets, bows and arrows, and all manner of valuable things which denoted their grief. They kept this fire burning all night and when morning came there were still coals in the pit. They put the fire out with water and then filled the pit with earth. That

---

[225]This is the sort of sound made by people when they are swimming and playing about in the water.

[226]Informant: Mary Louie, Eastern Dialect.

[227]For further information concerning Pomo bear doctors see Univ. Calif. Publ., Amer. Arch. Ethn., XII, pp. 443-465, 1917.

evening they purified themselves by going to the sweat-house, building a big fire and sweating themselves thoroughly, after which they swam in the nearby stream.

During all of this Pelican was with them and showed signs of mourning the same as the others.

When they had returned from their swim they went back to the sweat-house where all the men congregated purposely, in order that they might tell stories, jokes and do everything possible to make everyone laugh. They did this in the hope that they might find out who was the murderer. Finally they began to joke at Pelican's expense. He hung his head and his lips were dry. This made people suspect that he was guilty.

Next morning as was always their custom they made a fire in the sweat-house before breakfast and after sweating they went down to the stream for a swim. When they came back they sat about the sweat-house talking and joking as usual.

They watch Pelican very closely. He laughed loudly and tried to behave as naturally as possible. In laughing he opened his mouth wide so that his teeth were bare and they noticed the flesh and blood of Falcon about his teeth where he had bitten Falcon. This proved conclusively the guilt of Pelican. They set upon him with bows and arrows and with clubs and shot and beat him to death. Then they took his body out and burned it in the very same spot where they had burned the body of his victim.

On the following morning when they assembled in the sweat-house, they placed in front of it a bead belt so that Falcon could return and walk upon it without touching the ground. Falcon's spirit presently arrived, walked in on this belt and sat down with his back against the center pole, facing the fire.

Meadowlark was in the sweat-house at the time and he was always saying something that he shouldn't. Presently he spoke up and said, "hu^{n}———, it does not smell right here. It smells as though something has burned."

Hearing this remark Falcon slumped down where he was sitting and began to weep. He felt very badly indeed as Lark continued, "I would never have come back here if all my relatives had burned me up with a big fire."

Everyone felt very glad that Falcon had come back to them and the remark of Meadowlark made them so angry that someone picked up a mush paddle and struck at Meadowlark. Meadowlark dodged and the paddle came down on his tail and cut about half of it off. That is why Meadowlark's tail is so very short at the present time.

What Meadowlark did at this time makes it so that people cannot come back to life any more after they have died. If Meadowlark had not said what he did people would be coming back to life again after they have been cremated.

99—WOODRAT IS REFUSED FOOD BY HIS BROTHER-IN-LAW[228]

Characters: 1. Woodrat, 2. Woodrat's sister, 3. Red-headed-woodpecker.

Woodrat (Bayók) and his sister were both married. His sister's husband was Red-headed-woodpecker (Katák). The two families lived in separate houses and had, of course, separate stores of food. All the year round, Red-headed-woodpecker had plenty of acorns. Woodrat also had saved up a large store of acorns, but during the winter his store became exhausted. He heard his sister pounding acorns to make mush so he went over to visit her. After she had pounded the acorns into meal, she took it home and leached it in the usual manner.

When she placed the meal in the basket and commenced to cook the mush with hot rocks. Woodrat thought he had better wash his hands so he could eat some of the mush when it was cooked. He did this and sat down on the opposite side of the fire and waited. Presently, however, Red-headed-woodpecker who was a very stingy man came home. Woodrat's sister had, at times before this been generous and given Woodrat something to eat but Red-headed-woodpecker would give him nothing.

Woodrat sat there and watched them eat but got no food himself. Then he began to weep and he wept so long that his eyes became red and his eye-lids swelled until they nearly closed his eyes, so that he has had very small eyes ever since. When his sister began to cook mush he thought he was going to eat some, so he went out and washed his hands very thoroughly and this is the reason why he has always had white hands ever since.

[228]Informant: Bill James, Garcia River, Central dialect.

100—WASP REFUSES WOODRAT FOOD[229]

Characters: 1. Woodrat, 2. Wasp.

Woodrat traveled a very long time. He was nearly starved. Finally he came to the home of Wasp who lived near a spring. To Woodrat's request for food Wasp replied that he never ate anything himself. "Do you not see how thin my legs and my body are? I only drink water." Woodrat traveled on.

Wasp never talks much. He only answers questions when people ask them.

MISCELLANEOUS TALES

101—THE GIRL WHO MARRIED RATTLESNAKE[230]

Characters: 1. A girl, 2. Rattlesnake, 3. Four rattlesnake children.

At a place called "Cō'bōwin" there was a large rock with a hole in it and there were many rattlesnakes in this hole. At Kalē'sīma there was a village with four large houses. In one of these large houses which had a center pole there lived a girl. This was in the spring of the year when the clover was just right to eat. This girl went out to gather clover and one of the rattlesnakes watched her. When she had a sufficient amount of this food she took it home and gave it to her mother.

Rattlesnake went to the village and when he had approached very near to the house he transformed himself into a young man with a head-net on his head and fine beads about his neck. He made himself look as handsome as possible. Then he climbed up onto the top of the house and came down the center pole. He went to this girl and told her that he wanted to marry her and he remained there with the family. The following morning he went home again. This he did for four days. On the fifth evening he came back but this time he did not change his form. He simply went into the house and talked just as he had before. The girl's mother said that there was someone over there talking all the time. She made a light and looked over in the place where she heard the sound and there was Rattlesnake. He shook his head and frightened her terribly. She dropped the light and ran.

On the following morning Rattlesnake took the girl home with him and she remained there. Finally this girl had four children and as they

[229]Informant: Lee Peters, Central dialect.
[230]Informant: Charley Brown, Northern dialect.

grew up, whenever they saw any of the people from the village, they would say to their mother, "We are going to bite those people." But she would say, "No, you must not do that. Those are your relatives," and they would do as she told them.

Now these four rattlesnake boys were out playing around one day as they grew a little older. Finally they became curious. They came in and asked their mother, "Why do you not talk the way we do? Why are you so different."

To this she replied, "I am not a rattlesnake. I am a human being. I am different from you and from your father." Then the boys inquired if their mother was not afraid of their father to which she answered that she was not.

Then the oldest of the Rattlesnake boys said that he heard something, said that he had heard the other Rattlesnakes talking and that they too thought it strange that she was so different from them and that they were going to investigate and see just why it was that she was so different. They were going to crawl over her body and find out why she was so different from themselves. She was not at all afraid and when the rattlesnakes all came they crawled over her and she was not alarmed in any way.

Then she said to her oldest boy, "It is impossible for you to become a human being and I am not really a human being any longer so I am going back to my parents and tell them what has happened." She did go home and she said to her parents, "This is the last time that I shall be able to talk to you and the last time that you will be able to talk with me." Her father and mother felt very sad about this but they said nothing. Then the daughter started to leave but her mother ran after her and caught her right by the door, brought her back into the house and wept over her because she was so changed. Then the girl shook her body and suddenly she was gone. No one knew how or where she went, but she really went back to Rattlesnake's house where she has lived ever since.

102—WASP AND WILDCAT[231]

Characters: 1. Wasp, 2. Wildcat.

Wasp was burning down a dead tree by applying firebrands to it. Wildcat came along and saw him at work. He asked Wasp why he did

---

[231]Informant: Mary Louie, Eastern dialect.

this. Wasp replied that he had no other way to get wood. Wildcat put down his blanket, food and beads. Then he broke up a whole arm full of wood and gave it to Wasp.

Wildcat had had a difference with his wife and had left home. He came upon Wasp at the spring over at Bana'xaia. Wasp was not really trying to cut down a tree but a weed, called tsūma (E) (tcīma') (C), but it was a very great undertaking for him.

Wildcat asked Wasp if there were any people living around there. Wasp said that there were people living way over toward the east. He said that he had not seen them but that he had heard about them.

NOTE: This is only an incident in a long story of the doings of Coyote, and of the wanderings of Wildcat, toward the east to Sacramento Valley, thence southward, thence westward, thence northward and finally back to the point whence he started. Finally he went by canoe out into the ocean toward the west.

103—COYOTE KILLS TWO FAWNS[232]

Characters: 1. Coyote, 2. Bullfrog (wife of Coyote).

Coyote and Bullfrog were married. One morning Coyote told his wife he was going out hunting. He took a deer-head mask, his bow and arrows and other hunting paraphernalia. He traveled on until he saw two fawns, which had been born only a few moments before, lying under a pepperwood tree on a small rocky knoll. He then commenced to sing the following song and put on his deer mask.

I am handling the deer-head's face (Repeat 4 times)
I shall take (handle) the face to the Alder Bunch (Repeat 4 times)
I am handling the deer-head's face
I shall take the face to the Standing Wood (Repeat 4 times)
I am handling the deer-head's face.[233]

He then crawled up toward the fawns until he had come so close that he was within range. Then he shot and killed both. He made a carrying sling, bound them up and started to return home. As he approached the house, he called out to his wife, "You had better come out, so that you can watch me carry these deer. I killed two big deer." She

---

[232]The Pomo title of this myth is "Iwī' a ce'mī danō-kawō yadjōl-īdūdama mentsība nwatc katic tcide'n-idūmal mūn ke matū de," Coyote ancient times bull-frog was married fawn spotted shot that my story.
Informant: Bill James, Garcia River, Central dialect, 1906.
[233]Bīcē' cīna dē'dū ūī; (Repeat 4 times)
    Gatcitī tcīmawanī dē'dū ūī; (Repeat 4 times)
    (Repeat first line).
    Bīcē cīna dē'dū ūī eūhai tōwanī dē'dū ūī; (Repeat 4 times)
    (Repeat first line).

did this and he brought the deer in and laid them down in front of the house. They held the two deer on the fire and singed their hair and scraped it off with a flint knife. Then they finished cooking the deer without even removing the entrails. When they were cooked, the man and his wife ate them.

104—MOUNTAIN-LION GOES HUNTING[234]

Character: 1. Mountain-lion.

One night Mountain Lion went hunting. He climbed up into a tree to wait for the deer to come along the trail. As he sat there, along about midnight, the tree shook violently though there was no wind to make it do so. Shortly after this Mountain Lion felt something wet on his back and, looking around, he saw that from the trunk of the tree at a point a little above him there ran a small stream of clear water. Soon this turned to a stream of muddy water, next to a stream of red water, and finally to some other kind of a stream the name of which the informant said he could not recall.[235]

105—THE ORIGIN OF THE SUL-KE OR VULTURE DANCE[236]

Characters: 1. Man, 2. Woman, 3. Vulture, 4. Magic tree, 5. Kūsū't, 6. Oak-ball.

There was a village. In this village there was but one house, in which a man and his wife, his father, mother and sisters lived. Away over east of this house there was a big redwood tree, on which there was a limb which pointed toward the south. One day while this man was out, he saw a large fine-looking bird sitting on this limb.

He went home and told his people about the bird, saying that he was going to try to catch it, so he took his wife over east and told her what to do. When they arrived near the tree, he removed all of his clothing and chewed up some angelica root (djomatku) and rubbed this all over his body. While he was doing this, he sang constantly. He taught his wife how to sing the song and she removed all her clothing and rubbed angelica root all over her body, in the same manner. He then said to his wife that she must sing and dance back and forth, constantly, on the

---

[234]Informant: Tom Mitchell, Eastern dialect, 1902.
[235]The informant stated that this incomplete myth had something to do with menstrual regulations, but that he was unable to recall any more of it.
[236]The Pomo title of this myth is "Cĕ'mī sūl ūyū tcmaū makō'ya i dumal mūnke matū de," Old time Vulture high sitting found it my story.
Informant: Bill James, Garcia River, Central dialect, 1906.

south side of the tree. The song she sang was "negice hulahaita yahaitaka", repeated over and over again.

While she thus sang and danced, he started to climb the tree; but when he had gone about half way, he slipped and fell to the ground, unconscious. His wife stopped dancing, chewed up some more angelica root and rubbed it on him and threw water on his head, thus bringing him again to consciousness.

He said, "You did not sing loud enough or dance hard enough. That is the reason why I fell."

She sang again more loudly, while he again climbed up the tree. This time he succeeded in reaching a point a little above the middle of the tree but again fell to the ground, unconscious.

His wife revived him as before and they tried again. They did this way three times, but the fourth he endeavored to climb the tree, he succeeded.

He then climbed out on the limb and caught the bird by one leg but the bird rose and flew away with the man.

The bird flew far to the east and finally came to a big, dead redwood tree, which as it approached, split open so that the bird flew inside. Then the tree closed. This tree which had opened in this manner, was the bird's home. When the bird and the man were inside, they fought together for a long time with the result that the bird was finally killed.

The woman ran home and told her people that her husband had been killed; that he had climbed up the tree, and had caught the bird, but had been carried off eastward. They all mourned over the man's death. They took all their beads out to where the woman had danced and scattered them there, while they cried loudly. They also made a fire and burned off their hair, scratched their faces and otherwise exhibited their great grief. Then they returned home.

After four days, however, the man returned and the bird with him; the bird all dried. He had dried it completely, leaving all its feathers, and with the wings extended, in order that he might be able to take hold of them and dance around so that he would look like this bird while dancing. The dance which he was going to dance in this manner is called the Sūl-ke or the Vulture Dance. No one knows just where or how he learned this dance but when he returned with the dried bird-skin, he knew all about this dance. He did not know what kind of a bird this was. He never had seen this kind of a bird before but he decided that it should be called "Sul."[237] When he came home, he asked his people why they had burned off their hair, and had scratched their faces and in every other way shown signs of mourning. They told him they had done this because they thought him dead and never expected to see him again. This made him feel sorry for them.

He then started over toward the east to dance with the people there. When he came to the first large valley, he stopped and dressed up, so that he might show his new dance costume to the people. He made red paint out of marrow and powdered red stone. He striped his face with this and when he was all prepared he began to sing:

"A he hi yaka hi yaha hoi poni ce he."

He repeated this song continually as he ran around in the valley.

As he approached the village, Kusūt, the watchman or lookout saw that someone was approaching. He then called Oak-ball (Poloce) out to look, for Oak-ball could see farther than anyone else. He saw this man coming and knew who it was and what sort of dance he was dancing. He then told the people that this man was coming and that he was going to dance the Sul or Vulture Dance and that everyone must go into the sweat-house and prepare to receive him.

When he arrived at the sweat-house, he ran four times around it on the outside in a counter-clockwise direction, then four times around it in a clockwise direction, then four times forward and back at the door. He then entered the house and repeated the circling and dancing forward and back, with the fireplace as the center.

When he had finished dancing, the chief told the people to go home and bring beads as a present to the man. This, they all did, for, if they had not made the present to such a visitor, he would then have had a right to kill the head chief and the female chief of the village. They also brought acorn mush and food and everyone enjoyed a good feast.

After this, he went north, then he went west then south, in all of which places he did the same as in the east. He went all around the country this way in order to introduce this dance and teach it to the people, for this was the first time that this dance had ever been known. Then he came home.

---

[237]California vulture, Cathartes Californicus, Shaw.

106—THE ORIGIN OF THE LEHUYA-KE OR KA-TCAHA-KE, THE WHISKEY DANCE[238]

Characters: 1. A man, 2. His brother's ghost, 3. The Ghost-people.

A man lay down by his brother's funeral pyre and refused everything offered him. He refused to eat and said that he intended to die there. He did this way for four days and four nights until, at last, his brother appeared. He rose directly out of the ashes of the funeral pyre.

The man endeavored to catch hold of his brother but he found that he was unable to grasp anything solid about him. His brother then started off toward the east and he followed, constantly trying to take hold of him. He finally followed his brother into a dark place in the east. He walked around in this dark place for a long time until finally, he saw a spot of light that looked bright like a small star. He went to this place and passed through it and finally came into a large level place in the timber where there were many people and everything was bright and pleasant.

These people were all hunting in the timber. They smelled something strange and collected around the man to see who he was. He smelled strange to them because he was a live person and they were dead people. Among them were some of the relatives who had died long before and they asked the Ghosts not to kill him, for he was a relative.

They then took him into the sweat-house and gave him food. Then everyone danced in order that he might learn and return to this world and teach the people this dance. They danced the Lehuye-ke or Ka-tcaha-ke. They taught him all the songs and everything about the dance and then sent him back home to this world.

He came home and told about what he had found; he told how he had seen his brother rise up out of the ashes of the funeral pyre and how he had endeavored to catch him but could not. Then he taught the people the dance which he had learned in the east.

[238]The Pomo title of this tale is "Cĕ'mī ma makŏya," Old time world found. Informant: Bill James, Garcia River, Central dialect, 1906.

107—THE ORIGIN OF THE POMO BEAR DOCTORS

As elsewhere fully discussed,[239] there formerly existed among the Pomo a secret group of Bear Doctors[240] to whom were credited many malevolent acts. There was apparently no organized society and while the various bear doctors knew each other they never met in a body. A very circumstantial myth accounting for the origin of this organization is given by informants. It is given in full in the above mentioned paper (pp. 445-451) and is again recounted by Gifford and Block,[241] and need not be repeated here.

Further, in my paper above mentioned[242] there is also given an account of the acquisition of this power by a young hunter who was taken by an old bear to her hiding place and taught the songs and ritual of the bear doctors.

108—MYTHS CONCERNING BASKETRY

Purdy[243] records two short myths relating to the "dau" or opening in the patterns on Pomo baskets. These are as follows:

THE MYTH OF THE DAU

When the world-maker, the coyote spirit, had concluded his work of creating the world and man, he seated himself to rest, congratulating himself upon the many good works he had done. At this juncture the Pika Namo, or basket spirits, came before him and petitioned him to give them a village or home to be theirs always. The coyote spirit graciously acceded, and said to them, that there, on the surface of baskets, they might have a home which should be theirs always, and then addressing the basket spirits, said, "You basket spirits, young men and young women, old men and old women, children all, here is a good home for you all, to be yours always. If you die, you will lie in the ground four days here, then you will ascend to the upper sky to live forever, where there is no sickness, where it is always day, where all are happy.

"The door (dau) of the basket will always keep swinging for you to escape through when you die."

But the basket spirits were discontented and kept crying out as if in pain.

"What are you doing down there?" the coyote spirit asked. "We said noth-

[239]Barrett, 1917a, pp. 443-465.
[240]Loeb prefers the name "man bear" to "bear doctor", and considers them to be purely mythological, but admits that the Pomo in general firmly believe in these bear doctors. (Loeb, 1926, p. 335.)
[241]Pp. 287-296.
[242]Pp. 453, 454.
[243]Purdy, Carl, The "dau" in Pomo Baskets, Out West, Vol. 18, pp. 319-325, 1903, Los Angeles.

ing," they said. "We talk good; we speak discourses to the dead ones. Now we basket spirits are going to do good; you have spoken wisely to us and we will remember it. We will stay in this home you have given us until we die and can go to the sky home."

This myth shows clearly that they believe a particular race of spirits inhabited the baskets, and that they needed the dau, or door, to escape through when the basket was destroyed. As to what this door, which should always swing open, is, our illustrations best explain. In baskets in which the design is circular, there is an intentional break in the continuity of the design. Follow the circle and there is a design or alternation of designs repeated again and again, but at the dau an altogether different design is inserted. A dau may be very small or inconspicuous, so much so that the untrained eye fails to note it; but it is usually very plain, and often the most beautiful part of the design. Where the design is in a number of circles, there is not always a dau in each circle, and if the design is spiral, there is no need of a dau. If a basket has a number of designs, each forming a circle, there is not always a door in each circle, although there may be. It has been suggested by some students of basketry that the dau originated in the fact that sometimes a repetition of a design did not form a complete circle, but left a gap which the weaver filled in with some sort of figures; and that the myth or superstition was a second thought. It is easily to be shown that this supposition is absolutely groundless. In the first place, christianized Indians make baskets without daus, and still more pertinent is the fact that a woman may make a small dau, a very large dau, or none at all, in the successive circles of one basket, showing that she is complete master of the situation.

Many Indian women are Catholics or Protestants, and some are quite intelligent; but there are few who will omit the dau from a basket. The following myth explains this. To one who believed it, it must have carried a terror sufficient to preserve the custom.

THE LEGEND OF KALTOI

There was a woman in Gravelly Valley, near Kaltoi, who had failed to make a dau on a basket. To her appeared the spirit of the basket, saying, "You have always neglected to make a door for our spirits to escape by. You shall never go to the home above over there, I say to you. Good women never fail to make daus, I tell you. I will myself cause you to die; this instant shall you die.

Then the Kaltoi woman said, "O, my basket spirit, spare me now, and after this I will never fail to make daus in my baskets. When I die I will meet you in the sky-home above, where we will always be good, where day always stays, where you and I will live together. O, basket spirit, my heart is good now. My brain will stay good. If I die now, you will come to me afterwards and we will live friends forever."

Then the world-maker said, "It is good. I accept this woman's life as a sacrifice, and you may live in the sky home together."

Then the woman, weeping, accepted her fate and died.

In both of these short myths there are certain modernistic elements which remove them from the realm of the true, old-time Pomo myths, but they carry a certain amount of authenticity and indicate a belief in the mind of the Pomo that these spirits did exist.

ABSTRACTS AND NOTES

1—FALCON BRINGS FOOD FROM ACROSS THE OCEAN

(Page 45)

I.   Falcon kills geese with a magic sling.

II.   He next travels in a magic canoe across the western ocean in search of food, leaving four tokens to guide his return. These western people post guards who fall asleep. Falcon enters their houses and braids the hair of each person to that of his neighbor. He then takes acorns, bread and other foods and returns home, guided by his own tokens. Falcon demonstrates his superior strength by carrying all his sacks full of food.

III.   Coyote causes a large sweat-house and many dwellings to be built. He then creates people out of feathers after four days. All feast, sweat and dance.

IV.   Putrid-Man plays witcili with Falcon and wins. Falcon makes a journey toward the east. He finally transforms himself into an elk. Kī'lak comes and gambles with Elk. Elk wins and eats Kī'lak's beads. The Kī'laks toll Elk to their home with beads. They finally kill Elk.

V.   Falcon finally returns to the village, where Blue Jay is now chief. Blue Jay is offended because the people disagree with him. He leaves. The people then decide, each for himself, what he wants to be and each is transformed into his own kind and leaves the village.

NOTES

The salient features of the first three incidents of this myth are: the use of the magic sling, Coyote's dreams, the securing of food from the outer world, the journey by means of the magic canoe and with the aid of tokens, and finally the creation of people from feathers.

In the last two incidents we have an entirely different idea entering. The gambling of Putrid-man is a very unusual feature. He is usually pictured as a very incidental and minor character. The transformation of Falcon into Elk and his use of beads for food are extraordinary, as is also the method employed by Kī'lak to get Elk to his home. Finally we see Elk transformed back into Falcon without any word of explanation. The ultimate change of people into animals is quite the usual thing.

Here we find the use of the sacred number quite frequently. Duality occurs several times. Most unusual, however, is the sending of the people out in groups of twenty to secure the various materials required for building the roof of the sweat-house.

2—HAWK STEALS FOOD FROM THE MINKS AND
COYOTE CREATES PEOPLE
(Page 53)

I. Coyote lay starving and his son, Black Hawk, starts out to see what he can find. He attempts to make a magic raft to cross the ocean; upon the fourth trial and fourth sacrifice he succeeds.

Leaving a quiver on shore as a token, he sails westward on this magic raft. Half way across the ocean he leaves a skewer as a token. He finally arrives at the Mink village, and causes very dense darkness.

The people are cooking quantities of food. Then all dance in the dance-house. Black Hawk goes ashore. The people become suspicious and he again pushes off from shore. He then wills that all shall sleep. He then returns ashore and steals all the food, after which be braids the hair of each dancer to that of his neighbor. He then shoots one man, whose outcries wake up all others.

Black Hawk's tokens guide him on the return journey. When he arrives at the shore he goes to recover his quiver token. One of the pursuers has outdistanced him and shoots at him. Black Hawk, however, kills this Mink. Then he returns home. At first he brings Coyote only a piece of white-oak acorn bread.

II. Coyote decides to create people. He cuts his body open to attract birds from which he secures feathers. He then instructs Hawk in building houses and placing feathers in them.

With his magic flute Coyote causes Mole to make beds. His flute causes houses to be built. Next they build a sweat-house. At dawn people appear.

III. Coyote and Hawk next create fish from sticks, again aided by the magic flute.

IV. Coyote places people in their respective localities, east, north and south. He designates what trees and foods shall be found in each locality. None are sent to the west because the ocean lies there.

V. Coyote creates the various vegetal foods, again aided by his magic flute.

NOTES

This is a myth with a purely coastal setting.

The use of the magic flute, in the processes of creation is most unusual. Duality occurs in the playing of the flute.

The entrapping of birds by Coyote's opened body is unusual, as is the detailed designation of the spots where people shall live, and the creation of specific vegetal foods.

A most unusual feature is the building by the hero of his own means of magic transportation and the use of sacrifices of beads in order to produce the proper magic which will enable his raft to perform as he wishes it to do. Again the return trip is made possible through the use of the tokens as guides.

3—WOLF AND COYOTE CREATE PEOPLE

(Page 61)

I. Coyote and Wolf live together. Wolf feigns illness and refuses Coyote's proffered aid. Wolf catches deer in a magic wier but does not share his food with Coyote so Coyote makes him leave.

II. Wolf builds a big sweat-house and tries to create people out of pieces of tule, but fails after four days. He then succeeds in making people out of willow sticks after another four days. Coyote then moves over to Wolf's village and eventually creates people in the same way.

III. The two peoples play against eachother for four days. Coyote's players always win. Wolf creates two grizzly bears from buckeye root, using mountain mahogany for teeth. He stations them near Coyote's goal and they kill several of the Coyote people. In retaliation Coyote creates rattlesnakes out of rawhide, using gooseberry thorns for fangs. So the people play on, until all have been killed by the bears and the rattlesnakes.

IV. Coyote then leaves and goes to live under the rocks in the mountains.

NOTES

This is a particularly fully detailed myth. Here we see Coyote deceived by Wolf and his magic wier, and Wolf's feigned illness.

The creation of people is accomplished first by Wolf and next by Coyote. Each tries to create people out of green tule and fails. They finally succeed when willow sticks are used.

Grizzlies are created out of buckeye root, using mountain mahogany for teeth. Rattlesnakes are created out of strips of deer hide, using gooseberry thorns for fangs.

The sacred number, four, is used repeatedly and double the sacred number once. Duality is also present.

A rare element here is the pronouncement by Wolf of a formal curse upon Coyote.

4—CREATION OF PEOPLE BY WOLF AND COYOTE
(Page 69)

I. Wolf, while pretending illness, builds a magic wier for catching food, fully prepared, but does not share it with Coyote, who does his best to care for Wolf. When the deception is discovered Coyote drives Wolf away. Coyote tries to use this magic wier but fails. Coyote takes his boy, Pestle, and moves away.

II. Wolf creates people by placing maple sticks out in the mountains. Coyote visits Wolf and asks how to make people and after three failures he succeeds.

III. Coyote's and Wolf's people play shinney. Wolf creates grizzlies and Coyote creates rattlers to kill people. Rattlers have gooseberry-thorn fangs and maple-leaf rattles.

IV. Coyote's boys play with two abalone-shell balls regurgitated by Coyote. Wolf causes them to go east. The boys follow and are killed by the Sun-people, who make a sack out of these Coyote skins. They fill it with light and hang it up.

V. Coyote searches for his sons. Arriving at the sweat-house of the Sun-people, he finds there only two children. He transforms himself into an old man and learns the fate of his sons. The people return toward evening and dance. Coyote dances the people to sleep and braids their hair together, while two mice ascended the center pole and cut the lashing of the sun-sack.

Red-headed-woodpecker liberates the people and they pursue Coyote. When Fog catches up with him, Coyote shoots him with a sling. The others finally catch up with him. Rabbit now appears and takes the sun sack from Coyote and runs on with it. As Fog catches up with Rabbit the latter strikes the sun sack on a large rock and liberates the light.

Crow finally succeeds in hanging the sun up in the sky.

NOTES
This is a composite myth with some parts very fully detailed.

Wolf's magic wier catches food, fully cooked. Wolf deceives Coyote, this time with the nub of a deer antler.

The creation of people by Wolf is immediately successful, but he fools Coyote three times before Coyote succeeds in creating his people.

Again we see the two peoples contesting and killed by grizzlies and rattle-snakes. The latter are created by Coyote from strips of deer hide. Their fangs are made of gooseberry thorns and their rattles of maple leaves.

Finally two of Coyote's boys journey to the land of the Sun-people, are killed, and their skins are used in making the "daylight sack."

Coyote induces sleep by means of his dancing. He ties the hair of the long-haired ones together, while pitch and string are used on those with short hair. Coyote is assisted by two mice instead of four.

The sun is finally liberated and placed in the sky by Crow, but no details are given.

We find the sacred number, four, used a number of times and duality appears frequently. Here again we see a curse pronounced by Wolf.

Throughout the trickster element is quite pronounced.

5—COYOTE CREATES MAN BUT LIZARD GIVES HIM PROPER HANDS

(Page 80)

Coyote creates people with hands like his own. Lizard causes them to have hands like his. Coyote tries to talk to one of the newly created people. Lizard decrees that there shall be differences in speech.

NOTES

This very fragmentary myth contains the usual item accounting for the form of man's hand and an unusual one accounting for the fact that different tribes have different speech.

6—WATERDOG AND LIZARD CREATE HUMAN BEINGS AND GIVE THEM HANDS

(Page 80)

Coyote, Lizard and Waterdog contest in the creation of people. Waterdog fails. Lizard succeeds in all except the hand. Coyote creates people with paws. Lizard causes people to have hands like his own.

NOTES

This is a fragmentary myth, but of interest in that it brings Waterdog into the creation. Lizard succeeds in his creation except for the hand, but when Coyote creates people with impossible hands Lizard changes them.

7—PEOPLE ARE TRANSFORMED INTO ANIMALS
(Page 81)

As the hunters are out snaring deer, Thunder takes their chief, Panther, up into the sky. He is finally brought back by Coyote who ascends to the Upper World by means of Spider's web.

After celebrating the return of the chief, Coyote announces that the people will be transformed into various kinds of animals. On the following morning he designates what each shall be and the transformation takes place.

NOTES

This seems to be a rather abbreviated version of the familiar transformation of humans into animals.

One very interesting feature is the way in which Spider ascends to the Upper World and fastens his web there. This is an incident which is frequently met with in Pomo mythology but in almost every case Spider is represented as living up there, as the guard of the Zenith Gate, who comes down on his web and takes Coyote or others up into the Upper World.

No mention is made of a contest to overcome Thunder in order to get Panther back again. Further, it will be noted that three Thunders are mentioned. Both of these are very unusual and we may assume that they are due to error.

8—PEOPLE ARE TRANSFORMED INTO BIRDS BY FOX
(Page 83)

Coyote creates the "first people" from feathers. They spend much time in dancing and feasting.

Fox assembles all kinds of feathers and as each person selects the feather he prefers he is transformed into that particular kind of bird and flies away. The three brothers of Fox become Mallard ducks, but Fox himself is unable to change his form and fly.

All the people, now transformed, fly down the river to Tomales Bay and thence disperse over the world. Fox follows along crying because he is unable to fly and cannot keep up with the birds.

NOTES

This myth contains at the outset a very brief account of the creation of people from feathers. Then there is a rather mixed account of the transformation of these people into birds, the important feature of which is the transformation of each into the particular kind of bird desired according to the feathers he himself selects.

A very unusual feature is the regulation of this matter by Fox. That this is the informant's actual intention, and that he has not confused Fox with Coyote, seems probable because at the outset he has Coyote creating people.

The whole is evidently abbreviated and in its full form probably would contain additional features which would add very much to its clarity.

One of the most peculiar features of this myth is that all the rest of the people are transformed into birds, including the three brothers of Fox. He himself is unable to change his form and to fly despite repeated trials.

9—COYOTE GIVES PEOPLE IMPLEMENTS AND FOODS

(Page 84)

Coyote first creates people. Then he creates for them everything, both good and bad. He tells people just what they can and cannot eat, and gives them the various implements needed for catching their food.

He also teaches them how to cure bites, and sickness, and teaches them how to make the paraphernalia for dances and for doctoring.

He then makes Wolf hunting-chief, and gives him a charm. The people become dissatisfied and are later transformed into birds and mammals, chiefly into deer. Wolf's son is returned to human form by his father.

Wolf's son disobeys. Both father and son are transformed into deer. Then the son goes to hunt for his mother. His magic song enables him to find his mother with whom he remains thereafter.

NOTES

This myth is especially interesting on account of the elaborateness and detail with which the plants, birds, mammals, and fishes, and their uses are given, also for the details with which implements and their uses are outlined, and for the fullness of the song sung by Wolf's son when in search of his mother.

A very unusual feature is the return of Wolf's son to human form because of faith in his father. The penalty for the son's gazing at his father while he is hunting is that both are transformed into deer.

10—COYOTE'S CREATIONS

(Page 87)

I. Coyote is very poor and lives with the wealthy inhabitants of the eastern end of the world. He creates sickness as a means of gaining wealth through doctoring.

II. Coyote creates grizzly bear to harm people. When hunters go to their deer snares a grizzly kills one of their number.

III. Coyote institutes cremation and prescribes its details.

IV. Coyote creates rattlesnake to bite women who go out to harvest foods during their menstrual periods.

V. Coyote creates elk as human food.

VI. Coyote creates "Indian potatoes" and instructs the people in their use.

VII. Coyote institutes divorce.

NOTES

This is patently an assembly of a variety of short, etiological tales accounting for conditions which we find at present. They are fairly well joined together into a continuous tale but lack the close bonding of incident to incident which is usually found in the regulation composite myth.

11—COYOTE CREATES THE OCEAN

(Page 91)

Coyote creates the ocean and makes it too rough. He then modifies its action so that sea-foods can be secured by the people.

NOTES

This is an extremely abbreviated etiological tale accounting for some of the present conditions found in the ocean.

12—COYOTE INSTITUTES DEATH

(Page 91)

Coyote causes the death of the chief's daughter through a rattlesnake bite, and then refuses to allow her to be brought back to life. The chief, in retaliation, poisons Coyote's daughter and refuses his plea for revivification. Thus is death instituted in the world.

NOTES

This is a fragmentary myth, one which appears as an incident in other composite myths, though in slightly different form. It is a variant of the trickster-tricked idea.

13—CREATION OF SALMON

(Page 92)

A wooden image of a fish is carved and placed in the river. It immediately changes into a salmon.

NOTES

A very fragmentary account.

14—COYOTE CREATES THE SUN, MOON AND STARS AND PEOPLES THE EARTH

(Page 93)

Coyote creates the sky and the sun. The sun and the moon cause Coyote to create stars, including the morning star. Next darkness is created. Moon causes the earthquake.

Coyote then creates plants and animals and designates where each shall reside. He next creates supernatural beings. Presumably also he creates man. Coyote finally disappears in a very dense fog.

NOTES

This myth, while it is decidedly fragmentary, is interesting. It accounts for the creation of the sky by Coyote who threw water up into the heavens. This produced clouds which came eventually together and overspread the earth, producing the sky.

It is also interesting as accounting for the creation by Coyote of the sun from an oak-ball and of the moon from blue clay. Also he creates the stars, including the morning star, from coals. Darkness is also created.

Also it carries a very large list of the various mammals, birds, foods, supernatural beings, etc., created by Coyote. This list is all given in Indian terms and is not included in this myth as here transcribed.

Interesting as this myth is, it must be viewed with caution. It is too radically different from the general run of Pomo myths to dispell the suspicion that it is in various of its details fabricated by the individual informant, and that it shows an attempt in places to incorporate at least some of the things he has learned from whites.

Incidentally, this particular informant is one of whom just this sort of thing might be expected.

15—THE BURNING OF THE WORLD AND THE CREATION OF CLEAR LAKE

(Page 95)

This myth, which originally appeared in the Journal of American

Folklore (Vol. XIX, pp. 35-51) was there abstracted. It is reprinted here in full. For the abstract, therefore, see pages 108 and 109.

NOTES

This myth is one of the best examples of the Pomo tendency to compound a complete myth out of a number of incidents which are, of themselves, distinct and each of which, in many cases at least, forms a complete and finished unit by itself, but which may, on the other hand, be joined together in such a way as to make a connected story.

Here Coyote is seen first as a trickster, then as a vengeful destroyer of the world, then as a creator of Clear Lake and various streams, together with the water-life in them, then as a creator of human beings, then as the giver of light, and finally as a transformer.

One of the most striking features of this myth is the great exactness with which the different officials and their duties are designated, and this same exactness persists in the last section of the myth where Coyote indicated the habits and food of each bird or other animal at the transformation.

The story of the theft of the sun is told here in much detail, as is also that of the destruction of the world by fire.

The sacred number is less used than might be expected in a myth where other details are so exactly recounted.

There is a very unusual localization of the abode of Kū′ksū at Kūcá-danó-yō. He is usually supposed to live at the southern extremity of the world.

No mention is made, for some reason, of the pursuit of Coyote and his people after stealing the sun.

16—COYOTE DESTROYS THE WORLD BY FIRE

(Page 109)

1. Coyote tunnels into a mountain and sets fire to the earth. He then escapes burning, by ascending a rope into the Upper World. He also saves his two children by carrying them in his hunting sack. He refuses the entreaties of the other people to save them.

II. After four days he returns to earth, remodels and repeoples it. He eats meat roasted by the world-fire. He searches for water, is denied a drink by Frog, and finally drinks from the ocean. He makes the ocean rough but limits it by establishing the shore-line. He makes Clear Lake, also fish. He then makes creeks.

III. He lives at Yō′būꞇūī. Aided by Duck, he builds a dance-house, and creates people, the present Indian race, from feathers. He also creates vermin. He instructs the new race and gives them the feather dance. He then ascends again to the Upper World by means of the rope.

NOTES

This is one of the characteristic composite myths of the Pomo. It consists of three distinct myth incidents: the destruction of the world by fire, the creation of Clear Lake, and the creation of the present race. The detail of the myth is, on the whole, very incomplete, very much indeed being left to the imagination of the auditor. No explanation is offered for the presence of the two Coyote children, no motive is assigned for the burning of the world. The manipulation of the rope which took Coyote to the sky, and many other points are not explained, as they are in the more fully detailed and more perfect of these accounts.

Coyote is, as usual, here made to play the double role of a masterful and almost all-powerful deity, who can create at will, and of the ordinary impotent individual who must, when refused a drink of water by Frog, pass without a protest, or who must first obtain the consent of the people of the vicinity before he dares to create Clear Lake. There is here, however, none of the trickster element in Coyote's nature.

Two separate creations of people are here given: one immediately after Coyote's return to the earth following the great world-fire, and the other after the creation of Clear Lake. It would appear that in the first case the creation was that of a bird-people similiar to, if not identical with, the bird-people who existed prior to the world-fire, while the second was that of the present Indians.

The conclusion of this myth, in which Coyote returns to the Upper World after his creations, is quite unusual. In most cases Coyote becomes provoked at the actions of the people he has created and transforms himself into the animal coyote which we know at present and goes off into the hills to live. In the present case, however, he seems to retain his human attributes to the last.

Another unusual feature is the mere finding of Duck. He is usually dug from the ground.

The creation of fleas and lice by Coyote from grass seeds is an incident which is very rarely mentioned in Pomo mythology.

The sacred number does not appear to any extent in this myth, in fact it is used but once, when Coyote's stay in the Upper World is mentioned.

17—COYOTE BURNS THE WORLD IN REVENGE FOR THE ILL TREATMENT OF HIS CHILDREN

(Page 113)

I. The people of Maiyï' abuse Coyote's children after he has been deserted by his wife. Coyote therefore goes east and sets fire to the world. As the fire comes near the village the people become alarmed and beg Coyote to save them, but he refuses to save even his wife who had deserted him. As the fire is about to burn up the village Coyote ascends with his two children to the Upper World.

II. When Coyote returns to the earth he becomes thirsty and searches for water. This he finds at the ocean. He drinks this water which is not then salty. He dislikes the stillness of the ocean and makes it wavy and its water salty. He marks the shore-line.

III. Coyote then starts to return to the Clear Lake vicinity. He sees water at a spring near Philo. He drinks this water and becomes ill. He reaches Kaba'i and is doctored by a girl. The water he drank forms Clear Lake. He then pulls out the snakes he had eaten on his return from the ocean and transforms them into fish. He then creates the various creeks about Clear Lake, in order that the fish might have a place to run up at spawning season.

Obsidian-man goes up Kelsey creek with the fish and succeeds in killing all of the people at Nō'napōtī. He then goes down to Calistoga and lives in the sulphur springs there.

NOTES

In this story Coyote's children are a boy and a girl. No mention is made of their miraculous birth. Twelve days, one period of eight days, the other a period of four days, are required here for the preparations for burning the world. Coyote's means of escape in this case is a feather rope, no spider being mentioned.

Coyote here appears to become thirsty immediately upon his return to the earth and before eating any of the roasted meat. He drinks ocean water, but the chief object of his visit to the ocean seems to be to make the water salty and to establish the shore-line, after he has made the water rough. He later drinks water from a spring. Also upon the return journey he eats meat, snakes only being mentioned, though whether it was before or after drinking the water from the spring is not stated.

As usual he reaches Kabái. Sickness is inferred and Coyote is doctored, this time by a girl who slyly approaches and jabs him just below the floating ribs with a cane. After the water has all run out of his belly he pulls the snakes out and transforms them into the various species of fish, the species being named here.

The encounter between Obsidian-man and the people of Nō'napōtī is an unusual feature. Obsidian-man, when this encounter is over, goes to Calistoga to live in the sulphur springs.

18—COYOTE CREATES PEOPLE, BURNS THE WORLD AND MAKES CLEAR LAKE
(Page 117)

I. Coyote creates two boys, one for himself and one for Wolf.

They play shinney. Coyote's boy wins and Wolf's boy kills him. The body is burned and then Coyote creates a grizzly to kill Wolf's boy. After four days Wolf proposes that the boys shall be brought to life again but Coyote refuses to allow this because it would soon cause too great a population on the earth.

II. Coyote starts to dig the pit for a dance-house and discovers Chub Duck who helps him and they finish the house the same day. Coyote then calls a large number of houses into being. He then procures feathers and places these around in the sweat-house and in the dwelling houses. He then wishes four times that these feathers shall become people and they do so. He creates his father, mother and two wives. His wives give birth to twins and people think him supernatural.

III. He leaves the village and the people abuse his children. He sets fire to the world. People beg him to save them but he refuses. A spider-web is let down from the sky and he ascends to the Upper World.

IV. Coyote returns to this earth and eats all sorts of roasted meat. Then he drinks water from the ocean. Kū'ksū doctors him at Red Mountain. Coyote creates Clear Lake. Madū'mda then sends Coyote to the under world to be Coyote-fire-man.

NOTES

The creation of boys from earth is an unusual feature.

When the two boys play shinney it is more usual for one of their elders to create something which kills one of them than for the loser of the game to himself kill his opponent, as in this instance.

The creation of a grizzly from a small, round stone is unusual. Other versions have the creation of or placing of a rattlesnake in this incident.

The extremes to which Coyote goes in order to show his grief at the death of Wolf's son are exceptional, particularly in his jumping onto the funeral pyre.

The fact that Coyote refuses to allow Wolf to catch fish but secretly arranges matters so that he catches ducks instead seems to be in a way irrelevant and has no direct bearing on the attendant events except perhaps to show that Coyote is more powerful than Wolf and that he can resort to trickery to gain an end.

Here again Coyote refuses to allow people to return to life for the reason that the world would soon be too full of people.

The way in which the narrator disposes of Wolf is a little out of the ordinary. Usually any superfluous character simply drops out of sight with no account being given of his whereabouts. People are created from feathers. All that is necessary is for Coyote to wish four times that these feathers should be transformed. The whole of the creation in this story is of extremely short duration. It takes only one day for Wolf and Coyote to part, for Coyote to make a speech announcing his intention to build the dance-house, to dig the pit, discover Duck, finish the sweat-house, procure feathers, and create the people.

Not much prominence is given to Duck here.

The creation by Coyote of his own relatives and wives is not usually related.

The birth of twins to Coyote's two wives is an unusual cause for Coyote's relatives to distrust him. The marvelously quick birth is the usual cause and it may be that this was the cause assigned in the original version of this story.

An unusual feature is the creation of fleas from milkweed chaff.

Here Coyote simply sets fire to the world and does not have to go to the trouble of digging a tunnel and procuring pitch, etc., to start the fire.

Here it is a spider-web but not a spider which takes Coyote to the Upper World. Also his children are not saved.

Further, it is from the summit of Red Mountain that Coyote ascended to the Upper World, and not from the village itself.

The creation of Clear Lake is here very curtailed, only the barest facts being mentioned.

It is very unusual for Madū'mda to step in, as at the end of this myth, and direct what Coyote shall do. Here, however, he does this and consigns him to the Lower World as a sort of ruler there. This whole idea of Coyote-fire-man and of Coyote's going to an under world is entirely foreign to Pomo thought. It is patently an adaptation of missionary notions to Pomo terminlogy.

19—COYOTE BURNS THE WORLD AND CREATES CLEAR LAKE

(Page 121)

I. Originally there was no fire. Coyote creates the fire-drill.

II. People offend Coyote and he causes the destruction of the world by fire, killing all living beings and burning off the mountains.

Coyote escapes, with his two sons, by jumping over the world fire.

III. Coyote and his sons eat roasted meat and search for water, which Frog has hidden away. The two boys finally die, but Coyote finds water and drinks a great deal. He becomes ill and finally stabs himself in the belly with an awl. This lets the water out and forms Clear Lake. Fish are also created. Coyote prescribes that if people are not good the fish-bones will stick in their throats.

NOTES

This myth appears to be an abbreviated version, though it has some features not mentioned in the other versions.

I. The World is first seen without fire. This is provided by Coyote through the creation of a fire-drill which he makes out of elderberry wood. Buckeye is actually used by the Indians in later times.

II. In time Coyote becomes angered by the actions of the people and notifies them that the world will shortly burn up. Nothing is said as to the origin of the fire in this instance. The world-fire burns not only all living things but also the mountains as well. Here Coyote places his two boys in his hunting-sack and escapes the fate of the others by jumping over the fire instead of ascending to the sky as he does in most versions.

III. As usual Coyote eats inordinately of the roasted meat left by the world-fire and becomes thirsty. In this case, however, his two boys do the same and all three hunt for water, the two boys dying before it is found. Here again the water in one place is hidden from them by Frog who sits on it. Coyote does not go to the ocean to get water. He finally finds it down in Big valley.

As always this water makes Coyote ill and he lies down, but in this case he doctors himself by puncturing his own belly with an awl instead of being doctored by someone ele. Also he seals his wound and cures it with pitch. The water from Coyote's belly forms Clear Lake. The bald statement is made here that the different fishes came out of Coyote's belly at this time, though the real origin of these fish is not explained as in a number of other instances. Coyote designates that these fish are placed in this lake in order that the people may catch them, but at the same time he prescribes a severe punishment in case of disobedience on the part of the people.

20—COYOTE BURNS THE WORLD

(Page 123) ₁

The people abuse Coyote's two boys. He places pitch in the ground in the four cardinal directions and finally burns the world, escaping with his two boys to the sky by means of a magic rope. Upon returning to the earth Coyote seeks water. He finds some in a spring guarded by Frog who refuses him a drink. He then goes over to Clear Lake.

One of the boys has some basket-willow rods which he throws into the lake. Coyote tells him to go and hunt for some more willow rods. The boy finds nothing but snakes wherever he goes. Coyote had vomited and produced these snakes.

These later turn into fish and the people do not know what to do with them until an old woman tastes of them and finds that they are good food.

NOTES

This very abbreviated version of the usual theme of the destruction of the world by fire shows a few unusual features. Here Coyote places pitch in the ground in all four of the cardinal directions instead of in the east only. There is no visit by Coyote to the ocean and there is no creation of Clear Lake. Coyote's vomiting simply creates snakes which later turn into fish, though there is no explanation of the cause or the method of this transformation. The incident of the old woman tasting the fish to determine whether it is suitable for food is not found in other versions of this myth.

21—COYOTE CREATES CLEAR LAKE

(Page 124) .

I. The world is burned. Coyote searches for water. He finds Frog and Waterdog making baskets at Philo. They deny that they have any water there. Frog and Waterdog place a half-finished burden basket in Blue Lakes which, if seen by menstruating women, causes illness.

II. Coyote passes on to the coast and drinks ocean water. He returns to the Clear Lake region. He lies down to rest and his belly is cut open by Kū'ksū so that the water forms Clear Lake. The waters of Clear Lake always have waves on this account.

NOTES

This very fragmentary myth is essentially the usual myth of the destruction of the world by fire, the devouring of the roasted meat by Coyote, and the subsequent search for water and the creation of Clear Lake. It also contains two important features not often mentioned: (1) accounting for the waves on Clear Lake by reason of the fact that the water was originally ocean water, and (2) the mention made of the unfinished burden basket of Blue Lakes. This is somewhat extraneous in this myth, its only connection being that it was made by Frog and Waterdog at this time. This basket was in early times much dreaded by the people, particularly by menstruating women, and formed one of the terrors, so to speak, of the Blue Lakes vicinity, which made this a place to be shunned by all. The narrator of this myth avers that she saw this basket at one time and was ill for a long period thereafter, but was finally cured by proper doctoring.

22—THE BURNING OF THE WORLD AND THE CREATION OF CLEAR LAKE

(Page 125)

I. Coyote burns the world and all in it except Blacksnake, who is a very good man.

II. Coyote gorges himself on roasted snakes and lizards. He then drinks water in Big Valley, becomes ill, and is doctored by Bullfrog. The water from Coyote's belly forms Clear Lake. Fish are created.

III. Coyote creates people from sticks.

IV. People are killed by grizzly bears and rattlesnakes.

V. Coyote creates plants.

NOTES

The narrator seems to have the features of this myth badly mixed.

Coyote has four children walking with him, of whom two die. The remaining boy is Wolf, who builds a sweat-house in which Coyote creates people from sticks.

Bullfrog hides water from Coyote, but after he finds it and drinks excessively, Frog doctors him. Clear Lake and fishes are created.

No details of the contest are given but the creation of bears and rattlesnakes is mentioned but reversed.

Coyote creates trees, bushes and grass.

23—THE DELUGE AND THE ESCAPE OF FALCON

(Page 126)

I. Water covers the world. Falcon and the swimming birds only escape. As the water rises the swimming birds dive to the bottom of Clear Lake and bring up blue clay and water-logged tule stems with which material they build up Mt. Kanaktai and thus keep the peak of the mountain high enough so that Falcon has a resting place. Ducks finally succeed in bringing fire from their house under the water and after the rain ceases they build a fire from some dry grass which Falcon has brought with him. Then some birds catch fish while others bring acorn mush and bread from their house under the water and all feast. The water subsides and all return to their former homes.

II. Falcon hunts ducks and mud-hens with a miraculous sling and easily carries a great load home.

NOTES

Protracted rain usually causes the deluge among the Pomo. The flight of Falcon for a long period before he finds a resting place on the summit of Mt. Kanaktai is a very unusual incident. Also the building of Mt. Kanaktai in advance of the rising water, thus accounting for its present comparatively great altitude is very interesting. The ducks bring fire and food from their houses under the water. No explanation of the fact that the fire existed here despite the deluge is given, though difficulty is experienced in getting the fire to the surface.

Falcon's magic sling is emphasized. By proper songs he reduces the weight of a large load so that he is able to carry it home very easily.

24—COYOTE CAUSES A DELUGE TO DESTROY THE WORLD
(Page 129)

I. Through a dream Coyote is able to tell the people of the approaching deluge. Since there are no mountains on earth the people seek refuge in the tree tops. Coyote makes a log by breaking off a tree and he and several others are saved by floating on it.

II. Coyote pays Mole a large fee in magnesite beads to create hills and mountains. Then the water subsides. This requires several days.

III. Coyote then makes a large dance-house and spends four days splitting small sticks of willow and elder wood from which people are created through ceremonies performed by him. He then divides them up into groups, giving each full instructions as to what it should do and prescribing penalties for failure to follow instructions.

IV. Finally Coyote creates all manner of animals from certain specified things.

NOTES

This myth contains several rather unusual features:

Coyote does not cause the deluge but knows of its approach by means of a dream.

Coyote and a few others escape by floating on a log.

Mole creates mountains while the world is still covered with the water of the deluge.

People are created from small sticks made by Coyote from willow and elder wood.

Penalties are prescribed by Coyote for disobedience of the people to his rules.

Animals are created by Coyote, not by transforming people into animals, but from certain specific objects, some animate and some inanimate.

25—THE THUNDER CHILDREN ESCAPE THE DELUGE AND FLY TO THE SKY
(Page 131)

I. Thunder-people eat trout from a spring and are transformed into deer. Three children, two boys and a girl are the only people who eat none of the trout and are therefore saved.

II. These children go north to live on a high mountain. It rains for a long time and the world is covered with water, all except a very small area. As the water rises nearly to where the children are the rain stops and after four days an old man appears. During the night he causes the water to disappear.

II. He then creates angleworms from sinew and instructs the girl in their use. Then he disappears.

IV. The elder brother makes a thunder suit which enables him to fly. The glint of the sunlight upon this suit produces lightning. He flies off to the north and while he is gone it turns very cold. When he returns it is again warm. He then makes suits of the same kind for his brother and sister. The three fly to the sky, one to the north, one to the south, and one to the east.

NOTES

In this story there are five themes: (1) the transformation of people into animals, (2) the miraculous escape of three children, (3) the deluge and the subsidance of the water, (4) the creation of angleworms, and (5) the flight and other actions of the Thunder children.

The cause of the transformation of the people into animals is usually the eating of or at least the capture of some supernatural being. Several myths mention a snake-like being, but in this one supernatural fishes are the cause.

The deluge is here caused by a protracted rain. The only land not covered by the water is, in this case, indefinitely located in the north instead of being some definite local mountain, as is usually the case.

The creation of angleworms from sinew and the giving of a method of capturing them is an interesting, though rather extraneous incident.

The flight of the Thunders by means of miraculous suits is the usual method. It is unfortunate that a more detailed description of the suits could not be given by the informant. The lightning produced by these suits and its effect upon certain natural objects is interesting. It should be noted that there are but three of these Thunders instead of the usual sacred number, four, and that the elder brother goes south, the younger goes north, and the sister goes east. Especially interesting is the fact that no Thunder is located in the west. In most myths where Thunder appears, the abode is somewhere toward the west, on the coast or across the ocean.

26—GOPHER SECURES FIRE AFTER THE DELUGE

(Page 135)

Gopher, the only survivor of the deluge, goes to the top of Mt. Kanaktai. He digs down into the center of the mountain and secures fire for the world.

NOTES

This very fragmentary myth is most unusual in that it depicts Gopher as the sole survivor of the deluge. Gopher is an individual of no importance ordinarily.

The securing of fire by digging down into the center of Mt. Kanaktai is most unusual, especially in view of the volcanic origin of the mountain, though it is not to be presumed that the Indians had any knowledge of such an origin.

27—THE THEFT OF THE SUN

(Page 135)

The world is in complete darkness. Lizard hunts with torches, going very far toward the east. He finally sees light in the east, but his people refuse to believe its existence and send messengers to investigate. Finally all journey eastward and visit the Sun-people, whom they find living in a large sweat-house. On its center pole hang four sacks containing respectively snow, wind, rain and the sun.

The Sun-chief, Gilak, and Falcon gamble and the Sun-chief is killed.

Four mice gnaw the string which holds the sun sack. The sun is liberated and rolled westward. The Sun-people give chase and so many arrows are shot that we now find arrow-heads everywhere.

The Crow brothers finally succeed in placing the sun up in the sky.

NOTES

In this version of the theft of the sun Lizard discovers the sun and all the people go to get it. Usually Coyote does the stealing. In this instance the Gī'laks are definitely identified as the keepers of the sun. Their chief is killed as a result of losing a grass game to Falcon. Four mice gnaw the string holding the sun sack and liberate it. Usually Coyote accomplishes this by causing the Sun-people to fall asleep.

We next have the usual pursuit by the Sun-people, but here we find arrow-heads accounted for.

As usual the Crow brothers succeed in placing the sun up in the sky. The reason here given is that they can go longer without water than anyone else.

28—COYOTE STEALS THE SUN

(Page 137)

I. Lizard sees light in the east. Coyote takes mice and goes after the sun. He braids the hair of the Sun-people together, except one whose hair is too short. He then dances while the mice gnaw the string which ties the sun sack to the center pole. The short-haired man gives the alarm but Coyote escapes and brings the sun home.

II. The Bird-people place it in the sky. Red-headed-woodpecker is appointed special watchman and announcer for this event. He looks so long and so steadily at the sun that his eyes are now shiny. Crows succeed in putting the sun in place. They are well paid by the people.

III. Then Coyote places them in Blue Lakes, where they make people ill. Coyote refuses to allow them to break through the adjacent mountain.

NOTES

This is the usual sun-theft myth but is quite abbreviated. When Lizard discovers light he mourns because he thinks that it is from the funeral pyre of a relative. Coyote goes alone to steal the sun. He uses a sleep charm and a ritual to put the Sun-people to sleep. Here we find the sun hung up in an elk-skin bag. It is a short-haired man who gives the alarm when Coyote steals the sun.

After the Crow brothers have hung the sun in the sky Coyote places them in Blue Lakes where they frighten people. This is a most unusual incident added to the sun-theft myth. Also these Crows wanted to break through the mountain to the northwest of the lakes. This really has an etiological tinge for there is at this point a very low gap which forms part of the watershed between the Clear Lake and Sacramento River drainage on the one hand and that of the Russian River on the other. For a fuller explanation of the geology of this locality see footnote 96, page 197.

29—THE STEALING OF THE SUN SACK
(Page 139)

I. Lizard discovers light in the east.

Coyote climbs Mt. Kanaktai to verify Lizard's statement. Crane takes Coyote across the lake.

The sun is kept in a bag consisting of four thicknesses of elk hide and is tied to the roof of the house with four ropes. The Sun-people are absent but the sun is guarded by some children. Coyote carries four birds and some shells, which he gives to the children.

With the sun-sack are seven others, holding rain, snow, cloud, cold, fog, wind and frost. The sun is in the largest sack. Coyote learns about it from the children.

Coyote returns home and brings over his people for a dance. Finally, all the Sun-people, except Salmon-trout, sleep. Coyote brings eight mice who go up and gnaw off the ropes which hold the sun-sack. It falls to the floor but is so hot no one can touch it, nor can they cool it off with water. They drag it home by means of a rope.

II. Coyote sends Hummingbird and others to hang up the sun. Red-headed-woodpecker is the announcer. Finally Crows succeed. One of the Crow brothers remains up with the sun.

III. Coyote instructs the sun in its future movements so that people can have light.

As a reward for hanging the sun up they remove Crow's vermin.

IV. The Sun-people are the Bagils. They come to live in various bodies of water and scare people.

NOTES

This version of the myth of the theft of the sun shows some interesting variants.

Coyote himself goes to verify Lizard's discovery of light in the east. Coyote is "carried across Clear Lake by Crane." We may presume that this is by means of the usual Crane-bridge.

There are eight sacks: the rain, snow, cloud, cold, fog, wind, frost, and sun sacks respectively. The sun-sack is the largest, consisting of four thicknesses of elk hide, in which there are two holes through which light is emitted. The sun-sack is suspended by four lashings. The elaborate detail concerning this feature is most unusual.

No mention is made of Coyote's having transformed himself into an old man but we find the two Sun-children willing to give him information because he is so very old.

It is interesting that Coyote makes this first investigational trip alone. He then goes home and returns with his people to steal the sun. Eight mice are used in this instance.

No sleep-charm is used by Coyote and there is no hair-tying incident. The Sun-people all fall asleep, except Salmon-trout. He gives the alarm, but no pursuit is mentioned.

The sun is so hot that no one can touch it. Nor can it be cooled with water. They have to drag it home.

In placing the sun in the sky we find some unusual details. An attendant accompanies the one who attempts to put the sun up. He carries a red-feathered basket filled with water for the carrier to drink on the way. Also a pond is made for the carrier to fall into when he comes down out of the sky. Crow is a vermin-ridden outcast. When all others fail he is invited to try. He succeeds. His younger brother remains up in the sky with sun. As a reward for his services the people dip Crow into hot water and remove his vermin.

Perhaps the most unusual feature of this myth is the identification of the Sun-people with the Bagils. They come and inhabit our bodies of water where they frighten people.

The use of numbers in this myth is very interesting. The sacred number, four, is frequently employed. Eight sacks, and eight mice are mentioned. Duality is also present in several instances.

30—COYOTE STEALS THE DAYLIGHT SACK AND LIBERATES THE SUN

(Page 143)

I. Coyote's nephews and two Grizzly-bear boys play shinney. Near the goal posts are bears and rattlesnakes to bite them. The ball finally rolls far to the east into another country. The Coyote boys follow and are killed and skinned by the eastern people. Coyote mourns.

II. Lizard discovers light in the east. Coyote, with two mice, goes to investigate. He transforms himself into a very old man with a cane. The Sun-people are dancing. Coyote lies down in the rear of the dance-house and soon sees the skins of his two nephews made into a sack to hold the sun. Finally Coyote turns young and dances, telling the people to lie down with their heads together. When all are asleep he braids their hair together so that none can pursue him.

His two mice meantime have cut the ropes which hold the sun sack. He runs out with the sun sack and is seen by a one-eyed old woman, the only person not attending the dance. She gives the alarm but the people are unable to pursue Coyote until the old woman brings a flint knife and cuts their hair.

Finally Fog brothers nearly overtake Coyote, but he breaks open the sack and liberates the sun.

NOTES

Here we have duality strongly emphasized. Two nephews of Coyote play shinney with the two Grizzly-bear boys. Two mice gnaw the lashings of the sun sack which is made of two Coyote skins. Two of each kind of the Sun-people pursue Coyote.

We see Coyote transforming himself into an old man and then back into a young dancer. He gets his dancing paraphernalia by magic.

The usual sleeper's-hair incident is told, but it is a one-eyed old woman who gives the alarm and who finally cuts the people loose so that they can pursue Coyote.

The sun is simply liberated and automatically ascends into the heavens. No one places it there.

31—COYOTE STEALS THE MORNING SACK, CONTAINING THE SUN, MOON AND PLEIADES

(Page 146)

I. Black Lizard discovers light over in the east. Black Lizard, Coyote and Turtle go to secure it. Coyote transforms himself into an old man. The Sun-people dance and finally Coyote dances. His mice cut the strings holding the morning sack, which Coyote takes as he runs away. Turtle guards the door and is shot at by the Sun-people, after Blue Jay gives the alarm. Dove and Fog pursue Coyote but he breaks open the morning sack.

II. The Crow brothers succeed in hanging the Sun, Moon, and Pleiades up in the sky.

NOTES

Here we have a decided variation from the usual theft-of-the-sun idea. In this case it is the "morning sack", containing the sun, moon, and Pleiades.

As usual Coyote journeys to the house of the Sun-people, but this time he is accompanied by Lizard and Turtle. While they dance the four mice which Coyote has brought as his aides gnaw the lashings of the morning sack. However, the Sun-people do not fall asleep. Coyote at the proper juncture leaps us, pulls the morning sack down and makes his escape. His confederate, Turtle, is stationed in the doorway. As the Sun-people shoot, the arrows glance off Turtle's shell. Hence the streaks across the shell.

Finally we find the Crow brothers placing the sun, moon and Pleiades in the sky. No mention is made of reward or other details.

32—THE HUMMINGBIRD BROTHERS RESCUE PEOPLE HELD IN THE SUN VILLAGE

(Page 148)

I. The acorn crop fails about Clear Lake.

Messengers hunt north, east, south and west, but only in the east are there any acorns at all. Everyone journeys thither to the harvest.

After passing two villages, they reach the abode of the Sun-people. In a fanning contest Sun-man kills all the men. The women become the wives of the Sun-men.

II. Turtle-woman and the Hummingbird brothers only are left at the original village. By and by, the boys grow and practice with bows and arrows. They kill a gray squirrel, a rabbit, and two deer. They then take a hornet's nest, some grasshoppers, a yellowjacket's nest and some fish. They gather some angelica shoots and killed a bear.

III. The Hummingbird brothers secure bows, arrows and costumes from Mink, and practice at war. Then they journey eastward to the Sun village. They are hidden by their mother, but are discovered by Sun-man. The elder brother goes to meet Sun-man, is bound to the center pole and killed by the excessive heat, but comes to life again. Next he eats food by means of his elderberry tube. Finally both Hummingbird brothers go rabbit hunting. They are attacked by bears, which they kill by means of yellowjackets. They then join the other hunters and eat rabbit meat by means of their magic tubes. The Sun-people then attack them. The boys again transform themselves into hummingbirds and kill all the Sun-people, except the boy who had warned them.

They then assemble the people from the west, take all goods and return to their original home. Again the yellowjackets kill the people of another village on the way.

While the Hummingbird brothers are away Turtle-woman brings together food for a feast and all rejoice at the return of the people.

NOTES

This is a very detailed myth of the composite type and contains some unusual features. The original cause for action is a famine which is a most unusual theme.

We find here the killing of all the men of the visiting party by the Sun-people and the incorporation of the women as wives of the Sun-people.

The Hummingbird brothers travel to the east to contest with the Sun-people and rescue their relatives. These contests are not the usual sort of shooting contests, though the preparation of the heroes is entirely a war preparation.

After undergoing several trials they overcome and kill all the Sun-people through their yellowjacket allies.

One of the most interesting features is the training of these Hummingbird brothers by their grandmother, Turtle, who teaches them what various foods are and in detail how to take them.

33—THE SUN PEOPLE ARE KILLED BY YELLOWJACKETS
(Page 160)

At a village where nothing ever grows live an old woman and her two grandsons. She gives them bows, arrows and quivers and they start on a journey to the village of the Sun-people. They pass one village after another.

Arriving at the Sun village they find their mother. The elder of the boys buries the younger in the floor to secrete him.

Sun-man burns the elder brother but he comes to life again. Meanwhile the mother instructs the younger brother.

Sun-man sends the boys hunting and they are attacked by grizzly bears, which they kill with yellowjackets.

Then the yellowjackets kill all the Sun-people. All those who have been killed by the Sun-people come to life again and accompany the boys back home.

The baskets of food and other valuable things from the Sun village roll along with them.

During a celebration in honor of their return everyone becomes ill and dies. Their bodies, together with the houses, implements, etc. of the village turn into water and flow into Clear Lake.

NOTES

Here two supernatural boys journey to the Sun village and after undergoing certain tests, they kill all the Sun-people by means of their yellowjacket allies. Thereupon all the people whom Sun-man had killed return to life, and all start on a journey to their old home. Enroute the boys kill, with their yellowjackets, a large number of people for no reason.

They cross Cache Creek by means of a Crane bridge, though no such crossing is mentioned in the outward journey.

A most unusual ending is found when all these returned people sicken and die. Their bodies, together with the houses, implements, etc., in the village all turn to water which flows into Clear Lake. This, however, has no connection with the origin of this lake.

34—FALCON KILLS THE KILAK FAMILY

(Page 164)

I. Coyote discovers Duck from whom he takes feathers and creates human beings. They build a dance-house and have a great feast. Duck is made chief.

II. Coyote marries one of the young women and the people kill Coyote's mother in retaliation. Coyote buries his mother.

III. Coyote removes his mother's heart and from this he constructs a sleep-producing wand. With this he causes everyone to sleep and finally burns the dance-house. He then eats the roasted meat.

IV. Coyote then searches for water which he finally finds hidden by Frog.

Coyote goes to the grave of his mother and mourns. She is finally resurrected. Coyote creates Falcon whom he makes chief.

V. Falcon and Coyote start eastward to gamble with Kī'lak. They are warned by several whom they meet as to the dangers they face. Coyote, by his magic, knows just how to contest with the Kī'laks, and causes Falcon to win by killing the four Kī'lak brothers. They then kill the father and mother of the Kī'laks. They recover all that the Kī'laks have taken from the people and also rescue the last woman that the Kī'laks have brought home. She becomes Falcon's wife.

NOTES

Coyote's loneliness prompts him to create people. Chub Duck is dug from the ground and is made chief which is very unusual. The choking of Coyote's mother with a hot rock is very unusual, as is also Coyote's burial of the body.

Coyote takes his mother's heart and makes a sleep charm. With this he takes revenge by causing all the people to sleep and then burning the sweat-house.

He then eats some of this roasted meat and searches for water which is hidden by Frog. The meat eating and search for water are usually incidents of the World-fire myth. Here however his search for water is given in great detail.

From a single feather Coyote next creates Falcon who insists, despite repeated warnings, upon going to the home of the Kī'laks. In these warnings we have good descriptions given of the home of the Kī'laks.

We find that here there are six Kī'laks who live in a house whose door is guarded by a mechanical trap. No rattlesnakes are mentioned. Also there is no mention of Bottle-fly.

There is the usual dangerous food served and the usual sham eating. We find Coyote possessing an inexhaustible supply of beads and there is given a very detailed description of the gambling, with the fire, shooting, etc.

One very unusual touch is the smoking by one of the Kī'laks of his magic pipe.

In this myth Coyote and Falcon do not take back any people. The last woman victim brought in by one of the Kī'laks becomes the wife of Falcon. They do, however, take home all the wealth which the Kī'laks have taken from people.

35—FALCON IS TAKEN BY KILAK

(Page 177)

I. Falcon is taken into the Upper World by Kī'lak. Vulture is called to find him through his sense of smell and finally locates him. Spider takes Coyote up to the Zenith Gate on his web and there calls to his grandfather who opens the gate.

Coyote and Spider then go to Kī'lak's house where they find Falcon's body. Coyote hides Spider and sets an arrow-head trap for Kī'lak and finally succeeds in killing him. He then takes everything from the house and returns with Falcon's body after burning the house.

Coyote then puts Falcon into a basket of water, puts a rope around it and attaches it to his arm. Falcon finally comes to life and orders everyone to dance in celebration.

II. Night Owl has two garrulous daughters, one of whom journeys toward the south and marries Wind-man. Night Owl pays his daughter a visit.

III. Wind-man makes human beings out of vulture feathers. He instructs Coyote how to do this but Coyote does not follow his instructions and is killed. Blue Jay and Screech Owl doctor Coyote and bring him back to life.

IV. Coyote is very much disgusted with his failure and everyone is transformed into animals.

NOTES

This rather full myth shows several interesting variants of details. Here we find the dead body of Falcon, which has been carried up to the Upper World by Kī'lak, located through Vulture's sharp sense of smell.

The Spider who takes Coyote up to the Zenith Gate on his web is not the gate-keeper himself. The gate-keeper is another spider who is the grandfather of the one who takes Coyote up to the Upper World.

Coyote arrives at the home of Kī'lak, while he is absent. After hiding Spider, Coyote places arrow-heads around in various parts of the house in order to trap and kill Kī'lak. When Kī'lak comes in there is no contest between him and Coyote in the ordinary sense of the term. He simply attacks Coyote and the latter by artful and careful dodging causes Kī'lak to run onto these arrow-heads and cut himself to pieces.

Blue-fly is rather fully described in this myth.

Upon returning home with the body of Falcon, Coyote places it in a basket of water and places a rope around it which he attaches to his arm in order that he may know when Falcon has come to life.

Then follows something entirely unrelated. Night Owl's garrulous daughter runs away toward the south and becomes the wife of Wind-man who is able to create human beings from vulture feathers.

Wind-man instructs Coyote but Coyote bungles the task and is killed through his own stupidity.

He is brought to life by Blue Jay and Screech Owl, instead of by Blue Jay alone.

36—FALCON AND EAGLE JOURNEY TO GILAK'S HOME

(Page 180)

Falcon and Eagle journey far to the north to the home of Gī'lak. They have to pass through a magic rock, the opening in which closes and kills people. Through the magic of Eagle, however, they are able to pass this dangerous spot successfully.

Eventually they reach the home of Gī'lak who is finally killed by Eagle because he has killed her brother.

On the return journey Falcon shoots at and breaks the dangerous rock so that they can pass through safely.

NOTES

In this myth we find the home of Gī'lak located far to the north instead of at the eastern edge of the world as in some cases, or in the Upper World as in others.

Here also we find mention of the magic rock, the hole in which closes and traps travelers.

Gī'lak's home is as usual described as of a glistening white, due to the many bones of humans whom he has eaten. There is no contest with Gī'lak. Eagle is welcomed by Gī'lak. She watches her chance and by a surprise attack cuts Gī'lak to pieces with her sharp claws.

On the return journey we find Falcon doing a great service to the world by destroying the deadly rock which kills people.

37—QUAIL DESERTS HER HUSBAND AND GOES TO GILAK'S

(Page 183)

Quail deserts her husband, Hawk, and goes to the home of the Gī'laks. Hawk and his brother follow her. Hawk conceals his brother in his hair. The Gī'laks kill Hawk, but the body is recovered by his brother.

The people prepare to make war upon the Gilaks. Bat makes arrow-points by magic. Hummingbird revivifies Hawk. Upon arrival at the Gī'laks' house the medicine of Blue Jay and Red-headed-woodpecker cause the Gī'laks' bow-strings to break. Fisher and the Gī'laks gamble and both of the Gī'laks are killed.

The people return home but Hawk refuses to do so because he has been dead.

NOTES

This myth shows us some very unusual features.

Quail walks upon the ocean waves in order to hide her trail. However, when she reaches two different rivers she can not walk across these but must dry them up by her magic before crossing. Later her husband has no trouble in tracking her on top of the waves.

Gi'lak's house, located far to the south, is quite fully described. The watchman stationed on top of the house is an unusual feature. There are two of the Gi'laks.

When Hawk arrives Gi'lak shoots him as he enters. There is no contest. Hawk's brother, a midget whom Hawk has brought along in his hair, carries the body back toward home. Before revivification is possible, Hummingbird travels throughout Hawk's alimentary canal to purify him.

Preparations are made to avenge Hawk's death. Particularly of note is the manufacture of arrow-heads by magic. Bat swallows a block of obsidian and vomits great numbers of arrow-heads.

Another unusual feature is the use of powerful magic medicine to break the bow-strings of the Gi'lak brothers. Then follows the usual contest in which both Gi'laks are finally killed.

We have an unusual feature in Hawk's own refusal to return with the others because he has about himself the odor of the dead. We often find some one other than the revivified person himself offering this objection.

38—GAMBLING LUCK IS GIVEN BY GILAK
(Page 186)

A man who loses in gambling puts on a deer mask and transforms himself into a deer.

Gi'lak takes him to his home in the sky and feeds him beads.

The man returns to earth and wins every time.

The people complain and Blue Jay transforms them into birds.

NOTES

Here we find the abode of Gi'lak located in the sky. He is not given any cannibalistic attributes, but takes this deer home as a pet.

The supernatural food, beads, which the deer eats gives him gambling luck.

Here it is Blue Jay who transforms people into animals.

The whole idea that the usually cannibalistic Gilak can be a benevolent being, giving good luck, is very extraordinary.

39—THE ABODE OF THUNDER UNDER THE OCEAN
(Page 188)

A little boy is refused food by his aunt. His father is also similarly refused. This angers the man who walks out into the ocean and disappears. Thunder now originates at this point.

Thunder controls the fish which run up the Garcia river. He also produces thunder and lightning.

NOTES

Refusal of food causes a man to walk out into the ocean north of Point Arena where he now, as Thunder, lives in his dry, crystalline, underwater abode. Little description is given of his appearance, but the sound of thunder is produced by his movements and lightning is the glint from an object he carries under his arm. He controls fish. His house is filled with them and if he pulls the great lever which controls the door to his house great numbers of fish will run up the streams.

This whole conception of Thunder. is quite extraordinary.

40—FLOWER-MAN KILLS THUNDER

(Page 190)

An unsuccessful fisherman, Flower-man, weaves a fish basket out of snakes. He catches many whales, sharks, etc. Coyote becomes ill when he sees this. Flower-man prepares to cook his fish in an underground oven. Discovering that Coyote has deceived him he places him in the oven and kills him. Then he punishes his wife by throwing her into the ocean. Coyote returns to life and Bullsnake crawls up onto a rock out in the ocean.

Flower-man finally induces his wife to return, but she leaves again and he weds the Duck sisters who take him to their home across the ocean. They take him through a magic rock which opens and closes. He then destroys this death trap. The father of the Duck sisters is Thunder who lives in a house filled with snakes. Thunder tests Flower-man: fishing, getting fire-wood, with rattlesnakes and with grizzlies, and finally in a shooting contest. Flower-man kills Thunder, who again comes to life.

Next Flower-man is tested with the magic swing beset with spears but escapes death. The swing then kills Thunder.

All the people whom Thunder had killed then came to life.

NOTES

We first see Flower-man catching whales and other large sea creatures in a fish basket woven of snakes. His revenge upon Coyote is to bake him in an underground oven. The wife of Flower-man is Bullsnake, a character almost never encountered in Pomo Mythology. No mention is made of her transformation into a seal.

With his magic songs he attracts two new wives who take him across the ocean to the home of their father, Thunder. The journey is not made in a canoe or on a raft but the two ducks swim beside him and help him across. They have to pass through an opening and closing gate trap.

Thunder's house is filled with snakes of all kinds. Thunder subjects his son-in-law to various trials. After being killed and coming to life, Thunder is finally killed permanently by his own magic swing. This swing has spears set all around it. Flower-man is able to control these spears by his magic, but Thunder is not and is pierced by them. This swing is mentioned elsewhere but never with the field of spears connected with it.

41—THUNDER KILLS COYOTE AND CREATES ALL FORMS OF SEA LIFE

(Page 193)

Thunder has a fish-trap and a net made of snakes in which he catches whales. Coyote tricks Thunder's wife. Thunder roasts Coyote and kills him. He kicks his wife into the sea and she becomes a seal. The sticks and stones which he throws at her become various forms of sea-life.

With his lover's-flute Thunder calls other women to him and finally chooses Mallard.

NOTES

Here we find Thunder's fish-trap and net made of snakes. Coyote tricks Thunder's wife by causing her burden basket to remain where she has set it down. Thunder roasts Coyote to death. Thunder turns his own wife into a seal and creates all forms of sea-life.

42—TCODOK KILLS GUKSU

(Page 195)

I. The Eagle sisters have miraculous sons, the Gū'ksū boys. The chief, Eagle, challenges Gū'ksū to a fire-fanning contest, but is killed. Tco'dok follows Gū'ksū to his abode and kills him with a sleeping medicine.

II. The Gū'ksū children doctor their father and bring him back to life.

The people rejoice and have a big feast in honor of Tco'dok.

NOTES

In this myth we have an unusual incident in which Gū'ksū kills Eagle. Gū'ksū is usually a benevolent and powerful medicine-man who is called in to cure the sick or bring someone back to life. In this instance he takes on the attributes usually assigned to Gilak.

Here we see Diver giving a traveler a tule boat to cross San Francisco Bay. When the southern ocean is reached, however, the travelers wade across it. Usually it is Crane who has to assist travelers to cross the water by making a bridge of his neck, or leg.

Here again we have revivification of the dead. This time by throwing the remains into the water.

43—BAKI'L IS CREATED AND PLACED IN CLEAR LAKES

(Page 197)

Tsaa't is miraculously born and has himself placed in a spring where he is transformed into Baki'l. He gives his uncle songs which cure people frightened by seeing supernatural beings.

Creator causes him to enlarge the spring and create Blue Lakes.

Baki'l gives regulations for people passing Blue Lakes and other places where supernatural monsters reside.

NOTES

Here we have the miraculous creation of the supernatural monster, Baki'l, also the giving of medicine-songs to cure people who have seen supernatural monsters. Blue Lakes are created and the conduct of people in respect to Blue Lakes is established.

This detailed account of the origin of Baki'l is very different from one other which states that the numerous Baki'ls were originally the Sun-people. When the sun was stolen and liberated they moved over to Clear Lake but were later transferred by Coyote to the ocean whence they dispersed and now live in many bodies of water.

44—THE MONSTER OF BLUE LAKES

(Page 200)

Crow makes his brother into a monster and places him in Blue Lakes to scare people. Then he restricts him to the frightening of menstruating women and their husbands. The Bagil goes into the mountainside and creates a great spring. He may still be seen at times and consequently people shun these lakes because of the Bagil's power to cause illness.

NOTES

In this myth we see a new explanation of the water monster of Blue Lakes. Crow is represented as placing his brother in the northernmost of these lakes and as causing him to lengthen until his tail touches the southern shore of the second of the Twin Lakes. Then he places horns and decorations on this serpent and created the creature which has since made these lakes a most dreaded spot.

A very unusual explanation for the fact that this monster is not seen at all times is found in his having crawled inside of a nearby mountain, from which a great spring now gushes.

The proscription against menstruating women and their husbands approaching Blue Lakes is fully laid down here.

45—BAGIL IS CAUGHT IN A RABBIT SNARE

(Page 201)

A man catches a Bakil in his rabbit snare. He is made ill but is cured by his younger brother.

NOTES

This very short myth is of interest chiefly for the fact that the procedure in doctoring a case of Bagil sickness is given quite in detail. Also this description of the Bagil is quite full and we see a very different creature from the long water-serpent usually portrayed.

46—COYOTE CREATES OBSIDIAN-MAN FROM AN ARROW-POINT

(Page 202)

I. Coyote steals fish from the trap of a neighboring tribe and is shot. The arrow-head remains in his body and he becomes very ill. He finally extracts the arrow-head and from it he creates Obsidian-man.

II. The people of the village endeavor to kill Obsidian-man on account of his supernatural abilities but he succeeds in killing them all.

III. Obsidian-man then takes Coyote and Frog and starts on a journey. He finally places Frog in a spring which it is now very dangerous for people to visit. He places Coyote on a mountain and also selects his own abode.

NOTES

Starting with quite a circumstantial account of the theft by Coyote of fish from the dam of a neighboring tribe, we next see Coyote creating Obsidian-man from the arrow-head which he has carried in his wound for four days.

Then follows a series of contests and trials by the people, in which Obsidian-man is always victorious and finally a great battle in which all the people are arrayed against Obsidian-man. Obsidian-man is victorious and all his opponents are killed. Obsidian-man's feeling of remorse at having killed all the people is quite unusual.

Also an unusual feature is the subordination of Coyote. Obsidian-man assigns a home to Coyote. Usually it is Coyote who does all such assigning.

This myth also accounts for the fact that a certain spring is a very dangerous place for humans to visit.

47—THE STORY OF ARROWPOINT YOUNG MAN

(Page 208)

Coyote steals fish from the fish dam of a neighboring village. He is finally shot. The arrow-head remains in his body and turns into a young man.

Coyote trains this young man and when he grows up he contests with the people. The sharpness of his body enables him to gather clover and wood more rapidly than others. He escapes death when the people try to shoot him because his body is of obsidian and the arrows glance off. When the people bind him to burn him in the sweat-house, he easily cuts his lashings with his sharp body.

Finally, growing weary of these repeated attempts on his life, he kills all the people.

NOTES

In this myth we have the usual theft of fish by Coyote, but here the arrow-point turns into a young man while still in Coyote's body.

We here have Obsidian-man winning all contests and surviving all tests as usual. Very strong emphasis is laid upon the sharpness of his entire body. We see him escaping the fire test and other trials by cutting his bonds. His body is of obsidian and he can therefore cut with any part of it.

Also we see him here as invulnerable. Arrows glance off his body and do him no harm.

The myth is incomplete because the informant could not recall the details of the killing of the people of Obsidian-man.

48—OBSIDIAN-MAN KILLS THE FOUR THUNDER BROTHERS

(Page 210)

I. While stealing fish, Coyote is shot and killed. Blue Jay revivifies him.

Obsidian-man is created from the arrow-head which killed Coyote. After his revivification he places this arrow-head in the body of Frog.

II. Coyote and Obsidian-man go to the home of the Thunders, despite four warnings on the way. Coyote hits the water of the river with a polishing stone and it dries up so that they can cross.

Obsidian-man kills the bears who guard Thunder's house. Then Coyote springs the trap at the door. Coyote disposes of all the deadly food offered by Thunder.

Thunder tries to kill Obsidian-man when they go for wood.

Obsidian-man builds a fire which flies up on him. He has an ice garment and a frog-tube and escapes unharmed. Then they compete by pouring live coals over each other. Obsidian-man's ice coat and fog tube protect him and, after four trials each, alternately, he finally kills Thunder with coals and his own heated obsidian arms.

One of the three remaining Thunders takes Obsidian-man as his son-in-law. Coyote kills the rattlesnakes which protect Thunder's daughter.

Thunder then sends Obsidian-man to a fish dam made of snakes, to a forest where there are monster serpents, to a magically growing tree, to a rattlesnake-infested rock, and to a bear-infested hunting ground. Obsidian-man is successful in all these trials.

Fire comes but Obsidian-man kills him.

Again the Thunders try to kill Obsidian-man, who kills two of them. He spares the last of the Thunder brothers.

Then each displays his special magic. Thunder makes it rain. Obsidian-man makes it very hot. Next Thunder produces hail. Then Obsidian-man causes a shower of small stones. Next Thunder produces snow. Then Obsidian-man causes a shower of fire. Thunder next produces a near deluge. Obsidian-man finally causes a shower of large boulders and crushes Thunder.

Obsidian-man burns the house, including Blue-fly and Thunder's daughter.

Obsidian-man goes home and everyone rejoices because the Thunders are dead.

NOTES

This myth is one replete with details of many kinds and is primarily concerned with a subject rather rarely encountered in Pomo mythology, the four Thunder brothers, whose home is here localized near the mouth of Big River on the Mendocino coast.

We start out with the usual theft of fish by Coyote, and the creation of Obsidian-man from an arrow-head which is shot into Coyote. Here, however, we find Coyote dying from his wound. He is revivified by Blue Jay. He takes the arrow-head and inserts it into the body of Frog where it is transformed into the young man who becomes the hero of the story. There are no contests between Obsidian-man and the people of the village, but the young hero immediately journeys westward to contest with the Thunders. He is accompanied by Coyote who is his protector and adviser. They take along another young man, but he plays no part in the adventures.

Interesting incidents of the journey are the encountering of four different people along the way each of whom advises against the journey, and also the drying up of a stream by Coyote's magic polishing stone in order that the party may pass dry-shod to the other side.

Obsidian-man first kills the many bears who guard Thunder's house. When they finally reach the house, Coyote again uses his magic bead-polisher, this time to spring the trap at the door of Thunder's house.

We have Coyote using some device in his mouth (presumably the usual magic tube) which enabled him to dispose of the dangerous food proffered by Thunder.

Here we see Obsidian-man depicted as having arms with serrated edges which enables him to overcome many obstacles. With these he catches arrows shot at him. He uses them to kill bears, cut down bushes and trees and for various other similar purposes. In his fire contests he heats these saw-toothed arms of stone and kills his opponents.

One of the most unusual features of these fire contests is the pouring of red-hot coals on an opponent, using a seed-beater for the purpose. Obsidian-man is specially protected in these fire contests by a garment of ice and by a tube which runs down to the ocean and through which fog pours up to envelope and help him.

There are four of these Thunder brothers. When the first one has been killed by Obsidian-man, one of the others recognizes Obsidian-man as his son-in-law and offers him his daughter as a wife. This is, of course, only another attempt upon the life of Obsidian-man, for this girl's whole body is covered with rattlesnakes. Coyote goes in and kills all these snakes and makes her a safe mate for Obsidian-man.

Then follows a series of further tests for Obsidian-man, each of which is supposed to kill him but he is successful in overcoming all these dangers. These are a fish-dam woven of snakes, some monstrous serpents, a growing tree, many rattlesnakes, many bears, and finally a forest fire, personified. In these contests he is aided by certain benevolent assistants. He kills Forest-fire by shooting him in a vulnerable spot.

There then follows the killing of two more of the Thunders, thus leaving only one. Ordinarily this last one also would have been killed at once, but Obsidian-man, curiously enough, spares his life. In return this Thunder proceeds to show Obsidian-man his magic. It is not done as a matter of instruction, but the two alternately display their respective powers, first Thunder and then Obsidian-man. They are rain versus heat, hail versus a shower of small stones, snow versus a shower of fire, and finally a deluge versus a shower of boulders. This shower of boulders crushes Thunder.

Finally Obsidian-man burns Thunder's house, including Bottle-fly and Thunder's daughter, before he returns to his own home.

49—OBSIDIAN-MAN CONTESTS WITH THE KILAKS

(Page 220)

I. Coyote is shot while stealing fish from the traps in a fish·weir. He remains in the water for four days but is finally revivified by Blue Jay. As he emerges from the water, the arrow-point which has gone into his body falls out and he takes it home and feeds it to his wife, Frog.

The following morning Obsidian-man is sitting on the opposite side of the fire.

II. The people of the village invite Obsidian-man to contest with them and they try very hard to kill him, but he always wins in the contests. Finally they propose a war and he, with his magic arrows, kills each group of warriors who come against him on four successive days.

III. He then takes his father and mother, Coyote and Frog, and journeys northward to visit the home of the Kī'laks. He meets four bears successively on the way and shows his power to be greater than theirs.

Arriving at the house of Kī'lak, the party enters after springing two traps near the door. The two elder Kī'laks are at home and the other four Kī'laks arrive from the four cardinal points shortly thereafter. In the contest which follows the four younger Kī'laks are killed by Obsidian-man. He then burns their house, together with Bottle-fly, who lives there.

IV. The three then return southward, again meeting the four bears and finally, when they reach Upper Lake, Obsidian-man places Coyote and Frog in their respective environments.

Obsidian-man then goes on over Mt. Kanaktai and finally breaks up his body on the southern slope of the mountain.

NOTES

This myth, which comprises several incidents, contains some interesting details. Here we find the birth of Obsidian-man from the usual arrow-head, which has been shot into Coyote's body, but in this case we find the arrow-head taken home and swallowed by Coyote's wife.

Again we find the home of the Kī'laks located in the far north and in the journey to this home, the party meets successively four different bears.

Here we find that the four younger Kī'laks arrive from the four cardinal points, but we find that each has his own particular smoke-hole on his side of the house.

Here again we find Coyote disposing of the food offered him by the Kī'laks through the magic flute he carries in his hunting sack. The contest between Obsidian-man and the Kī'laks is of the usual flying and shooting sort, but here we have mentioned a special kind of fan used to blind the contestants with smoke and dust.

In this myth we find mentioned Bottle-fly as one of the residents of Kī'lak's house.

We find here also that it is Obsidian-man who places Coyote and Frog in their respective elements and gives them their particular calls.

Obsidian-man finally breaks up his body on the southern slope of Mt. Kanaktai by trying to free himself after his hair is caught in the bushes.

50—THE CONTEST BETWEEN OBSIDIAN-MAN AND MOUNTAIN-MAN

(Page 226)

I. The Bird-people hold a race, using the shores of Clear Lake and its subsidiary lakes as a race-course. One bird of each species is entered in this race and Crane is stationed on the top of Mt. Kanaktai to announce the progress of the race. All of the runners make three complete laps around the lake, but about the middle of the fourth round nearly all of them become exhausted and drop out of the race. The only two left are Loon and Mud-hen. Mud-hen finally wins.

II. Everyone rejoices over this race and a great celebration is held, to which all are invited except Obsidian-man. This incenses him so that he, in company with Coyote, leaves the village and journeys far to the south.

They finally meet Mountain-man, a giant with whom Obsidian-man contests. Each first displays his powers and then they enter into a contest to the death, Obsidian-man cutting down trees and Mountain-man knocking them over. Finally, after all the trees in the vicinity have been felled in this way, Obsidian-man escapes toward the ocean and Mountain-man pursues him hotly. Finally Obsidian-man takes refuge on top of a rocky peak which Mountain-man breaks into pieces.

Obsidian-man then runs on to a place near the coast where he climbs a large redwood tree. Mountain-man is unable to fell this tree as he has the others so he builds a great fire at its base, determined to burn the tree down.

Obsidian-man is at this point helped by all of the birds who bring water to prevent the tree from burning and this tree still stands to this day, and from a point about thirty feet above the ground a spring still issues.

Finally Mountain-man wearies and falls asleep. Obsidian-man comes down, lifts a large abalone shell with which Mountain-man has covered his heart and runs his spear into Mountain-man's body and kills him. Mountain-man's body breaks up into boulders which roll down into the ocean.

Obsidian-man then returns to Mt. Kanaktai, but in ascending the mountain his hair is caught in some brush and his body breaks into many pieces, thus accounting for the great number of pieces of obsidian now to be found on the southern slope of Mt. Kanaktai.

NOTES

In this myth we have two important elements. First there is a race among representatives of the different species of birds in which Mud-hen, a very slow-moving individual, finally wins.

In the second element we have a lively contest between Obsidian-man and a giant, called Mountain-man, in which Obsidian-man finally wins by piercing the heart of Mountain-man.

Here also we have explained the presence of great numbers of boulders and pieces of obsidian now to be found on the southern slope of Mt. Kanaktai. These are the body of Obsidian-man which broke into these pieces as he was returning to the top of Mt. Kanaktai.

Here the indestructibility of the redwood is explained.

51—THE CONTEST BETWEEN ROCK-MAN AND GRAY SQUIRREL

(Page 231)

Gray Squirrel meets Rock-man and they contest by testing each other's bows. When Gray Squirrel breaks his opponents bow he is pursued. Being a good dodger, Gray Squirrel escapes by scurrying up trees, each of which is promptly cut down by Rock-man. Gray Squirrel escapes westward with Rock-man rolling after him.

Finally they reach the coast, where Gray Squirrel takes refuge in a large redwood tree. Rock-man cannot cut this great tree down so he tries to burn it down. Gray Squirrel causes a spring to flow from the side of the tree and thus prevent it from burning.

NOTES

This short story is in abbreviated form about the same as the one immediately preceding it. Here, however, Gray Squirrel is substituted for Obsidian-man and Rock-man for Mountain-man.

The ability to cut down trees is here ascribed to Rock-man, and Gray Squirrel is given none of the attributes of Obsidian-man, except his agility and ability to dodge.

Rock-man is depicted as rolling along instead of walking or running.

Here again we find the pursued one taking refuge in a big redwood tree, and we see this tree as indestructible, due to the fact that a spring flows from its side.

This spring is wished into existence.

52—THE DEATH OF MUYAMUYA

(Page 232)

The giant, Mū'yamūya, is always trying to induce people to gamble with him, and is very much disliked by the people. They make several attempts to kill him, but he always revivifies himself. He warns the people that if they ever kill him they will all be transformed into animals. They finally pound him up completely and in so doing they come upon a tiny kernel under the nail of the great toe on his right foot. Examination shows that this contains his heart. When they destroy this all are transformed into animals. Before this happens they have thrown the fragments of his body over the cliff and have rolled rocks down on them. This accounts for the presence of the boulders now at this point.

NOTES

Mū'yamūya, the giant, is quite fully described. He proves indestructible until the hard kernel under his toe nail which contains his heart is discovered.

His warning proves correct and when his heart is destroyed the people are transformed into animals.

This myth also accounts for the presence of boulders at the base of a certain cliff.

53—MUYAMUYA
(Page 233)

Mū'yamūya takes from the people whatever he wants and people try to kill him. He refuses to attend the funeral of his own mother.

Finally the people pound up Mū'yamūya completely, this time mashing the small kernel under his toe-nail and he never comes to life again.

NOTES

This very short myth is quite similar to the one immediately preceding and accounts for the death of a giant by the discovery of his vulnerable spot.

There are two new features in this version, the fact that Mū'yamūya took from the people whatever he wanted, and the fact that he would not even attend the funeral of his own mother.

54—HUK TRANSFORMS PEOPLE INTO DEER
(Page 234)

Upon visiting a spring a boy and his sister find a deer-like animal caught in a snare. The people of the village eat its meat and are transformed into deer. The boy, his sister and his grandmother do not partake of this meat and are saved by Coyote.

NOTES

This very abbreviated myth has one point of special interest, the transformation of Hūk into a deer in order that he may deceive the people.

The wisdom displayed by the small boy is also encountered elsewhere, but usually there is an elder brother whom he guides and saves. In this case it is an elder sister and a grandmother.

The entry of Coyote at the end and his causing a fog to roll in and bear these three away in an unusual touch, though there seems a considerable possibility that this idea may be a modernization.

55—BAGIL TRANSFORMS PEOPLE INTO DEER
(Page 235)

A boy catches a Bagil in a trap. He recognizes it as a dangerous being and through his magic song protects his sister, his grandmother and himself. They do not eat any of the meat. The rest of the people of the village eat of this meat and all are transformed into deer.

NOTES

This myth is quite similar to the one immediately preceding, except that here it is a Bagil instead of a Hūk which transforms himself into a deer in order to deceive people.

Here everyone except the small boy, his sister, and his grandmother are transformed into deer. These three continue to live on in the village as before. Finally the boy discovers the home of the deer and thereafter secures meat easily.

56—THE WATER SPIRIT IN BLUE LAKES

(Page 236)

Water-man lives in a big assembly house in Blue Lakes. He is the only one saved from the great World-fire. After the fire Coyote created fish and now people go to Blue Lakes for fishing luck which is granted them by Water-man.

NOTES

In this myth we see the abode of Water-man beneath the waters of Blue Lakes, where he lives entirely on fish. His friend Vulture lives entirely on shellfish. It appears that when the world-fire came Water-man was the only one spared because he lived under the water. Fish are created by Coyote from snakes.

Here we have also the giving of fishing luck by Water-man to those who come to him with the proper ritualistic procedure.

57—FALCON IS STOLEN BY KILAK

(Page 237)

I. Falcon hunts geese and is stolen by Kï'lak.

Falcon's wife, Blackbird, follows his tracks and finds where he disappeared.

Blackbird, accompanied by Coyote, journeys far to the east and then to the south and rescues the body of Falcon from Kï'lak's house and brings it back to their own village. Here Coyote doctors Falcon and causes him to return to life. Everyone rejoices.

II. When the Falcon children grow up they repair to the mountains and practice the maneuvers of bears and finally succeed in transforming themselves into bears. They then journey to the home of Kï'lak which they burn. He is destroyed in the fire. They then return to their own home and retransform themselves into human beings.

NOTES

This myth seems to be rather abbreviated in certain of its phases. We are left to infer that Falcon hunts with a magic sling. No clear notion is given of just how Gï'lak stole Falcon. The journey of Blackbird and Coyote to the east is apparently lacking in some details.

Certain unusual features are present. When the revivified Falcon returns he complains of being cold. The Falcon children become bears, in fact they become "bear-doctors" capable of changing from human to bear and back again by putting on and taking off their bear suits. There is no contest with Gi'lak (one only is mentioned). He is killed when he returns, finding his house afire, and attempts to enter it to save some of his possessions. Nor is there any contest when originally Blackbird and Coyote visit Gi'lak's house. They simply take the body of Falcon and return home.

Coyote's manifestation of mourning is not often encountered.

Here we find the revivification of Falcon by Coyote accomplished by placing Falcon's body in the creek for four days.

58—THE ORIGIN OF THUNDER

(Page 240)

Coyote creates Thunder on Redwood Mountain and sends him over to Big River, there to live in a house under the water. The sound of thunder always travels from west to east and back again.

NOTES

Obviously an extremely abbreviated myth accounting for the fact that the sound of thunder always rolls from the west to the east and back again.

59—COYOTE TRICKS HIS MOTHER-IN-LAW

(Page 241)

Coyote tricks his mother-in-law who returns to the village with four children. The people kill the children.

NOTES

Here Coyote appears as a trickster. He causes his mother-in-law to bring to the village four children.

Here we have mentioned the "children's trail".

60—COYOTE KILLS HIS SISTER-IN-LAW, SKUNK

(Page 242)

I. Coyote kills his sister-in-law, Skunk, by holding her foot in the fire. Eagle eats Skunk and tricks Coyote by throwing the offal into his mouth.

II. Coyote's wife is Skunk's elder sister. She pretends to be ill and

Coyote tries to doctor her. She kills Coyote with her scent. She then mashes up Coyote's body and throws it outside. Blue Jay revivifies Coyote.

NOTES

Here we see Coyote as a trickster killing his sister-in-law. He is next tricked by Eagle and finally by his wife, who kills him with her scent. As usual Coyote is revivified by Blue Jay. He objects to being awakened from his slumber.

61—COYOTE TRICKS SOME GIRLS

(Page 244)

The women of the village go out to gather buckeyes. Coyote transforms himself into a very old woman and follows them. He builds a small house and causes it to rain in order that he may trick the young women.

NOTES

Coyote here plays the trickster role, changing his form in order to fool some women. He can by his magic change his form at will and can cause it to rain very hard.

62—COYOTE TRICKS TWO GIRLS

(Page 245)

Here Coyote transforms himself into a dead fish in order to trick his victims, who are two sisters. They follow the dead fish out into the lake until suddenly he transforms himself back into Coyote. Ten Coyote children are miraculously born, but are killed by the mother of the girls.

NOTES

Here we have an unusual transformation of Coyote into a dead fish in order to trick two girls. The result is the miraculous birth of ten children. Five is here used as the number instead of the usual four.

63—COYOTE IS TRICKED BY GROUND SQUIRRELS

(Page 246)

I. Kabada*te'tes* steals Duck. When he is rescued by ten medicinemen sent by Coyote for the purpose he has a human head.

II. Coyote changes himself into a young woman and marries Hawk in order to obtain the latter's hunting secrets. By this magic he catches ground squirrels but is not satisfied and takes a large number so the ground squirrels pull Coyote's arm off. Coyote produces a new arm from a mush-oak limb.

The people build a dance-house in which to celebrate Coyote's magic recovery. They dig up Chub Duck. Duck gathers all the manzanita growing on Cow Mountain.

Coyote causes all the Ground-squirrel-people to sleep. He ties their hair together and then sets fire to the house. Meadowlark escapes to a field, Blue Jay to a tree, and Duck to the lake.

Coyote gathers up the roasted ground squirrels and gives one each to the Bullfrog-women who are constantly weaving tule baskets.

Coyote goes off to gather poles to build a house in which to store the rest of the squirrels. He makes a great noise on his return which revivifies the squirrels.

III. One of the Bullfrog women had eaten so heartily of the squirrels that she died, but after four days she comes to life again. Meadowlark objects to Bullfrog's return to life. Blue Jay throws hot coals upon him. Coyote arranges matters so that people will not come back to life after death.

IV. Coyote creates Kelsey Creek and fish follow up the stream. Coyote makes fish-traps. He then invites people to come here to fish and establishes the custom of inviting people here during the hītc run.

NOTES

This is a typical composite myth containing several very distinct elements.

The magician, Kabadate'tes, appears at the outset. He is a character not mentioned elsewhere.

The rescue of Duck by the ten medicine-men is accomplished by means of a sleeping charm.

Coyote appears as a trickster, as a dupe who is tricked, as a creator, and as a giver of customs. His ability to make for himself a new arm out of an oak limb shows his magic power. We find Coyote taking revenge for the loss of his arm by putting all the Ground-squirrel-people to sleep with his sleep charm. Then he braids their hair and burns the house.

Revivification through noise is shown when Coyote brings the willow poles and the Ground Squirrels come to life.

We here have explained why almost no manzanita is now to be found on Cow Mountain.

Dug-from-the-ground again appears in this myth in the person of Chub-duck.

The regulation of death, as here given, is rather unusual. As usual it is

Meadowlark who interposes objections to the return of the dead. He is punished by Blue Jay for his remarks, not in the usual manner, by having his tail clipped off, but this time by having live coals poured over him. His objections, however, prevail and death is made permanent.

The creation of Kelsey Creek, in order that the fish may run up it, is attended by the establishment of the custom of inviting neighboring tribes over for the fish-run each season.

An interesting feature is the weaving in place on the bushes of fish-baskets, two for each person invited.

64—GROUND-SQUIRRELS STEAL COYOTE'S ARM TO MAKE A RATTLE

(Page 251)

I. Coyote learns from Falcon how to catch ground squirrels. The squirrels tear Coyote's arm off. He plugs the wound with moss and replaces the arm with an elderberry stick.

II. Coyote digs up Duck in building a dance-house.

III. The Squirrel-people come to Coyote's house for a dance, bringing rattles made of Coyote's arm-bones. Coyote becomes angry and ties the hair of the squirrel-people to the feet of their neighbors. Duck takes all the manzanita bushes from the slope of Cow Mountain. Coyote burns the house and roasts all the squirrels.

IV. Coyote plans to store the meat. When he prepares to dry it, the squirrels come to life. Meantime, however, the blind Crow-women steal a few squirrels. Coyote eats the offal and upbraids the women for not having taken more.

NOTES

First of all Coyote is tricked and loses his arm. He is next shown building a dance-house and discovering Duck, whose prodigious carrying power accounts for the fact that there are no manzanita bushes on Cow Mountain.

Coyote is seen retaliating by tying the hair of the Squirrel-people and roasting them. This hair-tying is different from the usual version of this incident. Here the hair of the long-haired ones is tied to the feet of the short-haired ones.

Contrary to Coyote's instructions the blind Crow-women take some meat. After the rest of the squirrels have come to life Coyote scolds because they did not take more. All that Coyote has to eat is the offal of the few squirrels stolen by the blind crows.

65—COYOTE IS TRICKED BY THE SKUNK BROTHERS

(Page 254)

Coyote eats the hunting sacks of the Skunk brothers, and then takes them deer hunting, using them as deer drivers. He deceives the Skunk boys and feeds them deer viscera and pieces of burned meat. He himself eats the best meat.

The Skunk boys finally steal what is left of the meat in order to trick Coyote. Coyote hunts for the boys and finally finds a rock with smoke issuing from it. Here he breaks his bow and arrows endeavoring to shoot into the rock.

Coyote pulls on the deer-skin which the boys had stuffed with refuse, and finally breaks his back. The Skunks pound Coyote up and throw his body away.

Blue Jay revivifies Coyote, who calls for a doctor.

Crow brothers go to investigate, after dressing themselves in full ceremonial costume. They try to doctor Coyote but are repulsed. The same is the result when Kingfisher brothers, Buzzard brothers, Vulture brothers and others try to doctor Coyote.

Finally Coyote calls the Kŭ'ksŭ brothers. They are able to cure him.

NOTES

Coyote here appears both as a trickster and as a foolish fellow who is killed by those whom he has deceived.

He is awakened by Blue Jay but is still helpless. He calls for help and a pair of each kind of bird tries unsuccessfully to cure him. Finally the Kŭ'ksŭ brothers succeed.

An unusual feature is the devouring by Coyote of the hunting sacks as well as their contents. Also the rooting of Coyote to the earth by a grape-vine, through the wish of the Skunk brothers. Another is the sending by Coyote of the Skunk brothers repeatedly after binding material.

The sacred number, four, is very much used, but duality is even more prominent.

66—THE SKUNK BROTHERS TRICK COYOTE

(Page 260)

Coyote, who is a great hunter, shows the Skunk brothers the deer which he has killed and asks them to prepare it to be carried home. Coyote searches for something with which to carry the meat. The

Skunks steal the meat. They trick Coyote into pulling out the stuffed deer-skin. Coyote becomes angry and challenges the Skunks to a shooting contest. They kill him. He returns to life.

NOTES

This is a variant of a familiar theme in which Coyote goes out to hunt the tying material. Usually he sends the Skunk brothers after it. The Skunk brothers do not kill Coyote in the actual pulling out of the stuffed deer-skin, but later in a shooting contest. Coyote comes to life but nothing is said about how this is accomplished.

67—COYOTE IS TRICKED AND KILLED BY SKUNK BROTHERS

(Page 261)

Coyote and his nephews, Skunk brothers, live together. Coyote sets snares and catches a large buck. He weaves a net of tule to carry the game home. When he tires he lays down his burden and leaves the Skunk brothers for a while. The smaller Skunk carries the load. They wish that Coyote should not be able to proceed. In attempting to rise he pulls out his intestines and fills the cavity with moss. Meantime the Skunk brothers reach their home. Coyote finally arrives at Skunk's home, pulls to get the deer out, falls over and is stunned. The Skunk boys then beat him to death.

Coyote is revivified by Blue Jay.

NOTES

In this myth the Skunk boys appear as Coyote's nephews.

They trick Coyote and kill him after causing great difficulty in following them. They cause him to become rooted to the ground. Coyote finally pulls out his entrails and plugs the cavity with pendant moss.

As usual Coyote upbraids Blue Jay for making so much noise and waking him up.

68—COYOTE IS TRICKED BY THE SKUNK BROTHERS AND AGAIN BY SMALL BIRDS

(Page 262)

I. Coyote kills a deer and sends the Skunk brothers repeatedly to get some kelp. He finally goes for it himself and the Skunk brothers take the meat home. Coyote is angry and searches for the Skunk brothers. He finally arrives at Skunk's house where he is tricked into pulling the meat out through the very small door. He pulls very hard and falls over into the canyon and is killed.

Coyote is finally revivified by Blue Jay.

II. Coyote then meets many small birds who trick him into trying to fly into the bushes. He puts out an eye. Tree gives him some moss to put in his eye socket and Blue Jay later cures him. Then he advises Coyote to give a feast.

NOTES

Coyote is tricked by the Skunks and killed, not by Skunk's scent, but by a pulling contest and by falling into a canyon.

Coyote loses an eye through being tricked by small birds.

Blue Jay shows himself to be a great doctor first by revivifying Coyote and then by curing Coyote's eye.

Coyote is here shown as the one tricked in both incidents, instead of being the one who tricks others as is so often the case.

This myth has a decided coastal tinge, as is shown by the location of the action and also by the kelp binding-material.

69—COYOTE IS TRICKED BY SAPSUCKER
(Page 266)

I. Sapsucker instructs Coyote how to make string and weave a head-net, but Coyote is incredulous, so Sapsucker tells Coyote to use pitch and dust to hold his hair in place.

Coyote does so and joins in a fanning contest with the result that his head hurns and people make fun of him.

II. Sapsucker correctly instructs Coyote in the method of getting wood, but, on account of Coyote's incredulity, Sapsucker gives him wrong information. On the fourth day Coyote falls and is badly hurt. He is carried home and his wife mourns over his bad luck. To this he objects.

III. The people of the village hear someone approaching singing. Coyote and his wife are starving and are coming to dance. Their costumes are made of flowers, leaves, etc. The people bring food and Coyote eats prodigiously.

IV. Falcon is untrue to his wife, Fish Hawk, who leaves. She arrives at Kūcádanōyō when a dance is in progress. Next day she travels northward arriving at Sun-man's house, north of Witter Springs. Falcon follows her, springs the rattlesnake trap at the door and enters.

Kī'lak who lives with Sun-man challenges Falcon to a shooting contest. Falcon is protected by his bead-grinding stone and finally kills Kī'lak. Next evening Sun-man and Falcon contest and Sun-man is killed. The people rejoice at Sun-man's death.

V. Barn Owl loses his head in gambling. When Falcon tries to pull his head off he finds it impossible. The head snaps back down into Barn Owl's shoulders. Hence his present form.

VI. Wildcat is successful at hunting. By her nudity she attracts deer. This offends her husband, Fox, who leaves home, taking his son. He stops at two villages. He meets Wasp and procures wood for him. He journeys to a village in Long Valley and then to Sacramento Valley. Here he gives the boy to Crane's wife. He meets Frog. Finally he visits the Mosquito village.

He reaches the coast, builds a canoe of kelp and crosses to a Sea Lion island, where he is killed in a fanning contest.

The Sea Lions escape through holes in the floor.

NOTES

This is an excellent example of a composite myth.

It starts off with the tricking of Coyote by Sapsucker, first in the use of pitch in his hair and again in wood gathering.

Next, Coyote and his wife come to a village and dance for food. Their costumes consist of flowers, leaves and branches and the dancing is in a summer dance-house of brush.

Next comes the incident where a wife leaves home because of the infidelity of her husband. The husband pursues his wife and kills Kī'lak and Sun-man in contests. These two live together at a point near Witter Springs.

Here we see Sun-man as a cannibal but on friendly terms with his neighbors, a most unusual feature.

Next Barn Owl loses his head in gambling. Hence the present form of Barn Owl.

Finally Fox becomes incensed at his wife's way of hunting and leaves, journeying very far and having many experiences.

He meets Wasp and cuts wood for him.

He builds a kelp canoe and visits the Sea Lions' island where he is killed in fanning. The Sea Lions escape through holes in the floor.

The use of a bead-polishing stone first to rid the door trap of its snakes and then as a breast-plate protection in a shooting contest is quite interesting.

70—OSPREY AND MINK FOOL COYOTE

(Page 280)

I. Osprey tricks Coyote into breaking his own leg. Coyote heals his leg and departs.

II. Mink tricks Coyote into burning off all of his own hair.

NOTES

In both incidents in this myth Coyote is shown to be a credulous and foolish fellow and is ridiculed. In each case he cures himself and leaves in disgust.

71—OAK-BALL, HAWK AND OWL TRICK COYOTE

(Page 281)

I. Coyote tries to float like Oak-ball, but is killed. He is revivified by Blue Jay.

II. Hawk tricks Coyote in catching ground squirrels. Coyote is bitten by a rattlesnake and dies but is revivified by Blue Jay.

III. Coyote tries to imitate Owl, but a tree closes and imprisons him. He dies. Red-headed-woodpecker opens the tree and throws out Coyote's bones. Blue Jay revivifies him.

NOTES

In each of these myth incidents Coyote is killed by trying to imitate someone else. In each instance Coyote is revivified by Blue Jay.

In the last incident an unusual element is introduced when Woodpecker opens up the tree in which Coyote's bones are imprisoned. The closing of the tree on Coyote is in itself a very unusual incident.

72—COYOTE FALLS FROM A TREE

(Page 283)

Woodcock is very successful in getting wood and tells Coyote how to do it. Coyote fails and is seriously injured by falling from a tree.

Frog, Coyote's wife, bewails his fate, but Coyote upbraids her for not singing about his success.

Lizard makes love to Frog while Coyote is ill.

NOTES

Here Coyote appears as a foolish person, unable to accomplish what he sets out to do.

The love-making of Lizard and Coyote's wife, during Coyote's illness, is an unusual element.

Woodcock is rarely mentioned in Pomo myths.

73—GRAY SQUIRREL TEACHES COYOTE HOW TO RUN UP A TREE
(Page 285)

Coyote envies Gray Squirrel her ability to run up a tall tree and to jump from tree to tree. He tries to do the same but fails and is killed.

NOTES

This very short myth is not of the usual trickster-tricked variety for, as here given, Coyote gets no incorrect instructions. It merely demonstrates his inability to do everything that he sees others doing. The mention of Gray Squirrel's clapping her hands really refers to the chattering so commonly heard from squirrels in trees.

74—COYOTE IS TRICKED BY LITTLE BIRDS
(Page 285)

Birds trick Coyote who tries to imitate them by jumping into the water, but the water disappears and Coyote lands in the mud so that only his hind legs are visible. He calls upon Kū'ksū to save him. Buzzard dresses fully in his doctor's suit and doctors Coyote. Coyote recognizes the deception. Next comes Blue Jay and then Crow with the same result. Finally Gī'lak, the proper or real Kū'ksū, comes and saves Coyote.

NOTES

Here Coyote is tricked by birds into jumping into mud.

He calls upon Kū'ksū to save him. Three impostors, Buzzard, Blue Jay and Crow, come but finally the real Kū'ksū, Gī'lak, comes and cures Coyote.

75—COYOTE IMITATES THE WILLOW
(Page 288)

Coyote is tricked into trying to imitate Willow, but is drowned. He is revivified by Blue Jay.

NOTES

Here Coyote envies Willow who stands out in the water and trembles constantly. He is tricked into trying to do the same thing. As usual he dies and is revivified by Blue Jay.

76—BLUE JAY KILLS COYOTE'S MOTHER WITH A HOT ROCK

(Page 288)

Blue Jay kills Coyote's mother with a hot rock, and misinforms Coyote as to how it is used. Coyote tries to retaliate but is himself killed. Blue Jay revivifies Coyote.

NOTES

This short myth shows Coyote as a credulous fool who follows instructions in the use of a hot rock and is killed as a result.

77—COYOTE GETS MAGIC BLACK BREAD FROM THE SUN

(Page 289)

I. Coyote learns how to snare birds from an expert hunter. As usual he gets things mixed and succeeds in catching only one bird. This he roasts.

II. He calls to Sun for some black bread. Sun throws down a small piece of bread which makes a great noise as it falls through the air. Coyote tries to pick it up but the bread moves away. Coyote finally succeeds in catching the bread by driving it into a net made of tule. He and the Bird-people find that this bread is not good. The people throw the bread into the water and leave.

Coyote slips away and tries to get the bread again. He is discovered and is killed by the Bird-people. Then the Turtle brothers are told to take care of the bread. They dive down and hide most of the bread, bringing up only a small piece of it. For this the people decide to kill the Turtles. They propose to burn them but are warned that if they do so the smoke will kill all the people. Finally they decide to drown the Turtles, who are enabled thereby to escape. Blue Jay revivifies Coyote. He then goes around and finds that the birds are all afraid of him.

III. Coyote finally induces them to come out and play with him. Each bird gives him a feather. With these he covers his body and learns to fly, but in attempting to escape from Hawk he flies into a bush and loses an eye. He makes a bead eye for himself and leaves that place.

NOTES

Coyote is shown here throughout as a dupe, first in snaring birds, then in getting black bread from the sun, and finally in trying to learn to fly.

The people are tricked by the Turtle brothers, whom they try to drown.

Coyote, as usual, is revivified by the cry of Blue Jay, to which he objects.

His ability to replace one of his eyes by an eye which he makes from a shell bead is interesting.

78—TULE BOY

(Page 292)

Coyote is tricked into rubbing pitch into his hair to make it look nice. He joins in a fanning contest and the pitch takes fire. He plunges into the water but all his hair is burned off and he becomes very ill. His wife, Frog, doctors and cures him.

NOTES

This myth again shows Coyote as one who is incredulous and is easily duped. The point of chief interest, however, in this myth is the presence of Tsĭkólkol, a character usually placed in the second Upper World and depicted as having nothing whatever to do with earthly matters. Here he is depicted as an ordinary mortal net-weaver.

79—COYOTE BRAGS OF HIS WEALTH

(Page 293)

Coyote and Kalkalmáptseu brag about their wealth. The latter defecates pure beads and proves his superiority.

NOTES

Here Coyote appears as a fool on account of his bragging and because of the superiority of his opponent.

80—WOODRAT, THE TRICKSTER

(Page 294)

I. Woodrat is refused food by his sister, Woodpecker, whose husband is very stingy.

II. Woodrat finds Pine-nut-man who digs a hole in which to kill Woodrat but Woodrat leaves a token and escapes. Pine-nut-man tracks Woodrat and his body is pierced as he tries to enter the dance-house. All the pine-nuts run out of his body. Gray Squirrel recognizes pine-nuts as a food.

III. Woodrat reaches the Crow village. They are all blind. They are deer-hunting so Woodrat tricks them by rolling a boulder down the hillside. Toad, a one-eyed old woman, discovers the deception and warns the Crows. Woodrat next eats the food of the Crow-people. Toad again gives warning. Next Woodrat joins the men in a fanning contest. Toad again gives warning. Finally Woodrat steals all the food at the feast of the blind crows, but is apprehended by Toad.

When the Crows attempt to kill Woodrat he places their own chief so that he is killed while he himself finally escapes.

IV. Woodrat arrives at a point where lives a woman who induces him to climb a magic tree. Woodrat, however, escapes, returns and burns the woman and her son.

V. Woodrat meets the swinging girls, escapes their swing and kills one of them with it.

VI. Woodrat encounters Fire-man and finally kills him.

VII. Woodrat encounters Basket-people and destroys them.

VIII. Woodrat encounters Putrid-man and kills him.

IX. Woodrat encounters Spider-woman and kills her.

X. Sharp-heel is next killed.

XI. Woodrat is joined by Mouse. They overcome Bear by means of dummies.

XII. Woman kills deer with magic pestle. Mouse causes pestle to break. This offends Woodrat, who leaves, followed by mouse.

XIII. Woodrat and Mouse are transformed.

NOTES

This myth is a most extraordinary one in that it contains such a great variety of incidents.

Here we find the refusal of food because of stinginess, the use of tokens and dummies in tricking an adversary, the growing tree and the magic swing, both of which are outwitted by the hero, and the use of a magic pestle in killing deer.

Then there are a number of very unusual characters: Pine-nut-man, the blind Crows, the one-eyed Toad-woman, Fire-man, Baskets, Putrid-man, Spider-woman, Sharp-heel.

This is the only myth thus far encountered where Mouse appears.

Usually Coyote appears as the great trickster but here Woodrat takes over this role completely.

81—WOODRAT KILLS MORNING-STAR WITH A MAGIC SWING

(Page 305)

Morning-star protects his daughter with thorns but Woodrat finally marries her.

Morning-star challenges Woodrat to a contest in his magic swing. Morning-star is finally killed by his own swing.

NOTES

Here the jealous father-in-law protects his daughters with thorns instead of rattlesnakes. The successful suitor overcomes this obstacle but is subjected to the swing trial by his father-in-law. He finally succeeds in killing the father-in-law with his own swing.

A most interesting feature is Morning-star's game-fence with which he catches people. All nimble persons escape but he captures the old and crippled ones.

82—SKUNK KILLS DEER WITH HER SCENT

(Page 306)

Skunk tricks Deer and kills him with her scent. When the fourth deer becomes suspicious and refuses to go to doctor Skunk she goes over to the home of the deer and kills them all with her scent.

NOTES

This myth emphasizes the great death-dealing power of the scent of the skunk.

83—THE GROWING ROCK

(Page 307)

I. The Bluebird children fall asleep on a rock which Crow causes to grow up into the sky. Various people try to climb this rock to rescue them. Finally Measuring Worm succeeds, and is honored and rewarded.

II. All the fires in the village had gone out during this rescue. Bat insists that he can see fire. Oak-ball also sees fire. Many people try to get fire but fail. Finally Jackrabbit steals fire and eventually hides it by sitting upon it, hence his white rump.

III. Bluebird journeys to the south, and the boys track her. Blue Jay cares for the boys. Crow befriends them and provides them with bows and arrows. Arriving at Mink's house they are given more arrows. The boys practice at war. Arriving at Chicken Hawk's house the boys are given still more arrows. The younger brother kills a deer and a grizzly and they make quivers out of the skins. The boys encounter Wind-man, who demonstrates his power. They journey still farther toward the south and meet Stone-woman, and here they find their mother. The younger brother kills her. The boys are pursued by a magic basket and a magic pestle. They escape through a stone wall which closes on and kills Stone-woman. They contest with Arrow-man, and kill him. Then they are attacked by a whole village and kill all. Then they return home.

NOTES

This composite myth is most interesting because of the range it covers. First there is the rescue by Measuring Worm of the children who are carried up into the sky by the growing rock. Next comes the theft of fire by Jackrabbit and finally the circumstantial and detailed account of the journey of the Bluebird brothers in search of their mother.

The younger of these brothers is always the victorious contestant. Here also we have the escape of these boys from a magic basket and a magic pestle and their escape through a stone wall which opens and closes.

84—QUAIL ASCENDS INTO THE SKY ON A MAGIC CANE

(Page 315)

Quail goes out hunting clover. A magic cane comes down from the heavens and when she takes hold of the cane it transports her up through the Zenith Gate and to the house of Kī'lak. The people hunt for her and find a blood-red line leading from the point where she left to the Zenith Gate.

Coyote causes a magic tower to grow up to the Zenith Gate and within this the Meadowlark boys ascend into the Upper world and then journey to Kī'lak's house.

Quail springs the rattlesnake trap in the tunnel of Kī'lak's house so that the boys may enter safely. She then hides them until Kī'lak returns. When Kī'lak returns with a victim he throws it into the house through the smoke-hole. Blue-fly breaks its shin-bones and sucks out the blood and marrow. Kī'lak's return is indicated by a token.

The Meadowlark boys contest with Kī'lak and kill him. Then they carry their mother back home with them.

NOTES

In this myth we have a very detailed description of Ki'lak's house and of the trap in its tunnel. Also of Ki'lak's method of procedure in handling his victims.

Particularly full is the description of the part played by Blue-fly. Here also we have two magic methods of ascending from the earth to the Upper World, one by means of a magic cane which takes Quail up to Ki'lak's house, and the other by means of a magic tower which enables the Meadowlark brothers to fly up.

85—A MAGIC TREE KILLS FALCON

(Page 319)

Falcon's wife is Quail. With them lives his sister-in-law. In this same village live Coyote and Cĕ'tata, who is a nobleman.

Falcon goes to catch some doves which live in a magic tree which grows to a prodigious height. Falcon is blown out of the tree and killed.

Falcon's wife finds some of his hair from which Coyote brings Falcon back to life again.

The people are celebrating this occasion when Meadowlark objects to the odor of the dead and Falcon leaves.

Blue Jay is angered and strikes at Meadowlark with a club, cutting off part of his tail.

NOTES

In this myth we see Falcon killed by a magic growing tree, which carries him up to a prodigious height. A strong wind blows him out and blows him to bits.

Coyote revivifies him from a little of his hair, using the "water in a basket" method.

Meadowlark objects to the odor of the dead and has his own tail cut short. Had he not raised this objection people would now come to life four days after death.

We have a fairly detailed reference to the nobility.

86—SWAN FISHES IN HER STONE CANOE

(Page 322)

Swan lives at Sulphur Bank with her husband, Bear, and with her two daughters (Swans).

Swan has a magic stone canoe with which she fishes. She starts at the upper end of the lake and with a tremendous fish-net she fishes all the way down to the narrows leading from Clear Lake into East and Lower lakes.

Falcon crosses Clear Lake on a fog bridge from Mt. Kanaktai to Bald Hill and then journeys down to the home of Swan where he marries her two daughters.

Bear tries repeatedly to kill Falcon by setting traps for him. Falcon escapes every time and finally he tires of these attempts upon his life and returns home, again crossing by means of the fog bridge, but he dies before reaching his own home.

NOTES

In this myth we have two very interesting incidents — the crossing of Clear Lake by means of the fog bridge and the use of a magic stone canoe. Minor incidents are the several attempts upon the life of Falcon by Bear, and the upbraiding of Bear by Swan. We have also the use of a magic fish-net in conjunction with the stone canoe.

87—BEAR KILLS HER OWN DAUGHTER-IN-LAW, DEER
(Page 327)

I. Falcon gives rancid meat to his mother, Bear. She becomes angry and tries to kill Falcon. Tree opens and receives Falcon. She then kills Deer while removing vermin from her hair. The Deer boys allow a basket to float down-stream. Bear follows it.

II. The Deer boys kill the Bear boys in a fanning contest. Bear pursues the Deer boys, who escape toward the east. Net-maker, Log and small birds try to protect the boys, but Bear gains on them. The elder brother then creates Blue Lakes to impede Bear's progress. Arriving at Clear Lake the boys cross by the Crane's-neck bridge. When Bear attempts to cross they kill her with a hot rock.

III. The boys journey eastward in quest of their mother. They contest with and kill a poison-man. The Loon-people take the boys across the lake, passing them from island to island. They finally reach the landing place of the Sun. The mother of the boys conceals them in Sun-man's house. He knows they are there and proposes a race. They finally kill Sun-man with their magic bows.

IV. The boys then carry their mother homeward but allow her to touch the ground and she disappears. Two grape-vines now mark the spot where this happened.

NOTES

This is a rather fully detailed account of the Deer and Bear children. It has some incidents of special note.

Bear does not succeed in killing Falcon. His grandfather, Tree, opens and receives him. The Bear children are set up in the smoke-hole as if alive. The elder of the Bear boys carries his younger brother, who serves as a lookout to the rear. The boys enlist the aid of a net-maker, a log and some small birds. Bear questions these three but they keep the secret of the Deer boys. When Bear tries to kill the small birds they are so small that they easily escape between her teeth. The crossing by the Crane bridge and the killing of Bear with the hot rock are the usual thing.

We next see these boys provided with two magic stone bows. Anything is caused to burn up simply by pointing the bows at the object to be destroyed. The long journey in relays across the lake takes these boys over to the extreme eastern edge of the world where Sun resides.

The contest with Sun this time takes the form of a foot-race. Sun is killed with the magic bows.

The bringing of their mother back is finally unsuccessful because they allow her to touch the ground whereupon she vanishes. This is an unusual feature.

88—THE DEER AND THE BEAR CHILDREN

(Page 334)

Deer is trapping birds and small mammals and gives his mother, Bear, some of the poorer meat. She becomes incensed at this deception and lies in wait for Deer along the trail and kills him.

Bear then invites Deer's wife, Wildcat, to go out to gather greens. Bear asks Wildcat to remove the vermin from her hair. Wildcat finds that this vermin is not the ordinary kind but consists of lizards and snakes which she throws away and does not eat. This incenses Bear and she undertakes to remove the vermin from Wildcat's head and kills Wildcat by decapitating her.

Wildcat has left a token at her house to notify her children when she is killed.

Pursuant to their mother's instructions the younger of the Deer brothers gets a fine basket and allows it to float down the river. Bear pursues this basket and while she is gone the Deer boys kill the two Bear girls.

The Deer boys then leave home, journeying in each of the cardinal directions for some distance. It turns red wherever they walk. Finally they place tokens in the four points of the compass to answer for them when they are called and, taking with them a magic medicine given them by Owl, they start on a long journey toward the south.

On feathers their grandfather blows them far to the south. They reach a point on the creek opposite Crane's village. He helps them across. Bear pursues them. Crane kills Bear by throwing her off of the bridge which is made of his neck.

Flea sings for the dance while the Deer boys are playing outside. The younger brother hears his mother's voice over in the east and the two brothers journey thither to rescue their mother whom they find decapitated in Sun-man's house. They attempt to carry her back home but contrary to instructions they allow her to touch the ground and she disappears.

NOTES

This is a very full and detailed myth of the adventures of the Deer and Bear children. Quite prominent here are the tokens, one of which advises the Deer boys of their mother's death and the others answer for these boys when they are pursued by Bear. The Deer boys kill the Bear girls in revenge and do this by a regular fanning contest, something which is never indulged in by women in real life.

Very unusual features are the "feather of safety", the lengthening of the day by a wish, the introduction of the character "Grandmother Flea", who is a great singer, the headless-woman ghost, and the penalty for touching the ground.

The grandfather, Putrid-man, places the boys on feathers and blows them in the direction in which they wish to travel. In fact the grandfather assists the Deer boys at every turn in killing the Bear girls, and in making their escape.

Crane uses his neck as a bridge, here quite fully described, and succeeds in killing Bear.

The Deer boys go to the house of Sun-man to rescue their mother. They find her there, a headless ghost, and in attempting to bring her home they allow her to touch the ground and she disappears.

In this myth there is very little given in the way of description of the house of Sun-man and nothing is said concerning the people inhabiting that house, or of a contest between Sun-man and the visitors.

The use of numbers is worthy of notice. There are two each of the Deer and Bear children. The Deer boys place two sticks in each of the cardinal directions at their play ground to serve as tokens. Bear goes out four times to see Deer's snares before she kills him.

The indestructibility of Putrid-man is emphasized.

89—THE THUNDER AND BEAR CHILDREN

(Page 344)

I. Bear's son, Thunder, gives her bad meat. Her children discover this deception and Bear becomes angry. Leaving a dummy, she herself goes out to Thunder's traps and kills him.

Thunder's wife knows what happened' by the action of a token left by Thunder.

Thunder's wife, Deer, and Bear louse each other and Bear kills Deer, taking her eyes for food.

Another token indicates to Deer's children that their mother is dead. They escape toward the west and are pursued by Bear. Their grandfather, Blue Heron, allows them to pass safely across the ocean on his neck. He also offers to take Bear across but when she reaches the middle he throws her into the ocean, where she drowns.

The children return and the girl hears her mother crying over in the east. The children journey thither meeting a mouthless man on the way.

They finally reach the village of the Sun-people where they find their mother, who is now headless.

When Sun-man returns the boy kills him with hot rocks which burn him almost completely.

II. The Crow brothers finally place the sun in the heavens.

The boy attempts to carry his mother back to the west, grows tired, puts down his burden and Deer turns into a rock.

NOTES

In this myth we have certain features not found in other versions. Bear uses a dummy to deceive Thunder. In his endeavor to escape Thunder runs into a hollow tree and then into a hollow rock. Neither closes and protects him so that Bear finally kills him. There is no recovery of Thunder's remains. A token gives notice of Thunder's death. When Deer is killed another token notifies her children. The only parts of Deer taken by Bear are her eyes which are eaten by Bear. There is no retaliation by the Deer children. They simply flee. This time they escape by means of the Crane bridge to the western shore of the ocean. Bear is drowned by falling from the Crane bridge. We find here that the Deer children are a boy and a girl and the Bear children are two girls.

When the Deer children journey eastward in search of their mother they encounter a mouthless man.

Their mother is found to be headless. Sun-man produces light by opening his mouth and darkness by closing it. The Deer children kill Sun-man by throwing hot rocks into his mouth. This causes his body to burn up almost completely. Finally someone puts out this fire with water, thus saving a small bit of Sun-man's body, which is placed in the sky and becomes the sun.

In taking their mother home the Deer children allow her to touch the ground and she is transformed into a rock.

90—GRIZZLY BEAR KILLS HER DAUGHTER-IN-LAW
(Page 350)

Deer deceives his mother, Bear, by giving her inferior meat. Bear inspects Deer boy's teeth and discovers the deception. She goes out to a snare, digs a pit, secretes herself here and kills Deer.

When she arrives home she cooks venison and gives a shoulder to one of Deer's sons.

Meadowlark chides the boy for gnawing his own father's bones. Bear tries to kill Meadowlark but only chops off his tail.

Bear cleans vermin out of Deer-woman's hair and kills her. Deer's head pronounces a curse upon Bear.

Meadowlark advises the Deer boys how to escape. Bear gives the boys a sun-basket which they set adrift in the river. Bear pursues it to the ocean.

The Deer boys journey northward. They meet Wasp, who is cutting down a tree with an elk-horn wedge.

Next they meet a man burning a log in two.

Next they come to the great stream at the northern edge of the world. Crane makes a bridge of his neck and the boys cross over. There they find Yellowhammer.

Bear pursues the boys. She comes to Wasp and Tsaṯī'. Both deny that they have seen the boys. She kills both but each came to life again. Finally she comes to Crane who puts his neck bridge across for her. She crosses with mouth open and eyes closed. Yellowhammer kills Bear with a hot rock.

NOTES

In this rather abbreviated tale of the Deer and Bear children we find Meadowlark chiding the Deer children for eating the flesh of their father and then advising them how they may escape. There is no retaliation by the Deer boys. They flee northward to the end of the world. Here we see Wasp chopping down a tree with an elk-horn wedge and Tsaṯī' burning a log in two. These are two unusual incidents.

When Bear crosses the Crane bridge she is admonished, not only to close her eyes, but also to keep her mouth open. It is Yellowhammer who heats the rock and kills Bear.

There is a total lack of tokens in this version.

Revivification is found in the case of Wasp and Tsati' The Deer boys do not return home but continue to reside at the northern extremity of the world.

91—THE RACE BETWEEN MUDHEN AND OTHER BIRDS
(Page 354)

The Bird-people engage in a race around the shores of Clear Lake and its associated lakes. Two of each species of bird enter the race and at first the Mud-hens are left far behind. However, they eventually win the race.

Blue Heron is stationed at the foot of Mt. Kanaktai to announce the progress of the race. He shouts his announcements very loudly and the jar made by his voice causes the eastern side of the mountain to break off in great boulders, which accounts for the precipitous eastern slope of this mountain and the great boulders along the shore of the lake at its foot.

NOTES

In this myth we have a very detailed account of the race of the Bird-people around the shore of Clear Lake. The names of the various points they pass and the exact progress of the race are carefully detailed by the narrator.

Here Mud-hen, who is an extremely slow-moving person, finally wins the race.

The most striking feature of this myth is the manner in which it accounts for the precipitous eastern side of Mt. Kanaktai and for the boulders at the foot of the precipice. These were caused by the loud voice of Blue Heron as he announced the progress of the race.

92—THE RACE BETWEEN DEER AND MUD-HEN
(Page 355)

At a gathering, Deer boasts of his ability as a foot-racer. He is finally challenged by Mud-hen. Goose is stationed on the top of Mt. Kanaktai to announce the progress of the race. Mud-hen finally wins and Deer is so chagrined that he offers to forfeit his own horns and hide. Mud-hen is a very generous man and refuses them.

NOTES

This myth is one showing that boasting is a very bad thing and that a swift man like Deer can be outdistanced by a slow and awkward fellow like Mud-hen.

93—WOLF KILLS DEER BY MAGIC

(Page 356)

During a famine Chicken Hawk is too famished to move. Wolf kills Deer by magic. After three days Chicken Hawk grows stronger. He becomes suspicious, watches his wife, and is angered by her actions. He leaves home and journeys eastward. His wife follows and tries to induce him to return but he rebuffs her. On his return next day he avoids his wife, collects his possessions and journeys northward. The people present him with beads which he places in his magic sack.

Again Wolf comes to try to induce her husband to return, but without success. Again he journeys northward where he receives more beads which he places in his magic sack, and again his wife comes after him. He journeys on to another village where the same thing happens again, but this time his wife brings such fine presents that he returns home with her.

Chicken Hawk finally recovers from the famine and is able to hunt in the regular way.

NOTES

This myth is chiefly notable for the detail with which the journeys of Chicken Hawk are given. An interesting feature is that he journeys east and then returns home to get his bead-sack, etc., before making his main journey which is toward the north. This is a tiny magic sack. When anything is placed in this sack it is immediately transferred to the home of the owner.

Oak-ball is here shown as a far-seeing lookout.

The repeated visits of Hawk's wife, each time bringing presents of increasing value are fruitless, until finally she brings such fine presents that Hawk consents to return.

Here again we find famine as the initial cause of action in this myth.

94—PANTHER'S WIFE KILLS DEER BY MAGIC

(Page 360)

Panther's wife goes hunting. By divesting herself of her clothing and singing a magic hunting song she succeeds in killing deer. Curiosity eventually prompts her husband to spy upon her. He becomes angry at her methods and leaves home. She obliges him to take their son along. He gives the boy to a woman in another village.

He journeys on until he reaches the coast. There he makes a canoe and journeys out to an island offshore. The people here build such a hot fire in the dance-house that everything and everyone is burned up.

NOTES

This rather pointless story recounts how Panther's wife does the hunting and secures deer by a magic song sung while she lies divested of her clothing. This procedure meets with disapproval from her husband who leaves and after making a very long journey, arrives at a village located on an island. The sweat-house finally burns and destroys everything in the village.

It is quite evident that this is an incomplete myth. Other versions of a similar myth recounts the pursuit of Panther by his wife and her endeavors to induce him to return. Furthermore the journey out to the island in the ocean indicates that this element is really intended for the journey to the Sea Lion island which is fully detailed in myth No. 69 of this series.

95—BLACK HAWK LEAVES HOME BUT IS INDUCED TO RETURN
(Page 363)

Black Hawk is very ill and weak. His wife, Panther, kills Deer for him by her charms. Upon the fourth time he discovers her methods, becomes jealous and journeys eastward to a big village.

After trying four times, Panther induces her husband to return home.

Shortly he dresses for dancing and journeys northward to a great village. The people give him beads which he places in his magic purse and journeys farther.

Again after four trials his wife induces him to return home.

NOTES

Here we have in rather abbreviated form about the same tale told in myths 93 and 94.

Here, however, we find that Black Hawk is induced to return two different times, and that it takes four trials in each case before he can be brought back.

96—THE PEOPLE ARE UNABLE TO KILL TURTLE
(Page 368)

Turtle goes visiting but the people capture him and debate as to how he shall be killed. He warns them not to burn him as it will bring death to everyone. They then shoot at him but the arrows glance off and only make streaks on his shell.

Then they throw him into the deepest pool to drown him. Turtle laughs at them as he makes his escape.

NOTES

This is an etiological tale accounting for the streaks on Turtle's shell and also a trickster tale which shows Turtle escaping by duping the people.

97—TURTLE TRICKS THE PEOPLE

(Page 369)

Turtle, who is caught shooting people, is about to be put to death and cautions his executioners not to burn him or to mash him up because it will kill everyone in the village. They finally decide to throw Turtle into the water, to which he agrees. He, of course, escapes completely.

NOTES

This is a simple trickster story in which Turtle tricks people into trying to drown him and thus escapes death.

98—FALCON DIES AND RETURNS TO LIFE

(Page 370)

Pelican, who is chief, is deposed and Falcon is installed in his place. Pelican is a "Bear Doctor" and kills Falcon. The people finally discover Pelican's guilt through his actions and the presence of some of Falcon's blood and flesh in Pelican's teeth. They kill Pelican.

People place a bead belt in the door of the assembly house. Upon this the returning Falcon enters. Meadowlark objects to the odor of the dead. His tail is clipped short. His objection makes death permanent.

NOTES

Here we find certain unusual features. Pelican is brought in as a character. Bear Doctors are mentioned. Methods of cremation and of detection of crime are detailed. Also the placement of a bead belt at the door as a means of bringing a returning spirit back.

Meadowlark's objection to the return of the dead and the penalty of having his tail clipped off are frequently met with.

99—WOODRAT IS REFUSED FOOD BY HIS BROTHER-IN-LAW

(Page 372)

Woodrat is refused food by his stingy brother-in-law, Red-headed-woodpecker.

Woodrat had washed his hands preparatory to eating. Hence his hands are now very white. Woodrat weeps and therefore has small, reddish eyes.

NOTES

This is an etiological tale accounting for Woodrat's white hands and for his small, reddish eyes.

100—WASP REFUSES WOODRAT FOOD

(Page 373)

Wasp refuses Woodrat food, and says that he himself never eats. In evidence he shows how thin his legs and body are.

NOTES

An etiological tale accounting for the thinness of Wasp.

101—THE GIRL WHO MARRIED RATTLESNAKE

(Page 373)

Rattlesnake sees a girl gathering clover. He transforms himself into a young man, goes to her house and marries her. Eventually he takes her to his home. She prevents her children from biting people. Eventually she is transformed into a rattlesnake herself.

NOTES

This short myth shows transformation through long association. This girl lives with the rattlesnakes and finally is herself transformed into one.

102—WASP AND WILDCAT

(Page 374)

Wasp in trying to burn down a tree. It is really a weed, not a tree, but to the tiny Wasp it is just the same as a tree would be to a man.

Wildcat comes by and helps him by cutting down a whole armful of these weeds for him.

In return Wasp gives Wildcat the information he desires.

NOTES

This is a minor incident in a long and detailed myth of the wanderings of Wildcat.

103—COYOTE KILLS TWO FAWNS

(Page 375)

Coyote goes hunting with a deer mask and kills two fawns. On his way home he calls his wife, Bullfrog, to come out and see him bring in the game. He then cooks the fawns and the two eat them.

NOTES

This very short myth shows Coyote as a braggart, boasting over the "big deer" he has killed, whereas they are two helpless little fawns.

104—MOUNTAIN-LION GOES HUNTING
(Page 376)

Mountain Lion climbs up into a tree to lie in wait for deer. A spring gushes from the side of this tree. The water of this spring changes its nature four times.

NOTES

This fragmentary tale recalls the more elaborate ones of the redwood tree over on the coast which has a spring running from its side at a point many feet from the ground. See myths Nos. 50 and 51, pages 226 and 231.

105—THE ORIGIN OF THE SUL-KE OR VULTURE DANCE

(Page 376)

A large vulture is sitting on the limb of a redwood. While his wife dances and sings at the base of the tree, a man climbs the tree. On the fourth trial he succeeds. The vulture flies away with him to another redwood which splits open to admit them. Then it closes. After a long battle inside this tree the bird is finally killed.

After four days the man returns with the vulture completely dried and brings with him the Vulture dance.

Then he travels about introducing this new dance everywhere.

NOTES

This myth gives a rather circumstantial account of the origin of the Vulture dance and of its introduction among the people of this region.

106—THE ORIGIN OF THE LEHUYA-KE OR KA-TCAHA-KE, THE WHISKEY DANCE

(Page 379)

A man remains at the funeral pyre of his brother until the spirit rises. Then he follows it to the land of the dead. The ghosts teach him the Lehuya-ke.

NOTES

This short myth accounts for the origin of one of the Pomo dances.

THE USE OF NUMBERS IN POMO MYTHS

Among almost every people there is something in the nature of a sacred number, and this is very likely to be used frequently in myths. Among the Pomo, this number is four. It is used incessantly. Four persons, like the Gilaks or the Thunders, are encountered in a contest. In making a journey, four bears are encountered, or similiar experiences are met with four successive times before success is attained. Four mice assist Coyote in stealing the sun, which is kept in a bag of four thicknesses of elk hide. A person, on arrival at a ceremonial house, must perform a succession of movements in groups of four before and upon entering. There are four smoke-holes in the house of Gilak. So we might compound example after example of the employment of the number four throughout Pomo mythology. It is the most frequently occurring and important number found.

A very marked feature of Pomo mythology also is duality. In fact, its use is only a little less frequent than that of four. We frequently find two persons undertaking a certain thing instead of one. They are usually two brothers or two sisters. The two Thrasher brothers are watchmen, two Crows put the sun up in the sky, two Bluebird brothers are carried up by the growing rock and have a long series of other experiences. Coyote makes two rattlesnakes out of rawhide, and regurgitates two abalone-shell balls for his two children, who are then killed in the east, where Coyote finds the sun sack made out of their two skins. A myriad of such examples of duality, particularly in the characters themselves, is found.

One of the finest examples of duality among the Pomo has been pointed out by de Angulo and Freeland. This is commented upon at length elsewhere in this paper.[244]

Other numbers also are used but in much fewer instances. Three, five, six, twenty and forty are each encountered upon a very few occasions. Sometimes they occur in connections which cause us to wonder whether these were really the original numbers employed in each of these cases. However, they are now used and must be accepted at face value at this time.

In the case of eight, which is double the sacred number, we find a dozen or so places where this number is employed, and in such connections as to leave no doubt that their use is intentional.

One interesting feature is the variation in the numbers used in the several variants of the same idea. For instance in the rodent allies, the mice who assisted Coyote in his Theft of the Sun, we find in the several versions of this myth incident the numbers one, two, four, and eight used. There seems therefore to be no rigid rule in respect to the use of such numbers, the changing of such features being apparently within the province of the individual narrator.

The basic numbers are however unquestionably two and four, wherever a number greater than one is deemed necessary, and the abundant use of duality is a rather unique feature of Pomo Mythology.[245]

CATCHWORDS IN POMO MYTHOLOGY

In order to facilitate comparisons of the mythologies of different tribes it is very desirable to have short, easily handled *catchwords,* or perhaps more properly speaking, *catch phrases,* by which each important element may be designated. Several attempts have been made to work out such lists, notably those by Lowie[246] and by Kroeber.[247]

Some of these are based upon Old World mythology and their application to American Indian mythology is in some instances rather an approximation than an exact application. In preparing the present list of *Catchwords in Pomo Mythology* therefore it has seemed expedient to make certain changes which are, in this particular case more exact

---

[244]See pages 480, 481.
[245]The myths here recorded are from the Northern, Central and Eastern dialectic divisions of the Pomo. It is interesting to note that de Augulo and Freeland have noted this same duality among the Southeastern Pomo also (*See* de Augulo and Freeland, 1928, pp. 249-252).
[246]1909, pp. 24-27.   1910, pp. 332-333.
[247]1909, pp. 222-227.

and more nearly descriptive of the ideas involved. For instance instead of using *Babel* with all its connotation, we have preferred the simple term *Differences in speech*. This much more correctly expresses the simple etiological idea underlying the Pomo element, which merely attempts to account for the fact that different peoples speak differently, and which in no way carries the Biblical notion of Babel. Another good example is the substitution of the term *Ogre's scent* for *Feefofum*.

In the following list of catchwords no attempt is made to list up and account for the minor elemental features of Pomo mythology. Only the major elements are listed. For the sake of convenience, the page reference where some of the examples of these myth elements may be found are here given. This is done despite the fact that these "catchwords" are also included in the index to this work.

CREATION

Under this caption are included also: ideas of remodeling the world; creation of people, animals, plants, implements; the institution of customs; and also transformations.

Earth-diver: An animal is sent to dive for mud, which is transformed into the earth, or with which a mountain is heightened. 127.

Remodeling of the world: A culture here or other person remodels the world or some feature of it; such as the roughness and saltiness of the ocean, forms of mountains, streams, and the like. This is fundamentally an etiological concept. 91, 98, 110, 111, 115, 117, 130, 199, 250.

Water from belly: Water or a lake originates from the pierced or burst belly of one who has over-drunk. 99, 111, 116, 120, 122, 125, 126.

Creation of People: This creation is usually from some pre-existing material, though it may be simply by the will of the creator. Among the Pomo we find people created from wood, feathers, or earth. 49, 59, 65, 67, 73, 75, 80, 83, 100, 110, 112, 117, 119, 126, 130, 165, 170, 179.

Lizard-hand: The human hand is fashioned on the lizard's. 80.

Separation of nations: People are separated into groups and assigned to their localities of abode. 130.

Differences in speech: Differences in speech are accounted for.

An etiological idea. This has been referred to by others as *Babel*.[248] 60, 80.

Creation in a vessel (under cover) : Creation of man or animals, in a basket, from a bundle, or under a blanket. Among the Pomo this is usually accomplished by placing an object (an arrow-head, some hair, or the like) in a basket of water with another basket inverted over it. 204, 321.

Creation of animals: From certain things animals are actually created, in contradistinction to "people transformed into animals." 60, 68, 76, 84, 85, 88, 89, 90, 92, 94, 100, 111, 116, 118, 122, 123, 126, 131, 133, 194, 237.

Creation of plants: Different plants, particularly food-plants, are created; or the culture-hero stipulates what plants may be utilized. 61, 84, 90, 126.

Creation of implements: Implements, weapons and the like are created and given to the people. 121.

Creation of Vermin: Vermin are created from some pre-existing substance, such as seeds or chaff. 112, 119.

Customs instituted: People are instructed in customs to be followed, foods, etc., to be used, and the like. 84, 89, 90, 101, 113, 122, 131, 133, 200, 250.

Medicine practices established: Man is given medicines and instructions in methods of curing illness. 85, 88.

Ceremonies established: Man is given ceremonies and instructions concerning them and the paraphernalia required. 376, 379.

People transformed into animals: A race of "first people" is transformed into animals, either at the direction of some individual, or of its own volition, each individual choosing what he prefers to be. 53, 68, 82, 83, 85, 86, 107, 132, 168, 180, 186, 187, 198, 226, 232, 236, 239, 304.

Transformation, self: A person transforms himself into something else, either animate or inanimate, in order to make a journey, gain admission, or accomplish some other specific purpose. 51, 77, 78, 96, 140, 144, 146, 147, 158, 159, 234, 239, 244, 245, 247, 251, 373, 374.

---

[248]The term, *Babel,* implies a purposeful confusion of tongues in order to confound people. This is not the idea in California mythology. Here it has a much simpler etiological significance. It merely accounts for existing differences in speech, without any idea of the punishment of man.

Transformation of an animal into a man: An animal is transformed into a man or given human attributes. 112, 187.

DESTRUCTION

World-fire: A great conflagration destroys the surface of the earth and its inhabitants. 96, 97, 110, 114, 117, 120, 121, 123-125, 168, 237.

Deluge: A deluge covers the earth and destroys its inhabitants. 127-130, 132, 133, 135.

SUN AND FIRE

Theft of the sun: The earth was formerly in darkness. The sun (luminaries, light) is kept by a foreign people or by the Sun-people. It is stolen for the benefit of the human race. 78, 137, 138, 141, 143, 145, 146, 272.

Sun placed in sky: The placement of the sun in the sky after its theft from its keepers is such a special feature that it deserves separate consideration. 79, 105, 137-139, 141, 147, 349.

Theft of fire: Fire is kept by a foreign people and is stolen by some one for the benefit of man. 127, 135, 309, 310.

DEATH

Death made permanent: Originally someone objects to the return of the dead. When, however, his own relative (usually son) dies he wishes to change the arrangement but is overruled. Thus death is made permanent.[249] A form of the trickster-tricked idea. 92, 118, 249, 322, 372.

Objection to return of dead: A dead person returns but someone objects to the odor of the dead, or to the fact that with this arrangement the world will become overpopulated. 186, 249, 271, 321.

Death thought sleep: A dead person revivified thinks he has only slept. 180, 210, 221, 243, 256, 258, 262, 265, 282, 283, 288, 289, 291.

Revivification: A dead person is revivified from bones or other parts of the body, or by other means. This revivification may be accomplished in any one of the following ways:

---

[249]This is very closely related to the idea carried in "originator of death the first sufferer", but is slightly different.

1. By placing in a stream or lake. 196, 239.

2. By placing in a basket of water. 179, 321.

3. Self revivification. 140, 157, 163, 192, 232, 241, 330, 353.

4. By the call of Blue Jay or other animal. 180, 184, 190, 193, 210, 221, 243, 258, 261, 262, 265, 282, 283, 288, 289, 291.

5. Unintentional. 168, 249, 254.

Dissolution of body. The body of a supernatural being breaks up upon his death. Mountain-man and Obsidian-man are examples. 226, 230, 231.

Purification of dead: The body of a dead man is purified before it can be revivified. 184.

SUPERNATURAL BEINGS

The whole Pomo Mythological world was filled with supernatural beings. No attempt is here made to list these individual beings. They are fully detailed in the section of this paper dealing with the subject of "Supernatural beings" (see pages 21 to 41). The following elemental concepts, however should be noted:

Dug-from-the ground: A person with supernatural powers is dug from the ground. He may be a baby who grows rapidly and attains great power, or he may be, like the Pomo Chub Duck, a person who possesses all his attributes from the first. 119, 162, 248, 252.

Rolling man: A supernatural being who pursues his opponents by rolling along. Among the Pomo this is Rock-man. Closely related to Rolling-head among some other tribes. 231.

Water monster: Being (animate or inanimate) placed in a lake or other body of water to frighten people. 124, 139, 142, 198, 199, 200, 201, 235, 236.

Supernatural serpent: Dragon, giant lizard, horned serpent or other supernatural serpent-like creature. 142, 198, 199, 200, 235, 236.

Supernatural bird: Any giant bird-like creature. Usually steals and often devours people. Among the Pomo these are Gilak, Sun-people, Thunder, Huk, Bird-people. (See these subjects as listed in index.)

Personified sharpness: Obsidian-man among the Pomo personifies the sharpness of this rock. He was miraculously born from an arrow-point taken from Coyote's body. 205, 209, 214, 219, 222, 228.

Sharpened-leg: One who kills people with his sharpened leg or heel. 302.

Underwater abode: Abode of a being is underwater, in the ocean, a lake, or the like, where he has a house similar to those of mortals. 189, 199, 236, 240.

Invulnerable: A person is invulnerable. 202, 205, 208, 209, 210, 220, 226, 231, 232, 241.

JOURNEYS TO SUPERNATURAL PLACES, AND BY SUPERNATURAL MEANS

Journeys to the Upper World: A person makes a journey to the Upper World, usually to rescue a relative who has been stolen by one of the supernatural beings residing in the Upper World. (Sometimes referred to as *Sky Journey*). 81, 82, 97, 110, 113, 115, 120, 123, 178, 187, 315.

Zenith Gate: A gate located in the Zenith by which access to the Upper World is had. 97, 98, 178, 179, 315.

Sky-rope: A rope used to ascend to, or climb from, the sky. Often a basket or net is used in connection with this rope, which is frequently the web of Spider. 82, 97, 98, 110, 113, 115, 120, 123, 178, 179.

Journey to the Outer World: To the end of the known world in any one of the four cardinal directions. 46, 51, 55, 77, 104, 143, 149, 156, 161, 170, 179, 180, 188, 191, 195, 223, 238, 240, 258, 275, 311, 331, 343, 348, 352, 362, 365, 366.

Journey to the land of the dead: A journey made to the abode of the dead. 379.

Magic flight: Journey or escape is made by means of magic means of flight, or by causing by magic, some obstacle to arise in the path of the pursuer. 134, 145, 173, 174, 177, 224, 315, 330, 377.

Magic transportation: A hero or traveler is transported by a magic canoe, cane, or the like. 46, 48, 54, 279, 315, 322.

Feather of safety: The hero extricates himself from danger by wafting away on a magical feather. 340.

Growing tree: People killed by magically growing (swaying or springing) tree.[250] 215, 300, 320, 376, 377.

---

[250]This has been sometimes referred to as "heaven tree". This, however, implies that the tree grows up into the Upper World which is not the case among the Pomo.

Growing rock: A magically growing rock carries people up. 307, 308.

Growing tower: A growing tower (stone) carries people up or enables them to fly up into the sky. 315.

Hidden trail: A person purposely hides or obliterates his trail by walking on the water, over rocks, or otherwise. 183, 296.

Dry crossing: A person, by magic, causes a stream to dry up so that he can cross dry-shod. 183, 184, 212.

MAGIC DEVICES

Magic weapon: Magic sling, arrow, net, wier, or other device which enables a person to secure a large amount of food with little or no effort. 45, 63, 64, 69, 72, 73, 128, 129, 182, 190, 191, 193, 222, 247, 251, 283, 304, 306, 314, 319, 322, 331.

Hot-rock missile: A pursuer or ogre is killed with a heated rock. 166, 167, 331, 349, 354.

Door trap: The door of a building is guarded by a trap, either mechanical or of animate objects such as bears, snakes, or the like. 171-173, 212, 223, 272, 273, 316, 332.

Gate trap: An opening in a great stone wall opens and closes in such a way as to catch people who attempt to pass through. 181, 182, 191, 313.

Closing tree: A hollow tree grows together imprisoning or saving a refugee. 328, 377.

Swing trick or Magic Swing: A magic swing is used to kill victims. Usually a hero kills the owner of the swing with it. 192, 300, 301, 305, 306.

Sham eating: By means of a magic tube, flute, or other implement a hero is able to apparently devour prodigious quantities of food or food which would ordinarily prove fatal. 157, 158, 172, 174, 185, 212, 213, 224.

Magic flute: Music from a magic flute is used to accomplish some purpose, such as the creation of people, etc. 59, 60, 61.

Magic pipe: Tobacco pipe possessing magic powers. 175.

Superior Strength: Hero lifts or carries prodigious weight with ease. 48, 253, 261, 308.

Inexhaustible: A person has a container filled with inexhaustible wealth. 46, 75, 172, 174, 185, 224, 358, 366.

Magic bag: A tiny bag which will hold an impossible quantity. It sometimes has a magic connection with the owner's home and anything placed in it is immediately transported thither. 75, 224, 359.

Diminution of load: Hero causes a great load to contract so that he can carry it with ease. On arrival it returns to its original size. 48, 56, 97, 127, 128, 129, 151, 159, 178, 319, 359, 368.

Diminution of distance: Through a wish or by other means a traveler causes the distance between two places to be shorteneed. 105.

Alteration of time: Through magic, a person causes either the shortening or the lengthening of time, thus causing something to happen more quickly, or allowing a greater length of time to accomplish some purpose, such as a journey. 343.

Crane bridge: Characters cross water on bridge made of the neck or leg of crane. 140, 164, 171, 331, 342, 347, 352.

Fog bridge:[251] Characters cross water on a bridge made of fog. 323, 327.

TOKENS

Life tokens: An object is left which gives a sign when a person dies. 328, 337, 338, 345, 346.

Assistant tokens: An object is left to assist a person on his return journey or to enable him to make his escape. 46-48, 55, 57, 296, 317, 328, 332, 340, 341, 345.

CONTESTS

Advice disregarded: A person making a journey or entering a contest is advised against the procedure. He disregards the advice and succeeds in his perilous undertaking. 161, 170, 172, 180, 211, 267, 332.

Boy and grandmother: All his kin having been destroyed, a boy is brought up by his grandmother alone, finally avenging his relatives. 132, 150, 160.

Powers displayed: Two characters display alternately their powers

---

[251]No mention is made of a rainbow bridge in Pomo mythology, though such a bridge is sometimes encountered in the myths of some other American tribes.

of strength, magic, or the like. One finally overcomes the other. 211, 218, 219, 228, 229.

Hare and tortoise: Race between animals in which the naturally slow-moving one finally wins. 170, 227, 354, 355.

Midget adviser: A midget is secreted by the hero and gives advice on a journey or in contests. Sometimes designated as *Tom Thumb*. 183, 184.

Contestant-Conqueror: A young man (or men) wins back property or people lost in gambling or stolen. He may do so by gambling or by any other form of successful contesting. 160, 163, 170, 274, 333.

Ogre overcome: An ogre is killed or otherwise overcome by a mortal. 137, 175, 178, 182, 192, 196, 218, 225, 301.

Ogre's scent: The ogre scents the presence of a human being. 156, 173, 174, 224, 317, 333.

Outcast children: Children, either orphans or others, are outcasts and are subjected to abuse. They perform miraculous feats or are the cause of others doing so. 96, 113, 119, 123.

Outcast succeeds: One who is a despised outcast is the only one who is able to accomplish a certain feat. 142.

Sleeper's hair: The hair of sleeping people is fastened together, before an attack or flight. 47, 56, 78, 138, 145, 249, 253.

Vulnerable spot: A person is vulnerable in a single spot.[252] 217, 228, 230, 232-234.

THE DEER AND BEAR CHILDREN

Deer and Bear children: Bear kills Deer. The Deer children retaliate by killing the Bear children and then make their escape. 327, 334, 342, 344, 350.

MARRIAGE

Licentious Coyote: A variant of the "trickster tricks others" group of myths. 190, 194, 241, 244.

Flute-attracted bride: By means of his flute a man is able to attract one or more brides. Based on custom, but in the myth the girl has usually rejected many previous suitors. 190, 195.

Miraculous birth: Birth in a phenominally short time, of an un-

---

[252]This has also been referred to by others as *Achilles heel.*

usual number of children, or birth which displays any other unnatural feature. 96, 119, 125, 190, 194, 195, 198, 210, 221, 241, 246.

TRICKSTER

Trickster tricks others: A person succeeds in gaining his end through trickery. 62, 69, 74, 96, 193, 241, 242, 244, 245, 247, 251, 252, 254, 291, 295, 297-299, 369, 370.

Trickster tricked: A person tries to do as others and fails or he follows wrong directions. He is killed or, at least, is made ridiculous. 180, 242, 246, 252, 256, 257, 260-263, 265, 276, 269, 280-283, 285, 288, 289, 292, 300.

Sham illness: Feigned illness gains desired end. 62, 69, 243.

Auto trap: In order to catch birds, or the like, a person uses his own body as the trap or as bait. 58.

Eye-opening prohibition: A person is forbidden to open his eyes because it will injure himself or others if he looks while something is being done. 86, 182, 242, 257, 260, 265, 280, 281, 353.

TESTS

Evil father-in-law: A father-in-law, either before or after the marriage of the hero to his daughter, causes the young man to undergo various tests and dangers. 191, 214, 216, 305, 324.

Armed vagina: With teeth, flint, rattlesnakes, but made harmless. 214, 305.

Fire test:[253] Competition with fire: (1) Pouring live coals on opponent. (2) Fanning heat on opponent. (3) Binding and burning opponent. 149, 157, 162, 205, 209, 212, 214, 217, 218, 222.

Ground-touching prohibition: A rescuer is prohibited from letting his load touch the ground on penalty of its disappearance. 343, 349.

---

[253]Other tests less frequently met with are:
1. The Hunting test. A person is sent to some dangerous spot to hunt, usually one infested with bears.
2. The Fishing test. A person is sent to some dangerous spot to get fish, such as a wier or basket woven of snakes.
3. The Wood-gathering test: A person is sent to some dangerous spot to gather wood.
4. The Pitch-gathering test. A person is sent to gather pitch from a miraculously growing or otherwise dangerous tree.
5. The Obsidian-gathering test. A person is sent to a dangerous spot to get obsidian. Usually it is a rocky place infested with rattlesnakes.

ASSISTANTS

Benevolent assistant: A person is assisted in accomplishing a test, or the like, by friendly animals. 192, 215, 216, 229, 298, 340, 341, 354.

Rodent ally: A rodent (mouse, etc.) aids a hero. 78, 104, 105, 137, 138, 141, 144, 146, 147.

Insect allies: Yellowjackets or other insects assist a hero in overcoming opponents. 158, 159, 160, 163.

Malevolent assistant: Creation or placement of bears, rattlesnakes, or the like, in order to kill opponent or opponent's people. 68, 76, 85, 88, 89, 91, 94, 118, 126, 143, 158, 163, 214, 220, 225, 334.

Ogre's assistant: An assistant or slave of an ogre. Such as Bottlefly, who is the assistant of Gilak. 178, 183, 185, 186, 220, 225, 317, 334.

Sleeping guard: Someone who is supposed to be especially wakeful is posted as a guard, but falls asleep. 47.

NUMBERS

Certain numbers recur with great frequency in myths, particularly the sacred number four. Duality is used with almost equal frequency among the Pomo. For further details concerning this see the special treatment of "numbers", (pp. 453-454).

MEDICINE

Magic clothing: Clothing, the wearing of which gives a person supernatural power, such as flight, or the like. 134, 145, 173, 174, 177, 224, 377.

Gambling luck: Secured by supernatural means. 187.

Hunting luck: A charm, usually with ritual, is given by the culture-hero, or obtained through contact with some supernatural being. 85.

Sleep Charm: A special wand or tuft of feathers has the power to cause opponents to sleep soundly. 56, 103, 105, 138, 167, 168, 196, 247, 249.

Curse: A curse is pronounced upon someone. 64, 72, 256.

Skunk's scent: Skunk feigns illness and when a shaman attempts to cure, shoots the shaman with his scent. 243, 306.

FOOD

Original food: A culture-hero secures original food from a distant land or by some supernatural means. 46, 55.

Supernatural food: A person refuses all other foods and eats only beads, or something of the kind, which is not normal food. 51, 186, 290.

Food refused: A relative refuses someone food and thus starts a chain of events. 188, 272, 295.

Hoarded game: All the game (or fish) is originally kept by a single being. 189, 306.

Famine: A condition of famine exists as the initial cause for the action in a myth. 53, 148, 160.

Cannibal: Supernatural being who devours people. 174, 272, 316.

Hidden-water: Water is hidden by Frog or someone else, from a thirsty searcher. 110, 116, 120, 122-125, 168.

ETIOLOGY

Etiological tale: Any tale rationalizing and accounting for the present condition of things, color or shape of animals, and the like. 115, 117, 125, 136, 137, 139, 147, 165, 226, 230, 233, 240, 248, 253, 275, 310, 322, 329, 351, 355, 369, 372.

RELATION OF POMO MYTHOLOGY TO THAT OF OTHER TRIBES OF THE CENTRAL CALIFORNIA AREA

Very early in the present work we pointed out the "Position of Pomo Mythology in the California Area", noting that it logically falls into the northern sub-area of the Central California area and that it presents features closely allied to the mythologies of tribes of this main unit of California.[254]

At the same time it presents certain features not found in other tribes. It will now be quite appropriate to consider the more striking of these various features, special attention being given to similarities to the mythologies of other tribes.

In analyzing and comparing the characters and incidents of the Pomo myths here presented it will be the author's endeavor to make

---

[254]See pp. 11-13 of this paper.

comparisons with published material on the tribes of the Central California area only. Affiliations with the myth systems of other California tribes may be pointed out but there will be no attempt, except incidentally to carry these comparisons farther afield. Many of the incidents and characters found among the Pomo have a rather wide distribution, particularly over western North America, but for our present study it seems most expedient to confine our attention to the Central California area only. In making these studies it will be our endeavor to follow as nearly as possible the order in which the myths in the preceding pages are treated.

CREATION[255]

Among the Pomo, as we have seen, the creation of the world appears to be less emphasized than among some other tribes of this area, yet we do have here our non-animal creator in the person of Madumda, who, however, with some informants, is so closely allied to Coyote that we are led to conclude that they were originally identical. Their names and works are in some accounts interchangeable, while in others we find Coyote more or less as an assistant of the creator. At the same time we do not have a world creation as clearly defined here as we do among some of the other tribes. In fact the world transformation is much more prominently featured by the Pomo.

When we come to the closely related ideas, the creation of human beings, we find much greater detail and exactness among the Pomo. Here Coyote is the chief factor in creation though we find certain others, like Wolf, taking a hand, either by creating human beings independently or in company with Coyote.

The importance of creation in the Central California mythological concept has already been pointed out. These tribes are, as a rule, not content to merely assume that the world always existed. They must account for its coming into being. This is done among the Maidu[256] and other tribes in the northeast by assuming the power of Earth-Initiate to cause the world to spring into being largely by his will, though he has to have something concrete from which to begin. This is furnished by mud which Turtle brings up from the bottom of the primeval ocean.

---

[255]Compare the interesting series of California myths concerning "The Origin of the World and of Man" assembled by Gifford and Block (pp. 79-117).
[256]Dixon, 1912, Maidu Texts, pp. 4-68. 1902, Maidu Myths, pp. 39-51.

Among the Yuki we have a very different conception of creation.[257] Originally there was only water overspread by grayish mist. In the foam, which floated on the water like down, Taikomol came in human form spontaneously into existence, leapt from the water and stood. Coyote hung onto Taikomol. Taikomol took out of his own body, sewing materials and implements and finally made the earth by sewing as one makes a basket, making it finally firm and strong with pitch. He then created the ocean, and established the shore-line. From four whale skins he made the sky. Finally he created human beings out of sticks. Then he established certain customs and ceremonies and created other peoples with different languages. At last he went, with his two sons, up into the sky to live.

The spontaneity of this Yuki creation is unusual, for among most of the Central California tribes we find a very definite creation of our present world from some pre-existing substance, brought up from the depths of a primeval sea. The details of this creation vary considerably.

We have already discussed the creation concept among the Pomo, in which this particular feature is largely lacking, so far as the original creation of the world is concerned, though we do find the idea of diving during the deluge in order to secure mud with which to add to the height of Mount Kanaktai.

Their near neighbors, the Coast Miwok, according to Merriam,[258] show Coyote arriving from across the ocean to the west. The only land above the water's surface is the summit of Sonoma Mountain. Coyote places his raft (made of tules and split sticks) on top of the mountain and thus forms the world.

From the Yokuts we have the following versions of creation: One version[259] tells us that the world was covered with water except for one mountain-top. The people ate this for food. Mud-hen dove and brought up mud. Eagle mixed this with seeds and created the world. Mountains were created, and finally people were made by sending the animals off to become people, which is the reverse of what usually happens in myths.

In another version[260] Turtle dives for the earth from which Eagle and Coyote make the world. They also make from this earth six men

[257]Kroeber, 1932, pp. 907-918. Gifford and Block, 1930, p. 82.
[258]1910, pp. 203-205.
[259]Kroeber, 1907B, pp. 209-211.
[260]Kroeber, 1907 B, pp. 218, 219.

and six women. A slightly different version from another branch of the Yokuts is given by the same author.[261]

In still another version[262] Falcon and Raven cause one of the ducks to dive and bring up some sand. This Falcon mixes with tobacco. He divides this mixture and he and Raven fly over the water dropping it little by little. This causes the water to boil up and the earth to form.

Powers[263] gives a Yokuts creation myth, accounting especially for the creation of the Coast Range and the Sierra Nevada Mountains by Hawk and Crow from mud brought up by Duck.

From the immediate neighbors of the Yokuts, the Sierra Miwok, we have very similar versions of the creation myth. In one,[264] Coyote sends one of the ducks to dive for earth from which he then makes the world. In another,[265] a myth from the Southern Sierra Miwok, we find this earth brought up by Frog instead of Duck.

From the Western Mono, Gifford[266] records a creation myth in which Grebe dives for sand from which Prairie Falcon and Crow succeed in creating the world.

Very little has been preserved to us from the coastal region of the state but we find that among the Rumsien there was apparently no true creation myth. In the beginning everything is covered with water except certain peaks. Eagle, Hummingbird and Coyote are on one of these peaks. When the water subsides they repopulate the earth.[267]

Closely related to this idea of the creation of the world is that of the creation of people. In most instances we find the human race created from either sticks or feathers. In a few cases earth is employed. Among the Pomo, sticks or feathers chiefly are used.

Among the Maidu,[268] Earth-initiate creates people out of earth.

Among the neighboring Yana, sticks are employed. Sapir[269] records a myth, collected by Dixon among the Yana, which recounts the creation of people from sticks. In this version the creation is by Lizard,

[261] Ibid. pp. 229-231.
[262] Ibid. pp. 204, 205.
[263] 1877, pp. 383, 384.
[264] Kroeber, 1907 B, p. 202.
[265] Barrett, 1919, pp. 4, 5.
[266] 1923, pp. 305, 306.
[267] Kroeber, 1907 B, pp. 199, 200.
[268] Dixon, 1902, pp. 41, 42.
[269] Sapir, 1910, pp. 209, 210.

Gray Squirrel and Coyote. In another version[270] the creation was effected by Cottontail Rabbit and Lizard.

Among the Yuki the creation of people is from sticks, by Taikomol or by Coyote.[270a]

Among the Wintum[271] we find Wolf creating his sons and daughters from sticks.

Among the Lake Miwok, people were created from goose feathers by Coyote and Falcon, according to Merriam.[272]

According to de Angulo and Freeland,[273] the Lake Miwok and Southeastern Pomo state that Coyote made people by carving them out of wood of many different kinds.

Merriam records two Coast Milwok versions of this creation of people. According to one,[274] sticks of many different kinds were employed by Coyote. According to the other version[275] Coyote created people by throwing feathers up into the air. This idea of throwing the feathers into the air is quite unusual.

Powers[276] recounts the belief of the Southern Wintun, that Coyote created people from sticks, after the great world-fire.

A Yokuts[277] myth says that Eagle sent off to different places the animals which were with him at the time the world was created. These animals became the present race of people.

According to the Sierra Miwok,[278] people were created by Coyote and Falcon, from the feathers of the buzzard, the crow and the raven. Another version of this myth[279] from the Southern Sierra Miwok is exactly the same except that only the feathers of the crow and the buzzard are mentioned.

Powers[280] recounts a Miwok myth of creation which seems a very unusual Indian conception. The various animals held a council. Each described the attributes man should have. They could not agree so each

[270]Sapir, 1910, pp. 76, 77.
[270a]Kroeber, 1932, pp. 909, 911, 926.
[271]Curtin, 1898, pp. 243-247.
[272]1910, pp. 146, 149.
[273]1928, p. 237.
[274]Merriam, 1910, p. 159.
[275]Ibid., p. 204.
[276]1877, p. 227.
[277]Kroeber, 1907 B, pp. 209-211.
[278]Merriam, 1910, pp. 83-87.
[279]Barrett, 1919, pp. 8, 9.
[280]1877, pp. 358-360.

started to model from earth a human being after his own ideas. All except Coyote fell asleep over the task. Coyote finished his man and then went around and destroyed the work of all the others.

The shape of man's hand seems to have been a matter of considerable concern. We find that wherever the matter is taken up it is argued by Coyote and Lizard, the latter insisting that man must have a hand like his own, with fingers, in order to work properly. This is the case among the Pomo.

Among the Yana we find a most detailed account. The Yana[281] state that originally people had no fingers. Coyote and Lizard argued about the shape of man's hand. Finally Lizard took a fragment of flint and cut his own hand and made fingers. The people liked his hand so much that, one after another, they asked him to cut their hands and make fingers for them. He, however, refused to make fingers for Coyote.

In other tribes we find that Lizard merely prevailed in the argument over the shape of man's hand and that he was spontaneously provided with a five-fingered hand. This is the case among the Yuki,[282] the Pomo, the Yokuts,[283] and the Miwok.[284] In the Yokuts version above mentioned we find Coyote disgruntled over the fact that man did not have a hand like his own. In retaliation, therefore, he causes death to be permanent.

In various of the myths in our present series we find the Pomo recounting the circumstances under which the people of the original race were transformed into animals. In some instances Coyote designates what each shall be and how and where each shall live. In others each animal chooses his own form.

We find the same idea prevalent among the Yuki,[285] among the Miwok,[286] and among the Yokuts.[287] In this last instance Eagle designated what each was to become.

In another Miwok version recorded by Merriam[288] the first people were prevented from becoming the present human race and became

[281]Sapir, 1910, pp. 89-91.
[282]Kroeber, 1932, p. 926.
[283]Kroeber, 1907 B, p. 231.
[284]Merriam, 1910, pp. 61, 115. Barrett, 1919, p. 5.
[285]Kroeber, 1932, pp. 926, 927.
[286]Merriam, 1910, pp. 171, 172.
[287]Kroeber, 1907 B, pp. 223, 224.
[288]1910, p. 132.

actual animals instead, because of the fact that Meadowlark objected to
the return of the dead to life.

THE WORLD FIRE

The belief in the destruction of the world by a great conflagration
seems fairly general though it is perhaps more prominently featured
in Pomo myths than in any of the others which have been recorded.
The cause of the World-fire is variously given by different tribes.
Among the Pomo it is usually ascribed to Coyote's retaliation for the
abuse of his children by the people.

Among the Maidu there is no recorded version of a real World-fire
similar to that of the Pomo. The closest approximation to it is perhaps
the story of "The Loon Woman,"[289] which contains various of the
same elements incorporated in the Pomo world-fire myths.

The Yana[290] believe that the World-fire was caused by Coyote who
dropped the firebrand at the time of the theft of fire from the south.

The Yuki version of the World-fire is a mere incident in the theft
of fire.[291] In the dissemination over the earth of the fire stolen by
Dove, a world conflagration was caused. In order to escape destruction
the people took refuge in a pond. There was not sufficient room for all
to submerge themselves so that some were scorched. That is why the
head of the red-headed woodpecker and the shoulders of the red-winged
blackbird are now red.

The Lake Miwok and the Southeastern Pomo[292] relate that the
World-fire was caused by a theft of beads from Weasel. Hawk steals
these beads and Weasel sets the world afire in revenge.

Another version by these same authors[293] collected among the Lake
Miwok and Southeastern Pomo states that Snipe caused the World-fire.

Gifford and Block[294] give two Lake Miwok myths of the World-fire
which differ very greatly from the tales of this destruction as given by
the Pomo. In one of these we see Snipe setting fire to the world by
throwing a magic stone about in the north. Wherever the stone struck
a fire started. Then the stone would come back to Snipe and he would

[289]Dixon, 1902, pp. 71-76.
[290]Gifford and Block, pp. 129-132.
[291]Kroeber, 1932, p. 920.
[292]de Angulo and Freeland, 1928, p. 232.
[293]de Angulo and Freeland, 1928, p. 242.
[294]1930, pp. 145-149.

throw it in another direction. In the second of these myths we find Weasel burning the world in revenge for the theft of his store of shell beads by Hawk.

Powers[295] records the following myth of the Southern Wintun. A man is in love with the Magpie sisters, who scorn him. He journeys far to the north and sets the world on fire. He then makes a tule boat and escapes on the ocean. Coyote lives far to the south. He runs north-ward and finally extinguishes the World-fire with honey-dew. He places honey-dew in a hole in a creek and again the world has water. His two boys are lonesome so he builds a Sweat-house in which he creates people from sticks.

Another Wintun version of the destruction of the world by fire is told by Curtin[297]. Here we see Swift destroying the world in revenge for the theft of obsidian from him. Olelbis, the Creator, then calls upon Wind and Water to come down from the north and extinguish the World-fire. This combination of the World-fire and the Deluge in a single incident is rather unusual.

According to the Sierra Miwok[298] the great fire which destroys the world comes as a result of the death of Gilak in a contest with Coyote.

THE DELUGE

Among the Pomo the Deluge is a very important myth incident. No special reason is assigned for it. It simply rains incessantly. Falcon takes refuge on the top of Mt. Kanaktai. Assisted by some of the water-birds he succeeds in building the top of this mountain higher and higher and thus escapes drowning. When the water subsides the world continues about the same as before. It is in this heightening of Mt. Kanaktai that we encounter the "earth-diver" element in Pomo mythology. The birds not only dive for mud and other materials with which to build up this mountain top, but they also dive down and bring up food from their old homes. One of them also dives down and brings fire in a tube made of a water-lily root.

The Shasta[299] version of the flood is as follows: Coyote forewarns people of the flood but they pay no attention to him. When the water

[295]1877, p. 227.
[297]1898, pp. 9-25.
[298]Merriam, 1910, pp. 81, 82.
[299]Farrand, 1915, pp. 210, 211.

rises, Coyote and two companions take refuge on a very high mountain.
Being fearful that they also will perish he inquires of parts of his body
and is assured that these three will be saved. After the flood subsides
all the people return to life spontaneously. Then Coyote designates
what animal each shall become.

According to the Lake Miwok and Southeastern Pomo the Deluge
is caused by Coyote in order to extinguish the World-fire.[300] This is a
rather novel idea since the Deluge and the World-fire are usually entirely separate incidents.

According to the Coast Miwok[301] the Deluge resulted from the
revenge of Coyote upon Falcon with whom he had quarreled.

ASCENT TO THE SKY

Reaching the sky by means of a rope and through the agency of
Spider seems to be a feature of the north central sub-area. We find it
prominently featured among the Maidu, the Yana and the Yuki, as well
as among the Pomo. More complete data will probably show it among
other tribes of this sub-area. Among the Pomo we find this ascent as
one of the important incidents connected with the great World-fire.

According to the Yana, Spider takes people, in this case the
daughters and sons-in-law of Moon, to the sky in his basket by means
of a rope which he has attached to the sky.[302]

An interesting variant of this incident is also found among the
Yana.[303] Spider has a great basket in which she places Wildcat and his
people in order to save them from Loon. Spider climbs nearly to the
sky with this basket, when Coyote's curiosity causes him to make a tiny
hole in the bottom of it in order to see what is going on down on the
earth. This rends the basket and all fall into the fire which Loon in her
rage has made by burning the sweat-house.

Another variant of this same tale, as recorded from the Achomawi,
has been recently published by de Angulo and Freeland.[304] Here we
find the spider-rope shot up and attached to the sky by the arrow of
Giant Lizard. Then those who try to escape do so by climbing individ-
ually. Coyote looks down and causes the rope to break.

---

[300]de Angulo and Freeland, 1928, p. 233.
[301]Merriam, 1910, p. 157.
[302]Curtin, pp. 293, 294.
[303]Curtin, pp. 309-410. Gifford and Block, p. 131.
[304]1931, pp. 125-130.

Among the Maidu,[305] Spider carries people up to the sky in a net. Lizard makes a hole in the net to peep through. The net tears and all are precipitated into the burning house below. This is one of the incidents in the story of Loon-woman.

Among the Yuki we find a similar idea of Spider serving as the means of transportation between earth and sky.[306]

The Yokuts[307] mention a descent from the sky by means of a rope made of down feathers. The descent is through a hole in the sky, presumably in the zenith.

THE SUN

The importance of the Sun is so great that the concepts of it should be carefully compared with those of adjacent tribes, particular attention being given to myths concerning the theft of the sun. We have already given quite fully the Pomo concepts concerning the Sun, the Sun-people and their abode.[308] So closely related are the ideas of fire and the theft of daylight, that they should be here considered together. In some tribes we find the liberation of the sun coming as a direct result of the theft of fire, and throughout there seems to be a very close connection between the three ideas. The idea that the sun and light and fire were formerly jealously guarded by a foreign people, way back in those days when our known world was all in darkness, is very prevalent.

To secure these highly essential items for man was one of the great achievements of the "first people". How it was accomplished is variously recounted in different tribes.

Among the Pomo we find Coyote, assisted by some mice (usually four), accomplishing this theft of the sun from its keepers at the eastern edge of the world.

Goddard[309] records among the Lassik a tale of the theft of daylight from the people in the east, which has several points of similarity to the Pomo versions.

Gifford and Block[310] give a Kato myth of the theft of the sun by Coyote assisted by three mice.

A clear distinction is made by the Yuki between the theft of fire and

---

[305]Dixon, 1902, pp. 73, 74.
[306]Kroeber, 1932, pp. 932, 933.
[307]Kroeber, 1907 B, p. 209.
[308]See pp. 21-25 of this paper.
[309]1906, pp. 136, 137.
[310]Pp. 153-154.

the theft of the sun.[311] The Sun is kept by two old women. Coyote causes them to sleep soundly. The Sun is covered by a pile of skin blankets, which Coyote removes. He then places the Sun in his net sack and starts homeward, pursued by many of the Sun-people. These people overtake Coyote and question him three different times. Each time he successfully throws them off by evasive answers. The fourth time, however, the people are suspicious of Coyote. Just as they are about to seize him he dashes the Sun against a rock, willing that the Sun's eyes and brains shall lodge in a crack in the rock. After the Sun-people have killed Coyote he revivifies himself, and takes the Sun's eyes and brains out of this crevice and resumes his journey westward. There he causes the Sun to reconstruct itself and to be as it was before and finally he succeeds in making it rise and in regulating its movements. Among the Yuki we also have the familiar incident in which a child refuses to give Coyote information as to the container carrying the moon and the morning star.[312]

According to the Lake Miwok and Southeastern Pomo, the Sun was stolen by two Doves. They shot Sun's house with their slings and Sun rose directly up into the sky and remained there.[313]

A fragmentary but unusual version of the theft of the sun is recounted by Merriam[314] from the Coast Miwok.

Among the Miwok,[315] the Sun and Fire were kept by the people of the Sierra region, and were guarded by Turtle. Coyote finally succeeded in stealing the sun and in regulating its movements so that it would give light for both the valley and the mountain people. In a second version of this myth Coyote steals the Morning, which is obviously synonymous with sun. Though this theft by Coyote does not specifically account for fire, we may assume that fire was obtained by him at the same time.

Among the Southern Sierra Miwok[316] we find an account of the theft of the sun by Coyote, who transformed himself into a crooked stick in order to gain admission to the abode of the Sun.

[311]Kroeber, 1932, pp. 918-920 and 922-924.
[312]Kroeber, 1932, p. 924.
[313]de Angulo and Freeland, 1928, p. 236.
[314]1910, p. 201.
[315]1910, Merriam, 35-46.
[316]Barrett, 1919, pp. 19, 20.

JOURNEYS TO THE ABODE OF THE SUN-PEOPLE

Myths which recount journeys to the abode of the Sun and contests with the Sun-people, but which have nothing directly to do with the theft of the sun are recorded. They have to do usually with attempts to rescue some one who has been stolen by the Sun-people. Several such accounts are found among the Pomo.

A Yana version of the journey to the home of the Sun and of contests imposed by the Sun is recorded by Curtin.[317]

The Wintun, according to Curtin,[318] place the abode of Sun far toward the east. It is surrounded by the bones of human victims and is thoroughly guarded by grizzly bears and rattlesnakes. When Dug-from-the-ground arrives at Sun's house, his two dogs, Panther and Fox, kill the grizzlies and snakes and make his entry safe.

THE THEFT OF FIRE

When we turn to myths concerning the theft of fire we find the following interesting comparative material among the Central California tribes.

The theft of fire among the Pomo is accomplished by Coyote.

The Shasta[318a] version of the theft of fire is as follows: Formerly people obtained heat by piling rocks together. Coyote becomes tired of this proceedure and goes to the house of a shaman who has regular fire. Only the children are at home and through trickery Coyote obtains a firebrand and runs away with it. Returning at this juncture, the shaman gives chase. Coyote has stationed his people to run in relays with the fire. It is finally given to Turtle who, finding himself hotly pursued, places the fire in his arm-pit and plunges into the water, thus saving it for the people. A Shasta version of the theft of fire is told by Burns also.[319]

Among the Yana[320] we learn that fire is stolen from the fire-keepers in the south, while they sleep. Coyote induces Fox to allow him to carry the fire. It burns his hands and he drops it, thus setting the world on fire. Spider undertakes to take the people up to the sky in his tule

[317]1898, pp. 281-294.
[318]1898, pp. 121-160.
[318a]Farrand, 1915, pp. 309, 210.
[319]1901, pp. 132-133.
[320]Sapir, 1910, pp. 31-35.

basket. Coyote wants to look down and see the World-fire so he makes
a small hole in the basket. This becomes a wide opening and all fall
back to earth and are burned. Spider alone remains up in the sky.

Sapir[321] also gives, in text and translation, Curtin's Northern Yana
myth of "The Finding of Fire." This is as follows: Fire was discovered in the south, and was stolen from the Fire-people by Wolf,
Coyote and Dog. Dog finally succeeded in escaping with fire hidden in
her ears, despite the fact that the Fire-people sent Flood, Hail, Wind
and Snow in pursuit.[322]

The Maidu[323] say that people formerly had fire which was stolen
from them by Thunder. Lizard discovers fire which is then stolen by
Mouse in his flute. Dog carries fire in his ear, Deer carries it on his
hock. They are pursued by Wind, Rain, and Hail.

Powers[324] gives a Southern Maidu account of the theft of fire. The
people have no fire but there is plenty of it over in the west. Bat sends
Lizard to steal some. On the way home he has great difficulty to keep
people from stealing it from him. One night he encounters a lot of
Sand-hill Cranes. To save his fire Lizard sets the grass on fire and it
burns its way across the great valley to the Sierra Nevada Mountain
country.

Among the Yuki "the theft of fire" has an interesting version
according to Kroeber.[325] Here the discovery of fire is made by Jackrabbit who, in those early days when the earth was in total darkness
and everyone ate his meat raw, was an abused orphan crying outside the
ceremonial house. He sees intermittent flashes of fire. The fire is held
down by Spider who is squatting on it. Upon the arrival of Coyote and
his party they succeed in causing Spider to raise his belly while laughing
at the antics of Mouse. Dove at this juncture succeeds in stealing fire
in some rotten wood. With this he escapes, though hotly pursued by
Spider, and he succeeds in disseminating fire over the world.

According to the Lake Miwok,[326] Coyote sends two Shrews to the
house of Crow, very far to the east, to steal fire. Assisted by Firefly
they succeed. Coyote then puts fire in the buckeye.

[321]Sapir, 1910, pp. 160-174.
[322]Curtin, 1898, pp. 365-370
[323]Dixon, 1902, pp. 65-67. Also Dixon 1912, pp. 165-171.
[324]1877, pp. 343, 344.
[325]Kroeber, 1932, pp. 918-920.
[326]Merriam, 1910, pp. 149-151.

The Lake Miwok and Southeastern Pomo says that fire was stolen by the two Mouse brothers, at the request of Coyote. They obtain it from the people at the extreme southern end of the world. They do not use their flutes but catch the sparks directly on some punk.[327]

The Coast Miwok[328] relate how Coyote sent Hummingbird to steal fire from the east. He carries it under his chin and hence has the "blaze there to this day." This theft of fire gave both fire and light again to the people.

A Yokuts[329] myth recounts that the people of the foothills have no fire. It is all kept by a man out in the valley region to the west. Finally Jackrabbit steals the fire and when pursued he makes a burrow in the brush and crouches down over it, holding it in his hands. Hence the palms of his hands are black.

In another Yokuts[330] myth Eagle sends Crow out to search for fire. He discovers it in the north. Roadrunner, Fox, Coyote and Crow then go to steal fire which they carry in a net bag.

According to the Sierra Miwok,[331] we find Turtle sitting on the fire and concealing it. Coyote turns himself into a stick of wood and steals the fire. The Sierra Miwok, according to Merriam,[332] relate how Lizard discovered fire down in the valley region. White-footed Mouse puts the Fire-people to sleep by his flute playing and then conceals the fire in his flute. He later hides the fire in the buckeye, but finally takes it to his people. Another and very different version of the theft of fire is given by this same author.[332a] Hummingbird steals a spark of the fire kept in the east by the Star-women. He carries it under his chin, hence his "ruby throat." Again fire is placed in the buckeye.

In another myth collected by Merriam[333] we find fire in possession of the Valley people. It is stolen for the Mountain people by White-footed mouse who escapes with it by hiding it in his flute. When he reaches the mountains he ties his fire into a small bundle which Coyote in turn tries to steal, but when he tries to swallow it, the fire shoots up into the sky and becomes the Sun. The small amount of fire still remaining is

[327]de Angulo and Freeland, 1928, pp. 234, 235.
[328]Merriam, 1910, pp. 153, 154.
[329]Kroeber, 1907 B, p. 219.
[330]Kroeber, 1907 B, pp. 211, 212.
[331]Kroeber, 1907 B, pp. 202, 203.
[332]1910, pp. 61-63.
[332a]Ibid., pp. 89, 90.
[333]1910, pp. 49-53.

then put into the buckeye and the incense-cedar from which it can still be obtained.

Merriam[334] gives a Miwok reason for the diversity of languages. It is related that when Coyote nearly extinguished the newly acquired fire through his greed, those people near the fire were the only ones whose speech was normal and correct. Those farther away from it were so cold that their teeth chattered. Hence the imperfection of their speech and the origin of language differences.

Several versions of the theft of fire as this idea is incorporated in the mythology of various California tribes are also given by Gifford and Block.[335]

SUPERNATURAL BEINGS

The supernatural beings of the Pomo mythological world are very numerous. Some personify great forces of nature, others are of very minor importance. Most of them are considered as malevolent and capable of doing man much harm. A few are benevolent. These have been quite fully described in appearance, abode and attributes under the head of "Supernatural Beings" in the early part of this present paper.[336]

Certain of these are found among neighboring tribes: Gilak, Thunder and others.

While Gilak appears to be a very important character among the Pomo, it would seem that he does not occur among many of the neighboring peoples. In fact outside of the Miwok we do not find this character specifically mentioned. The proximity of the Lake Miwok to the Pomo would easily account, of course, for their knowing this character, and the probable visiting relation between these people and the Sierra and Valley Miwok might easily account for the fact that he is mentioned by these southern members of the Miwok family, where Merriam[337] records that Gilak lives in the north and relates a tale in which Falcon visits him and is killed in a contest. Later Coyote kills Gilak.[338] The World-fire is the result.

Among the Lake Miwok[339] we find a rather interesting conception

---

[334]1910, pp. 63, 64.
[335]Pp. 129-141.
[336]See pp. 21-40.
[337]1910, pp. 75-82.
[338]It is interesting that this giant could only be killed by hitting a vulnerable spot, a white spot on the under side of his arm.
[339]de Angulo and Freeland, 1928, p. 245.

of the Gilak family. The Gilaks live in a village in the high mountains.
There are two brothers and a sister. The latter is Log-drum. As her
brother brings home his human victims she chews them up and spits
forth the bones. There is a circle of these bones all around the house.
The guards of the outer door of the tunnel are two bears and two snakes.
Gilak's elder brother has only one leg because once, when this elder
Gilak forgot to set the trap at the inner door, Gilak became very angry
and cut off one of his legs. Should a visitor get by the outer guards this
trap catches him, hurls him against the center pole, and breaks his back.
Bumble-fly is the watchman who is stationed on the roof. Once he went
to sleep and Gilak gouged out one of his eyes as a penalty.

The Lake Miwok give a very interesting account[340] of a visit of
Coyote to the home of the Gilaks for the purpose of recovering the
bones of his grandson, Hawk. Accompanied by the two Flint brothers,
the two Bluebird brothers and the two Brownbird brothers, Coyote goes
to the home of the Gilaks, which is located in the high mountain country.
He lights punk and blows the smoke into the entrance tunnel. This
blinds the four guards, two bears and two snakes. With a flat stone he
springs the trap at the inner end of the tunnel. All seven visitors then
enter. They play the hand game but the guessing is done by shooting an
arrow at the ones holding the bones. The Bluebirds have a "medicine"
which they can shoot all around in any direction. It will zigzag all
through the house. When the younger Gilak takes his bones to play he
flies and darts about everywhere in the house. With their special medicine the Bluebirds shoot and kill Gilak. They hit him in a special vulnerable spot. Next they shoot the elder Gilak brother. Then they feed
both bodies to the sister, the Ceremonial-drum. Then Coyote and his
men start to dance. The Brownbirds, drumming for them, finally break
the ceremonial drum. Coyote then sends his six companions out of the
house. He takes the bones of Hawk and ties them to his own ear. Then
he goes to sleep. His ear twitches four different times and then Hawk
comes to life. Coyote proposes to burn the house of the Gilaks but
Bumble-fly, who is Gilak's watchman, persuades him to leave the house
so that he may continue to live there. Coyote then takes Hawk and his
wife, Quail, and all start home. As they approach the village Meadow-

[340]de Angulo and Freeland, 1928, pp. 244-249.

lark sniffs and remarks about the odor of the dead. This makes Hawk so ashamed that he and his brother refuse to go farther.

They start off on another trail. When Coyote misses them he starts to track them, but finally comes to a place where the trail forks. Now, one of the brothers had taken one fork, while the other took the other fork. Coyote does not know which to take because if he follows one of the brothers the other will think that Coyote esteems his brother most. Finally Coyote throws his walking stick up into the air. As it comes down it cleaves him in two so that he can follow both of the Hawk brothers.

After recounting this and a number of other myths from the Lake Miwok and the Southeastern Pomo, de Angulo and Freeland[341] call particular attention to a special feature of these myths, namely the dual characters. Instead of there being a single individual the characters come in twos, as two Dove brothers, two Flint girls and the like. Perhaps one of the most interesting instances of this dualization is the one just recounted, where Coyote encounters the fork in the trail and, in order that he may follow both forks, finds it necessary to split himself in two. Merriam also records several myths from both the Coast and the Lake Miwok where duality occurs.

It may be here remarked that this dualization of personages also very frequently occurs in the myths of the Northern, Central and Eastern dialectic groups with which our present work deals. It would seem from the instances of dualization recorded by these authors and those noted in the present work that this device is a characteristic of Pomo and Miwok mythology. It is a feature rarely noted among other tribes so far as the present literature shows.

Merriam[342] describes, among the Southern Miwok, another giant bird, called Yellokin, who devours people, and who is evidently very much like the Pomo Gilak in his various attributes.

It is interesting to note that the deity, Thunder, is not given very considerable prominence in other California mythologies. We have already shown that Thunder as such is of minor importance among the Pomo, but that this character is given attributes in some instances so

---

[341]de Angulo and Freeland, 1928, pp. 249-252.
[342]1910, pp. 163-167.

similar to those of Gilak that we may well suspect that these two characters were at one time identical in the Pomo mind.

The Shasta[343] have an interesting myth in which Thunder tries to destroy his son-in-law (1) by sending him to spear salmon, (2) by sending him into a rattlesnake-infested sweat-house, (3) by sending him up a precipice to get bird's eggs, and (4) by playing the game of spring-board. In all these trials the son-in-law is successful and in the last he throws Thunder up into the sky where he remains.

The Lake Miwok recount that Thunder formerly devoured people. He was killed by Wild-oats-man.[344]

Among the Southern Miwok Merriam[345] records the origin of Thunder. One of the great man-eating giants devours all the people of a certain village except two small boys. These children save all the feathers of the birds they kill and make themselves into giant birds and finally become the thunderers and reside in the sky.

Lightning is encountered among the Yana[345a] in the person of Ilhataina. He was originally dug from the ground as a tiny baby. After a miraculous growth, and certain miraculous adventures and contests he becomes lightning and goes to the sky in a black cloud. Rain is water running from his rabbitskin robe. This importance of lightning is very unusual in Central California and contrasts markedly with the Pomo conceptions of lightning.

One of the adventures of Ilhataina is his overcoming of the Giant Lizard who has killed all of Ilhataina's relatives. He kills the Lizard by shooting him in a special vulnerable spot. He visits the home of Lizard and recovers their bones and revivifies them.

Such rescues, either of the living or of parts of the dead from which people are then revivified are rather frequent in Pomo myths. They are usually effected by the hero from Gilak, or the Sun-people.

Similar ideas are also found among some of the other California tribes.

Among the Southern Miwok we find Oowellin[346] a great giant who travels about devouring people. Finally the few survivors find him

[343]Farrand, 1915, pp. 211, 212.
[344]de Angulo and Freeland, 1928, p. 244.
[345]1910, pp. 173-178.
[345a]Curtin, 1898, pp. 313-322.
[346]Merriam, 1910, pp. 169-172.

asleep. Fly bites him from head to foot to discover his vulnerable spot, and finally locates it in his heel. He is then killed by the people.

Very many of the other supernatural beings mentioned by the Pomo have no real counterparts in neighboring tribes and vice versa, for instance a character which occurs among the Maidu,[347] and the Yana,[348] but which is not even mentioned at all by the Pomo is Rolling-head or Cannibal-head. The Pomo mention, however, that Rock-man travels by rolling along like a rolling boulder.

For several Pomo characters, such as, Mountain-man, Brush-man, Fire-man, Putrid-man and various others, there are no real counterparts in the recorded myths of these neighboring tribes. It seems quite possible, however, that larger series of myths from these other tribes might bring to light other characters similar or identical to these.

In some instances we find certain similarities but no real identity. A good example is Dug-from-the-ground.

This character, which is quite important in Wintun[348a] and Yana[348b] mythology, has no real counterpart among the Pomo. There are two characters each of which has some of the attributes of Dug-from-the-ground. Chub Duck, it will be recalled, is dug up when Coyote starts excavating for the sweat-house in which he creates people. Duck assists in this creation but otherwise is apparently of no special importance.

So far as miraculous birth, growth and exploits are concerned, probably Obsidian-man among the Pomo is more nearly similar to Dug-from-the-ground than any other Pomo character, though the resemblance is not really very close.

TRICKSTER STORIES

One of the most popular types of myths is that in which the trickster element enters, and in which the chief actor plays a trick upon someone in order to gain his end or in which this same chief actor is tricked and duped by an opponent in some way. In most instances these stories center around Coyote, though we do find Woodrat, Fox and others as tricksters among the Pomo, to a certain extent.

---

[347]Dixon, 1902, pp. 97, 98.
[348]Curtin, 1898, pp. 325-335.   Sapir, 1910, pp. 115-128.
[348a]Curtin, 1898, pp. 121-160.
[348b]Curtin, 1898, pp. 313-322.

Among other tribes of the Central California area we find Coyote similarly depicted.

Dixon[349] has recorded an interesting series of sixteen Coyote tales, which show Coyote (1) as a clever person and (2) as a fool, who is easily duped by others. The details differ quite markedly in most instances from those found in Pomo tales of Coyote, but the same trickster elements prevail in many of them. The same author[350] has also recorded four Coyote stories from the Maidu in a paper entitled "Some Coyote Stories from the Maidu Indians of California."

An incident in which Coyote is tricked by Crow into using burning pitch to beautify his hair is told by the Yuki.[351] Also an interesting variant of the idea of Coyote falling from a tree is found among the Yuki.[352] A version somewhat different from that told by the Pomo, of the trickster incident of wood gathering is told by the Yuki. On the advice of Crow, Coyote tries to break off the branches of manzanita for firewood but only succeeds in breaking his legs and arms.[353] Also a version of Coyote breaking his own leg with a stone is found among the Yuki.[354]

Among the Southeastern Pomo there is a myth of Coyote's being killed while trying to imitate blackbirds in flying.[355]

One myth collected by Kroeber[356] among the Yokuts contains several incidents in which Coyote is tricked.

Gifford and Block,[357] have brought together a number of Coyote stories of various kinds from various parts of California.

Two of these are from the Western Mono. In one Coyote is killed by the swing trick. This time the swing is a springy sapling. In the second we see Coyote as a licentious individual who is thwarted and killed by his own son, Grasshopper.

One of these myths is from the Shasta and shows Coyote tricked by the Yellowjackets.

Of the three remaining myths in this group two are of Karok and

---

[349]1902, pp. 83-94.
[350]Dixon, 1900, pp. 267-270.
[351]Kroeber, 1932, p. 936.
[352]Kroeber, 1932, p. 937.
[353]Kroeber, 1932, pp. 936, 937.
[354]Kroeber, 1932, p. 938.
[355]de Angulo and Freeland, 1928, p. 343.
[356]1907 B, pp. 231-240.
[357]Pp. 167-182.

one of Hupa origin, and belong, therefore outside the Central California area.

COYOTE REVIVIFIED

Closely related to the trickster stories is a series which has to do with the revivification of Coyote. In most instances where Coyote is persuaded to undertake something and does it incorrectly the result is death to Coyote. He lies there for a time, but always comes to life again. This is, among the Pomo, usually accomplished by Blue Jay who flies over, giving his characteristic, shrill call, "tsai, tsai, tsai." Coyote then rouses himself and complains that Blue Jay is always making a noise and waking him up from his pleasant dreams.

In rare instances Coyote revivifies himself. Whether his return to life is spontaneous or through the help of someone else, he usually returns fully healed and normal in every respect.

A few instances are mentioned where he is revivified but where he must still be doctored in order to bring him back to a normal state.

Usually, also when Coyote is injured he must be doctored, but there are several instances where he put a stick in place of a lost arm and thus grows a new one, where he inserts moss into a wound to heal it, or where a lost eye is replaced by one made from a shell bead.

We find this revivification of Coyote among some of the neighboring tribes also.

Among the Yuki we have an interesting variant of the revivification of Coyote. He revivifies himself without the assistance of anyone else. As he is being killed he wills that his blood shall adhere to the under sides of the sunflower leaves and that his bones shall be scattered under these same plants. He later brings these together and rebuilds himself, using sunflower stalks as a framework. He stabs with a stick at gophers as they come from their holes. This causes him to come to pieces again. Then he rebuilds himself again, this time using digging-stick wood as a framework. This time he is successful.[358]

Among the Southeastern Pomo, Coyote is brought to life by a being called "Skoykyo" who, from the description given, is undoubtedly Kuksu.[359]

---

[358]Kroeber, 1932, pp. 923, 925, 937.
[359]de Angulo and Freeland, 1928, p. 243.

MAGIC DEVICES

Among the Pomo we find several magic devices in use. The growing rock, the growing tower, and the growing tree may be grouped together as variants of one fundamental idea. This idea prevails among some of the other Central California tribes.

The growing of El Capitan to its present great height (3300 feet above the floor of Yosemite Valley) and the rescue by Measuring Worm of the bones of the two bear cubs which were carried up by this rock as it grew is told by the Southern Sierra Miwok.[360]

Powers[361] records this same myth, but here Measuring Worm rescues the two boys who had been carried up by this growing rock. Galen Clark[362] recounts the same tale.

In the magic cane which takes Quail up into the sky we have here in Pomo mythology an idea closely related to the magic arrow which is shot up into the zenith and by which the ascent to the sky is made among the Maidu,[363] and among the Achomawi.[364]

Among the Pomo we find also the growing tree or spring tree by which victims are killed. This tree sometimes simply grows up into the sky and sometimes it grows very high and then lashes back and forth in a strong gale. One instance is mentioned in which the trunk of this tree is very slippery.

Among the Yana, the son of Rainbow contests with Moon by means of the latter's springing pole. He finally wins and throws Moon up into the sky where he remains.[365]

Among the Maidu[366] we have a very novel variant of this idea. Here we find a swaying tree of solid ice. The hero, pursued by a bear, (one of the tests to which he was subjected by Thunder) arrives at this tree just in time to catch hold of its top as it dips down to the ground. The ice tree carries him up and then stops swaying. Finally he hits the bear in his vulnerable spot and thus wins in his contest with Thunder.

Among the Wintun the spring tree is again encountered[367] in the

---

[360]Barrett, 1919, p. 22. Gifford and Block, p. 264.
[361]1877, pp. 366-367.
[362]1904, pp. 92-95.
[363]Powers, 1877, pp. 341-343.
[364]de Angulo and Freeland, 1931, pp. 125-130.
[365]Curtin, 1898, pp. 291-293.
[366]Dixon, 1902, pp. 70, 71.
[367]Curtin, pp. 152-160.

story of Dug-from-the-ground, who finally overcomes the Sun with Sun's own spring tree, throwing him up into the sky where he splits and becomes both Sun and Moon.

The magic swing of the Pomo, which throws its victims out into the ocean or onto an area filled with spears, is also found among some of the other tribes of Central California.

We find certain spots where, according to the Pomo, passage is only possible through an opening which opens and closes suddenly and thus crushes its victims. For instance, at the south end of the world there stands a wall of solid rock which reaches to the sky. A similar wall and gate are located at the western margin of the world. Also, one of these gate traps was given a local position a short distance from Upper Lake. It was destroyed by the magic sling of one of the heros.

Passage through one of these gate traps was possible only by virtue of the great skill and quickness of the hero, a form of magic.

A rather unusual version of the closing trap is recorded by Curtin[368] among the Wintun. Dug-from-the-ground, in journeying eastward to find the home of Sun, meets up with a gigantic stone cliff with but a single opening. In this opening stood "a great sugar pine, and in the pine was a cleft large enough to let a person pass easily. When anyone was passing, and half way through the cleft, the pine closed and crushed him." It is usually the rock itself which closes as the trap instead of a tree standing in the opening in the rock wall.

In the journey of the Mouse brothers to the southland to steal fire as recounted by the Lake Miwok and Southeastern Pomo, they have to pass and repass through the south "sky door" which automatically opens for them and closes after them.[369] Here we have the reverse of the usual order of things. Such an opening and closing gate is usually a malevolent trap having for its object the killing of the person who attempts to pass. Here, however, we have a benevolent feature introduced which is most unusual.

In the journey of Falcon, as told by the Mountain Miwok,[370] we find that the south hole in the sky is a trap which closes quickly and kills anyone who tries to pass.

---

[368]1898, pp. 133, 134.
[369]de Angulo and Freeland, 1928, pp. 234, 235.
[370]Merriam, 1910, pp. 183, 184.

The Southern Sierra Miwok[371] tell of a journey of Falcon to the south end of the world in which it is necessary to pass through a stone doorway which suddenly closes to crush its victims.

The magic sling is found among the Pomo. It carries a projectile which passes from one to another of a flock of geese, for instance, and when it has killed all it returns to its owner.

This same killing of many geese by means of a magic sling is recounted by the Lake Miwok.[372]

Among magic devices mentioned by the Pomo should be recorded the magic flute or tube used by certain heroes who are called upon to devour great quantities of dangerous foods, by Gilak, by the Sun-people or others. By means of such a magic tube the hero or his protector, Coyote, is able to dispose of this food and win the contest.

Another magic object is the small inexhaustible sack, from which the hero brings forth all the beads necessary to "top the bets" of the supernatural beings with whom he is contesting. A similar sack is sometimes used as the container of the great winnings of the gambling hero. It is supposed by some to have some magic means of immediately transporting to the home of its owner whatever is placed in it. In this same connection may be mentioned the magic bags filled with yellow-jackets with which the Sun-people are annihilated in one myth.

Most of these magic aids are found in one form or another in the myths of most of the Central California tribes.

THE DEER AND BEAR CHILDREN

The prevalence of this theme of the Deer and Bear children, especially throughout Central California mythology, has been remarked by Dangel who has brought together in tabular form the elements and published references on the subject in convenient arrangement for comparison.[373]

It is a theme counted among the Pomo as one of first importance and is one which was very frequently recounted. We give four different versions, varying only in minor details one from the other.

Among the Sinkyone[374] we find the usual story of the Deer and

[371]Barrett, 1919, pp. 12 and 14.
[372]Merriam, 1910, pp. 139, 140.
[373]Dangel, 1929, pp. 307, 308.
[374]Kroeber, 1919, p. 349.

Bear children in which the Deer children kill the Bear children and make their escape by means of the Crane's neck bridge.

Goddard[375] records, from the Lassik, a version of the myth of the Deer and Bear children quite similar to that told by the Pomo. As usual the Deer children escape by the Crane's neck bridge.

Sapir[376] gives us the Yana version of the Deer and Bear children myth.

Dixon[377] has recorded three Maidu versions of this myth, all quite similar to these of the Pomo.

Powers[378] gives a Southern Maidu version which contains certain additional incidents. Bear cuts Deer's head off and takes her eyes home in her basket of clover. The Deer children entice the Bear children into a cave and there roast them to death. When Bear pursues the Deer children they take refuge on a rock which grows nearly to the sky. When Bear tries to climb up this rock the Deer children kill her with a hot rock. Then the Bear children build a ladder on up to the sky which they enter by means of a hole in the sky made by shooting an arrow through it. There they find their mother but are not able to get to her. They are finally drowned up there in the sky.

This familiar tale extends as far south as the Sierra Miwok.[379] It is interesting to observe that here the Deer children later become the Thunders. This same tale is found in Gifford and Block's[380] collection of myths.

Merriam[381] records from the Miwok two versions of the myth of the Deer and Bear children.

The Western Mono[382] have a version of this story which is quite similar to those told by the Pomo, except that the Deer children make their escape into the Underworld, whither they are pursued by Bear. One of the Deer children is killed by Coyote. The other is helped across a river by Measuring Worm (not by Crane) who later dumps Bear into the stream.

---

[375] 1906, pp. 135, 136.
[376] Sapir, 1910, pp. 207, 208.
[377] 1902, pp. 79-83.
[378] 1877, pp. 341-343.
[379] Kroeber, 1907 B, pp. 203-204.
[380] Pp. 237-240.
[381] 1910, pp. 103-112.
[382] Gifford, 1923, pp. 357-359.

THE ORIGIN OF DEATH[383]

Two reasons for the permanence of death are given by the Pomo. In one we find Coyote objecting to the proposal that people shall come to life after death on the ground that the world would soon become too densely populated. The second person to die was Coyote's own son. He then thought better of the revivification idea, but the others would not then agree. In the second we find someone brought back from the afterworld. Meadowlark objects to the odor of the dead. This offends the one who has returned and death thereafter becomes permanent.

The Shasta[384] account for the origin of death as follows: Coyote and Spider lived together. Each had a boy. Spider's boy died but Coyote objected to his returning to life. Soon Coyote's boy died and he tried to induce Spider to consent to having both boys return to life, but Spider pointed out that this could not be because his own boy was "now all spoiled".

The Yana[385] account for the origin of death, as follows: Coyote proposed to Lizard, Cottontail Rabbit and Gray Squirrel that they should cause people to die. He prevailed and prevented the first man who died from returning to life. In revenge a rattlesnake was created and placed where it would bite Coyote's son. Coyote then besought Lizard and the others to let his son return to life but they refused. Thus permanent death came into the world.

Among the Maidu[386] we find Coyote as usual objecting to the return of the people to youth and life. Soon thereafter Coyote's own son is killed by Rattlesnake. Coyote then tries in vain to have his own regulation repealed.

Curtin[387] records an interesting myth from the Wintun in which Coyote interferes with the arrangements being made by the Creator for perpetual life for the world. Coyote is himself the first to die.

Among the Lake Miwok and Southeastern Pomo we find Meadowlark objecting to people returning to life after death and thus causing death to be permanent.[388]

---

[383]Compare myths on "The Origin of Death" assembled by Gifford and Block, (pp. 121-126).
[384]Farrand, 1915, p. 209.
[385]Sapir, 1910, pp. 91-93.
[386]Dixon, 1902, pp. 41-44, 46, 47.
[387]Pp. 163-174.
[388]de Angulo and Freeland, 1928, p. 241.

Coyote wishes to revive people after death, but Meadowlark (not Coyote) objects and permanent death is the result (Sierra Miwok[389]).

The Yokuts[390] say that it was the objection of Meadowlark to the odor of the dead and his suggestion that the body be cremated that gave rise to this custom instead of the revivifying of the dead after three days.

Merriam[391] also gives us a Miwok version of Meadowlark's objection to the return of the dead.

CONCLUSION

In the foregoing pages we have a fairly extensive and a fully representative series of myths, all collected so long ago that they retain their truly aboriginal essence and show practically none of the modernized notions which so often creep into such material. They can, therefore, be taken at face value, and may be considered as typical in every respect of this phase of Pomo culture. The mythological picture drawn from them, therefore, may be accepted as a correct basis of Pomo religious thought as it existed before the coming of the white man, and we find it quite in keeping with the general cultural level of the Pomo.

Comparison of the salient features of Pomo mythology with those of surrounding tribes clearly places them, as might be expected, in the northern sub-area of the Central California culture area.

The most characteristic features of Pomo mythology are the following:

1. The Pomo universe comprised the known world, and the outer worlds lying in the four cardinal directions. Those on the north and south were separated from the known world by relatively narrow bodies of water. That toward the west lay beyond the Pacific ocean, and that to the east had no separation from the known world at all. There were also the first and second Upper Worlds. Access to the first was by means of the Zenith Gate. The second was a nebulous place to which no one ever journeyed and about which very little was known.

2. The existence of this universe is largely assumed and there is, therefore, no true creation story accounting for the details of its origin, as there is among a number of the other Central California tribes.

---

[389]Kroeber, 1907 B, p. 203.
[390]Kroeber, 1907 B, p. 205.
[391]1910, pp. 131, 132.

There is, however, a creator, Madumda, identified with Coyote, at least to a considerable extent.

3. The conditions which originally obtained required, as is usually the case in mythology, considerable alterations. All was originally in darkness and the sun had to be stolen and placed in the sky. Fire had to be secured. The ocean had to be made salty and wavy and a shore-line had to be established. Clear Lake had to be created and certain creeks had to be made.

4. A great world fire and a deluge have destroyed the surface of the earth at different times.

5. A considerable variety of different supernatural beings inhabited the world. Most of these were malevolent creatures inimical in every way to the human race.

These ogres were to be found everywhere: flying through the air, walking upon the land and swimming in the waters of the lakes and rivers. Some caused illness when seen, others stole people whom they kept as prisoners while still others were dreaded cannibals.

6. Man's creation from sticks or feathers is very important. These first people are referred to as the "bird people " They were later trans-formed into actual birds and mammals. There was then another crea-tion of the present human race.

7. The myth characters are of two kinds. On the one hand we find these same "bird people": birds, mammals, reptiles and a large variety of the creatures of animate nature. On the other, the supernatural beings, with whom the "bird people" were constantly contesting. The myths are replete with such contests, with journeys and adventures of many kinds, and these are interspersed with the simple experiences of daily life.

In these contests and adventures magic devices of many kinds were employed, the growing rock, tree and tower, the magic eating tube, magic clothing, the door trap and the gate trap, the magic sling and many others are mentioned.

8. The trickster element is very prominent. In the main these trickster stories center around Coyote. He carries a double role. On the one hand, he is the cunning person who gains his end by some artifice. On the other, he is the simple dupe who is the victim of some most obvious trick. In connection with this group of trickster myths,

as well as in various other series, we find revivification of the dead victim very strongly emphasized.

9. Etiological tales are fairly numerous and explain the reasons why many things are as they are in the world today.

10. In addition to the frequent use of the sacred number, four, we find duality very prominently featured.

11. Perhaps the most characteristic single feature of Pomo mythology is found in the composite nature of many of the myths. The manner in which incident after incident appears linked together to form a single myth is almost unique. In some instances the component parts bear little relation one to another, but in most cases we find these stories so arranged that the incidents are in a fairly logical sequence with one or more of the characters carrying the action through from one incident to the next.

Pomo myths, like those of most of the peoples of the world, were handed down from father to son by word of mouth, and the ability to recount these stories in full was considered an accomplishment. They constituted the literature, unwritten to be sure, of the Pomo, upon which their beliefs were based and the recounting of these tales did much to insure the continuity of Pomo culture from generation to generation.

GLOSSARY[392]

POMO-ENGLISH; ENGLISH-POMO

[(N)=Northern dialect; (C)=Central dialect; (E)=Eastern dialect]

abalone-shell: hwi'l (C,E).
    abalone-shell blanket: hwi'l-stīt (C).
    abalone-shell pendant: hwi'l (E).
Abalone-shell-small-piece, daughter of Coyote: hwi'l-biyūmen (C).
Abode of the Dead: tca'dūwel-ma (E).
acema'ikatīte (N): maple [?].
acorn: būdū (N,E); pdū (C).
    acorn bread: ka'sī-lasoi (N,C); karo (C,E).
    acorn cache: maa'cūwit (N).
    acorn storage basket: ditīr (E).
ai (C,E): an exclamation.
algae, green, such as grows on water: ka'kasū (C).
ama'la (C); berē'mal (E): flea.
amīgi (N): elder brother.
amphibians,
    frogs:
        frog: sapō' (N); kawō' (N,C); tsa'watak (N,C,E); mītsa'-
            karai, xawō' (E).
        bullfrog: tsawa'tak-matō (N); danō'-kawō (C,E).
        toad: bata'k (N).
    salamander, waterdog: ca'kawōLō (N,C); masan-kalīts (E).
    unidentified: hisīndata (E).
    see also reptiles.
angelica: batcō'a (N,C); djomatku (C); bakō (E).
approval: o! o! idīemūl (C) [*lit.* Yes! yes! that is good].
arrow, or throwing-stick: mlū'i, tsū (N,C); batī' (E).
Arrow-man, a supernatural being said to inhabit the outer world to the
        south: tsū'-tca (C,E).
arrow-point, or other projectile point: katca' (C); xagᶜa' (E).

---

[392]For phonetic values of characters used in recording Pomo words see Barrett, 1908,
pp. 51-54.

Arrowpoint-young-man, a supernatural being: xagᶜa'-cela (E).

see also Obsidian-man.

aū'aū (N); a species of crow.

awl, bone: ya (N,C); ser (C); hīya (E).

baba' (C): a root food plant.

baby, supernatural: see tsaa't.

baca' (C): buckeye.

baca'badalat (E): butter-ball duck.

ba'c-kōt (C): raspberries.

bada'bada (N,C): 1. Wood duck, a mythical character. 2. a bird.

badī'uk (C): rope.

badō'n (C,E): island.

badō'n-baten (E): Bloody Island, a relatively large island near the eastern shore, at the northern end of Upper Lake.

bagī'l (E): A supernatural being, usually in the form of a great horned serpent. There are many of these large monsters and they live in various bodies of water, but particularly in Blue Lakes. There is a large one which renders this place extremely dangerous. The term *bagil* really signifies *long*, hence its application to the horned serpent.

same as bakī'l.

bagō' (E): old or dry tule.

bagō'l-tca (C): a sad man; i.e. one who is treated so badly by his people that he wants to go away and die.

bahe' (C): pepperwood.

baiya'k (C): fish-net.

baiyō'k (N,C); bayo'k (C): 1. Woodrat, a mythical character. 2. a mammal.

bakai' (C): manzanita.

baka'ka (C,E): 1. Woodcock, one of the Bird-people, a poison doctor. 2. a species of bird.

baka'm (C): chemese.

baka'mōla, baka'mōlaū (C) [lit. chemese pointed down]: a place mentioned in a myth. It is located very far to the north.

baka'r, baxa'r (E): a wood-gathering hook.

bakī'l (E): see bagī'l.

bakō'yō (C): rattlesnake.

Bald Eagle, 1. a mythical character; 2. a bird: cai (N,C,E).

Bald Hill: kītsī'danōyō (E).

balō-kai (N,C): Potter Valley.

bal wa sin (C): an ejaculation, meaning "what is the matter here?"

bamū' (C): a food plant.

bana (C): a canyon on the mountain east of Boonville.

bana'xaia (E): a place where Wasp lived, as recorded in one of the
    myths. It is near a large spring.

basket: pīka (N); ōnma (C); cadi (E).

    acorn storage basket: ditīr (E).

    openwork storage basket: tīt (C).

    burden basket: būdjī, bitcī (N); ptcī (C); būgᶜū (E).

    common type of flaring basket: stū'ptcī (C,E).

    "sun basket", a red-feathered basket: ta'sītōl (C,E).

basket willow tree: tsūba'ha (E).

Bat, 1. a mythical character; 2. a mammal: hō'cmatala, hō'smatalak
    (C) [lit. fire-ear-lop-down].

bat (N): obsidian knife.

bata'k (N): 1. Toad, a mythical character. 2. an amphibian.

bata'l (E): pestle.

batca'l (N,C): 1. Fish Hawk, a mythical character. 2. a bird.

batcō'a (N); djomatku (C): angelica.

batī (E): arrow, or throwing-stick.

batsīya (N): 1. Yellowhammer, a mythical character. 2. a woodpecker.

batsō'm-danō (N) [lit. black oak mountain]: Sanhedrim Mountain.

batū'm (C): a root food plant.

baxa'r, baka'r (C,E): a wood-gathering hook.

bayo'k (C): 1. Woodrat, a mythical character. 2. a mammal.

bead, shell: kal, kaia (N); talēya (C); catane (E).

——, magnesite: pō, pokal (N); pō (C); pōl (E).

    beads, thick white shell: na'mūlī, wina'mūlī (N,C).

    bead belt: cbū (C,E).

    bead measure mentioned in myths: būgū (E) [lit. burden basket].

    bead neck-ornament: kē'ya cbū (C).

    bead neck-band: na'mūle (E).

    bead wrist-band, with pendants: talē'ya-kūtsī (C,E).

bead-grinding stone: tcūwī'u-kabē, tūwī'u-kabē (C); ca*t*ane-gūwī-kabē (E).

Bear, Grizzly Bear, 1. a mythical character; 2. a mammal: bita' (N,C, E); pta'ka (C); būra'kal (E).

Bear-fly: *see* Blue-fly.

Beaver, 1. a mythical character; 2. a mammal: kage (N,C); tīhnū'r (E).

bed, made of poles and raised from the floor, used only by the nobility: xai'dasōtī (E).

bee: *see* insects.

behem (N,C); behep (E): pepperwood.

belt: *see* bead belt *and* feather belt.

berē'mal (E); ama'la (C): flea.

   berē'mal-līha''mīle (E): Grandmother Flea, a mythical character.

berries: *see* foods.

bīce' (N,E): 1. Deer, a mythical character. 2. all kinds of meats.

bīcē'bila (N): a species of lizard.

bīce'cīna (N): deer-head mask.

bicē-dakō (N): a magic pestle.

bīce'-gaūk (E): Deer-man, a supernatural being.

bīce'-gaūk-kedī (E): a place on the eastern shore of Clear Lake, about half a mile south of Bloody Island.

bicē-*t*aba-dawente (N): two girls, mythical characters, visited by Woodrat.

bicē-ūi-saale (C): 1. Green Lizard, a mythical character. 2. a reptile.

bida'mīwīna (E): a village on the western bank of Kelsey Creek.

big-head head-dress: kū'ksū-kaiya (C,E).

Big River: bū'l-pda (N,C).

Big Valley: yō'gakoi (E).

bīke' (N): 1. Ground Squirrel, a mythical character. 2. a mammal.

bilī'ya (N): blackbird.

binding material, grapevine: ce, ctīn (C,E).

birds,

   birds in general: *t*a (C,E); tsi*t*a (N); tsīya (E).
   small birds: tsī*t* (E).
   blackbird: bilī'ya (N); tsilī' (C); tsūLi (E).
   bluebird: tcō'tcō (N); madjō'djō (N,C); tsa'pū (C).

birds *cont.*

blue jay: *see* jay (under birds).

butter-ball: *see* duck (under birds).

buzzard: kawē'na, kīwē'na, kūwe'na (N,C,E): tcitcī', tutcī' (C);
gūkī, kūkī, xūkī (E).

condor: *see* vulture (under birds).

coot, mud-hen: katsī'ya (N,C); xatsī'ya (E).

crane: makō' (N,C,E).

white crane: kala'k (N).

see also heron (under birds).

crow: kaa'i (N,C,E); aū'aū (N).

dove: maiyū', mayū, mayū'kūtcū (C,E).

duck:

butter-ball: baca'badalat (E).

chub duck: *t*ana' (C,E).

daylight duck: kaa'-kaiyan (C,E).

mallard: kaiyan (N,C); xaiyan (E).

wood-duck: bada'bada, wada'wada (N,C); wa*r*a'wa*r*a (E).

eagle, bald or golden: cai (N,C,E).

falcon: *see* hawk (under birds).

flicker: batsīya (N); katsīya (C); tīyal (E).

geese: dala' (N); yala', koto'c (C).

see also duck (under birds).

hawk,

chicken hawk: kabē'kat, kabē'katc, kabē'ukatc (N,C); ī'lil (E).

falcon: ta'ta (N,C,E).

fish hawk: batca'l (N,C); kīca (E).

night-hawk: natō'tō (C,E).

Western Red-tail Hawk: tciya' (N,C,E); kīya (E) [also called
chicken hawk].

heron,

blue heron: kala'k (N); kalē'yaka, kalē'yagaū, klē'yaka (C).

shitepoke: kaka'ū (C,E).

see also crane (under birds).

hummingbird: tsū'dūyūn (N,C); tsū'dīyūn (N,C,E); tsū'īdūn
(C,E); tele (C).

j̇ay, blue jay: tsai (N,C,E).

kingbird: kapin*t*ada'*t*adaū (C,E).

birds *cont.*
    kingfisher: tca'dadaū (C,E).
    loon: kok (C,E).
    mallard: *see* duck (under birds).
    meadowlark: djīcī'l, djucī'l, gecī'l (N,C): xūcī'li (E).
    mockingbird: *see* thrasher (under birds).
    mud-hen: *see* coot (under birds).
    osprey: kaca' (C).
    owl;
        barn owl: sīya'k (N); masī'k! (C); masī't (E).
        great horned owl: makū'gū, makū'kū (C); matsīgīrī (E).
        night owl: dzi'gīnī, tsīki'nī (N).
        screech owl: cadō'dō (N,E).
    pelican: kala'i (E).
    pigeon: tca'batbat (N).
    quail, valley: caka'ka (N,C,E); cagᶜax (E).
    robin: tsīto'ktok (N); tsatō'tō (C); tsītō'tō (E).
        mountain robin: sī'wa, sū'wa, tsū'wa (C).
    sapsucker: *see* woodpecker (under birds).
    shitepoke: *see* heron (under birds).
    swan: ko*r* (E).
    see also ducks, geese (under birds).
    vulture, California Vulture: sūl (N,C,E).
    woodcock: baka'ka (C,E).
    woodpecker:
        red-headed woodpecker: kata' (N); kata'k (C); ka*r*atc (E).
        sapsucker: kale'tsat (N,C,E); kanabatī'ltīl (E).
        yellowhammer: batsī'ya (N); katsī'yō (C); tīya'l (E).
    unidentified birds:
        būra'kal bakaiūkke, tco'dok, tco'dûk (E): a small bird with a
            top-knot.
        ce'tata (C,E): a large species of hawk.
        cma'ikadōkadō (C,E): an owl.
        cna-batcū'dūk, cina'batcōdok (C): a duck.
        daka't (C,E): a small hawk.
        dīkū'būhū (C,E): a wading-bird.
        kabada*te*'tes (E): a small bird.
        kaba'ltū (N): a small bird.

birds *cont.*

    kaba′nasiksik (E) : a small bird.

    kabē′djicīl (C) : a small bird.

    kalē′cakcak (C) : a small bird.

    kalē′tata (N) : a hawk.

    ka′nakaūkaū (E) : a water-bird.

    kato′ (C) : a duck.

    kūsū′t (C) : a small bird.

    nanhwa′ (E) : a water-bird.

    tcitcī′ (C) : a hawk.

    tcū′tkil, tsū′tkil, tsū′tkilbek (E) : a diving-bird.

    tsatī′ (C) : a small gray bird about the size of a robin.

    tco′dok: *see* būrakal bakaiūkke.

    xagū′nūbek (E) : a water-bird.

    xa′gūnū″la (E) : a duck.

bird story: *ta*′-matū (C).

bita′ (N,C,E) : 1. Grizzly bear, a mythical character. 2. a mammal.

bita′ka-tsamō (C,E) : *same as* bita′-tsamō.

bita′-pōpō (N) : place where Bear-woman lived.

bita′-tsamō (C) *lit.* bear-fly: Bottle-fly, or Blue-fly, a servant of the Gilaks, a mythical character.

bi*te*′rk (E) : feather tuft.

bīyū′tkūi (N) : sugar pine.

blackberries: tī′tō-nō′ō (C).

blackbird: bilī′ya (N) ; tsilī′ (C) ; tsuLi′ (E).

Black Chicken Hawk: *see* Chicken Hawk.

blackfish: caka′l (C,E).

    "blackfish mountain", Mount Kanaktai: caka′l-gūnal (C,E).

Black Hawk: *see* Chicken Hawk.

Black Lizard, 1. a mythical character; 2. a reptile: xa-du′nutal (E).

Blacksnake, 1. a mythical character; 2. a reptile: mīca′kala (N).

"black oak mountain", Sanhedrim Mountain: batsō′m-danō (N).

blanket: s*tī*t (C).

    abalone-shell blanket: hwi′l-s*tī*t (C).

Blind-man, a supernatural being: ūī-nasai (C,E) ; ūī-bagō (E).

Bloody Island: badō′n-baten (E).

Bluebird: 1. a mythical character; 2. a bird: tcō′tcō (N) ; madjō′djō (N,C) ; tsa′pū (C).

Bluebottle-fly: *see* Blue-fly.

blue clay: maca'la (N); bor' (E).

Blue-fly, a mythical character, a servant of the Gilaks: 1. bita'-tsamō, bita'ka-tsamō (C,E); būra'gal-tsamal, tsamal (E) [*lit.* bear-fly]; 2. pcē'-tsamō (C) [*lit.* deer-fly].

Blue Heron; 1. a mythical character; 2. a bird: kala'k (N); kalē'yaka, kalē'yagaū, klē'yaka (C).

Blue Jay, 1. a mythical character; 2. a bird: tsai (N,C,E).

Blue Lakes,

   Upper Twin Lake: xa'-cīnal (C,E) [*lit.* water head].

   Lower Twin Lake: dīlē'-xa (C,E) [*lit.* middle lake].

   Wambold's Lake: xa'-sīli'u (C,E); xala'-xatū (E) [*lit.* clam lake].

bōamalī (E): a place on the western shore of Clear Lake.

bōa'nū (C): Pine Ridge, a village east of the Devil's Elbow near Ukiah.

bōca' (C): buckeye.

Bodega Bay: xam-*t*ara (C); lakō'ka-wina (E).

bō'dehase, bō'dīhase (E): ceremonial name for "tule".

bodono (C): a village on Robertson Creek, about five miles west of Yokaia.

bōka'pcū*t*, bō'l-kapcū*t* (C): a very small mammal, the size and color of a mouse. It lives underground, and feeds at night. Possibly a shrew, or a meadow mouse.

bō'lmakī (E): head-net.

bō'na ka'ce (C): ceremonial name for "kelp".

bōō (E): 1. Elk, a mythical character. 2. a mammal.

Boonville: pda'*t*eyama (C).

bor (E): a bluish mud found especially on lake bottoms.

bo'tcimat: a place located on the McNab Ranch, south of Hopland.

Bottle-fly: *same as* Blue-fly.

bow,

   common bow: ha'ia-cim, ha'i-cim (C).

   very fine bow: manamkī (C).

bōwa'l (C): eel.

Bow Sun, a place near Upper Lake: cūhnī'la (E).

bō'ya (C): Cliff Ridge, a place in the north.

bread, acorn: ka'sī-lasoi (N,C); karo' (C,E).

brother, elder: amīgi (N); kīdī, kīde (C); mexa (E).

brush house, a dance-house: se'hmarak (E).

Brush-man, a supernatural being: see'-baiya, seē'-tca (C); se-gak (E).

buckeye: baca', bōca' (C); kaba'i (E).

    buckeye-field: kaba'i-gagō (E).

būdū (N,E); pdū (C): acorn.

būgū (E): mentioned in myths as a measure used for beads, *lit.* burden basket.

Bullfrog, 1. a mythical character; 2. an amphibian: tsa'watak-matō (N); danō'-kawō (C,E).

    see also amphibians.

Bullsnake; 1. a mythical character; 2. a reptile: kakō'ī (N,C); ka'baōyel (E).

bū'l-pda (N,C): Big River.

bulrush, *Scirpus maritimus*: tsīwi'c (N,C,E).

būra'gal-tsamal, tsamal (E): *see* Blue-fly.

būra'kal (E): Grizzly Bear, a mythical character.

būra'kal bakaiūkke, būra'kal būkaiūkke (E): 1. Tcodok, a mythical character; 2. a small bird with a top-knot.

burden basket: *see* basket.

bū'tsike (E): old man.

Butter-ball Duck, 1. a mythical character; 2. a bird: baca'badalat (E).

Buzzard, 1. a mythical character; 2. a bird: kawē'na, kīwē'na; kūwē'na (N); tcitcī', tūtcī' (C); gūkī, kūkī, xūkī (E).

cabakle (C): hazel.

cache, acorn: maa'cūwit (N).

cadō'dō (N,E): 1. Screech Owl, a mythical character. 2. a bird.

cagᶜax (E): valley quail.

cai (N,C,E): 1. Eagle, a mythical character; 2. the bald or golden eagle.

ca'kabē, ca'xabē (E): Cow Mountain, a short distance from Upper Lake.

caka'ka, caka'kaiya (N,C,E): 1. Quail, a mythical character. 2. valley quail.

caka'l (C,E): blackfish.

cakaleyo (E): Echo, a village.

caka'l-gūnal (C,E) [*lit.* blackfish mountain] : Mount Kanaktai, also
    called Uncle Sam Mountain.
caka'-tca (E) : a supernatural being.
caka'tci (N) ; caka'tciu (C) : a walking-stick or cane.
ca'kawōLō (N,C) : 1. Salamander, a mythical character. 2. Waterdog,
    a mythical character. 3. an amphibian.
cakō' (N) : grasshopper.
cakōdō (N) : 1. Jackrabbit, a mythical character. 2. a mammal.
cakō'ik (E) : 1. official staff of Kuksu doctors. 2. walking-stick or cane
    of any kind.
cakō't (C) : 1. Mouse, a mythical character. 2. a mammal.
cakū-kattciū (C) : Whittled-leg-widow, a mythical character.
cala'm (C) : sunflower.
California Vulture, *Cathartes californicus*: sūl (N,C,E).
Calistoga: La'lnapō, hlal-napō (C,E) [*lit.* goose-village].
ca'lnis, shalnis (E) : a supernatural being, residing in the east.
ca'mītce (E) : a conical fish-trap.
cane, or walking-stick, not used for digging: caka'tcī (N) ; caka'tciu
    (C) ; cakō'ik (E) ; macū' (N,C).
capa'l (C) : pike, a fish.
capa'lawel-danō (N) : Redwood Mountain, near Calpella.
Carex barbarae, sedge: kūhū'm (N,C,E).
carrying sack: maa'tc (N,C).
ca*t*ane-gūwī-kabē (E) : bead-grinding stone.
Cathartes californicus, vulture: sūl (N,C,E).
ca'xabē, ca'kabē (E) [*lit.* fish rock] : Cow Mountain.
cbū (C,E) : 1. a root food plant. 2. belt ornamented with beads or
    feathers.
ce (C,E) : split grapevine, for binding.
cēla/ (E) : young man.
cĕ'mī (C) : *see* myth terms.
ce'mtūlū (C) : 1. Green Lizard, mythical character. 2. a reptile.
ce'tata (C,E) : 1. a mythical character. 2. a large hawk.
charcoal: masik (E).
    charcoal paint: pūī (E) [ceremonial term].
chemese: baka'm, gōnhō', gōnō', kanō' (C).

Chicken Hawk (also called Black Chicken Hawk, and Black Hawk),
1. a mythical character; 2. a bird: tcīya' (N,C,E); kabē'kat,
kabē'katc, kabē'ukatc (C); ī'lil (E).

chief (head-man or captain): tca'-kalik (E); xaxalik (E); tcakale
(N); tcaedūl (C).

head chief: tca'-yedūl-bate (C,E).

female chief: mata-kalitc (C,E).

Chub Duck: tana' (C,E).

cī (N): a large mammal with black fur.

cī (E): 1. Buzzard's way of saying "yes" in myths. 2. cry of buzzard.

cī'gōm (E): an old village on the northeastern shore of Clear Lake,
at a place now called "Morrison's Landing".

cīna'batcōdok (C): 1. a mythical character. 2. a species of duck with
red bill and head, and an erect top-knot.

cīta' (N): hornet.

cī'wa (E): a village on Upper Lake.

cīya'kale (N): a species of pine tree.

cīye' (N): sweet pine.

cīyō-gak (E): Shade-man, a supernatural being.

cīyō'-ptakal (E): a magic feather-suit.

cka'le (C): a root food plant.

Clam Lake, Wambold's Lake, one of the Blue Lakes: xala'xatū (C);
xa'silīū (C,E).

clay, blue: maca'la (N); bor (E).

Clear Lake Region: cōka' (C).

Cliff Ridge, a place in the north: bō'ya (C).

cloud: kaba' (C,E).

Cloud-man, a supernatural being: kaba'-tca (E).

Cloud-sack, a mythical sack: kaba'-hola (C).

cma'ikadōkadō (C,E): 1. a mythical character. 2. an owl.

cma'kasak (E): bone ear-plugs.

cma'kapa (C): a place west of the McNab Ranch, near Hopland, where
the wind never stops blowing.

cna-batcū'dūk (C): 1. a mythical character. 2. a duck.

cna'ganō (N,C): head- or hair-skewer.

cō'bōwin (N): a place where there is said to be a large rock which
has a hole filled with rattlesnakes.

cō cō pīlīdjai cō pīlīdjai (N) : a phrase signifying a very long journey
    to the east.

cō'da-yō (C) : abode of the Sun.

cō'ka (N,C) : grass-game, or grass-game bones.

cōka' (C) : the Clear Lake Region.

cokai (N) : a place east of Gravely Valley.

cō'laiya, cō'laiyō (E) : the land of the Sun-People in the far east.

cold : kasī' (C).

    Cold-sack, a mythical bag : kasī'-hola (C).

cō'ma hamda (C) : the eastern end of the world, in myths.

    cō'ma hamda ke tca (C) : the people who lived at the eastern end of
        the world.

cō'mtūlū (N) : a small spotted lizard.

cō'l-danō (N) : Snow Mountain.

Condor (also called Vulture), 1. a mythical character; 2. a bird : sūl
    (N,C,E).

Coot (also called Mud-hen), 1. a mythical character; 2. a bird : katsī'ya
    (N,C,E).

Cottontail Rabbit, 1. a mythical character; 2. a mammal : makī'ū (C).

Cow Mountain, near Upper Lake : ca'kabē, ca'xabē (E).

Coyote, 1. a mythical character; 2. a mammal : dīwī' (N) ; īwī', dūwī'
    (C) ; gūnū'la (E).

    Coyote Creator, a supernatural being : īwī' madū'mda (C).

    Coyote-fire-man, a supernatural being : īwī'-hō-tcatc (C).

    Coyote-head-chief, a mythical character : dīwī'-tca'kale (N).

    Coyote-old-man, a mythical character : gūnū'la-būtsīke, gūnū'la-
        būtcīke (E).

    coyote-skin quiver : īwī' ka*t* (C).

Crane, 1. a mythical character; 2. a bird : makō' (N,C,E).

    see also Blue Heron.

    crane-dance : makō'ma-ke (E).

    crane-sack; a sack made of crane skins : makō'-ye*t* (C).

crazy people : diwi' (C) [so named for Coyote because of his crazy
    actions at times].

Creator, the chief deity : madū'mda, īwī' madū'mda (N,C,E).

Crow, 1. a mythical character; 2. a bird : kaa'i (N,C,E) ; aū'aū (N).

cta-hai (N) : a wood used in making hair-skewers.

ctīn (C,E): split grapevine, for binding.

cūhnī'la (E) [*lit.* bow sun]: a point on the eastern shore of Upper Lake, and about half a mile southeast of Bloody Island.

curling around something: parī*t*kī (E).

currants, wild: kō'tȯ (C).

cūta'nnomanok (E): a place about two miles west of Lower Lake.

da' (N,C): the Sun.

dagaū-xatūs (E): small pestle.

da'gō-tca kĕmīge (C): place where the Sun rises.

da'-hola (C): Sun-sack, in myths.

da'idūl (C): a place on the coast near Greenwood.

daka'lak, daka'dalak (N): 1. Woodrat, a mythical character; 2. a mammal.

daka't (C,E): 1. a mythical character. 2. a small hawk.

dako (N,C): 1. Pestle, a mythical character. 2. an implement.
    dako-batal (C). a small pestle.

dakōl-baiya (C): Insanity-man, a supernatural being.

dakō'-tcūwak (C): a supernatural being who walks about on white oak trees, just as though he were on the ground.

dala' (N,C): geese.

dala'dalaū (E): Mosquito-people, in myths.

dalō'm (C,E): 1. Wildcat, a mythical character. 2. a mammal.

da'-ma*t*a (C,E): Sun-woman, or Sun Girls, supernatural beings.

da'-matū (C,E): Sun-dreamer, a supernatural being, the judge of the dead.

damō't (N,C,E): 1. Panther, a mythical character. 2. a mammal.

dance-house, brush: se'hma*r*ak (E).

dancing-ground or area: ke'male (C,E).

dancing-wand: kaa'i-tcil (N,C).

danō'-baiya (C): Mountain-man, a supernatural being.

danō'-batin (E): Mount Kanaktai.

danȯ-'gak (E): Mountain-man a supernatural being.

dano'-kawō (C,E): 1. Bullfrog, a mythical character. 2. Pond-woman, a mythical character. 3. a species of frog.

danō'-matū (C,E): Mountain-prophet, a supernatural being who takes the ghosts of good people.

danō'-tca (C): Mountain-man, a supernatural being.
danō' xa (E): a village visited by Fox in one of the myths.
data'lalī (C): a supernatural being who steals babies.
    data'lalī kamabem (C): an expression used when someone is constantly dropping something he is trying to hold.
da'-tca (E): Sun-man, a supernatural being.
da'-tcatc (E): Sun-messengers, supernatural beings, servants of Sun-man.
da'-tcma (E): Sun-executioners, four supernatural beings, servants of Sun-man.
da'tsim (E): a place on the western shore of Clear Lake.
da'wai (C): salmon-berries.
dawente (N): see bicē-taba-dawente.
Daylight Duck, a supernatural duck: kaa'kaiyan (C,E).
Deer, 1. a mythical character; 2. a mammal: bīce' (N,E); pcē (C).
    magic dwarf deer: pcē'-stū (C).
    magic white deer: pcē'-dam (C).
    fawns: nū'watc (C); nwatc (C); nōhwak (E).
Deer-fly: see Blue-fly.
deer-head mask: bīce'cīna (N).
deer-horn, nub at the base of: kamīla't! (N,C).
Deer-man, a supernatural being: pcē'-tca (C); bīce'-gaūk (E).
Deer-sweathouse, a mythical place: pcē'-cenē (C,E).
Devil's Elbow, a formation on Pine Ridge near Ukiah: po'kal (C).
diaper, shredded tule: kato'lī (E).
digging-stick: macū' (N,C); wacū' (E).
dīkū'būhū (C,E): 1. a mythical character. 2. a wading-bird.
    i'ts dīkū'būhū: the cry of this bird.
dilē'-xa (C,E): Lower Twin Lake, one of the Blue Lakes.
dīsa'hwai (E): a place near Upper Lake Landing.
Disease-man, a supernatural being: ītal-baiya (C); gak-kalal (E).
dita' (C): perch, a fish.
ditīr (E): acorn storage basket.
Diver, 1. a mythical character; 2. a species of water-bird: tcū'tkil, tsū'tkil, tsū'tkilbek (E).
diving-birds: see birds.
dīwī' (N,C): 1. Coyote. 2. crazy people.

dīwī'-tca'kale (N) : Coyote-head-chief, a mythical character.
djicil (N,C) : 1. Meadowlark, a mythical character. 2. a bird.
djomatku (C) : angelica root.
djo'mī (N,C) : a place in Anderson Valley on the Navarro River.
djucī'l (C) : 1. Meadowlark, a mythical character. 2. a bird.
djūhū'la-ma-ye (N) : the north end of the world in myths.
doctor's wand : kalū'l (E).
dol (E) : the number "four".
Dove, 1. a mythical character. 2. a bird : maiyū', mayū', mayū'kūtcū (C,E).
down, feather : te (C,E).
Dream-man, a supernatural being : marū (C,E).
drummer, a person who drums : tsīlo'-tca (C).
dūcī' (C) : hazel.
duck : *see* birds.
dūka'r (E) : a species of wading-bird.
dūla'dūlaū (E) : 1. Mosquito-people, mythical beings. 2. an insect.
dū'ōka (C) : the number "four".
dūtcī', dūtsī' (C) : live-oak tree.
dūwē'ga (E) : grass game.
dūwē'-gak (E) : Night-man, a supernatural being.
dūwī' (C) : Coyote.
dzi'gīnī (N) : night owl.

Eagle, 1. a mythical character; 2. a bird : cai (N,C,E).
ear-plugs, bone : kē'ya-cma"tcakle (C) ; cma'kasak (E).
Earth Occupant, a supernatural being : ka'i-matūtsi (E).
earthquake : mā'cīlē (N) ; mā-cweū (C) ; xai-yihek (E).
Eastern End of the World, a mythical place : cō'ma hamda (C).
    Eastern-end-of-the-world-people : cō'ma hamda ke tca (C).
Echo, a place : cakalēyō (E).
eel : bōwa'l (C).
Eel River Valley : tcidī'ū (N,C).
elderberry : kalū'l (E).
    elderberry tube : kitē'cato"lo (N).
Elem, an old village on Sulphur Bank Island in East Lake : elem (C).
Elk, 1. a mythical character; 2. a mammal : kasī'zī (N,C) ; bōō (E).

Elk Creek, two miles south of Greenwood: ya′kōda-pda (C,E).
elk-horn hair-skewers: kasī′zī-kanō′ (N,C).
　　elk-horn wedge: p!ō′ma (C).
e′ma (C): frost.
　　e′ma-hola (C): Frost-sack, in myths.
　　e′ma-tca (C,E): Frost-man, a supernatural being, one of the six
　　　　servants of Madumda.
Emerson's Point, a place on the western shore of Upper Lake: pū-
　　li′ts-ūwī (E).
exclamation, general: ai (C,E); ha (E).
　　approval: o! o! idīemūl (C) [lit. Yes! yes! that is good].
　　disgust: he——, hehe′, ya (E).
　　displeasure: ha——ha—— (C).
　　pain, from burns: hō′tōtōtōtōi (C).
　　surprise: bal wa sin (C) [lit. what is the matter here?].
excrement or anything putrid: pa′ (N,C,E).
　　Excrement-man, a supernatural being: pa′-tca (N,C,E).
　　Excrement-old-man, a supernatural being: pa′būtsigᶜe, pa′-būtsike
　　　　(E).

Falcon, 1. a mythical character; 2. a bird: ta′ta (N,C,E).
　　also called Hawk, and Black Chicken Hawk.
fan, used in fanning contests: ī′plūk (C).
fat, any kind of: pūī (E).
fawn (young deer): nū′watc, nwatc (C); nōhwak (E).
feast, for the recovery of a friend who has been dangerously ill: maa′i-
　　kako-bako (E).
feather,
　　feather belt: cbū (C).
　　down: te (C,E).
　　rope: yū′lūk (C,E).
　　skirt: xaicī′gī (E).
　　stick, used in kuksu kaiya: gī (E).
　　suit: cīyō′-ptakal (E).
　　tuft: bite′rk (E).
　　sleep-producing tuft: sma-kaa′itcil (C,E).
　　red-feathered basket: ta′sītōl (E).

fiber plant: kō'lōlō, kotohlo (E).
field: gagō (E).
fire: hō (N,C,E); xō (E).
    fire-blanket, Gilak's suit: hō'-bata (N).
    fire-dance: hō'-ke (C,E).
    fireʏ-drill: kalū'l (E).
    fire-ear-lop-down: *see* Bat.
    Fire-man, a supernatural being: hō'-tca (N); hō'-baiya (C);
        xō-gak (E).
    Fire-prophet, a supernatural being: hō'-matū (E).
    Fire-sweathouse, a mythical place: hō'-canē (E).
    fire-tender: la'imōc (N,C,E).
    Fire-village: hō'-napō (N).

fish: ca (N,C,E).
    blackfish: caka'l (N,C,E).
    eel: bōwa'l (C).
    flatfish: tsawa'l (C).
    hardmouth: kōnō'*t*ōnō*t*ō (C).
    perch: dita' (C).
    pike: capa'l (C).
    silversides: mi'ya (C).
    sucker: kōm (C).
    thunder-fish: makē'la-ca (C).
    trout: ca-lawem (N); lawem (C); mala'k (C); mala'x (E).
    whitefish: tsūLītsūLīū (C).
    unidentified species:
        hī'tc (C,E).
        stīli'c (C).
Fisher, 1. a mythical character; 2. a mammal (mink?): slīl (C).
Fish Hawk, 1. a mythical character; 2. a bird: batca'l (N,C); kīca (E).
fish-net: baiya'k (N,C); waiyak (E).
fish rock: *see* ca'xabē (E).
fish-trap: ca'mītce (E).
flatfish, a fish: tsawa'l (C).
Flea, 1. a mythical character; 2. an insect: ēmala (N); mala, ama'la
    (C); berē'mal (E).
    Grandmother Flea, a mythical character: berē'mal-līha"mīle (E).

Flower-man, a supernatural being: tcīdō'-tca (N,C).
flute: wo'lwol (C).
flying squirrel: tala'k (N,C).
fog: pōt (N,C); xaba (E).
    Fog-man, a supernatural being: pō't-tca (E).
    Fog-sack, a mythical sack: pō't-hola (C).
food: maa' (C).
    meat: bīce' (N,E).
food, vegetal:
    berries:
        blackberries: tī'tō-nō'ō (C).
        currants (wild): kō'tō (C).
        elderberry: kalū'l (E).
        gooseberries: lū'm-maa'i (C,E).
        huckleberries: ka'kai (C).
        raspberries: ba'c-kōt (C).
        salal-berries: tō'ltōl (C).
        salmon-berries: da'wai (C).
        strawberries: ma'mūl (C).
    leaves, and tender shoots:
        angelica: batcō'a (N); djomatku (C).
        bamū' (C).
        ho'mtca (C).
        kaca'iyū (C).
        kala' (C).
        kala'kū (C).
        masī'l (N): greens.
        nak!a' (C).
        pabō' (E): greens.
        t!ala' (C).
        tcawa'iya, tcawa'iyū (C).
        teca', tece' (C).
        tule: tībē' (E).
    nuts and seeds:
        acorn: būdū (N,E); pdū (C).
        acorn bread: ka'sī-lasoi (N,C); karō' (C,E).
        buckeye: baca', bōca' (C); kaba'i (E).

foods *cont.*
> kahe' (C) : a long nut from the mountains.
> pine-nut: kūtī' (N).

roots; and tubers:
> baba' (C).
> batū'm (C).
> cka'le (C).
> cbū (C).
> hō'bū (C).
> kakō'bū (C).
> mtīt (C).
> pūtī' (C).
> tala'bū (C).

> *see also* birds, mammals, fish, insects, plants, trees.

Food-village, a mythical place: maa'napō (C).

four, the number: tak (N); dū'ōka (C); dol (E).

Fox, 1. a mythical character; 2. a mammal; k!aū (C); kaka'ū (E).

Frog, 1. a mythical character; 2. an amphibian: tsawa'tak (N,C,E);
> kawō' (N,C); sapō (N); mītsa'karai, xawō' (E).

> *see also* amphibians.

frost: e'ma (C).
> Frost-man, a supernatural being: ema'-tca (C,E).
> Frost-sack, in myths: ema'-hola (C).

gac gagᶜoi (E) : a place far to the east.

gagō' (E) : a field or open valley.
> gagō'-gak (E) : Valley-man, a supernatural being.

gak-dagōl (E) : Insanity-man, a supernatural being.

gak-kalal (E) : Disease-man, a supernatural being.

gallinipper, an insect: kū'ksū (E).

gambling, wagering, betting: *see* games.

games,
> grass game: cō'ka (N,C); dūwē'ga (E).
> guessing game: wi'tcilī (N,C).
> shinney game: kapī'yem (N,C); pīkō'taik, pkō'stil (C); pīkō'taina
> (E).
> throwing-stick game: tsū'-kat, tsū'dūyen (N).
>> throwing-sticks: mlū'ī (N,C); tsū, tsūdūyen (N); batī (E).
> women's gambling staves: kada'ika (C,E).

gapa'-baiya (C); gapa'-gak (E): Spring-man, a supernatural being.

gano'sai (E): a place near Upper Lake.

Garcia Village: pdaha'ū-kēya (C).

gecil: *see* djicil.

geese: *see* birds.

ghost, human soul after death: tca'dūwel, xa-hlūī-xak (E).

Ghost-sweathouse, a mythical place: tca'dūwel-canē (E).

gī (E): 1. a feather stick used in the kuksu-kaiya; 2. head-louse.

giant: *see* Gilak, Mountain-man, Muyamuya.

gᶜigᶜi (E): otter.

gī'lak (N,C,E): an important supernatural being. One of the six attendants of Madumda. Also identified by some with the keeper of the Sun. A cannibal whose home is variously located by different informants.

same as kī'lak.

golden eagle: cai (N,C,E).

gōnhō', gōnō' (C): chemese.

gōnhō'yō (C) [*lit.* chemese under]: a place where Wolf and Chicken Hawk lived, in myths.

Goose, 1. a mythical character; 2. a bird: koto'c (C) [a large species]; yala' (C) [a small species].

Goose-village, Calistoga: La'lnapō, hla'lnapō (C,E).

gooseberry bush: lū'm-maa'i (C,E).

Gopher, 1. a mythical character; 2. a small mammal: lamō' (N); lam (C); lami (E).

gō'tekale-kahwe (E): soft pine pitch.

grandfather: maba'ts (C); ma'tīle (E).

Grandmother Flea, a mythical character: berē'mal-līha"mīle (E).

grapevine, split for binding: ce, ctīn (C,E).

grass, coarse, used in drying fish: mūtī'p (E).

grass game: *see* games.

grasshopper: cakō' (N, C); cagᶜō (E).

grass valley: *see* Gravely Valley.

Gravely Valley: katsa-gokai (N) [*lit.* grass valley].

Gray Squirrel: *see* mammals, Obsidian-man.

Great Horned Owl, 1. a mythical character; 2. a bird: makū'kū (C); makū'gū (C,E); matsīgīri (E).

Green Lizard; 1. a mythical character; 2. a reptile: bīce-ūī-saale, ce'mtūlū (C).

Green Measuring Worm, a mythical worm: mtca'-tsīmūl (C).

greens (vegetal food): pabō' (E); masī'l (N).

   see also foods.

Grizzly Bear: *see* Bear.

Ground Squirrels; 1. mythical characters; 2. small mammals: bīke' (N); gūma'r, īge', mkē (C); xōma'r (E).

   see also mammals.

Gualala, a river in south-central Pomo territory.

gū'bahmūi-bida (C): *see* kū'ba-hmūi-bida.

gūca'l (E): a kind of plant.

guessing game: *see* games.

gūkī' (E): 1. Buzzard, a mythical character; 2. a bird.

gū'ksū (E): a supernatural being, and great doctor. He presides over the Abode of the Dead at the southern end of the world. *Same as* kū'ksū.

   gū'ksū-doctor's wand: cakō'ik, kalū'l (E).

gumar (C,E): 1. Ground Squrrel, a mythical character; 2. a mammal.

gūnū'la (E): 1. Coyote, a mythical character. 2. a mammal.

   gūnū'la-būtcike (E): Coyote-old-man.

ha (E): an exclamation, "look" or "there you are".

ha——ha—— (C,E): an exclamation of surprise, displeasure, or ex-ultation.

ha'i cim, ha'ia cim (C): common bow.

hailstones: yū'ksū (C).

hair-net: *see* head-net.

hair-skewer: kanō' (C,E); cna'ganō (C) [*lit.* head-skewer].

   hair-skewer wood: cta-hai (N).

haiū kalel (C) [*lit.* tree white]: a mountain where magic deer lived.

hardmouth, a fish: kōnō'tōnōtō (C).

haūbala (C): 1. Lizard, a mythical character. 2. a reptile.

hawk: *see* birds.

hazel: dūcī, cabakle (C).

he—— (E): an exclamation of disgust.

head-chief: tca'-yedūl-bate (C,E).

head-dress, feather: kesan (C), kūtcū'n (E).
  big-head head-dress: kū'ksū-kaiya (E).
head-louse: gī (E).
head-net: sūlē' (N); bō'lmakī, kala'i (E).
  head-net of human hair: talē'ya-kala'i (C).
head singer: ke'ūya (C,E).
head-skewer: see hair-skewer.
Heaven, Upper World: xalī'wīnaūna (E).
hehe' (E): an exclamation.
heron: see birds.
hīyek bētsba (E): see myth terms.
hisīndata (N): 1. a mythical character, friend of Bullfrog. 2. an
    amphibian.
hītc (C,E): a species of fish.
hla'l-napō (E): see La'l-napō (C).
hma'r-danō (E): a mountain about a mile and a half east of the town
    of Upper Lake.
hō (N,C,E): fire.
  hō'-baiya (C): Fire-man, a supernatural being.
  hō'-bata (N): the flame blanket used, according to some informants,
    by Gilak to enable him to fly about in search of his human prey.
  hō'-bū (C): a root food plant.
  hō'-canē (E) [lit. fire-sweathouse]: the abode of departed souls, a
    large assembly-house at the southern extremity of the world.
  hō'-cmatala (C): see hō'smatalak.
  hō'dūdū"dū (N): milksnake.
  hō'-ke (C,E): the fire-dance.
hōm (N): nettle.
hō'-matū (E): Fire-prophet, or Fire-dreamer, a supernatural being.
ho'mtca (C): a food plant.
hō'-napō (N) [lit. fire-village]: a mythical place.
hook, for gathering wood: baka'r, baxa'r (C,E).
hornet: cīta (N).
hō'smatalak, hō'cmatala (C) [lit. fire-ear-lop-down]: 1. Bat, a mythical
    character. 2. a mammal.
hō'-tca (N); Fire-man, a supernatural being.
hō'tōtōtōtōtōi (E): an exclamation of pain from burns.

huckleberries: ka'kai (C).

hūk (N,E): a supernatural being.

Hummingbird, 1. a mythical character; 2. a bird: tsū'dīyūn (N,C,E);
 tsū'dūyūn (N,C); tsū'īdūn (C,E); tele (C).

hunting sack: ye*t* (N,C,E); maa'tc (N,C); tcū'lū (E).
 large hunting sack: makō'-ye*t* (C) [*lit.* crane-sack].

hwil (C,E): abalone-shell, abalone-shell pendants.
 hwi'l-biyūmen (C): Abalone-shell-small-piece, a mythical character.
 hwi'l-s*tīt* (C): abalone-shell blanket; *i.e.* a blanket or net profusely
 ornamented with abalone-shell.

idīemūl (C): "that is good".

īge' (C): 1. Ground Squirrel, a mythical character. 2. a mammal.

īhība (E): *see* mīnba īhība.

ī'lil (E): 1. Chicken Hawk, a mythical character. 2. a bird.

īmō'waiyax (E): sinew net.

Insanity-man: dakōl-baiya (C); gak-dagōl (E).

insects:
 bear-fly: bita'-tsamō, bita'ka-tsamō (C); būra'gal-tsamal, tsamal
 (E).
 deer-fly: pcē'-tsamō (C).
 flea: ama'la (C); berē'mal (E).
 "gallinipper": kū'ksū (E).
 grasshopper: cakō' (N).
 hornet: cīta' (N).
 lice:
 louse: pere'c (C).
 head-louse: gī (C).
 mosquito: tsamū'l (C); dala'dalaū, dūla'dūlaū (E).
 spider: mīca' (N,E); mtca (C); to'-cbū (C,E).
 wasp: ma'nkitsī (C); ta*r*a (E).
 yellowjacket: tcoo, tcoowī (C).

ī'plūk (C): a bird-wing fan. This is used to raise a ʿ.ust, and to fan
 smoke toward an opponent during a fanning-contest, in order to
 blind him.

island: badō'n (C,E).

ītal-baiya (C): Disease man, a supernatural being.

ï'ts-bida, ï'ts-pda (C): Kelsey Creek.

īwē-baiya (C): Night-man, a supernatural being.

īwē'-tca: a supernatural being residing in the mountains.

īwī' (C,E): Coyote.

īwī'-hō-tcatc: Coyote-fire-man, a supernatural being.

īwī' kat (C): coyote-skin quiver.

īwī' madūmda, īwī' medu'mda (C,E): Coyote Creator, a supernatural
   being.

Jackrabbit, 1. a mythical character; 2. a mammal: cakōdō (N); maka'la,
   maga'la (C); mō'hya (E).

jay: *see* Blue Jay.

Judge of the Dead, a supernatural being: da'-matū (C,E).

kaa'i (N,C,E): 1. Crow, a mythical character. 2. a bird.

kaa'i-tcil (N,C): 1. top-knot. 2. dancing-wand.

kaa'-kaiyan (C,E): Daylight Duck, a mythical character.

kaa'pūlū (N,C): wormwood.

kaa'-tōltōl (N,C): Morning Star, a supernatural being.

kaba' (C,E): cloud.

kabadate'tes (E): 1. a mythical character. 2. a bird.

kaba'-hola (C): Cloud-sack, in myths.

kaba'i (C,E): 1. a village about two miles north of Lakeport on Clear
   Lake. 2. buckeye.

   kaba'i-danō (C,E): Wild Onion Mountain, a bald hill on the western shore of Clear Lake.

   kaba'i-gagō (E) [*lit.* buckeye-field]: a place near Upper Lake.

ka-baiya (C): Water-man, a supernatural being.

kaba'ltū (N): 1. a mythical character. 2. a small bird.

kaba'nasiksik (E): 1. a mythical character. 2. a small bird.

ka'baōyel (E): 1. Bullsnake, a mythical character. 2. a reptile.

kaba'-tca (E): Cloud man, a supernatural being. One of the six servants of Madumda.

kabē'-baiya (C): Rock-man, a supernatural being.

kabē'bot: a magic place, south of the McNab Ranch, near Hopland,
   dangerous to hunters.

kabē'djicīl (C): 1. mythical character. 2. a bird.

kabē'-hō (C): a mythical place visited by Chicken Hawk.

kabē'kat, kabē'katc (C): 1. Chicken Hawk, or Black Chicken Hawk, a mythical character. 2. a bird.

kabe'kki-kanō (E): a skewer used to fasten ornaments to the hair.

kabe'l (E): a place on the western shore of Upper Lake, Rocky Point.

kabē'-mata (C,E): Stone-woman, or Rock-woman, a supernatural being living at the southern extremity of the world.

kabē'-mata-tca (C,E): Stone-woman's house.

kabē'napō (E): a place on the western shore of Clear Lake.

kabē'ndōlaū (C): a place just north of Rock Pile, on the North Fork of the Gualala River.

kabe'ū-katc (C): see kabē'kat.

ka-bita'ka (C); ka'būragal (E): sea-lion.

kaca' (C): osprey.

kaca'iyū (C): a food plant.

kaca'yama (C): Stewart's Point.

ka'ce (C): kelp.

bō'na ka'ce (C): a ceremonial term for kelp.

kacī (E): a grass-like material similar to tule. One mythical character uses *kaci* in making a canoe.

kada'ika (C,E): woman's gambling staves.

kadjī (C): pendant tree moss.

kage (N,C): 1. Beaver, a mythical character. 2. a mammal.

kagō' (E): valley.

kagō'mōrī (E): valley with waving fields of tall grass.

kahe' (C): a long nut, from a tree which grows in the mountains.

kahwē (E): pine pitch.

kahwē-le's: soft, pine pitch.

kahwa'latī, kahwa'lalīkē (C): the mouth of the Russian River.

kahwa'laū (C): a town, Pieta.

ka'iamot (C): a dangerous, mythical being, living in Blue Lakes, and known as "water-cat", or "water panther".

ka'ī-matūtsi (E): Earth Occupant, "earth occupation", a supernatural being, the diety of the Underworld.

kaiya'n (N,C,E): 1. Mallard Duck, a mythical character. 2. a bird.

kaiyē'bīdas (E): a pond near the western shore of Upper Lake.

ka'kai (C): huckleberries.

ka'kaiyaū (E) : the entire Upper Lake Region.

ka'kasū (C) : a green algae such as grows in water.

kaka'ū (C,E) : 1. Fox, a mythical character. 2. a mammal. 3. the shite-poke, a species of small heron.

kakō-baiya (C) : Valley-man, a supernatural being.

kakō'-bū (C) : a root food plant.

kakō'ī (N,C) : 1. Bullsnake, a mythical character. 2. a reptile.

kakū'l (C) : a species of small post oak.

kala' (C) : a food plant.

kala'i (E) : 1. Pelican, a mythical character. 2. a bird. 3. a head-net.

kala'k (N,E) : 1. Blue Heron, or White Crane, a mythical character. 2. a species of heron.

kala'kū (C) : a food plant.

kalē'cakcak (C) : 1. a mythical character. 2. a bird.

kalē'kol (E) : 1. Worm, a mythical character. 2. a species of worm which lives on wood.

kalē'tata (N) : 1. a mythical character. 2. a bird.

kalē'tsat (C,E) : 1. Sapsucker, a mythical character. 2. a bird.

kalē'yagaū, kalē'yaka (C) : 1. Crane, or Blue Heron, a mythical character. 2. a bird.

kalī (E) : the number "one".

kalīmata'ūta (N) ; kalī-matoto (E) : Thunder.

kalī-matūtsi (E) : Sky Occupant, "sky occupation", a supernatural being, the deity of the Sky.

kalī'mīnaū (E) : the first Upper World, the abode of Madumda.

kalkalma'ptseū (C) : a supernatural being, whose feces consists of beads.

ka'ltciū (C) : menstrual period.

kalū'l (E) : 1. a Kuksu doctor's wand. 2. elderberry wood. 3. fire-drill.

kama-sīlī-dūket-mīya (E) ; kama-sili-dūketya (N) ; Whittled-leg-widow, or Sharp-heel, a supernatural being.

kamīla't! (N,C) : the nub at the base of a deer horn.

kanabati'ltil (E) : 1. Sapsucker, a mythical character. 2. a bird.

ka'nakaūkaū (E) : a species of water-bird.

Kanaktai: see Mount Kanaktai.

kanō' (C,E) : 1. hair- or head-skewer. 2. chemese.

kapa'-kū (E) : Spring-baby, a supernatural being.

   kapa'-tca (E) : Spring-man, a supernatural being.

kapin*t*ada'tadaū (C,E) : 1. Kingbird, a mythical character. 2. a bird.

kapī'yem (N,C) : shinney, a game.

kapohol (C) : McGough's slough, a place west of the St. Turibius Mission, in Big Valley.

ka*r* (E) : the dry limb of a tree.

   baka*r* (E) : a wood-gathering hook.

ka*r*a' (C) : small pond or lake.

ka*r*atc (E) : 1. Red-headed-woodpecker, a mythcal character. 2. a bird.

karo' (C,E) : acorn bread.

kasī' (C) : cold.

   kasī'-hola (C) : Cold-sack, in myths.

kasil (N) : the redwood, *Sequoia sempervirens.*

ka'sīlasoi (N,C) : acorn bread.

kasī'zī (N,C) : 1. Elk, a mythical character. 2. a mammal.

   kasī'zī-kanō' (N,C) : elk-horn hair-skewers.

kata' (N) ; ka*t*a'k (C) : 1. Red-headed-woodpecker, a mythical character. 2. a bird.

ka*t*a's (E) : trembler plumes.

ka'-tca (N) : Water-man, a supernatural being.

katca' (C) : arrow-head.

ka-tcaha-ke (C) : the Whiskey-dance.

katca'-tca, katca'-tcatc (C,E) : Obsidian-man, Gray Squirrel, or Arrow-point-young-man, a mythical character.

kate' (C) : whale.

ka'*t*-matcū-pda (C) : a place mentioned in myths.

kato' (C) : ducks.

katō'l (N) : 1. Oak-ball, a mythical character. 2. a nut-gall.

kato'la (E) : shredded tule.

   kato'lī (E) : a diaper of shredded tule.

ka'tsa (C) : the purple lupine.

katsa-gokai (N) [*lit.* grass valley] : Gravely Valley.

katsa'mtiu (C) : a person so starved that he cannot get about to get food.

katsa'mūkal (C,E) : an old village about two miles north of Lakeport.

katsi'l-gago (E) : a supernatural and very dangerous spring, located at a place called Cold Creek, about seven miles from Kelsey Creek, on the Lower Lake road.

katsī'ya (N,C,E) : 1. Coot, or Mud-hen, a mythical character. 2. a bird.

katsī'yō (C) : 1. Yellowhammer, a mythical character. 2. a bird.

katū'lūtūdūk (E) : a snake.

katū'nūtal (E) : 1. a mythical character. 2. a mountain lizard.

k!aū (C) : 1. Fox, a mythical character. 2. a mammal.

kaūbala (C) : 1. Lizard, a mythical character. 2. a reptile.

kaū'ca (C) : a village on the coast, south of Greenwood.

kawē'na (N,E) : 1. Buzzard, a mythical character. 2. Sulphur Bank.
     3. a bird.

kawīna (N) : 1. Turtle-woman, a mythical character. 2. a turtle.

kawin tsala (C) : a white stone or pebble.

kawō' (N,C) ; xawō' (E) : 1. Frog a mythical character. 2. an amphi-
     bian.

kawolwol (N) : a very large species of snake.

kedī (E) : *see* bīce-gaūk-kedī.

kelp : ka'ce (C) ; bō'na ka'ce (C) [ceremonial term].

Kelsey Creek : ī'ts-bida, ī'ts-pda (C).

ke'male (C,E) : dancing-area or -ground.

kesan (C) : feather head-dress.

ke'ūya (C,E) : head singer.

kē'ya-cbū (C) : bead neck-ornaments.

kē'ya-cma″tcakle (C) : beautiful bone ear-plugs.

kīca (E) : 1. Fish Hawk, a mythical character. 2. a bird.

kīdē, kīdī (C) : elder brother.

kī'lak : *see* gī'lak.

kilem (C) : a place just south of Rocky Point near Kucadanoyo.

Kingbird, 1. a mythical character; 2. a bird : kapintada'tadaū (C,E).

Kingfisher, 1. a mythical character ; 2. a bird : tca'dadaū (C) ; tca'dada,
     tcadada'ū (E).

kīnō (C) : an expression used when seeing something for the first time,
     "something never seen before, but which will bring good luck".

kitē'cato″lo (N) : elderberry tube.

kītsī'danōyō, kitsīdanō (E) : Bald Hill, on the eastern shore of Clear
     Lake.

kīwē'na (N,C) : 1. Buzzard, a mythical character. 2. a bird.

klē'yaka (C) : 1. Crane, or Blue Heron, a mythical character. 2. a
     wading-bird.

knife, obsidian: bat (N,C); xaga (E).

kō (N,C): the number "two".

kō'batap (E): a place on the western shore of Clear Lake.

kodalau (C): an old village on Brush Creek.

kok (C,E): 1. Loon, a mythical character. 2. a diving-bird.

kōkō (E): a tump-line.

k!ol (N,C): a flat slab of pine-wood.

kolaha' (N): 1. Lizard, a mythical character. 2. an amphibian.

kō'lōlō (E): a plant from which fiber-string is obtained.

kōm (C): sucker, a fish.

kōmaka' (N): a species of long-nosed lizard.

kō'mka: a magic place on the McNab Ranch, near Hopland, where
    there is always a very bad odor.

kō'mtil (N,C): a village on the Big River.

kōnō'tōnōtō (C): hardmouth, a fish.

kōō (N): snakes in general.

k!op (E): water-logged tule.

kor (E): a swan.

kō'tata (N): a place on the Grover Ranch, in Potter Valley.

kō'tō (C): wild currants.

koto'c (C): 1. Goose, a mythical character. 2. a bird.

kōtōhlō (E): a plant from which fiber-string is obtained.

kōwa'nnō (C): a place east of Rock Pile and somewhere between
    Cloverdale and Yorkville.

kū'bahmūi, gūbahmūibida (C): a place to the south of Rock Pile.

kūbu'kbul (C): a place just north of the town of Ukiah.

kūca'danōyō (E): a village at the foot of Kucadano.

    kūca'danō (E): a small hill south of Upper Lake and about half-
    way between Clear Lake and Tule Lake.

kūca'l (E): a kind of plant.

kūhla'napō (E): a village in Big Valley.

kūhū'm (N,C,E): sedge, *Carex barbarae*.

kūkī (E): 1. Buzzard, a mythical character. 2. a bird.

kū'ksū (C): an insect, the gallinipper. *See also* gū'ksū.

    kū'ksū-kaiya (C,E): the big-head head-dress.

kūLa' (E): water-lily.

kūma'r (E): 1. Ground Squirrel, a mythical character. 2. a mammal.

kū'sūt (C): 1. a mythical character. 2. a bird.
kūtcū'n (E): a large, feather head-dress.
kūtī' (N): pine-nut.
    kūtī'-tcūlīya (N): 1. Pine-nut-man, a mythical character. 2. a mammal that eats pine-nuts.
kūwē'na (N): 1. Buzzard, a mythical character. 2. a bird.
kū'ya (E): the spirit or soul of a human being.
    kū'ya-canē (E) [lit. spirit-sweathouse]: a mythical place.

la (E): the Sun.
    la'-gaūk (E): Sun-man, a supernatural being.
la'imōc (N,C,E): fire-tender.
lakō' (C): a shell.
lakō'ka (E): Tomales Bay.
    lakō'ka-wīna (E) [lit. water-top]: Bodega Bay.
lala'i (E): the Sun.
La'lnapō (C); hla'lnapō (E) [lit. goose-village]: Calistoga.
lamō' (N); lam (C); lami (E): 1. Gopher, a mythical character. 2. a mammal.
latcū'pda (C): an old village on the North Fork of the Gualala River.
leaves and greens: see foods.
lehūya-ke (C): the Whiskey Dance.
lē'ma (C): an old village near Hopland.
lībū' (E): a single whistle.
lice: see insects.
live oak: dūtsī, dūtcī' (C).
lizard: see reptiles.
lok nis an baset (C): "you are very ugly looking".
Loon, 1. a mythical character; 2. a bird: kok (C,E).
Louse, 1. a mythical character; 2. an insect: pere'c (C).
    head louse: tcī (N,C); gī (E).
lūm (C,E): gooseberry thorns.
    lu'm-maai (C): gooseberries.
lupine, purple: ka'tsa (C).
lynx: wīk!a' (E).

maa' (C): food.
    maa'cūwit (N): acorn cache.

maa'i kako bako (E): a feast celebrating the recovery of someone dangerously ill.

maa'ī tūnī (N): a village, the same as masū't-napōl (N).

maa'napō (C): a mythical village visited by Black Hawk; *lit.* "food-village".

maa'tc (N,C): hunting sack, or carrying sack.

maba'ts (C): grandfather (father's father).

maca' (C,E): milkweed bark and fiber.

maca'la (N): blue clay.

ma'cbū (C): a name for coyote.

ma'cīlē (N): earthquake.

macū' (N,C): a cane, or walking-stick; 2. a digging-stick.

macū'm (N): mountain mahogany wood.

madjō'djō (N,C): 1. Bluebird, a mythical character; 2. a species of bird.

madū'mda (N,C,E): Creator, a supernatural being, the chief deity. *See also* ca'lnis.

    īwī' madū'mda; Coyote Creator.

mag'a'la (C): 1. Jackrabbit, a mythical character. 2. a mammal.

magic wand: yū'lūk (C).

    magic pestle: bicē-dakō (N).

    magic sleep charm: sma'kaaitcīl (C,E); sīma'koo (E).

magnesite: po (C).

mahogany, mountain mahogany wood: macū'm (N); kanō'-hai (C).

maiyī (E): an old village site near Upper Lake.

maiyū' (E): 1. Dove, a mythical character; 2. a species of dove.

maka'la (C): 1. Jackrabbit, a mythical character; 2. a mammal.

makē'la (C): thunder.

    makē'la-ca (C): thunder-fish, a fish something like a trout.

    makē'la-pda (C): a creek south of Bridgeport, where thunder-fish are found.

ma'kesil, ma'kīsil (C): Red Mountain.

makīla (N): Thunder.

makī'ū (C): a cottontail rabbit.

makō' (N,C,E): 1. Crane, a mythical character; 2. a species of wading-bird.

    makō'ma-ke (E): Crane-dance.

makō'ya (C) : rattlesnake.

makō'-yet (C) : crane-sack, a large hunting sack.

makū'gū (C,E) : 1. Great Horned Owl, a mythical character; 2. a bird.
    makū'gū kaaitcil (N) : "owl topknot", an ornament on a skewer.

makū'kū (C) : 1. Night Owl, a mythical character; 2. the Great Horned
    Owl.

mala'k (C) ; mala'x (E) : 1. a species of trout (fish) ; 2. a mythical fish
    created by Coyote and in turn, according to one informant,
    creator of all other fish.

Mallard Duck, 1. a mythical character; 2. a species of duck: kaiya'n
    (N,C,E) ; xaiya'n (E).

mammals,

    bat: hō'cmatala, hō'smatalak (C).

    bear: bita' (N,C,E) ; pta'ka (C) ; būra'kal (E).

    beaver: kage (N,C) ; tīhnū'r (E).

    cottontail: *see* rabbit.

    coyote: dīwī' (N) ; īwī', dūwī', ma'cbū (C) ; gūnū'la, tībē'cela (E).

    deer: bīcē' (N,E) : pcē' (C).

    elk: kasī'zī (N,C) : bōō (E).

    flying squirrel: *see* squirrel.

    fox: k!aū (C) ; kaka'ū (E).

    gopher: lamō' (N) ; lam (C) ; lami' (E).

    jackrabbit: *see* rabbit.

    lynx: wīk!a' (E).

    mink: sīli'l (N) ; slīl (C) ; stīlī'stīlīū (C,E).

    mole: wūn (N,C).

    mountain lion: *see* puma.

    mouse: bōka'pcūt, bō'lkapcūt, cakō't (C).

    otter: gᶜigᶜi' (E).

    panther: *see* puma.

    puma: damō't (N,C,E) ; yamō't (C).

    rabbit:

        cottontail: makī'ū (C).

        jackrabbit: cakō'dō (N) ; magᶜa'la, maka'la (C) ; mō'hya (E).

    sea-lion: ka-bita'ka (C) ; ka'būragal (E).

    skunk: mpē (C) ; nūpe'r (E).

    squirrel:

mammals *cont.*

> flying squirrel: tala′k (N,C).
> gray squirrel: tcīma′t (N); tcūma′t (C); saka-lahlai (C,E).
> ground squirrel: bīke′ (N); mkē (N,C); īge′, yīke′ (C); gūma′r (C,E); kūma′r, xōma′r (E).

whale: kate′ (C).

wildcat: dalō′m (C,E).

wolf: tsūmē′wa (N); smē′wa (C,E).

woodrat: daka′lak, daka′dalak (N); baiyō′k (N,); bayo′k (C).

unidentified:

> cī (N): a large animal with black fur.
> kūtī′tcūlīya (N): a small animal that eats nothing but pine-nuts.

ma′mūl (C): strawberries.

man (human being): tcūlī′ya (N); tca (E); ba (N); baia (C); xak (E).

> old man: bū′tsike (E); būsa (N); tcayim (E).

manamkī (C): a very fine bow.

manē (N): quiver.

ma′n-kitsī (C): 1. Wasp, a mythical character; 2. an insect.

manzanita: bakai′ (C).

maple: acemai′katīte (N).

marrow: pūī (E).

marū′ (C,E): 1. Dream-man, a supernatural being; 2. "an old story".

marū′mda (E): same as madū′mda.

masanr-kalits (E): 1. Salamander, a mythical character; 2. an amphibian.

masik (E): charcoal.

masī′k! (C); masī′t (E): a species of barn owl.

masī′l (N): a kind of greens (vegetal food).

mask, deer-head: bicē′cīna (N).

masū′t-napōl (N): a village two and a half miles north of the town of Calpella.

ma′ta-kalitc (C,E): female chief.

mati′l (E): a place on the eastern shore of Upper Lake.

ma′tīle (E): paternal grandfather.

matsīgīrī (E): 1. Great Horned Owl, a mythical character. 2. a bird.

matū′ (C): same as marū′ (E).

> matū′matū (C): telling a story.

matu'xal (E) : a place near the Hopper Ranch on Cold Creek.

mayī' (N) : same as maiyī'.

mayū' (N,C) : same as maiyū'.

    mayū'kūtcū : a species of dove.

McGough's Slough: kapohol (C).

mcīk (C) : sling.

Meadowlark, 1. a mythical character; 2. a bird: djicī'l, djucī'l (N,C); xūcīli (E).

meat (all kinds) : bīce' (N,E).

medze (N,C,E) : a stakeholder in a game.

mee'ū (C) : a place a short distance from Latcupda; it was never inhabited by any but Bird-people.

men (plural of man) : tcatc (E).

menelī (C) : a village at the southern extremity of the world (in myths).

menstrual period: ka'ltciū (C).

meta'sin (E) : an ejaculation meaning "what is the matter here?".

mexa (E) : elder brother.

mīca' (N,E) : 1. Spider, a mythical character; 2. a species of spider.

mīca'kala (N) : 1. Blacksnake, a mythical character; 2. a reptile.

Middle Lake, one of the Blue Lakes: dilē'-xa (C,E).

milkweed (bark and fiber) : maca' (C,E).

minawel (N,C) : a place far to the north (in myths).

mīnba īhība (E) : "I saw it".

Mink, 1. a mythical character; 2, a mammal: sīli'l (N) ; slīl (C); stīlīstīlīlīū (C,E).

min xaēlība (E) : "that is the way they say it was".

    min xaē'li dok (E) : "Once upon a time there was".

mitī' (N) : 1. Rattlesnake, a mythical character; 2. a reptile.

mītsa'karai, mītsa'kara (E) : 1. Frog, a mythical character; 2. an amphibian.

mīxō't-pīle" (N) : spider-web.

mi'ya (C) : silversides, a fish.

mkē' (N,C) : 1. Ground Squirrel; a mythical character. 2. a mammal.

mlū'i, tsū (N,C) ; batī' (E) : arrow or throwing-stick.

Mockingbird, 1. mythical character; 2. a bird: wo'cwoc (N,C,E).

mō'hya (E) : 1. Jackrabbit, a mythical character. 2. a mammal.

Mole, 1. a mythical character; 2. a mammal: wūn (N,C).

mōrī' (E): a waving field of grain or grass.

Morning Star, a supernatural being: kaa'-tōltōl (N,C).

mosquito: tsamō-bītamta (N); tsamū'l (C); dūla'dūlaū (E).

Mosquito-people, a mythical race: dala'dalaū, dūla'dūlaū (E).

moss, a pendant tree-moss: kadjī (C); xalē'sībū (E).

    floating-moss (acquatic): xa'sībū (E).

Mount Kanaktai: caka'l-gūnal (C,E); danō'-batin (E).

mountain-lion: *see* panther.

mountain lizard: katū'nūtal (E).

mountain mahogany: kanō'hai (C).

Mountain-man, a supernatural being: danō'-baiya, danō'-tca (C); danō'-gak (E).

Mountain-prophet, a supernatural being, who takes the ghosts of good people: danō'-matū (C,E).

mountain robin: sī'wa, sū'wa, tsū'wa (C).

Mouse, 1. a mythical character; 2. a mammal: cakō't (C).

mpē (C): 1. Skunk, a mythical character. 2. a mammal.

mtca (C): a species of spider.

mtca'-tsīmūl (C): 1. Green Measuring Worm, a mythical character; 2. a worm.

mtīt (C): a root food plant.

mtū'lū (N,C): 1 Lizard, a mythical character; 2. a reptile.

mud, a bluish mud from the lake bottom: bor (E).

Mud-hen, 1. a mythical character, 2. a water-bird: katsī'ya (N,C); xatsī'ya (E).

mush oak: ūcī' (C).

    mush-oak limb (branch): pa'lo (E).

mūtī'p (E): a coarse grass used in fish-drying.

mū'yamūya (C): a supernatural, indestructible giant.

myth terms,

    cē'mī (C): "in olden times", "once upon a time".

    hiyek bētsba (E): "this is the last time I shall see you". A form of farewell and a formal myth ending.

    īhība, mīnba īhība (E): "I saw it".

    marū', matū' (C,E): "an old story".

    matū'matū (C): telling "an old story".

min xaë'lī ba (C) : "that is the way they say it was".
min xaë'lī dok (E) : "once upon a time there was".
ta-matū (C) : "bird story".
xaë'lī (E) : "I have heard".

nak !a' (C) : a food plant.
na'mūle (E) : bead neck-band.
na'mūlī (C) ; wina'mūlī (N,C) : thick white shell beads.
nanhwa' (E) : a species of water-bird.
napa (E) : a valley in Napa County.
natō'tō (C,E) : 1. Night Hawk, a mythical character; 2. a species of
     hawk.
na'wek (E) : a village in Long Valley, east of Clear Lake.
neck-band (bead) : na'mūle (E).
nemehī-napō : a place far to the south where Wind-man resides.
net : sīma' (E).
     fish-net : baiya'k (C) :
     sinew net : īmō'waiyax (E).
     tule net : tībē'-patsō-waiyox (E).
Net-maker, a supernatural being : pa'-tca.
nettle : hōm (N).
Night Hawk, 1. a mythical character; 2. a bird : natō'tō (C,E).
Night-man, a supernatural being : īwē-baiya (C) ; dūwē'-gak (E).
Night Owl, 1. a mythical character, 2. a bird : dzi'gīnī (N) ; makū'kū
     (C).
Noble (a man who is of high rank and so wealthy that he never does
     any work; he lives in a fine house, wears fine clothes, has a
     "chair", and does not even get water for himself; a servant
     brings him water and food, wherever he sits) : tsīdī'man,
     tsīdī'mal (E).
nōhwak (E) : fawn.
nō'napōti (C,E) : a village near Kelseyville.
Northern End of the World, a mythical place : djūhū'la-ma-ye (N) ;
     tcūlama'-ham-napō (C).
nub, (at the base of a deer-horn) : kamīla't! (N,C).
nūpe'r (E) : 1. Skunk, a mythical character. 2. a mammal.
nuts : see foods.
nū watc, nwa'tc (C) : fawn.

oak: *see* trees.

Oak-ball, 1. a mythical character; 2. a kind of very light gall on oak trees: katō'l (N); pacai ka*t*alak, palō'cai, paloce, poloce, pōtō'ce (C); ˌpatō'l (E).

obsidian: katca-kabe (N,C); xagᶜa-xabe (E).

obsidian knife: bat (N).

Obsidian-man, a supernatural being: katca'-tca (C,E).

Old man: bū'tsike (E).

one, the number: tca (N); ta'tō (C); kalī' (E).

o! o! idīemūl (C): "yes! yes! That is good".

ōpe'bō (C): a swelling of the jaw.

osprey, a bird: kaca' (C).

otter, a mammal: gᶜigᶜi' (E).

owl: *see* birds.

pa' (N,C,E): any putrid substance, excrement.

pabō' (E): greens (vegetal food).

pa'-būtsīke, pa'-būtsigᶜe (E): Putrid-old-man, a supernatural being.

pacai ka*t*alak (C): 1. oak-ball, a mythical character. 2. a nut-gall.

pa'lo (E): the limb of a mush oak tree.

palo'cai, paloce (C): 1. Oak-ball, a mythical character. 2. a nut-gall on an oak tree.

pa'-napō (N): the place where Putrid-man lived (in myths).

Panther, Mountain Lion: 1. a mythical character; 2. a mammal: damō't (N,C,E); yamō't (C).

parī*t*kī (E): an expression meaning "curling around something".

pa'-tca (N,C,E): Putrid-man, a supernatural being.

patō'l (E): 1. Oak-ball, a mythical character; 2. a nut-gall from a white oak tree.

pa'tolka (C): a name invented by Meadowlark, to be used instead of "ta sītōl" when asking for a "sun-basket".

pcē (C,E): deer.

   pcē'-cenē (C,E): "deer-sweathouse", the house of magic deer (in myths).

   pcē'-dam (C): White Deer, a supernatural being.

   pcē'-stū (C): dwarf deer, a supernatural being.

   pcē-tca (C): Deer-man, a supernatural being.

pcē-tsamō (C) : 1. an insect, *lit.* "deer-fly"; 2. Bottle-fly, or Blue-fly,
a mythical character.

pcī (C) : a small shell like the periwinkle.

pdaha'ū, pdaha'ū-keya (C) : Garcia Village, an old village east of Man-
chester, on the Garcia River.

pda'-*t*eyama (C) : Boonville (village).

pdū (C) ; būdū (N,E) : acorn.,

pendant of abalone-shell: hwil (C,E).

Pelican, 1. a mythical character; 2. a bird: kala'i (E).

pepperwood: behem (N,C) ; bahe' (C) ; behep (E).

perch, a fish: dita' (C).

pere'c (C) : 1. Louse, a mythical character. 2. an insect parasite.

pestle, a utensil: daxō (N) ; dako (C) ; dag^ōn (E).

    bata'l (E) : an ordinary pestle.

    bicē-dakō (N) : a magic pestle.

    dako (N,C) : 1. an ordinary pestle; 2. Pestle, a mythical character.

    dako-batal (C,E) : small pestle.

    dagaū-xatūs (E) : small pestle.

    tsī'lo (E) : Sun-man's pestle.

Pieta, a town on the Russian River: kahwa'laū (C).

Pigeon, 1. a mythical character, 2. a species of bird: tca'batbat (N).

pīka'-napō (N) : a place (in myths) where the Basket-people lived.

pike, a fish: capa'l (C).

pīkō'taik (C) ; pīkō'*t*aina (E) : a game, shinney.

pine: *see* trees.

pine-nut: kūtī' (N).

    Pine-nut-young-man, 1. a mythical character; 2. a mammal: kūtī'-
tcūlīya (N).

pine pitch: kahwē (E) ; gō'tekalē-kahwē, kahwā-le's (E) (soft pitch) ;
sī (E)) (hard pitch).

Pine Ridge, a place near Ukiah: bōa'nū (C).

pkō'stil (C) : shinney, a game.

plants,

    algae: ka'kasū (C).

    Carex barbarae (sedge) : kuhu'm (N,C,E).

    chemese: baka'm, gōnhō', gōnō, kanō' (C).

    elderberry: kalū'l (E).

plants *cont.*

    grape-vine: ce, ctīn (C,E).

    kelp: ka′ce, bō′na ka′ce (C).

    lupine, purple: ka′tsa (C).

    milkweed: maca′ (C,E).

    moss: kadji (C); xa′sībū, xalē′sībū (E).

    nettle: hōm (N).

    Scirpus maritimus (bulrush): tsīwi′c (N,C,E).

    soaproot: a′msūla (N).

    sunflower: cala′m (C).

    tule: bagō′, k!op, bō′dehase, bō′dīhase, tībē, xa ci (E).

    water-lily: kūLa′ (E).

    wormwood: kaa′pūlū (N,C).

    unidentified:

        gūca′l, kūca′l (E).

        kacī′ (E): a grass.

        kō′lōlō, kōtōhlō (E): a fiber plant.

        mūtī′p (E): a coarse grass.

        tcīma′, tsūma′ (C): a weed.

        tsū′kale (C): a shrub.

    see also foods, trees.

plumes: ka*t*a′s (E).

po (C): magnesite.

po′kal (C): The Devil's Elbow, a rock formation, on Pine Ridge near Ukiah.

poloce (C): 1. Oak-ball, a mythical character. 2. a nut-gall found on oak-trees.

po′lpol (E): a village in the Sacramento Valley.

p!ō′ma (C): an elk-horn wedge.

pond: ka*r*a′ (C).

Pond-woman, a supernatural being: danō′-kawō (C,E).

post oak: kakū′l, wjū, ūyu (C).

pōt (C,E): fog.

    pōt-hola (C): Fog-sack (in myths).

pōtō′ce (C): 1. Oak-ball, a mythical character; 2. a nut-gall found on oak trees.

pō′t-tca (E): Fog-man, a supernatural being, one of the six servants of Madumda, the creator.

Potter Valley: balō'kai (N,C).

pta'ka (C): 1. Grizzly Bear, a mythical character. 2. a mammal.

ptcī (C): a type of burden basket.

pū—— (N): an expression used in games, meaning "I shot you".

pūī (E): 1. fat of any kind; 2. charcoal paint; 3. marrow.

pūli'ts-ūwī (E): a place, called Emerson's Point, on the western shore
    of Upper Lake.

Puma: *see* Panther.

purple lupine: ka'tsa (C).

pūtī' (C): a root food plant.

Putrid-man, a supernatural being: pa'-tca (N,C,E).

Putrid-old-man, a supernatural being: pa'būtsīke (E).

putrid substance (any): pa' (N,C,E).

pūyemlī (C): an expression translated as "looking around".

Quail, 1. a mythical character; 2. a bird: caka'ka (N,C,E); caka'kaiya
    (C); cag^cax (E).

quiver: manē (N).

rabbit: *see* mammals.

rain: bicema (N); tce' (C); kīke (E).

   Rain-sack, in myths: tce'-hola (C).

raspberries: ba'c-kōt (C).

rat: *see* Woodrat.

rattle *verb*: tīli'm, tīhli'm (E).

Rattlesnake, 1. a mythical character; 2. a reptile: mitī' (N); makō'ya,
    bakō'yō (C); xas (E).

Red-headed-woodpecker, 1. a mythical character; 2. a bird: kata' (N);
    kata'k (C); karatc (E).

Red Mountain: ma'kesil, ma'kīsil (C).

redwood tree, *Sequoia sempervirens;* kasil (N).

Redwood Mountain, near Calpella: capa'lawel-danō (N).

reptiles,

    turtle: kawīna (N).

    lizard:

        black lizard: xa'dūnū"tal (E).

        green lizard: bicē-ūi-saale (C).

reptiles *cont.*

    other lizards (unidentified):

        bīcē'bila (N): has black back and green belly.

        ce'm*t*ūlū (C): a green species with striped back and white belly.

        co'mtūlū (N): a small spotted species.

        haūbala, kaūbala (C): a species.

        ka*t*ū'nūtal (E): a mountain lizard.

        kolaha' (N): a species with a mouth at both head and tail.

        kōmaka' (N): a long-nosed species.

        mtū'lū (N,C): a species.

    snakes:

        blacksnake: mīca'kala (N).

        bullsnake: kakō'ī (N,C); ka'baōyel (E).

        milksnake: hō'dūdū"dū (N).

        rattlesnake: mi*t*ī (N); makō'ya, bakō'yō (C); xas (E).

        unidentified species:

            ka*t*ū'lū*t*ūdūk (E): a reddish species with black stripes and a strong odor.

            kawolwol (C): a very large species.

            tcūwa'dū (C): a species.

Robin, 1. a mythical character; 2. a bird: tsīto'ktok (N); tsatō'tō (C); tsītō'tō (E).

    see also mountain robin.

Rock-man, a supernatural being: kabē-baiya (C); xabē-gak (E).

Rock-woman, a supernatural being, living at the southern extremity of the world: kabē-ma*t*a (C,E).

    Rock-woman's house: kabē-ma*t*a-tca (C,E).

Rocky Point, on the western shore of Clear Lake: kabe'l (E).

roots: *see* foods.

rope: badī'uk (C); yū'lūk (E). *see also* Feather rope.

Russian River, mouth of: kahwa'lalīkē, kahwa'latī (C).

saka-lalai (C,E): 1. Gray Squirrel, a mythical character. 2. a mammal.

salal-berries: tō'ltōl (C).

Salamander, 1. a mythical character; 2. an amphibian: ca'kawōLō (N.C): masan-kalits (E).

salmon-berries: da'wai (C).

Sanhedrim Mountain: batsō'm-danō (N).

sapō (N): 1. Frog, a mythical character. 2. an amphibian.

Sapsucker, 1. a mythical character; 2. a bird: kalē'tsat (C,E); kanabati'ltil (E).

Scirpus maritimus: tsīwi'c (N,C,E).

Screech Owl, 1. a mythical character; 2. a bird: cadō'dō (N,E).

sea-lion, 1. a mythical people; 2. a mammal: ka'bitaka (C); ka'būragal (E).

seaweed: *see* kelp.

sedge, *Carex barbarae:* kūhū'm (N,C,E).

see'-baiya (C): Brush-man, a supernatural being.

seeds: *see* foods.

se-gak (E): Brush-man, a supernatural being.

seē'-tca (C): Brush-man, a supernatural being.

se'hmarak (E): a large brush dance-house.

sē'napō (C): a village east of Cache Creek.

Sequoia sempervirens: kasil (N).

ser (C): bone awl.

serpent, supernatural: *see* bagī'l.

Shade-man, a supernatural being: cīyō-gak (E).

sha'lnis: *same as* ca'lnis.

Sharp-heel, a supernatural being: kama-silī-dūketya (N).

shell,

 lako' (C): a species of shell.

 pcī (C): a small shell like a periwinkle.

 see also abalone.

 shell beads: wina'mūlī (N,C); na'mūlī (C).

shinney, a game: kapī'yem (N,C); pīkō'taik, pkō-stil (C); pīkō'taina (E).

shredded tule: kato'la (E).

shrew (?): bōka'pcūt (C).

sī (E): hard pine pitch.

sī'bō (C): the number "three".

sī"kala'la (C): smoke-hole.

sīli'l, slīl (N,C): 1. mink, a mythical character; 2. a small amphibious mammal.

silversides, a fish: mi'ya (C).

sīma' (E): net.

sīma'koo (E): a sleep-producing wand (in myths).

sinew net: īmō'waiyax (E).

singer: ke'ūya (C).

sīnwa nō balma (C): an expression meaning "what have you come here for?".

sīto'ktok: 1. Robin, a mythical character; 2. a bird.

sī'wa: mountain robin.

sīya'k (N): 1. Barn Owl, a mythical character; 2. a bird.

skewer, head-: cna'gano (C); kanō', kabē'kki-kanō (E).

    elk-horn skewer: kasī'zī-kanō (N,C).

Skunk, 1. a mythical character; 2. a mammal: mpē (C); nūpe'r (E).

Sky Occupant, "sky occupation", a supernatural being, deity of the Sky: kalī'matūtsi (E).

sleep charm: sma'-kaa'itcīl, sīma'koo (C,E).

slīl (C): 1. Mink, or Fisher, a mythical character; 2. a mammal.

sling: mcīk (C).

sma'-kaa'itcīl (C,E): sleep charm, or wand.

smē'wa (C,E): 1. Wolf, a mythical character. 2. a mammal.

smoke-hole: tcabū'ma (N,C); sī"kala'la (C).

snake: see reptiles.

snow: yū (N,C); hūl (E).

    Snow-man, one of Madumda's six servants: yū'-tca (E).

    Snow-mountain: cō'l-danō, yū'danō (N).

    snow-sack (in myths): yū'-hola (C).

soaproot, dried tops of: a'msūla (N).

sol (N): a flat slab of pine.

soul, or spirit of living persons: kū'ya (E).

Spider, 1. a mythical character; 2. an insect: mīca' (N,E), mtca (C), to'-cbū (C,E).

spider-web: to'cbū (C,E); mīxō't-pīle" (N).

spirit: kū'ya (E). see soul and ghost.

    spirit-sweathouse, a mythical place: kū'ya-canē (E).

Spring-baby, a supernatural being: kapa'-kū.

Spring-man, a supernatural dwarf: gapa'-baiya (C); gapa'-gak (E); kapa'-tca.

squirrel: *see* mammals.

staff,

 official staff of the Kuksu doctors: cakō'ik (E).

stake-holder, one who holds the bets in a game: medze (N,C,E).

starved person, one so starved that he cannot get food for himself:
 katsa'mtiu (C).

Stewart's Point: kaca'yama (C).

stīli'c (C) : a fish.

stīlīstīlīū (C,E) : 1. Mink, a mythical character; 2. a species of mammal.

s*t*īt, (C) : blanket.

 hwi'l-s*t*īt (C) : abalone-shell blanket.

Stone-woman: *same as* Rock-woman.

storage basket: *see* basket.

strawberries: ma'mūl (C).

stretcher, an apparatus for carrying the injured or dead: xaitsa'k (E).

string snare: *t*a'-slēma (C).

stū'ptcī (C,E) : a large flaring basket.

sūbū (N) : "three", the number.

sucker, a fish: kōm (C).

sūl (C,E) : 1. a mythical character, referred to as both Vulture and
 Condor; 2. a species of vulture, the California Vulture, *Cathartes
 californicus,* Shaw.

sūlē' (N) : head-net, or hair-net.

sūl-ke (C) : Vulture-dance.

Sulphur Bank: kawē'na, xa-wīna (E).

sūlūmōī (N) : a place near Upper Lake.

sun: da (N,C) ; la,lala'i (E).

 sun-basket, a mythical red-feathered burden basket (unfinished):
 ta'sītōl, pa'tolka (C).

Sun-dreamer, a supernatural being: da'matū (C).

Sun-executioners, four servants of Sun-man, who kill erring mortals
 with invisible arrows: da'-tcma (E).

sunflower, a wild flower: cala'm (C).

Sun-girls, daughters of Sun-man: da'-ma*t*a (C,E).

Sunland, abode of the Sun: cō'da-yō (C) ; cō'laiyō (E).

Sun-man, a supernatural being who carries the Sun: da'tca (C,E); la'-gaūk (E).

Sun-messengers, servants of Sun-man, who accompany him on his journeys: da'-tcatc (E).

Sun-prophet: *same as* Sun-dreamer.

sun-sack (in myths): da'-hola (C).

Sun-women, *same as* Sun-girls.

supernatural beings, *see* section on Supernatural beings, pp. 21-41.

sūū'padax (E): a supernatural being, Whirl-wind; the deity of the North.

sū'wa (C): mountain robin.

swan, a species of: kor (E). *See also* birds.

sweat-house: cane (N); cane, cene (C); 'xōma*r*ak (E).

*t*a (C,E): birds of any kind.

taa'ya-xa (E): a place on the eastern side of Clear Lake.

tak (N): the number "four".

t!ala' (C): a food plant.

    tala'-bū (C): a root food plant.

tala'k (N,C): 1. Flying Squirrel, a mythical character; 2. a mammal.

*t*alē'ya-kalai (C): a beautiful hair-net made from human hair.

    *t*alē'ya-kūtsī (C): bead waist-band, with pendants.

*t*a'-matū (C): "bird story".

*t*am-nōyō (C): a place about one mile east of the village of Hopland.

tan oak: ūtce'c (C).

*t*ana' (C,E): 1. Chub Duck, a mythical character; 2. a bird.

*t*a'napō (N): a "bird-village" near Upper Lake.

ta*r*a (E): 1. Wasp, a mythical character; 2. an insect.

ta'sītōl (C,E): "sun-basket", red-feathered basket.

*t*a'-slēma (C): string snar*e*s.

ta'ta (N,C,E): 1. Falcon, a mythical character; 2. a bird.

ta'tō (C): the number "one".

tca (N): the number "one".

tca (E): "man".

    tcatc (E): "men" (plural of tca).

tcaba'tbat (N): 1. Pigeon, a mythical character; 2. a bird.

tcabū'ma (N): smoke-hole, an opening in the roof of a dance-house.

tca'dadaū, tca'dada, tcadada'ū (C,E): kingfisher.

tca'dūwel (E): ghost, the spirit of the human after it reaches the Abode of the Dead.

tca'dūwel-canē (E) [*lit.* ghost-sweathouse]: a large assembly-house for ghosts (in myths), at the southern extremity of the world.

tca'dūwel-ma (E): Abode of the Dead, a mythical place, at the southern extremity of the world.

tca'i-bidame (E): a creek five or six miles from Kelseyville.

tca'-kalik (C,E): chief, head man.

tca'*t*-batē (C): a place about two miles south of the mouth of the Gualala River.

tcawa'iya, tcawai'yū (C): a food plant.

tcawī-a-kabe (C): a rock for grinding beads.

tca'-yedūl-bate (C,E): head-chief.

tce' (C): rain.

tce'-hola (C): Rain-sack, in myths.

tcidī'ū (N,C): Eel River Valley.

tcīdō'-tca (N,C): Flower-man, a supernatural being.

tcīma' (C): *same as* tsuma (C).

tcīma't (N): 1. Gray Squirrel, a mythical character. 2. a mammal.

tcitcī' (C): 1. Hawk, a mythical character; 2. a bird.

tcīya' (N,C,E): 1. Chicken Hawk, a mythical character; 2. Western Red-tail Hawk.

tcma'-ke (C,E): war-dance.

tco'dok, tco'dūk (E): 1. a supernatural being, *same as* būra'kal būkaiūkke (E); 2. a small species of bird with a top-knot.

tcōm (N): a species of pine.

tcoo, tcoowī (N,C): yellowjacket, an insect.

tcō'tcō (N): 1. Bluebird, a mythical character; 2. a species of bird.

tcūlama'-ham-napō (C): a mythical place, the northern end of the world.

tcūlī'ya (N): "young man".

kūtī'-tcūlī'ya: Pine-nut-young-man.

tcūlū' (E): hunting sack.

tcūma't (C): a gray squirrel.

tcū'*t*kil (E): 1. Diver, a mythical character; 2. a diving-bird.

tcūwa-dū (C): a snake.

tcūwī'u-kabē (C) : a bead-grinding stone.

te (C,E) : feather down.

teca', tece' (C) : a food plant.

tele (C) : 1. Hummingbird, a mythical character, 2. a species of bird.

thorns,

    gooseberry thorns: lūm (C,E).

Thrasher, 1. a mythical character, 2. a species of bird: wo'cwoc (C,E).

three, the number: sūbū (N); sī'bō (C); xōmka (E).

throwing-stick: mlū'ī, tsū (N,C); batī' (E).

    throwing-sticks, a game: tsū'dūyem, tsū-kat (N).

Thunder, 1. a supernatural being; 2. a natural phenomenon: kalīmata'-ūta, makīla (N); makē'la (C); kalī-matoto (E).

    thunder-fish: makē'la-ca (C).

tībē' (E) : young edible tule.

    tībē'-cela (E) [lit. tule-young-man] : Tule-boy (Coyote), a supernatural being and a mythical character.

    tībē'-patsō-waiyax (E) : tule net.

tīhēma-pda (C) : place where Grizzly Bear lived.

    tīhēma (C) : an ejaculation used when someone is always doing something you do not like.

tīhnū'r (E) : 1. Beaver, a mythical character. 2. a mammal.

tīhlim, tīli'm (E) : to rattle.

tīt (C) : an openwork storage basket.

tī'tō-nō'ō (C) : blackberries.

tīyal (E) : 1. Yellowhammer, a mythical character. 2. a bird.

Toad, 1. a mythical character; 2. an amphibian: bata'k (N).

tō'cbū (C,E) : 1. Spider, a mythical character. 2. an insect. 3. a spider-web.

tō'ltōl (C) : salal-berries.

Tomales Bay: lakō'ka (E).

tō'mkai (N) : an old village site about three miles below Traveler's Home.

top-knot: kaa'itcīl (N,C).

    owl top-knot: makū'gū kaa'itcīl (N).

trees,

    hazel: cabakle, dūcī' (C).

    manzanita: bakai' (C); kaiye (N,C); xaiye (E).

trees *cont.*

    maple: acema'ikatīte (N).

    mountan mahogany: macū'm (N); kanō'-hai (C).

    oak:

        black oak: dicī (N); ūcī (C); līcūī (E).

        live oak: dūtcī', dūtsī' (C).

        mush oak: ūcī' (C).

        post oak: wjū, ūyu, kakū'l (C).

        tan oak: ūtce'c (C).

        white oak: tsīpa (N,E); tsapa' (C).

    pepperwood: behem (N,C); bahe' (C); behep (C).

    pine:

        sugar pine: bīyū'tkūi (N).

        sweet pine: cīye' (N).

        other pines:

            cīya'kale (N).

            tcōm (N).

            kō'tekale (E).

    Sequoia sempervirens: xasīl (N,E); kasīl (C).

    willow, "basket": kalal (N); kalal-nō (C); tsūba'ha (E).

    unidentified: cta-hai (N) (skewer-wood).

trout, a fish: mala'k, mala'x (C,E).

tsaa't (C): a supernatural baby (who became Bakil and who now lives in Blue Lakes).

tsai (N,C,E): 1. Blue Jay, a mythical character. 2. a bird.

tsa'mal (E): 1. Blue-fly, a mythical character; 2. an insect.

tsamū'l: mosquito.

tsapa' (C): white oak.

tsa'pū (C): 1. Bluebird, a mythical character, a magician and poison-man; 2. a small bird.

tsa*tī*' (C): 1. a supernatural being; 2. a small gray bird about the size of a robin.

tsatō'tō (C): 1. Robin, a mythical character; 2. a small bird.

tsawa'l (C): flatfish, a fish.

tsawa'l-xabē (E): a place on the eastern side of Clear Lake.

tsawa'tak (N,C,E): 1. Frog, a mythical character; 2. an amphibian.

    tsawa'tak-matō (N): 1. Bullfrog, a mythical character. 2. an amphibian.

tsīdī'mal, tsīdī'man (E) : Noble *q.v.*

tsīki'nī (N,E) : great horned owl.

tsīko'lkol (E) : Madumda's younger brother, a supernatural being and
the ruler of the second Upper World.

tsili' (C) : blackbird.

tsīli'tsīlīū (C,E) : 1. Mink, a mythical character ; 2. a small mammal.

tsī'lō (E) : a pestle used by Sun-man for breaking the shin or leg-bones
of his victims.

  tsīlō'-tca (C) : a drummer (one who beats a drum).

tsī*t* (E) : all kinds of small birds.

tsitīt (E) : the noise made by Kilak's house when the owner is coming.

tsīto'ktok (N) ; tsītō'tō (E) : 1. Robin, a mythical character ; 2. a bird.

tsītū'mpa (E) : a term used in calling for Kuksu or any other magician.

  tsītū'mpahe——, tcīhūī hūūyū——, tsīhūī hūūyū (E) : a meaningless expression, said to be the regular call for Kuksu in ceremonies.

tsīwi'c (N,C,E) : bulrush (*Scirpus maritimus*).

tsiya'gago (E) : a small wet-weather lake on the side of Mount
Kanaktai.

tsīya'-kabē (E) : a mythical place about two miles north of Witter
Springs, where Sun-man lived.

tsō'lōpa (E) : a yellowhammer-feather forehead-band.

tsū, mlū'ī (N,C) ; batī' (E) : arrow or throwing-stick.

tsūba'ha (E) : a tree, the "basket" willow.

tsū'dīyūn (N,C,E) ; tsū'dūyūn (N,C) ; tsū'īdūn (C,E) : 1. Hummingbird, a mythical character ; 2. a tiny bird.

tsū'dūyen (N) ; 1. a game, throwing-sticks ; 2. a throwing-stick.

tsūka' (N) : war-feathers.

tsū'kale (C) : a shrub.

tsū-kat (N) : a game, throwing-sticks.

tsuLī' (E) : blackbird.

tsūLītsūLīū, tsūLītsūLī (C) : whitefish, a fish.

tsūma (E) : a kind of weed.

tsūmē'wa (N) : 1. Wolf, a mythical character ; 2. a mammal.

tsū'-tca (C,E) : Arrow-man, a supernatural being.

tsū'*t*kil, tsū'*t*kilbek (E) : 1. Diver, a mythical character ; 2. a water-
bird

tsū'wa (C): mountain robin.

tubers: *see* foods.

tule,

    batcō (N,C); bagō' (E): green or dry tule.

    bō'dīhase (E): ceremonial term for "tule".

    kato'la (E): shredded tule.

    k!op (E): tule which has become water-logged and has sunk to the bottom of the lake.

    tībē' (E): the young edible tule, much esteemed as food.

    xa ci (E): a special kind of tule, something like *carex*.

Tule-boy, another name for Coyote: tībē'-cela (E).

Tule Lake, a lake northwest of Clear Lake.

tule net: tībē'-patsō-waiyox (E).

tump-line: kōkō (E).

turtle: kawīna (N,C); kanadīhwa (E).

Turtle-woman, a mythical character: kawīna (N).

tūtcī' (C): 1. Buzzard, a mythical character; 2. a bird.

tūwī'u-kabe (C): a bead-polishing stone.

Twin Lakes: *see* Blue Lakes.

two, the number: kō (N,C); xōtc (E).

ūcī' (C): mush oak.

ūī-nasai (C,E); ūī-bagō (E): Blind-man, a supernatural being.

Ukiah Valley: yō'kaia-ma (C).

Uncle Sam Mountain: *see* Mount Kanaktai.

Upper Lake Region: ka'kaiyaū (E).

Upper World, the abode of Madumda: kalī'mīnaū (E).

ūtce'c (C): tan oak.

ūyu (C): a species of large post oak.

valley, any valley (general term): gagō', kagō' (E).

    Gravely Valley: katsa-gokai (N) [*lit.* grass valley].

    Napa Valley: napa (E).

valley blue jay: tsai (N,C,E).

Valley-man, a supernatural being: kakō-baiya (C); gagō-'gak (E).

valley quail: caka'ka (N,C); cagᶜax (E).

Vulture, 1. Vulture, a mythical character; 2. a bird: sūl (N,C,E).

    vulture-dance: sūl-ke (C).

wacū' (E): a digging-stick.
wada'wada (C,E): 1. Wood-duck, a mythical character; 2. a bird.
walking-stick: *see* cane.
Wambold's Lake, one of the Blue Lakes: xa'-silī'ū (C).
wand, Kuksu's: cakō'ik, kalū'l (E).
wara'wara (E): Wood-duck, a mythical character; 2. a bird.
war-dance: tcma-ke (E).
   war-feathers: tsūka' (N).
Wasp, 1. a mythical character; 2. an insect: ma'n-kitsī (C); tara (E).
watchman, Gilak's lookout: kūsū't (C).
Water-cat, a supernatural being living in Blue Lakes: ka-iamot (C).
Water-dog, 1. a mythical character; 2. a batrachian: ca'kawōLō (N,C).
"water-head": xa'-cīnal (C,E).
water-lily, an acquatic plant: kūLa' (E).
Water-man, a supernatural being: ka'-tca (N); ka'-baiya (C); xa'-gak
   (E).
Water Occupant, "water-occupation", a supernatural being, the deity
   of the West: xa'matūtsi (E).
"water-top", Pomo name for Bodega Bay: lakō'ka-wīna (E).
wave, waving field of grain or grass: mōrī (E).
wedge, elk-horn: p!ō'ma (C).
weed, a species of: tcīma' (C); tsūma' (E).
Western Red-tail Hawk: tcīya' (N,C,E).
whale, a cetacean: kate' (C).
Whirl-wind, a supernatural being, the deity of the North: sūū'padax
   (E).
Whiskey-dance: ka-tcaha-ke, lehūya-ke (C).
whistle (single): lībū' (E).
white,
   white bread (acorn meal): ka'sī-lasoi (N,C).
   White Crane, a mythical character: kala'k (E).
   whitefish, a fish: tsūLītsūLīū (C).
   white oak-ball: patō'l (E) (nut-gall from a white oak).
   white oak (tree): tsapa' (C).
   white rock (pebble): kawin tsala (C).
Whittled-leg-widow, a supernatural being: cakū-kattciū (C); kama-
   sīlī-dūket-mīya (E).

wīk!a' (E): 1. Panther, a mythical character; 2. a mammal, possibly the lynx.

Wildcat, 1. a mythical character; 2. a mammal: dalō'm (C,E).

Wild Onion Mountain: kaba'i-danō (C,E).

Willow, 1. a mythical character; 2. a tree, the "basket" willow: tsūba'ha (E).

wina'mūlī, na'mūlī (N,C): large shell beads.

wind: ya (N,C); hīya (E).

> Wind-man, a supernatural being, one of Madumda's six servants: ya'tca (N,E); ya-tcatc (C); yai-kī (E).

> Wind-sack, in myths: ya-hola (C).

wi'tcilī, wi'tclī (N,C): a guessing game.

wjū (C): a species of large post oak.

wo'cwoc (N,C,E): 1. Thrasher, or Mockingbird, a mythical character; 2. a bird.

Wolf, 1. a mythical character; 2. a mammal: tsūmē'wa (N); smē'wa (C,E).

wo'lwol (C): flute.

wood,

> dry wood, a special kind, high up in the trees, one in which wood-peckers have stored acorns: kaℓ, xaℓ (E).

> skewer wood (used for making hair-skewers): cta'hai (N).

> wood-hook, a hook used for gathering fire-wood: baka'ℓ (E); baxa'ℓ (C,E).

Woodcock, 1. a mythical character, a poison doctor; 2. a species of bird: baka'ka (C,E).

Wood Duck, 1. a mythical character; 2. a duck: bada'bada (C); wada'-wada (C,E); waℓa'waℓa (E).

Woodpecker: *see* birds.

Woodrat, 1. a mythical character; 2. a mammal: daka'lak, daka'dalak (N); baiyō'k (N,C); bayo'k (C).

Worm, 1. a mythical character; 2. a species of worm which lives in wood: kalē'kol (E).

worms:

> green measuring worm: mtca'tsīmūl (C).

> a species that lives in wood: kalē'kol (E).

wormwood, an herb: kaa'pūlū (N,C).

wrist-band (bead): talĕ′ya-kūtsī (C,E).

wūn (N,C): 1. Mole, a mythical character; 2. a species of rodent.

xaba′i (C,E): an old campsite on the western shore of Clear Lake; *same as* kaba′i.

xabē-gak (E): Rock-man, a supernatural being.

xabe′l (E): a place at Rocky Point on the northwestern shore of Clear Lake.

xa ci (E): a special kind of tule something like *carex*.

xa′-cīnal (C): 1. "water-head", Upper Twin Lake, one of the Blue Lakes. 2. the head of any lake.

xa′-du′nutal (E): 1. Black Lizard, a mythical character; 2. a reptile.

xaĕ′lī (E): a term meaning "I have heard".

xagᶜa′ (E): a projectile-point, an arrow-head.

xagᶜa′-cela (E): Arrowpoint-young-man, a supernatural being; identical with Obsidian-man.

xa′-gak (E): Water-man, a supernatural being.

xagū′nūbek (E): a species of water-bird.

xa′-gūnū′la (E): 1. a mythical character; 2. a small duck.

xa-hlūī-xak (E): a ghost, or spirit of the dead.

xa′ibahlaū (E): a wooden implement.

xaicī′gī (E): a feather skirt.

xai′dasōtī (E): a raised platform or bed upon which Nobles recline.

xaitsa′k (E): a stretcher for carrying the injured or dead.

xaiya′n (E): 1. Mallard Duck, a mythical character; 2. a duck.

xalaxak (E): a small pond on the western shore of Clear Lake.

xala′-xatū (E): "clam lake", Wambold's Lake, one of the Blue Lakes; *same as* xa′silīū.

xalĕ′-sībū (E): a tree moss.

xalī′wīnaūna (E): the Upper World.

xa′-matūtsi (E): "water occupation", Water Occupant, a supernatural being, the deity of the West.

xam *t*ara (C): Bodega Bay.

xa*r* (C): a special kind of dry wood, *see* wood.

xas (E): rattlesnake.

xa′sibū (E): a kind of floating moss.

xa′-silī′ū (C,E): Wambold's Lake, one of the Blue Lakes.

xatsī'ya (E) : 1. Mud-hen, a mythical character; 2. a species of water-bird.

xa-wīna (E) [*lit.* water-on-top-of] : Sulphur Bank Village; so called because the village seems to be located on top of the water.

xawō' (E) : 1. Frog, a mythical character; 2. a batrachian.

xōdeē'lim (E) : a place on the eastern shore of Upper Lake.

xō-gak (E) : Fire-man, a supernatural being.

xōma'ʳ (E) : 1. Ground-squirrel-people, mythical characters; 2. a mammal.

xō'maxa (E) : a pond in the hills, where Wildcat hunted deer by magic.

xōmka (E) : "three" the number.

xōtc (E) : "two" the number.

xūcīli (E) : meadowlark.

xūkī (E) : buzzard.

ya (C,E) : 1. wind; 2. an exclamation of disgust.

    ya'-hola (C) : Wind-sack (in myths).

yai-kī (E) : Wind-man, a supernatural being.

ya'katapopo (N) : a mythical place, where the Kabaltu Girls lived and had a magic swing.

ya'kōda-pda (C,E) : a creek now called "Elk Creek", about two miles south of Greenwood.

yala (C) : a small species of goose.

ya'mō : a place near the head of Potter Valley, the abode of Wind-man.

yamō't (C) : 1. Panther (sometimes called Mountain-lion), a mythical character; 2. a mammal.

ya'-tca (N,E) : Wind-man, a supernatural being; one of the six servants of Madumda.

yellowhammer, 1. a mythical character; 2. a bird: batsīya (N); katsī'yō (C); tīyal (E).

    yellowhammer-feather forehead-band: tsō'lōpa (E).

yellowjacket, 1. a mythical character; 2. an insect: tcoo (N,C); tcoowī (C); xalō (E).

ye*t* (N,C,E) : a hunting or carrying sack.

yīke' (C) : 1. Ground Squirrel, a mythical character; 2. a mammal.

yō'butiū (C,E) : a place about three-quarters of a mile south of the present town of Upper Lake, and about one-half of a mile south of Kucadanoyo.

yō'ga-koi (E) : Big Valley.

yō'kaia-ma (C) : Ukiah Valley.

yōma-hamke (C) : a place at the southern end of the world.

young man : tcūlīya (N) ; cēla (E).

yū (C) : snow.

    yū'-danō (N,C) : Snow Mountain, a mountain south of Round Valley.

    yū'-hōla (C) : Snow-sack (in myths).

    yū'ksū (C) : hailstones.

yū'lūk (C,E) : 1. feather rope; 2. magic wand.

yū'-tca (E) : Snow-man, a supernatural being, one of Madumda's six servants.

BIBLIOGRAPHY

Alexander, H. B.
     1916, The Mythology of All Races, (Vol. X, North America),
     Boston.

Angulo, see de Angulo.

Bancroft, H. H.
     1875, The Native Races of the Pacific States, III, 88.

Barrett, S. A.
     1906, "A Composite Myth of the Pomo Indians", Journ. Amer.
     Folk-Lore, XIX, 37-51.
     1908, "The Ethno-geography of the Pomo and Neighboring
     Indians", Univ. Calif. Publ., Amer. Arch. Ethn., VI, 1-332.
     1917A, "Pomo Bear Doctors", Univ. Calif. Publ., Amer. Arch.
     Ethn., XII, 443-465.
     1917B, "Ceremonies of the Pomo Indians", Univ. Calif. Publ.,
     Amer. Arch. Ethn., XII, 397-441.
     1919, "Myths of the Southern Sierra Miwok", Univ. Calif. Publ.,
     Amer. Arch. Ethn., XVI, 1-28.

Benson, see de Angulo and Benson.

Boas, Franz.
     1914, "Mythology and Folk-Lore of the North American In-
     dians", Journ. Amer. Folk-Lore, XXVII, 374-410.

Burns, L. M.
     1901, "'Digger Indian Legends", (Scott Valley Shasta), Land
     of Sunshine, XIV, 130-134, 223-226, 310-314, 397-402.

Chambers, G. A.
     1906, "Tradition Formerly Obtained at Chico."
     (Fragment of a Mermaid Story from the Chico Maidoo),
     Journ. Amer. Folk-Lore, XIX, 141.

Clark, Galen.
     1904, Indians of Yosemite Valley, Chapter VII, pp. 76-100.
     Yosemite Valley, Calif. [Southern Miwok].

Curtin, Jeremiah.
    1898, Creation Myths of Primitive America, Boston. [Wintun and Yana].
    1909, "Achomawi Myths" (Edited by R. B. Dixon), Journ. Amer. Folk-Lore, XXII, 283-287.

Dangel, R.
    1929, "Bear and Fawns", Journ. Amer. Folk-Lore, XXXXII, 307, 308.

de Angulo, J. and Freeland, L. S.
    1928, "Miwok and Pomo Myths", Journ. Amer. Folk-Lore, XXXXI, 232-252.
    1931, "Two Achomawi Tales", Journ. Amer. Folk-Lore, XXXXIV, 125-136.

de Angulo, J. and Benson, W. R.
    1932, "The Creation Myth of the Pomo Indians", Anthropos, XXVII, 261-274, 779-795.

Dixon, R. B.
    1900, "Some Coyote Stories from the Maidu Indians of California", Journ. Amer. Folk-Lore, XIII, 267-270.
    1902, "Maidu Myths", Bull., Amer. Mus. Nat. Hist., XVII, 33-118.
    1905, "The Mythology of the Shasta-Achomawi", Amer. Anthrop., VII, 607-612.
    1908, "Achomawi and Atsugewi Tales", Journ. Amer. Folk-Lore, XXI, 159-177.
    1910, "Shasta Myths", Journ. Amer. Folk-Lore, XXIII, 8-37, 364-370.
    1912, "Maidu Texts", Publ., Amer. Ethn. Soc., IV.

Farrand, Livingston.
    1915, "Shasta and Athapascan Myths from Oregon", Journ. Amer. Folk-Lore, XXVIII, 207-242.

Gatschet, A. S.
    1890, "The Klamath Indians of Southwestern Oregon", Contr. N. A. Ethn., II, part 1.

Gifford, E. W.
    1917, "Miwok Myths", Univ. Calif. Publ. Amer. Arch. Ethn.,
        XII, 283-338.
    1930, "Western Mono Myths", Journ. Amer. Folk-Lore,
        XXXVI, 301-367.

Gifford, E. W. and Block, G. H.
    1930, California Indian Nights Enchantment, Glendale, Calif.,
        Pp. 323.

Goddard, P. E.
    1906, "Lassik Tales", Journ. Amer. Folk-Lore, XIX, 133-140.
    1909, "Kato Texts", Univ. Calif. Publ. Amer. Arch. Ethn., V,
        65-238.

Hudson, J. W.
    1902, "An Indian (Yokut) Myth of the San Joaquin Basin",
        Journ. Amer. Folk-Lore, XV, 104-106.

Johnson, Adam.
    1854, "Fragment of a 'Po-to-yan-te' Yokut Creation Myth",—
        in H. R. Schoolcraft's "Indian Tribes", IV, 224-225.

Kroeber, A. L.
    1904, "Types of Indian Culture in California", Univ. Calif.
        Publ. Amer. Arch. Ethn., II, 81-103.
    1905, "Wishosk Myths", Journ. Amer. Folk-Lore, XVIII, 85-
        107.
    1907A, "The Religion of the Indians of California", Univ. Calif.
        Publ. Amer. Arch. Ethn., IV, 319-356.
    1907B, "Indian Myths of South Central California", Univ. Calif.
        Publ. Amer. Arch. Ethn., IV, 167-250.
    1909, "Catch-words in American Mythology", Journ. Amer.
        Folk-Lore, XXI, 222-227.
    1911, "Languages of the Coast of California North of San
        Francisco", Univ. Calif. Publ. Amer. Arch. Ethn., IX, 273-
        435.

1919, "Sinkyone Tales", Journ. Amer. Folk-Lore, XXXII, 346-351.

1925, Handbook of the Indians of California, Bur. Amer. Ethn., Bull. 78.

1932, "Yuki Myths", Anthropos, XXVII, 905-939.

Kroeber, Henrietta Rothschild.

1908A, "Wappo Myths" (The Two Brothers; The Coyote and the Frog), Journ. Amer. Folk-Lore, XXI, 321-323.

1908B, "California Indian Legends" (The Pleiades, a "Southern California" Myth; The Theft of Fire, a Yokut Myth), Out West, XXVIII, 66-69.

Loeb, E. M.

1926A, "Pomo Folkways", Univ. Calif. Publ. Amer. Arch. Ethn., XIX, 149-405.

1926B, "The Creator Concept Among the Indians of North Central California", Amer. Anthr., XXVIII, 467-493.

1932, "The Western Kuksu Cult", Univ. Calif. Publ. Amer. Arch. Ethn., XXXIII, 1-137.

1933, "The Eastern Kuksu Cult", Univ. Calif. Publ. Amer. Arch. Ethn., 139-232.

Lowie, R. L.

1909, "Catch-words for Mythological Motives", Journ. Amer. Folk-Lore, XXI, 24-27.

1910, "Additional Catch-words", Journ. Amer Folk-Lore, XXII, 332-333.

Merriam, C. Hart.

1910, The Dawn of the World, Cleveland, Ohio.

Powers, Stephen.

1877, Tribes of California, Contr. N. A. Ethn., III.

Purdy, Carl.

1903, "The 'Dau' in Pomo Basketry", Out West, XVIII, 319-325.

Sapir, Edward.
  1909, "Takelma Texts", Univ. Penn. Anthr. Publ. of the Univ. Mus., II, No. 1.
  1910, "Yana Texts", Univ. Calif. Publ. Amer. Arch. Ethn., IX, 1-235.

Spencer, D. L.
  1908, "Notes on the Maidu Indians of Butte County California", (The Buumo Myth-Battle of Coyote and the Bat), Journ. Amer. Folk-Lore, XXI, 242-245.

Stewart, G. W.
  1906, "A Yokuts (Wiktchumne) Creation Myth", Journ. Amer. Folk-Lore, XIX, 322.
  1908, "Two Yokuts Traditions", (Fragments of Tachi tales on the Origin of Fire, and the Turtle), Journ. Amer. Folk-Lore, XXI, 231-239.

INDEX

[(C)=Catchword.　(T)=Title.　(I)=Incident.　(H)=Heading]

Key to abbreviations used in "terms of relationship".

A.	Aunt.	GF.	Grandfather.	Ne.	Nephew.
B.	Brother.	GM.	Grandmother.	S.	Son.
BL.	Brother-in-law.	GS.	Grandson.	Si.	Sister.
D.	Daughter.	H.	Husband.	SiL.	Sister-in-law.
DL.	Daughter-in-law.	M.	Mother.	SL	Son-in-law.
F.	Father.	ML.	Mother-in-law.	U.	Uncle.
FL.	Father-in-law.	N.	Niece.	W.	Wife.
GD.	Granddaughter.				

ARROW-POINT, Coyote Creates Obsidian-man from an, (T) 202.
ARROW-POINT-YOUNG-MAN: son of Coyote, 208. *See also* OBSIDIAN-MAN.
——, The Story of, (T) 208.
ASCENT to the sky, 473.
ASSISTANT, BENEVOLENT: (C) 192, 215, 216, 229, 298, 340, 341, 354, 464.
ASSISTANT, MALEVOLENT: (C) 68, 76, 85, 88, 89, 91, 94, 118, 126, 143, 158, 163, 214, 220, 225, 334, 464.
ASSISTANT, OGRE'S: (C), *see* OGRE'S ASSISTANT.
ASSISTANT TOKEN: *see* TOKEN.
AUTO TRAP: (C) 58, 463.
AVENGE His Death, Falcon's Children, (I) 239.

BAGIL: 21, 142, 199; bice, 236; capture of, 201, 235; cure of illness caused by, 202; described, 38; 197, fn. 94; in Blue Lakes, 200; of Blue Lakes, explanation of, 38; origin of, 142, 198; regulation of, 143, 199; restrictions concerning passing Blue Lakes, 200; songs, 198; transforms himself into Deer, 236; *same as* Bakil.
—— Is Caught in a Rabbit Snare, A (T) 201.
—— Transforms People into Deer, (T) 235.
BAGILS, Origin of the (I) 142.
baiyō'k: *see* WOODRAT.
BAKIL Is Created and Placed in Blue Lakes, (T) 197.
BARN OWL: form explained, 275.
—— Gambles, (I) 275.
BASKET: becomes water monster of Blue Lakes, 124.
BASKET-PEOPLE: 301.
——, Woodrat and the, (I) 301.
BASKETRY, Myths Concerning, (T) 380.
BASKET-VILLAGE: 302.
BAT: arrow-maker, 184; sees fire, 309.
batca'l: *see* FISH HAWK.
BEADS: eaten by Elk, 186; sacrificed to safe ocean journey, 54.
BEAD-GRINDING STONE: serves as armor, 273; used to spring door-trap, *see* DOOR-TRAP.
BEAR: 107, 118, 223; cook's Deer's Eyes, 346; created by Coyote, 85,

BEAR cont.

88, 94, 126, 131; created by Wolf, 76, 118; follows magic basket, 329, 339, 347, 352; gets meat from between Deer Boys teeth, 350; gives Deer Boys meat from their own mother, 329; killed by Crane Bridge, 347; killed with hot rock, 331, 354; kills Deer, 328, 336; 346, 350, 351; kills Thunder, 345; kills Wildcat, 336.

> *Relationships of*: F. of Swan Sisters, 322; GM. of Deer Boys, 327, 329, 334; GM. of Thunder Children; 344; H. of Swan, 322; M. of Bear Boys, 327, 329; M. of Bear Girls, 334; M. of Deer, 334, 350; M. of Falcon, 327, 329; M. of Thunder, 344; M. of two girls, 303; ML. of Deer, 327, 329, 344; ML. of Wildcat, 334; W. of Blue Jay, 334.

—— Kills Deer, (I) 327.

—— Kills her own Daughter-in-law, Deer, (T) 327.

——, Woodrat and Mouse Kill, (I) 303.

> *see also* GRIZZLY BEAR.

BEAR BOYS: (two), 143, 327, 329.

——, The Deer Boys Kill the, (I) 329.

BEAR BROTHERS: children of Falcon, 239.

BEAR CHILDREN: *see* DEER AND BEAR CHILDREN.

——, Myths of the Deer and, (T) 334.

——, The Deer and, (T) 334.

——, The Thunder and, (T) 344; (I) 344.

BEAR AND DEER CHILDREN (C): *see* DEER AND BEAR CHILDREN.

BEAR DOCTOR: Pelican, 370.

BEAR DOCTORS: Pomo, 41, 240.

——, The Origin of the Pomo, (T) 380.

BEAR-FLY, *see* BLUE-FLY.

BEAR GIRLS: (two)

> *Relationships of:* A. of Deer Boys, 334; A. of Thunder Children, 344; D. of Bear, 303, 344; D. of Bear and Blue Jay, 334; Si. of Deer, 334; Si. of Thunder, 344; SiL. of Deer, 344; SiL. of Wildcat. 334.

BEAR VILLAGE: 303.

BEAVER: 164, 197.

BED: 319.

BENEVOLENT ASSISTANT: *see* ASSISTANT.

bēre'mal-līha"mīle: *see* FLEA, GRANDMOTHER.

BULLFROG-WOMEN: 249.
BULLSNAKE: chief, 203; W. of Flower-man, 190.
būra′gal-tsamal: *see* BLUE-FLY.
būra′kal-bakaiūkke: 289.
BURNING OF THE WORLD, The, (H) 95.
——, and the Creation of Clear Lake, The, (T) 95, 125.
BURNS the Dance-house, Coyote, (I) 167.
——— the Ground-squirrel-people, Coyote, (I) 252.
——— the World and Creates Clear Lake, Coyote, (T) 121.
——— the World and Makes Clear Lake, Coyote Creates People, (T) 117.
——— the World, Coyote, (T) 123; (I) 96, 113, 119, 121.
——— the World in Revenge for the Ill Treatment of His Children, Coyote, (T) 113.
BUTTERBALL: 354.
BUZZARD: 79, 81, 137, 170, 195, 203, 286, 308, 310; breaks open the Sun-sack, 137.
BUZZARD BROTHERS: doctors, 259.
BUZZARD-PEOPLE: 161.
BUZZARD-VILLAGE: 161.

cai: *see* EAGLE.
caka-tca: 38.
ca′kawōLō: *see* SALAMANDER.
CALIFORNIA AREA: mythology of, 11.
CALNIS: 14, 30.
CANNIBAL: (C) 174, 272, 316, 465.
CANNIBALISM: 174, 272, 316.
CANOE: kelp, 279; stone, 322.
CARDINAL DIRECTIONS: 14.
CATCHWORDS IN POMO MYTHOLOGY: 454.
ce′mtūlū: *see* LIZARD.
CEREMONIES: origin of, 376, 379.
CEREMONIES ESTABLISHED: (C) 376, 379, 456.
ce′tata: 105, 319.
CHARM: diminution of load, 129; sleep, 56, 196, 247.

Coyote *cont.*

heals self; dreams, 46, 48, 71, 73; drinks ocean water, 98, 110, 115,
120, 124; drinks water in Big Valley, 122, 126; eats roasted meat,
see WORLD-FIRE; escapes Deluge, *see* DELUGE; establishes the fish
run, 117; establishes the shore-line of the ocean, 116; gives hunting
charm, 85; heals arm with elderberry stick, 252; heals arm with
oak limb, 248; heals eye with shell bead, 292; heals own leg, 280;
heals own wound with grass, 256; heals own wound with moss, 252,
262, 266; heals own wound with pitch, 122; heals self, 122, 204, 281;
importance of, 9; institutes dances, 112; is rooted to the ground by
curse of Skunk Boys, 256; journeys to Upper World, *see* JOURNEYS
TO UPPER WORLD; jumps over the World-fire, 121; killed by rattlesnake bite, 283; makes a trap by opening his own body, 58; makes
it rain, by wishing, 241; makes ocean wavy, 111, 115; makes shore-
line, 111; makes sleep charm from his own mother's heart, 167;
objects to pity, 270; punctures his own belly with an awl, 122; puts
Sun-people to sleep with charm, 138; regurgitates abalone-shell
balls, 77; rescues Panther from the Upper World, 82; revivified,
485; revivified by Blue Jay, 180, 210, 258, 265, 282, 283, 288, 289,
291; revivified by Screech Owl, 180; revivifies Falcon, 179; revivifies himself, 190, 261; revivifies his mother, 170; revivifies people
unintentionally, 168; roasted by Flower-man, 190; rooted to the
ground by the wish of the Skunk Brothers, 262; secures costume
by magic, 145; secures feathers from which to create people, 58;
sends Skunk Brothers for building material, 261; springs door-trap;
see DOOR-TRAP; steals fish, 203, 208, 210, 220; steals the Sun, *see*
THEFT OF THE SUN; sticks in the mud, 286; summons doctors, 258;
ties hair of Ground-squirrel-people together, *see* THEFT OF THE
SUN, ORIGINAL FOOD; transforms Chub Duck into man, 112; transforms people into animals, 180; transforms self into dead fish, 245;
transforms self into old man, 77, 140, 144, 146; transforms self into
old woman, 96, 244; transforms self into original form, 251; transforms self into young man, 78, 144, 147, 245; transforms self into
young woman, 247; tricked, 13; tricked into breaking own leg, 280;
tricked into burning own hair, 281; tricked into jumping into water,
285; tricked into putting pitch onto hair, 268, 292; tricked in snaring
birds, 289; tricked in wood-gathering, 269; tricked by birds in flying,
265, 292; tricked by birds in jumping into water, 285; tricked by

Coyote *cont.*

Blue Jay, 288; tricked by Eagle, 242; tricked by Gray Squirrel in tree-climbing, 285; tricked by Hawk in hunting ground squirrels, 283; tricked by Mink, 281; tricked by Oak-ball in floating, 282; tricked by Osprey, 280; tricked by Owl, 283; tricked by Sapsucker, 267, 269; tricked by Skunk Brothers, 257, 260, 263, 265; tricked by Tsikolkol, 292; tricked by Osprey in spear-making, 280; tricked by Willow in water, 288; tricked by Woodcock, 283; tricks Falcon, 251; tricks girls, 244; tricks ground squirrels, 248; tricks Hawk, 347; tricks mother-in-law, 241; tricks Skunk, 242; tricks Skunk Brothers, 254; tricks Thunder's Wife, 193; trickster, 11, 13, 91, 95, 96, 98, 103, 106, 109, 110, 193, 241, 242, 244, 245, 247-254, 257, 260, 263, 265, 267, 269, 280-283, 285, 288-293, 347; Tule Boy, 292; weaves fish traps, 250; wise man, 82, 133.

> *Relationships of:* B. of Wolf, 69, 72, 76, 77; F. of Abalone-shell-small-piece, 113, 115, 116; F. of Arrowpoint-young-man, 208; F. of Black Hawk, 53, 58, 60, 61; F. of Falcon, 237; F. of Louse, 113; F. of Obsidian-man, 202, 205, 207, 210, 211, 220, 222, 223, 226; F. of Pestle, 69, 72, 76, 77; F. of Thunder, 193; F. of Wolf, 125, 126; FL. of Blackbird, 237; GF. of Falcon, 45, 46, 48, 164, 166-168, 170, 177-180, 273; GF. of Flower-man, 190; H. of Bullfrog, 375; H. of Frog, 202, 205, 207, 210, 211, 220, 222, 223, 226, 267, 269, 271, 283; H. of Skunk, 242, 243; H. of Wood Duck, 113, 115, 116; Ne. of Wolf, 62, 66, 68; U. of Skunk Brothers, 261.

——, Bird-people Trick, The, (I) 291.

—— Brags of his Wealth, (T) 293.

—— Builds a Dance-house, (I) 252.

—— Builds Kelsey Creek and establishes Fishing Customs, (I) 250.

—— Burns the Dance-house, (I) 167.

—— Burns the Ground-squirrel-people, (I) 252.

—— Burns the World, (T) 123; (I) 96, 113, 119, 121.

—— Burns the World and Creates Clear Lake, (T) 121.

—— Burns the World in revenge for the Ill Treatment of his Children, (T) 113.

—— Catches Ground Squirrels by Magic, (I) 247.

—— Causes a Deluge, (I) 129.

—— Causes a Deluge to Destroy the World, (T) 129.

Coyote *cont.*
—— Is Tricked by the Skunk Brothers and again by Small Birds, (T)
    262.
—— Is Tricked by Small Birds, (I) 265.
—— Kills His Sister-in-law, (I) 242.
—— Kills His Sister-in-law, Skunk, (T) 242.
—— Kills Two Fawns, (T) 375.
—— Loses His Arm, (I) 251.
——, Mink Tricks, (I) 281.
——, Oak-ball, Hawk, and Owl Trick, (T) 281.
——, Oak-ball Tricks, (I) 282.
—— Obtains Black Bread from the Sun, (I) 290.
——, Osprey and Mink Fool, (T) 280.
——, Osprey Tricks, (I) 280.
——, Owl Tricks, (I) 283.
—— Places People, (I) 60.
—— Regulates Death, (I) 249.
—— Regulates the Ocean, (I) 115.
—— Rescues Duck (I) 246.
——, Sapsucker Tricks, in Getting Wood, (I) 269.
——, Sapsucker Tricks, in Hair-dressing, (I) 266.
——, Skunk Brothers Trick, The, (T) 260.
——, Small Bird Tricks, A, (I) 289.
—— Steals the Daylight Sack and Liberates the Sun, (T) 143.
—— Steals the Morning Sack, Containing the Sun, Moon, and
    Pleiades, (T) 146.
—— Steals the Morning Sack, (I) 146.
—— Steals the Sun, (T) 137, (I) 77, 140, 143.
——, Thunder Kills, and Creates all forms of Sea Life, (T) 193.
—— Transforms People, (I) 180.
—— Transforms People into Animals, (I) 106.
—— Tricks His Mother-in-law, (T) 241.
—— Tricks Some Girls, (T) 244.
—— Tricks Two Girls, (T) 245.
Coyote and Frog Dance for Food, (I) 270.
——, Obsidian-man Assigns Homes to His Father and Mother, (I) 226.
——, Obsidian-man Places, (I) 207.
Coyote and Wolf: *see* Wolf and Coyote.

CREATE *cont.*
—— Human Beings and Give Them Hands, Waterdog and Lizard, (T) 80.
—— People from Maple Sticks, Wolf and Coyote, (I) 72.
—— People from Willow Sticks, Wolf and Coyote, (I) 65.
—— People, Wolf and Coyote, (T) 61.
CREATED, Bakil is, and Placed in Blue Lakes, (T) 197,
——, Clear Lake is, (I) 124.
CREATES all forms of Sea Life, Thunder Kills Coyote and, (T) 193.
—— Clear Lake, Coyote, (T) 124; (I) 116, 122.
—— Clear Lake, Coyote Burns the World and, (T) 121.
—— the Elk, Coyote, (I) 90.
—— Fish, Coyote, (I) 60.
—— Grizzly Bear, Coyote, (I) 88.
—— Human Beings, Coyote, (I) 164.
—— "Indian Potatoes," Coyote, (I) 90.
—— Man but Lizard Gives Him proper Hands, Coyote, (T) 80.
—— Obsidian-man, Coyote, (I) 202, 210, 220.
—— Obsidian-man from an Arrow Point, Coyote, (T) 202.
—— the Ocean, Coyote, (T) 91.
—— People, Burns the World and Makes Clear Lake, Coyote, (T) 117.
—— People from Feathers, Coyote, (I) 48, 58, 100, 111, 118.
—— People, Hawk Steals Food from the Minks, and Coyote, (T) 53.
—— People, Wind-man, (I) 179.
—— the Rattlesnake, Coyote, (I) 89.
—— Sickness, Coyote, (I) 87.
—— the Sun, Moon and Stars and Peoples the Earth, Coyote, (T) 93.
—— Various Things, Coyote, (I) 126.
—— Vegetal Foods, Coyote, (I) 61.
CREATION: 13, 15, 17, 466; (C) 455; of birds, 94; of Blue Lakes, 139; of Clear Lake, 100, 111, 116, 122; darkness, 94; of the Earth, 16; elk, 90; fish, 92, 122, 237; fish from sticks, 60; foods, 94; grizzly bears, 68; human beings, 12, 45; human hair and eyebrows, 80; mammals, 94; moon, 93; morning star, 94; motifs, 12; people, 16; people by Lizard, 80; people by Waterdog, 80; people by Wind-man, 179; people, *see also* COYOTE CREATES, *and* WOLF CREATES; plants, 94, 126; salmon, 92; shell fish, 194; sky, 93; snakes by Thunder, 214; snakes from sticks, 123; stars from live coals, 93; sun from

CREATION *cont.*

oak-ball, 93; supernatural beings, 94; vermin from grass seeds, 112; vermin from chaff of milkweed bark, 119; water animals, 100; of the World, 12; *see also* COYOTE CREATES.

—— of Angleworms, (I) 133.

—— of Clear Lake, The, (I) 98, 110, 120, 125.

—— of Clear Lake, The Burning of the World and the, (T) 95, 125.

—— of the Fire-drill, (I) 121.

—— of Mammals, Birds, etc., (I) 131.

—— of Mountains, The, (I) 130.

—— of People, (I) 126, 130.

—— of People by Wolf and Coyote, (T) 69.

—— of Salmon, (T) 92.

—— and Transformation of Human Beings, Myths of, (H) 45.

CREATION OF ANIMALS: (C) 60, 68, 76, 84, 85, 88, 89, 90, 92, 94, 100, 111, 118, 116, 122, 123, 126, 131, 133, 194, 237, 456.

CREATION OF IMPLEMENTS: (C) 121, 456.

CREATION OF PEOPLE: (C) 49, 59, 65, 67, 73, 75, 80, 83, 100, 110, 112, 117, 119, 126, 130, 165, 170, 179, 455.

CREATION OF PLANTS: (C) 61, 84, 90, 126, 456.

CREATION OF VERMIN: (C) 112, 119, 456.

CREATION IN A VESSEL: (C) 204, 321, 456.

CREATIONS, Coyote's, (T) 87.

—— and Regulations, Miscellaneous Myths of, (H) 84.

CREATOR: madū'mda, 97, 120.

CREMATION: instituted by Coyote, 89, 370.

——, Coyote Institutes, (I) 89.

CRIME: detection, 371.

CROW: 79, 101, 105, 107, 307; a doctor, 287; an old man, 81, 137, 139, 311; has great endurance, 101; places Sun in Sky, 79; remains in sky accompanying sun, 142.

—— Is Rewarded, The Sun is Regulated and, (I) 142.

CROW BROTHERS: 142, 147, 200, 258, 349; place sun in sky, 105, 349.

CROW-PEOPLE: 171, 297.

CROW-VILLAGE: Woodrat at the (I) 297.

CROW-WOMEN: 251-253.

CULTURE HERO: 11, 21; Coyote, 15.

CURSE: (C) 64, 72, 256, 464; pronounced by Deer's head, 351.

CUSTOMS: *see* CREMATION, DIVORCE.
——, Coyote Builds Kelsey Creek and Establishes Fishing, (I) 250.
CUSTOMS INSTITUTED: (C) 84, 89, 90, 101, 113, 122, 131, 133, 200,
    250, 456.

daka't: *see* HAWK.
dako: *see* PESTLE.
dakō'-tcūwak: 37.
da'ma*ta*: 24.
da'matū: 22, 23.
damō't: *see* PANTHER.
DANCE for Food, Coyote and Frog, (I) 270.
——, The Origin of the Lehuya-ke or Ka-tcaha-ke, the Whiskey-, (T)
    379.
——, The Origin of the Sul-ke or Vulture, (T) 376.
DANCE COSTUMES: of flowers, leaves and branches, 271.
DANCE-HOUSE, Coyote Builds a, (I) 252.
——, Coyote Burns the, (I) 167.
danō'-matū: 24.
danō'-tca: 32; *see also* MOUNTAIN-MAN.
DARKNESS: caused by wish, 55; creation of, 94.
da*ta*'lalī: described, 39.
da'-tca: 21.
da'-tcatc: 22.
da'-tcma: 22.
DAU, The Myth of the, (T) 380.
DAY: lengthened by wish, 341, 343.
DAYLIGHT: caused by wish, 57.
DAYLIGHT SACK, Coyote Steals the, and Liberates the Sun, (T) 143.
DEAD: disposal of the, 82; *see also* ABODE of the Dead.
DEAD, OBJECTION TO RETURN OF: (C) 186, 249, 271, 321.
DEATH: (C) 457; the origin of, 490.
——, Coyote Institutes, (T) 91.
——, Coyote Regulates, (I) 249.
——, Falcon's Children Avenge his, (I) 239.
—— of Muyamuya, The, (T) 232.
DEATH MADE PERMANENT: (C) 92, 118, 249, 322, 372, 457.

DEATH THOUGHT SLEEP: (C) 180, 210, 221, 243, 256, 258, 262, 265, 282, 283, 288, 289, 291, 457.

DEER: 107, 186, 355; boasts of his racing ability, 355; taken by hunter's nudity, 276.

> *Relationships of:* B. of Bear Girls, 334; DL. of Bear, 327, 332, 334, 345, 349; F. of Deer Boys, 334, 350; F. of Skunk, 306; GF. of Skunk Boys, 306; H. of Deer, 350; H. of Wildcat, 334; M. of Deer Boys, 327, 332, 334; M. of Thunder Children, 345, 349; SiL. of Bear Boys, 327, 332, 334; SiL. of Bear Girls, 345, 349; S. of Bear, 350; S. of Bear and Blue Jay, 334; W. of Falcon, 327, 332, 334; W. of Sun-man, 327, 332, 334; W. of Thunder, 344, 345, 349.

——, Bagil Transforms People into, (T) 235.

——, Bear Kills, (I) 327.

——, Bear Kills her own Daughter-in-law, (T) 327.

——, Huk Transforms People into, (T) 234.

——, Panther's Wife Kills, by Magic, (T) 360.

——, Skunk Kills, with her Scent, (T) 306.

——, The Thunder-people Are Transformed into, (I) 131.

——, Wolf Catches, in a Magic Weir, (I) 62.

——, Wolf Kills, by Magic, (T) 356.

——, A Woman Kills, with her Magic Pestle, (I) 304.

DEER AND BEAR CHILDREN: 488, (C) 327, 334, 342, 344, 350, 462.

——, Myths of the, (H) 327.

——, The, (T) 334.

DEER AND MUD-HEN: The Race between, (T) 355.

DEER BOYS: given their own mother's flesh to eat, 338, 351.

> *Relationships of:* GS. of Blue Jay, 334; GS. of Crane, 327, 329, 331, 334; GS. of Grizzly Bear, 327, 334, 350; GS. of Loons, 327, 329, 331, 334; Ne. of Bear Boys, 327, 329, 331, 334; Ne. of Bear Girls, 334; S. of Deer, 350; S. of Deer Wildcat, 334; S. of Falcon and Deer, 327, 329, 331, 334.

—— Attempt to bring their Mother Home, The, (I) 334.

—— Kill the Bear Boys, The, (I) 329.

—— Kill Sun-man, The, (I) 331.

DEER HOUSE: 306.

DEER-MAN: 41.

Escape *cont.*

—— the Deluge and Fly to the Sky, The Thunder Children, (T) 131.

Establishes Fishing Customs, Coyote Builds Kelsey Creek and, (I) 250.

Ethnographic Areas of California: 12.

Etiological Tales: 12; (C) 115, 117, 125, 136, 137, 139, 147, 165, 226, 230, 233, 240, 248, 253, 275, 310, 322, 329, 351, 355, 369, 372, 465.

Etiology: (C) 465.

Evil Father-in-law: (C) 191, 214, 216, 305, 324, 463.

Excrement-man: *same as* Putrid-man.

Eye-opening Prohibition: (C) 86 ,182, 242, 257, 260, 265, 280, 281, 353, 463.

Falcon: chief, 50, 100, 102, 105, 108, 127, 136, 148, 170, 321, 370; contests with Kilak, 170; contests with Sun-man, 274; created out of feather, 170; escapes Deluge, 127; exhibits superior strength, 48; famous hunter, 251; hunts with magic sling, 128; kills Sun-man, 275; rescued by Coyote, 178; tata, 79, 127, 128.

   Relationships of: B. of Bear Boys, 327; B. of Cetata, 319; F. of Deer Boys, 327; GS. of Coyote, 45, 46, 50, 51, 52, 170, 177; GS. of Coyote-old-man, 272, 275; GS. of Tree, 327; H. of Deer, 327; H. of Eagle, 180; H. of Fish Hawk, 272, 275; H. of Quail, 177, 319; H. of Swan Sisters, 323; S. of Bear, 327; S. of Coyote, 237.

—— Brings Food from across the Ocean, (T) 45.

——, The Deluge and the Escape of, (T) 126.

—— Dies and Returns to Life, (T) 370.

—— Hunts with a Magic Sling, (I) 128.

—— Is Stolen by Kilak, (T) 237.

—— Is Stolen by Gilak and later Rescued, (I) 237.

—— Is Taken by Kilak, (T) 177; (I) 177.

—— Kills Geese with a Magic Sling, (I) 45.

—— Kills Kilak and Sun-man, (I) 272.

—— Kills the Kilak Family, (T) 164.

—— Kills the Kilaks, (I) 170.

—— A Magic Tree Kills, (T) 319.

—— Secures Food from across the Ocean, (I) 46.

Falcon *cont.*

—— Transforms Himself into an Elk and Goes to Kilak's House (I) 51.

Falcon and Eagle Journey to Gilak's Home, (T) 180.

Falcon and Putrid-man Gamble, (I) 50.

Falcon's Children Avenge His Death, (I) 239.

Falcon's Wife: prey of Kilak, 176.

Falls from a Tree, Coyote, (T) 283.

Famine: 45, 271, 356, 363; (C) 53, 148, 160, 465.

Fan: used in fanning contest, 225, fn. 113.

Fanning Contest: 102, 149, 195 (fn. 93), 196, 268, 279, 293, 298, 329, 340.

Fawns, Coyote Kills Two, (T) 375.

Feast: after recovery from illness, 321.

Feathers, Coyote Creates People from, (I) 48, 58, 100, 111, 118.

Feather of Safety: (C) 340, 459.

Feather Rope: 20; *see also* Sky Rope.

Fire: (C) 457; discovered by Bat, 309; fanning, *see* Fanning Contest; impersonated as monster, 217; secured from within Mount Kanaktai by Gopher, 135; tube, 128; *see also* World-fire, *and* Theft of Fire.

——, Coyote Destroys the World by, (T) 109.

——, Gopher Secures, after the Deluge, (T) 135.

——, The Theft of, by Jackrabbit, (I) 309.

Fire-drill, Creation of the, (I) 121.

Fire-man: 301, 310; described, 34.

——, Woodrat Kills, (I) 301.

Fire-sweathouse: 23.

Fire-tender: 78; Blue Jay, 49.

Fire Test: (C) 149, 157, 162, 205, 209, 212, 214, 217, 218, 222, 463.

Fire-village: located in the north, 301.

Fish: created by Coyote, 126, 237; created from snakes, 116, 124; created from roasted meat, 122, 126; dam made of snakes, 214; source of, 189; taking of, 152; trap made of snakes, 190.

——, Coyote Creates, (I) 60.

Fish Hawk: batcal, 47; kīca, 272.

Fisher: 184.

Fishes in Her Stone Canoe, Swan, (T) 322.

FROG *cont.*

    221-223, 226; W. of Coyote, 202, 205, 207, 210, 221-223, 226, 268, 270, 271, 285, 293, 375; W. of Tule-boy, 293.

FROG AND COYOTE: *see* COYOTE AND FROG.

FROST-MAN: 18.

FUEL: carried in hair, 127, 128.

GALLINIPPER: 29.

GAMBLE, Putrid-man and Falcon, (I) 50.

GAMBLES, Barn Owl, (I) 275.

GAMBLING LUCK: (C) 187, 464; given by Gilak, 187.

—— Is Given by Gilak, (T) 186.

GAME: drive used to catch people, 305; lured by nudity, 357; throwing stick, 49, 157; witcili, 50, 186.

GATE: *see* ZENITH GATE.

GATE TRAP: (C) 181, 182, 191, 313, 460; at south end of the world, 32.

GEESE, Falcon Kills, with a Magic Sling, (I) 45.

GHOST: 23; brother of Man, 379; disappears when allowed to touch the ground, 343, 349.

GHOST-PEOPLE: 379.

GHOST-SWEATHOUSE: 23.

GIANT: Mountain-man, 228; Muyamuya, 232, 233; Rock-man, 231.

GILAK, Falcon is Stolen by, and later Rescued, (I) 237.

——, Gambling Luck Is Given by, (T) 186.

GILAK'S, Quail Deserts Her Husband and Goes to, (T) 183.

—— Home, Falcon and Eagle Journey to, (T) 180.

GILAKS: 14, 18, 19, 21, 24, 51, 137, 177, 181-183, 186, 240, 316; abode of, 26; attacks Coyote, 178; brings home human for food, 174, 178; described, 25; family, 176; fire blanket of, 177; food of, 27, 223, 224; friend of Kuksu, 287; home of, 272; home in the north, 223; home in the south, 183; home in the Upper World, 316; house burned, 186; house in the Upper World, 178; house has four smoke-holes, 222; house near Witter Springs, 181; human prey of, 51; identified as Kuksu, 287; keeps the Sun, 173; killed by arrowhead-trap, 178; killed by Eagle, 183; killed by sons of Falcon, 240; kills Hawk, 184; lives in same house with Sun-man, 273; mother of, 52;

HORNETS: taking of, 151.
hō'smatalak: *see* BAT.
hō'-tca: 34.
HOT ROCK MISSILE: (C) 166, 167, 331, 349, 354, 460.
HUK: described, 36; hūk, 234.
—— Transforms People into Deer, (T) 234.
HUK DEER: 235.
HUMAN BEINGS: creation of, 12; transformation of, 45.
——, Coyote Creates, (I) 164.
——, Myths of Creation and Transformation of, (H) 45.
——, Waterdog and Lizard Create, and Give Them Hands, (T) 80.
HUMMINGBIRD: doctor, 101, 105; doctors Hawk, 184; medicine-man, 184; tele, 184; thunder and lightning creator, 105; tsū'dīyūn, 101, 105; tsūdūyūn, 79; tsūīdūn, 141.
HUMMINGBIRD BROTHERS: tsū'dīyūn, GS. of Turtle, 150, 154, 160.
—— Are Instructed by their Grandmother Turtle, The, (I) 150.
—— Rescue People Held in the Sun Village, (T) 148.
—— Win Contests by means of their Yellowjackets, The, (I) 154.
HUNTING: by trickery, 247.
——, Mountain-lion Goes, (T) 376.
HUNTING LUCK: 276, (C) 85, 464.
HUNTS with a Magic Sling, Falcon, (I) 128.
hwi'l-biyūmen: *see* ABALONE-SHELL-SMALL-PIECE.

ICE GARMENT: 212, 218.
ī'lil: *see* CHICKEN HAWK.
IMITATES the Willow, Coyote, (T) 288.
IMPLEMENTS AND FOODS, Coyote Gives People, (T) 84.
INDESTRUCTIBLE REDWOOD: 230, 232.
INDIANS OF CALIFORNIA: religion of, 12.
INDIAN POTATOES, Coyote Creates, (I) 90.
INEXHAUSTIBLE: (C) 46, 75, 172, 174, 185, 224, 358, 366, 461.
INFERIOR FOOD: given away, 327, 334, 344, 350.
INSANITY-MAN: 41.
INSECT ALLIES: (C) 158-160, 163, 464.
INSTITUTES Cremation, Coyote, (I) 89.
—— Death, Coyote, (T) 91.

INSTITUTES *cont.*
—— Divorce, Coyote, (I) 90.
INSTRUCTED by their Grandmother Turtle, The Hummingbird Brothers are, (I) 150.
INSTRUCTION: by grandmother, 150.
INVULNERABLE: (C) 202, 205, 208-210, 220, 226, 231, 232, 241, 459.
ïwē'-tca: described, 38.
ïwī': *see* COYOTE.
ïwī' madū'mda: 21.

JACKRABBIT: 81; maka'la, steals fire, 310; *see also* RABBIT.
——, The Theft of Fire by, (I) 309.
JOURNEY: across the Pacific Ocean, 46, 55; in the four cardinal directions, 340; of Fox, 275; of Woodrat, 294; to the abode of the Sun-people, 476; to land of the Sun, 104; to south edge of the world, 195.
—— to Gilak's Home, Falcon and Eagle, (T) 180.
JOURNEY BY SUPERNATURAL MEANS: (C) 459.
JOURNEY TO LAND OF THE DEAD: (C) 379, 459.
JOURNEY TO OUTER WORLD: (C) 46, 51, 55, 77, 104, 143, 149, 156, 161, 170, 179, 180, 188, 191, 195, 223, 238, 240, 275, 348, 311, 331, 343, 352, 365, 366, 358, 362, 459.
JOURNEY TO SUPERNATURAL PLACES: (C) 459.
JOURNEY TO UPPER WORLD: (C) 81, 82, 97, 110, 113, 115, 120, 123, 178, 187, 315, 459.

kaa'i: *see* CROW.
kaa-toltol: *see* MORNING STAR.
kabadate'tes: magician and kidnapper of Duck, 246.
kaba'ltū: chief, 149; sisters, owners of magic swing, 301.
kaba'nasiksik: brothers, 259.
kaba'ōyel: *see* BULLSNAKE.
kaba'-tca: 18.
kabē'bot: 41.
kabē'kat: *see* CHICKEN HAWK.
kabē'katc: *see* CHICKEN HAWK, *and* BLACK HAWK.
kabē'-mata: 32; *see also* STONE-WOMAN.
kabē'ukatc: *see* BLACK HAWK.

ka'imatūtsi: 14.
kaiya'n: *see* DUCK.
kaka'ū: chief fisherman, 102.
kakō'ī: *see* BULLSNAKE.
kalai: *see* PELICAN.
kala'k: *see* BLUE HERON.
kalē'kol: 196.
kalē'yagaū: *see* CRANE.
kalī'matūtsi: 14.
kalkalma'ptseū: 293.
KALTOI, The Legend of, (T) 381.
kama-sili-dūketya: *see* SHARP-HEEL.
kana'batiltil: *see* SAPSUCKER.
kapa'-kū: 37.
kapa'-tca: 37.
kapintada'tadaū: *see* KINGBIRD.
kata'k: *see* RED-HEADED-WOODPECKER.
kata'-tca: 30.
ka-tca: *see* WATER-MAN.
KA-TCAHA-KE the Whiskey Dance, The Origin of the Lehuya-ke or, (T) 379.
katca'-tca, katca'tcatc: *see* OBSIDIAN-MAN.
katsī'ya, ka'tsiya: *see* MUD-HEN, COOT.
katsī'yō: *see* YELLOWHAMMER.
kawē'na: *see* BUZZARD.
kawīna: *see* TURTLE.
kawō': *see* FROG.
kawolwol: 215.
KELSEY CREEK, Coyote Builds, and Establishes Fishing Customs, (I) 250.
kīca: *see* FISH HAWK.
kī'lak: *see* GILAK.
KILAK, Falcon Is Stolen by, (T) 237.
——, Falcon Is Taken by, (T) 177; (I) 177.
KILAK AND SUN-MAN, Falcon Kills, (I) 272.
KILAK FAMILY, Falcon Kills the, (T) 164.
KILAKS, Falcon Kills the, (I) 170.

LOOKOUTS: Blue Jay Brothers, 47; Kusut, 366, 378; Oak-ball, 358, 359, 360, 366; Red-headed-woodpecker, 79, 101; Red-headed-woodpecker Brothers, 47; Thrasher, 101; Thrasher Brothers, 47.

LOON: kok, 103, 107, 128, 197, 227.

LOON-PEOPLE: 332.

LOSES His Arm, Coyote, (I) 251.

LOUSE: pere'c, Coyote's son, 113.

LUCK Is Given by Gilak, Gambling, (T) 186.

madjō'djō: *see* BLUEBIRD-PEOPLE.

madū'mda: 13, 14, 16, 18, 21, 30, 199; *see also* CREATOR.

MAGIC, Coyote Catches Ground Squirrels by, (I) 247.

——, Panther's Wife Kills Deer by, (T) 360.

——, Wolf Kills Deer by, (T) 356.

MAGIC AIDS: 13, 218.

MAGIC ARROW: 223.

MAGIC BAG: 75, 224; (C) 75, 224, 359, 461; passes beads to home of owner, 359.

MAGIC BASKET: 314, 346; floats away, 339, 352; unfinished, 124, 197.

MAGIC BEAD-GRINDING STONE: 212, 214, 223, 273, 274.

MAGIC BLACK BREAD: 290.

—— from the Sun, Coyote Gets, (T) 289.

MAGIC BOW: 331.

MAGIC CANE: 315.

——, Quail Ascends into the Sky on a, (T) 315.

MAGIC CANOE: 46, 48, 322.

MAGIC CLOTHING: (C) 134, 145, 173, 174, 177, 224, 377, 464.

MAGIC DEVICES: (C) 307, 460, 486.

——, Myths of, (H) 307.

MAGIC DOVES: 320.

MAGIC FEATHERS: carry Deer Boys away, 340.

MAGIC FISH-NET: 322.

MAGIC FLIGHT: (C) 134, 145, 173, 174, 177, 224, 315, 330, 377, 459.

MAGIC FLUTE: (C) 59-61, 460.

MAGIC FOG BRIDGE: 323.

MAGIC FOG TUBE: 213.

MAGIC FOOD: 171, 224.

PANTHER'S WIFE Kills Deer by Magic, (T) 360.

pa'-tca: 34; *see also* PUTRID-MAN.

pcē: *see* DEER.

pcē'dam: described, 37.

pcē'-stū: described, 37.

pcē'-tsamō: *see* BLUE-FLY.

PELICAN: kalai, a chief, a bear doctor, 370.

PENALTY: prescribed, 131; prescribed by Coyote, 122.

PENDANT MOSS: used in healing, 252, 262, 266.

PEOPLE: assigned their abodes, 60; creation of, 16, 45; killed by Sun-people, return to life, 163; rescued from abode of the Sun, 163; turn into water, 164.

—— Are Transformed into Animals, (T) 81.

—— Are Transformed into Birds by Fox, (T) 83.

—— Are Unable to Kill Turtle, The, (T) 368.

——, Bagil Transforms, into Deer, (T) 235.

——, Coyote Creates, Burns the World and Makes Clear Lake, (T) 117.

——, Coyote Creates, Hawk Steals Food from the Minks and, (T) 53.

——, Coyote Creates, from Feathers, (I) 48, 58, 100, 111, 118.

——, Coyote Gives, Implements and Foods, (T) 84.

——, Coyote Places, (I) 60.

——, Coyote Transforms, (I) 180.

——, Coyote Transforms, into Animals, (I) 106.

——, Creation of, (I) 126, 130.

——, Creation of, by Wolf and Coyote, (T) 69.

——, Huk Transforms, into Deer, (T) 234.

——, The Hummingbird Brothers Rescue, Held in the Sun Village, (T) 148.

——, Obsidian-man Wins Contests with the, (I) 221.

——, Turtle Tricks the, (T) 369.

——, Wind-man Creates, (I) 179.

——, Wolf and Coyote Create, (T) 61.

——, Wolf and Coyote Create, from Maple Sticks, (I) 72.

——, Wolf and Coyote Create, from Willow Sticks, (I) 65.

PEOPLE TRANSFORMED INTO ANIMALS: (C) 53, 68, 82, 83, 85, 86, 107, 132, 168, 180, 186, 187, 198, 226, 232, 236, 456.

PEOPLES the Earth, Coyote Creates the Sun, Moon and Stars and, (T) 93.

pere'c: *see* LOUSE.

PERSONIFIED SHARPNESS: (C) 205, 209, 214, 219, 222, 228, 458.

PESTLE: dakō, son of Coyote, 72; used to simulate swelling, 63.

PIGEON: tcaba'tbat, 79.

PINE-NUTS: run out of the body of Pine-nut-man, 297.

PINE-NUT-MAN: kūtī'tcūlīya, H. of Woodpecker, BL. of Woodrat, 295.

——, Woodrat Tricks, (I) 295.

PITCH: used by Coyote as hair-dressing, 268, 281, 292.

PITCH AND STRING: used on short-haired people, 78.

PLACED in Blue Lakes, Bakil is Created and, (T) 197.

—— in the Sky, The Sun Is, (I) 147.

PLACES Coyote and Frog, Obsidian-man, (I) 207.

—— People, Coyote, (I) 60.

PLACING the Sun in the Sky, (I) 138, 141, 349.

PLEIADES: placed in the sky by Crow Brothers, 147.

——, Coyote Steals the Morning Sack, Containing the Sun, Moon and, (T) 146.

POISON: removed by doctor passing through alimentary canal of patient, 184.

POISONERS: 100, (fn. 64) 141, 184, 185, 331.

POMO BEAR DOCTORS, The Origin of the, (T) 380.

POMO DIALECTS: 7, 8.

POMO ENVIRONMENT: 7.

POMO LANGUAGE: 8.

POMO MYTHOLOGICAL SYSTEM: 43.

POMO MYTHOLOGY: position of, 11.

POMO MYTHS: characteristics of, 9; classification of, 10; composite nature of, 9; recording of, 8; subject matter of, 10.

POMO RELIGION: 14.

POMO RELIGIOUS CONCEPTS: 13.

POMO TERRITORY: 7.

POND: created for people to alight in after trying to place the Sun in the Sky, 79, 141.

POND-MAN: 41.

pō't-tca : 18.
Powers Displayed : (C) 211, 218, 219, 228, 229, 462.
Presents : to visiting dancers, 378.
Property : divided between man and wife, 276.
Purification of Dead : (C) 184, 458.
Putrid-man : pa'tca, a gambler, 50; arrow-maker, 302; net-weaver, 338; described, 34.
    Relationships of: GF. of Deer and Bear Girls, U. of Blue Jay, F. of Bear, 335.
——, Woodrat and, (I) 302.
Putrid-man and Falcon, Gamble.
Putrid-old-man : pa'būtsīke, firetender of Sun-man, 273.
Putrid Village : 302.

Quail : M. of Meadowlark Brothers, 315; W. of Black Chicken Hawk, 183; W. of Falcon, 177, 319.
—— Ascends into the Sky on a Magic Cane, (T) 315.
—— Deserts Her Husband and Goes to Gilak's, (T) 183.

Rabbit : runs with Sun-sack, 79; sits on fire, hence his white rump patch, 310; *see also* Jackrabbit.
Race between Deer and Mud-hen, The, (T) 355.
—— between Mud-hen and other Birds, The, (T) 354.
Race-course : shores of Clear Lake, *see* Hare and Tortoise.
Rain : causes Deluge, 132.
Rattle : made of Coyote's arm-bones by Ground Squirrels, 252.
——, Ground Squirrels Steal Coyote's Arm to Make a, (T) 251.
Rattlesnake : children, 373; creation of by Coyote, 68, 76, 85, 89, 91, 94; guards at door of Sun-house, *see* Theft of the Sun; husband of Girl, 373; protectors, 214; transforms himself into a young man, 373; tooth trap, 332.
——, Coyote Creates the, (I) 89.
——, The Girl Who Married, (T) 373.
Rattlesnakes, Wolf and Coyote Create Grizzlies and, (I) 67, 76.
Red-headed-woodpecker : far-sighted man, 79, 101, 105, 107, 139, 141; has shiney eyes, 139; husband of Woodrat's Sister, 372; liberates Coyote, 283; lookout, 78, 101; poison-man, 184; stingy man, 372.

·

Sun-man *cont.*

party, 149; house of, near Witter Springs, 272; open mouth produces light, 349; la'gaūk, 272; smells out hidden visitors, 156; tests
visitors, 163; trickster, 290.

> *Relationships of:* H. of Deer, 348; H. of Fish Hawk, 272;
> Step-father of Deer Boys, 322.

——, Falcon Kills Kilak and, (I) 272.

——, The Deer Boys Kill, (I) 331.

Sun-messengers: 22, 104.

Sun-people: 14, 25, 78, 104, 137, 138, 141, 143, 144, 147, 149, fn. 47;
are birds, 77; become Bagils, 142; described, 21; kill visitors with
fire, 157, 162; put to sleep by Coyote, 105; warned by Trout, 141.

—— Are Killed by Yellowjackets, The, (T) 160.

——, The Coyote Boys Are Killed by the, (I) 76, 143.

——, Men Are Killed by the, (I) 148.

Sun-prophet: 24, 22.

Sun Sack: of coyote skins, 77, 143, 146; of four thicknesses of elk
hide, 140; has two holes for emission of light, 141.

——, The Stealing of the, (T) 139.

Sun Village, The Hummingbird Brothers Rescue People Held in the,
(T) 148.

Superior Strength: (C) 48, 253, 261, 308, 460.

Supernatural Beings: 11, 14, 21, 479; (C) 458.

——, Myths of, (H) 164.

Supernatural Bird: (C) 458; *see* Gilaks, Huk, Sun-people,
Thunder, *also* Bird-people.

Supernatural Food: (C) 51, 186, 290, 465.

Supernatural Serpent: (C) 458.

Supernatural "Spring Trout": 132.

sūū'padax: 14.

Swan: W. of Bear, 322.

—— Fishes in Her Stone Canoe, (T) 322.

Swan-people: 238.

Swan Sisters: two, D. of Swan and Bear, W. of Falcon, 322.

Swaying Tree: escape of Woodrat from, 300; *see also* Growing
Tree.

Sweathouse: Ghost, Spirit, Fire, 23.

Swing Trick: (C) 192, 300, 301, 305, 306, 460.

tala′k: 148.
TALES, Miscellaneous, (H) 373.
*t*ana: *see* CHUB DUCK.
ta*r*a: *see* WASP.
ta′ta: *see* FALCON.
tcaba′tbat: *see* PIGEON.
tca′dūwel: 23.
tca′dūwel-canē: 23.
tca′dūwel-ma: 23.
tcīdō′-tca: *see* FLOWER-MAN.
tcitcī′: *see* HAWK.
tcīya′: *see* HAWK, CHICKEN HAWK.
tco′dok: 41; N. of Diver, 195, 197.
TCODOK Kills Guksu, (T) (I) 195.
tcō′tcō: *see* BLUEBIRD.
tcū*t*kil: *see* DIVER.
tele: *see* HUMMINGBIRD.
TESTS: (C) 463; berry picking, 324; deer hunting, 325, 326; fire, 205, 212; fishing, 191; foot-racing, 333; hunting, 158, 216; obsidian gathering, 215; pitch gathering, 192, 215; wood gathering, 191, 212, 215.
THEFT OF FIRE: 476; (C) 127, 135, 309, 310, 457.
—— by Jackrabbit, The, (I) 309.
THEFT OF THE SUN: (C) 78, 137, 138, 141, 143, 145, 146, 272, 457.
——, The, (T) 135; (I) 103, 138.
THRASHER: wo′cwoc, a lookout, 47, 101.
THUNDER: 15, 25, 131, 135, 189, 191; abode of, 28, 189; cause of, 189; causes freezing, 134; clothing of, 134; creation of, 240; described, 28; fish weir and net of, 193; gives poor meat to Bear, 344; guards at house of, 212; home of, at western edge of the world, 191; killed by his own magic, 193; killed by Flower-man, 192; killed by shower of boulders, 219; magic of, 218, 219; refused food by his sister, 188; roasts Coyote, 194; subjects son-in-law to tests, 191; takes Panther to Upper World, 81; three, go to north, east and south, 135.

    Relationships of: F. of Duck Sisters, 191; FL. of Flower-man, 191; husband of Deer, 344; H. of Seal, 193; S. of Bear, 344; S. of Coyote, 193.

ya'kōda: dangers of, 231.

ya'kōda-pda: 42.

yamot: *see* PANTHER.

ya-tca: 18, 34; *see also* WIND-MAN.

YELLOWHAMMER: katsīyō, 353.

YELLOWJACKETS: 158, 163; aid heroes, 160; allies, kill people, 160; allies, kill Sunpeople, 159, 163; allies, kill bears, 158, 163; taking of, 152.

——, The Hummingbird Brothers Win Contests by means of their, (I) 154.

——, The Sun People Are Killed by, (T) 160.

YOUNGER BROTHER: braver than elder, 312, 313.

yū'-tca: 18.

ZENITH GATE: 19, 26, 27; keeper of, 20; (C) 97, 98, 178, 179, 315, 459.

CPSIA information can be obtained
at www.ICGtesting.com
Printed in the USA
LVOW11*2203120517

534377LV00020B/608/P